One-Time
Online
Access Code
Included

Third Edition

Straight Talk about
COMMUNICATION
RESEARCH METHODS

Christine S.Davis
Kenneth A. Lachlan with
contributor Robert Westerfelhaus

Kendall Hunt
publishing company

Book Team

Chairman and Chief Executive Officer *Mark C. Falb*
President and Chief Operating Officer *Chad M. Chandlee*
Vice President, Higher Education *David L. Tart*
Director of Publishing Partnerships *Paul B. Carty*
Senior Developmental Coordinator *Angela Willenbring*
Vice President, Operations *Timothy J.* Beitzel
Senior Production Editor *Sheri Hosek*
Senior Permissions Editor *Caroline Kieler*
Cover Designer *Faith Walker*

Screen shots on these pages are used with permission of Microsoft: 259, 260, 261, 263, 268, 270, 271, 272, 273, 275.

Cover image © Shutterstock.com

Kendall Hunt
publishing company

www.kendallhunt.com
Send all inquiries to:
4050 Westmark Drive
Dubuque, IA 52004-1840

BRIEF CONTENTS

Appendices 435

Index 447

CONTENTS

Chapter 2: Metatheoretical Considerations, Research Perspectives, and Research Paradigms   27

Chapter 11: Quantitative Analysis of Text and Words: Content and Interaction Analysis   221

Chapter 15: Social Science Qualitative Approaches to Communication Research   345

Chapter 16: Social Constructionist and Arts-Based Qualitative Approaches to Communication Research   389

PREFACE

Welcome to *Straight Talk about Communication Research Methods*! Through this textbook we hope you will catch our excitement with research. Your authors are researchers who—amazingly enough—love doing research. We may be crazy, and we may be academic nerds, but that's not why we love research. We think research is FUN! We feel investigating, following leads, and solving puzzles is exciting.

It is our hope that in this book we give you enough information about the foundations of research methods, the choices we as scholars make, and the methodological decisions driving communication scholarship to balance your desire to know and inquire into interesting communication questions while instilling an enthusiasm about the process!

Research is like being a detective. Both researchers and detectives are trying to find out something. Both are asking and answering questions. Both are trying to put together a puzzle to come up with a solution. In both, answering questions leads to more questions. And, in both, seeing patterns is crucial to solving the puzzle.

There is much about the social world that most of us think we know already; yet, there is also much left to learn. This book will ask you to question what you know, why you know what you know, and where that belief came from. While much of the material here is sometimes difficult to understand, we tell our students that their struggle with this material will allow them a place to store the other knowledge about communication and society. We also suggest that when your head begins to hurt, you have really begun the work of thinking about this material. Research Methods may not be an "easy A" class, but it's worth it! You'll learn a lot in this class—perhaps more information you'll use the rest of your career than many other classes. Our students would tell you that we also encourage them to talk with each other about this material. As communication scholars, we often overlook the powerful learning tool of discussing informally what we learn in the classroom. As you learn to talk about these conceptual ideas, you will begin to crystallize your understanding of both communication research methods and theory.

We hope that through this course you'll discover your own joy in conducting research. Some communication students are intimidated when they first encounter research methods, and we'd like to lessen the intimidation factor for you. To do this, we want to introduce to you a model of the stages of learning (Dubin, 1962; Howell & Fleishman, 1982; Kirkpatrick, 1971).

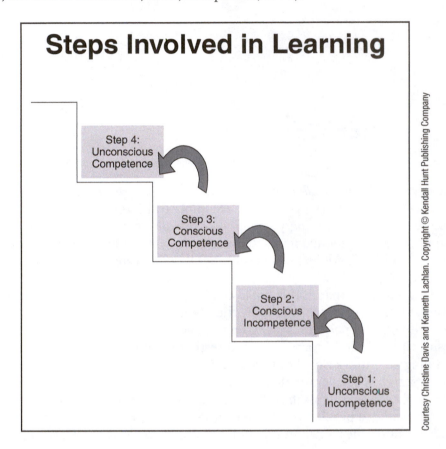

Courtesy Christine Davis and Kenneth Lachlan. Copyright © Kendall Hunt Publishing Company

You're in Step 1 right now—Unconscious Incompetence. That means you know so little, you don't even know what you don't know! This is a pretty blissful place to be ("ignorance is bliss"), but we're about to move you out of your comfort zone. We're about to move you to Step 2—Conscious Incompetence. We're about to tell you what you don't know. We're going to teach you how to do things, which will move you to Step 3—Conscious Competence, and you will spend much of the semester moving between Steps 2 and 3. We'll teach you something, and you'll be very conscious of the fact that you're learning something new. By the end of the semester, you will have mastered many skills and competencies, and you will be in Step 4—Unconscious Competence for much of the course content. These stages are always uncomfortable because new learning feels awkward. Remember when you were first learning how to drive a car? There was a time when you had to remind yourself to push in the brake, and check your rear view mirror, and for a while that felt very uncomfortable. Luckily for you (and your parents), that stage didn't last long, and soon you were in the stage of Unconscious Competence in your driving—you could get in the car and drive without even thinking about it! We promise that by the end of the semester, you will be in this final stage for research. You will be able to do things that, right now, you don't even know exist! And, you'll enjoy it!

We've based the structure of this textbook on adult learning theory. Adult learning scholars suggest that learning for adults must be experiential—taking into account the learners' experiences, and integrating the materials into their own lives, combining active experimentation with theory and practical life skills as participants learn both formally and informally through application of course materials to experiences (Dinmore, 1997; Knowles, 1984). Research has also shown that adult learners best remember concepts given to them as spaced repetition—repeated in intervals over time (Spieler & Balota, 1996). In this textbook, we give you information in small chunks that build upon each other, repeating then expanding knowledge. We'll give you multiple passes over concepts—introducing you to concepts in early chapters; then telling you more about those concepts in subsequent chapters. That's why it's going to be important for you to keep up with the material throughout the semester—you don't want to miss any of the early passes over the information.

In this third edition of *Straight Talk about Communication Research Methods*, we've made quite a few substantive changes. Of course, we've updated the information and the examples. We added sections and material on conducting research on, and involving, social media and digital media. Remembering that not all students might be planning to attend graduate school, and to show how research methods are relevant to all students, we added many more examples of how students might use Communication research methods in business and industry jobs after graduation. We greatly rewrote and expanded the qualitative methods section, and included much more detailed information about each method. We included an introductory overview of all qualitative methods (Chapter 14) for those students or classes who don't want to go into as much detail for each of the various qualitative methods. We then follow this with four chapters giving comprehensive instructions on how to conduct a number of different qualitative methods, from social science based qualitative methods (e.g., focus groups and grounded theory), to social constructionist-based qualitative methods (e.g., autoethnography and feminist ethnography), arts-based qualitative methods (e.g., ethnodrama and visual ethnography), and rhetorical criticism (e.g., Burkean criticism and narrative criticism). This edition includes many qualitative methods not included in the previous editions of the textbook as well as additional details about how to conduct each method.

When you graduate with a degree in Communication, your academic department is certifying you are properly socialized into our field. We are indoctrinating you into our community of knowledge—and, like every community of knowledge, we have ways of knowing, ways of seeing the world, ways of thinking, and ways of deciding. We require that you take classes in Communication Theory so you will learn how we in our community think about things. We require that you take classes in Research Methods so you will learn how we know things, describe things, and decide if something is true or not. You're probably had quite a few courses in our field by the time you take this course. You've been told a lot of things about the world, given a lot of facts, and memorized a lot of theories. Have you ever wondered where all these things, facts, and theories came from? Did someone just make them up so you could have something to be tested on? We know sometimes it feels that way, but this semester you'll learn how to do the same type of research that communication scholars before you have done. You'll see firsthand how theories (and other research questions) begin as a curiosity—an "I wonder if . . ."—and how these musings and wonderings turn into full-blown research, then into facts, knowledge, and theories. Who knows? You might discover that you're the next George Herbert Mead, Barnett Pearce, Kenneth Burke, Elisabeth Noelle-Neumann, or Marshall McLuhan!

You'll also learn how people in our community prove a point. You'll learn that not everything you read or hear is true, and, as we said, you'll learn how to question what you hear and believe, and how to determine if you want to continue believing it. You'll learn how to make credible claims and how to back them up with evidence so other people will believe what you have to say.

By the way, throughout this textbook we are using the term Communication, or Communication Studies, to refer to our field of study. The field of Communication or Communication Studies is incredibly diverse. In most universities, our community of scholars can include people in fields as varied as health communication, interpersonal communication, organizational communication, cultural studies, rhetoric, mass media, public relations, broadcasting, and film studies, to name only some. At some universities, study of Communication is under an umbrella of Communication Studies; and at other universities, study in a field called Communication Studies is under an umbrella called Communication. When we use either term—Communication or Communication Studies—we are using the term to be inclusive of all scholarship in all forms of human communication—mediated or interpersonal, organizational or rhetorical.

Confused—or curious? For now, don't worry about what you don't yet know. Just sit back, relax, and enjoy the ride!

▼ Student-Oriented Pedagogy

Because we recognize the importance of assessing student learning, we have included features in each chapter that facilitate student learning and help instructors measure learning outcomes.

- Chapter Outlines serve as a map to guide you through the content of the text and focus on key points.
- Key Terms list shows important terms to focus on as you read the chapter.
- Chapter Objectives help you focus on the overall concepts, theories, and skills discussed in the chapter.
- Running Glossary provides the definition of a key term in the margin for quick clarification when reading the material.
- So What? chapter summary reviews the key points explored in the text.

- Chapter Glossary serves as a helpful reference tool at the end of each chapter.
- References list documents the research cited within the chapter.

. . . .

Instructional Online Enhancements ▼

Both students and instructors have access to online content that is integrated chapter by chapter with the text to enrich student learning. The Web access code is included on the inside front cover of the textbook.

Look for the Web icon in the text margins to direct you to various interactive tools.

. . . .

References ▼

Dinmore, I. (1997). Interdisciplinary and integrative learning: An imperative for adult education. *Education, 117*(3), 452–468.

Dubin, P. (1962). *Human relations in administration.* Englewood Cliffs, NJ: Prentice-Hall.

Eves, H. W. (1987). *Return to mathematical circles: A fifth collection of mathematical stories and anecdotes.* Prindle, Weber, and Schmidt.

Howell, W. C., & Fleishman, E. A. (Eds.). (1982). *Human performance and productivity: Information processing and decision making.* Hillsdale, NJ: Erlbaum.

Kirkpatrick, D. L. (1971). *A practical guide for supervisory training and development.* Reading, MA: Addison-Wesley.

Knowles, M. (1984). *Andragogy in Action.* San Francisco, CA: Jossey-Bass.

Spieler, D. H., & Balota, D. A. (1996). Characteristics of associative learning in younger and older adults: Evidence from an episodic priming paradigm. *Psychology And Aging, 11*(4), 607–620. doi:10.1037/0882-7974.11.4.607

ACKNOWLEDGMENTS

The authors wish to gratefully acknowledge the support and encouragement by Kendall Hunt for this book, especially Paul Carty and Angela Willenbring. We would also like to thank and acknowledge the hard work and help of graduate assistant Rebecca Bubp.

Many people have helped and supported us while we worked on this book. Christine Davis acknowledges the memory of Horace Kelly and of Buddy Goodall, who both taught me and mentored me to be a much better researcher. I also want to express gratitude for Carolyn Ellis, Art Bochner, and Ken Cissna, who also mentored and supported me as a scholar. I also must mention the help and encouragement given to me by my husband, Jerry, without whose love and support I would never have achieved anything of significance; and colleagues Deb Breede, Jon Crane, Dan Grano, Shawn Long, and Maggie Quinlan, whose support was especially invaluable to me while I was writing this book. I also want to thank my co-author Ken Lachlan and our contributor Robert Westerfelhaus, both of whom have always been delightful collaborators.

Ken Lachlan would like to thank his graduate school mentors, Bradley S. Greenberg, Chuck Atkin, Stacy Smith, and in particular Ron Tamborini. I would also like to thank Patric Spence for his friendship and collaboration, and thank our frequent collaborators Jennifer Burke, Nick Bowman, Autumn Edwards, Chad Edwards, Donyale Griffin, Xialing Lin, J. J. McIntyre, Lin Nelson, Matt Seeger, Tim Sellnow, Ashleigh Shelton, Stephen Spates, and David Westerman. Finally I extend my deepest thanks to my wife, Heather Gallant-Lachlan. Words cannot adequately express my gratitude for her ongoing love, support, patience, and encouragement.

ABOUT THE AUTHORS

Christine Davis is Professor at the University of North Carolina at Charlotte. Her area of academic expertise is in Communication Studies, specializing in the intersection of family, culture, and health communication. Dr. Davis publishes regularly on topics such as children's health, end-of-life communication, disability, and qualitative research methods. Her preferred methodologies are autoethnography, narrative, and critical ethnography. She has over 30 years of research and corporate consulting experience, including as owner of a national marketing research firm and executive director of a nonprofit for older adults. She obtained all three of her degrees in Communication Studies. Her BA is from Virginia Polytechnic Institute and State University (more commonly known as Virginia Tech), her M.A. is from the University of North Carolina–Greensboro, and her Ph.D. is from the University of South Florida. Christine has a loving husband, a wonderful daughter and son-in-law, the most adorable grandson ever, and an awesome Sheltie named Maggie. In addition to conducting research and teaching, she loves to sail, hike, jog, and swim.

Ken Lachlan is Associate Professor at the Department of Communication at the University of Connecticut. Prior to his academic career, he worked in public radio and television promotions for several years. His research interests include the psychological effects of mass media, health and risk communication, social robotics, and new media technologies. Recent publications have appeared in the *Computers in Human Behavior, Media Psychology*, and the *Journal of Applied Communication Research*, to name a few. Ken considers himself mostly a quantitative scholar, preferring experimental and survey methodologies in investigating his areas of interest. He has also served as a consultant statistician for various companies and government agencies. He holds a dual B.A. in Communication and Sociology from Wake Forest, an M.A. in Mass Communication from Bowling Green State University, and a Ph.D. in Communication from Michigan State. An avid jogger and diehard hockey fan, Ken lives in Hartford, CT with his wife and their cat.

Robert Westerfelhaus, contributor, is a professor in the Department of Communication at the College of Charleston (South Carolina, USA). He received his Ph.D. and M.A. from Ohio University, and earned his B.A. from Ohio Dominican University (ODU). He has published numerous articles, book chapters, and encyclopedia entries regarding the mythic and ritual elements shaping American popular culture, examining how these elements reflect, inform, and perpetuate culturally constructed depictions of ethnicity, gender, race, religion, sexual orientation, and socio-economic class. In 2009–2010, he was a Fulbright Fellow at the Instytut Anglistyki of the Uniwersytet Marii Curie-Sklodowskiej in Lublin, Poland.

INTRODUCTION TO COMMUNICATION RESEARCH

PART **1**

WHAT IS COMMUNICATION RESEARCH?

1

CHAPTER OUTLINE

KEY TERMS

A priori

Authority

Communication researchers

Epistemology

Experience

Health communication scholars

Hypotheses

Interpersonal communication

Media research

Organizational communication

Research

Scientific reasoning

Social research

Tenacity

Theory

CHAPTER OBJECTIVES

1. To introduce the concept of communication research
2. To explain the ways of thinking behind communication research
3. To explain what exactly it is that communication researchers do
4. To give examples of communication research

▼   ### What Will You Do with the Information You Learn in this Course?

Imagine you're in your first job after college, a Research Assistant for an advertising and marketing research company. You've been working there for about six months, and one day you find yourself standing in front of a room of corporate executives. Your company has conducted advertising testing for its products, and the executives are waiting anxiously to hear you discuss the results. The information you're about to give them will help them make some major corporate decisions: Should they keep the same advertising agency or hire another? Should they change their marketing slogan or continue using the same one they've been using? Should they change the language or images in their ad? And, finally, they want an answer to their most important question: Does their advertising really make a difference in their product sales? This is the day you've been waiting for. You've been training for this presentation for years. You took Public Speaking as a college freshman, and you feel confident as you prepare to begin your presentation. You took Research Methods, and you know how to explain and justify the methods your company undertook to test the advertising. You also took Communication Theory, Persuasion, Mass Media, and Public Relations in college, and you understand the theories that explain why the consumers reacted the way they did to the advertising. You understand the importance of this presentation—the corporate executives will make million-dollar advertising decisions based on your presentation. This is not simply a made-up scenario—one of your book's authors (Christine Davis) actually faced this situation in her first job out of college.

> *I had no idea when I graduated from college with an undergraduate degree in Communication Studies that I would end up taking a job as a market researcher. I just wanted a job that would let me use what I had learned in my major—communication—the conveyance of symbols and information from one party to another in order to elicit a particular response. When I took my* **Communication Research** *Methods course as an undergraduate, I didn't realize how much I would end up using what I'd learned in my career. Yet, my Communication Research Methods course got me my first job and my first career.*

communication researchers
Scholars and professionals who study communication.

It might get you your first job, too, or it might be responsible for your first promotion or a pat on the back from your boss. You might, for example, get a job with an Internet consulting company and be asked to study the ways people deceive others when using e-mail and Facebook. You might end up working for a political candidate, helping him or her understand the rhetorical strategies used by political pundits in advancing his or her agendas. You might work for a public relations company using information on the ways people may respond to accidents and public crises by turning to different news outlets under different conditions. You might be hired by a major television network and use research about the declining ratings of reality programming and to understand what this might mean for the television industry. You might be hired by a retailer to head up their social media efforts.

Some of your classmates might decide they want to use their knowledge of communication research methods to change the world for the better. They might join a social marketing firm and use research findings to develop campaigns to convince students to practice safe sex or make more healthful lifestyle choices. They might get a job working for a health department in which they study or use different intervention strategies and effective ways of convincing people to get tested for HIV infection. They might work for a research think tank and focus on communication with, and understanding of, people from different cultures or with different needs than their own.

Communication, as a field, is exceptionally diverse. Those who dedicate their careers to either researching or using research on the conveyance of meaning do so in a number of ways. Some use surveys to measure opinions and behavior. Some conduct experiments using human participants, examining people's attitudes and opinions before and after receiving messages. Others conduct long interviews and look for themes that may emerge from people's responses, or they may immerse themselves in certain social interactions as participant-observers. Some conduct focus groups to listen to consumers deliberate about a product launch.

Still others are more interested in what the information looks like, as opposed to how people will respond. They may try to systematically analyze the content of a particular program, genre, or network. They may try to identify certain rhetorical devices and argumentation strategies to figure out *how* influence may occur. They may even be more concerned with the underlying biases and issues of power that make information look a certain way.

There are literally dozens of approaches to the study of communication as a discipline. While communication researchers often engage in spirited academic debate about the pros and cons of looking at things in different ways, there is really no right or wrong approach. Rather, the prevailing wisdom in our field is that different approaches to communication research are appropriate for different research questions.

What Is Research?

Research

Research is the activity of conducting intellectual investigations into the observable world. Researchers are generally concerned with discovering and investigating the means by which things work, in order to advance human knowledge with the goal of better understanding our world. Generally speaking, research involves

research
The activity of conducting intellectual investigations into the observable world.

the asking and answering of questions. These questions may be derived from observations of the world, a lack of understanding of observed phenomena, or the questioning of previously held assumptions about the ways in which something may work. Research is often driven by a desire to improve the human condition, as one of its fundamental motivations is the assumption that more and better knowledge can only serve to help humanity.

Very often, when we think of research, our minds first turn to research in the natural sciences. As a matter of fact, when we say research, your mind might go back to your eighth-grade Science Fair project. You can probably think of dozens of examples of research in physics, chemistry, biology, and engineering that have served to advance human knowledge. For example, in recent years, much attention (and controversy) has surrounded research concerning the viability of using human stem cells to cure a wide array of physical ailments. Advances in biomedical research have extended the life expectancies associated with certain types of cancers, while early twentieth century research in inoculations for childhood diseases has dramatically reduced infant mortality rates in the Western world. Research in engineering has helped make our automobiles, planes, and working environments far safer than they were fifty years ago and has allowed people with disabilities to live lives that were inconceivable a decade ago. Computer science research has allowed us to carry cell phones that are more powerful than computers that took up entire buildings during the 1970s. The list goes on and on.

Communication as Social Research

social research
This research focuses less on the observable world in which human beings interact, and more on the interactions themselves, how they come into existence, how they function, and how they affect the human experience. Research in communication, psychology, sociology, economics, political science, and anthropology are typically classified as social research.

Perhaps less well known is the process of **social research**. Social researchers are more concerned with human interactions and the ways in which human beings make sense of their world. This research focuses less on the observable world in which human beings interact, and more on the interactions themselves, how they come into existence, how they function, and how they affect the human experience. Research in psychology, sociology, economics, political science, and anthropology are typically classified as social research.

Communication research can also be classified as social research. Communication researchers study parts of the observable world as it interacts with us—symbol-producing and symbol-using humans. We study the ways in which human beings use information and symbols to create meaning among ourselves. This process will be discussed at great length throughout this text, but in basic terms, social science communication researchers often attempt to solve problems and answer questions associated with the exchange of information between human beings.

Communication as Humanities Research

Many communication researchers conduct research that could be classified as research in the humanities, rather than a social science. Rather than looking at how we exchange information per se, communication humanities scholars tend to look at how we co-construct meaning through communication. Performance studies scholars, for example, create and present performances that exemplify societal or interactional phenomena to help both themselves and their audiences understand the communication phenomena at a deep level. Other communication scholars use novelistic elements to write narratives that pull the reader into the story and evoke meaning and understanding. Others use poetry, art, or music to more deeply understand a communication act or culture.

Communication as Critical or Cultural Research

There are other scholars in the field of communication studies who look at the construction, use, and abuse of power and control in a culture, situation, organization, or community. They might look at how communication perpetuates or reifies power, or how communication is used by marginalized groups to resist power by dominant groups in a society. Other scholars might study how communication creates identity within a culture, or how cultures use communication to construct meaning.

How Is Research Knowledge Distributed? ▼

Academic Publishing

Of course, answering these questions is not a particularly useful endeavor if no one knows about it. In both the natural sciences and in social research, the most common way of distributing the answers to the questions asked by researchers is through academic publishing. As you will see in Chapter 3, there are a number of scholarly journals in the field of communication that provide an outlet for the distribution of these findings. Communication scholars often publish books and volumes of selected studies that report the findings of their research. They are also known to publish their work in journals and volumes outside the field, or in collaboration with scholars from other disciplines. Communication scholars frequently publish alongside psychologists, sociologists, management scholars, and public health researchers, just to name a few.

One common misconception surrounding academic publishing is the notion of the ivory tower. People often think that social researchers, such as communication scholars, sit around mulling over grand ideas that have little bearing on the real world. Many people would also say no one outside of academia reads scholarly research, or places much value in its findings and conclusions.

Social Dialogue and Public Policy

Nothing could be further from the truth. Social researchers and communication scholars, in particular, have a long history of contributing to social dialogue on the relevant issues of the day. Government agencies, policymakers, and businesses frequently look to research published in academic journals to inform their decision making.

Take this example: A hotly contested social issue is the unrealistic portrayal of body image on television. Public health officials, psychologists, and communication researchers have become increasingly concerned with the abundance of dangerously thin people in mainstream media, and in particular, what impact this may have on self-esteem and eating disorders among adolescents. Further, they have become concerned with the ways in which television may influence our perceptions of people of varying sizes and how this may contribute to various forms of stereotyping. In 1999, a team of communication researchers led by Bradley S. Greenberg decided to examine television characters in terms of both their body sizes and the ways in which they were portrayed. Generally speaking, they found that a little less than a third of the women on television can be classified as dangerously underweight, while larger characters on television are often ridiculed or presented in other unflattering ways.

The article was presented at an academic convention in Quebec and was eventually published in the *American Journal of Public Health* (Greenberg, Eastin, Hofshire, Lachlan, & Brownell, 2003). However, realizing that there may be a wider market that could use this information, Greenberg's research team created a press release and distributed it to varying media outlets. This press release caught the attention of *USA Today*, which promptly ran a story on the findings. Thus the findings of the study were made available not just to other scholars interested in the subject matter, but to the general public, policymakers, parents, and activists.

There are numerous other examples of communication research being disseminated not only to those in academic circles, but also to the general public and to those in positions of authority. Communication researchers have even *testified before Congress* regarding the implications of their findings. Notably, a large number of communication researchers played a pivotal role in the 1972 Surgeon General's Commission Report (U. S. Surgeon General's Scientific Advisory Committee on Television and Social Behavior, 1972), on television violence and aggressive behavior. Communication researchers have presented testimonies on the influence and impact of alcohol advertising on young consumers, tobacco advertising, violence in video games, sexual television content, and numerous others.

Here's another, very different example. The May 26, 2009, edition of the *Charlotte Observer* reported on a play put on by a writing company, a university professor, and staff and residents of a residential maternity home. The play, performed for the public, depicts—through the use of drama and performance—stories and experiences of the home's clients—pregnant women, children in foster care, and at-risk adolescents. The purpose of the play is to inspire empathy (Toppman, 2009, p. 5D), and it's a great example of performance studies being used for social dialogue.

Communication in the Popular Press

Communication scholars often release the results of their academic work to the popular press in hopes that it will draw the attention of those in business and government. Our field even has an online publication—*Communication Currents*—that makes recent communication research accessible to the general public. You can access this publication at: http://www.natcom.org/CommunicationCurrents/. A recent issue reported on negative body talk, communication opposing genetically modified food, online dating, and a documentary about reconciliation and hope following the Rwandan genocide.

Other communication scholars have published books based on their research that made their way to the popular press. H. L. Goodall, for example, conducted an autoethnographic exploration of his father's work for the CIA and published a novel titled *A Need to Know: The Clandestine History of a CIA Family* (Goodall, 2006).

How Do We Know What We Know?

▼

Where Does Knowledge Come From?

Of course, in order to answer these and other questions, we are forced to confront difficult issues concerning knowledge itself. These aren't likely to be questions that you ask yourself every day. Most of us, communication researchers included, go through our everyday lives with a fairly comfortable understanding of what is and what is not. Our view of the world may come from a variety of sources, and we generally don't stop to think about what those sources may be. We certainly don't often stop to ask ourselves the question: Where does knowledge come from?

The study of knowledge itself is known as **epistemology** (Babbie, 1995). Before examining communication research, the questions it asks, and methods of exploring those questions, it may be helpful to think about different ways of understanding what it is that we know to be true. This serves to illustrate both how we make sense of our world, and how scholarly inquiry into communication and other social phenomena may deviate from these means of gathering knowledge. The philosopher Charles Peirce identified four methods of knowing: tenacity, authority, a priori, and science (Buchler, 1955). We'll discuss these plus a few others—personal experience; traditions, customs, and faith; magic, superstition, and/or mysticism; and intuition or hunches.

epistemology
The study of knowledge.

We should begin to learn about knowledge building by considering how it is we come to know something in our everyday life. Much communication research is dedicated to things that we see in our everyday lives, the functionality of everyday interactions, and ways in which we make sense of the world around us. In fact, if we think about it for a minute, there are countless examples of everyday behaviors that can be informed by communication research.

When you go home after class, there is a good chance you turn on the television. Why do you watch what you watch? There are entire programs of communication research dedicated to uncovering the motives for your media consumption. Maybe you have very general reasons for selecting certain programs, like desiring entertainment or needing a score in the big game. Maybe there are far more specific reasons, like needing to relax when you are stressed or excitement when you are bored. Communication research can answer this question.

Maybe you are walking across campus one day, and someone approaches you and asks if you would like to buy some raffle tickets for a local charity. While you don't mind helping a good cause, you realize that before you knew it your wallet was out and you were handing over cash. How was this person so convincing? Why were you so willing to comply?

You get into an argument with your significant other. You don't feel that he is spending enough time with you, while he thinks he is doing the right thing by not trying to smother you or monopolize your time. How did this disconnect take place? How can two people in a relationship see that relationship so differently?

Let's say you go to your doctor for your annual checkup. There is nothing to worry about, you are in perfect health, and everything is fine. But for some reason you walk away with a strange feeling. You have been going to this doctor for years, but you feel as though she was completely unsympathetic to your questions and barely knows who you are. Why do you not feel as though you and your doctor are on the same page?

Perhaps you are at work and your boss is being very demanding. Your boss constantly rides you about how you need to spend more hours at your job and how you don't seem particularly dedicated to it. You don't understand because you think you take your job seriously and do it well. Then you find out that your boss's supervisor has been criticizing him about his performance. Why is your boss taking it out on you? And why didn't you know that people further up the ladder had concerns about your boss's performance?

While communication research can help inform issues of policy, activism, and government, it is also very useful in understanding our everyday interactions and in helping us make sense of the world. These are only a few examples of real-life questions that can be informed by communication research. Almost every interaction you can possibly have—be it with mediated information or in a face-to-face setting—can be informed by the study of the conveyance of meaning.

experience
A common way of understanding the social world.

Experience. One of our best teachers is often personal **experience**. Many of us learn much of understanding of the social world by experiencing. The easiest example of this type of knowledge conforms to the adage that sometimes we have to learn the hard way. Touching a hot stove with your hand is a pretty good teacher. Not many experiences with a hot stove are necessary before you have complete knowledge of what will happen if you touch another hot item. Our experience with people is no different. We may have had previous experiences with specific people, similar people, or situations that we can then use as a guide to anticipate and interpret a new experience and/or situation. This is known as generalizing and it is an important aim for some scientific research. The value of this type of knowing is that it can be a fruitful beginning upon which we build to gain knowledge.

Tenacity. Think of some things about the world that everybody knows. For example, "everybody knows" that if you toss a coin off the Empire State Building, it will kill whomever it lands upon. Likewise, "everybody knows" that a dog's mouth is actually cleaner than a human's; bad guys in the Old West always wore black hats; and when you cross the equator, toilets begin flushing in the opposite direction.

There is just one problem with all of these statements: None of them are true. A coin tossed off a skyscraper does not have enough mass, relative to resistance from the air below it, to accelerate to a speed that could kill someone. Think about how you bathe and how your dog bathes. Lawmen and outlaws in the Old West wore hats that came in a variety of colors. Toilets will flush in the direction that water enters them (usually counterclockwise), whether they are in New York or Melbourne. So how, then, do statements such as those above become accepted as "facts"?

tenacity
The assumption that something is true because it has always been said to be true.

Part of the reason may be our tendency to rely on **tenacity** as a method of knowing. Tenacity is simply the assumption that something is true because it always has been said to be true. Knowledge is passed from person to person and generation to generation through cultural norms and assumptions. You may believe that the sun rises in the morning because the sun god Ra wills it so; if you do, chances are it's because that's what your parents, grandparents, and great-grandparents believed. Furthermore, consensus plays a critical role in tenacity as a source of knowledge: the frequent repetition of these so-called facts makes them seem more likely to be true (Kerlinger, 1992). Even in the face of conflicting information, people will hold onto their beliefs and rationalize away evidence that flies in the face of what they already hold to be true.

Of course, tenacity is not inherently bad as a means of knowing. It comes in handy in a variety of different scenarios, mostly because, as humans, we don't have the time or energy to consider all possible explanations for every observation we ever make. And very often, it provides us with knowledge that is useful and accurate. We don't really need to formally test the notion that stepping out in front of traffic is a bad idea, or that it is more likely to rain if it is cloudy outside, or that your lawn will grow if you water it. These are things that most of us have always accepted as being true, have heard repeated over and over, and for the most part are correct.

Authority.   Another important instructor in everyday knowledge is **authority**. Authority is when we turn to experts to help us make sense out of a particular situation. Authority has less to do with the repetition of information and more to do with the perceived credibility of the source of that information. Very often, people realize they are not experts on a given subject, to the extent that they may not even be able to comprehend or make sense of their observations. In these instances, they often rely on someone in a position of power to tell them what is factual. This power may be derived from a variety of places, such as expertise, political power, religious authority, or interpersonal trust.

Consider this common example. Many people, including this author (Ken), have a geek. This is the person they go to for information about anything having to do with computers, software, or technology. This person may have been assembling and disassembling computers since he was a child, or he may be more of a programmer type who enjoys cracking the source code on various software applications. In any case, this person can probably tell you how to turn on the computer, as this will be child's play given their level of expertise. This person could tell you practically anything, and you would assume it to be true (at least until you try it out, and even then you might assume that you are not following his or her instructions correctly, since he or she, after all, is the expert).

Advertisements using celebrity spokespersons are good examples of how authority guides our knowledge building. If Michael Jordan tells us to purchase Hanes underwear, then we think we should since we have trust in him. After all, Michael wouldn't lie to us, would he? Authority only works as a source of knowledge if I have faith in the authority figure or she has some control over me. For example, one of your authors once served on a jury. One of the experts brought in to testify in the case was a drug specialist for the state of North Carolina. Her job was to explain to us the laboratory tests conducted on the white substance found in the defendant's car and convince us that it was, in fact, crack cocaine. Due to her experience, her education, and the way in which she

authority
The reliance upon someone in a position of power to determine what is factual. This power may be derived from a variety of places, such as expertise, political power, religious authority, or interpersonal trust.

presented herself, the jury never debated over whether the substance was actually crack cocaine. Her authority created knowledge for us.

Consider another example: Most of us have experienced our parents' authority, and you can probably remember how smart your parents were when you were a small child and how stupid they became when you reached adolescence! If they haven't already, they'll become much smarter in your eyes as you move through college and into adulthood. You probably believed your parents' authority when they told you that vegetables were good for your health, and you might someday use your mom's advice for making stock market picks!

Authority has value, if we believe the authority to be reliable, because it saves us time from having to find out everything for ourselves. What's the downside of relying on information from an authority without checking it out for ourselves? Authorities are sometimes wrong, or they may have biased information or opinions. I (Christine) once worked as executive director for a nonprofit organization that served older adults. One of our older adult volunteers asked me how to do something, and I gave her instructions. Several hours later, it became apparent that my instructions were wrong, and she commented, "That didn't sound right when you told me!" I asked her, "Then why in the world didn't you question me?" and she replied, "You sounded so sure of yourself when you told me!" What she didn't understand was that I'm a communication expert and I'm trained to sound confident, even when I'm clearly wrong! Her mistake was relying on my perceived authority.

Traditions, Customs, and Faith. Traditions, customs, and faith are also great teachers. **Health communication scholars** are experts at understanding the role that traditions, customs, and faith play in communicating health information. A perfect example is the adage "an apple a day keeps the doctor away." An adage is a type of tradition, and while we all know eating one apple a day really will not ensure our not getting sick, we also know that eating a healthy diet, including fruits, does increase the likelihood of living a healthy life.

health communication scholars
Communication scholars who look at the interpersonal exchanges between doctors and patients, public health campaigns, the flow of information in public health organizations, and other health issues.

Think about the things you've come to know by the traditions your family followed and the knowledge passed down from one generation to the next. Take the tradition of the Easter basket. In a recent conversation with another mother, who is a friend of one of your authors, we were discussing Easter baskets for our daughters. She detailed her search for just the right basket this year, as she couldn't reuse last year's basket, or her daughter might catch on. I responded that at our house the Easter bunny uses the basket that we already have, which I place out in the house for decoration during the Easter season. What our daughters know about the Easter bunny is based upon the traditions each family follows. Her daughter is convinced the Easter bunny is wealthy, while my daughter knows that the Easter bunny is concerned with the environment! Another great example comes from the same friend. She grew up in the South during the 1960s and 1970s and loved Pepsi. It was a treat not often allowed in her youth. Because her family expected each child to drink a glass of milk with each meal, Dianne would guzzle down her glass of milk, hoping for a chance to have her cherished beverage. However, Dianne's mother explained to her that drinking Pepsi after milk would upset her stomach and cause her to be sick. It was not until she was away at college that Dianne realized she had been duped. This demonstrates how we know or believe things to be true because we've been told or taught by others to believe them early in life. While the latter examples may not ring true, many customs, such as eating an apple a day, are based upon solid evidence.

Magic, Superstition, and/or Mysticism.

Another way we believe we know is through magic, superstition, and/or mysticism. When you study for an exam, are you superstitious? Do you have a lucky item of clothing, a particular feeling about some numbers, a routine that if deviated from undermines your confidence? If so, then you already have a clear understanding of how we can come to know something through magic, superstition, and/or mysticism. Some of us have been known to change clothes during a Panthers football game, as it seems that some t-shirts are luckier than others, and we know that what we wear influences how our team performs! How many of you know your sign and read your horoscope, swearing it is accurate? No, we are not here to argue about its accuracy, rather to point out that we like to believe we gain knowledge of the world around us through these particular mechanisms. We experience some things that are unexplainable; we often attribute these things to mystery. If we struggle to find a clear understanding, we often chalk it up to magic, mysticism, or superstition. The value of this method of knowledge is that, in fact, there are some things we cannot know scientifically.

Intuition or Hunches.

Most of us also have some form of knowledge we believe is based upon intuition. Intuition is that feeling we get that we often call our *gut feeling*. It is some internal-based instinct we have about a situation, issue, or experience. It is not unusual for us to accept certain things as true, just because they make sense. Some people see intuition as a "leap of insight." Again, intuition can produce useful ideas, but since we are unable to explain why, it can be difficult to investigate.

A Priori Reasoning.

The **a priori** way of knowing has its roots in early philosophers contemplating epistemology, such as Immanuel Kant. A priori knowledge refers to ways of knowing that are independent of empirical observation, that are known through personal reasoning or judgment.

For lack of a better way of putting it, a priori reasoning is based on logic, or the fact that there are some things you just simply know to be true. Based on universal truths, you might know something is true even if you haven't tested it.

For example, let's say you are trying to move an enormous couch into your apartment. It weighs about 300 pounds, and you and your roommate have been trying to get it up a stairwell for half an hour. It isn't working. You look over and see a large freight elevator. A priori knowledge tells you that using the elevator to move the couch will greatly increase your success. You don't have to test the hypothesis or conduct an engineering test of the elevator—it's a universal truth that elevators reduce effort.

Of course, it's possible that the elevator is broken. This illustrates the major shortcoming of a priori reasoning: exceptions to logic. While accumulated experience in related matters may lead to an assumption about a specific experience, there is always the possibility that this particular scenario deviates from past experiences.

a priori
This form of reasoning is based on personal reasoning or logic, or the fact that there are some things you just simply know to be true.

▼ What's Wrong with Everyday Ways of Knowing?

While the everyday ways of knowing we have detailed above do provide a starting point for building knowledge, there are numerous problems inherent in these ways of knowing. People tend to place more trust in their beliefs from personal experience than from evidence that may be contrary to their own experience. We must consider some of these problems with everyday ways of knowing.

Accuracy

First, all in all, the majority of us are not very accurate at making observations. We tend to be pretty casual observers. Think back for a minute to the last person you saw before reading this textbook. Who was that person? What was he or she wearing? What kind of shoes? Do you remember the details? Most of us do not.

Overgeneralization

Another problem with our everyday ways of knowing is overgeneralization. As individuals, we prefer our world to be orderly and, as such, we tend to generalize our knowledge to a broader reach. This can be problematic when we base this knowledge on just a few experiences or observations. For example, we might generalize that people with college degrees are less likely to get divorced. However, what if our experience is atypical? We need to be cautious when it comes to generalizing based on limited data in any form.

Cognitive Conservatism

Yet another difficulty with everyday knowing is that, once we believe something, we tend to pay special attention to experiences and situations that are consistent with our beliefs, and disregard those that are inconsistent with our beliefs. This is called **cognitive conservatism**, the idea that how we view the world is often based upon our prior beliefs. Allport and Postman (1945) conducted a series of studies that demonstrate how cognitive conservatism works. In this research, they played a game called "Rumor," where a message is given to the first person who then must whisper in his or her neighbor's ear, each in turn, until the message is shared aloud by the last participant. For their study on racial prejudice, they showed white subjects a picture of a fight between a white man and a black man on a train. The white man was holding a razor to the black man in the picture. What do you suppose participants experienced? Yes, that's right; the razor typically changed hands. Allport and Postman noted information that does not fit the predisposition of a perceiver is likely to be forgotten or changed in memory.

cognitive conservatism *The idea that how someone views the world is often based upon his or her prior beliefs.*

Contradictory Knowledge

Everyday ways of knowing can lead to contradictions in what we know. For example, if you've ever been in a long-distance relationship, you've likely heard the expression "absence makes the heart grow fonder," and that makes logical sense. However, you might have also experienced the effects of "if you can't be with the one you love, love the one you're with." So you know that both could be true. Your parents or other authorities (including your friends) might have given you advice on one side or the other about that reality, and they could probably cite everyday evidence to support each claim.

Scientific Reasoning

▼

This leads us to the final way of knowing, identified by Charles Pierce and cited by Buchler (1955): science. The scientific method attempts to address the problems with these everyday ways of knowing. **Scientific reasoning** begins with a priori assumptions, but goes a step further—it includes *self-correction* (Kerlinger, 1992). Under the method of science, one has an idea about how things ought to be, then tests this by making observations. As you will see in Chapter 6, these ideas are often called **hypotheses,** or educated guesses, about a social phenomenon based on prior observations. Scientists propose hypotheses and then make observations in order to test them.

scientific reasoning
A way of knowing where one has a hunch about how things ought to be, then tests that hunch by making observations.

hypotheses
Educated guesses about a social phenomenon based on prior observations.

One major misconception of science as a way of knowing is that science *proves* things. Scientific reasoning by its very nature is skeptical, and scientists don't make claims about the truth in black-and-white terms. Rather, scientists are more likely to talk about *probability* and confidence in their conclusions. They discuss their conclusions in terms of the likelihood of their explanations and observations being true. In fact, the process of scientific reasoning is largely concerned with the *disproving* of a priori statements, as opposed to looking for ways of finding out that they are correct (which we will discuss in further detail in Chapters 10 through 13). Scientists start from a position of skepticism, assuming their hunches to be wrong, and evaluate their observations in terms of how they may refute or fail to refute their hypotheses. They then repeat their procedures in order to build more confidence in these conclusions. In order to do so, science must remain objective, without the biases, values, or attitudes of the scientist interfering with the interpretation of this data.

The most useful advantage to scientific thinking is the ability to *predict.* Of course, science can be as a cumbersome way of understanding our everyday experiences. Using our example earlier, if you are lugging a couch up a stairwell, you don't have time to conduct a series of tests to determine the best course of action; you just need to move the couch. If your hard drive crashes, you probably don't want to conduct a series of tests of different procedures that may fix the problem; you just want it fixed immediately! If a conclusion drawn from tenacity or authority accomplishes this task, then so be it.

Science is, however, very useful in the understanding of more complex social phenomena such as communication. The repeated testing of hypotheses in an academic or applied research environment or an in-depth exploration to understand a phenomenon on a detailed description of a communication act may lead to the basic goal of science: the development of **theory.** Accumulating these statements over time may lead to the formation of a theory, otherwise known as "a set of interrelated constructs, definitions, and propositions that present a

theory
A set of interrelated constructs, definitions, and propositions that present a systematic view of phenomena by specifying relations among variables, with the purpose of explaining and predicting the phenomena.

systematic view of phenomena by specifying relations among variables, with the purpose of explaining and predicting the phenomena" (Kerlinger, 1992, p. 9). In plain terms, this is to say that systematically seeking to answer questions and understand phenomena can lead to useful heuristics (techniques to answer questions and address problems) and allow us to make informed predictions and understandings about social behavior under different circumstances. Theoretical work derived from academic research can then serve to inform everyday problems and issues.

▼ What Do Communication Researchers Do?

What Specific Areas Do Communication Researchers Study?

Now that we have established an epistemological framework for the systematic study of communication, let us turn our attention to some of the more specific subject areas that communication researchers study. The following pages will detail some of the phenomena that communication researchers address using assumptions and techniques derived from a scientific or humanistic approach to the study of human interactions.

As stated earlier, communication as a discipline deals fundamentally with the use of symbols and information to convey meaning to others. The conveyance of meaning can exist in several contexts. For example, communication researchers may be concerned with the impact of mediated information—transmitted through media channels such as film, television, and the Internet—on public opinion, attitudes, and behaviors. Others may be more concerned with communication in interpersonal contexts, such as face-to-face interactions, conversations between family members, or those in romantic relationships. Still others may study the ways in which information is transmitted through different levels of organizations and businesses.

Scholarly Research

scholarly research
Primary research conducted by academic researchers and distributed through academic publications with the desire to build theory.

Generally speaking, communication researchers draw a distinction between *scholarly research* and *applied research*. When we speak of **scholarly research**, this usually refers to primary research conducted by communication professors and academics and distributed through academic publications. As stated above, scholarly research is often driven by the desire to build or explain *theory*. Those conducting scholarly research are typically concerned with the theoretical implications of their findings and building or contributing to theories.

Let's take one well-known example of the development of a theory that is widely used in both communication and psychology research: the Theory of Reasoned Action (Ajzen & Fishbein, 1980). Frustrated with past research in persuasion, Ajzen and Fishbein began conducting a series of experiments during the 1970s and 1980s looking at other things they thought might be important in the process of compliance. Through numerous studies, they came to the conclusion that while there is a link between attitude change and actual behaviors, there are other things that are important as well. Most notably, they identified people's intentions as a critical factor that had been overlooked. The Theory of Reasoned Action argues (to put it in the simplest terms possible) that attitudes don't directly affect people's behavior; they affect people's intentions to behave in a certain way, which then may or may not result in a change of behavior.

For example, a commercial advocating that people stop smoking might be effective in changing a person's attitude toward smoking (e.g., "Okay, now we see that smoking is a bad idea"), but this does not necessarily mean she will quit. Instead, the Theory of Reasoned Action would argue that not only does she have to realize that it is a bad idea, but also actually *decide* that she is going to quit before doing so. Of course, there are a number of reasons why things might break down; the person in question may or may not actually decide to quit, and then may or may not actually do it.

Still, something was missing. Adding a person's intentions into the equation did a better job of explaining persuasion, but did not explain it completely. As Ajzen and Fishbein continued these experiments throughout the 1980s and 1990s, they came to the conclusion that an important consideration might be people's belief that they could actually get it done. They (and others) have called this "behavioral control." In fact, they found that attitudes were more likely to drive intentions, and intentions were more likely to drive behavior, if people actually believed that they could successfully perform the behavior in question. To tie it in to our smoking example above, a person may experience a shift in her attitude toward smoking; this attitude shift is much more likely to lead her to attempting to quit if she *believes* that she can quit. Likewise, if she tries to quit, she is more likely to actually do so if she believes she can. The committed smoker, who has been doing it for years and years and has given up on the idea of ever quitting, may form an increasingly negative view of the habit, but she will not likely try to quit, and if she does try, she will likely fail.

By adding in a person's behavioral control to the theory, Ajzen and Fishbein modified their original theory and gave it a new title: Theory of Planned Behavior (TPB) (Ajzen, 1995). Through decades of fine tuning and adjustment, the results of their studies led to a well-informed and commonly applied theory that has been used to explain persuasion in a variety of contexts, including smoking, drinking, signing up for treatment programs, using contraceptives, dieting, wearing seatbelts or safety helmets, exercising regularly, voting, and breast-feeding (Fishbein, Middlestadt, & Hitchcock, 1994).

Applied Research

Fishbein and Ajzen's work has proved to be a major contribution to communication thinking. Developing their framework through scholarly research has helped inform not only theoretical development on the topic of persuasion, but also numerous studies evaluating the utility of the theory in real-world contexts.

Such research is often labeled *applied research*. Communication scholars, like other social, behavioral, and humanities researchers, will take the theoretical lessons learned in their academic studies and further apply them to varying real-life contexts. **Applied research** is typically concerned with investigating

applied research
Research that takes the theoretical lessons learned in academic studies and applies them to varying real-life contexts.

whether theoretical developments can be taken outside of the academic setting and used to solve more tangible social problems. While applied research can often be found in the same journals and texts as theoretical research, the goal of applied research is quite different—to test theory in the field to see if it can be used to solve problems.

Often, applied research addresses very specific concerns. For example, Roberto, Krieger, Katz, Goei, and Jain (2011) tested the Theory of Reasoned Action, as described above, to see if it could be applied to pediatricians' likelihood to encourage parents to get their daughters vaccinated for the HPV virus. After mailing out a survey measuring attitudes, norms, perceived control, intentions, and behaviors, the authors analyzed the links between these data points to see if TPB held in this context. They report that it did, and that positive attitudes toward the vaccine, subjective norms regarding its use, and perceptions of behavioral control all combined to predict the likelihood that the subjects would encourage parents to get their daughters the vaccine. Thus, the authors offered evidence that this theory was effective in explaining one highly specific, real-life problem.

Nothing as Practical as a Good Theory

Let's think about this a little further. Communication scholars and other social researchers are quick to draw a line between scholarly and applied research. Yet at the same time, applied research is defined as that which takes theoretical work and tests it in the field. We do this so that we can have more confidence in our theories, and also so that we may witness the contributions of theory in solving real-life problems.

Might it be the case that this distinction is not as stark as we make it out to be? Certainly, the theoretical insights offered by academic research can be useful in applied contexts. By the same token, if we test our theories in the field, and they do not work so well, then we need to refine them just as we would with results from a laboratory. Further, we frequently build theories from applied research; in fact, in the example above, Ajzen, Fishbein, and colleagues conducted research that could be classified as both scholarly and applied, using these criteria.

It really depends on how we piece together our studies. Sometimes we start with theories and then go out and test them. Other times we build our theories from a number of observations, without preexisting ideas of what might happen. But that is a discussion for Chapter 2.

· ·

What Are Some Examples of Communication Research?

Where Do Communication Researchers Study?

Now that we have talked a little bit about both theoretical and applied research, let's look at some examples of each across a wide range of communication subject areas. The examples below don't go into a great deal of detail, nor are they all-inclusive by any stretch, but a few examples of different research topics are presented to give you an idea of the range of subject matter in which communication researchers may be interested.

In Businesses and Organizations.

Organizational communication, as a subfield, is dedicated to studying the ways in which people exchange information in order to accomplish group or individual goals (Miller, 2005). The exchange of information in organizational contexts can take on a variety of different forms, including relationships between managers and subordinates, relationships with constituents outside the organization, different ways that organizations deal with crises and emergencies, and so on.

Here are a few examples of studies that illustrate the diversity of communication research in organizations. Coombs and Holladay (2004) developed a means of measuring how tolerant employees are of aggressive behavior in their organizations, hoping that this tool could be used to improve relationships between employees and managers. Daft and Lengel (1986) looked at the role of media richness in computer-mediated work teams, and the impact it would have on productivity. Sellnow, Seeger, and Ulmer (2002) examined emergency messages surrounding the 1999 Red River floods, arguing that these messages hindered the goals of those organizations responding to the crisis. Ehrlich and Shami (2010) explored the use of microblogs such as Twitter inside and outside the workplace as a form of information gathering within the workplace. James and Minnis (2004) looked at the role of organizational storytelling in corporate leadership. Stohl and Stohl (2005) examined communication networks associated with the founding of the United Nations and the Universal Declaration of Human Rights. Real and Putnam (2005) examined organization-employee relationships by looking at the message strategies of a group of airline pilots who went on strike. Mignerey, Rubin, and Gordon (2005) examined the processes through which new employees reduce uncertainty upon arriving in organizations and their exposure to organizational assimilation processes. Davis (2008) used an ethnographic method to look at the role of leadership in interorganizational peer-led teams. Organizational communication may include the study of individuals, organizational entities, groups, or messages themselves and how they serve to meet certain goals. Bochantin studies how employees and organizations use communication to manage work-family boundaries (see, for example, Bochantin & Cowan, 2016).

In Media.

Some communication researchers explore research questions and hypotheses related to the mass media. Again, these research questions can take on a variety of different forms. Much attention in the media literature has been paid to the influence of media messages on attitudes and behaviors, such as persuasion, aggressive behavior, attitudes toward sexuality, and political opinion. Other research has focused more on what it is that people choose to watch, and their motivations for seeking out different types of information that meet different needs. Other studies are more concerned with the *content* of media, analyzing the messages themselves to look for different types of messages that might be important.

Media research relies heavily on several different methods that will be discussed in this volume. It uses surveys, laboratory experiments, and content analysis to answer questions about our uses of and responses to mediated information. Whether the information in question is used for entertainment purposes,

organizational communication
This field of communication studies the ways in which people exchange information to accomplish organizational goals. The exchange of information in organizational contexts can take on a variety of different forms, including relationships between managers and subordinates, relationships with constituents outside the organization, different ways that organizations deal with crises and emergencies, and so on.

media research
This type of research uses surveys, laboratory experiments, and content analysis to answer questions about the uses of and responses to mediated information. It can be useful in understanding how humans convey meaning.

acquiring information, or facilitating social interactions, examining mediated information can be useful in understanding how humans convey meaning.

Katz, Blumler, and Gurevitch (1973), for example, conducted a long program of research exploring the reasons why people choose to use different types of media, select different channels, and what they get out of the experience on the whole. McCombs and Shaw (1972) explored the role media coverage plays in highlighting specific political issues that people consider when voting. Gerbner, Gross, Morgan, and Signorielli (1986) studied the ways in which heavy television viewers tended to believe that the real world looks like that on television, and in particular whether the presence of violence and policing on television made people more fearful; similarly, Lowry, Nio, and Leitner (2003) compared the extent of network crime reporting to FBI crime statistics, revealing a disconnect between people's fears and their actual likelihood of becoming a victim. The National Television Violence Study (Wilson et al., 1998) quantified not only the amount of violence on mainstream television, but also how often violence was presented in a way known to lead to aggression, fear, and desensitization among viewers. Dixon and Linz (2000) explored the underrepresentation of Latinos and African Americans in mainstream television. Raney (2002) examined the relationship between moral judgment and enjoyment of crime dramas. Nabi, Moyer-Guse, and Byrne (2007) explored the relationship between televised political humor and attitude change. Both Ledbetter et al. (2011) and Greenhow and Robelia (2009) have examined the way in which Facebook affects our communication. Ledbetter et al. (2011) found support for the idea that our self-disclosure and social connections were directly related to both our Facebook communication and relational closeness. Plotnick studies the relationship between humans and technology to understand the politics and meaning behind the taken-for-granted use of communication technologies (see, for example, Plotnick, 2015).

In Health Care. Communication researchers are increasingly turning their attention to the role of information exchange in the context of health care. This research also tackles a wide range of subject matters. Some health communication scholars look at the interpersonal exchanges between doctors and patients or how an illness or disability affects family communication. Others look at public health campaigns designed to encourage healthy behaviors or how our culture constructs ideas of health, wellness, and illness. Still, others look at the flow of information in public health organizations, just to name a few.

For example, a number of studies have looked at the ways in which people can be scared into engaging in healthy behaviors (like quitting smoking or practicing safe sex); these fear appeal studies, such as Dillard, Plotnick, Godbold, Freimuth, and Edgar (1996), have looked at the extent to which audiences can be scared into compliance and any unintended effects associated with this fear. Other campaign studies have looked at the effectiveness of health messages in very specific contexts, such as sun protection (Silk & Parrott, 2006), gun safety (Meyer, Roberto, & Atkin, 2003), or bicycle helmets (Witte, Stokols, Ituarte, & Schneider, 1993). Still other studies have examined the role communication plays in the experience of social support for cancer survivors as they return to their workplace (Yarker, Munir, Bains, Kalawsky, & Haslam, 2010). Laura Ellingson (2005) used ethnography to examine *backstage* communication in a health-care setting. Carolyn Ellis used a technique called *autoethnography* to examine her relationship with her colleague and husband Gene Weinstein as he died from emphysema (1995). Christine Davis co-constructed a narrative with her sister Kathy Salkin (Davis & Salkin, 2005) to describe and explain the experience of being and having a sibling with a disability. Davis and Crane (2015) examined horror films to understand how they construct cultural ideas about the end of life.

In Interpersonal Interactions.

Perhaps the most diverse subset of communication research is research in interpersonal exchanges. The exchange of information in face-to-face settings has fascinated communication scholars for nearly a century. Along the way, interpersonal scholars have developed areas of study too numerous to cover in their entirety. However, there are a few major areas of focus that should be mentioned.

A large body of **interpersonal communication** research has been devoted to the study of compliance gaining and social influence, or of persuading people to adopt certain attitudes or behaviors. Relational scholars have looked at the dynamic and exchange of information between those in romantic relationships or members of families; Burleson and MacGeorge (2002), for example, explored the ways in which people in relationships effectively provide social support during difficult times. Segrin, Woszidlo, Givertz, Bauer, and Murphy (2012) examined the role "helicopter parenting" has on parent child communication and the relationship between overparenting and adaptability and entitlement attitudes in adult children. They found that lower quality parent-child communication is associated with overparenting and that this was a significant predictor of adult children's sense of entitlement. Powell (2011) explored the dissolution of her marriage through a retrospective analysis of letters she wrote to her husband.

Deception scholars have long studied the use of both verbal and nonverbal cues to indicate when someone is lying. In a study conducted by Dunleavy, Chory, and Goodboy (2010), they found that liars who withhold information rather than distort it are perceived as being more competent and of higher character within the workplace, while coworkers perceived as having the highest character and being most trustworthy are colleagues who told the truth rather than lied.

Nonverbal scholars study the use of gesture, inflection, and other forms of self-presentation in conveying meaning to others. Okora and Washington (2011) examined the connection between faculty attire and students' nonverbal behaviors and attitudes. They explored the idea that faculty attire functions as a form of nonverbal communication, impacting student perception of quality of instruction. Conversation analysts study the patterns of verbal exchanges between individuals. Others study conflict negotiation and resolution between individuals in both everyday and political contexts. The list goes on and on.

interpersonal communication
The study of compliance gaining and social influence; persuading people to adopt certain attitudes or behaviors; establishing identity, information gathering, building understanding with each other, and creating and maintaining relationships in a variety of contexts.

So What?

In summary, the field of communication is exceptionally diverse. Communication researchers are in the business of answering questions related to these and dozens of other matters. The prevailing theme throughout all aspects of communication research—to reiterate the opening of this chapter—is that communication researchers seek the answers to questions regarding the use of symbols and information to convey meaning. This volume will give a basic overview and explanation of the ways in which these questions are formulated, how they are explored, and how the answers to these questions are reported. It is a how-to guide on the practice of communication research.

Glossary

A priori
This form of reasoning is based on personal reasoning or logic, or the fact that there are some things you just simply know to be true.

Applied research
Research that takes the theoretical lessons learned in academic studies and applies them to varying real-life contexts.

Authority
The reliance upon someone in a position of power to determine what is factual. This power may be derived from a variety of places, such as expertise, political power, religious authority, or interpersonal trust.

Cognitive conservatism
The idea that how someone views the world is often based upon his or her prior beliefs.

Communication researchers
Scholars and professionals who study communication.

Critical or cultural research
Research that looks at the construction, use, and abuse of power and control in a culture, situation, organization, or community.

Epistemology
The study of knowledge.

Experience
A common way of understanding the social world.

Health communication scholars
Communication scholars who look at the interpersonal exchanges between doctors and patients, public health campaigns, the flow of information in public health organizations, and other health issues.

Humanities research
Research that uses performative or artistic elements to look at how we co-construct meaning through communication.

Hypotheses
Educated guesses about a social phenomenon based on prior observations.

Interpersonal communication
The study of compliance gaining and social influence; persuading people to adopt certain attitudes or behaviors; establishing identity, information gathering, building understanding with each other, and creating and maintaining relationships in a variety of contexts.

Intuition
An internal-based instinct that people have about a situation, issue, or experience.

Media research
This type of research uses surveys, laboratory experiments, and content analysis to answer questions about the uses of and responses to mediated information. It can be useful in understanding how humans convey meaning.

Organizational communication
This field of communication studies the ways in which people exchange information to accomplish organizational goals. The exchange of information in organizational contexts can take on a variety of different forms, including relationships between managers and subordinates, relationships with constituents outside the organization, different ways that organizations deal with crises and emergencies, and so on.

Overgeneralization

A problematic way of knowing in which individuals base their knowledge on just a few experiences or observations.

Research

The activity of conducting intellectual investigations into the observable world.

Scientific reasoning

A way of knowing where one has a hunch about how things ought to be, then tests that hunch by making observations.

Scholarly research

Primary research conducted by academic researchers and distributed through academic publications with the desire to build theory.

Social research

This research focuses less on the observable world in which human beings interact, and more on the interactions themselves, how they come into existence, how they function, and how they affect the human experience. Research in communication, psychology, sociology, economics, political science, and anthropology are typically classified as social research.

Tenacity

The assumption that something is true because it has always been said to be true.

Theory

A set of interrelated constructs, definitions, and propositions that present a systematic view of phenomena by specifying relations among variables, with the purpose of explaining and predicting the phenomena.

References

Ajzen, I. (1995). Attitudes and behavior. Beliefs. Theory of reasoned action. Theory of planned behavior. In A. S. R. Manstead & M. Hewstone (Eds.), *The Blackwell dictionary of social psychology*. Oxford, UK: Blackwell.

Ajzen, I., & Fishbein, M. (1980). *Understanding attitudes and predicting social behavior*. Englewood Cliffs, NJ: Prentice-Hall.

Allport, G. W., & Postman, L. J. (1945). The basic psychology of rumor. *Transactions of the New York Academy of Sciences, 8*, 61–81.

Babbie, E. (1995). *The practice of social research*. Belmont, CA: Wadsworth.

Bochantin, J. E., & Cowan, R. L. (2016). Acting and reeacting: Work/life accommodation and blue-collar workers. *International Journal of Business Communication, 53*(3), 306–325.

Buchler, J. (1955). *Philosophical writings of Peirce*. New York: Dover.

Burleson, B. R., & MacGeorge, E. L. (2002). Supportive communication. In M. L. Knapp & J. A. Daly (Eds.), *Handbook of interpersonal communication* (3rd ed., pp. 374–424). Thousand Oaks, CA: Sage.

Coombs, T., & Holladay, S. J. (2004). Understanding the aggressive workplace: Development of the workplace aggression tolerance questionnaire. *Communication Studies, 55*(3), 481–497.

Daft, R. L., & Lengel, R. H. (1986). Organizational information requirements, media richness, and structural design. *Management Science, 32*, 554–571.

Davis, C. S. (2008). Dueling narratives: How peer leaders use narrative to frame meaning in community mental health care teams. *Small Group Research, 39*(6), 706–727.

Davis, C. S., & Crane, J. L. (2015). A dialogue with (un)death: Horror films as a discursive attempt to construct a relationship with the dead. *Journal of Loss and Trauma, 20*(5), 417–429. doi: 10.1080/15325024.2014.935215

Davis, C. S., & Salkin, K. A. (2005). Sisters and friends: Dialogue and multivocality in a relational model of sibling disability. *Journal of Contemporary Ethnography, 34*(2), 206–234.

Dillard, J. P., Plotnick, C. A., Godbold, L. C., Freimuth, V. S., & Edgar, T. (1996). The multiple affective consequences of AIDS PSAs: Fear appeals do more than scare people. *Communication Research, 23*, 44–72.

Dixon, T. L., & Linz, D. (2000). Overrepresentation and underrepresentation of African Americans and Latinos as lawbreakers on television news. *Journal of Communication, 50*, 131–154.

Dunleavy, K. N., Chory, R. M., & Goodboy, A. K. (2010). Responses to deception in the workplace: Perceptions of credibility, power, and trustworthiness. *Communication Studies, 61*, 239–255.

Ehrlich, N., & Shami, S. (2010). Microblogging inside and outside the workplace. USA Proceedings of the Fourth International AAAI Conference on Weblogs and Social Media. May 23–26, 2010. Washington DC. Association for the Advancement of Artificial Intelligence.

Ellingson, L. L. (2005). *Communicating in the clinic: Negotiating frontstage and backstage teamwork.* Cresskill, NJ: Hampton Press.

Ellis, C. (1995). *Final negotiations: A story of love, loss, and chronic illness.* Philadelphia: Temple University Press.

Fishbein, M., Middlestadt, S. E., & Hitchcock, P. J. (1994). Using information to change sexually transmitted disease-related behaviors. In R. J. DiClemente & J. L. Peterson (Eds.), *Preventing AIDS: Theories and methods of behavioral interventions.* New York: Plenum Press.

Gerbner, G., Gross, L., Morgan, M., & Signorielli, N. (1986). Living with television: The dynamics of the cultivation process. In J. Bryant & D. Zillman (Eds.), *Perspectives on media effects* (pp. 17–40). Hillsdale, NJ: Lawrence Erlbaum Associates.

Goodall, H. L. (2006). *A need to know: The clandestine history of a CIA family.* Walnut Creek, CA: Left Coast Press.

Greenberg, B. S., Eastin, M. S., Hofshire, L., Lachlan, K. A., & Brownell, K. (2003). Portrayals of overweight and obese individuals in commercial television. *American Journal of Public Health, 93*(8), 1342–1348.

Greenhow, C., & Robelia, E. (2009). Old communication, new literacies: Social network sites as social learning resources. *Journal of Computer-Mediated Communication, 14*, 1130–1161.

James, C.H., & Minnis, W.C. (2004). Organizational storytelling: It makes sense. *Business Horizons, 3*, 23–32.

Katz, E., Blumler, J. G., & Gurevitch, M. (1973). Uses and gratifications research. *Public Opinion Quarterly, 37*(4), 509–523.

Kerlinger, F. (1992). *Foundations of behavioral research.* Fort Worth, TX: Harcourt Brace.

Ledbetter, A. M., Mazer, J. P., DeGroot, J. M., Meyer, K. R., Mao, Y., & Swafford, B. (2011). Attitudes toward online social connection and self-disclosure as predictors of Facebook communication and relational closeness. *Communication Research, 38*, 27–53.

Lowry, D. T., Nio, T. C., & Leitner, D.W. (2003). Setting the public fear agenda: A longitudinal analysis of network TV crime reporting, public perceptions of crime, and FBI crime statistics. *Journal of Communication, 53*, 61–73.

McCombs, M., & Shaw, D. (1972). The agenda-setting function of mass media. *Public Opinion Quarterly, 36*(2), 176–187.

Meyer, G., Roberto, A. J., & Atkin, C. K. (2003). A radio-based approach to promoting gun safety: Process and outcome evaluation implications and insights. *Health Communication, 15*(3), 299–318.

Mignerey, J.T., Rubin, R.B., & Gorden, W.I. (2005). Organizational entry: An investigation of newcomer communication behavior and uncertainty. *Communication Research, 22*, 54–85.

Miller, K. (2005). *Organizational communication: Approaches and processes.* Boston: Thomson Wadsworth.

Nabi, R. L., Moyer-Guse, E., & Byrne, S. (2007). All joking aside: A serious investigation into the persuasive effect of funny social issue messages. *Communication Monographs, 74*(1), 29–54.

Okoro, E., & Washington, M. (2011). Communicating in a multicultural classroom: A study of students' nonverbal behavior and attitudes toward faculty attire. *Journal of College Teaching and Learning, 8*, 27–38.

Plotnick, R. (2015). What happens when you push this?: Toward a history of the not-so-easy button. *Information & Culture, 50*(3), 315–338. doi: http://dx.doi.org/10.7560/IC50302

Powell, H. L. (2011). Letters to Louis: Marital dissolution through the social construction of lived experience. *Journal of Divorce & Remarriage, 52*, 19–32.

Raney, A. A. (2002). Punishing criminals and moral judgment: The impact on enjoyment. *Media Psychology, 7*(2), 145–163.

Real, K., & Putnam, L. L. (2005). Ironies in the discursive struggle of pilots defending the profession. *Management Communication Quarterly, 19*(1), 91–119.

Roberto, A. J., Krieger, J. L., Katz, M., Goei, R., & Jain, P. (2011). Predicting pediatricians' communication with parents about the Human Papillomavirus (HPV) vaccine: An application of the theory of reasoned action. *Health Communicaiton, 26*(4), 303–312.

Segrin, C., Woszidlo, A., Givertz, M., Bauer, A., & Murphy, M. T. (2012). The association between overparenting, parent-child communication, and entitlement and adaptive traits in adult children. *Family Relations, 61*, 237–352.

Sellnow, T. L., Seeger, M. W., & Ulmer, R. R. (2002). Chaos theory, informational needs, and natural disasters. *Journal of Applied Communication Research, 30*(4), 269–292.

Silk, K. J., & Parrott, R. L. (2006). All or nothing . . . or just a hat?: Farmers' sun protection behaviors. *Health Promotion Practice, 7*(2), 180–185.

Stohl, M., & Stohl, C. (2005). Human rights, nation states, and NGOs: Structural holes and the emergence of global regimes. *Communication Monographs, 72*(4), 442–467.

Toppman, L. (2009, May 26). Mothers' bare emotions burst out in "Miracle Kick." *Charlotte Observer,* pp. 1D, 5D.

U.S. Surgeon General's Scientific Advisory Committee on Television and Social Behavior. (1972). *Television and growing up: The impact of televised violence* (DHEW Publication No. HSM 72-9086). Washington, DC.

Wilson, B. J., Kunkel, D., Linz, D., Potter, W. J., Donnerstein, E., Smith, S. L., et al. (1998). *National television violence study: Vol. 1. Violence in television programming overall: University of California–Santa Barbara study*. Thousand Oaks, CA: Sage.

Witte, K., Stokols, D., Ituarte, P., & Schnieder, M. (1993). Testing the health belief model in a field study to promote bicycle safety helmets. *Communication Research, 20,* 564–586.

Yarker, J., Munir, F., Bains, M., Kalawsky, K., & Haslam, C. (2010). The role of communication and support in return to work following cancer-related absence. *Psycho-oncology, 19,* 1078–1085.

METATHEORETICAL CONSIDERATIONS, RESEARCH PERSPECTIVES, AND RESEARCH PARADIGMS

2

CHAPTER OUTLINE

1. What Are the Goals and Methods of Communication Scholars and Everyday Observers?
2. Metatheoretical Considerations
   a. Ontology
   b. Epistemology
   c. Axiology
3. Research Perspectives and Paradigms
   a. Positivism
   b. Interpretivism
   c. Critical Perspective
4. Types of Research
   a. Proprietary Research
   b. Scholarly Research
      i. Characteristics of Scholarly Research
5. Two Logical Systems
   a. Inductive Model
   b. Deductive Model
   c. Model of Deduction/Induction
6. Qualitative and Quantitative Research
   a. Qualitative Research
   b. Quantitative Research
7. So What?

KEY TERMS

Axiology

Critical perspective

Deductive model

Epistemology

Hermeneutics

Inductive model

Interpretivism

Metatheory

Nominalist

Objectivist

Ontology

Positivism

Proprietary research

Qualitative research

Quantitative research

Realist

Scholarly research

Social constructionist

Subjectivist

CHAPTER OBJECTIVES

1. To explain metatheory and its primary components
2. To understand the differences between the research perspectives and paradigms discussed in this chapter
3. To understand how our beliefs, values, and the ways we see the world influence our research choices
4. To become familiar with the different types of research

▼ # What Are the Goals and Methods of Communication Scholars and Everyday Observers?

The primary goal of both social scientists and humanities scholars is to understand the world around us. Communication scholars are interested in questions and ideas relating to how we communicate. These goals have grown out of everyday concerns, a type of common sense allowing us to better understand the world in which we live. From an early age, we observe things in our everyday life as they occur around and to us. Many of us try to understand why these things happen to or around us. We wonder about specific happenings, while also making general conclusions about why we behave as we do, as well as why others are the way they are.

Consider this example: We observe teenagers waiting in line at an amusement park speaking rudely to one another, yet they appear to be friends. We want to know why they speak to each other in this manner. What would you do? We could ask them; we could observe their behavior before and after the incident; we could ask an expert in teenage behavior. We may conclude that speaking rudely to one another in conversation is a way to demonstrate affiliation and to project identity. To reach some conclusion about the experience we have observed, we must formulate a research question and/or hypothesis, gather data, and draw conclusions until we are satisfied with the conclusion we've drawn.

▼ # Metatheoretical Considerations

All forms of communication research are built upon researchers' own unique metatheoretical considerations, which are inherent in the research question(s) and/or hypotheses at study. **Metatheory** is theory about theory and allows us to understand the philosophy driving our decisions about research methods, design, and even analysis. Metatheory is a tool allowing us to recognize what aspects about the social world we think about and study. There are three primary components of metatheory: ontology, epistemology, and axiology. These three components are inherent within all of us—researchers and even students. It may be you have never identified or studied your beliefs about the world yet; we invite you to do so here.

metatheory
Theory about theory that allows people to understand the philosophy driving their decisions about research methods, design, and analysis.

Ontology

First, we need to consider the metatheoretical consideration, called ontology. **Ontology** is simply the study of the nature of reality. It answers the question: How do we know about the world around us? What we believe exists in the world and how we know it exists are the crux of our ontological perspective. As with all metatheoretical considerations, a continuum of knowing about the reality of the world exists. Some scholars take a **realist** stance; they believe the world exists out there and is tangible. This is an objective perspective, because they believe there is an objective reality independent of anything else. These scholars are at one end of the continuum of ontology. At the opposite end of the continuum we find scholars who take a **nominalist**, or **social constructionist** position. They believe that there is no universal truth and that ideas about the way things are, are constructs of our individual or cultural ways of seeing the world.

Sometimes, it's helpful to take a realist view of the world. If I am a medical student, I may need to learn how to identify cancer cells. I simply need to know, at the cellular level, do these cells exhibit the characteristics of cancer cells? A realist viewpoint would be most appropriate in this instance. However, once I've identified a cancer cell, I have to break the news to a patient. Sometimes the presence of cancer cells indicates a long, slow, painful death. Other times, cancer is easily treated and requires a short recovery time. How my patient reacts to the news depends on his/her prior experience with cancer, and if this is his/her first time being diagnosed with cancer, if he/she has a family history of cancer and what that experience was like. How I react to giving the news might depend on how I personally feel about cancer, how successful I've been in breaking bad news to patients in the past, and how comfortable I am with a patient expressing emotion to me. A social constructionist, or nominalist viewpoint, would help me understand the myriad of ways the conversation about cancer might go.

Epistemology

Our second metatheoretical consideration, called **epistemology**, is simply the study of the nature of knowledge. It answers the questions: What can we know? Or, how do I approach studying the world as a scholar? As with all metatheoretical considerations, a continuum of belief about knowledge exists.

Some scholars take an **objectivist** position, which believes it is possible to know and explain the world. They search for regularities and patterns to communication behavior. They are most often interested in global understandings of life. Many individuals taking an objectivist epistemological perspective prefer a separation between the researcher and the subject, with the goal of not interfering with the outcome. People with this epistemology believe they know by discovery. They believe there is an objective reality outside of humans that can be observed by all. They believe they can study this objective reality in an unbiased, precise (accurate), systematic, and reliable manner through repetition, generalization, and discrimination.

On the other end of the continuum of epistemology is a **subjectivist** perspective. These scholars believe knowledge is relative and can be understood only from the point of view of the individual involved. They are most often

ontology
The study of the nature of reality.

realist
The belief that the world exists and is tangible.

nominalist
The belief that there is no universal truth and that ideas about the way things are, are constructs of our individual or cultural ways of seeing the world.

Social constructionist
The belief that our ideas about reality are constructed through societal and interpersonal communication.

epistemology
The study of the nature of knowledge.

objectivist
The belief that it is possible to know and explain the world.

Subjectivist
The belief that knowledge is relative and can be understood only from the point of view of the individual involved.

interested in local understandings of life within a specific context. People with this epistemology believe they know by interpretation—that more than one reality can be known, so they use interpretation to guide their understanding of the different perspectives.

Axiology

axiology
The study of values.

The third metatheoretical consideration, called **axiology**, is the study of values. While scholars once believed it was possible to separate our value system from influencing scientific exploration, most scholars have come to realize that, in fact, it is a matter of how values influence our science. Some researchers believe, for example, that it is important for a researcher to be objective and that the researcher is the expert authority on his or her research. Others believe it is important to make sure multiple perspectives of participants are heard and that authority comes from all research participants, including the people in the group or culture being researched. What we value in research determines what research questions we ask, what types of studies we conduct, how we design those studies, and how we analyze the data. Essentially, it is impossible to eliminate the influence of values from scholarship. More importantly, many argue we should not separate values from scholarship and that good scholarship is based upon our values and ethics, which will be discussed in Chapter 5. As research is bounded in context, it is unlikely and unwise to ignore the values embedded within that context. However, as we have suggested about both our ontological and epistemological perspectives, a continuum of axiological perspective still exists. This reflects how strongly a researcher feels these values should be considered as part of the research.

▼ ## Research Perspectives and Paradigms

From our metatheoretical considerations, we can build a composite picture of several different perspectives and paradigms we might take in conducting research. Our metatheoretical considerations are the foundation on which we build research, while research perspectives and paradigms are the overarching principles we use to conduct research. They are a way of experiencing and acting upon reality, to study communication. Like other areas of research, communication studies utilize a paradigm to determine the rules of gathering data and evidence and how such data should be interpreted. These might also be considered common boundaries established for what constitutes legitimate research practices. Research paradigms are shared by scholars across academic fields and agreed upon as a shared language within each paradigm. As they are understood across a community, they are jointly constructed by the intellectual community. Some scholars have suggested that paradigms enforce a particular view of the world. We prefer to think of paradigms as different views of the world that inform our research.

While our metatheoretical considerations tend to be intuitive and learned through everyday ways of knowing, early in our lives, research paradigms are more often taught. We learn research paradigms through our formal education. The academic community, through trial and error, has found research paradigms to be more useful than the everyday ways of knowing we discussed earlier. As research paradigms have been created through an intellectual community based on education, it is possible that research paradigms can be revised and changed through new discoveries and knowledge. Each research paradigm commits itself to its own standards and rules, including what problems can and cannot be addressed and studied. While a research paradigm is an important concept for understanding research methods, the idea is not free from disadvantages. Communication does not come neatly in one research paradigm or another. It is inherently messy and difficult to carve up. Some scholars become so entrenched in their own research paradigm that they may not see what does not fit into their own paradigm. We will talk about three research perspectives and paradigms: positivist, interpretivist, and critical.

Positivism

Positivism is most often thought of as the most traditional research perspective. Individuals who identify themselves as preferring this perspective believe scientific evidence is superior to other types of knowing. They tend to prefer empirical data and formal theoretical perspectives as the way to gain knowledge about the physical and social world. In terms of their metatheoretical considerations, they are usually realists in their ontology, yet many recognize the possibility that multiple realities may exist. Objectivists in their epistemology believe social regularities exist. The social world, such as communication, occurs in patterns and can and should be studied using the tenets of social scientific methods. While original positivists would have argued for the exclusion of values in research, meaning that the researcher's values had no place contaminating data collection, most modern postpositivists recognize that our values, if in no other way, impact our research by the choices we make in what to study. If it had no value, why would we study it (Miller, 1986)?

Positivism
The most traditional research perspective with the belief that scientific evidence is superior to other types of knowing.

Positivism as a research perspective began with scholars in the social sciences during the 1920s and 1930s (Miller, 1986). These researchers were interested in verifying social science through analysis and often experiments. Eventually, researchers using the verification approach recognized the difficulty of proving any particular fact and switched gears. They decided instead that what they should be doing is ruling out alternatives; in other words, attempting to prove that something is not true, rather than true. This is known as falsification and differentiates classic positivism from postpositivism, which most scholars taking this approach use today. This is also where we get the notion of the null hypothesis, which will be addressed later. It is also the reason most communication research methods instructors we know cringe when a student uses the word *prove*, because what we are really doing is ruling out alternatives.

A postpositivist approach to research often attempts to explore research questions concerned with explanation, prediction, and/or control of communication phenomena. We can answer questions about why something will happen (explanation), forecast what will happen under similar circumstances (prediction), and attempt to create particular outcomes (control). For example, if a positivist or postpositivist scholar wanted to study relationship development, he or she might develop a hypothesis (see Chapter 6) predicting that the longer the relationship, the more time couples spend together. He or she might design a study considering people in three groups: those in relationships fewer than six months, those in relationships between six months and five years, and those in relationships over five years. The researcher might ask the study participants to keep a journal of their time spent together, then might conduct a statistical analysis to determine if there is a causal relationship between time in relationship and time spent together.

Positivists know by discovery. These scholars believe they must come to understand the world and the communication within it from an objective stance of observation. They feel strongly about precision and conduct research with an eye toward the systematic procedures of data collection and analysis and the ability to replicate their findings. These scholars tend to use experimental design and survey research to study communication.

Interpretivism

interpretivism
A research perspective in which understanding and interpretation of the social world is derived from one's personal intuition and perspective.

Interpretivism as a research perspective began with scholars such as Immanuel Kant and Max Weber. Both were pioneers contributing to a new understanding of the social world. Kant argued our understanding of the social world begins with intuition and a subjective spirit—a sense, essentially, that we are interpreting the world through our own perspective. Weber similarly advocated for moving to a more interpretive social science, which allowed room for studying the subjective reality of all individuals involved in interaction, rather than just knowing an objective reality. A term often connected with interpretive approaches to research is *phenomenology*. Phenomenology is most often considered an ontological consideration concerned with the essence of what we experience from an individual's first-person perspective. It is an intentional analysis of lived experience. Again, the reason for this viewpoint is the emphasis on the importance of understanding from each person's perspective. This perspective provides primacy to an individual's own perceptions and interpretations of their experience. If we take this perspective to research, individual consciousness is the source of knowledge. Here we experience ourselves and others through the act of communication or dialogue.

In understanding what it means to take an interpretivist lens to research practice, we must also understand the metatheoretical commitments inherent within this choice. The epistemological position associated with interpretivism is that of a subjective stance, emphasizing that we can only understand reality from the person living it. In order to access this type of data, scholars taking this perspective are comfortable with minimal distance between themselves and their research participants. Interpretivism is based upon the epistemological consideration that knowledge is created in individual consciousness. Therefore, meaning will depend upon our own perceptions, backgrounds, and life experience. For example, consider your own perception when we ask you to consider a cat. How many of you picture a soft, cuddly kitty cat that you would love to pet and hold? How many of you think of a cat as a mean, independent, and smelly creature that you wish would stay away from you? Do any of you experience swelling throat, burning eyes, a tight chest, and trouble breathing when you are around cats? When we say "cat," do any of you think about the cats we might encounter at a zoo or circus? Our knowledge of cats is influenced by whether we like animals, whether we had a bad experience with a particular cat, whether we are allergic to cats, or whether we grew up with a cat we loved. Scholars who take this approach to research are truly interested in the individual perspective and meaning embedded within that experience. Based on what you know so far, what do you think an interpretive scholar's ontological tendencies are? Are they a realist or a social constructionist? Most likely they have nominalist leanings. A social constructionist stance on ontology preferences individual frames of reference and understanding. Interpretive scholars utilize this axiological approach in their work, while acknowledging that they see the world through their own biases and perspective. As such, they encourage their values to be part of the discussion and the analysis, rather than striving toward an artificial attempt to eliminate their own value system.

Scholars who follow interpretive perspectives believe that more than one reality can be known and that interpretation is their guide to understanding. These scholars tend to use qualitative research techniques such as ethnography (described fully in Chapters 14–18). An interpretive scholar might study relational development by looking at his own relationship and, perhaps, write a narrative about the history of that relationship. He might also want to include the perspective of his partner and co-construct a narrative written by both of them. Interpretive scholars might also include the perspectives of other significant people in their lives—perhaps other family members and close friends might contribute to the narrative as well.

Critical Perspective

The third perspective, known as the **critical perspective**, essentially questions the primary goals associated with positivist and interpretivist perspectives. Remember that positivists' primary goal in research is explanation, while interpretivists are interested in understanding. Critical scholars think both of these representations are lacking. According to critical tradition, they see research methods as a tool to challenge unjust discourse and communication practices. There are several foundations of this perspective. One comes from the German Frankfurt School, which embraced Karl Marx's tradition of critiquing society. Another comes from French philosopher Michel Foucault, whose work was especially important in understanding power and deviance as it is experienced and conveyed in everyday practices, discourses, and discursive rules, and in understanding how discourses and associated practices come to be accepted as true or legitimate (Deveaux, 1994; Foucault, 1965, 1972, 1973, 1995).

As they are critical of contemporary society and the practices found within our social structure, critical theorists typically challenge three components of contemporary society that are particularly useful to communication students. First, the structure and control of language perpetuates power imbalances in our society. Second, individuals become less sensitized to repression through

critical perspective
This perspective uses research methods as a tool to challenge unjust discourse and communication practices, with the goal of using knowledge as a tool to create social change.

the role of the mass media. Third, they suggest we have relied too heavily on the scientific method and accept all empirical findings, without adequate critique. The goal of most critical scholars is to use knowledge as a tool to create social change. Most of them are crusaders and/or activists of sorts working actively in reforming and changing the world with their research. Critique was originally suggested as a way to focus on the ways in which we alienate people.

What are the metatheoretical considerations of the critical perspective? Hopefully, by now, you are starting to see how the metatheoretical considerations of epistemology, ontology, and axiology begin to guide our choices of perspective. What might be most interesting about critical scholars is that they have some unique characteristics in terms of their metatheoretical considerations. They range from one side of the epistemological perspective to the other; being both positivistic in ways, while also exhibiting social constructionist tendencies, and even sometimes nominalist beliefs. Let me explain. Jürgen Habermas (1968) suggested that critical theory is a form of **hermeneutics**. Hermeneutics is essentially a way to study textual data through interpretation to create meaning. In other words, hermeneutics is a way to gain knowledge via interpretation. As the focus in these instances is upon explanation and interpretation, it could be considered as having a realist or social constructionist epistemological stance. However, other scholars taking the critical approach call into question the values and norms of a society, exploring how society adopts and reinforces dominant power structures. These scholars see realization of these dominant power structures and subsequent change as the goal of research. They clearly take a more nominalist stance, believing that knowledge comes from the cognitive process of recognizing the flaws of the society we live within. Similarly, in terms of their ontology, scholars taking the critical perspective can range from an objectivist stance to a more subjectivist stance. However, it is most common for contemporary communication scholars who take the critical perspective to reside more on the subjective side. As the goal for all critical theorists is identifying the power structures that bind our communication, they would argue that values not only are part of scholarship, but that they should drive scholarship. Critical theorists would suggest that values are the motivation behind their research, since they use research to be agents of societal change.

Many critical scholars are interested in work related to cultural studies. This work explores the idea of culture as a viable framework for understanding how one's values and beliefs are woven together and guide their experience of the world. Still other critical scholars ground their work in feminist theory, which recognizes gender as among the most important defining features of social life. It is their belief that women throughout social life have been silenced or muted. This type of scholarship highlights the oppression women face in our society.

Scholars following the critical perspective believe that everything about how we communicate is shaped by values. The world is socially constructed and critical theorists study it through understanding knowledge for the purpose of bringing about social change. These scholars use different types of research, such as rhetorical criticism and critical ethnography, to understand the communication of our world.

hermeneutics
A way to study textual data through interpretation to create meaning; knowledge gained via interpretation.

Critical scholars might study relational development by asking a question such as: How do traditional relationships marginalize women or constrain the empowerment of women? They might use mixed methods such as observation, in-depth interviews, and perhaps focus groups to gather information that will help them understand how social relationships construct power among people of different genders.

The following chart (Table 2.1) summarizes the different research perspectives and paradigms. In summary, postpositivists typically conduct research using strict scientific methods with bias-free inquiry as the goal, using objective methods. Their analysis is conducted at the conclusion of data collection as a separate step of the research process. Interpretivists, on the other hand, prefer to conduct research driven by empirical observation—in other words, grounded in the theory, with their primary goal to understand, rather than measure or explain. Unlike postpositivists, their data analysis occurs throughout the data collection process. They are guided by the question: Does this research provide in-depth understanding? Critical scholars conduct research using a variety of methods, as you will see throughout this book. However, most important is the idea that they are warriors on an ethical agenda of identifying with human suffering and working toward changing the human condition.

Table 2.1. Current Research Perspectives and Paradigms in Communication Studies

		Ontological Assumptions (What do we believe about reality?)	Epistemological Assumptions (What can we know and study?)	Axiological Assumptions (What do we value in research and knowledge?)
Realist ↕ **Nominalist/ Social Constructionist**	Positivism/ Postpositivism	Reality is orderly, fixed, and measurable.	We can know and study objective reality.	We value research that is objective and researchers who are expert authorities.
	Critical/Cultural	May believe reality is orderly, measurable, objective. May believe reality is subjective.	We can know and study reality that is either objective or subjective. We can know and study reality that is interpreted or observed as it is.	We value research that includes marginalized voices. We value research in which the researcher shares power with participants.
	Interpretivism	Reality is both orderly and chaotic. Reality is subjective.	We can know and study subjective reality as it is constructed, mediated, and biased.	We value research in which all participants are equal authorities and in which all perspectives are represented.

▼ Types of Research

As we have considered the metatheoretical foundations, research perspectives, and possible paradigms guiding scholarly research, we have yet to consider the characteristics of research. In other words, how do we conduct research? Research involves disciplined inquiry; we study communication in a systematic or planned approach. We take a scientific approach to research, no matter our metatheoretical considerations, our paradigm, or our method. We work to avoid the problems we encounter in our everyday ways of acquiring knowledge. There are two types of research: proprietary and scholarly. Most of you at one point or another will be responsible for or involved in both types of research.

Proprietary Research

proprietary research
Research that is conducted for a specific audience, which is not shared beyond the intended audience.

Proprietary research is research conducted for a specific audience, which is not shared beyond the intended audience. Many corporations and businesses conduct research to examine anything from their business practices, to satisfaction with employee benefits programs, to marketing new products and services within potential client or consumer groups. When one of your authors (Christine Davis) worked for a market research consulting firm, she conducted proprietary research for clients. Many of you may end up doing this type of research for your career.

Scholarly Research

scholarly research
Research conducted to contribute to generalizable knowledge for public consumption.

Scholarly research is research conducted for the goal of contributing to knowledge for public consumption. While most research methods courses focus on scholarly research, it is important to realize that the steps, methods, and/or approaches for how to conduct research don't change, regardless of what type of research you are conducting.

Characteristics of Scholarly Research.
Research is question-oriented. Academic scholarship is always interested in answering interesting questions. For communication scholars, the crux of our questions must involve questions related to communication. These questions are remaining questions about communication that, to date, remain unanswered. Questions come in all forms, from a variety of places. Sometimes we come up with questions through our experience and other everyday ways of knowing, recognizing the limitations of this type of knowledge. This is often a good way to come up with questions, but is only a starting point. Other questions come about from reading scholarly work and recognizing questions left unanswered from previous research.

Research is methodological. As we suggested earlier, without fail research involves planning and following a systematic approach for data collection and analysis. Regardless of the research questions or the area of communication studies we study, research follows rules. These rules may differ depending upon the research methodology we choose; yet, there are rules nonetheless.

Research is creative. This is often a characteristic of research that many students fail to recognize about research. We are in the process of creating new knowledge or adding to existing knowledge, and there are a variety of ways we can do this. Selecting (or inventing!) the best ways to know is a delightfully creative process.

Research is self-critical. As researchers, we are obligated to examine our own work from a critical vantage point. We should always be the first critic of our own work, fairly assessing the strengths and weaknesses of our scholarship. It is imperative that we remember there is no *perfect* research study; there is always more to learn. Good scholarship acknowledges the limitations of the work as a method of advancing our understanding. This self-critical view also suggests areas of future research.

Research is public. As we discussed earlier, academic research is conducted for public consumption. Researchers typically view scholarship as a mechanism for serving useful social purposes. If you ask most scholars what they most love about conducting research, it is the idea that they can work toward scholarship that may be useful to someone.

Research is both cumulative and self-correcting. All research is built upon previous scholarship. Good scholarship begins with the ability to gather scholarly research and critically assess the results of the work. This provides researchers the opportunity to correct mistakes made in other work. While we often think of correcting others' research, scholars often have the opportunity to improve upon their own previous research.

Research is cyclical. All research occurs in stages. The stages are determined first and foremost by the type of research question(s) we ask. The research question(s) determine the methodological design of the research project and the way we analyze the data we gather. Ultimately, while research answers questions, it also generates new questions that need to be answered.

Two Logical Systems ▼

The purpose of social science, including communication research, is to build knowledge that contributes to our understanding of communication behaviors. In some cases, we hope to be able to predict communication behaviors and even control these behaviors. However, in order to explain, predict, and/or control communication behaviors, we collect data and gather evidence to evaluate our understanding of these behaviors. There are two logical systems that allow social scientists to do just that. It is important to remember that the type of question determines which logical system we use. Neither is better than the other; in fact, they are merely different entry points into the same system.

Inductive Model

One system is the **inductive model**. This approach to research is often referred to as grounded theory, and it is often appropriate when we know little about a topic. Inductive methods can help create theory that can be tested with deduction (our second system). With inductive methods, instead of starting out with a theory and testing the theory, communication scholars begin the research process by gathering data, observing patterns and idiosyncrasies within the data, and developing theory based upon that data. Most scholars who prefer this method of inquiry use qualitative research methods. It is said that inductive reasoning moves us from the specific (the research study) to the general (the theory), while deductive reasoning moves us from the general (the theory) to the specific (the research study).

inductive model
This approach to research is often referred to as grounded theory. Communication scholars begin the research process by gathering data, observing patterns and idiosyncrasies within the data, and developing theory based upon that data. Most scholars who prefer this method of inquiry use qualitative research methods.

One interesting example of induction comes from a study on physicians' disclosure of confidential patient information. Maria Brann (2006) wondered how physicians balanced families' caregiving needs for information with patients' confidentiality rights. Using grounded theory, she interviewed physicians and used a detailed thematic coding process. Her findings theorized that the nature and severity of the patient's impairment influenced physician disclosures. She determined that federal privacy laws (HIPAA regulations) did not seem to discourage physicians from disclosing information, primarily because they were motivated by concern for the patient and belief in their own judgment. In other words, she developed a theoretical conclusion based on her research findings, which is an inductive approach.

example of inductive →

Deductive Model

deductive model
This model is typically referred to as theory driven. Communication scholars preferring a deductive approach begin with a theory and gather evidence to evaluate that theory. Most scholars who prefer this method of inquiry use quantitative research methods.

The other system is the **deductive model**. This model is typically referred to as theory driven. Communication scholars preferring a deductive approach begin with a theory and gather evidence to evaluate that theory. Most scholars who prefer this method of inquiry use quantitative research methods.

One example of a deductive approach is Geddes' 2001 study on the impact of speech style such as gender/power on the perception of employee satisfaction and speaker effectiveness. She created both male- and female-delivered messages with one of three speech styles: powerless, powerful, and a mix of powerless and powerful. Union members were asked to evaluate one of these speech styles reporting on the effectiveness of the manager's speech style, as well as the employee satisfaction they experienced viewing the message. Geddes (2001) found that both male and female managers using the mixed speech style were rated both most effective and elicited the most satisfaction. This study demonstrates a deductive approach.

Another example of a deductive approach is Mark Morman's 2000 study on the use of fear appeals to motivate men to practice testicular self-exam (TSE) to detect cancer. Building on Witte's Extended Parallel Process Model (EPPM), Morman designed and tested alternative messages to motivate men to perform TSE. His findings supported the EPPM, which suggests that messages that create fear by communicating perceived severity of the threat and perceived susceptibility to the threat (the reaction will be bad and I could get it) and that communicate perceived efficacy (I can do something effective about it) are the most effective to motivate action. Morman started with an existing EPPM, developed a study to test it in a specific context, then evaluated the model in that new context. This is also a deductive approach.

An interesting example of a deductive approach using qualitative methods is Alexander Lyon's research (2007) on Merck's marketing of the pain medication Vioxx. Building on Deetz's theory about systematically distorted communication, Lyon used a multiple case study approach to analyze Merck's corporate communication. He determined that Merck used neutralization, topic avoidance, and disqualification to reduce the amount of open information patients and physicians received about the drug, and to thus stifle their decision-making ability. Lyon used a deductive approach—starting with Deetz's theory, developing a study to apply that theory, then evaluating the theory in the context of Merck's communication.

Model of Deduction/Induction

Although we have discussed these two types of systems as separate and different, in reality, they are really two parts of the same process. Another way to think about them is that they both begin at different points in the process. All social scientific research proceeds in a circular fashion. You can see how this would work because if we looked back to the EPPM study, someone might pick up after this experiment and start researching this from a deductive stance. For example, we might say, "Well, if the EPPM is true, then women who believe they could get breast cancer and who think they can prevent it through breast self-exam (BSE) should be more likely to practice BSE." So, we conduct a survey and if it is true, then the EPPM receives further support.

We can also start with inductive reasoning and ask, "Why do some women practice BSE and some don't?" We might conduct interviews or focus groups with women to examine their beliefs and practices, and might use grounded theory to come up with a model or theory (perhaps much like the EPPM) to determine what might make women more likely to practice BSE.

Qualitative and Quantitative Research   ▼

Finally, to conclude our discussion of research perspectives and paradigms, we must consider the overarching concepts of qualitative and quantitative research. It is paramount that you understand what the differences are, as well as understand that the research question we ask must always drive our methodological decision making. Therefore, if we ask a question best suited to qualitative methods, even though we prefer quantitative methods, we have to consider whether we are both able and willing to step outside our comfort zone to answer the question appropriately. We suggest to our students that a good scholar will, despite her own individual preferences, come to appreciate and understand the utility of both qualitative and quantitative methods. Neither method is a better method; they just address different questions using different methods, all contributing to our understanding of the world around us.

One way to distinguish between qualitative and quantitative research is to think: Is the research what you might call *art-based* or is it *science-based*? Qualitative research is sometimes thought of more like art, while quantitative research is more like science.

Qualitative Research

Qualitative research methods embrace a naturalistic, interpretive paradigm typically conducting research from an inductive discovery based point of view. Here they often seek to answer research questions that consider how our reality is constructed in interaction. They are less concerned with generalizing to a wider population or other cases; rather they tend to focus on studying the way in which their research participants understand, describe, and see the world. Qualitative research methods are best used when there is not much previously known about the topic, when the topic is personal, and when you want to know more in great

qualitative research
Research, usually studying words or texts, that uses methods which embrace a naturalistic, interpretive paradigm typically from an inductive discovery based point of view.

detail about a small unit or event. Some of the research tools that qualitative researchers make use of include: observation, participation, interviews, focus groups, reviewing documents, gathering life histories, exploring one's own life, field notes, transcripts, and narrative forms of coding data. Qualitative research strives toward the goals of preserving human behavior, analyzing its qualities, and representing different worldviews and experiences. Qualitative researchers see themselves as part of the process of creating knowledge and meaning through understanding what's going on. Another important point about qualitative research that differentiates scholars using these approaches from those taking a quantitative approach is that qualitative scholars not only see themselves as observing the meaning behind communication, but also see themselves as actually being part of the process of meaning making (Krauss, 2005).

Quantitative Research

quantitative research
Research, usually studying numerical data (or reducing words to numerical data), that uses methods which embrace a postpositivist paradigm typically from a deductive explanatory based point of view.

Quantitative research methods embrace a postpositivist paradigm, typically conducting research from a deductive explanatory based point of view. Here they often seek to answer research questions based on the premise that reality is knowable and measurable. Scholars taking the quantitative approach are most interested in generalizing to a wider audience, and they believe that knowledge is something objective that is found and measured. Quantitative methods are best used when you seek to learn something about a lot of people and/or when you are interested in generalizing from your sample to a larger group of people; or when you seek to generalize to a similar situation. Some of the research tools that qualitative researchers make use of include experiments, questionnaires, surveys, interviews, statistical methods, theory testing, secondary data analysis, and numerical coding. The primary goals of quantitative research include representing and explaining objective reality with the overarching goal of simplifying, organizing, predicting, and controlling human behavior.

Table 2.2 is a summary of the basic differences between qualitative and quantitative research:

Table 2.2. Basic Characteristics of Qualitative and Quantitative Research

Qualitative	Quantitative
Impressionist	Realist
Inductive	Deductive
Goal is to discover, preserve form and content of human behavior, represent different world views, create knowledge and meaning, understand what's going on.	Goal is to explain, subject the world to statistical transformations, predict and control, represent and explain objective reality.
Assumption is that reality is constructed in interaction.	Assumption that reality is objective and measureable.
Believes that knowledge is created.	Believes that knowledge is found and received.

Qualitative	Quantitative
Generalizes research findings to other cases or similar phenomena.	Generalizes research findings as widely as possible.
The purpose is to understand, describe, get close to those studied, to understand how participants see the world.	The purpose is to measure relationships among variables, test hypotheses, predict, and control.
Is appropriate when you want to know a lot about a small unit, where not much is known about the topic, when the topic is something you can be immersed in, when you have a desire to make the strange familiar or the familiar strange.	Is appropriate when you want to know something about a lot of people, when you want to generalize from your sample to a large group.

Using our previous language on ontology, epistemology, and axiology, quantitative researchers tend toward the realist end of the spectrum, while qualitative researchers tend toward the nominalist or social constructionist end of the spectrum (Table 2.1).

		Ontological Assumptions (What do we believe about reality?)	Epistemological Assumptions (What can we know and study?)	Axiological Assumptions (What do we value in research and knowledge?)
Realist QUANTITATIVE ↕ **Nominalist/Social Constructionist QUALITATIVE**	Positivism/ Postpositivism	Reality is orderly, fixed, and measurable.	We can know and study objective reality.	We value research that is objective and researchers who are expert authorities.
	Critical/ Cultural	May believe reality is orderly, measurable, objective. May believe reality is subjective.	We can know and study reality that is either objective or subjective. We can know and study reality that is interpreted or observed as is.	We value research that includes marginalized voices. We value research in which the researcher shares power with participants.
	Interpretivism	Reality is both orderly and chaotic. Reality is subjective.	We can know and study subjective reality as it is constructed, mediated, and biased.	We value research in which all participants are equal authorities and in which all perspectives are represented.

As we've said several times in this chapter and book, the method you choose depends entirely on your research question—different methods are most appropriate for answering different research questions. However, as you've seen, because qualitative and quantitative research methods represent different ontologies, epistemologies, and axiologies, researchers tend toward one or the other. In other words, since how you see the world determines the type of research questions you ask, this influences the type of research methods you tend to use. So, for fun, let's see where you fall on the spectrum of beliefs and methods.

You might be a qualitative researcher if you:

Like ambiguity and complexity.

Like to ask questions.

Like to interact/be with people.

Like to analyze immediate experience.

Fantasize about what goes on behind people's windows/phone calls.

Concentrate on episodic, emotional aspects of social life.

Question authority.

You might be a quantitative researcher if you:

Like to simplify, organize, manage the world, categorize the world.

Like math and formulas.

Usually think there's a separate, objective reality to be captured.

Concentrate on rational, patterned order of social life.

Write in authoritative, declarative sentences.

So What?

 As you can see, both quantitative and qualitative research methods answer interesting questions and help us come closer to understanding both the world around us and the people within it. And while some researchers claim that one method is better than another, there are benefits to both methods. It is our goal to objectively consider the strengths and limitations with all types of research practices. Remember that the research question and/or hypotheses drive our decision about how to pursue our research and the research methods we follow.

Glossary

Axiology
The study of values.

Critical perspective
This perspective uses research methods as a tool to challenge unjust discourse and communication practices, with the goal of using knowledge as a tool to create social change.

Deductive model
This model is typically referred to as theory driven. Communication scholars preferring a deductive approach begin with a theory and gather evidence to evaluate that theory. Most scholars who prefer this method of inquiry use quantitative research methods.

Epistemology

The study of the nature of knowledge.

Hermeneutics

A way to study textual data through interpretation to create meaning; knowledge gained via interpretation.

Inductive model

This approach to research is often referred to as grounded theory. Communication scholars begin the research process by gathering data, observing patterns and idiosyncrasies within the data, and developing theory based upon that data. Most scholars who prefer this method of inquiry use qualitative research methods.

Interpretivism

A research perspective in which understanding and interpretation of the social world is derived from one's personal intuition and perspective.

Metatheory

Theory about theory that allows people to understand the philosophy driving their decisions about research methods, design, and analysis.

Nominalist

The belief that there is no universal truth and that ideas about the way things are, are constructs of our individual or cultural ways of seeing the world.

Objectivist

The belief that it is possible to know and explain the world.

Ontology

The study of the nature of reality.

Positivism

The most traditional research perspective with the belief that scientific evidence is superior to other types of knowing.

Proprietary research

Research that is conducted for a specific audience, which is not shared beyond the intended audience.

Qualitative research

Research, usually studying words or texts, that uses methods which embrace a naturalistic, interpretive paradigm typically from an inductive discovery based point of view.

Quantitative research

Research, usually studying numerical data (or reducing words to numerical data), that uses methods which embrace a postpositivist paradigm typically from a deductive explanatory based point of view.

Realist

The belief that the world exists and is tangible.

Scholarly research

Research conducted to contribute to generalizable knowledge for public consumption.

Social constructionist

The belief that our ideas about reality are constructed through societal and interpersonal communication.

Subjectivist

The belief that knowledge is relative and can be understood only from the point of view of the individual involved.

References

Brann, M. (2006). The influence of illness factors on physicians' likelihood of disclosing confidential health information to relatives of patients. *Communication Studies, 57*(3), 259–276.

Deveaux, M. (1994). Feminism and empowerment: A critical reading of Foucault. *Feminist Studies, 20,* 223–248.

Foucault, M. (1965). *Madness and civilization: A history of insanity in the age of reason.* New York: Random House.

Foucault, M. (1972). *The archaeology of knowledge and the discourse on language.* New York: Pantheon Books.

Foucault, M. (1973). *The birth of the clinic: An archaeology of medical perception* (A. M. S. Smith, Trans.). New York: Pantheon Books.

Foucault, M. (1995). *Discipline and punish: The birth of the prison* (A. Sheridan, Trans.). New York: Random House.

Geddes, D. (2001). Sex roles in management: The impact of varying power of speech style on union members' perception of satisfaction and effectiveness. *The Journal of Psychology, 126,* 589–607.

Habermas, J. (1968). The idea of the theory of knowledge as social theory. In J. Habermas, *Knowledge & Human Interest.* Cambridge, UK: Polity Press.

Krauss, S. E. (2005). Research paradigms and meaning making: A primer. *The Qualitative Report, 10,* 758–770.

Lyon, A. (2007). "Putting patients first": Systematically distorted communication and Merck's marketing of Vioxx. *Journal of Applied Communication Research, 35*(4), 376–398.

Miller, T. G. (1986). Goffman, positivism, and the self. *Philosophy of the Social Sciences, 16*, 177–195.

Morman, M. T. (2000). The influence of fear appeals, message design, and masculinity on men's motivation to perform the testicular self-exam. *Journal of Applied Communication Research, 28*(2), 91–116.

DISCOVERING WHAT'S ALREADY KNOWN: LIBRARY RESEARCH

3

CHAPTER OUTLINE

KEY TERMS

Academic journals

Applied research

Body of knowledge

Boolean search

Databases

Peer review

Primary research

Secondary research

Study objectives

CHAPTER OBJECTIVES

1. To explain reasons to conduct library research
2. To explain how to evaluate data sources
3. To explain how to use library research in your own research

▼ # What Are the Purposes of Library Research?

Throughout your scholarly career (from elementary school through college), you've likely had to write a lot of research papers and conduct a lot of library research to do so. In this chapter, we'll help you understand how library research is part of the bigger process of scholarly research. We'll teach you to move from your academic research to library research and back again. We'll explain how to find and evaluate sources, and perhaps most importantly, how to actually read, understand, and use a journal article. One main purpose of this research you've been doing since possibly elementary school was to learn more about the subject you were studying. That's still one main purpose of the library research you're going to conduct in your Communication Research Methods course, and it's still one main reason that all scholars conduct library research. However, it's not the only purpose.

There are five main purposes of library research:

1. To determine what's already known about the topic and related topics.
2. To define the problem and formulate possible solutions. The assembling and analyzing of available secondary data will almost always provide a better understanding of the problem and its context, will frequently suggest solutions not considered previously, and will identify gaps in the body of knowledge for which research is needed. In addition, you don't want to duplicate what's already been done (Hart, 2001).
3. To plan the collection of primary data. You can examine the methods and techniques used by previous research efforts in similar studies, which will be useful in planning your present study. Also, this may be of value in establishing classifications that are more compatible with past studies, so that you can more readily analyze trends.
4. To define the population and select the sample in your primary information collection. This may be valuable in helping you choose areas for most productively interviewing participants.
5. To supply background information that will fill out what you find in your primary research. You may also find information against which you can compare your own findings and experience.

purpose

One basic premise of academic research is that it creates, and builds upon, a **body of knowledge**. There is very little (if anything) that has not been studied in some way, by some person. Your job as a scholar is to build on the research that has already been done by contributing to it, updating it, replicating it, and/or extending it (Booth, Colomb, & Williams, 1995; Rossman, 1995). In order to find out what's already been done, you conduct library research.

body of knowledge
Research that has already been conducted.

▼ # Types of Research

As we explained in Chapter 1, research is the way we find answers to questions. One good way to discover what you're interested in is to listen to the voice in your head that says, "I wonder. . . ." What types of things do you find yourself wondering about? You might be sitting around your apartment talking to friends and wonder, "Why don't guys call when they say they're going to?" or "How many people my age have issues with their parents telling them what to do?" Or, perhaps, you're reading a newspaper and ask, "Why do women in abusive relationships refuse to leave the relationships?" or "What causes people to become homeless?" or "How do movies depict smoking behaviors?" Regardless of how you attempt to find the answer, your method of answering your question is research. As Booth and colleagues said, "Research is simply gathering the information you need to answer a question and thereby help you solve a problem" (Booth et al., 1995, p. 6). Your research may be systematic and valid, or it may not be, but it's still research. If you ask a few friends if they have the same issues with their parents, you're conducting research. If you do a Google search on the Internet to identify the causes of homelessness, you're conducting research. The purpose of this book is to teach you how to conduct research that is considered, in our field (and related fields), to be valid (defensible). Defensible research is planned and conducted in an organized, orderly, methodical manner (Alberts, Hecht, Buley, & Petronio, 1993).

When you ask your friends questions, you're actually conducting what's called primary research; you are generating your own data. If you look up information on the Internet, you're conducting what's called secondary research; you're looking at other people's data.

Primary Research

If you were answering a question with **primary research**, you would be conducting a study to specifically answer that question. Primary research is research that is conducted to answer a specific problem or question. A primary source is the original, or first, published account of research findings (Galvan, 2006). Most research papers you read in journals are examples of primary research (unless it is a synthesis of the literature), so, don't get confused. When you are writing a literature review, you will be reading published articles reporting on primary research. Those articles include a literature review section, which is secondary research (because it summarizes and reports on other people's research). Consequently, your literature review is secondary research, because it summarizes and reports on other people's research.

primary research
Research that is conducted to answer a specific problem or question and produces original data.

Secondary Research

Secondary data is information that has been collected or conducted previously. If you were answering a question with **secondary research**, you would be looking for the answer in papers or books that summarize other studies, or you would be looking at the other studies yourself. Textbooks are classic examples of secondary research. This textbook gives you lots of information, and all of it is taken from other sources, from research previously conducted (and published) by other people. Other examples of secondary research are literature reviews. When you write the results of your library research into a paper, you're writing a literature review. By the way, if you're writing a review of the literature for a class project,

secondary research
Research that has been previously collected or conducted.

you're actually conducting secondary research. When a stand-alone literature review is published in a journal, it's often called a *synthesis of the literature*, and that's another example of a secondary research report. An additional example is the literature review *sections* of research reports.

No research project should ever be conducted without first searching secondary information sources. Why? Because all scholarly research builds upon the scholarly community's body of knowledge, and you have to conduct secondary research to find out what that body of knowledge is. Think of research like a conversation. When you are conducting research, you are entering into a scholarly conversation. You'd never walk up to a conversation and just start talking without finding out what the other people are talking about, right? In the same way, to enter a scholarly conversation, you need to find out what the conversation is about.

▼ Phases of Research

This chapter assumes that you have (or want to have) a research question for which you want to find the answer. Let's say your instructor has given you a research assignment for a class, or you want to do an independent study research project on a topic that's intrigued you. When you decide you want to conduct a research project (or when your instructor gives you a research assignment for a class), the first thing you need to do is come up with a topic. Sometimes you have a specific topic in mind, sometimes you have a vague idea of what your topic might be, and other times you have no idea of where to even begin when choosing a topic!

Since this is a book on communication research methods, the first thing to do is to make sure your topic is *communication* related. That's not necessarily as easy as it sounds. Remember, from Communication Theory or other communication classes you've taken, the scholarly definition of communication: "Communication is a transactional process involving a cognitive sorting, selecting, and sending of symbols in such a way as to help a listener elicit from his or her own mind a meaning or response similar to that intended by the communicator" (Ross, 1977, p. 11). What does that mean exactly? It's a process that is ongoing, circular, and continual, and it consists of give-and-take messages and feedback, feedback and messages. Since it's a process, it has no definite beginning or end point, so it's a complicated process. It's also about using symbols to create meaning. Words are symbols; gestures are symbols; language, pitch, and tones are symbols. Because messages are transmitted through nonverbal means, and because communication is an ongoing process, you cannot not communicate; all behavior is potentially communication, because there is the potential for transmission of meaning, regardless of intent. This meaning or interpretation is based on each of our filters—our individual ways of seeing the world, based on our experiences, culture, history, and so on—and noise—those voices in our head that distract us, or beliefs we have that convince us we're wrong, and so forth. Why are we reminding you of all this? Because pretty much any element in the communication process is subject to communication research. You can create a communication-related research question about the message sender or receiver, the message, feedback to the message, meaning, channel (medium) of the message, noise, context, culture, and so on.

Therefore, you can pretty much study any behavior, but you have to study it in the context of transmitting meaning. For example, you may be interested in exercise behavior. Studying how jogging leads to weight loss has nothing to do with communication. However, studying what jogging (as the *message*) communicates to others does. Or, studying how you can use communication to persuade people to jog is, obviously, about communication. Communication research answers questions about the sender, receiver, message, meaning, or channel that describe, explain, and/or predict communication related behavior (Alberts et al., 1993).

We'll come back to your research question in a minute. First, let's talk about the phases of research. The first phase is called *conceptualization*—forming an idea. Ideas are built on the body of knowledge that's already been created. Your idea builds on the research that's already been done on your topic or related topics.

Once you've formed an idea for your research project, you've got to plan it. You've got to determine exactly what you're looking at and decide how you're going to define your terms. This is called *operationalization*—defining your terms as you're using them in your research project. You often operationalize your data based on how other people have operationalized the same variables—you find this out based on your library research. You've got to decide how to study it and what research methodology to use to collect your data. You've got to know how you're going to analyze your data. One step in planning your research and methodology is to look at what other people have done with the same or similar projects—what worked for them, what didn't work, and what they recommended to do differently.

Then, when you're done planning, you've got to carry out the research. When you write up your research, you do what's called *reconceptualization*—you reconnect it back to the larger body of knowledge.

So, before conducting any type of research, there are two things you must do: determine exactly what information is already known about your topic and determine exactly what you want to know. You have to have a starting point. You have to start with knowing the assumptions the community of knowledge already has and build your information on that. You don't want to spend time, money, and energy gathering information that's already been gathered. Funding agencies won't fund research that's "so what" research, and publications won't publish it. One of the characteristics of academic research is that it builds on a *body of knowledge*—other research that has already been done on your topic or on related topics. So, the first use of library research is to determine what background information already exists about your topic.

• •

Using Library Research to Come Up with Your Research Question   ▼

By the time you're ready to plan your library research, you'll need to be able to articulate a statement of the problem ("The topic of this study is____"), the objective of the study ("This research will determine_____"), and the questions to be answered (Rossman, 1995).

How do you find possible research topics when your mind is blank? Here's where library research can help you. We recommend you start by browsing through your textbooks. Did you especially like Interpersonal Communication? Or Mass Media? Or Public Relations? Pull out your old textbook and look at what topics interest you. Delve a little deeper in the topic by searching the Internet (Booth et al., 1995). Or browse newspapers or magazines to see if there's a topic or story that interests you. Once you have a general topic, you can conduct a library search (we'll explain how to do this later in this chapter) on that topic to see what research other people have done on the topic to help you refine your objective and decide your ultimate research question.

study objectives
What it is that researchers hope to answer through their research. Good researchers refer back to the objectives every step of the way, and insure that everything they are doing answers these objectives. Usually, there are one main objective and several related secondary objectives.

Next, you need to determine your **study objectives**—what do you want to answer with this research? This is probably the most important step of any research study. All other steps stem from the objective. Good researchers refer back to the objectives every step of the way, and ensure that everything they are doing answers these objectives. Usually, there is one main objective and several related secondary objectives. Your objectives should be precise and specific.

Finally, a well defined objective might take the form, "I am studying X because I want to find out [who/what/when/where/whether/why/how] . . ." (Booth et al., 1995, p. 43). Your research question may be what's called *pure* research, in that you just want to know something that is not already known. Or it may be what's called **applied research**, in that what you find out will result in some sort of specific action (Booth et al., 1995). So, you might want to formulate a pure research question about domestic violence, "I wonder if family communication patterns affect levels of domestic violence?" Or you might want to formulate an applied research question about domestic violence, "I wonder how we can persuade women to leave violent relationships?"

applied research
Research that tests theory in real life contexts to see if it can be used to solve problems.

By the time you've finished your library research and are ready to begin collecting your own data, you'll need to be able to articulate the theoretical or conceptual framework for the research (how this issue relates to other issues or other research, or how it explains or adds to existing theories), the questions to be answered (they will be more developed or refined at this point and will usually be either in the form of a research question or a hypothesis), and the significance of the study (Why is my research important to society? How does my research idea fit into the body of knowledge that already exists?) (Rossman, 1995).

Once you have a good problem statement and objective, you're ready to conduct library research. You're done with your library research when you have a theoretical or conceptual framework, a well-defined research question or hypothesis, and when you fully understand the significance of your study.

▼ ## Research Sources

Let's say you have a vague idea of a general topic area, but aren't sure how to narrow your idea from there. The first thing you might want to do is browse journals and books in your topic area to get ideas from what other people have studied. There are many sources of literature for your library research; some are more suited to academic purposes than others:

- Books—often give the original (or primary) information on a topic or theory, but typically are more out-of-date since there is a much longer lag time from writing to publication.
- Articles—in scholarly journals, tend to be up-to-date and therefore often cutting-edge; in peer-reviewed journals, have met academic standards.
- Governmental statistical data—often available online, usually up-to-date and available (Hart, 2001).
- Other sources, such as magazines, newspapers, and websites—typically not appropriate for a scholarly review of the literature.

There are several good sources of secondary research in Communication Studies: handbooks, textbooks, edited books, and journals. Scholarly type books consist of monographs (often published by communication associations or key publishers in our field), anthologies or edited books, textbooks, and reference books (Hart, 2001). Books are more difficult than journals to identify as scholarly versus nonscholarly, but one good rule to evaluate books is to look at their references—if the book itself cites scholarly references, then it is likely a scholarly book.

Scholarly Journals

The key journals in the field of Communication Studies are published by communication associations:

→**The International Communication Association (ICA) publishes six journals:**

- *Journal of Communication*—publishes primary research reports on all aspects of communication.
- *Human Communication Research*—publishes primary research reports on human communication with a social science focus.
- *Communication Theory*—publishes articles and essays introducing, suggesting, critiquing, or extending communication theory; publishes articles based on both primary and secondary sources.
- *Journal of Computer-Mediated Communication*—publishes primary research reports related to communication via the Web.
- *Communication, Culture, and Critique*—publishes primary research reports that are related to media and cultural studies topics.
- *Annals of the International Communication Association*—publishes interdisciplinary and international communication-related research.

→**The National Communication Association (NCA) publishes 11 journals:**

- *Communication and Critical/Cultural Studies*—publishes both primary and secondary research-based articles related to criticisms of cultural power and issues of class, race, ethnicity, marginalization, and so on.
- *Communication Education*—publishes primary research related to communication instruction.

- *Communication Monographs*—publishes primary research articles on interpersonal, group, organizational, cultural, and media communication.
- *Communication Teacher*—publishes teaching and classroom suggestions for Communication courses.
- *Critical Studies in Media Communication*—publishes primary research in mass media topics.
- *Journal of Applied Communication Research*—publishes primary research on applied communication topics, often related to organizational, group, and health communication.
- *Journal of International and Intercultural Communication*—publishes primary research related to cultural and international contexts.
- *Quarterly Journal of Speech*—publishes primary research that specifically uses different forms of rhetorical analysis as the methodology.
- *Review of Communication*—an online journal that publishes reviews of other communication-related publications.
- *Text and Performance Quarterly*—publishes primary research that is related to communication performance, communication-as-performance, and "Performance Studies."
- *First Amendment Studies*—publishes essays related to free speech law and rhetorical analysis of judicial rhetoric.

There are several regional communication associations, each of which also publishes journals:

- The Southern States Communication Association (SSCA) publishes a journal called *Southern Communication Journal* (SCJ), which includes articles on primary research from a wide variety of communication contexts and topics.
- The Central States Communication Association (CSCA) publishes *Communication Studies*, which also includes primary research from a variety of communication areas.
- The Western States Communication Association publishes two general communication journals, *Western Journal of Communication* and *Communication Reports*.
- The Eastern Communication Association (ECA) publishes two general communication journals, *Communication Quarterly* and *Communication Research Reports*, and one journal that focuses on qualitative research, *Qualitative Research Reports in Communication*.

In addition, most states have communication associations that publish journals or yearbooks. Carolina's Communication Association, for example, publishes *The Carolina Communication Annual*.

→The Association for Education in Journalism and Mass Communication (AEJMC) publishes three journals:

- *Journalism and Mass Communication Quarterly*—publishes primary research on journalism and mass communication.

- *Journalism and Mass Communication Educator*—publishes teaching and classroom suggestions for journalism and mass communication courses.
- *Journalism and Communication Monographs*—publishes primary research on journalism and mass communication and theory-related topics.

The Public Relations Society of America (PRSA) publishes the *Public Relations Journal* which includes primary research on public relations related topics.

→**The American Marketing Association publishes four journals in the field of advertising and marketing:**

- *Journal of Marketing*
- *Journal of Marketing Research*
- *Journal of International Marketing*
- *Journal of Public Policy and Marketing*

The Advertising Educational Foundation publishes an online journal called *Advertising and Society Review*, and the Advertising Research Foundation publishes the *Journal of Advertising Research*.

There are also many specialized and interdisciplinary journals that may be of interest to students in our field:

- The Organization for Research on Women and Communication publishes *Women's Studies in Communication*, which includes primary research on gender and feminist issues.
- Students interested in health communication (and related areas) may want to look at general and specialized journals such as *Journal of Health Communication: International Perspectives, Health Communication, Journal of Loss and Trauma, Journal of Qualitative Health Research,* and *Disability Studies Quarterly.*
- Students interested in looking at qualitative research could browse *Qualitative Inquiry; Qualitative Research; Journal of Contemporary Ethnography; International Review of Qualitative Research; Storytelling, Self, and Society;* and *Qualitative Communication Research.*
- Students interested in interpersonal and family communication could look at *Symbolic Interaction, Journal of Family Communication, Journal of Loss and Trauma, Journal of Social and Personal Relationships,* and *Journal of Divorce and Remarriage.*
- Students interested in cultural studies should check out the journals *Cultural Studies* and *Cultural Studies* ↔ *Critical Methodologies.*
- Students interested in public relations should also investigate *Public Relations Quarterly, Public Relations Review,* and *Journal of Public Relations Research.*
- Students interested in rhetoric and advocacy could look at *Rhetoric and Public Affairs* and *Rhetoric Society Quarterly.*
- Students interested in mass communication should look at *Critical Studies in Media Communication.*

- *Howard Journal of Communication* publishes research related to culture and ethnicity.
- Students interested in organizational communication might want to look at management journals such as *MIT Sloan Management Review, Management Communication Quarterly, Journal of Business Communication, Small Group Research,* and *Journal of Organizational Behavior.*

How Do You Access Scholarly Journals?　Now you've got lots of names of journals, but how do you access the journals? If you Google the journal name, you will likely be able to access a table of contents and maybe a list of abstracts. Perhaps this is all you need to begin forming ideas. For example, let's say you think you might be interested in family communication. Google the *Journal of Family Communication* (http://www.tandfonline.com/toc/hjfc20/current). The first listing gives you the Web page for the journal.

When you click on that link, it takes you straight to the listing for the current issue of that journal. Notice that this listing gives "volumes" and "issues." The volume represents a year for the journal; for example, in the *Journal of Family Communication,* 2016 journals are all Volume 16. Within a year, each journal is represented by an issue. The *Journal of Family Communication* publishes four issues per year.

Take a look at the page for the current issue: Volume 16, Issue 4.

You get a list of the eight articles in that issue. The first one ("Grief Communication and Privacy Rules: Examining the Communication of Individuals Bereaved by the Death of a Family Member," by Basinger, Wehrman, and McAninch, 2016) sounds interesting. Let's see if you can get more information about it. Click the link for the abstract.

The abstract is a short description (usually 100–300 words) of the article. If you're only looking for general ideas, the abstract may be all you need for right now. But let's say you're intrigued and want to read the actual article. This is as far as you're allowed to go on the Internet without subscribing to the journal. However, you haven't really hit a dead end.

Your university library subscribes to many of these journals. Let's see if your library subscribes to this one. Go to the Web page for your university library. It probably has an opening screen with a place to search the library catalog for books, then a tab for articles, and a tab for journals. Since you're looking for a journal, click the link for journals.

Let's see what happens when you type in the journal title, *Journal of Family Communication.*

You're in luck if the library subscribes to it and it's available online.

If your library doesn't subscribe to the journal, you can order the article through Interlibrary Loan. Interlibrary Loan (sometimes called ILL) usually takes a few days to a few weeks to arrive, so you'd have to allow time for that in your schedule.

If your library does have this journal, you'll come to a listing of volumes for the journal. Remember that you were looking for an article in Volume 16, Issue 4. And remember that Volume 16 was 2016, so look at 2016, then select Issue

4. This time, when you click on the article from the list, it will open the article. For right now, you can either print it or read it online.

Finding Research Sources Using Search Strategies

Now let's say through browsing journals and the Internet, talking to friends, and reading the newspaper, you've decided on your communication-related topic: "grief communication." Your study objective is: "This research will determine how people communicate when they are bereaved over the death of a loved one." Your next step is to find out what other research has been done on this and related topics. Let's identify the key concepts in this objective: "bereavement communication" and "grief communication." Before you start searching, think of alternative or related concepts you can use if you need them. For example, you might also search for simply "bereavement" or "grief," or perhaps "death," or "death of loved ones."

You would use your library Web page to search for journal articles on the topic. You conduct this search through **databases**—sources that search through many journals at a time. There are many databases you can use, and there are a few that tend to work best for the field of communication studies. Some of our favorites are "Academic Search Complete," "Web of Science," and "Communication and Mass Media Complete." While Google is an inappropriate search engine to use for academic research, Google Scholar might yield useful information because it includes peer-reviewed papers and articles (Munger & Campbell, 2007). Google Scholar also might include some sites that aren't appropriate for academic research, so you'll need to be a bit more discerning if you search through that source.

You can start your search in a specific database or in all databases. You would start by choosing a search term. If you combine "bereavement" and "communication," you would type in: "bereavement AND communication." The word "AND" is in all caps because it is a **Boolean search** term, and you are using it to connect the two concepts. You are telling the search engine that you want only articles that have both of your terms in the keywords. It's really important to make sure you also check the box for "scholarly (peer-reviewed) journals" because you are only interested in scholarly or **academic journals** for this research project.

Your search should yield a list of articles that relate to your term. If you have too few "hits," you can broaden your search by eliminating one or part of your terms or by choosing a different search term. If you have too many "hits," you can narrow your search by adding additional search terms or choosing a different one.

Once you've found an article you think might fit your research needs, you click the title of the article to access the record. On the article record page, you will see options to access the PDF full text to pull up the article just as you would see it in a print journal.

Evaluating Research Sources

Not all sources are created equal. As Booth and colleagues (1995) said, "One good source is worth more than a score of mediocre ones, and one accurate summary of a good source is sometimes worth more than the source itself" (p. 71). The

databases
Sources that search through many journals at a time.

Boolean search
A search function that is used to connect two or more concepts in a search engine. Common Boolean search operators are "and" (narrows the search) and "or" (expands the search).

academic journals
Collections of published, peer-reviewed scholarly research that are often consulted by academic scholars, government agencies, policy makers, and businesses to inform their decision making.

first step in evaluating your source is to read it—all of it. And read it slowly and carefully (Booth et al., 1995).

First of all, make sure it really is an article in a scholarly journal. You selected that check box, but databases sometimes make errors, so you need to make sure it's really a scholarly journal you're reading. If you recognize the journal name from the list earlier in the chapter, you're in luck. All of the names we gave you are scholarly journals. The reason that this is an important distinction is because scholarly research falls under the practice of **peer review**—a "self regulatory practice designed to protect against the publication of flawed research or unsound scholarship, and to recognize and promote innovative and cutting-edge studies," says Art Bochner, NCA President (Bochner, 2008, p. 3). In other words, peer review is the way a scholarly field determines which research is acceptable, sound, and valid, and which is not. Make sure you understand the requirements of your assignment, but for most literature reviews or library research assignments for college classes, your professor will either prefer or require that you use scholarly sources. If you don't recognize the name of the journal, how else can you tell? Simply put, many journals have the word "journal" in their name. Many will state that they are published by a scholarly association. It's sad to say, but you can also use this general rule: If it looks as if it's fun to read, it might not be a scholarly journal. If it looks like a magazine article with lots of glossy pages, color pictures, and white space, it's probably a magazine article, and not a journal. If it is more dense, with more complex language, usually with footnotes, endnotes, references, and citations, it's more likely to be a scholarly journal. Watch out here, though. Some people publish what look like scholarly articles on websites that are not peer reviewed and are not in scholarly journals. Don't be fooled. You want to use articles that are in recognized peer-reviewed journals, unless otherwise instructed by your professor.

In some cases, you might need additional information that is not available from academic sources. For example, suppose you are doing library research on domestic violence and you want to provide statistics on the number of people who were killed by spouses last year. An academic journal would not likely have up-to-date information on that subject, but the Internet very likely might (Munger & Campbell, 2007). You have to be careful with Internet sources, however. Anyone can create a website or post to a blog, and the Internet has no standards under which posted messages must fall. Look at who the sponsor of the site is and try to determine where the information came from (Munger & Campbell, 2007).

Just like not all sources are equal, not all journals are equal either. As a general rule, international journals are rated more highly than national journals, which are rated more highly than regional journals, which are rated more highly than state journals.

There are several other criteria to evaluate sources. The most straightforward is the year of publication. How current is the research? In most cases, the more recent, the better. For some reason, certain topics have peaks and valleys; some years there is a lot published on a topic, and in other years, not so much (Rossman, 1995). You may find this to be the case. Notice how the

peer review
The way in which a scholarly field determines which research is acceptable, sound, and valid, and which is not.

research has evolved in each peak—the topic likely has a slightly (or largely) different focus from one peak to another. Make sure you know which focus you're interested in. Knowing when the study was done will help determine if replicability is needed or warranted. Maybe the research you're looking at is old—does it need to be updated? If you're suggesting updating outdated research, then you should go ahead and cite the research you're updating. Generally, though, this textbook was published in 2017, and we probably wouldn't cite any sources older than 2010. The exception would be if you are citing a source that is considered a *classic* in the field of communication studies. For example, if you're talking about the concept of symbolic interactionism, you'd need to cite Blumer, who wrote the original book on the topic, *Symbolic Interactionism: Perspective and Method*, in 1969.

Another consideration is the reputation of the author. How well known is this person? How much has this person published? How prestigious are the journals or publishers of this person's work? How often have the author and this article been cited? You may not have been in this field long enough to know the answers to all of these questions, but if you have a few communication classes under your belt, you may have heard some names related to some of the key theories or concepts in our field. If they're in your textbook, and if you're studying them in a general survey class of communication theory, they're important names. So, for example, if you're citing symbolic interactionism, you might want to cite what someone currently said about it, but you'd definitely want to cite what Blumer (1969) said as well.

Other evaluation variables concern how the research was conducted. Is it relevant to you? How does the research topic relate to your topic? How was the population sampled? How does this population relate to your objectives? Is the perspective of the article local, regional, national, or international? Why was the study conducted? What problem was the researcher addressing?

Finally, is this a primary or secondary source? For most of the literature reviews you are writing, you will be synthesizing primary sources, that is, you will be reporting on primary research reports that describe actual research studies. Occasionally, however, you might, in the course of your library research, find that someone has published a synthesis of the literature on your topic. Feel free to use this, but use it properly. If the synthesis says anything new, such as commenting on, critiquing, or extending the literature they're reviewing, cite that source. Otherwise, to cite the sources they are citing, you must go to the primary source. In other words, if someone named Smith cites Blumer, you must go directly to Blumer to cite Blumer. You cannot count on Smith properly explaining and summarizing Blumer. It is very bad form and lazy research to stop at the secondary source. Booth and colleagues (1995) suggest that you cite both the primary and secondary sources and reiterate that you must go to the primary source and read it before you use it. Booth and colleagues (1995) also say, "You will soon discover that you cannot trust researchers to quote reliably. It is intellectually lazy not to look up an important quotation in its original context if that source is easily available" (p. 75). Instead of relying only on the secondary source, use it to point you in the right direction. Feel free to look up references, and once you've read them yourself, then you can use them.

• •

▼ How to Read a Journal Article

We've said that you need to read the journal article thoroughly. But how do you read a journal article? If you start reading at the beginning and move through it, for most articles, you'll get bogged down in the "Findings" section before figuring out what you're reading.

Papers differ slightly in their headings and organization, but most articles have the following sections in roughly this order: Abstract, Introduction, Literature Review, Findings, Discussion, Limitations, and Conclusion. We suggest you read them out of order. We know this may feel odd, but we have a good reason to suggest this. We generally read research articles in this order:

1. Abstract
2. Introduction
3. Conclusion
4. Discussion
5. Literature Review
6. Method
7. Findings
8. Limitations
9. References

Read to gather the following information, in this order:

1. What is the *research topic*?
2. What are the *main points* and *findings*?
3. What *claim* is this article making?
4. What is the *evidence* for that claim?
5. Is this *basic* or *applied* research?
6. Does this have a *research question* or a *hypothesis*? What is it?
7. How highly *regarded* is the journal?
8. How *recent* is the research?
9. What is the *methodology*? Is it clearly detailed?
10. How *in-depth* was the research?
11. How recent are the *sources*?
12. What *relevant quotes* might you use from this in your own literature review?
13. What other *sources* should you look up from the article's literature review?

If, at any point answering these questions, you find that the article is not appropriate for your library research, move on to another article; don't waste any more time on one that's not relevant to your needs.

Let's consider the article we found above in the *Journal of Family Communication* by Erin D. Basinger, Erin C. Wehrman, and Kelly G. McAninch (2016) called "Grief Communication and Privacy Rules: Examining the Communication of Individuals Bereaved by the Death of a Family Member." Under the title and names of the authors, the first thing you see is the abstract. The abstract is always found directly after the title, before the body of the paper begins. It is often in italics, centered, or otherwise set apart from the rest of the text. Perusing the abstract tells you that the article is about communication about grief, communication privacy management theory, and how people who are bereaved navigate discussions about death and the deceased. Sounds interesting so far.

From the abstract, this appears to be **applied research**, although you don't yet know the research question or hypothesis. You also know that this is a highly regarded journal (if nothing else, you know we gave you the name of the journal in the list earlier in the chapter of scholarly journals in our field), and that it is a recent article.

To find out more, you'll have to read further. Jump to the Introduction. The paper starts off with these two sentences:

> *The loss of a loved one can be a life-altering experience, and grief can have devastating effects, including increased levels of anxiety, anger, and depression (Asai et al., 2010; Holland & Neimeyer, 2010). Due to its complex nature, grief can continue for long periods of time as the bereaved work through stages of grief toward accepting their loss (Kübler-Ross & Kessler, 2005) (p. 285).*

Right up front, you know that this is a significant problem for society because grief can be life-altering, devastation, complex, and long-lasting.

The Conclusion section tells you:

> *The goal of this investigation was to examine grief communication through the lens of three processes identified in communication privacy management theory: privacy ownership, privacy control, and privacy turbulence (Petronio, 2013). Bereaved individuals indicated that they think of their grief as something that they own (RQ1), and they described three types of rules that govern how they interact with others about their loved one: selectivity rules, avoidance rules, and positivity rules (RQ2). In spite of their rules, however, participants also indicated that they had some turbulent exchanges with family members, friends, and romantic partners (RQ3). The types of turbulence they experienced were primarily boundary rule mistakes, dissimilar privacy orientations, and intentional rule violations (Petronio, 2002). The results of the study support assumptions in CPM about the processes that regulate the sharing or withholding of private information, and they resonate with extant research on grief communication that describes the complexity of losing a loved one (pp. 299–300).*

The Conclusion summarizes the study. From the conclusion, you now know that grief feels very personal and private to people who are experiencing it; that people communicate their grief with others while following very specific social rules related to with whom they do and do not share their grief and preferences for focusing on positive aspects of the deceased; and, finally, grief communication can be turbulent.

You will want to move to the Discussion section and here you can find additional information about, for example, privacy rules and turbulence. From the Discussion section, you know that turbulent communication involved violations of privacy expectations and information sharing, and occurred over many interactions.

Now that you know what Basinger, Wehrman, and McAninch found in their research, you might decide that this paper is relevant to your own research. Take a step back and look at the first three paragraphs of their "Literature Review" to begin to get a sense about what's known thus far (before Basinger, Wehrman, and McAninch's research) on these topics:

As we observed before, loss and grief can be life-altering and devastating (according to Asai et al., 2010, and Holland and Neimeyer, 2010). Grief is complex and long-lasting (according to Kübler-Ross and Kessler, 2005). The second paragraph of the literature review also tells us that communicating about grief can be helpful in that it can help ease the emotional distress of grief (according to Rosenblatt and Elde, 1990 and Sedney, Baker, and Gross, 1994); strengthen relationships (according to Hooghe, Neimeyer, and Rober, 2011, and Shapiro, 2008); obtain social support (according to Golish and Powell, 2003, and Kübler-Ross and Kessler, 2005); help the survivors renegotiate their identities and roles in light of their loss (according to Gilbert, 1989); and lower depression and stress (according to Calvete and De Arroyabe, 2012, and Kaunonen, Tarkka, Paunonen, and Laippala, 1999). The downside of sharing about grief is that some experiences are difficult to share because of discomfort or fear of stigma (according to Brierley-Jones, Crawley, Loman, and Ayers, 2014–2015, and Maguire et al., 2015); and because of responses from others that are not helpful (according to Breen and O'Conner, 2011).

As you keep reading through the Literature Review, you'll see that it also provides the different concepts, theories, and definitions the authors are using to design this study, and you'll note that Basinger, Wehrman, and McAninch use the literature to inform their Research Questions.

Next, take a look at the Methods section and see how Basinger, Wehrman, and McAninch did what they did. "Participants" tells who they interviewed, where and how they found the people to interview, and describes the participants:

Method. *We conducted individual interviews with college students who had lost a parent or a sibling. We used analytic techniques from grounded theory methodology (Charmaz, 2006; Corbin & Strauss, 2008), guided by concepts from CPM theory. Our analyses centered on how the bereaved conceptualized ownership of information about their grief, how they enacted privacy rules surrounding information about the death of their family member and their grief, and how they experienced turbulence when their privacy rules were breached.*

Participants. *We interviewed 21 individuals whose father (n = 11, 52.4%), mother (n = 4, 19.0%), brother (n = 4, 19.0%), or sister (n = 2, 9.5%) had died. All participants* *were college students from a variety of majors at a large Midwestern university. Participants' ages ranged from 19–28 years (M = 21.24), and a majority were female (n = 15, 71.4%). Over half of the interviewees identified their race/ethnicity as European American/White (n = 13, 61.9%), and other participants were African American/Black (n = 6, 28.6%), Asian American (n = 1, 4.8%), and Pakistani (n = 1, 4.8%). Most family members died from health-related issues (n = 17, 81.0%), whereas others died because of accidents (n = 2, 9.5%) or were murdered (n = 2, 9.5%). Family members' deaths occurred an average of 7.17 years prior to the interview (SD = 6.06), ranging from 1 month to 20 years (pp. 288–289).*

As Basinger, Wehrman, and McAninch move through the Methods section, they describe their study procedures, consent process, and analysis process.

Finally, in the Results section, Basinger, Wehrman, and McAninch tell how they came up with their findings—how they analyzed their data and drew their conclusions. While you may not yet be familiar with the procedures they use in this paper, you can still begin to form opinions as to whether their methods seem appropriate, or if they make sense to you.

The last thing to look at is their references. You are looking for two things in the "Reference" section. First, how old are their sources? They range from 1984 to 2016, but most are from the past five years. Some of the oldest ones are classics. Perhaps you've heard of Argyle and Henderson's (1984) friendship rules in your interpersonal communication class. So, while a few of their references are older, the older ones are the classic sources, and this tells you that they are extending and applying these concepts and theories. You have to evaluate the age of their sources with the rest of their research—was it conceptually, methodologically, and analytically sound? Perhaps you could discuss your opinions of that in class. You'll learn more specifics about how to critique research throughout this textbook.

The second reason you want to look at the reference list is to *mine* their sources. Perhaps from the Literature Review, you find the concept of social support particularly useful for your study. Basinger, Wehrman, and McAninch cite Golish and Powell's 2003 article about social support, but if you want to cite Golish and Powell, you'll need to read it yourself. Think of the reference list as an additional database of potential sources for you to look up.

• •

Taking Notes on Research   ▼

You've read an article and have begun to critique it. You've gotten to the point where you think this article will be a great one to include in your library research and literature review. Now you have to take notes on it. You're taking notes for two purposes: to make sure you have the information you need to use in your paper (to make sure you have it down thoroughly and accurately) and to make sure you have the information you need to properly cite your source.

In order to make sure your notes give you enough information to understand and remember what you've read, Booth and colleagues (1995) suggest that you write down not only the single idea you want to use, but also the paragraph or several paragraphs around it so you can fully understand the concept or argument the author is making.

Many students find it helpful to use "old-fashioned" bibliography notes written on index cards. Other students type out the information on their word processor. There is also software available to categorize information, such as Endnotes, and Munger and Campbell (2007) suggest creating a personal blog (blogger.com or livejournal.com) to capture your information. However you capture the information, it's a good idea to put the information for each citation on separate pages or index cards so you can sort and resort through them later as you're organizing your synthesis. At a minimum, you want to put down your citation information, the abstract, a summary of the findings, and the key points from the discussion. To avoid unintentional plagiarism (we'll discuss plagiarism in Chapter 4), make sure you are clear about summarizing, paraphrasing, or quoting (Booth et al., 1995). If you're using quotes, make sure you put down the page number for the quote, and make sure you put the quote in quotation marks so you remember it's a direct quote. We'll talk about citations in Chapter 4, but at this point, you need to know that you must cite your sources accurately to avoid charges of plagiarism. Plagiarism can ruin careers, derail graduations, and cause students to fail courses.

Take a look at the APA, MLA, or Chicago Manual of Style citation requirements to make sure you're getting all the information you need for your citation. There's nothing worse than wanting to use a source, but not being able to because you left off an important piece of citation information and can no longer find the article or book to get it again. When you put down the citation information for a book, for example, you'll need first and last names of all the authors (in the same order listed on the book cover), year of publication, exact name, publication location, and publishing company. When you put down the citation information for a journal article, you'll need the first and last names of all the authors (in order), year of publication, name of journal, volume number, issue number, and page numbers of the article. If you've accessed the article via the Web, it would also be helpful to put the URL so you can find it again, if necessary (Munger & Campbell, 2007).

When you're taking notes on the findings or main points, make sure you get the exact quotes and page numbers for direct quotations. Make sure you correctly read the article so that you understand it and are getting the context and claim right. If you used a source to go to one of their sources, make sure you are properly differentiating between primary and secondary sources.

When taking notes, you might find it helpful to follow this format, answering each question:

- What is the correct citation for the article?
- What is the purpose statement?
- What is the research question or hypothesis?
- What are the key concepts or variables under study?
- What is the method of data collection?
- What are the key findings or conclusions?
- What are other key pieces of information you found in the article that might be relevant to your research?

So What?

In this chapter, we've shown you how to conduct library research and how to choose and use databases, journals, and scholarly articles from our field of Communication Studies. We've shown you how to evaluate and read scholarly research. In short, we've shown you how communication scholars begin their scholarship. Communication scholars use systematic, scholarly, scientific methods to conduct research from the minute they get a research idea to the publication of that research idea. In Chapter 4, we'll show you the next step in the scholarship process—what to do with your library research.

Glossary

Academic journals
Collections of published, peer-reviewed scholarly research that are often consulted by academic scholars, government agencies, policy makers, and businesses to inform their decision making.

Applied research
Research that tests theory in real life contexts to see if it can be used to solve problems.

Body of knowledge
Research that has already been conducted.

Boolean search
A search function that is used to connect two or more concepts in a search engine. Common Boolean search operators are "and" (narrows the search) and "or" (expands the search).

Databases
Sources that search through many journals at a time.

Peer review
The way in which a scholarly field determines which research is acceptable, sound, and valid, and which is not.

Primary research
Research that is conducted to answer a specific problem or question and produces original data.

Secondary research
Research that has been previously collected or conducted.

Study objectives
What it is that researchers hope to answer through their research. Good researchers refer back to the objectives every step of the way, and insure that everything they are doing answers these objectives. Usually, there are one main objective and several related secondary objectives.

References

Alberts, J., Hecht, M., Buley, J., & Petronio, S. (1993). Methods for studying interpersonal communication research. In S. Petronio, J. Alberts, M. Hecht, & J. Buley (Eds.), *Contemporary perspectives on interpersonal communication* (pp. 18–24). Dubuque, IA: Wm. C. Brown.

Argyle, M., & Henderson, M. (1984). The rules of friendship. *Journal of Social and Personal Relationships, 1*, 211–237. doi:10.1177/0265407584012005

Asai, M., Fujimori, M., Akizuki, N., Inagaki, M., Matsui, Y., & Uchitomi, Y. (2010). Psychological states and coping strategies after bereavement among the spouses of cancer patients: A qualitative study. *Psycho-Oncology, 19*, 38–45. doi:10.1002/pon.1444

Basinger, E. D., Wehrman, E. C., & McAninch, K. G. (2016). Grief communication and privacy rules: Examining the communication of individuals bereaved by the death of a family member. *Journal of Family Communication, 16*(4), 285–302. doi: 10.1080/15267432.2016.1182534

Bochner, A. (2008, May). The case against the anonymous culture of peer review. *Spectra, 44*(5), 3.

Booth, W. C., Colomb, G. G., & Williams, J. M. (1995). *The craft of research*. Chicago: University of Chicago Press.

Breen, L. J., & O'Connor, M. (2011). Family and social networks after bereavement: Experiences of support, change and isolation. *Journal of Family Therapy, 33*, 98–120. doi:10.1111/j.1467-6427.2010.00495.x

Calvete, E., & De Arroyabe, E. L. (2012). Depression and grief in Spanish family caregivers of people with traumatic brain injury: The roles of social support and coping. *Brain Injury, 26*, 834–843. doi:10.3109/02699052.2012.655363

Galvan, J. L. (2006). *Writing literature reviews: A guide for students of the social and behavioral sciences*. Glendale, CA: Pyrczak.

Golish, T. D., & Powell, K. A. (2003). Ambiguous loss: Managing the dialectics of grief associated with premature birth. *Journal of Social and Personal Relationships, 20*, 309–334. doi:10.1177/0265407503020003003

Hart, C. (2001). *Doing a literature search: A comprehensive guide for the social sciences*. London: Sage.

Holland, J. M., & Neimeyer, R. A. (2010). An examination of stage theory of grief among individuals bereaved by natural and violent causes: A meaning-oriented contribution. *Omega: Journal of Death & Dying, 61*, 103–120. doi:10.2190/OM.61.2.b

Hooghe, A., Neimeyer, R. A., & Rober, P. (2011). The complexity of couple communication in bereavement: An illustrative case study. *Death Studies, 35*, 905–924. doi:10.1080/07481187.2011.553335

Kaunonen, M., Tarkka, M., Paunonen, M., & Laippala, P. (1999). Grief and social support after the death of a spouse. *Journal of Advanced Nursing, 30*, 1304–1311. doi:10.1046/j.1365-2648.1999.01220

Kübler-Ross, E., & Kessler, D. (2005). *On grief and grieving: Finding the meaning of grief through the five stages of loss*. New York, NY: Scribner

Munger, D., & Campbell, S. (2007). *What every student should know about . . . researching online*. New York: Pearson Longman.

Rosenblatt, P. C., & Elde, C. (1990). Shared reminiscence about a deceased parent: Implications for grief education and grief counseling. *Family Relations, 39*, 206–210. doi:10.2307/585725

Ross, R. S. (1977). *Speech communication: Fundamentals and practice*. Englewood Cliffs, NJ: Prentice-Hall.

Rossman, M. H. (1995). *Negotiating graduate school: A guide for graduate students*. Thousand Oaks, CA: Sage.

Sedney, M. A., Baker, J. E., & Gross, E. (1994). "The story" of a death: Therapeutic considerations with bereaved families. *Journal of Marital and Family Therapy, 20*, 287–296. doi:10.1111/j.1752-0606.1994.tb00116.x

Shapiro, E. R. (2008). Whose recovery, of what? Relationships and environments promoting grief and growth. *Death Studies, 32*, 40–58. doi:10.1080/07481180701741277

WRITING A LITERATURE REVIEW

4

CHAPTER OUTLINE

KEY TERMS

American Psychological Association (APA) style

Annotated bibliography

Chicago style

Literature review

Modern Language Association (MLA) style

Plagarism

CHAPTER OBJECTIVES

1. To understand the purpose and use of a literature review
2. To understand how to synthesize literature
3. To understand how to write a literature review, using appropriate grammar, style, and organization
4. To understand how to use citations properly in a literature review

▼ # What's the Purpose of a Literature Review?

literature review
Summary of existing literature on a given topic.

This chapter assumes you are writing a stand-alone **literature review** that serves the express purpose of synthesizing the existing literature on the topic. In Chapter 3, we taught you how to find good-quality research. In this chapter, we'll teach you how to use it—we'll discuss the definition and purposes of a literature review. Then we'll teach you how to synthesize the literature and how to write up the literature review: how to organize it, use proper citation to avoid plagiarism, and use appropriate writing and citation styles.

You may later write a literature review that becomes part of another project, such as a research proposal or a research paper, but we're assuming for now that your literature review will specifically be a summary and critique of the previous (usually academic) literature on a given topic, organized thematically or topically (Rossman, 1995). Its purpose is to give the reader a clear overview of what is known about the topic, point out common themes in existing research, and draw conclusions about what knowledge there is in the topic area. Literature reviews such as these are often called a *synthesis of the literature* because they combine and blend what's already been researched on a topic.

There are other purposes for conducting a literature review that you should be aware of, however. You might also write a literature review as part of a research proposal. This type of literature review not only summarizes existing literature but also builds your argument on why your study is necessary to be done, in the way you are proposing to do it. You might also write a literature review as part of a research paper reporting on your research findings. This type of literature review also summarizes existing literature, explains why you did the research the way you did it, and also shows the theories and concepts on which you built your study (remember the deductive paradigm) and the prior research that influenced the ways you operationalized (defined) and measured your variables. Often, with a literature review, you are building your case for your research study, so your literature review will provide evidence of what important questions remain to be explored and why your study can address those questions. This is why all research reports and proposals begin with a literature review, because a literature review shows your expertise and knowledge about your topic area, and shows you are up-to-date on the literature (Rossman, 1995).

In this chapter, we will discuss the elements of a good literature review; how a literature review is differentiated from another similar assignment that students frequently confuse it with—annotated bibliographies; specific skills related to writing a literature review such as synthesizing the literature and organizing the paper; and other writing elements related to writing literature reviews, such as proper citation, avoiding plagiarism, and avoiding common grammatical mistakes. In short, in Chapter 3 we told you how to find your literature. In this chapter, we will tell you everything you need to know to write up your findings.

What Is a Literature Review?

A literature review is not a list of separate summaries of your various sources; that would be a form of an **annotated bibliography**. Instead, a literature review is a single summary, of several things: research conclusions previously made on your topic, the various methods that have been used to investigate your topic, and what areas still remain to be investigated on your topic. Your literature review places your research in the context of current and past studies. It compares your proposed research with what others have done—what they've studied and what they haven't, and what problems and successes they had in their design and methodology (and how they addressed any problems they had). Your literature review will help you decide what design and methodology you should use based on what has worked and has not worked for other people.

Your literature review gives you the ammunition to argue for your research: how is your study different from and/or better than other research that's already been done? It lets you justify the importance of your topic area. Finally, your literature review will help you decide on the theoretical or conceptual framework on which you will be basing your research (Rossman, 1995).

In Chapter 3, we suggested it might be helpful to think of your literature review as a way to enter the scholarly conversation. A conversation about Communication scholarship has been going on for decades. Just like joining any conversation, you want to know what is being said before you interject. You have to listen before you can contribute something, and your literature review is your way of listening to what's being said.

annotated bibliography
A list of separate summaries of various sources.

Annotated Bibliography versus Synthesis of the Literature

The number one problem students have in writing literature reviews is synthesizing the literature. Many first-time literature reviews read like annotated bibliographies— a listing of summaries of research studies, one at a time, with no link or connection between them. Here's an annotated bibliography that was published in a journal, *Technical Communication Quarterly*, to describe specific research published about organizational culture. Notice how, even though the research studies are compared to each other, the bibliography summarizes the research one study at a time, keeping each of the summaries separate from each other.

Paige, Michael. *Education for the Intercultural Experience.* Yarmouth, ME: Intercultural Press, 1994.

In this edited collection, Paige compiles articles and essays from the field of intercultural communication. These articles address the ways in which individuals are affected by and react to the different cultural dimensions encountered in international

Continued

From "Organizational & Intercultural Communication: An Annotated Bibliography" by H. Constantinides, K. St., Amant & C. Kampf, *Technical Communication Quarterly*, *10(1)*, 2001; reprinted by permission of the publisher, (Taylor & Francis Ltd, http://www.tandfonline.com).

Continued

and intercultural immersion experiences. They discuss in more depth many of the issues raised by Adler with respect to cross-cultural managers, such as culture shock, intercultural adjustment, and reentry. However, the articles also address other topics such as Milton Bennett's model of intercultural sensitivity, the effects of intercultural experience on the individual, methods for preparing individuals to live in another culture, and ways to recognize and deal with the stress inherent in intercultural communication.

In contrast to Adler, the articles in this book focus exclusively on the personal aspects of and preparation for intercultural experiences. As such, they are useful for helping individuals develop empathy for people from other cultures, people whom they may encounter as co-workers, audiences, and clients in international business contexts. These essays also can help global employees prepare for assignments that immerse them in different cultures.

Storti, Craig. *Cross-Cultural Dialogues: 74 Brief Encounters with Cultural Differences*. Yarmouth, ME: Intercultural Press, 1994.

Storti gives examples of intercultural miscommunication for the reader to

In contrast, look at the literature review section of the article "Cultural Identity Tensions in a Post-Acquisition Organization" by Pepper and Larson, 2006, in the *Journal of Applied Communication Research*.

From "Cultural Identity Tensions in a Post-Acquisition Organization" by G.L. Pepper & G.S. Larson, *Journal of Applied Communication Research, Vol. 34, No. 1*, January 2, 2006, reprinted by permission of the publisher (Taylor & Francis Ltd, http://www.tandfonline.com).

Identification and Disidentification with Cultural Premises

When people experience identity tensions, what they are wrestling with are cultural premises. Organizational culture refers to "patterns of human action and its recursive behaviors (including talk and its symbolic residues) and meanings" (Eisenberg & Riley, 2001, p. 294). Thus, organizational culture includes practices, as well as organizationally embedded values, assumptions, and expectations (Pacanowsky & O'Donnell-Trujillo, 1982, 1983; Schrodt, 2002).

Organizations are multi-cultural (Nicotera, Clinkscales, & Walker, 2003), and these multiple cultures are held together by what Parker (2000) refers to as "stabilizations of meaning" (p. 81). Culture and organization construct each other, resulting in both fragmentation and unity (Alvesson & Berg, 1992; Koene, Boone, & Soeters, 1997; J. Martin, 2002). Thus, "organizations are collective but also divided — not either one or the other" (Parker, 2000, p. 223). Organizational culture is a composite reflection of stakeholder stories (Mills, Boylstein, & Lorean, 2001) that represent the sensemaking (Weick, 1995) of groups as diverse as managers, founders, salespeople, and customers. And, as shown at the opening of this paper and elsewhere (Dukerich, Golden, & Shortell, 2002; Lampe, 2002), culture can have both a positive and negative impact on both employees and organizational performance.

Because of the large potential impact of organizational culture, managers and organizational leaders will try to create and manipulate culture in ways consistent with corporate profit and success. These efforts at creating uniform values, beliefs, and behaviors are often futile because culture, especially in complex organizations, is difficult to manage from the top (J. Martin, 2002; Parker, 2000; Turner, 1999).

The relationship between identification and organizational culture is crucial to understand when trying to discern acquisition success and failure. Strong cultures often produce highly identified employees, which may then lead to highly committed workers and concertive control (Barker, 1999; Tompkins & Cheney, 1983).

Notice how different this synthesis is from the annotated bibliography. Especially notice how the different references have been merged together, discussed under a common topic or finding. For example, in the second paragraph, notice the line that says: "Culture and organization construct each other, resulting in both fragmentation and unity (Alvesson & Berg, 1992; Koene, Boone, & Soeters, 1997; J. Martin, 2002)." This sentence references three different studies, all of which talk about how culture and organizations both fragment and unify each other. They have been merged, or synthesized, into this one idea.

The next sentence merges in a related thought from another research study, and uses a direct quote from that study to make their point: "Thus, 'organizations are collective but also divided—not either one or the other' (Parker, 2000, p. 223)."

This next sentence continues to talk about what organizational culture is, pulling together two more related-yet-different thoughts from two other references:

Organizational culture is a composite reflection of stakeholder stories (Mills, Boylstein, & Lorean, 2001) that represent the sensemaking (Weick, 1995) of groups as diverse as managers, founders, salespeople, and customers.

Here are more examples of synthesis of sources. First, here are three separate sources discussing communication competence. This first is from Query and James (1989):

human communication to create, maintain, and terminate relationships. The task portion of the continuum refers to how the interactants communicate job-related information to one another.

The preceding examination of communication competence has two implications for the present study. First, communication competence is a multidimensional concept. Second, communication competence is contextually bound. For the present study, *communication competence* is defined as the perceived ability to communicate one's view as well as to understand another's perspective across a variety of situations. Similar to the view of social skills previously advanced by Heller (1979) and by B. R. Sarason et al. (1985), this definition encompasses social support reception and provision. Addressing social support reception, individuals have to be able to symbolically influence interaction in order to mobilize their support group or social network. Concerning social support provision, social actors must be able to interpret another person's situation to render satisfactory social support.

From "The Relationship Between Interpersonal Communication Competence and Social Support Groups in Retirement Communities" by Jim. L. Query & Anita C. James, *Health Communication, Vol. 1, No.3*, January 7, 1989; reprinted by permission of the publisher, (Taylor & Francis Ltd, http://www.tandfonline.com).

Next is an excerpt from Cegala, Socha McGee, and McNeilis (1996) also discussing communication competence:

From "Components of Patients' and Doctors' Perceptions of Communication Competence During a Primary Care Medical Interview" by Donald J. Cegala; Deborah Socha McGee; Kelly McNeilis, *Health Communication, Vol. 8, No. 1,* January 1, 1996; reprinted by permission of the publisher (Taylor & Francis Ltd, http://www.tandfonline.com).

guage-in-use), and it all but ignores the role of context. As an alternative, we propose an approach to research on competence that is grounded in communicative behavior and, as such, is inherently context-bound (see Cegala & Waldron, 1992). Our approach is by no means adverse to striving toward a general theory of communication, but it assumes that such a theory is likely to evolve from deep understanding of what competence is within several different contexts.

Finally, here is an excerpt from McNeilis (2001) also discussing communication competence:

From "Analyzing Communication Competence in Medical Consultations" by Kelly McNeilis, *Health Communication, Vol. 13, No. 1,* January 1, 2001; reprinted by permission of the publisher, (Taylor & Francis Ltd, http://www.tandfonline.com).

promise of the CACS is its ability to provide assessments of linguistic communication competence at the dyadic level. On the basis of the results of the coding system applied to these data, some conclusions about communication competence in the medical consultation are made here.

Competence Assessments

Results of this coding scheme provide some insights into health communication processes between physicians and patients regarding their use of specific linguistic strategies for accomplishing various goals. In particular, the use of continuers and other similar strategies by physicians (and patients) were observed as a recurring pattern within information exchange portions of the consultation.

Now, here's a paragraph synthesizing those three sources:

Davis, C. S., Massey, O. T., Armstrong, M., Vergon, K. S., & Smith, R. B. (2008). *Refinement of an instrument to measure mental health literacy among caregivers and providers and a qualitative examination of interventions to enhance mental health literacy.* Tampa, FL: Louis de la Parte Florida Mental Health Institute. University of South Florida.

The concept of communication competence has been defined as "the perceived ability to communicate one's view as well as to understand another's perspective across a variety of situations" (Query & James, 1989, p. 171), and, as Cegala, Socha McGee, and McNeilis (1996), McNeilis (2001), and Query and James (1989) point out, communication competence is bound by context, situation, and goals.

Notice how important it is, when you are synthesizing your literature, to take the time to read thoroughly so you can fully understand what the research claims and does. It would be impossible to merge and synthesize research articles without a thorough knowledge of what each article claims.

Organizing the Literature Review ▼

Synthesizing your literature is easier if you organize your paper according to your synthesis. In your literature review, you are making an argument, a claim (Booth, Colomb, & Williams, 1995). Your claim answers your research question (RQ), which for your literature review might be along the lines of: "What have other researchers found out about _____ ?" (Your claim for that RQ would state: "Other researchers have discovered these three things: _____.") If you synthesize the literature within each element of the claim, both your synthesis and organization will flow naturally.

Here's how you do that. Since you are making a claim, you should start your paper with that claim. You will be building your argument on this claim, and you will offer evidence from your literature review to support your claim. In other words, you will claim that "these things are known," and then provide the literature that supports that claim (Booth et al., 1995).

Typically, you will follow this organizational pattern:

1. Introduction: Introduce the topic and provide a preview of what is to follow
   a. Claim: Briefly describe what this research will show
2. Literature Review: Organize around your claim
3. Conclusion: Restate your claim and summarize your main points

You will likely organize your literature review topically: "These three things are known." You might also organize it chronologically: "We used to think this, but now we think this," or comparatively: "It's done this way in Europe, but this way in the United States." Let your data tell you how to best organize it. As you read through your sources, ask yourself how they are best grouped—what are the areas in which they are similar or different? Where do topics overlap and what are the most important findings to come out of all the research you have read? What are the trends, themes, or key ideas the literature indicates?

Know your organization scheme (and claim) before you begin writing, and as you are writing your literature review, make sure your organization follows your claim. For example, if your claim states that "three things are known," your literature review should have three distinct sections—one for each of the three themes. Make sure you use clean, smooth transitions between each of the themes. This can be as easy as saying: "Unlike this first theme, this next theme does_____," or "The next main area of research is_____."

You'll state your claim in the introduction, and you'll develop it in the literature review section, talking about each separate theme one at a time, making (in a sense) mini-claims for each theme. You'll cite the studies you read as illustrations or examples for each claim, and you'll use this literature to develop each point of your claim. You'll show how the studies are connected and how they relate to the themes. You can also critique the validity of the research, if possible, so if you read a study that didn't make sense to you or didn't seem to be conducted in a valid manner, you can say that in your literature review.

▼ # Citations

As you are synthesizing your literature and writing up your findings, you need to remember to cite your sources properly. We'll talk about citation styles in a minute, but let's go back to the Pepper and Larson example and take a look at how they cited their sources. Note that they've listed all the authors (we'll discuss exceptions to that in a minute) in all the papers they are citing. Look at this example:

> *Culture and organization construct each other, resulting in both fragmentation and unity (Alvesson & Berg, 1992; Koene, Boone, & Soeters, 1997; J. Martin, 2002).*

They are citing three different studies. The first was a 1992 study written by two authors, one with the last name of Alvesson and one with the last name of Berg. They are listed in that order (Alvesson first, and Berg second) because that's the order they were in the paper they cited. This is very important! Authorial order is important, and it's political and negotiated. At some universities, for example, first author position counts more toward tenure for a faculty member than second or subsequent positions. First author position implies that the first person listed is the one who spearheaded the research and took charge of writing and revising it. The order of subsequent positions is negotiated between the authors based, at various times, on amount of effort, work performed, and seniority on the project and in the organization. Teams of researchers who do many studies together may decide to rotate order of authorship. The point you should understand is that the authors did not take this order lightly and neither should you. Always list authors in the order they have listed them.

The second study was one published in 1997 and written by three authors: the first, a person with the last name of Koene, the second, with the last name of Boone, and the third, with the last name of Soeters. The third study was one published in 2002 and was written by J. Martin. The first initial is listed here to differentiate the author from another author with the same last name.

Do you see what order the three studies are listed? No, not chronological (although that would also be true for this example). They are ordered alphabetically—Alvesson comes before Koene, and Koene comes before Martin.

How do we know they're citing three different studies and not one study with six authors? There are two clues. First, there are three years, which indicate three different publishing dates. And, second, while commas separate the names of authors in a single article, semicolons separate the articles.

▼ # Avoiding Plagiarism

plagiarism
The failure to properly cite sources, which results in taking credit for someone else's words or ideas.

Why are we telling you how to cite your sources? Failure to cite your sources properly is called **plagiarism**. It is illegal because it is a violation of copyright laws. It is a form of cheating and stealing because you are taking credit for someone else's ideas and words. It is serious. It can get you kicked out of school, or can cause you to flunk a class or get a zero on an assignment. It can prevent you from graduating or from getting a job or a promotion. It can ruin your career and cause you to incur fines or even face legal charges. Now that so many sources are available on the Internet, it's very easy to plagiarize. However, you should know that it's also very easy to get caught. There are as many ways on the Internet to catch plagiarism as there are to plagiarize. We've already said that it's a mark of a good scholar to build on the ideas of other people, so we're not suggesting that you *not use* sources, we're just insisting that when you do, you give them proper credit. Look at it this way, after you're done conducting your research study and writing up the findings, would you want other people to take your work and claim it as theirs?

Booth and colleagues (1995) say it well:

Intentional plagiarism is theft, but of more than words. By not acknowledging a source, the plagiarist steals some of the little reward that an academic community has to offer, the enhanced respect that a researcher spends a lifetime trying to earn. The plagiarism steals from his (or her) community of classmates by making the quality of their work seem worse by comparison and then perhaps steals again by taking one of the few good grades reserved to reward those who do good work. By choosing not to learn the skills that research can teach [him or] her, the plagiarist not only compromises [his or] her own education but steals from the larger society that devotes its resources to training students to do reliable work later. Most important, plagiarism, like theft among friends, shreds the fabric of community (p. 257).

Even if you didn't mean to do it, plagiarism is still plagiarism (Booth et al., 1995). Many plagiarism cases happen when students get in a hurry taking notes from their sources, then when writing up the paper, they can't read their notes or find they don't contain all the needed information (Davis, 2007). What, exactly, do you need to make sure you *avoid plagiarism*? According to Booth and colleagues (1995), it's plagiarism when you use someone else's *words*, but fail to credit him or her; use someone else's *ideas*, but fail to credit him or her; or use someone's *exact words*, but fail to put the quote in quotation marks or block indentation, and/or fail to put page number references for the quote. So what's the bottom line? Give proper credit to your sources!

Usually, you'll be paraphrasing someone's words. It's a poorly written literature review that consists of one quote after another. A good general rule is that you paraphrase unless you are so enamored with the words the person used that you just have to use them. Be careful when paraphrasing, though. Make sure you rewrite the information sufficiently so that you're not plagiarizing. Remember that simply changing one or two words is not sufficient. To paraphrase, you must understand the entire idea and then restate it in your own words. Write it as if you're explaining it to a friend when the original source is not in front of you (Booth et al., 1995).

Here, for example, is a proper paraphrase of a research article:

The role of the empowered consumer implies that patients take on a problem-solving, collaborative role in their own care. Reports of medical miscommunication resulting from patients' misunderstanding of medical terminology; different perceptions and understandings of their health problems and goals; and obstacles between patient and provider, support the importance of a communication competence view of health literacy (Young & Flower, 2001).

Here's one of the pages from the original article that yielded some of the information for the paraphrase:

From "Patients as Partners, Patients as Problem-Solvers" by Amanda Young & Linda Flower, *Health Communication, Vol. 14, No. 1,* January 1, 2002; reprinted by permission of the publisher, (Taylor & Francis Ltd, http://www.tandfonline.com).

A major frustration among health care providers is the lack of patient compliance. Yet, patients usually have logical reasons for their behavior—perhaps a specific treatment is too embarrassing, too painful, too costly, or too time-consuming. Perhaps the patient does not understand the providers' instructions. Perhaps the patient does not have the necessary coping strategies to endure a specific treatment. Patients with cystic fibrosis, for example, have often complained that doctors and therapists do not understand how sore they get from continual chest percussion or how much the treatment interferes with the whole family's schedule . . .

The same article states, later on the same page:

Creating a Partnership Between Providers and Patients

An optimal medical encounter is an experience that validates the expertise of both patient and provider and that dignifies the patient's needs throughout the entire sequence of treatment. In a problem-solving relationship, patients and providers concentrate on negotiation and shared agency, rather than on compliance. Instead of a patient being given a choice to simply comply or not, patients and providers can jointly develop a plan of care that recognizes the social, psychological, and financial constraints of the patient. This partnership is dependent, however, on a reciprocal relationship that incorporates the strategies of CI.

The *SAFE Program*[7] is a clear illustration of how to create a patient–provider partnership (see Figure 2). Young women at Children's Hospital of Pittsburgh are . . .

[7]SAFE is part of a 5-year longitudinal study directed by Melanie Gold, DO, at Children's Hospital of Pittsburgh. Young and Gold developed the computer program using the concepts of CI. The follow-up counseling is based on Miller's (1983) model of motivational interviewing.

You can see how this information (plus other information from the overall article) is properly paraphrased into the paragraph above. The general understanding and ideas came from this Young and Flower (2001) article, but it is rewritten in the author's own words.

• •

▼ Writing Styles

When you cite your sources and write your paper, you'll be following one of a few accepted *styles*. If you are writing a paper for a class, your instructor will let you know which style s/he wants you to use. In the field of Communication

Studies, you will likely be using one of three styles: **American Psychological Association (APA) style**, **Modern Language Association (MLA) style**, or **Chicago style**. Each of the different styles came out of different academic traditions, and each is best for different types of papers. Most social science and communication scholars use APA, so this is the style we will talk about most in this chapter. A few communication-related or interdisciplinary journals use MLA or Chicago, so we will talk briefly about these two styles, as well.

The style manuals instruct you how to format your paper, how to cite your sources in the text (in the body of your paper), and how to list your references and cite your sources in a list at the end of your paper. Each style manual differs on how you list the author's name, where you place the publication date, where and how you use marks such as italics, quotations, or capitalization, and where and how you list the publisher's name, among many other things (Weidenborner, Caruso, & Parks, 2005). You should refer to the original manuals for specific, detailed information about each of the styles, but following is some general information about them. We recommend that you use this chapter to help remind you what details you should attend to for each style. Please remember, however, that this chapter is not intended to replace the use of the original style manuals.

Regardless of the style, you must develop an eye for detail to adhere to the proper style. In your citations, the number of spaces between words and punctuation marks is important. When to italicize and when not to italicize is important. How to list an author's name, when to italicize, and when to capitalize is important. In writing your paper, you need to know exactly how wide your margins should be, what font should be used, as well as what font size should be used. In addition, you need to know the difference in citation style between a journal article, a book, and a chapter in an edited book.

Here are some tips for each of the styles used in our field:

American Psychological Association (APA) Style (6th edition, 2nd printing)

Many of the NCA journals (*Communication Education, Communication Monographs, Communication Teacher, Critical Studies in Media Communication, Journal of International and Intercultural Communication, Journal of Applied Communication Research*, and *Review of Communication*) use APA style.

Body of the Paper. First of all, for you journalism majors, APA is not the same as AP. They are extremely different styles. Written in APA style, your paper will have 1" margins top, bottom, right, and left. Your right margin will be nonjustified. You will use 12-point type, in Times New Roman font. You will have a title page, an abstract page (in most cases), the body of your paper, and a reference section.

Your title page will include a header line, which includes the "running head," flush left, then on the same line, the page number, flush right. The running head includes the words "Running head," then a colon, then (in all caps) a short version of your title. The title page is numbered page one. About one-half to one-third of the way down the page, you will have the long version of your title on one or two lines, your name on the next line, your university affiliation on the next line, and, depending on the needs of your paper, separate lines for your course name,

American Psychological Association (APA) style
The editorial style most commonly used by social science and communication scholars, this style features a list of references and specifies the names and order of headings, among other elements. (Please refer to the Publication Manual of the American Psychological Association for the most up-to-date style rules and guidelines.)

Modern Language Association (MLA) style
An editorial style sometimes used by communication scholars that features an alphabetical list of works cited and brief parenthetical citations in the text, among other elements. (Please refer to the MLA Handbook for Writers of Research Papers and the MLA Style Manual and Guide to Scholarly Publishing for the most up-to-date style rules and guidelines.)

Chicago style
An editorial style sometimes used by communication scholars that is useful for providing detailed information about sources, and features footnotes and endnotes, among other elements. (Please refer to the Chicago Manual of Style for the most up-to-date style rules and guidelines.)

instructor name, and contact information. All of these lines will be centered, and double-spaced. Here's a sample title page in APA style:

Running head: DUELING NARRATIVES   1

Dueling Narratives: How Peer Leaders Use Narrative

to Frame Meaning in Community Mental Health Care Teams

Christine S. Davis, Ph.D.

Assistant Professor

University of North Carolina at Charlotte

Department of Communication Studies

9201 University City Blvd., Colvard 5004

Charlotte, North Carolina 28223

704-687-6638

Fax: 704-687-6900

csdavis2@email.uncc.edu

From page two on, your header will consist of your running head (WITHOUT the words "running head") flush left, and the page number flush right. Your header is in all caps. Note that your header MUST be on the same line as your page number. You accomplish this in the "Insert Header" function in Word. Tip: In Word, within "Insert Header" go to "Edit Header," and check "different first page" to let you change the header from page one to two.

Page two includes your abstract. The abstract is (usually) a 100- to 250-word brief summary of your paper (Booth et al., 1995). It provides the RQ, key themes, and the main point of the research. It begins with a line centered that says, "Abstract." The abstract begins on the very next line, with *no* first line indent. If you have keywords, they go on the next line, right after the abstract, indent, with the word "keywords" in italics. From here, throughout the rest of the paper, you will double-space. Here's a sample abstract page:

DUELING NARRATIVES   2

Abstract

Successfully leading an interorganizational peer-led team, a team of people from different backgrounds and organizations that are at comparable hierarchical levels with the leader, is a challenge, as is leading such a group to a new model in which the traditionally dominant frame is no longer valid. This research, reporting on observations of 118 child and family team meetings in a community children's mental health system of care, looks at peer leaders' narrative discourse to reframe meaning and assume leadership of the team. Leaders' use of strong narratives to frame consistent, clear, and congruent messages leads to both narrative power and their own desired outcomes.

Keywords: Narrative power, Narrative discourse, Team leadership, Peer-led teams

The body of your paper begins on page three. The first line is the long title, centered. The second line begins your paper. In the prior version of APA (the 5th edition), you used to include a header called "Introduction," but in the newest 6th edition, you no longer have that initial header. In APA, there are no extra lines between headers or between headers and the body of your paper, anywhere in the paper. Here's a sample of the first page of a paper:

DUELING NARRATIVES   3

Dueling Narratives: How Peer Leaders Use Narrative

to Frame Meaning in Community Mental Health Care Teams

In this research, I examine peer leadership within children's community mental health

system of care child and family team meetings and specifically look at the acquisition of power

and leadership through team leaders' and members' use of narrative to frame and reframe

meaning.

This research contributes to current knowledge by studying an interorganizational peer-

led team—a team of individuals from different organizations, all of whom are at comparable

status levels to each other and to the official team leader. I specifically address the paradox of

power from a seemingly power-less leader, by describing and giving examples of narrative

Your *first* level of section heading is reserved for the main sections of your paper, usually "Literature Review," "Study Objectives," "Discussion," and "Conclusion," for example. This level of heading is on its own line, centered, and boldface, with the first letter of each word capitalized. Your *second* level of section heading is for your subheadings. For example, if you are making three main points within your "Literature Review" section, you would have three subheads—one for each point. As in the example below, this level of subhead is on its own line, boldface, and flush left. The first letter of each word is capitalized.

If you have a *third* level of header, it is on the first line of the paragraph, tabbed (1/2-inch tab), and boldface, with only the first letter of the first word capitalized, and a period at the end of the header. Your paragraph would continue on the same line.

DUELING NARRATIVES   8

through sensemaking--communicating, managing, constructing, and creating a shared understanding of experience (Drath & Palus, 1994; Lennie, 1999; Witherspoon, 1997).

This paper will show the child and family team leader, with no other formal source of power, must coordinate and direct team participants in a way that creates a new meaning that follows a system of care orientation. It will specifically discuss the team leaders' and members' use of narrative to frame and reframe meaning and acquire power and leadership of the team.

Literature Review

Narrative as a Framing Device

Definition of narrative. Narratives can be defined as "the discursive way in which we organize, account for, give meaning to, and understand, that is, give structure and coherence to, the circumstances and the events in our lives . . . for and with ourselves and others" (Anderson, 1997, p. 212). People use narratives or stories to organize, make sense of, interpret, direct, and create meaning from their experiences. Leaders use storytelling to enact meaning-making (Drath & Palus, 1994). Our narratives evolve through interaction, language, and conversation; come from our individual perspectives; and influence the way people behave and interact in society (Anderson, 1997; Freeman & Lobovits, 1993; Herman, 2001; Parry & Doan, 1994). Understanding the discourse in these child and family team meetings as narratives, as stories with a beginning, middle, and end, and with characters, history, action, and a plot, lets us examine the conversational way in which the team leaders—and members—attempt to frame the meaning in the meetings.

Stories as source of conflict. In fact, in these meetings, it is the stories—or the meanings stories assign to actions and discourse—which are the source of team conflict. It is most likely

Reference List. In APA, your citations differ greatly depending on what type of citation you're using. Let's start with the citations at the end of your paper. This is called the "Reference" page, and this page begins a new page after the last page of the body of your paper. Your reference list is in alphabetical order. Any reference in this list *must* be used and cited in the body of the paper, and any reference used and cited in the body of the paper *must* be in this reference list. Your reference list has a *hanging indent*, which you access in Word through the "indent" dialogue box, using a 1/2-inch hanging indent.

DUELING NARRATIVES   32

References

Anderson, H. (1997). *Conversation, language, and possibilities: A postmodern approach to therapy.* NY: Basic.

Avery, C. M. (1999). All power to you: Collaborative leadership works. *The Journal for Quality and Participation, 22*(2), 36-40. Retrieved from: http://www.asq.org/

Barton, L. (1996). Sociology and disability: Some emerging issues. In L. Barton (Ed.), *Disability and society: Emerging issues and insights* (pp. 3-17). NY: Longman.

Bastien, D. T. & Hostager, T. J. (1992). Cooperation as communicative accomplishment: A symbolic interaction analysis of an improvised jazz concert. *Communication Studies, 43,* 92-104. Retrieved from: http://associationdatabase.com/aws/CSCA/pt/sp/journal

Bateson, G. (1972). *Steps to an ecology of the mind.* Chicago: University of Chicago Press.

On your "Reference" page, for a citation from a book, you would put the author's last name, then a comma, then the author's initial(s) (use whatever initials the author gave in the article itself and separate initials with a space), followed by a period, then the publication year in parentheses, followed by a period. Next is the title of the book in italics. The only letters you capitalize are the first letter of the first word of the title, the first letter of the first word that follows a colon or period, or a proper noun. The title ends with a period, followed by the city/state or city/country of publication, a colon, the publisher name, and a period. A citation for a single-authored book looks like this:

> Anderson, H. (1997). *Conversation, language, and possibilities:*
> *A postmodern approach to therapy.* New York, NY: Basic Books.

If you have more than one author, you would put the author names in the order they have them in the article. You would have a comma between them, and a comma followed by an ampersand (&) before the last name:

> Drath, W. H., & Palus, C. J. (1994). *Making common sense: Leadership as meaning-making in a community of practice.* Greensboro, NC: Center for Creative Leadership.

The citation style for an article in a journal is very different. Notice that you start the same way, listing the authors' names using first initials, a comma between names, an ampersand before the last name, and the year in parentheses followed by a period. The title of the article is *not* in italics. The only letters you capitalize in the article title are the first letter of the first word of the title, the first letter of the first word that follows a colon or period, or a proper noun. The title ends with a period. This is followed by the journal title in italics with the first letter of each word capitalized (*except* prepositions, conjunctions, and the words *the*, *a*, and *an*, unless it is the first word of the title). The journal title closes with a comma, followed by the journal volume number, followed by an issue number in parentheses, followed by a comma, then the inclusive (all) page numbers of the article, followed by a period. Note that the volume number is also in italics, but the issue number and page numbers are *not* in italics:

> Bastien, D. T., & Hostager, T. J. (1992). Cooperation as communicative accomplishment: A symbolic interaction analysis of an improvised jazz concert. *Communication Studies, 43*(2), 92–104.

If the journal is available as a published (hard copy) journal but you accessed it online, you would add the DOI number to the end of the citation. DOI stands for Digital Object Identifier, and this is a new style guideline as of the new 6th edition of the APA style manual. This is a code consisting of numbers and/or letters, and it's easiest if you just cut and paste it from the article to your citation. The DOI number can be found either in the article itself or in the database record. If there isn't one, then instead add to the end of your citation: "Retrieved from [the home page URL of the journal]." Note that the term "doi" is all in lowercase letters, and there is no period after a DOI number.

> An, S. (2008). Antidepressant direct-to-consumer advertising and social perception of the prevalence of depression: Application of the availability heuristic. *Health Communication, 23*(6), 499–505. doi: 10.1080/10410230802342127
>
> An, S. (2008). Antidepressant direct-to-consumer advertising and social perception of the prevalence of depression: Application of the availability heuristic. *Health Communication, 23*(6), 499–505. Retrieved from http://www.erlbaum.com/Journals/journals/HC/hc.htm

If it's an online journal (a journal published *only* online), the citation is:

> Bounds, P. (2008, May). Beyond *Ways of Seeing:* The media criticism of John Berger. Retrieved from http://www.fifth-estate-online.co.uk/criticsm/P.Bounds.html

There is no period after a URL.

You also might cite a chapter in an edited book. Again, you start with the author's last name and first initial, but this time you start with the author of the *chapter* you are citing. This is followed by the publication year in parentheses. The title of the chapter is next, *not* in italics, with the only letters you capitalize being the first letter of the first word of the title, the first letter of the first word that follows a colon or period, or a proper noun. This is followed by the citation information for the book from which you took the chapter. The chapter title ends in a period, then you type "In [*book* editor's name]." Note that the book editors' names here are reversed—first initials followed by last name. Note that if there is more than one editor, you put an ampersand before the last one, but not a comma. Notice that after the last name there is no comma, and this is followed by the word "Ed." (one editor) or "Eds." (two or more editors). This is in parentheses, followed by a comma, followed by the title of the edited book (in italics). The only letters you capitalize in the book title are the first letter of the first word of the title, the first letter of the first word that follows a colon or period, or a proper noun. The title does *not* end with a period, but is followed by the inclusive page numbers of the chapter you are citing in parentheses. Note that the page numbers are preceded by the letters "pp" and a period. A period is also placed after the closing parenthesis and the citation ends with the city of publication, a colon, the name of the publisher, and a period:

> Charmaz, K. (2000). Grounded theory: Objectivist and constructivist methods. In N. K. Denzin & Y. S. Lincoln (Eds.), *The handbook of qualitative research* (pp. 509–535). Thousand Oaks, CA: Sage.

In the references, always include all authors' names regardless of how many there are. Remember, put them in the same order as they were in the original paper or book that you are citing.

Increasingly important is the proper citing of electronic sources such as websites and Web pages. When citing a Web page, your reference will begin with the author of the page in the same format you would use for a journal article or book. If no author is provided, the title of the page will be the first entry, followed by a period. The only letters you capitalize in the title are the first letter of the first word of the title, the first letter of the first word that follows a colon or period, or a proper noun. The year of publication, in parentheses, follows. If no date is available, use "n.d." inside the parentheses. A period is used on the outside of these parentheses, followed by a space. Complete the citation with "Retrieved on [date you retrieved it] from [insert URL]" (remember, there is no period after a URL).

> What's new in the sixth edition of the publication manual? (n.d.).
>
> Retrieved June 6, 2016, from http://www.apastyle.org/manual/
>
> whats-new.aspx

If you are citing an entire website, you need only to give the address in your in-text citation. No end-of-text reference is necessary.

> The APA style website is a great source for information on
>
> structuring your paper, grammar, and citation examples
>
> (http://www.apastyle.org).

In-Text Citations. In addition to putting your citations in the reference list at the end of the paper, you also must cite within the text, at the point at which you are referring to the source. This is called an in-text citation, and there are some different ways to do this. You might want to write your sentence making your claim without using the name of the author specifically. If you do this, you would put the citation in parentheses at the end of the sentence, such as in this example:

> Organizational theorists generally agree that, regardless of its
>
> source, leadership requires power or the ability to influence
>
> behavior (Stupak & Leitner, 2001).

Note that in-text you only list the author's last name. Notice that you have an ampersand, but no comma between the two names. You do, however, have a comma between the last name and the year. And your period to end the sentence is outside the parentheses, *not* within them.

Perhaps you want to use the source's name in your sentence. To do this, you put the publication year in parentheses after the name, as shown here:

> Anderson (1997) points out . . .

If you're citing two authors' names in your sentence, always use *and* rather than an ampersand:

> Smircich and Morgan (1982) suggest that framing the meaning of
>
> a team requires the acquiescence to power among other team
>
> members.

If you're citing something in-text that has one or two authors, you must cite the author's or both authors' names every time. If there are three to five authors, you list all the names the first time you cite it, then omit every name after the first in subsequent times and replace them with "et al.":

> (Anderson et al., 2003).

In text, you can use the less awkward sounding:

> Anderson and colleagues (2003) said . . .

If your text has six or more authors, you *always* (even the first time) only list the first name, then "et al." It is "et al." in the reference section also.

When citing websites or Web pages, there is often no author or editor listed. In these cases, you would begin the citation in parentheses at the end of the sentence with the title or abbreviated title of the Web page or article. This title should be surrounded by double quotation marks, with each word capitalized. A comma inside the quotation marks will separate the title from the year. Again, if no date is available, use "n.d." It is often helpful to include a paragraph number following the date. The date and paragraph number are also separated by a comma.

> ("What's New in the Sixth Edition," n.d., para 3).

There are many more details and other types of citations you may need; you should refer to the most recent edition of the *Publication Manual of the American Psychological Association* (American Psychological Association, 2009) for more information.

Modern Language Association (MLA) Style (8th edition)

One of the NCA journals (*Text and Performance Quarterly*) uses MLA style.

MLA differs from APA in many significant ways. For example, the references page is titled "Works Cited." It, too, is formatted with a hanging indent, with the works organized alphabetically, and the book or journal titles are also italicized. A journal article is placed in quotation marks. Instead of using the author's first initial, you spell out the first name. The first author is listed as "last name, first name, middle initial." Subsequent authors are listed as "first name, middle initial, last name." The publication year is placed at the end of the citation (in parentheses). The first letter of each word in titles is capitalized (*except* for articles such as *and*, *a*, and *the* in the middle of the sentence). In addition to the volume number, you also include the issue number. This is written as "vol. #, no. #". The three references we gave you earlier would look like this in MLA:

> Anderson, Harlene. *Conversation, Language, and Possibilities: A Post-
> modern Approach to Therapy*. Basic Books, 1997.

Bastien, David T., and Todd J. Hostager. "Cooperation as Communicative Accomplishment: A Symbolic Interaction Analysis of an Improvised Jazz Concert." *Communication Studies*, vol. 43, no. 2, 1992, pp. 92–104.

Charmaz, Kathy. "Grounded Theory: Objectivist and Constructivist Methods." *The Handbook of Qualitative Research*, edited by Norman K. Denzin and Yvonna S. Lincoln. Sage, 2000, pp. 509–35.

In-text, each of these citations would be referred to parenthetically (in parentheses) by name and page number (*not* by year), as follows:

Organizational theorists generally agree that, regardless of its source, leadership requires power or the ability to influence behavior (Stupak and Leitner 784–801).

Anderson points out. . . . (629).

Smircich and Morgan suggest that framing the meaning of a team requires the acquiescence to power among other team members (543).

Chicago Style (16th edition)

Two of the NCA journals (*Communication and Critical/Cultural Studies* and *Quarterly Journal of Speech*) use Chicago style.

Instead of using the parenthetical, in-text style used by APA and MLA, the Chicago style uses an endnote or footnote system. In text, each citation is given a footnote or endnote notation and a note that refers to the numbered endnotes at the end of the manuscript or footnotes at the bottom of each page.

The three references we gave you earlier would be listed both in endnotes or footnotes, and also in a separate Bibliography at the end of the paper. Following is the format for the endnotes or footnotes. Note that the Bibliography style is slightly different, as well:

1. Harlene Anderson, *Conversation, Language, and Possibilities: A Postmodern Approach to Therapy* (New York: Basic Books, 1997), 483.

2. David T. Bastien and Todd J. Hostager, "Cooperation as Communicative Accomplishment: A Symbolic Interaction Analysis of an Improvised Jazz Concert," *Communication Studies* 43, no. 5 (1992): 96.

3. Kathy Charmaz, "Grounded Theory: Objectivist and Constructivist Methods," in *The Handbook of Qualitative Research*, ed. Norman K. Denzin and Yvonna S. Lincoln (Thousand Oaks, CA: Sage, 2000), 509.

In the Bibliography, the citations would be in alphabetical order, would have a hanging indent, and would look like this:

Anderson, Harlene, *Conversation, Language, and Possibilities: A Post-modern Approach to Therapy*. New York: Basic Books, 1997.

Bastien, David T., and Hostager, Todd J. "Cooperation as Communicative Accomplishment: A Symbolic Interaction Analysis of an Improvised Jazz Concert." *Communication Studies* 43, no. 5 (1992): 92–104.

Charmaz, Kathy. *Grounded Theory: Objectivist and Constructivist Methods*. In *The Handbook of Qualitative Research*, edited by Norman K. Denzin and Yvonna S. Lincoln, pg. 15. Thousand Oaks, CA: Sage, 2000.

In text, the citations would look like this:

Organizational theorists generally agree that, regardless of its source, leadership requires power or the ability to influence behavior.[1]

Anderson[2] points out. . . .

Smircich and Morgan[3] suggest that framing the meaning of a team requires the acquiescence to power among other team members.

▼ Common Grammatical Errors

The final thing you need to pay attention to when writing your literature review is grammar and punctuation. Some students are naturally good writers, while other students simply are not. We have found that proper grammar and punctuation separates the "A" papers from the "B" and "C" papers, so we've included this section to give some tips to those of you who need them. You want to make sure your paper is correct in regard to grammar and punctuation. In this chapter, we do not intend to teach you basic grammar, but we want to help you avoid common errors that students often make in their papers.

Remember that all sentences must have a subject (noun) and a verb. A sentence without a subject and a verb is a fragment.

If you are writing a number between one and ten, spell it out. If you're writing a number over 10, use numerical figures (use "12," rather than "twelve"). If mixed numbers (between one and ten, and over 10) referring to the same type of object are in a single sentence, keep it consistent and use figures. Write fractions in figures (1½) unless they begin a sentence—numbers that begin a sentence are always spelled out. Write decimals in figures (.7).

Your subject and verb must agree. If one is singular, both must be singular; if one is plural, both must be plural. So, for example, "We are talking," but "She is talking."

You must keep your tenses consistent. This is a particular challenge when conducting literature reviews, because the tendency is to write using the tense of the paper we are reading, so if the tenses in our literature change, the tenses in our paper tend to change along with them. It's helpful to write in the present tense when reviewing literature ("Smith says that . . .") and in the past tense when you're talking about research you have conducted ("We interviewed 100 people."). This is such a challenge that we recommend that when think you are finished with your paper, make one proofreading pass specifically to check your tenses. While you're at it, make another proofreading pass to check APA and another to check grammar and punctuation.

"Its" is possessive (its scarf means the scarf belongs to it), while "it's" is a contraction that means "it is."

Pronouns should agree with the nouns they are replacing, so for a nonhuman noun, you'd use the pronoun "that," while you'd use "who" for a human noun. ("The class that," but "The teacher who").

Use nongender biased word choices, so do *not* use *mankind* to refer to *humankind*, or *men* to refer to *men and women*. Avoid the generic *he* by alternating between *he* and *she*, using *he/she* or *she/he*, or switching to plural nouns and pronouns ("people and their . . .").

So What?

Writing a good literature review requires good skills in synthesizing the literature, organizing your paper, giving proper credit to your sources in the citation style commonly accepted by your peers in your academic community, and communicating your findings effectively through proper grammar and punctuation. We suggest you treat each of these skills as a separate step in your writing process. Often, students spend the bulk of their time finding the literature and then throw together their findings at the last minute. Unfortunately, students' grades frequently represent this misallocation of time. Once you have found your literature, your work has really just begun. You need to read through the literature so that you can understand the claim to make. You then need to outline your paper, organizing the outline around that claim. Once you have an outline, you're ready to start writing. Many researchers suggest writing your introduction last—after you know what you're actually introducing. Some of us write the introduction first (sometimes it helps us to get started on the paper), but then rewrite it at the end, to make sure it fits with where our paper actually ended up going. This raises another suggestion—you should plan on making several *passes* through your paper. In other words, your paper should go through several drafts. Your first draft will simply get down the information as you fill in the details under each point of your claim. Your next draft will make sure your citations are complete. Your next draft will make sure your citations follow the correct style format exactly. Your next draft will check for grammar and punctuation, perhaps even specific elements for separate passes. For example, one of your authors, Christine Davis, struggles with keeping tenses consistent through my papers. I always take one editing pass specifically to check my tenses. You may know specific writing challenges you have—take the time for a separate editing pass for each one. Finally, we suggest you leave enough time for one final pass, after you've had a good night's sleep. Putting it aside for a few hours will let you come back to your paper with a more objective mind. You'll be surprised how you can identify areas in which you were unclear or disorganized when you look at it with fresh eyes. After all, you've gone to a lot of trouble to learn what there is to know about your topic. Take the time to communicate it to others effectively.

Glossary

American Psychological Association (APA) style
The editorial style most commonly used by social science and communication scholars, this style features a list of references and specifies the names and order of headings, among other elements. (Please refer to the *Publication Manual of the American Psychological Association* for the most up-to-date style rules and guidelines.)

Annotated bibliography
A list of separate summaries of various sources.

Chicago style
An editorial style sometimes used by communication scholars that is useful for providing detailed information about sources, and features footnotes and endnotes, among other elements. (Please refer to the *Chicago Manual of Style* for the most up-to-date style rules and guidelines.)

Literature review
Summary of existing literature on a given topic.

Modern Language Association (MLA) style
An editorial style sometimes used by communication scholars that features an alphabetical list of works cited and brief parenthetical citations in the text, among other elements. (Please refer to the *MLA Handbook for Writers of Research Papers* and the *MLA Style Manual and Guide to Scholarly Publishing* for the most up-to-date style rules and guidelines.)

Plagiarism
The failure to properly cite sources, which results in taking credit for someone else's words or ideas.

References

American Psychological Association (2009). *Publication manual of the American Psychological Association* (6th ed.). Washington, DC: Author.

Booth, W. C, Colomb, G. G., & Williams, J. M. (1995). *The craft of research*. Chicago: University of Chicago Press.

Cegala, D. J, Socha McGee, D., & McNeilis, K. S. (1996). Components of patients' and doctors' perceptions of communication competence during a primary care medical interview. *Health Communication, 8*(1), 1–27.

Constantinides, H., St. Amant, K., & Kampf, C. (2001). Organizational and intercultural communication: An annotated bibliography. *Technical Communication Quarterly, 10*(1), 31–58.

Davis, J. P. (2007). *The Rowman & Littlefield guide to writing with sources*. Lanham, MD: Rowman & Littlefield.

McNeilis, K. S. (2001). Analyzing communication competence in medical consultations. *Health Communication, 13*(1), 5–18.

Query, J. L., & James, A. C. (1989). The relationship between interpersonal communication competence and social support among elderly support groups in retirement communities. *Health Communication, 1*(3), 165–184.

Pepper, G. L., & Larson, G. S. (2006). Cultural identity tensions in a post-acquisition organization. *Journal of Applied Communication Research, 34*(1), 49–71.

Rossman, M. H. (1995). *Negotiating graduate school: A guide for graduate students*. Thousand Oaks, CA: Sage.

Weidenborner, S., Caruso, D., & Parks, G. (2005). *Writing research papers: A guide to the process*. Boston: Bedford/St. Martin's.

Young, A., & Flower, L. (2001). Patients as partners, patients as problem-solvers. *Health Communication, 14*(1), 69–97.

PREPARING TO CONDUCT RESEARCH

PART **2**

5

RESEARCH QUESTIONS, OBJECTIVES, AND HYPOTHESES

CHAPTER OUTLINE

KEY TERMS

Conceptual definition

Fact pattern

Hypothesis

Null hypothesis

Operational definition

Research question

CHAPTER OBJECTIVES

1. To understand the purpose of research questions
2. To explain the different types of research questions
3. To understand research hypotheses
4. To learn how to evaluate research questions
5. To consider the boundaries of research questions and hypotheses

▼ ## How Do You Design Good Quality Research through Appropriate Questions and Hypotheses?

If we do our job as instructors and mentors, by the time you graduate, you will know maybe the answers to some questions, but most importantly—how to ask good questions (Miller & Nicholson, 1976). In this chapter, you will consider the role of objectives, questions, and hypotheses construction in good research design. Your study objectives, the questions you ask, and the hypotheses you write are grounded in metatheory (see Chapter 2), and collectively they contribute to your understanding of communication theory. This chapter will focus on research objectives, questions, and hypotheses, how they are driven by our metatheoretical consideration, and subsequently, how these research objectives, questions, and hypotheses drive the methodological choices we make in research design.

▼ ## What Are the Functions of Theory, Research Objectives, Research Questions, and Hypotheses?

Recall from Chapter 2 that in the deductive paradigm, research questions and hypotheses are derived from theory. Theory, research questions, and hypotheses allow us to organize and summarize information, while simultaneously focusing our attention on important questions or ideas. They also give us a framework for developing and contributing to knowledge, and they function to explain, predict, and/or control. Specifically, theory, research questions, and hypotheses help to explain or make sense of reality, linking interrelated constructs and processes and essentially answering the question of "Why?" (see Barnlund, 1968; Bross, 1953; Dance, 1982; Hall & Lidzey, 1970; Hawes, 1975; Kaplan, 1964; Kuhn, 1970; Littlejohn, 1996; and Poole, 1990). Questions and hypotheses also allow us to predict or forecast what will happen in the future, essentially telling us what we can expect to observe when certain conditions are satisfied. In terms of control, once we understand how a process works, to some extent this understanding allows us to control it. Ultimately, the primary function of research questions, hypotheses, and theory is heuristic, allowing us to generate new knowledge, learning, and understanding. Notice that under this paradigm, research questions and hypotheses are built on existing theory—either extending, testing, or explicating a theory. This type of research falls under the positivist paradigm, using deductive reasoning, and researchers who conduct research in this paradigm believe that reality is fixed, measurable, controllable, orderly, and objective.

Also recall that research can be conducted under the inductive model, in which researchers seek to answer more open-ended questions and end up with, perhaps, a theory, or a deeper understanding of an extant phenomenon. This model of research falls under the interpretive paradigm, and researchers who subscribe to this metatheory tend to believe that reality is subjective, constructed, and chaotic. Note that theory—in terms of providing an organization or framework for knowledge, or understanding of reality—has its place in both paradigms and philosophies of research.

Theories begin with either a **fact pattern** or a question. A fact pattern is a factual relationship occurring repeatedly. A good example of a fact pattern in Communication is what we call *divergence* or *convergence*. Have you ever noticed how when you are in a conversation with someone you like, or perhaps someone you need to impress, you adjust your style of speaking to match hers? This is an example of convergence. What about when you are in a conversation with someone you feel dissimilar to or dislike in some way? Do you tend to match him? Research suggests you will maintain your own style of communicating. This is an example of divergence. Convergence and divergence provide the basis for Communication Accommodation Theory (CAT). Giles and his colleagues have studied CAT in a variety of contexts; for example, one study examined how we adjust our communication behaviors when interacting with the elderly (McCann & Giles, 2006). A researcher working out of the positivist philosophy might design a study to see if CAT affects the therapeutic value of medical communication. A researcher working with interpretivist assumptions might instead look at medical communication in a more open-ended sense, and might in the end use CAT to help explain what they found in their study.

Theories might also begin with a question—a search for an answer to why something happens. As Miller and Nicholson (1976) suggest, "People incessantly ask questions" (p. 10). This search for answers, via questions posed, is really at the heart of the process of inquiry, the search for understanding. In our case, we will focus on the process of communication inquiry, but that does not mean the process of writing and examining research questions we will discuss is inappropriate for other forums of inquiry. However, what is unique to our approach is our substantive vantage point; we are interested in human interaction via communication.

fact pattern
A factual relationship occurring repeatedly.

· ·

What Are Research Objectives?   ▼

Research objectives represent the reasons you give for undertaking your own research project. They are the step between your research topic, your "I wonder if . . ." musing, and your research questions or hypothesis. When you are given an assignment to conduct a research study, the first thing you will do is determine your general area of inquiry. Several of the previous chapters mentioned areas of inquiry in our field of study: organizational communication, health communication, interpersonal communication, mass media, or public relations. From your general area of inquiry, you would need to narrow your focus to a slightly more specific topic for your research. We would suggest you start with something that interests you most—keeping it related to communication, of course. You should work on narrowing your topic until you have something specific enough to build a research study on it.

Next, narrow it by adding modifying words and phrases to each of your topic ideas. For example, if you are interested in the general field of health communication, you might decide you are very interested in patient-provider communication. That's good, but not specific enough. Let's add some modifiers: What types of patients? How about terminally ill patients? What types of healthcare providers? How about physicians? What types of communication? How about giving the bad news about their terminal diagnosis? Ahh, so *now* we see it . . . you're interested in studying how physicians give terminal diagnoses to people with terminal illness. Now, *that's* a research topic! Always think in terms of narrowing down to very specific questions addressing very specific variables. The need for this specificity will become even more apparent in later chapters when we discuss measurement and research procedures. Beginner social scientists often try to answer questions that are too broad to be definitively addressed in a single study. If you find yourself asking, "is this too specific?" the answer is, "probably not."

Now, let's turn your topic into a research objective. Research objectives are your statements of what you ultimately want to accomplish through this research. For many studies, your research objective can be determined by filling in the blanks of this statement: "I am studying _____, because I want to find out [who/what/when/where/whether/how] _____ is, in order to understand _____" (see Booth, Colomb, & Williams, 1995). For the example above, your research objective may be stated as, "I am studying patient-provider communication, because I want to find out how physicians give terminal diagnoses to patients, in order to understand the different ways to break bad medical news." Notice that we added a new part: "in order to understand the different ways to break bad medical news." This last section answers a significance or "so what" element. All research studies should connect to a bigger picture in some way. In the example above, you might be developing a theory about terminal diagnosis communication, or you might be testing an existing theory within this specific context. You might be understanding something that's important to society, or you might be describing something that will have public policy implications, or you might be measuring something that will have financial ramifications. There are lots of ways your study should answer the "so what" question, but you should know—up front—the significance of your own research. Given our arguments above considering specificity, this means that you are likely addressing or informing one small part of a much larger question or phenomenon. That's okay, and it is the nature of scientific inquiry. We take on small questions and problems one at a time, and try to replicate them in different contexts and settings, in an attempt to contribute to the answers to these larger questions. Researchers from the interpretive paradigm might tackle broader questions or issues, but even these must have defined boundaries.

Research objectives are frequently turned into research questions or hypotheses, but qualitative researchers also frequently stop at the research objective stage when designing their qualitative study. Countless qualitative studies simply have one of these two objectives: to understand _____ or to describe _____. In some types of qualitative research, such research objectives are actually unstated. For example, in an autoethnographic narrative (we'll explain more about this in Chapter 14), Davis (2005) wrote a story about her experience with the last week of her mother's life. The unstated objective of that research was to describe that experience. Green's 2002 study of having a child with a disability is another good example of qualitative research that had the (unstated) objective to understand or describe an experience. In her paper, she says that:

> *This work offers a glimpse into the emotional and social experience of disability through the lens of my own experience of mothering a child with severe cerebral palsy. (p. 21)*

Johnson's 2002 essay (textual analysis) on the performance of black American gospel music by white Australian gospel choirs states his objectives in the abstract, as the objectives of his essay are to prove two points—his conclusions, in fact:

> *This essay examines how the medium of gospel music facilitates a dialogic performance of "blackness." This essay also addresses the politics of appropriation, highlighting the ways in which Australians explain their interest in and performance of gospel music and the ironies that underlie these explanations. (p. 99)*

What metatheoretical perspectives (see Chapter 2) do you think these researchers tend toward? Researchers "seeking to understand or describe" reality tend to lean toward the interpretivist tradition. They are using the open-ended study objective (rather than the more specific research question and even more precise hypothesis, to be explained in the next section) to study a reality they believe to be chaotic and subjective.

How Do You Ask Research Questions?

What is a **research question**? Research questions are questions scholars ask about the way things work. Just as research can be basic or applied (see Chapter 1), research questions can be either basic or applied. In our field, most research questions are about the nature of communication or about the relationship between two or more variables. We'll talk more about variables in Chapter 7, but for now you should know that when you are stating a communication research question that relates two variables, at least one of the two variables must be a communication variable, because we are scholars of the process of communication. More on that in Chapter 7.

research question
Questions scholars ask about the way things work.

While research *objectives* are used by communication researchers to design open-ended research about a topic, other communication researchers pose research questions when they want to find out certain information about a topic without making a prediction ahead of time. Research questions are good starting points for new areas of inquiry, as opposed to formal hypotheses (which we will discuss shortly).

Fundamentally, a communication research question must be concerned with communication, must be empirical (which means it can be experienced and is practical and/or pragmatic), and must have some level of specificity. Typically, research questions ask about the *who, what, when, where,* and *how* of communication. They ask about: *Who* is impacted by, or involved in, this communication act; *what* does this communication act look like; *what* are the parts of the communication act; *what* are the categories of the communication act; *what* is the outcome of the communication act; *when* do the parts of the communication act occur; *where* does the communication act occur—what is the environment and context of the communication; *how* does this communication act relate to other things (society, community, power, culture, outcomes, etc.); and/or *how* does this communication act happen?

Consider some examples of research questions about the nature of communication. How much violence is depicted during Saturday morning cartoons? What persuasive techniques are used on late night infomercials? How do couples use touch to signal relationship status in public? All of these questions are concerned with some basic question about communication behavior.

Now consider some examples of research questions exploring the relationship between two variables (remember one must be a communication variable). Do children who watch a lot of cartoons behave more aggressively on the playground? Are couples who touch less in public as happy as couples who touch more in public? How have persuasive techniques in late night infomercials changed over time? Remember, research questions are simply questions that scholars are seeking answers to; there is not a statement or assertion of what will happen, just a question the research attempts to answer.

The research question is symbolized as the capital letters RQ, followed with a numeric subscript (RQ_1). The numeric subscript refers to the number of the research question in a particular study. In a complicated study, you may have several research questions and numbering allows us to keep track of what research question is being analyzed and discussed. Here's an example of a research question from a quantitative study conducted by Segrin, Powell, Givertz, and Brackin (2003):

> RQ_1: Do members of dating couples exhibit symptoms of depression that are indicative of emotional contagion?

And, here's an example of research questions from a qualitative study conducted by Davis (2009):

> RQ_1: What reality does hospice construct for patients and families through communication?

> RQ_2: How does hospice use communication to construct this reality?

Notice that the first stated RQ, for the Segrin et al. 2003 study, reflects positivist tendencies, toward a reality that is observable and measurable, while the RQs for the Davis 2009 research reflect interpretivist tendencies, toward a reality that is constructed and subjective.

Types of Research Questions about Communication

Questions of Definition.
One common type of research question is a question of definition. There is some debate as to whether questions of definition are in fact research questions, because they are not empirical questions with definitive answers. However, these types of questions are important to the process of communication inquiry, so we will discuss them here. In fact, there is a very common question of definition that you have probably already wrestled with in prior coursework: how exactly do you define communication? Often in introductory communication courses, we debate all the possible forms and definitions of communication and what constitutes communication and what

does not. Most students of communication are familiar with Watzlawick, Beavin Bavelas, and Jackson (1967), whose statement, "one cannot not communicate" (p. 51) provides ongoing debate and ardor. In fact, because the boundaries of our field are so difficult to agree upon, most textbooks as a matter of course (including ours) stipulate their own definition for the term *communication*, so as to alleviate some of the likelihood of misunderstanding. This is true for other types of questions that concern communication. Consider the question, "What communication patterns cause conflict in marriage?" Before you even address this question, you must agree upon the definition of *conflict*. Many scholars have attempted to define conflict in organizations and relationships (e.g., Gottman & Notarius, 2004; Pondy, 1967; Schmidt & Kochan, 1972).

We should note that questions of definition are an important part of the process of communication inquiry (Miller & Nicholson, 1976). We are always concerned with the way in which we define the concepts we desire to study, and definitions have a huge impact on the ways in which we choose to measure our variables. In fact, we will discuss this at length in Chapter 7. However, it is necessary to understand that if you are unclear about your definition, your research questions will suffer, and as a result your research design will encounter problems. It all begins with asking a good question—your measurement and design decisions can only be as good as the place from which you begin. Writing a good research question is more difficult and arduous than it seems at first glance. If you don't believe us, trying writing one!

Questions of Fact.   Another common type of research question is the question of fact. Much communication scholarship focuses on questions of fact, wherein you ask questions regarding what has happened or will happen in the future. These questions concern what is going on in the world. For example, "Will your instructor give you a pop quiz next class period over your reading?" As you know, there is, in fact, an answer to that question that has yet to be determined. Interestingly, these types of questions can only be answered in the known external world. This should remind you of the metatheoretical considerations we discussed in Chapter 2. Doesn't it sound like an objectivist epistemology? These questions can be confirmed or disconfirmed, essentially locating an affirmative or negative answer, a simple yes or no. For example, "Do men interrupt in conversations more than women?" This is a question of fact, with a simple yes or no answer. As we pointed out earlier, the question itself drives from the decisions scholars make about how to design and conduct research. If you return to your pop quiz example, how can you determine the answer to your question, in other words, how do you research the answer? Well, the easiest way is to attend the next research methods class period and observe whether your teacher administers a pop quiz. How could you find the answer to your question about who interrupts in conversations more, women or men? Well, again, observation would be a likely candidate. It is unlikely that you could ascertain the correct answer utilizing surveys, for instance.

So far, the questions of fact we posed are quite simple. However, we don't want to suggest all questions of fact are so simple, because they can be much more complicated. Take for instance the following question: "Are fear appeals effective instruments of persuasion?" If you have already taken a persuasion course, you know this question is much more involved than it initially appears. Other message components must be considered as potential caveats to this question: the message source, for example, and the receiver's previous knowledge, beliefs, and attitudes, as well as personality. Further, it may be the case that a particular degree of fear may be ideal—enough to motivate a response, but not so much as to lead to hopelessness—and that this degree of fear may vary from one persuasive campaign to another. So, while this question is a question of fact, a simple yes or no answer is essentially impossible.

Here are two other examples of research questions—these are ones posed in a qualitative study. This research (Kramer, 2004) uses ethnography (see Chapter 14) to look at the dialectical tensions in group communication in a community theater group. Kramer asks:

RQ$_1$: What dialectical tensions are experienced by community theater group members as they communicate to produce a group performance?

RQ$_2$: How do members of a community theater group manage the dialectical tensions through their communication?

Note that both of these questions are questions of fact, even though they are very much open-ended questions based in the interpretivist tradition.

Here is another way to look at research questions. How many observations are necessary to make a valid conclusion about the answer? In the pop quiz example, you need only attend class on the next occasion to answer the question. With the questions about who interrupts more, whether fear appeals work in health messages, or how members of a theater group manage dialectical tensions, the number of observations necessary increase exponentially. So, again, you begin to see that the question you ask drives the research design process, including what methodology is an appropriate choice.

Research questions can ask about a relationship of association ("Do families with a child with a disability experience closed communication?"), or about a relationship of causation ("Does depression in a relational partner affect the number of conversational turns in a communication act?"). We'll talk more about those relationships in the next section and in future chapters.

●●●

▼ ## What Are Research Hypotheses?

hypothesis
A statement a researcher makes about the relationship between a dependent and an independent variable.

A research hypothesis is used when the researcher knows enough about the topic under study to make a prediction. A **hypothesis** is a statement the researcher makes about the relationship between at least two variables (a dependent and independent variable). It is often predictive, specifying how two concepts are believed to be related. Most of you are already familiar with the common definition of a hypothesis—an educated guess. And that's exactly what a hypothesis is: an educated guess about what will happen in a relationship between variables, based on what is known from existing theory.

This educated guess is based upon some previous knowledge and/or scholarship into related ideas. Frequently (since hypotheses fall under the deductive model), your hypothesis is based on a theory you found in your library research. Perhaps, for example, you want to study communication between hospice physicians and their patients. Your library research may have found Spiers' 2002 study on the interpersonal contexts within which care is negotiated between home care nurses and their patients. Spiers identified six communication contexts (territoriality, shared perceptions of the situation, an amicable working relationship, role synchronization, knowledge, and taboo topics) that affect the therapeutic value of the communication, and perhaps you think some of these contexts might be relevant to hospice communication as well. You might write a hypothesis based on this previous research: "When hospice physicians and patients share the same perceptions of the situation, communication is perceived by the patients as being more therapeutic."

The research hypothesis is symbolized by a capital letter H, followed with a numeric subscript (H_1). This numeric subscript refers to the number of the hypothesis in a particular study. In a complicated study, you may have several hypotheses and numbering helps you to keep track of what hypothesis is being analyzed and discussed. Some scholars add letters to denote related hypotheses (H_{1a}, H_{1b}, etc.), though we would discourage you from doing do; simply numbering the hypotheses in order is the easiest approach for most readers to follow. The symbol and numeric subscript is then followed with a statement concerning how you think the two variables will be related.

Here are some examples from Segrin et al. (2003):

H_1: There will be a negative association between depression and relational quality in dating relationships.

H_2: The poor relational quality associated with depression will be associated with increased loneliness.

Notice that both of these hypotheses have at least two variables: depression and relational quality, and depression and loneliness, respectively. Notice, also, that these Hs reflect positivist tendencies, studying a reality that is believed to be orderly, fixed, objective, observed, and measurable.

Consider these examples:

H_1: The more people watch soap operas, the more extramarital affairs they will have.

H_1: Adolescent males report greater enjoyment of slasher films than do adolescent females.

What are the two variables in each of these hypotheses? For the first hypothesis, the two variables are soap opera viewing and extramarital affairs; in the second hypothesis, the variables are gender and slasher film enjoyment. Can you identify the independent and dependent variables?

Null Hypotheses

Technically, although statistically testing your research hypothesis to see if it's true, you are actually testing whether your hypothesis is *not* true. In other words, the research hypothesis is always contrasted with a **null hypothesis**, which simply says the research hypothesis is wrong. In other words, there is no

null hypothesis
A statement that the research hypothesis is wrong. In other words, there is no (null) relationship between the variables that the research predicted.

(null) relationship between the variables that the research predicted. The null hypothesis, when written, is symbolized by a capital letter H, followed with a numeric subscript of zero (H_0). Consider the null hypotheses for the original hypothesis from Segrin, Powell, Givertz, and Brackin (2003):

H_1: There will be a negative association between depression and relational quality in dating relationships.

H_0: There will be *no association* between depression and relational quality in dating relationships.

And,

H_2: The poor relational quality associated with depression will be associated with increased loneliness.

H_0: The poor relational quality associated with depression will *not be associated* with increased loneliness.

Are you getting the idea? Simply substitute in the phrase "no relationship" or "no association" to turn a research hypothesis into a null hypothesis.

What are the null hypotheses for these research hypotheses?

H_1: The more people watch soap operas, the more extramarital affairs they will have.

H_1: Adolescent males report greater enjoyment of slasher films than do adolescent females.

The correct answers are as follows:

H_0: There is no relationship between exposure to soap viewing and extramarital affairs.

H_0: Males and females do not report different enjoyment of slasher films.

Although you should be familiar with the concept of the null hypothesis, it is implied from the research hypothesis and is almost never written out in actual research studies. However, as we move toward analysis and statistics, it is imperative that you understand the concept.

Forms of Relationships in Hypotheses

There are two key types of relationship specified in a hypothesis: relationship of association ("associational relationship") and relationship of causation ("causal relationship"). A relationship of association implies that where one variable is found, the other also will be found. For example, the format for a relationship of association in a hypothesis would be: If A, then B (A and B are different variables). An example of a relationship of association would be "interpersonal conversation and friends go together." We're not implying that having friends causes conversation, or that conversation causes a person to have friends, or even that the *more* conversation you have the *more* friends you have. We're just hypothesizing that the two occur together. It's entirely possible that a third variable (high intelligence, perhaps) causes both of these two variables to occur. Or that they co-occur for another reason. We don't know enough to make a causal statement about the two.

We're simply predicting association—that if one happens, the other also tends to happen. If we word our earlier hypothesis as "H_1: People who watch soap operas have extramarital affairs," it is an example of an associational relationship.

A causal relationship implies that one variable causes a change in the direction of the other variable. The format for a relationship of causation in a hypothesis would be: An increase in "A" causes an increase in "B." It could also be: A decrease in "A" causes a decrease in "B"; an increase in "A" causes a decrease in "B"; or a decrease in "A" causes an increase in "B." Or, simply, it could be "A" causes "B." Note that many words can be used in our hypothesis to mean "cause": results in, affects, creates, induces, and so on. If we word our earlier hypothesis as "H_1: Watching soap operas causes people to have extramarital affairs," this is an example of a causal relationship.

Possible forms of relationships include positive and linear relationship (as A increases, B increases), negative and linear relationship (as A increases, B decreases), and curvilinear relationships (U shape, inverted U shape, and other more complicated curves). A U curvilinear relationship implies that as A increases, B decreases for awhile, then B increases. (Perhaps the more you drink, the less inhibited you are up to a point; then if you drink enough, you will become more inhibited.) One of your authors (Christine Davis) once conducted research on children's mental health treatment team meetings and found that meeting communication was less dialogic (called "wraparound fidelity score" in the graph) as team leader experience rose—up to six to ten years of experience. Then, meeting communication became more dialogic as team leader experience rose past eleven years of experience.

An inverted U shape implies that as "A" increases, "B" increases for a while then decreases. Davis once conducted research that found that the more people in attendance at children's mental health treatment team meetings, the more dialogic the meeting communication was up to a point—7 to 10 attendees, in fact. After 10 attendees, the dialogic nature of the meeting communication decreased.

If you consider the previous work cited in this chapter by Segrin and colleagues (2003):

H_1: There will be a negative association between depression and relational quality in dating relationships,

this is predicting a negative and linear associational relationship, such that as depression increases, the quality of dating relationships will decrease; and

H_2: The poor relational quality associated with depression will be associated with increased loneliness,

indicates a positive and linear associational relationship. In other words, they predicted that more depression is related to more loneliness.

What about the form of the relationship in the following hypotheses?

H_1: The more people watch soap operas, the more extramarital affairs they will have.

H_1: Adolescent males report greater enjoyment of slasher films than do adolescent females.

In the first hypothesis, we have a positive and linear associational relationship, as we do in the second (males like slasher films more than females).

Now, what about those curvilinear relationships? An example of a communication study that considers a curvilinear relationship is the use of touch across relational stage. Guerrero and Andersen (1991) found that touch in public spaces follows a curvilinear relationship, such that couples that are either in the early stages or later stages of relationship development exhibit less touch than couples between these two stages. This is a curvilinear relationship—actually an inverted U.

Directional and Nondirectional Hypotheses

Another component of hypotheses that becomes increasingly important to you is whether the hypothesis is directional. Some hypotheses are written specifying the direction of the relationship. Consider stating, "People from the South speak more slowly than people from the North." This is an example of a directional hypothesis because of the specific nature of the relationship between the variables. If, however, you had said, "People from the North and South speak at different rates," you have not specified who you expect speaks faster or slower; thus you have not identified a direction. This is a nondirectional hypothesis. Again, both hypotheses are acceptable, but they should be based upon previous research and theory. Being able to identify a hypothesis as directional or not becomes important when we approach statistical analysis in subsequent chapters. Directional hypotheses are called *one-tailed*, because you know where you expect to find your result. This identifies which tail end of the distribution your result will be associated with—based upon what your hypothesis identifies. A nondirectional hypothesis tells you that you must consider a result that could occur on either end of your distribution—thus it is *two-tailed*. This is because you are unsure about where the result will occur. We will return to the notion of one and two-tailed inferences in later chapters.

▼ ## How Do You Set Up Good Research Questions?

While there are many possible ways to critique a research question, you need to keep in mind that the best way to define what makes a good research question is based on utility, not a sense of correctness or incorrectness. In fact, we try to avoid thinking in terms of correctness and incorrectness when formulating these research questions. In other words, is the research question helpful to use in advancing your understanding of a particular communication problem or issue? Does it allow you to get at an important, narrowly defined, unanswered question in the field? If it does, then you have a successful research question.

When we ask our students to write questions, they often struggle to write a solid research question. The most common mistake they make is writing a question that has already been answered. We suggest that they dig a little deeper, perhaps there's a new and interesting way to expand that area that they and other scholars have not considered; this is often accomplished through the narrowing down process we discussed earlier in this chapter. Another important tool for evaluating research questions is the concept of quality.

In other words, that you have quality variables and the relationship among your variables. While we will talk later about types of validity (or accuracy), the question of validity begins to be answered when you write your research question and/or hypothesis.

Conceptual Definitions

While we will discuss variables more completely in Chapter 7, there are some core components that should be addressed here because they bear on whether you have an accurate research question and/or hypothesis. A quality research question and/or hypothesis begins with a solid **conceptual definition**. A conceptual definition is how you define the concept or variable that you are going to study. This is not as easy as it sounds.

     Think of the concept as the pieces of the research question or the hypothesis. They are the nouns in the question or statement. For example, we like to ask our classes to define the word *violence*, something many of our mass media scholars are interested in pursuing as a variable. Remarkably, the definitions of this word vary a great deal from student to student. Some people see violence as an act or behavioral situation, while others more broadly define violence to include verbal attacks. We could likely debate the merits of each type of definition for a long time; however, that is not the point. Your conceptual definition must be clear and explain to other scholars what you consider violence to be. Most successful communication scholars will explore their variable's conceptual definitions somewhere within their literature review. Consider another example. Imagine that you believe people engage in matching behavior when they desire intimacy with another person. Your first consideration is to define, conceptually, what you mean by intimacy. What if you mean "romantic and sexual interest" when you talk about intimacy, and we mean "caring and giving concern" when we talk about intimacy? There are potentially as many conceptual definitions as there are people to define them. It is essential that you make sure you know what you mean when you talk about your concepts.

conceptual definition
How the concept or variable that is being studied is defined.

Operational Definitions

The second consideration you must make in determining whether you have a quality research question and/or hypothesis is how you define your variables operationally. An **operational definition** is how you plan to measure and/or observe the concept or variable of interest. In the violence example, you must specify how you plan to determine whether behavior in the television programs you watch is to be coded as violent. What do you count as violence? What are the categories you'll use? Do you code physical violence, the different types of physical violence, the outcome of the violence? Do you code the verbal violence? How will you do that exactly? Will it be just the verbal content that determines verbal violence, or will you also take into account nonverbal components of the message such as tone of voice, volume, and paralanguage?

     Operational definitions are important as they minimize confusion within our scholarly field, provide an opportunity for others to replicate your work, and provide some *control* over the variable you study. What about the intimacy

operational definition
How the concept or variable of interest is measured and/or observed.

example? Obviously, it depends upon what conceptual definition you agree upon. Then, based upon that definition, you need to create an operational definition that will determine what types of questions you ask or what you measure as you observe relational couples.

Both a solid conceptual definition and operational definition are necessary for a quality research question and/or hypothesis. Yet, the key is that conceptual and operational definitions need to match. A quality research question and/or hypothesis will be certain that they do. You can't write a conceptual definition about violence that includes verbal aggression and then not include it in your operational definition.

▼ What Are the Boundaries of Research Questions and Hypotheses?

Another important consideration for both research questions and hypotheses is whether you wish to impose any boundaries upon them. In other words, under which conditions do you suspect your research question and/or hypotheses may be true? If you expect there to be boundaries, you need to specify this information in the question and/or hypothesis. If you don't expect there to be boundaries, there is no need to include this type of information in the question and/or hypothesis. Time, place, people, and situations could all be boundaries you place upon your questions and hypotheses. For example, do you suspect that the age of the individual matters? We generally assume that most research is based in current time, but is there a reason to consider that history or time might have some effect? Place, which could be culture and/or location, may matter a lot, depending on the question and/or hypothesis. What about the situation? Is it possible that this communication behavior you are interested in only occurs in certain situations? We have a graduate student currently interested in the communication scripts that occur in a speed-dating situation. This type of event—speed dating—is very different than any other type of dating situation. This must be included in the question.

Essentially, here you are considering, what are the limits on your research question? The key is to consider boundaries that might influence the process of inquiry. This can even be an opportunity to generate new research questions. Is there something specific about communication students at UNCC or UCONN that will influence the outcome of your study? If so, this may be a limitation to generalization and an example of how boundaries can influence your process of inquiry. It does not mean that you shouldn't ask the question; rather it means that you need to be aware of the level of specificity you offer. As you will see later, when we discuss each methodology, no one methodology is perfect; rather they are types of inquiry rife with tradeoffs. What one method offers as its strength, another has as its weakness. That is why we insist our students be exposed to a variety of methodologies because no one method is right for every study. In fact, we want you to consider how the question and/or hypotheses you write actually influence the methodology you should use, and the type of analysis you will conduct.

How Is Metatheory Related to Research Questions and Hypotheses?

▼

While we detailed at length in Chapter 2 the important foundations of metatheory to understanding communication research methods, we always like to revisit the topic when we discuss research questions and hypotheses. This is because what we find most interesting about reading a variety of communication research questions and/or hypotheses is how much metatheory seeps out from beneath the question or hypothesis. What we mean is that even when students are still grappling with the abstract concepts of metatheory, once they begin writing research questions, these concepts become a little clearer to them. Both your epistemological and ontological entailments drive how you write a particular question. In other words, you approach any question or hypothesis you write with certain assumptions about the world.

So What?

In summary, your research objectives, questions, and hypotheses are driven by the way you see the world and the assumptions you make about reality; but they are also driven by your curiosities and interests, as well as the research other people have conducted, and the theories, concepts, and conclusions they have come to in your area of interest. In previous chapters, we have shown you how to begin your research search in the library—among the mounds and mounds of research that has come before you. In this chapter, we've shown you how to pull your unique research idea out of that history, find the important questions left to be explored, and formulate good, solid objectives, questions, and/or hypotheses that will result in good quality research. The next several chapters will help you further design your research study as we show you how every decision you make in the research process—from choosing your method to designing your study to analyzing your results—depends on the objectives, research questions, and/or hypotheses you set out to address.

Glossary

Conceptual definition
How the concept or variable that is being studied is defined.

Fact pattern
A factual relationship occurring repeatedly.

Hypothesis
A statement a researcher makes about the relationship between a dependent and an independent variable.

Null hypothesis
A statement that the research hypothesis is wrong. In other words, there is no (null) relationship between the variables that the research predicted.

Operational definition
How the concept or variable of interest is measured and/or observed.

Research question
Questions scholars ask about the way things work.

References

Barnlund, D. C. (1968). *Interpersonal communication: Survey and studies*. Boston: Houghton Mifflin.

Booth, W. C., Colomb, G. G., & Williams, J. M. (1995). *The craft of research*. Chicago: University of Chicago Press.

Bross, I. B. J. (1953). *Design for decisions*. New York: Macmillan.

Dance, F. E. X. (1982). Essays in human communication theory: A comparative overview. In F. E. X. Dance (Ed.), *Human communication theory: Comparative essays* (pp. 286–299). New York: Harper & Row.

Davis, C. S. (2005). Home. *Qualitative Inquiry 11*(2), 392–409.

Davis, C. S. (2009). *Death: The beginning of a relationship*. Cresskill, NJ: Hampton Press.

Davis, C. S., & Dollard, N. (2005). *Team process and adherence to wraparound principles in a children's community mental health care system of care*. Tampa, FL: Louis de la Parte Florida Mental Health Institute, University of South Florida.

Gottman, J. M., & Notarius, C. I. (2004). Decade review: Observing marital interaction. *Journal of Marriage and Family, 62*, 927–947.

Green, S. (2002). Mothering Amanda: Musings on the experience of raising a child with cerebral palsy. *Journal of Loss and Trauma, 7*, 21–34.

Guerrero, L. K., & Andersen, P. A. (1991). The waxing and waning of relational intimacy: Touch as a function of relational stage, gender and touch avoidance. *Journal of Social and Personal Relationships, 8*(2), 147–165.

Hall, C. S., & Lidzey, G. (1970). *Theories of personality* (2nd ed.). New York: Wiley.

Hawes, L. C. (1975). *Pragmatics of analoguing: Theory and model construction in communication*. Reading, MA: Addison-Wesley.

Johnson, E. P. (2002). Performing blackness down under: The café of the gate of salvation. *Text and Performance Quarterly, 22*(2), 99–119.

Kaplan, A. (1964). *The conduct of inquiry*. New York: Harper & Row.

Kramer, M. W. (2004). Toward a communication theory of group dialectics: An ethnographic study of a community theater group. *Communication Monographs, 71*(3), 311–332.

Kuhn, T. S. (1970). *The structure of scientific revolutions*. Chicago: University of Chicago Press.

Littlejohn, S. W. (1996). *Theories of human communication* (5th ed.). Belmont, CA: Wadsworth.

McCann, R., & Giles, H. (2006). Communication with people of different ages in the workplace: Thai and American data. *Human Communication Research, 32*(1), 74–108.

Miller, G. R., & Nicholson, H. E. (1976). *Communication inquiry: A perspective on a process*. Reading, MA: Addison-Wesley.

Pondy, L. R. (1967). Organizational conflict: Concepts and models. *Administrative Science Quarterly, 12*, 296–320.

Poole, M. S. (1990). Do we have any theories of group communication? *Communication Studies, 41*, 237–247.

Schmidt, S. M., & Kochan, T. A. (1972). Conflict: Towards conceptual clarity. *Administrative Science Quarterly, 17*, 359–370.

Segrin, C., Powell, H. L., Givertz, M., & Brackin, A. (2003). Symptoms of depression, relational quality, and loneliness in dating relationships. *Personal Relationships, 10*, 25–36.

Spiers, J. A. (2002). The interpersonal contexts of negotiating care in home care nurse-patient interactions. *Qualitative Health Research, 12*(8), 1033–1057.

Watzlawick, P., Beavin Bavelas, J., & Jackson, D. D. (1967). *Pragmatics of human communication. A study of interactional patterns, pathologies and paradoxes*. New York: W. W. Norton & Company.

UNDERSTANDING RESEARCH ETHICS

6

CHAPTER OUTLINE

KEY TERMS

Anonymity

Assent

Belmont Report

Beneficence

Confidentiality

Deception

Ethical research

Human subjects protection

Informed consent

Justice

Legitimation

Member checks

Nonmaleficence

Nuremberg Code

Participatory action research

Relational ethics

Representation

Research ethics

Respect for persons

Vulnerable populations

CHAPTER OBJECTIVES

1. To understand the standard, proper, and ethical way in which to conduct the many types of communication research
2. To understand how to conduct research that is respectful to participants, the research community, and society
3. To understand how to conduct research that has appropriate legitimation and representation and appropriately represents multiple voices

Why Do We Care about Human Subjects Protection?

research ethics
The specific principles, rules, guidelines, and norms of research-related behavior that a research community has decided are proper, fair, and appropriate.

ethical research
Research that is designed and conducted validly, reliably, legitimately, and representatively, and protects a research participant's rights.

human subjects protection
Ethical research rules that refer to the guidelines that are followed to ensure the protection of people (participants) being studied.

Research ethics refer to the specific principles, rules, guidelines, and norms of research-related behavior that a research community has decided are proper, fair, and appropriate. In short, **ethical research** protects a participant's rights (Murphy & Dingwall, 2001), but it does more than that. Ethical researchers also design and conduct research that is valid, reliable, legitimate, and representative. In this chapter, we will discuss the history of research ethics and human subjects' protection, provide examples of ethics breaches, discuss some major concepts behind research ethics, explain the role of Institutional Research Boards (IRBs), and teach you how to ensure that your research follows ethical guidelines. We'll discuss ethics from the points of view of both interpretive and positivist paradigms, and address the specific applications of ethical research principles in both qualitative and quantitative research.

The research ethics codes that are adhered to by most researchers were written as a result of abuses and violations of ethical principles by many researchers over many years, worldwide. You might hear these rules referred to as **human subjects protection**, which refers to the guidelines we follow to make sure we are protecting the people we are studying (people whom we, in communication studies, typically call our "research participants"). Our field of Communication also has its own ethical views, guidelines, and norms that are specific to the types of research we conduct, which we will discuss throughout this chapter.

The history of human subjects protection in research really begins with the Nazi medical war crimes during World War II. These abuses were particularly heinous, including—in the name of research and science—conducting medical experiments on concentration camp prisoners. These medical experiments included such appalling acts as injecting people with gasoline, live viruses, and poisons; forcing them to sit in ice water or freezing temperatures for hours; forced sterilization; depriving them of food and water; dissecting their brains; and burning them with bomb material. After the war, former Nazis were indicted before the War Crimes Tribunal at Nuremberg. One of the outcomes of this trial was the **Nuremberg Code**, which was the first set of principles outlining professional ethics for medical researchers, and which forms the basis for today's research ethics codes in both medicine and in the social sciences. The Nuremberg Code specifically required voluntary consent among research participants, and was the first international standard for the conduct of research (Annas & Grodin, 1995). We'll further discuss the ethical standards and principles for research shortly, but first let's take a look at some other examples of violations of rights of research participants in our own country.

The most famous violation in United States history might be the Tuskegee Syphilis Study, a long-term study of black males conducted in Tuskegee by the U.S. Public Health Services. This research began in the 1930s and continued until 1972. The researchers studied over 400 African-American men with syphilis and 200 without syphilis. They were recruited without informed consent

Nuremberg Code
The first set of principles outlining professional ethics for medical researchers, which forms the basis for today's research ethics codes. It specifically required voluntary consent among research participants, and was the first international standard for the conduct of research.

and were misled about the nature of the study and what procedures would be done on them. Most appalling, they were not informed of the complications experienced by others in the study. (The death rate among those with syphilis was twice as high as among the control group.) In addition, in the 1940s penicillin was found to be effective in treating syphilis; the study continued and the men were not informed about the possible treatment. Investigation into this research abuse led to the U.S. government's oversight of ethics for federally supported research projects (Thomas & Quinn, 1991).

In 1963, studies were conducted at New York's Jewish Chronic Disease Hospital to understand whether the body's inability to reject cancer cells was due to cancer or to debilitation. To test this, they injected live cancer cells into patients. The consent process did not inform the subjects that they were about to be injected with cancerous cells, because the researchers didn't want to "unnecessarily frighten them." The researchers were later found guilty of fraud, deceit, and unprofessional conduct (Edgar & Rothman, 1995).

From 1963 to 1966, at the Willowbrook State School in New York, an institution for "mentally defective children," researchers wanted to study the natural history of infectious hepatitis. Newly admitted children were deliberately infected with the hepatitis virus. Parents gave consent, but since the hospital was only admitting patients who were in this program, this wasn't really freedom of consent because parents didn't have an alternate choice if they wanted treatment for their children (Krugman, 1971).

Don't think all research abuses and dilemmas have taken place in medical research. There are many examples of ill-treatment of research participants in social science research as well. The most famous example may be the Milgram obedience to authority experiment, in which the researcher used bogus electric shocks to measure the extent to which people would submit to authority to inflict pain on another person. Since the shocks were not real, the ethical criticism was not about the physical pain seemingly inflicted on the recipient of the shock, but on the emotional pain and duress inflicted on the research participants, who were led to believe that they were inflicting severe pain on other people (Kelman, 1967).

In a study closer to what communication researchers might investigate, in 1955 researchers in Wichita studied jury deliberations in an attempt to examine group decision making and negotiating. This study was also ethically criticized because participants were not told they were being researched, observed, and videotaped, and, as part of the social institution of the jury process, had reason to believe their communication was private and confidential (Kimmel, 1988).

Many qualitative and ethnographic social science researchers have been criticized for covertly observing people without their knowledge or consent. Humphrey's (1970) study of homosexual encounters in public restrooms and Kotarba's (1979) study of sexual activity in a public jail visiting room are two striking examples, especially given the deeply personal nature of the behaviors under observation. Even seemingly innocuous observations of people's day-to-day lives can be criticized if people don't know, or forget, they are being observed. Carolyn Ellis, for example, published her research of two Eastern Virginia fishing communities in her book *Fisher folk: Two communities on Chesapeake Bay* (Ellis, 1986). While she had obtained informed consent at the onset of her research, she spent so long in the field (several years) that many community participants claimed they had forgotten she was researching them and had begun to think of her as simply a friend. As Ellis states later in many writings on the subject (see Ellis, 2007, for example), her experience requires her, and us, to question **relational ethics**—the value placed on the relationships between the researchers and those they are researching. We'll discuss this in more detail later in this chapter.

In response to various research abuses in the United States, especially in medical research, in 1979 the U.S. government crafted a document titled "Ethical Principles and Guidelines for the Protection of Human Subjects," commonly known as the **Belmont Report**. The Belmont Report serves as the cornerstone of ethical principles upon which federal regulations for the protection of human research participants are based. Our human subject protection guidelines are based on the three principles of the Belmont Report: respect for persons, beneficence/nonmaleficence, and justice (Murphy & Dingwall, 2001).

relational ethics
The value placed on the relationships between researchers and the people they are researching.

Belmont Report
This document serves as the cornerstone of ethical principles upon which federal regulations for the protection of human research participants are based.

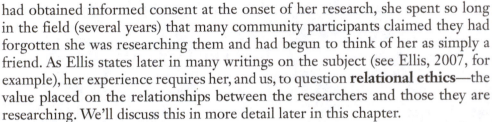

▼ How Do We Follow Research Ethics and Ethical Guidelines?

Respect for Persons and Informed Consent

The first principle, **respect for persons**, states that research participants should be treated as autonomous agents—that means they are independent, self-governing, and capable of making decisions for themselves as long as they are given sufficient information to make those decisions. This principle forms the basis for **informed consent**. In the consent process, people are to be given full information about the research, both risks and benefits, and allowed to make the decision for themselves if they will participate. A proper consent procedure should include the participant's right to withdraw from the study without penalty, the focus of the study and methods to be employed, statements surrounding confidentiality, and a signature of both the researcher and the participant (Creswell, 2007). The informed consent process assumes that the research participant is competent to consent—that, if he or she is given all relevant information, he or she will be able to comprehend the information and be able to agree to participate in a voluntary manner that is free from coercion. As part of the informed consent process, the researcher must disclose all relevant information to potential participants, including the purpose of the study, the nature of the research procedure, reasonable alternatives to the proposed intervention (if the intervention provides a service or treatment such as in medical research), and any risks, benefits, or uncertainties of the intervention. The process also insists that participants can change their mind and withdraw at any time (which can be more than a little nerve-wracking in long-term ethnographic research, in which the entire research study could be compromised if the participant changes his or her mind). However, withdrawing from research is always the participant's prerogative. We have included a sample consent form in Appendix B of this textbook.

respect for persons
Research participants should be treated as autonomous agents—that means they are independent, self-governing, and capable of making decisions for themselves as long as they are given sufficient information to make those decisions.

informed consent
This process assumes that the research participant is competent to consent—that, if he or she is given all relevant information, he or she will be able to comprehend the information and be able to agree to participate in a voluntary manner free from coercion.

There are a few exceptions to required informed consent, however. If the research could not possibly be carried out with informed consent, and if the risk to participants is minimal, it might be ethical to waive informed consent. An example in a communication studies project might be one in which participants are being interviewed about illegal drug use. In this case, signing a consent form (and putting their name on a legal document if their participation implies admission to drug use) would be more harmful than a waiver of consent. Typically, the researcher would obtain oral consent, but not signed consent. Sometimes, in an ethnographic research study, researchers are observing individuals in public places in which it would be impossible to obtain consent from everyone present. If the research was being conducted in a place sufficiently public that there is no reasonable expectation of privacy, consent is usually not required or obtained. Examples of this type of research might include studying anonymous chat room communication or observing nonverbal communication (from a distance) at a shopping mall. Of course, even if consent can be waived, this doesn't mean that the researcher is exempt from treating participants in an ethical manner.

There are also other types of communication research that are exempt from obtaining informed consent. Informed consent is, obviously, obtained from people who are research participants, typically defined as a living individual about whom a researcher obtains information through an interaction with the person. A research participant might also need to give consent to let the researcher have access to personally identifiable private information (e.g., medical records), or to let a third-party participant give information about him or her (e.g., if you are interviewing a doctor about a patient, the patient has to give consent to let the doctor talk about him or her) (Mertens & Ginsberg, 2008). In other words, when a communication scholar writes a rhetorical analysis of Barack Obama's latest speech, since Obama is a public figure, his speech is considered a public event, and if the researcher has not obtained that data through interaction with Obama, informed consent is neither possible nor necessary. Similarly, analysis of diaries or letters of a deceased historical figure does not require informed consent. However, analysis of letters from a person who is still alive might—or might not—require informed consent, as might a study of Internet blogs or videos posted to Facebook, if that study uses information in a way that identifies the author of the blog or video. In fact, the proliferation of blogs and other Internet-based communication raises new ethical considerations. Many scholars now say that if information is posted to an online community that is password protected, it should be considered private rather than public information (Parry, 2011). At the same time, some argue that social media posts on open-access platforms, such as Twitter, are tantamount to broadcasting—and as public information they are no more subject to informed consent than the content analyses described above. Many communication scholars are currently debating the issues of consent, confidentiality, and anonymity in online environments, and not all agree on what Internet-based information is public and what information is not.

In fact, the use of online information as data is a hot button right now. A 2011 article in the *Chronicle of Higher Education* (Parry, 2011) reported on the use by Harvard sociologists of 1,700 Facebook profiles of students at their university. On the "pro" side, researchers say that the research they are doing can lead to important social information about culture and communication and that steps were taken to minimize the risk of privacy violations. On the "con" side, critics of this research say that deceptive practices were used to access the Facebook information in the first place (research assistants added in people who had set restrictive privacy settings but were their own "friends" and so were available to them), and when the researchers shared the database of information with other researchers, the students' privacy was not sufficiently protected. Those with access to the report may have been able to figure out who some of the people were by comparing information from the Facebook profiles (hometown and major, for example) with the Harvard student database. Critics further say that the fact that people whose information was included were not informed of the project and didn't give consent is a breach of research ethics. Certainly, it's unclear whether information posted online in such settings is considered public or private information, but we suggest you always make your decision on the side of caution.

Therefore, we argue that there really is a bottom line issue here—if the information is publically available (published someplace, including online), and if there is not a reasonable expectation of confidentiality, you should obtain consent if possible, cite appropriately at all times, and maintain ethical standards when using the information. If the research participant can be identified by you, regardless of whether you keep that identification confidential, and if obtaining informed consent is possible, you should obtain it. If it's not possible to obtain consent, you must make sure risks are minimal and participants are treated ethically. Sometimes, this can be accomplished by using aliases or codenames, reporting information only in aggregate (combined with other people rather than individually), leaving out identifying information, or otherwise maintaining participant confidentiality when citing Internet-based communication. Of course, researchers must always abide by decisions on consent and exemptions from consent made by their Institutional Research Boards (IRBs). We will discuss the difference between confidentiality and anonymity shortly.

Third-party information is frequently obtained in health communication research, in which a health-care professional might be asked questions about a patient. In this type of research, consent must be obtained from both the provider and the patient. While somewhat beyond the scope of this textbook, there exists a whole other set of ethical guidelines concerning the handling of medical records. The privacy laws associated with the Health Insurance Portability and Accountability Act of 1996—or HIPAA (pronounced "hip-ah") —apply to the handling of medical records that may associated with health communication research and interventions. Researchers working in this domain or who collaborate with those in the medical field should consider reading up on HIPAA regulations concerning privacy, which in some instances are even more strict than the general standards associated with social research.

Sometimes, simply obtaining informed consent from participants isn't enough. As Ellis's study of fishing villages illustrates, when we are in the field for long periods of time, or when we are researching cultures in which we ourselves participate, we must also be attuned to our relationships with our research participants so that we don't use friendship to obtain information in ways that might be harmful or hurtful to them. As Ellis (2007) stated in musing about her experience, "the problem comes not from being friends with participants but from acting as a friend yet not living up to the obligations of friendship" (p. 10).

There are some potential participants who may not be fully able to decide for themselves if they want to take part in research. These people are referred to in human subjects protection terms as **vulnerable populations**, and they are defined as "persons with diminished autonomy" (NIH Office of Extramural Research, 2008). Children, people with cognitive impairments, older adults, people with severe health problems, employees, and students (yes, students) are considered vulnerable populations. Most of the characteristics are obvious, but why would employees and students be vulnerable populations? Both are susceptible to coercion—by employers or professors—to participate, and safeguards must be taken to make sure that their consent is truly optional. Some vulnerable populations, such as children, must be given additional protections in research, such as needing permission of a legal guardian overseeing their care in order to include them in research. However, researchers must give everyone, regardless of diminished autonomy, the opportunity to choose (to the extent they are able) if they want to participate in the research. This might mean that if you want to interview a person with Alzheimer's disease, you would first obtain legal consent from his or her guardian, then obtain **assent**—the permission of the person with Alzheimer's to conduct the interview just prior to doing so.

There are specific ethical challenges in conducting ethnographic, autoethnographic, and narrative research among certain vulnerable populations. Many autoethnographers have written about relationships with friends or relatives who are deceased. Obviously, it is impossible to obtain consent or assent from a person who is no longer alive, and IRB rules would exempt such studies from IRB oversight since the research subjects are not living participants. However, Ellis (2007) maintains that such writing should be held to even higher ethical standards. She reminds us that the dead cannot provide consent nor be libeled, and such research incites positive and negative emotions on behalf of the writer, as well as the audience.

Nonmaleficence and Beneficence

Nonmaleficence (no avoidable harm should be done to participants) and **beneficence** (the outcome of research should be positive and beneficial) maintain that research is ethical if the "benefits outweigh the potential for harm" (Murphy & Dingwall, 2001, p. 340). The types of risk-benefit analyses used in biomedical research would be helpful, but this is usually not feasible in communication research. Sometimes, participants may experience emotional or psychological harm that cannot be measured or may be delayed. The greatest risk in ethnography, for example, comes after publication, as a result of what is and what is not printed (Cassell, 1978; Murphy & Dingwall, 2001; Wax & Cassell, 1979). Unlike studies in more quantitatively oriented social science research, anonymity may not be possible in ethnography. It is difficult to gauge a subject's possible feelings of shame or embarrassment due to self-disclosure. To combat this phenomenon, it has been suggested that subjects have an opportunity to share in production of a work or be able to provide a response to printed material.

vulnerable populations
Persons with diminished autonomy; specifically, children, people with cognitive impairments, older adults, people with severe health problems, employees, and students.

assent
Permission obtained from individuals with limited capacity to consent (e.g., minors), allowing themselves to be included as participants in research studies. Assent occurs after informed consent (permission to participate) is obtained from a person who is responsible for the well-being of the participant, and should occur as near as possible in time to the research intervention.

nonmaleficience
No avoidable harm should be done to participants.

beneficence
The outcome of research should be positive and beneficial.

The principle of beneficence refers to making efforts to secure the well-being of research participants, or to maximize the possible benefits of the research and minimize its possible harm. The key to this principle is, since all research has both risks and benefits, to make sure they balance or that benefits outweigh potential harms. Benefits to research might include a monetary incentive for participation, a relationship with the researcher or other participants, knowledge or education gleaned from participation, or the opportunity to do good for society. The community of science also believes that it is important to make sure that the research is sound, and will make a sufficient contribution to knowledge that justifies any risks that may be incurred by the study participants.

The principle of beneficence says that no individual shall be intentionally injured in the course of the research. In communication studies research, we typically don't inflict physical harm on participants. However, our research might inflict emotional or social harm, such as embarrassment, shame, or stigma. Our research must always protect a participant's right to privacy through anonymity or confidentiality of responses, unless the participant gives permission to waive confidentiality. **Anonymity** means that no one, including the researcher, can connect the participant's responses with his or her identity. An example of anonymous research is a survey in which participants do not release their names or chat groups in which people don't use their real names. **Confidentiality** means that, although the researcher knows what each participant said (or can find out this information), the participant's identity is kept secret when reporting or writing up the findings. Sometimes, for example, participant confidentiality is ensured by providing aliases in the final report (Creswell, 2007). By many state and federal laws, a researcher must disclose information indicating a risk of harm to others (homicidal thoughts), a risk of harm to themselves (suicidal thoughts), or child or elder abuse. There may be instances in a research setting that require the interviewer/observer to report illegal activity divulged by a participant (Creswell, 2007), particularly if the information disclosed is pertinent to an ongoing legal investigation.

anonymity
No one, including the researcher, can connect a participant's responses with his or her identity.

confidentiality
The identity of participants is kept secret when researchers report or write up their findings.

There are times, especially when conducting qualitative research such as narrative or autoethnographic research, when anonymity and confidentiality are not possible or desirable. If this is the case, participants must be told this up front, and the researcher should follow two other related principles: Do no harm when publishing the results, and be attentive to causing discomfort in the study. There are times when a research finding *could* be reported but *must not* be reported if doing so could cause harm to a study participant.

Most researchers consider it highly unethical to deceive a participant for the purpose of gaining information, such as gathering information secretively (except when you are observing public behavior, as we discussed earlier) (Creswell, 2007). However, if an extreme instance makes it necessary to deceive the participants, you must lessen the adverse effects from the **deception** by, after the fact, dehoaxing them (tell them what you've done), debriefing them (discussing the research with them), and desensitizing them (if they have acquired negative information about themselves in the course of the research, make sure they know it is not true).

deception
A violation of the right to informed consent that may sometimes mislead participants as to the study purpose.

While researchers are rightly concerned about our research participants, we also might safeguard against potential harm done to researchers themselves. Researchers can be adversely affected by improper boundaries between themselves and their participants, and many qualitative researchers report ethical uneasiness with the levels of affinity they develop with study participants. These feelings of closeness to the subject of the study may lead to feelings of care and protectiveness, which may in turn bias interpretations of the behaviors under observation. Qualitative researchers must also balance their own self-disclosure to participants in interview situations. Some researchers report feelings of vulnerability, guilt, and emotional exhaustion resulting from their time in the field. Other researchers not directly involved with participants, but studying data about sensitive or disturbing topics, report experiencing emotional problems resulting from their research (Dickson-Swift, James, Kippen, & Liamputtong, 2007). Dickson-Swift and colleagues (2007) suggest that researchers vulnerable to these challenges utilize a support network of colleagues and researchers with whom to debrief their experiences.

Justice

The last tenet of the Belmont Report is the principle of **justice**. This principle takes a slightly different point of view of research participants, because it looks at who is included as research participants and who is excluded. This principle says that all classifications of people (race, ethnicity, gender, age, etc.) should receive equal treatment in terms of risks and benefits associated with the research. Certainly, including only people of one ethnicity in research that subjects them to harm is not just. However, excluding people of a certain ethnicity in research that might help them is equally unjust. Risks and benefits should be distributed fairly and without bias, and people should be included or excluded in research only for reasons that have to do with the research question or hypothesis.

justice
All classifications of people (race, ethnicity, gender, age, etc.) should be equally subjected to the risks and benefits of research, and people should be included or excluded only for reasons that have to do with the research question or hypothesis.

Like the Tuskegee study discussed earlier, medical experiments provide the most obvious examples of ethical breaches in this area. Bayer and Tadd (2000) reviewed research protocols of 155 medical studies that were relevant to elderly people and found that over half excluded people over a certain age without justification, failing to test medical interventions on sections of the very populations for which they were intended! In social science research, similar breaches can occur. Becker-Blease and Freyd (2006) argue that many policy decisions on child abuse are made on insufficient information because researchers are reluctant to interview survivors of abuse, for fear of causing emotional harm. They suggest that researchers are inflicting even more harm on abuse survivors by inadequately studying this experience.

Another consideration related to justice is including participants with physical or cognitive impairments in research, especially those participants whose impairments may affect their communication abilities, such as in the case of people with brain damage or neurological disease (Paterson & Scott-Findlay, 2002). It is often difficult to include people with communication impairments in research appropriately while overcoming those very impairments in the data collection process. In these instances, it is not unusual for proxies, such as nurses and family members, to assist in facilitating an interview. While the service of a proxy can be helpful, the proxy's own bias in making decisions for the subject is often unavoidable. Informed consent procedures may need to be modified so the research participant can understand the instructions. Researchers may also need to be attuned to participant distress, participant fatigue, misrepresentation of research questions, and irregular or conflicting responses from the participant.

In regard to justice, when designing a study and analyzing and writing results, researchers are dissuaded from prioritizing the perspective of the elite or privileged while downplaying the views of the less fortunate (Guba & Lincoln, 1989; Marshall, 1985; Murphy & Dingwall, 2001; Sandelowski, 1986; Silverman, 1985). It is important to depict accurately all parties involved (Murphy & Dingwall, 2001).

Including Participants in Co-Constructed Research

Researchers, especially those following the interpretive paradigm (see Chapter 2), are also concerned about issues of **legitimation** (Who can speak for these people?) and **representation** (How can you speak for these people?). Representation refers to understanding fully the lived experiences of research participants and including the multiple realities, interpretations, experiences, and voices emergent from all individuals and all angles. One challenge is to ensure that the people and context studied are adequately and sufficiently represented, and that rigorous attempts are made to include their own voices and interpretations. Methods that directly include—and help researchers more fully understand—participants' voices and interpretations might include interactive techniques such as interactive interviewing, interactive focus groups, co-constructed narratives, or close observation over a long period of time (which we will discuss later in this book), which allow study participants to give their own accounts of their own experiences. Other advantages of coauthored methods include the possible avoidance of obtaining consent (since participants are also researchers), alleviation of concerns about offending subjects, and less likelihood of research participants changing their minds about participating (Denzin, 2003; Ellis, 2007).

Qualitative researchers should also ensure that they are representing the voice of their participants by conducting **member checks** at the conclusion of their study. Member checks consist of a process of providing study participants with the research findings and giving them the opportunity to voice agreement or disagreement with the research as reported.

Social science researchers have been increasingly concerned about the moral ethics of conducting research among traditionally marginalized and stigmatized groups of people in ways that might exploit or take advantage of them. For example, some feminist researchers argue that proper interpretation can only be achieved by cooperation between the researcher and participant. Many feminist ethnographers, and others, subscribe to methods of reciprocity in researcher–participant relationships (Murphy & Dingwall, 2001). The traditional researcher–participant relationship is one of hegemonic power, in which the researcher holds power over the people he or she is studying, simply by virtue of the fact that the researcher is in charge of the study, the methodology, the analysis, and dissemination of the findings. In addition, in more traditional forms of research, researchers, in essence, speak for the participants, in effect silencing their voice and assuming a professional stance in which the researcher's opinion of the participant's point of view might be presumed to be more valid than the

---

legitimation
The question of who can represent another person in narrative writing.

representation
Fully understanding the lived experiences of research participants and including the multiple realities, interpretations, experiences, and voices emergent from all individuals and all angles.

member checks
The process of providing study participants with the research findings, and giving them the opportunity to voice agreement or disagreement with the research as reported.

participant's own opinions. In this context of "narrative privilege" (Adams, 2008, p. 180), researchers hold what's called "legitimate power" over non-researchers in their narratives. In other words, stories with stronger perceived cultural value—traditional researchers' stories—are considered to be more important or more valid than other types of stories—stories of people from marginalized groups. In addition, the narrative skills and ability traditional researchers have also hold legitimacy over people who cannot write or access textual forms.

More researchers are moving toward equalizing this power differential in their relationship with research participants by making a conscious effort to include the voice and feedback of all system of care participants, and by seeking to understand participants' own meanings and interpretations and using these interpretations of reality rather than their own. More recently developed methodologies represent multiple voices in a collaborative, co-constructed manner that lets research participants have a say in how the research is conducted by exerting or influencing control over the conversations. **Participatory action research** is an example of one methodology that attempts to break down power relationships between the researcher and the researched by letting the stakeholders define the problem and work toward solutions; inviting participants to formulate the original questions, design the methodology, facilitate the sessions, and lead the analysis efforts; and moving the research into the community. In a study by Ozer and Wright (2012), participatory action research was used to examine whether student-led participatory research increased autonomy in two urban secondary schools. It was suggested that this type of research led to unique interactions between students and adult faculty and expanded areas of student influence within these schools.

participatory action research
An example of one methodology that attempts to break down power relationships between the researcher and the researched by letting the stakeholders define the problem and work toward solutions; inviting participants to formulate the original questions, design the methodology, facilitate the sessions, and lead the analysis efforts; and moving the research into the community.

Ethics in Reporting Findings ▼

As you will discover in coming chapters, social scientists aim to test research questions and hypotheses through their observations and often times through the analysis of data. Scholars have argued over the years that academic journals tend to have a bias against non-significant findings —this is to say that when the analyses don't turn out as the researcher expects, this is sometimes interpreted as an indication that the work is deficient and the piece is deemed unpublishable by reviewers and editors. Rosenthal (1979) and others have called this the "file drawer" effect. Since non-significant findings often go unpublished, there may be a temptation to "massage" data in such a way as to suggest that they support certain positions. There may also exist the temptation to engage in "HARKing," or hypothesizing after results are known (Kerr, 1998). In such instances, researchers examine the data first, then pretend that they anticipated the results all along.

Do not do this. Both of these research practices are widely considered unethical, and can lead to serious academic and professional consequences. As we will see in later chapters, readers tend to have expectations of what good data reporting looks like. Dishonest reporting also produces knowledge that is fundamentally flawed, since the data don't actually support the claims made by the researchers. Data analytic issues are largely policed by journal editors and reviewers. When it comes to ethics in research procedures, ethical practices are supervised by entities called IRBs.

▼ ## Who Oversees Research Ethics? Institutional Review Boards (IRBs)

Most academic research is overseen by university IRBs (Institutional Research Boards). Simply put, IRBs act as gatekeepers to research conducted by researchers affiliated with their university. They have a three-fold purpose: to protect the university from legal repercussions of conducting research deemed unethical, to protect the university from financial (and legal) sanctions imposed by the federal government and other funders on research deemed unethical, and to protect research participants from unethical practices in research. IRB board members usually consist of a cross-section of university faculty, and might also include legal and administrative representatives. All faculty—and some student—research must be submitted to the IRB for approval before being conducted. Even if the IRB will consider the research to be exempt from human subjects protection, most university IRBs want to make that ruling themselves. Student research conducted as part of a class project is usually exempt from IRB oversight because the students are considered to be under the oversight of their professor. However, if the research may later be submitted for publication, since peer-reviewed journals usually require IRB oversight, IRBs usually recommend that it be submitted to them anyway. Student research conducted for thesis or dissertation purposes is usually required to be submitted to the IRB.

Even if you are not conducting research under the authority of a university, you might still be subject to IRB oversight. Hospitals, research institutes, community agencies, and other organizations that conduct research frequently have their own IRBs.

Often, IRBs approve research projects quickly and efficiently. Criticism of IRBs and the IRB process occur when they don't. IRBs, at times, require researchers to change their method or procedures, and some researchers see this as a threat to academic freedom and a form of censorship, especially since most university faculty are required to conduct and publish research (Lewis, 2008; Lincoln, 2000). Critics of IRBs and other research gatekeepers claim that such censorship serves to suppress more innovative forms of research (Lincoln, 2000; Lincoln & Cannella, 2004).

▼ ## How Do We Maintain Ethics through all Research Phases?

Ethical considerations in research do not stop when you are done with data collection—ethical researchers make ethical decisions at every stage of the research process, from study design to publication of findings. Booth, Colomb, and Williams (1995, pp. 255–256) address ethical decision making in all stages of the research process in their "7-commandments" of ethical research. They say that ethical researchers:

1. Do not steal by plagiarizing or claiming the results of others.
2. Do not lie by misreporting sources or by inventing results.
3. Do not destroy sources and data for those who follow.
4. Do not submit data whose accuracy they have reason to question.
5. Do not conceal objections that they cannot rebut.
6. Do not caricature those with opposing views or deliberately state their views in a way they would reject.
7. Do not write their reports in a way that deliberately makes it difficult for readers to understand them, nor do they simplify that which is legitimately complex.

To borrow from the NRA's (National Rifle Association) familiar saying about gun control: "Research doesn't harm, researchers do." Research findings, both qualitative and quantitative, can be manipulated, misinterpreted, and misrepresented. Despite the desire of quantitative positivist researchers to remain objective, researchers of all paradigms should admit that it is impossible to remain completely objective in any research. Quantitative researchers address this dilemma by designing studies that are as objective as possible. Qualitative researchers, in contrast, address it by admitting their subjectivity, and taking that into account when analyzing their results (Hewitt, 2007). All researchers use rigorous, acceptable, analytical methods to determine what their data means. Quantitative researchers use appropriate statistical and systematic techniques to analyze their data. Qualitative researchers take into account interpretation and context as they acknowledge their role in the construction of knowledge (Hewitt, 2007).

So What?

In summary, it is our responsibility as researchers to ensure that: our research is properly designed, scientifically sound, and yields valid results; we do what we say we're going to do; the study is approved by an IRB and conducted according to protocol; informed consent is appropriately obtained; the rights and welfare of the participants are monitored throughout the study; the risks and benefits of the research are positively balanced; participant anonymity and confidentiality are appropriately maintained; and all participants—including those from underprivileged and marginalized populations—have an opportunity to have their voices and interpretations fully represented. The bottom line: Researchers are accountable and must show respect to colleagues in their profession and society at large.

Glossary

Anonymity
No one, including the researcher, can connect a participant's responses with his or her identity.

Assent
Permission obtained from individuals with limited capacity to consent (e.g., minors), allowing themselves to be included as participants in research studies. Assent occurs after informed consent (permission to participate) is obtained from a person who is responsible for the well-being of the participant, and should occur as near as possible in time to the research intervention.

Belmont Report
This document serves as the cornerstone of ethical principles upon which federal regulations for the protection of human research participants are based.

Beneficence
The outcome of research should be positive and beneficial.

Confidentiality
The identity of participants is kept secret when researchers report or write up their findings.

Deception
A violation of the right to informed consent that may sometimes mislead participants as to the study purpose.

Ethical research
Research that is designed and conducted validly, reliably, legitimately, and representatively, and protects a research participant's rights.

Human subjects protection
Ethical research rules that refer to the guidelines that are followed to ensure the protection of people (participants) being studied.

Informed consent
This process assumes that the research participant is competent to consent—that, if he or she is given all relevant information, he or she will be able to comprehend the information and be able to agree to participate in a voluntary manner free from coercion.

Justice
All classifications of people (race, ethnicity, gender, age, etc.) should be equally subjected to the risks and benefits of research, and people should be included or excluded only for reasons that have to do with the research question or hypothesis.

Legitimation
The question of who can represent another person in narrative writing.

Member checks
The process of providing study participants with the research findings, and giving them the opportunity to voice agreement or disagreement with the research as reported.

Nonmaleficence
No avoidable harm should be done to participants.

Nuremberg Code
The first set of principles outlining professional ethics for medical researchers, which forms the basis for today's research ethics codes. It specifically required voluntary consent among research participants, and was the first international standard for the conduct of research.

Participatory action research
An example of one methodology that attempts to break down power relationships between the researcher and the researched by letting the stakeholders define the problem and work toward solutions; inviting participants to formulate the original questions, design the methodology, facilitate the sessions, and lead the analysis efforts; and moving the research into the community.

Relational ethics
The value placed on the relationships between researchers and the people they are researching.

Representation
Fully understanding the lived experiences of research participants and including the multiple realities, interpretations, experiences, and voices emergent from all individuals and all angles.

Research ethics
The specific principles, rules, guidelines, and norms of research-related behavior that a research community has decided are proper, fair, and appropriate.

Respect for persons
Research participants should be treated as autonomous agents—that means they are independent, self-governing, and capable of making decisions for themselves as long as they are given sufficient information to make those decisions.

Vulnerable populations
Persons with diminished autonomy; specifically, children, people with cognitive impairments, older adults, people with severe health problems, employees, and students.

References

Adams, T. E. (2008). A review of narrative ethics. *Qualitative Inquiry, 14*(2), 175–194.

Annas, G. J., & Grodin, M. A. (1995). *The Nazi doctors and the Nuremberg Code: Human rights in human experimentation.* New York: Oxford University Press.

Bayer, A., & Tadd, W. (2000). Unjustified exclusion of elderly people from studies submitted to research ethics committee for approval: Descriptive study. *BMJ [British Medical Journal], 321,* 992– 993.

Becker-Blease, K. A., & Freyd, J. J. (2006). Research participants telling the truth about their lives: The ethics of asking and not asking about abuse. *American Psychologist, 61*(3), 218–226.

Booth, W. C., Colomb, G. G., & Williams, J. M. (1995). *The craft of research.* Chicago: University of Chicago Press.

Cassell, J. (1978). Risk and benefit to subjects of field-work. *American Sociologist, 13,* 134–143.

Creswell, J. W. (2007). *Qualitative inquiry & research design* (2nd ed.). Thousand Oaks, CA: Sage.

Denzin, N. (2003). *Performance ethnography: Critical pedagogy and the politics of culture.* Thousand Oaks, CA: Sage.

Dickson-Swift, V., James, E. L., Kippen, S., & Liamputtong, P. (2007). Doing sensitive research: What challenges do qualitative researchers face? *Qualitative Research, 7*(3), 327–353.

Edgar, H., & Rothman, D. J. (1995). The Institutional Review Board and beyond: Future challenges to the ethics of human experimentation. *The Milbank Quarterly, 73*(4), 489–506.

Ellis, C. (1986). *Fisher folk: Two communities on Chesapeake Bay.* Lexington, KY: University Press of Kentucky.

Ellis, C. (2007). Telling secrets, revealing lives: Relational ethics in research with intimate others. *Qualitative Inquiry, 13,* 3–29.

Guba, E.G., & Lincoln, Y. S. (1989). *Fourth generation evaluation.* Newbury Park, CA: Sage.

Hewitt, J. (2007). Ethical components of researcher-researched relationships in qualitative interviewing. *Qualitative Health Research, 27*(8), 1149–1159.

Humphrey, L. (1970). *Tearoom trade: Impersonal sex in public places.* London: Duckworth.

Kelman, H. C. (1967). Human use of human subjects: The problem of deception in social psychological experiments. *Psychological Bulletin, 67*(1), 1–11.

Kerr, N.L. (1998). HARKing: Hypothesizing after results are known. *Personality and Social Psychology Review, 2,* 196–217.

Kimmel, A. J. (1988). *Ethics and values in applied social research.* Thousand Oaks, CA: Sage.

Kotarba, J. A. (1979). The accomplishment of intimacy in the jail visiting room. *Qualitative Sociology, 2,* 80–103.

Krugman, S. (1971). Experiments at the Willowbrook State School. *Lancet, 1*(7702), 749.

Lewis, M. (2008). New strategies of control: Academic freedom and research ethics boards. *Qualitative Inquiry, 14,* 684– 699.

Lincoln, Y. S. (2000). Institutional review boards and methodological conservatism: The challenge to and from phenomenological paradigms. In N. K. Denzin & Y. S. Lincoln (Eds.), *The Sage handbook of qualitative research* (pp. 165–181). Thousand Oaks, CA: Sage.

Lincoln, Y. S., & Cannella, G. S. (2004). Qualitative research, power, and the radical right. *Qualitative Inquiry, 10*(2), 175– 201.

Marshall, C. (1985). Appropriate criteria of the trustworthiness and goodness for qualitative research on educational organizations. *Quality and Quantity, 19,* 353–373.

Mertens, D. M., & Ginsberg, P. (2008). *The handbook of social research ethics.* Thousand Oaks, CA: Sage.

Murphy, E., & Dingwall, R. (2001). The ethics of ethnography. In P. Atkinson, A. Coffey, S. Delamont, J. Lofland, & L. Lofland (Eds.), *Handbook of ethnography* (pp. 339–351). London: Sage.

NIH Office of Extramural Research. (2008). Retrieved May 25, 2009, from http://phrp.nihtraining.com/users/login.php

Ozer, E. J. & Wright, D. (2012). Beyond school spirit: The effects of youth-led participatory action research in two urban high schools. *Journal of Research on Adolescence,* doi: 10.1111/j.1532-7795.2012.00780.x

Parry, M. (2011, July 15). Harvard researchers accused of breaching students' privacy: Social-network project shows promise and peril of doing social science online. *The Chronicle of Higher Education,* pp. A1, A8–A11.

Paterson, B., & Scott-Findlay, S. (2002). Critical issues in interviewing people with traumatic brain injury. *Qualitative Health Research, 12*(3), 399–409.

Rosenthal, R. (1979). File drawer problem and tolerance for null results. *Psychological Bulletin, 86*, 638–641.

Sandelowski, M. (1986). The problem of rigor in qualitative research. *Advances in Nursing Science, 8*, 27–37.

Silverman, D. (1985). *Qualitative methodology and sociology*. Aldershot: Gower.

Thomas, S. B., & Quinn, S. C. (1991). The Tuskegee Syphilis Study, 1932 to 1972: Implications for HIV education and AIDS risk education programs in the black community. *American Journal of Public Health, 81*(11), 1498–1505.

Wax, M., & Cassell, J. (1979). Fieldwork, ethics and politics: The wider context. In M. Wax and J. Cassell (Eds.), *Federal regulations: Ethical issues and social research* (pp. 85–102). Boulder, CO: Westview.

7

UNDERSTANDING VARIABLES

CHAPTER OUTLINE

KEY TERMS

Coextensive relationships
Conceptual fit
Confounding variable
Contingent relationships
Dependent variable
Deterministic relationships
Hawthorne effect
Independent variable

Interval level measurement
Irreversible relationships
Measurement
Multidimensional concepts
Necessary relationships
Nominal level measurement
Ordinal level measurement
Ratio level measurement

Reversible relationships
Self-report
Sequential relationships
Social desirability
Stochastic relationships
Substitutable relationships
Sufficient relationships
Unidimensional concepts

CHAPTER OBJECTIVES

1. To understand the function of variables
2. To explore the relationships that occur between variables
3. To understand confounding variables
4. To become familiar with the process of variable measurement

▼ ## What Is the Function of Variables in Communication Research?

measurement
A process of determining the characteristics and/ or quantity of a variable through systematic recording and organization of observations.

In this chapter, we will examine what variables are, how we think about variables, and how variables are used in communication research. We will consider the types of variables, both independent and dependent, while revisiting the importance of how we operationally define variables at the outset of our research. We will also explore, in depth, the types of relationships between variables. Additionally, we discuss problematic variables, called extraneous variables, that we should be mindful of as we design our research studies. Finally, we consider **measurement** theory, levels of measurement, and whether variables are unidimensional or multidimensional. Our focus will remain on how all of the decisions we make along the way inform the subsequent methodological choices we make.

▼ ## What Is a Variable?

Variables can be any concepts that have the ability to take on more than one value. In other words, a single object cannot be a variable because it is incapable of taking on more than one value. In communication, we are interested in concepts that can vary. They can vary from person to person, vary in time, and vary in intensity. Remember that we have suggested that the variables of the study are the nouns in our research question or hypothesis.

•••

Revisiting Conceptual and Operational Definitions

Although we discussed the concepts of conceptual definitions and operational definitions in Chapter 6 when we discussed research questions and hypotheses, we need to revisit our discussion on that topic, as that is an important consideration you make when choosing what variables to study in your research. Without a strong understanding of our conceptual and operational definitions we cannot establish variables that adequately answer our research questions and hypotheses.

Conceptual Definitions

Remember that a conceptual definition is simply how you define the variable you plan to study. In Chapter 5, we used the example of defining the word *violence*, illustrating that we might all have a slightly unique definition of what counts as violence. The goal of a conceptual definition is to delineate clearly what you mean, when you are identifying your variables of interest. It allows the reader of the research and others who wish to study the same construct to know without a doubt what you mean when you study a particular variable. The conceptual definition is really the written definition of the variables of the study. It allows you to define an often broad, obscure concept in terms of related, similar (often more concrete) concepts, and in some instances to establish the boundaries of what phenomena meet the definition you are using.

Operational Definitions

Operational definitions describe the observable characteristics of a concept, so that the characteristics can be measured or otherwise identified or represented. These definitions identify how the communication scholars plan to measure and/or observe the variable of interest. Having clear operational definitions allows researchers to replicate their studies and/or extend them into other domains, knowing that they are using the same procedures in terms of measurement. There are two types of operational definitions: measured operational definitions and experimental operational definitions. Both explore how you can measure a variable of interest, but they differ based on the methodological choices a scholar makes.

Measured Operational Definitions.   A measured operational definition describes how a researcher can measure the existence or quantity of a variable—for example, intelligence measured with an IQ test, class performance with a letter grade, risk perception with Lachlan and Spence's (2010) hazard scale, dialogic communication with discourse analysis, communicating power with a close textual analysis.

Measured operational definitions are important in descriptive research too. For example, if you wanted to examine the frequency and context of violence in slashers films, like Weaver (1991) did, you must identify what you will count and how. In Weaver's study, "Each scene was coded for (a) duration (in seconds); (b) the number, gender, and dramatic role (i.e., protagonist vs. antagonist) of all characters; (c) the general type of action depicted; (d) the specific nature of each action; (e) the resolution, if any, of each action; and (f) the involvement of nudity" (p. 387). Here he identifies exactly what will be coded. He then becomes even more specific, "Acts of aggression, for example, were coded as involving verbal abuse, an attempted attack, or an attack on a person or persons" (1991, p. 387).

Experimental Operational Definitions. Experimental operational definitions specify how the researcher can manipulate a variable in an experiment, in order to produce at least two values or levels of an independent variable. For example, a variable with an experimental operational definition would describe how we manipulate exposure to differing levels of media violence: *The Dark Knight* vs. *Mama Mia!*, or persuasive message presented by an attractive vs. unattractive speaker—Randy Johnson vs. Michael Jordan.

In both measured and experimental operational definitions, the goal is to create a kind of a guidebook for other scholars in your field. Good operational definitions allow others to replicate previous work, while at the same time providing some control over what you study. Operational definitions steer how you observe and measure your variable, thus functioning as guidelines for some of your methodological choice making. However, ultimately, the key of both conceptual and operational definitions is that they need to match. They define the variables of interest in any communication research study, and in order to have valid research we must actually measure what it is that we claim we are measuring.

▼ # Operationalizing: Matching Your Variables to Your Study

Conceptual Fit

One of the primary goals of this textbook and of communication research methods courses across the country is to teach you to be a critical consumer of research. As such, we are not only interested in teaching you to be critical of the results of empirical work, but also of the methodological choices the researcher makes in building their work. While there is clearly no such thing as a perfect study, we expect you to learn how to evaluate the components of all communication research. It is important that you give consideration to how to evaluate operational definitions. The biggest concern in defining a variable, operationally, is in the **conceptual fit** between what is measured and what you set out to measure. This conceptual fit is really designed to be certain that the meaning of both your conceptual and operational definitions is preserved throughout the research process. One important question you can ask is as follows: Is the operational definition adequate or complete; does it include all of the essential aspects of a

conceptual fit
How closely your operational definition matches your conceptual definition.

variable? For example, we might ask our students if they are comfortable with us determining whether they are a good student from their G.P.A. Not surprisingly, not all students are comfortable with this one measure having tapped into all of the aspects that should be considered when evaluating the relative success of a college student. Please recognize that while you strive to be as thorough as possible, most operationalizations are incomplete. It is nearly impossible to capture the complete meaning of some constructs with a single variable. The second question you should ask is: Is it accurate? In other words, do you agree with how the research measured the variable? Does it make sense? For example, you might ask whether hitting a Bobo doll (an inflatable child-size doll filled with sand and designed to be punched) is an accurate measure of aggression (see Bandura, Ross, & Ross, 1961; and Bandura, Ross, & Ross, 1963). Last, in evaluating both measured and manipulated operational definitions, the question you should ask is whether the researcher has made clear to us how the variable is measured or manipulated.

Measuring Variables

The last component of operational definitions we want to discuss has to do with the choices you make about the operational procedures for measured variables. There are three primary procedures you follow for measuring variables: self-report, other report, and observing behavior.

Self-Report.   **Self-report** procedures are familiar to most students. Think about the evaluation you make of professors and instructors at the end of each semester. Or perhaps, you find yourself consulting ratemyprofessor.com prior to enrolling in a class with a particular professor. These are good examples of self-report procedures (though despite students' beliefs to the contrary, one of these two methods is more accurate than the other; we will discuss sampling bias in Chapter 8). Self-report procedures are good at measuring an individual's beliefs, attitudes, and values, or in finding out about behaviors (after the fact) we might not be able to observe directly.

self-report
This procedure is good at measuring individual's beliefs, attitudes, and values, or in finding out about behaviors we might not be able to observe directly.

SOCIAL DESIRABILITY BIAS IN SELF-REPORT DATA.   Remember, research methods are about making the best choices with the tools at your disposal and none of the operational procedures for measured variables is without limitations. A well-documented limitation of self-report data collection is that it depends upon the participant's willingness to provide the information, as well as the ability to recall accurately something that has already happened. The most significant weakness of self-report is an issue we call **social desirability**. Social desirability is the idea that if you are asking participants to answer questions that are sensitive in nature, people might feel swayed to present themselves in a particular light, regardless of whether it is indeed true. An example of this can be seen in Oliver and Hyde's (1993) meta-analysis of sexual behavior by gender. This study found significant gender differences for sexual behavior, with eight of the nine measures reflecting greater experience for males. While this seems reasonable, the authors themselves note in the discussion that because all the studies they reviewed used self-report data, what they had found evidence of was "gender differences in reporting tendencies" (p. 45).

social desirability
The idea that if participants are asked to answer questions that are sensitive in nature, people will undoubtedly feel swayed to present themselves in a particular light, regardless of whether it is indeed true.

Other Report.   Another operational procedure for measured variables is an *other report*. In this method you ask others to report on the individual in question's behavior. The hope is that they may be more objective than an individual's self-report, eliminating your concern about social desirability.

LIMITATIONS IN OTHER REPORTS.   However, problems in asking people to rate others' behavior can include limited experience with the individual or limited prior exposure to her behavior. It is also possible that any kind of pre-existing relationship between subject and observer may bias the reporting of their behavior. Take for example the famous Bandura, Ross, and Ross's (1963) Bobo doll experiments. If you wanted to replicate these studies, you may want to measure children's aggression after viewing violent or nonviolent films by asking the classroom teachers to report on children's behavior. At the same time, it would be wise to pre-test the teachers making the observations to see if they have any existing biases toward identifying students who may be more or less inclined to exhibit violent behavior.

Observing Behavior.   The third operational procedure you can use for measuring variables is observing behavior. For example, your author Christine Davis observes children's mental health treatment team meetings to assess communication in the meetings. Students often like to observe communication behaviors in research settings such as bars, shopping malls, or restaurants. Other communication researchers prefer to do their observations in laboratory settings. They might use an observation lab, which is a room set up like a living room (or conference room) with video cameras and/or one-way mirrors. Researchers give participants communication tasks (such as, "talk to each other on this subject") and observe them while they are carrying out the behavior.

The major strength of observing behavior is that it can sometimes be more accurate than self-report or other report, especially if the observations are conducted in a naturalistic setting. Imagine that we ask you to rate your communication competence in a communication task you complete with your significant other. Are you likely to be an objective judge of either your own skills in communication or even of your relational partner's skills? Perhaps. However, to guard against inaccuracies, we often have trained researchers assess communication competence in strangers. They tend to be much more objective. However, observation is not without its own inherent limitations. You can only assess what people do—not why they may behave in a particular way, what they believe, or what they feel. Therefore, scholars must observe the behavior they believe most accurately represents the concept of interest. This can pose potential problems; it can sometimes be challenging to be certain that the behavior indicates what you think it does.

HAWTHORNE EFFECT BIAS IN OBSERVING BEHAVIORS.   Another potential limitation that occurs is the **Hawthorne Effect**. When you know others are observing you, do you change your behavior? Sure, most of us do alter our behavior slightly when we know that we are being observed. This is known as the Hawthorne effect. While the Hawthorne effect is most commonly associated with conscious observation, it should be noted that it can also occur

Hawthorne Effect
An effect where people alter their behavior because they know they're being observed.

in self-report and other-report studies too. Simply the awareness that someone will read your answers to a survey, or the suspicion that someone is looking at you from behind a one-way mirror in a laboratory setting, can be enough to induce Hawthorne.

Triangulation

As you can see, each type of operational procedure for measured variables has both strengths and limitations associated with it. As is often the case, there is no solution to the limitations presented. As such, one solution is to combine a variety of different methods for measuring the variable in question. Triangulation is defined as "the comparison of two or more forms of evidence with respect to an object of research interest" (Lindlof & Taylor, 2002, pp. 240–241). There are actually several different types of triangulation: you can triangulate *sources*— multiple interviewees, multiple field sites, multiple cases, multiple observations; *methods*—qualitative methods plus quantitative methods, observation plus self-report plus other report; or *researchers*—multiple interviewers or observers (Lindlof & Taylor, 2002). However, not nearly enough scholars employ this technique in their research studies, and it is often the case that triangulation has to take place across multiple studies and entire programs of research. Triangulation moves you closer to understanding the variable in question and enhances the validity of the findings. For example, you might study communication competence and triangulate the methods by measuring the variable in three different ways: self-report, other report (rating their conversational partner), and trained coders' observational ratings. Triangulation often yields interesting results and enhances study validity (see Chapter 9).

Measurement

Regardless of what method you use to gather the information to measure your variables (self-report, other report, or observing behavior), you might need to use a scale as a questioning device to obtain a fairly precise and consistent measurement. Measurement is the process of determining the characteristics and/or quantity of a variable through systematic recording and organization of observations. Often, when conducting research, you use a scale to assign numbers and/or symbols to the characteristics of variables. There are four levels of measurement, which you consider from least specific to most specific: nominal, ordinal, interval, and ratio.

Nominal Level Measurement.   **Nominal level measurement** makes use of unordered categories, classifying the variable into qualitatively different and unique categories. Nominal data does not have any true numerical value; the categories do not indicate any type of order or intensity of the degree to which a characteristic exists. Rather, they represent the potential categories of some variable of interest. For example, political party affiliation, religious affiliation, biological sex, and race are all variables measured at the nominal level. If you are unclear as to whether a scale is nominal, ask yourself whether there is some inherent order to the categories. If there is no order, the scale is nominal.

nominal level measurement
This type of measurement makes use of unordered categories, classifying the variable into qualitatively different and unique categories. These categories do not indicate any type of order or intensity of the degree to which a characteristic exists but represent the potential categories of some variable of interest.

There are two requirements for categorical representation: each category must be mutually exclusive and the list of categories must be exhaustive. Mutually exclusive categories have no overlap. You should be able to place an observation into one and only one category. One of the places you have likely encountered a categorical system that lacked mutually exclusive categories is when you have purchased music. Ever try to figure out what genre your favorite artist fits into? Is a CD by the Red Hot Chili Peppers likely to be found in Pop or Rock? Where do you look for a Taylor Swift CD, Country or Pop? In fact, Baccigalupo, Plaza, and Donaldson (2008) argue that genre is a fuzzy classification system for music, supporting our notion that genre is an example of a nominal categorical system violating the necessary mutually exclusive requirement of a categorical system. Second, the category system must be exhaustive. In other words, each category must represent the variable fully; each observation must be able to be classified by the measurement scheme. One of the ways scholars ensure that their category system is exhaustive is to identify the last category as *other*, thus ensuring that each observation will fit somewhere. For example, political party affiliation: Democrat, Republican, Independent, other.

Qualitative research frequently uses nominal measurements. Stephanie Houston Grey (2002), for example, analyzed the discourse of Japanese survivors of the Hiroshima and Nagasaki bombings in World War II as narratives of Christian transformation and meaning, redemptive knowing, and cultural authenticity. In another example, Warren and Kilgard (2001) studied a performance of Nathaniel Hawthorne's "The Birthmark" to understand the concepts (variables) of *whiteness*, *power*, and *privilege*—all nominal variables.

In quantitative research, nominal measurement is often used as a strategy to describe the sample of the study. For example, in their study on employee satisfaction with meetings, Rogelberg, Allen, Shanock, Scott, and Shuffler (2010) used nominal variables to describe participants' gender and organization type (publicly traded, privately held, private not for profit).

Ordinal Level Measurement.

ordinal level measurement
This type of measurement has ordered categories or rank, and it can be determined whether an observation is greater than, less than, or equal to other observations. However, this type of measurement does not indicate how much the difference is; the amount separating levels is not known.

Ordinal level measurement is an ordered category or rank. Here we can determine whether an observation is greater than, less than, or equal to other observations, which cannot be determined from nominal level measurement. However, ordinal level measurement does not indicate the magnitude of that difference. Further, the intervals between the numbers on the scale are not necessarily equal. Ordinal level measurement examples include television programs classified as high, medium, or low in violence; the top five college football teams; and the top ten finishers in a NASCAR race. Any measure that uses ranking is ordinal level measurement.

Ordinal level measurement is often seen in the corporate world in terms of performance evaluation. For example, sales organizations often rank order their employees based on sales production. A life insurance company may hold a competition for life applications and rank a group of agents by number of applications in a month.

Interval Level Measurement.

interval level measurement
This type of measurement specifies relative position and also establishes standard, equal distances between points on the scale.

Interval level measurement specifies relative position and also establishes standard, equal distances between points on the scale. Most rating scales used in research are interval level measurement scales. Teacher evaluations are a good example of interval level measurements. When researchers ask participants to use a 5 or 7-point scale Likert scale (see below), most researchers assume that people recognize that the distances between points on the scale are equal. A benefit of interval level measurement is that if the differences between the numbers are meaningful, calculations (such as addition and subtraction) can be done. However, remember that the zero point is meaningless, and as a result it is impossible to make proportional statements. In other words, take the IQ (intelligence quotient) test, which is considered an interval level measurement; while the points between numbers are thought to be equal, there is no such thing as an IQ of zero. As such, someone with an IQ of 150 is not twice as smart as someone with an IQ of 75. Other examples of interval level measurement scales are both the Fahrenheit and the Celsius scales of temperature. The difference between 80 and 90 degrees is the same as the difference between 50 and 60; but 80 degrees isn't twice as hot as 40 degrees, because zero degrees does not indicate a total lack of temperature.

Interval measurement is pervasive throughout quantitative research methods, allowing us to study communication in marriage, patient satisfaction, employee dissent, and even communication strategies in a deceptive encounter. In fact, most any consumer survey you receive from the local grocery store, telephone company, voter attitude phone survey, or even the Nielsen television ratings use interval level measurement.

Table 7.1. Top Grossing Films in the USA (2015)

An Example of an Ordinal Level of Measurement	
1. *Star Wars: Episode 7*	$742,208,902
2. *Jurassic World*	$652,198,010
3. *The Avengers: Age of Ultron*	$459,005,868
4. *Inside Out*	$356,461,711
5. *Furious 7*	$351,032,910

Retrieved July 18, 2016, from http://www.the-numbers.com/market/2015/top-grossing-movies

Because interval level scales are so prominent in research, we should consider three types of interval level scales: Likert's method of summated ratings, Osgood's semantic differential, and the Thurstone scale. All three of these scales measure participants' feelings or attitudes. The key difference between them is the way they get at obtaining this information. We should take a second to note that not all researchers consider these three scales to be interval—some consider them to be ordinal scales. The determining factor is whether you believe that everyone sees the difference between 1 and 2 on a semantic differential, or *agree strongly* and *agree somewhat* on a Likert scale as the same. Most researchers in our field are willing to make that assumption and treat these scales as interval data.

LIKERT SCALE.   The Likert scale is most common. You are probably already familiar with this interval scale, which measures participants' feelings or attitudes toward another person, issue, and event. The Likert scale is named after Rensis Likert (1932), an organizational psychologist who published a report detailing the use of this scale. Participants receive statements representing clear positions and are asked to indicate the extent to which they agree with each statement, usually on a 5- or 7-point scale (e.g., strongly agree, agree, neither agree nor disagree, disagree, strongly disagree). Often both positive and negative statements appear on the measure to be sure that participants are reading the questions, rather than responding without thought. Most human beings are quite patterned in their responses, so to avoid a response set, wherein they answer the same answer for each question, alternating the direction of a statement can alleviate this issue. Negative items are then reverse scored and scores are summed across the measure.

In their study on electronic multitasking in organization meetings, Stephens and Davis (2009, p. 71) utilized a Likert scale to measure the experience with technology variable. Participants were asked to rate their comfort with and skill with technology from "complete novice (1) to expert (7)."

Table 7.2.   Example of a Likert Scale

Listening Measure
Please indicate the degree to which each statement applies to you by indicating whether you:
Strongly Disagree = 1; Disagree = 2; are Neutral = 3; Agree = 4; Strongly Agree = 5
_____   **1.** I dislike speeches that don't interest me.
_____   **2.** Usually I can listen to a speech that doesn't interest me.
_____   **3.** I get restless and daydream when I listen to someone who doesn't interest me.
_____   **4.** I listen even when the information in a speech doesn't interest me.
_____   **5.** Listening to dull presenters about dull information makes me restless and causes me to daydream.
_____   **6.** I do listen to dull presenters about dull information.
_____   **7.** I don't usually listen to a presenter if there are distractions in the room.
_____   **8.** I do listen when there are distractions during a presentation.
_____   **9.** I listen to presentations that are not directed at me.
_____   **10.** I do not listen to presentations if they do not apply to me.
_____   **11.** If I have other things on my mind, I don't pay attention to a presenter.
_____   **12.** I listen to a presenter even if I have other things I'm thinking about.
_____   **13.** I usually will not listen to a presentation that does not have a clear agenda.
_____   **14.** I usually will listen even if a presentation has no clear agenda.
_____   **15.** I am accepting of a presenter who does not give continuous feedback.

_____ **16.** I am not accepting of a presenter who does not give continuous feedback.

_____ **17.** I listen to presenters who do not give continuous feedback.

_____ **18.** I will not listen to presenters who do not give continuous feedback.

_____ **19.** I will listen to a presenter who has different opinions than mine.

_____ **20.** I will not listen to a presenter who has different opinions than mine.

_____ **21.** I will listen to a presenter who does not explain his/her subject matter.

_____ **22.** I will not listen to a presenter if his/her subject matter is not defined.

SEMANTIC DIFFERENTIAL SCALE.   Osgood's semantic differential scale is another interval level measurement technique, which measures the meanings participants assign to some stimulus (e.g., groups, types of music, a person, an idea). This scale, named after Charles Osgood (Osgood, Suci, & Tannenbaum, 1957), was initially used to measure the connotative meaning of concepts. This scale presents a stimulus at the top of a list of scales, wherein the scales are anchored at either end by pairs of polar-opposite adjectives (active-passive; warm-cold). Participants check a single point on the scale expressing their perception of the stimulus. A graduate school friend of one of your authors was interested in the music used during public service announcements. To pretest different types of music, we listened to five clips of music and rated them using a semantic differential scale (happy-sad; calm-anxious; relaxed-fearful, etc.). In a study by Uhlmann and Swanson (2004), they used a semantic differential scale to have participants measure their own and others' association of aggression. In other words, they reported where they fell on a scale from −3 to +3. The scale anchors were aggressive-peaceful, fighter-quiet, and combative-gentle (p. 45).

Table 7.3.   Example of a Semantic Differential Scale

Group Behavior Inventory, Friedlander (1966)						
In this section, you are asked to judge the meaning of the concept Group Meeting (as it relates to _____ Department) in terms of each of the seven scales beneath it. Check one blank for each of the seven scales that best describes the meaning of the concept: _____ DEPARTMENT GROUP MEETINGS						
good						bad
weak						strong
active						passive
pleasant						unpleasant
deep						shallow
relaxed						tense
valuable						worthless

ratio level measurement
As the most specific type of measurement, it has all of the characteristics of an interval scale, but also a true, meaningful zero point.

Ratio Level Measurement. The most specific level of measure is the **ratio level measurement**, which not only has all of the characteristics of an interval scale, but also a true, meaningful zero point. Ratio scales also are assumed to be measured in equal intervals, and they can be mathematically measured, even to a decimal point or fraction of a point. Many variables have a true and meaningful measure of zero (e.g., age, heart rate, years at current address, the number of times you attended church in the last year, driving speed, income). The major advantage to ratio level measurement is that since there is a true, meaningful zero point, you can make proportional statements: Someone who is 50 is twice as old as someone who is 25 years of age. It is important to be able to identify whether a variable has been measured with a nominal, ordinal, interval, or ratio level of measurement, as the type of measurement level will determine the statistical techniques you can use to test your hypotheses and research questions.

Most often used in quantitative research studies, communication scholars use ratio measurement to examine relationships with a participant's age or measure a type of behavior of the participant. For example, Powell and Segrin (2004) used a ratio level to measure sexual behaviors, asking such questions as, "How many times in the last month did you engage in vaginal intercourse?" They also gathered the number of sexual partners over specific timeframes; this too, would constitute ratio level measurement.

Table 7.4. Practice with Levels of Variable Measurement

Is the variable measured or manipulated? If the variable is measured: is it nominal, ordinal, interval, or ratio?
1. Preferred news source (self-report): newspaper, TV, magazine, other, none.
2. Length of acquaintance: Ask married people to report number of months they knew spouse prior to marriage.
3. Personal relevance of issue: Freshmen hear message advocating comprehensive exams for seniors; some told to begin next year, some told it will begin after they graduate.
4. Personal relevance of issue: Ask people to rate how personally important an issue is to them on a 7-point scale ranging from not at all important to very important.
5. Compliance-gaining strategies: Ask people to describe how they tried to gain compliance on one occasion, classify strategies.
6. Ask how successful the strategy was: not at all, somewhat, very.
7. Instruct people to use one of four different strategies to gain compliance from others in the context of collecting door-to-door for a charity.
8. Record amount of money donated to the charity.
Answer key: (1) measured, nominal; (2) measured, ratio; (3) manipulated; (4) measured, interval; (5) measured, nominal; (6) measured, ordinal; (7) manipulated; (8) measured, ratio.

• •

▼ Types of Variables

Now that we've discussed levels of measurement, let's review certain types of variables. There are two basic types of variables in communication research projects that follow an experimental design: independent and dependent variables. It is necessary that we know the differences between the two.

Independent Variables

An **independent variable** is the variable that is thought to predict or determine the value in another variable. For example, consider two variables: the number of cigarettes a person smokes and the probability of getting lung cancer. Both are variables because they can take on different values. One might have smoked zero cigarettes or might have smoked 3,000 in his or her lifetime. Even lung cancer is a variable because it can vary—you can have lung cancer, or not. Thus, the concept has more than one value, making it a variable. In this example, which one is your independent variable? If you guessed the number of cigarettes smoked, then you are correct. Consider another example. If we assume that your ratio of fat to lean is a function of how much you exercise, what is your independent variable? This seems a little trickier; reread and think it through. The amount of exercise is your independent variable, because it is thought to predict the value of your fat/lean ratio.

independent variable
The variable that causes or determines the value in another variable.

Dependent Variables

While we have been discussing these examples, there are other variables present—lung cancer and our ratio of fat/lean. In both of these cases, they are the **dependent variable**. The dependent variable is assumed to depend on or be predicted by another variable. In the examples above, cancer is presumed to be predicted by or dependent on the number of cigarettes smoked, while the ratio of fat/lean depends upon the amount of exercise one engages in. An easy way to remember it: outcomes are called dependent variables, because they depend on what happens with the independent variable.

dependent variable
The variable that is assumed to depend on or be caused by another variable.

Examples of Independent and Dependent Variables.   Another way to think about the independent variable is that this variable is likely to be what the researcher manipulates or what the research manipulates, while the dependent variable is what the researcher measures. So, for the first example, you will measure whether the participant has cancer, while you select a variety of people (who undoubtedly smoke a variety of number of cigarettes). And in the second example, you select a variety of people who exercise to varying degrees, and measure their fat/lean ratio.

An unusual, yet effective way to think about independent and dependent variables comes from ballroom dancing. When two dancers are dancing, they are in a partnership. As Tony Prado, Owner of Queen City Ballroom in Charlotte, explained it: Both partners have a job to do—one, the male (think independent variable), is in charge of where the couple moves to on the floor; he is in the lead. However, his task depends upon the woman's ability (think dependent variable) to follow his lead. In this example, the independent variable (the male lead dancer) predicts—or determines—which direction the dependent variable (the woman) goes.

As one last example, let's imagine that you do a survey of current college students measuring both marijuana smoking and grades. Imagine that you find that the more pot an individual smoked, the lower his or her grades. What is the independent variable, and what is the dependent variable? In other words, what caused what? How many of you think that the amount an individual smokes is the independent variable, causing the student to have lower grades (dependent variable)? Is it possible that it works the other way around? Is it possible that an individual might have poor grades (independent variable) and as a result begin smoking more marijuana (dependent variable)? Here, there is no clear answer; it is up to the researcher to identify the answer with his or her research question and/or hypotheses. The research questions and/or hypotheses identify what variable is the independent variable and what variable is the dependent variable. In other words, you as the researcher determine which is the independent variable or the dependent variable when you set up your experiment.

Table 7.5. Practice with Independent and Dependent Variables

Identify the independent and dependent variables for each of the following hypotheses:

1. People with high levels of exposure to television news will report greater satisfaction with life than people with low levels of exposure to television news.

2. Communicators with formal debate training will report higher levels of assertiveness than communicators without formal debate training.

3. When people are exposed to fear-arousing messages, as opposed to non-fear-arousing messages, they will report increased levels of anxiety.

4. The older one is, the greater will be the levels of stress perceived in one's life.

5. Children who stutter will have higher self-esteem than children who do not stutter.

6. Subjects reading persuasive messages by attractive sources will experience greater attitude change than subjects reading persuasive messages by unattractive sources.

7. Individuals with low communication apprehension will report significantly more positive parental behaviors and attitudes toward communication than individuals with high communication apprehension. [HINT: There are two dependent variables.]

8. Alcohol use and misuse would increase across adolescence.

Extraneous Variables

Sometimes a third (or more) variable will make finding the *true* relationship between the independent and dependent variables difficult to determine, because this additional variable is another possible cause (other than the independent variable) of the effect on the dependent variable. This is called an extraneous variable. An extraneous variable is one that is typically thought of as being unpredictable and uncontrolled by the researcher, or as being a variable that is not part of the research design. When searching for extraneous variables, researchers sometimes talk about the *third variable problem*—an unseen or unmeasured variable that is accounting for the changes seen in both the independent and dependent variables.

confounding variable
An extraneous variable that muddies the relationship between the independent and dependent variable.

Confounding Variables.   A **confounding variable** is an extraneous variable that, because of its relationship to both the independent and dependent variables, cannot be distinguished from the independent variable in the analysis. Another way to define a confounding variable is when the effects of two variables cannot be separated from each other. For example, let's say a public speaking instructor not only asked students to practice their speeches an hour each day, but also suggested they visualize giving the speech before doing so. If the students were then rated as being better public speakers, there would be no way of knowing which of the two variables (practice or visualization) was responsible for the effect (better public speaking). These two actions likely had an effect on each other as well as on the dependent variable. Another commonly used example is as follows: imagine that you do a survey of various cities, and you measure two variables—crime incidence and ice cream consumption. You are going to discover that crime rates and ice cream consumption are strongly correlated. In this example, what are the dependent and independent variables? Do either one of these make sense to be dependent or independent? So, why is there a relationship between these two variables? The reason these are related variables in this instance is because both ice cream consumption and crime rates are dependent upon a third variable. This third variable is heat—hot weather drives people toward more outdoor interaction (and thus greater likelihood of confrontation). It also drives ice cream consumption, since ice cream is a cool, delicious treat on a hot day. Therefore, heat is the confounding variable, as it *muddies* the ability to detect the effect of the independent variable on the dependent variable. The relationship between the two variables, which is due to some confounding variable, is called a spurious correlation. When you design a research project and identify your variable, you need to attempt to anticipate potential confounds and eliminate them in the design of the study.

Table 7.6.   An Example of a Confounding Variable in "Much Ado about Nothing" from *The Simpson's*

Homer: Not a bear in sight. The Bear Patrol must be working like a charm.
Lisa: That's specious reasoning, Dad.
Homer: Thank you, dear.
Lisa: By your logic I could claim that this rock keeps tigers away.
Homer: Oh, how does it work?
Lisa: It doesn't work.
Homer: Uh-huh.
Lisa: It's just a stupid rock.
Homer: Uh-huh.
Lisa: But I don't see any tigers around, do you?
[Homer thinks of this, then pulls out some money.]
Homer: Lisa, I want to buy your rock.
[Lisa refuses at first, then takes the exchange.]

One of our favorite examples of a confounding variable is found in a newspaper article from June 11, 1984. The article, titled, "Ethel May Not Be Sexy, but She'll Do Better in Business than Cheryl," by Gary Dessler, reports on a master's thesis by Dorothy Linville. In this study, the author considered the question of whether the name of a woman would prevent her from landing management level positions. This particular research project utilized an experimental design. First, students rated the sexiness of 255 women's names on a scale of one to seven, with higher scores representing sexier names. Eight names receiving the highest scores were considered sexy, whereas the seven lowest scoring names were considered the least sexy. Keeping in mind that this study was done in the early 1980s, the sexy names were: Christine ($M = 5.08$), Candice ($M = 4.92$), Cheryl and Melanie ($M = 4.91$), Dawn, Heather, Jennifer, and Susan ($M = 4.83$). The least sexy names were as follows: Ethel ($M = 1.00$), Alma ($M = 1.08$), Zelda ($M = 1.16$), Florence, Mildred, Myrtle, and Esther ($M = 1.15$).

In the actual study, 100 college seniors and graduate students were asked to imagine being in the role of personnel managers. They received résumés of eight equally qualified women and were asked to rate them for management positions. Four of the résumés had unsexy names: Ethel, Myrtle, Mildred, and Esther; while four had high sexy names: Cheryl, Dawn, Jennifer, and Michelle. The results of this study indicated that men preferred hiring women with less sexy names for the management positions than did women. In fact, the article stated, "A new study finds that men are more likely to hire women with names they perceive as nonsexy for managerial positions, and give these women higher salaries. Women hiring other women are less influenced by the sound of a name" (Dessler, 1984). Is this really the conclusion one can draw based on the study as we have described it to you? Think for a minute about who you know with a name like Cheryl, Dawn, Jennifer, or Michelle. Then consider Ethel, Myrtle, Mildred, and Esther. Is it likely that these two groups of names come from two different generations? Therefore, there's a third variable going on here: perceived age of the applicant. Thus, it's highly possible that this is in fact age discrimination, not name discrimination. The key is that in this case there was another variable besides the sexiness of the name; therefore, it is incorrect to attribute the results to the sexiness of the woman's name.

There are two other types of variables that also have an effect on the dependent variable: mediating variables and moderating variables. These differ from extraneous variables in that they are typically predicted and controlled by the researcher.

Mediating Variables. With a mediating variable, instead of hypothesizing that A causes B directly, you might hypothesize that A causes M (mediating variable), which in turn causes B. An example of this might be that low communication apprehension (A) might cause a student to speak out more in class (M), which in turn might cause the student to get a better grade in class (B). Thus, while it may appear that low communication apprehension causes the student to get a better grade, it's only because of the mediating effect of speaking out more in class.

Moderating Variables. A moderating variable is a third variable that has an effect on both A and B. An example of this might be that an individual's overall health (M, moderating variable) affects both the individual's communication competence with his or her health-care provider (A) and the individual's satisfaction with his or her health care (B). Thus, it may appear that the individual's communication competence with his or her health-care provider causes the individual to be more satisfied with his or her health care, but it's actually that the individual's overall health affects both. We know that mediating and moderating variables sound similar to a confounding variable, but here's the primary difference—in the experiment, the researcher controls for the mediating and moderating variables and does not control for a confounding variable.

• •

The Different Types of Relationships between Variables ▼

In Chapter 6, we discussed how variables might have associational or causal, and directional or nondirectional, relationships with each other. As you have a better grasp on understanding the relationships between independent variables and dependent variables, and even how to look out for confounding variables, you must now consider the different types of relationships between the variables within the hypotheses you read and write.

Reversible and Irreversible Relationships

First, relationships between variables can be reversible or irreversible. **Reversible relationships** can go either way. For example, think about the pot-smoking example. Which comes first: pot smoking or grades? As you saw earlier, that relationship could go in either direction, thus it is a reversible relationship. Some are **irreversible relationships**, meaning the direction can only go one way. Think about the lung cancer and number of cigarettes smoked relationship. Can it go either way? No, thus it is an irreversible relationship.

Deterministic and Stochastic Relationships

Second, relationships between variables can be deterministic or stochastic. Relationships that are **deterministic** occur when the dependent variable must result from the independent variable. In communication studies, few relationships are deterministic; most are **stochastic**, which means probable. Again, think about the relationship between lung cancer and smoking. In fact, ask almost any smoker you know and he will tell you a tale of someone he knows who smoked like a fiend and died peacefully at an ancient age without ever getting lung cancer. That is because it is a probabilistic (stochastic) relationship, not deterministic. In other words, if a person smokes, she is more *likely* to get lung cancer (more probable), but smoking does not guarantee (determine 100%) lung cancer.

The above example is a classic case of what is sometimes referred to as an *individualistic fallacy*. When people fail to recognize the differences between stochastic and deterministic relationships, they may make inaccurate assumptions about the relationships between variables. It may very well be the case that the person in the example above knows someone who smoked his entire life and lived into old age in good health. There are always exceptions to rules. But in the aggregate, smoking will still damage your health and shorten your life. Rejecting this notion is an example of individualistic fallacy, rejecting a stochastic relationship based on a single observation.

reversible relationships
Relationships that can go in either direction or either way.

irreversible relationships
Relationships that can only go in one direction or one way.

deterministic relationships
Relationships that occur when the dependent variable must result from the independent variable.

stochastic relationships
Relationships that are probable.

sequential relationships
Relationships where the ordering of the variables is important and must occur sequentially, meaning chronologically or in order.

coextensive relationships
Relationships where the variables co-occur or happen simultaneously.

sufficient relationships
Relationships where the presence of or a change in one variable is enough to bring about a change in a second variable.

contingent relationships
Relationships where one variable is enough to bring about a third variable, if needed.

necessary relationships
Relationships where one variable must be present for a second variable to be present.

substitutable relationships
Relationships where other forces might bring about the same effect as a necessary relationship.

Sequential and Coextensive Relationships

Third, relationships between variables can be sequential or coextensive. In **sequential relationships**, the ordering of the variables is important and must occur sequentially, meaning chronologically or in order. The Bobo doll experiments are an example of relationships between variables that occur sequentially (Bandura, Ross, & Ross, 1961). The researchers exposed children to violent or nonviolent cartoons, then allowed them the opportunity to play in a room complete with Bobo dolls as a measure of violent behavior. Here the relationship between viewing violence and violent behavior is sequential. On the other hand, if they are **coextensive relationships**, the variables within the relationship co-occur or happen simultaneously. For example, if we feel happy, we will also be smiling. Marital dissatisfaction and depression often co-occur within distressed marriages.

Sufficient and Contingent Relationships

Fourth, relationships between variables can be sufficient or contingent. In **sufficient relationships**, one variable is enough to bring about a second variable, whereas, if a third variable is needed, those are considered **contingent relationships**. Consider the following example: Is viewing violent television sufficient to cause violence or does viewing violent television cause violent behavior when drugs are present, weapons are present, and violence is in the living environment? If other factors are involved, then the relationship is contingent. If other factors are not involved, the relationship between variables is sufficient.

Necessary and Substitutable Relationships

Fifth, relationships between variables can be necessary or substitutable. When one variable must be present for the second variable to be present, you have **necessary relationships**. If other forces might bring about the same effect, you have **substitutable relationships**. As you think about the following question, consider whether it is a necessary or substitutable relationship: Is unprotected sexual behavior necessary to contract human immunodeficiency virus (HIV)? No, HIV can be transmitted by other means, such as intravenous drug use; thus, it is a substitutable relationship. However, fire cannot occur without oxygen; therefore, the relationship between fire and oxygen is a necessary relationship. As communication scholars study human beings, it is highly unlikely that many of the variables you study will constitute a necessary relationship; rather, most of the variables you study in communication are substitutable relationships.

▼ # The Dimensions of Variables

Variables are concepts that can be described and understood from one dimension or more than one dimension. We're talking here about the complexity of the item you're measuring. Some items are not complex at all, and require only one question or series of questions to address. These are called unidimensional concepts. Other concepts require many different questions or ways to look at them. They are called multidimensional concepts.

Unidimensional Concepts

Some variables are **unidimensional concepts**; they contain only one dimension. A simple example of a unidimensional concept is education: What's the highest grade you've completed in school? An example of a unidimensional scale is Neuliep and McCroskey (1997)'s classic Intercultural Communication Apprehension Scale, which measures cultural and ethnic communication apprehension on one dimension: the fear and anxiety a person associates with interacting with people from cultural or ethnic groups that differ from their own.

> **unidimensional concepts**
> *Variables containing only one dimension.*

Multidimensional Concepts

On the other hand, **multidimensional concepts** are complex variables embodying more than one component or dimension. We're sure you're familiar with the concept of self-disclosure as a multidimensional concept (breadth and depth). Another example of a multidimensional concept is the SAT Reasoning Test (formerly Scholastic Aptitude Test and Scholastic Assessment Test). A college entrance exam testing writing, mathematics, and critical reading skills, each construct of the SAT is measured through more than one measure and then a composite score is created from the combination of the three area scores. The variable sensation-seeking is also a multidimensional concept, including boredom susceptibility, disinhibition, experience seeking, and thrill seeking.

> **multidimensional concepts**
> *Complex variables embodying more than one component or dimension.*

So What?

This chapter has considered variables from every possible angle. Beginning with independent and dependent variables, we revisited the importance of the significance of how you choose and define your variables within research. We also considered some important variables to watch for: confounding variables. We explored the typology of relationships between variables. Considering measurement theory, you must remember that measurement levels determine the type of statistical analysis that you can conduct. We discussed the difference between whether variables are unidimensional or multidimensional. Our goal in this chapter is to continue reinforcing the idea that within the research process, the decisions you make—from the variables you choose, define, and measure—determine the path you take, guiding the subsequent research methodology you choose from your toolbox.

Glossary

Coextensive relationships
Relationships where the variables co-occur or happen simultaneously.

Conceptual fit
How closely your operational definition matches your conceptual definition.

Confounding variable
An extraneous variable that muddies the relationship between the independent and dependent variable.

Contingent relationships
Relationships where one variable is enough to bring about a third variable, if needed.

Dependent variable
The variable that is assumed to depend on or be caused by another variable.

Deterministic relationships
Relationships that occur when the dependent variable must result from the independent variable.

Hawthorne effect
An effect where people alter their behavior because they know they're being observed.

Independent variable
The variable that causes or determines the value in another variable.

Interval level measurement
This type of measurement specifies relative position and also establishes standard, equal distances between points on the scale.

Irreversible relationships
Relationships that can only go in one direction or one way.

Measurement
A process of determining the characteristics and/or quantity of a variable through systematic recording and organization of observations.

Multidimensional concepts
Complex variables embodying more than one component or dimension.

Necessary relationships
Relationships where one variable must be present for a second variable to be present.

Nominal level measurement
This type of measurement makes use of unordered categories, classifying the variable into qualitatively different and unique categories. These categories do not indicate any type of order or intensity of the degree to which a characteristic exists but represent the potential categories of some variable of interest.

Ordinal level measurement
This type of measurement has ordered categories or rank, and it can be determined whether an observation is greater than, less than, or equal to other observations. However, this type of measurement does not indicate how much the difference is; the amount separating levels is not known.

Ratio level measurement
As the most specific type of measurement, it has all of the characteristics of an interval scale, but also a true, meaningful zero point.

Reversible relationships
Relationships that can go in either direction or either way.

Self-report
This procedure is good at measuring individual's beliefs, attitudes, and values, or in finding out about behaviors we might not be able to observe directly.

Sequential relationships
Relationships where the ordering of the variables is important and must occur sequentially, meaning chronologically or in order.

Social desirability
The idea that if participants are asked to answer questions that are sensitive in nature, people will undoubtedly feel swayed to present themselves in a particular light, regardless of whether it is indeed true.

Stochastic relationships
Relationships that are probable.

Substitutable relationships
Relationships where other forces might bring about the same effect as a necessary relationship.

Sufficient relationships
Relationships where the presence of or a change in one variable is enough to bring about a change in a second variable.

Unidimensional concepts
Variables containing only one dimension.

References

Baccigalupo, C., Plaza, E., & Donaldson, J. (2008). *Uncovering affinity of artists to multiple genres from social behavior data*. Presented at the International Conference on Music Information Retrieval, Philadelphia, PA.

Bandura, A., Ross, D., & Ross, S. A. (1961). Transmission of aggressions through imitation of aggressive models. *Journal of Abnormal and Social Psychology, 63*(3), 575–582.

Bandura, A., Ross, D., & Ross, S. A. (1963). Imitation of film-mediated aggressive models. *Journal of Abnormal and Social Psychology, 66*, 3–11.

Beck, A. T., Ward, C. H., Mendelson, M., Mock, J., & Erbaugh, J. (1961). An inventory for measuring depression. *Archives of General Psychiatry, 4*, 53–63.

Dessler, G. (1984, June 11). Ethel may not be sexy, but she'll do better in business than Cheryl. *Miami Herald*. Retrieved September 16, 2008, from News Bank on-line database (America's Newspapers) on the website: http://infoweb. newsbank.com

Friedlander, F. (1966). Performance and interactional dimensions of organizational work groups. *Journal of Applied Psychology, 50*, 257–265.

Grey, S. H. (2002). Writing redemption: Trauma and the authentication of the moral order in *Hibakusha* literature. *Text and Performance Quarterly, 22*(1), 1–23.

Lachlan, K.A., & Spence, P.R. (2010). Communicating risks: Examining hazard and outrage in multiple contexts. *Risk Analysis, 30* (12), 1872–1886.

Likert, R. (1932). A technique for the measurement of attitudes. *Archives of Psychology, 140*, 1–55.

Lindlof, T. R., & Taylor, B. C. (2002). *Qualitative communication research methods*. Thousand Oaks, CA: Sage.

Neuliep, J. W., & McCroskey, J. C. (1997). The development of a U.S. and generalized ethnocentrism scale. *Communication Research Reports, 14*(4), 385–398.

Oliver, M. B., & Hyde, J. S. (1993). Gender differences in sexuality: A meta-analysis. *Psychological Bulletin, 114*, 29–51.

Osgood, C. E., Suci, G., & Tannenbaum, P. (1957). *The measurement of meaning*. Urbana, IL: University of Illinois Press.

Powell, H. L., & Segrin, C. (2004). The effect of family and peer communication on college students' communication with dating partners about HIV and AIDS. *Health Communication, 16*, 427–449.

Rogelberg, S. G., Allen, J. A., Shanock, L., Scott, C., & Shuffler, M. (2010). Employee satisfaction with meetings: A contemporary facet of job satisfaction. *Human Resource Management, 49*, 149–172.

Stephens, K. K., & Davis, J. (2009). The social influences on electronic multitasking in organizational meetings. *Management Communication Quarterly, 23*, 63–83.

Thurstone, L. L. (1928). Attitudes can be measured. *American Journal of Sociology, 33*, 529–554.

Uhlmann, E., & Swanson, J. (2004). Exposure to violent video games increases automatic aggressiveness. *Journal of Adolescence, 27*, 41–52.

Warren, J. T., & Kilgard, A. K. (2001). Staging stain upon the snow: Performance as a critical enfleshment of whiteness. *Text and Performance Quarterly, 21*(4), 261–276.

Weaver, J., III. (1991, Summer). Are "slasher" horror films sexually violent? A content analysis. *Journal of Broadcasting & Electronic Media, 35*(3), 385. Retrieved August 28, 2008, from Communication & Mass Media Complete Database.

UNDERSTANDING SAMPLING

8

CHAPTER OUTLINE

KEY TERMS

Cluster sampling

Convenience sample

Data saturation

Extreme instance sampling

Generalizability

Maximum variation sampling

Network sampling

Nonrandom sampling

Proportional stratified sample

Purposive samples

Quota sampling

Random sampling

Refusal rate

Response rate

Sample size

Sampling frame

Simple random sample

Snowball sampling

Statistical power

Stratified sample

Theoretical construct sampling

Typical instance sampling

Unit of analysis

Volunteer sample

Chapter Objectives

1. To understand how we select the participants we include in our research
2. To know how to design the sample for a research study that is valid and representative
3. To be able to critique how representative a given sample is

▼ # How Important Is Sampling?

We cannot overstate how important sampling is to the quality, validity, and credibility of your research. You may have a solid study design, well written survey instrument or study protocol, and do an outstanding job in coding or statistical analysis, but if all that effort is devoted to a bad sample you are simply wasting your time. Proper sampling ensures that you are appropriately representing whomever you claim you're representing (we'll talk more about this in a minute). By the way, this is called *external validity*—are your findings valid among the population you're studying? (We'll discuss this in more detail in Chapter 9.) For now, just know that *whom* you study is just as important as *how* you study them.

This chapter will give you an overview of the theory behind sampling and will help you connect sampling strategies to different metatheories and research paradigms. We'll also talk about the basic concepts behind appropriate sampling, then we'll show you how sampling is done in both quantitative and qualitative research. We'll also discuss issues such as sample size and statistical power.

▼ # Sampling Theory

Generalizability and Representation

generalizability
Ensuring that a researcher's findings will apply to other people and situations that a study's sample supposedly represents.

First, let's explain a basic concept behind research design. In research, a *sample* of people is chosen to be included in the study as participants. This *sample* is expected to be *representative* of the entire *population* under study. Your *population* is the body of people you are claiming to generalize toward based on the sample. Populations can vary greatly in terms of breadth, though it should be noted that as scientists we seldom attempt to generalize to a population of *all* people. It is much more likely that we attempt to generalize to a populations specific to our research needs, such as "college students enrolled in a public speaking course," "elderly individuals in assisted care facilities," etc. If you carefully choose a *representative sample of one of these groups*, you can find out information about the *population* without having to interview the entire *population*.

Maybe you're asking, what's wrong with interviewing the entire population? Do you know what it is called when you actually interview an entire population? It's a *census*. It's so difficult to do that the federal government only does it once every ten years. Few researchers can afford to take a census of their entire population, and equally accurate data can be collected from a smaller sample when done correctly.

Unless you have an extremely small population, you would want to research a sample of your population. However, there is a trade-off in researching only a sample of your population: how well does that sample represent your population? Since you are not going to include everyone, the people you do include act as spokespersons for everyone else. In quantitative research, especially, this issue of representation is quite salient, as each study participant potentially represents the ideas or opinions of thousands of people. And in quantitative research, you are measuring and making predictions about those measurements, projecting them to your population. Obviously, if you are going to make predictions about your population based on the research you do of your sample, you want your sample to represent your population in a measurably accurate way. Representation is important in qualitative research also, by the way, but in a different way. We'll discuss that shortly.

So, let's talk about representation—how much of a problem is this? Wouldn't any group of people from your population represent your population? And how large should this group be? Five percent of the population? Fifty percent?

Let's look at an example. When your author Christine Davis was growing up, her parents had fairly conservative beliefs, while she and her sisters had fairly liberal beliefs. Suppose you wanted to survey them to determine how we felt about 10:00 PM Friday night curfews. Further, suppose you said her parents should represent their family—after all, they are the parents.

If you interviewed Christine's parents, you would be talking to 40 percent of her family. Surely this is a large enough sample to be representative, right? Wrong!

If you had sampled Christine's parents about their attitudes toward the curfew, you would probably have gotten 100 percent responses in favor of the curfew. Is this representative of the population? Let's take a census and compare:

- Mom—For
- Dad—For
- Cris—Against
- Kathy—Against
- Kelly—Against

The results of the census show that, in the population, only 40 percent were for the curfew, and 60 percent were against it.

Since that's the case, why did the sample differ so much from the census? Why wasn't interviewing 40 percent of the population enough?

It might have been, *if* it had been a representative sample.

In both quantitative and qualitative research, in order to derive a representative sample, there are several steps you would take.

You would first define your population. Your population may be as broad as all adults over the age of 18, but you still need to state the definition. More likely, your population will have some parameters, such as Communication undergraduates at your university (that's a pretty narrow definition), or all young adults between the ages of 18 and 24 (that's a fairly broad definition). If you're a rhetorical scholar, perhaps you study African American oratory. That's pretty broad. In order to conduct a research project, you would need to define which orators, which years, which speeches you plan to study, and so on. Perhaps you're an ethnographer, and you want to understand how a particular mental health treatment team interacts (see Davis, 2006), or how a specific street gang communicates (see Siegel & Conquergood, 1990). That mental health team or street gang would be your population, but then your sampling would be more concerned with representing their meetings or interactions. For example, you might want to observe student activities on campus; in this case, you're not sampling people, you're sampling observations (times of day, weeks, months, year, variety of locations, etc.). For example, you wouldn't only observe the library on Saturday morning during summer session—this likely is not representative of all student activities, and will likely produce very different data than observing the student center at lunchtime during fall semester. For your sample to be representative, you'd want to observe both, and probably more (more times, places, etc.).

Sampling Frame

sampling frame
A realistic version of your population; the ones you can identify and access.

Once you have defined your population, you have to determine how you will access them. The units to which you have access to are called your **sampling frame**. For example, if your population consists of all Communication undergraduates at your university, you might define your sampling frame as all Communication majors currently enrolled in classes. This will capture most of your population, but not all (for instance, there may be freshmen who intend to major in Communication, but have not yet taken coursework in the major). The sampling frame can be thought of as the realistic version of your population—the ones you can identify and access. Perhaps you want to study newspaper accounts of a particular event. You might define your sampling frame as the news stories available through the Lexis-Nexis database. If you're studying that medical team or street gang, your sampling frame might be the meetings or interactions you can access.

Unit of Analysis or Sampling Units

unit of analysis
Sampling units.

Your next step will be to define your **unit of analysis** or sampling units. For social researchers, more often than not the unit of analysis will be individuals— such as the individual students in our example above. Sometimes, however, your unit of analysis will be something other than individuals. For example, if you are studying couples' communication, your unit of analysis may be marital (or relational) dyads. If you are studying patient–provider communication, your unit of analysis may be patient–provider dyads. If you are studying group communication, your unit of analysis may be meetings, or groups themselves. Other units of analysis or sampling units might consist of sites, activities or events, times, or artifacts (documents, diaries, or texts). In a participatory action research study examining narrative as a method of transformation within emergency medicine, Eisenberg, Baglia, and Pynes (2006) defined their unit of analysis as an entire emergency department of an urban hospital.

Sampling in Quantitative Research   ▼

Sampling Methods

You have now identified your population by defining it, by identifying your sampling frame, and by defining your unit of analysis. Now you need to determine what sampling method you will use to represent your population. The sampling method you choose depends a lot on your study objectives, hypothesis, or research questions. Let's define the different types of samples used in quantitative research.

Random Sampling.   In quantitative research, in order to ensure that you have a representative sample, you sample *randomly*. This means that each person in the sampling frame has an equal chance of being interviewed as each other person. The laws of statistics and probability insure that, if you have a true random sample, it will be representative of your population. **Random sampling** is typically used by research in the positivist paradigm, because it helps ensure the objective reality being measured is being measured accurately. By the way, random samples are also called probability samples, because, based on probability theory, there is a measurable probability that the sample represents the population. Therefore, nonrandom samples are also called nonprobability samples.

Simple random sample.   The first sampling method, therefore, is called a **simple random sample**. Professional researchers (such as market researchers) who have sophisticated data collection technology do this by creating computer-generated random telephone numbers. A computer generates random seven-digit combinations of numbers, and these numbers are called. This allows an equal chance that people with unlisted numbers will be called, as well as those with listed numbers. Another alternative is to generate a list of random numbers through your computer (e.g., Excel has a function to do this). Number your sampling frame, giving the first name on the list a number of one, and so on. If you want a sample size of 100, generate a list of 100 random numbers. Choose the 100 people from your sampling frame who correspond to the random numbers.

Here's an example of how this works in real-life research. Mannion (2008) studied the effects of caring for people with Alzheimer's disease on informal caregivers. She used a:

> . . . *random representative group of caregivers registered with the Alzheimer Society of Ireland, Galway, or the Western Alzheimer's Foundation. The sampling frame was the list of caregivers registered with these organizations. The technique for the study was simple random sampling, which involved an employee from both voluntary organizations randomly selecting numbers from the list of registered caregivers until the required number of subjects was chosen. (p. 33)*

SYSTEMATIC RANDOM SAMPLE.   A variation on random sampling is known as the **systematic random sample**. In this type of sampling, a list of the entire sampling frame is assembled, and some seed number is chosen to make selections off of the list. For some reason, social scientists are fond of the numbers 7 and 11 (perhaps because they are prime numbers). If 7 is chosen, then

simple random sample
A basic sampling method where a group of subjects (sample) are selected for study from a larger group (population), and each member of the population has an equal chance of being chosen at any point during the sampling process.

systematic random sample
A variation on random sampling in which a list of the entire sampling frame is assembled, a seed number is chosen, and participants are selected based on multiples of that seed number (for example, every 7th person on the list is selected).

you would choose every 7th person on the list for inclusion in the sample—so person 7, person 14, 21, 28, etc. You would repeat this process until you attained a sample size appropriate for the study, which we will discuss in a few pages.

You can approximate this method yourself. Get a list of your sampling frame, perhaps a telephone book, or a list of every Communication major, or a course registration list. Pick every fifth name (or tenth, or twentieth, depending on the sample size you desire). Make sure you call people from the beginning of the book, the middle of the book, and the end of the book. You don't want Jonathan Abernathy to have a greater chance of being called than Benny Zimmerman.

Stratified sample. Sometimes you want more detail by subgroup than simple random sampling provides. Let's say you're not just interested in Communication Studies students in general, but you want to be able to compare students in Interpersonal Communication classes with students in Public Speaking classes, and students in Mass Media classes. You would choose to use a **stratified sample**. Interpersonal Communication students would be one stratum, Public Speaking students would be another stratum, and Mass Media students would be a third stratum. In this case, rather than sampling 100 students randomly, you might randomly sample 33 students in the first stratum, 33 in the second stratum, and 33 in the third stratum. In instances in which you want to make comparisons between or across groups, it may be wise to have equal proportions of individuals who fall into those groups.

Stratified samples are fairly common in content analytic research too. In a content analysis of newspaper radio schedules from 1930 to 1939 in three major Canadian cities to determine what percentage of the programming originated from the United States as opposed to Canada, MacLennan (2005) used a stratified random sample—taking three weeks' programming from each year. She had ten strata—each year was a stratum, and the strata had equal sample sizes (three weeks' programming in each).

Proportional stratified sample. Let's say you want to represent students from Interpersonal Communication, Public Speaking, and Mass Media, but you want to represent them proportionally to their occurrence in the population. For example, perhaps 40 percent of your students are Interpersonal Communication students, while 45 percent are Public Speaking students, and 15 percent are Mass Media students. In this case, you would take a **proportional stratified sample**. Since 40 percent of the students are Interpersonal Communication students, then 40 percent of your sample (out of your sample of 100, or 40 students) would be Interpersonal Communication students; 45 percent (or 45 out of 100) would be Public Speaking students; and 15 percent (or 15 out of 100) would be Mass Media students. Of course, this strategy is contingent on knowing what the proportions are across these categories in the population.

For example, in order to study the optimal channel distribution (theaters, home video, video on demand) of movies and media, Hennig-Thurau, Henning, Sattler, Eggers, and Houston (2007) used a proportional stratified random sample to represent movie consumers in three major movie markets: the United States, Japan, and Germany. They drew three random samples of a total of 5,094 consumers in the United States (n = 1,701), Japan (n = 1,802), and Germany

---

stratified sample
A type of sampling that uses a technique in which different subcategories of the sample are identified and then randomly selected.

proportional stratified sample
A type of sampling that uses a technique in which different subcategories of the sample are identified and then selected proportionate to their occurrence in the population.

(n = 1,591). Within each of these samples, they made sure that they had even gender distributions, and that the age breakdown for each sample was consistent with the population statistics for the country in which the data was collected.

Cluster sampling.

What if you can't get a sampling frame for your entire population? Let's say that you have defined your population as Communication Studies majors, but you can't access a list of all majors. You can, however, get several instructors to give you access to their class rosters. You could conduct what's called **cluster sampling**. In cluster sampling, you identify clusters, or groups (subsets of your population), that you think are representative of the entire population and sample randomly within each cluster, letting each cluster represent the population. In the example, you could use Dr. Smith's Public Speaking class as one cluster, and Dr. Jones' Interpersonal Communication class as another cluster. The trade-off for this method is obvious—if you cannot ensure that the clusters truly represent the population, you do not have a representative sample.

cluster sampling
A type of sampling method in which clusters, or groups (subsets of a population), are identified that are representative of the entire population, and are then sampled randomly within each cluster, letting each cluster represent the population.

Hilari and Northcott (2006) used cluster sampling to understand the role of social support in communication difficulties (called *aphasia*) after a stroke. Their clusters were three different speech therapy and rehabilitation sites, and they sampled randomly within each cluster.

Sarrafzadegan et al. (2009) evaluated the effects of a lifestyle intervention on diet, physical activity, and smoking in communities in Iran. They used cluster sampling in which they targeted three cities, and randomly sampled within each city. The cities each served as a cluster.

Nonrandom Sampling.

Sometimes, for logistical or convenience reasons, researchers use **nonrandom sampling** techniques. The most commonly used nonrandom samples in quantitative research are: convenience samples, volunteer samples, and snowball samples. While nonrandom sampling is often used by researchers with a positivist bent, the samples are used with an acknowledgment of the accuracy they're giving up by not using a random sample. Researchers from an interpretivist metatheoretical bent might be more comfortable with samples that are representative in ways that are different from orderly, fixed, predictable measurements.

nonrandom sampling
Sample that is not generalizable to the population; sample that is not a random sample.

Convenience sample.

A **convenience sample** is, simply, a group of people that is convenient to access—a Communication Studies class, for example, or patients of a particular doctor or medical clinic, or employees of a particular organization.

convenience sample
A group of people that is convenient to access.

Samp and Haunani Solomon (2005) sampled 106 dating couples to analyze their dyadic communication before and after they received certain types of problematic messages. This is clearly an experimental design (see Chapter 12), though the authors used a convenience sample of students solicited from "undergraduate communication courses at a large Midwestern university" (p. 30). Students were given extra credit or $10 to participate. Samp and Solomon's analysis does not discuss the limitations of their sample choice, but we can think of several. First, their sample is only representative of those 106 dyads. It's not necessarily representative of all communication students in that university, because students who participated may be different than students who didn't. Even if that wasn't an issue, it's also only representative of couples with the same demographics as the people in their sample—18 to 31 years old, and in relationships from 1 to 70 months. What other limitations to the sample can you think of? Nonetheless, it's published in a key communication journal (*Communication Monographs*), and this method of sampling is common in academic studies.

volunteer sample
Consists of people who are willing to volunteer for a study.

Volunteer sample. A **volunteer sample** is similar to convenience sampling—it consists of people who are willing to volunteer for a study, perhaps people who respond to a flyer you send out or post. Wilson, Morgan, Hayes, Bylund, and Herman (2004), for example, used a volunteer sample in a study to categorize mothers' child abuse potential based on observation of playtime interactions between mothers and children. They posted flyers advertising the study at two social service agencies, and when clients indicated an interest in participating, the researchers contacted them.

snowball sampling
This sampling method asks study participants to make referrals to other potential participants, who in turn make referrals to other participants, and so on.

Snowball sampling. **Snowball sampling** is the method of asking study participants to make referrals to other potential participants, who in turn make referrals to other participants, and so on.

Doerfel and Taylor (2004), for example, conducted a social network analysis (analysis of social networks) of Croatian organizations to understand how organizations and media in Croatia work together. They used snowball sampling to identify organizations to include in their sample. In their paper, they state:

> *Organizations for inclusion . . . were identified through interviews with USAID, IREX Pro-Media (1999), Soros, and the British Fund. These international donors identified active organizations in the 2000 parliamentary campaign that were also continuing to work on civil-society projects. (p. 381)*

Snowball samples can be useful in that they tend to generate a lot of data very quickly. Even with a fairly low response rate, if everyone who agrees to participate then recruits additional participants, the sample size will grow multiplicatively. They are also useful for getting data from organizations or groups that may be difficult to access—once a member of the organization participates, he or she can recruit additional individuals.

The major tradeoff, however, is a lack of control. You have no way of knowing who the individuals are who are being recruited, nor can you determine if they are representative of the population. In instances in which perfect generalizability is less important to the researcher than is generating a lot of data fast, or infiltrating a particular group, snowball samples work. If you are primarily concerned with perfect representativeness, they may not be the best solution.

network sampling
Using social networks to locate or recruit study participants.

NETWORK SAMPLING. **Network sampling** is using social or other networks (workplace, organizations, support groups, etc.) to locate and recruit participants.

Smith et al. (2008) sampled agricultural workers to assess brochures designed to inform them about the threat of hearing loss in their profession. They recruited participants through "seminars sponsored by the Michigan Farm Bureau . . . [and] through a pesticide certification meeting and by contacting the landscape departments of large organizations and local firms" (p. 204). This was network sampling—the networks being the Michigan Farm Bureau, the pesticide meeting, and the organizations and firms.

Research exploring the unique communication processes surrounding adoption within a family system requires creative use of both snowball and network sampling. Specifically, Harrigan and Braithwaite (2010) were interested in adoptions wherein it would be obvious to outsiders that an adoption had taken place due to differences in racial characteristics, a visible adoption. Here they describe their sampling decision:

> We used both network and snowball sampling procedures. Participants met three specific criteria. First, they were the age of majority in the state in which they resided. Second, they parented a visibly adopted child. Third, they self-identified as heterosexual. It is important to note that we do not deny the need for understanding salient communication in same sex families; instead adding this last criterion allowed us to focus on parents' communication regarding adoption and visible differences rather than same sex parenting. (p. 130)

ADVANTAGES AND DISADVANTAGES.   The advantages of nonrandom samples are obvious—they are easier (and often less expensive) to obtain than random samples, so research projects can be facilitated. The dangers to such samples are many, however. Research that gives a great deal of information about a nonrepresentative sample can be useless or at least misleading. It's important to know who or what your sample is representative *of*, and limit your conclusions to that population. Use of all samples must be done with the full knowledge of the limitations of the study.

Response Rate and Refusal Rate

Another factor in determining the representativeness of your sample is the **response rate**. The response rate is the proportion of people actually included in your sample, relative to the number of people you attempted to include. In other words, it's the number of people who agreed to participate, versus the number of people who refused participation (called the **refusal rate**). The higher the response rate, the better, and ideally you would want your response rate to be 60 percent or better (though this is quite rare). The problem with low response rates is that, if a lot of people are refusing to take part in your study, people who agree may be different in some way than people who refuse. In other words, there may be something consistent about the people who choose to respond that renders the obtained sample non-representative.

There are several things you can do about low response rates. The first set of suggestions involves ways to improve your response rate: Offer an incentive of some kind to get more people to agree to participate; follow up with people who refuse to participate to ask them again, hoping they'll change their mind the second time you ask; make your study easy to participate in (shorter surveys, for example), so they'll be less likely to refuse. The second suggestion is to determine if people who refused to participate have similar attitudes or characteristics than people who agreed. The only way to do this is to re-contact a sample of those who refused and try to get them to answer a few questions from the original survey, so that you can compare their responses with people who completed the entire study.

response rate
The proportion of people actually included in a sample, relative to the number of people who were attempted to be included.

refusal rate
The number of people who refuse participation in a study.

Sample Size and Power

Now that you know who to talk to, how many of them do you talk to? How many is enough to represent your population?

Let's do an experiment. You can do this yourself. Take a jar of marbles—some are black and some are white. You want to know how many black marbles are in this jar. You don't want to take the time to count them, so you take a sample.

Let's also say that you can draw out random handfuls of marbles.

In the first handful, you pull out five marbles—two of them are black (40%). You put them back and shake up the jar. Now, you pull out ten marbles—five of them are black (50%). You put them back and shake up the jar. Now, you pull out twenty marbles—eleven are black (55%).

Each time you increase your sample size, the number of black marbles you find in your sample is closer to what the actual number really is in your population. (Because you counted the marbles before you started the experiment, you know that 60% of the marbles are black).

The larger the sample you take, the more representative that sample is of the population. This is the "Law of Large Numbers."

So, you might wonder, what is large enough? That depends on what you want to do with the information after you get it.

Let's define two more terms: *confidence levels* and *margins of error*. You may have heard a television newscaster quote a political poll and say it had a 5 percent margin of error at a 95 percent confidence level. Statisticians talk about confidence levels of 80 percent, 90 percent, and 95 percent.

A confidence level of 95 percent means that, if you take 100 handfuls of marbles, 95 of those times you will come up with the same number of black marbles that are actually in the jar, within a margin of error, which we will define in a minute.

In other words, there is a 95 percent probability that your answer is pretty close to correct.

How close you are to correct is the margin of error. If you have a 5 percent margin of error, that means that your answer is within −5 or +5 percentage points of the true answer in the population.

In the case of your marbles, if you have a 5 percent margin of error, that means you count out between 55 percent and 65 percent black marbles.

If we tell you that at a 95 percent confidence level and a 5 percent margin of error, there are 60 percent black marbles in the jar, we are telling you that there is a 95 percent probability that there are between 55 percent and 65 percent black marbles in the jar.

Using a more real-life example, if we tell you that at a 95 percent confidence level and a 5 percent margin of error, your advertisement has 80 percent consumer recall, we are telling you that there is a 95 percent probability that your advertisement has consumer recall somewhere from 75 percent to 85 percent.

If you're right 95 percent of the time, that's not bad odds, is it? What confidence level you choose to use depends on what you are going to do with the information. For example, if your doctor is choosing a medicine to treat you for cancer, you surely want your doctor to choose a drug that was tested with a pretty high confidence level—99 percent, preferably (100% is impossible).

If you are making a go/no-go decision on spending your life savings to open a business, you would probably want a fairly high confidence level. Other decisions only warrant an 80 percent confidence level—being right 80 percent of the time isn't always bad. In social science research, like the quantitative research Communication Studies scholars conduct, most studies are conducted at the threshold of 95 percent confidence level with a desired margin of error at ±5 percent.

So, you may ask: What does all this have to do with sample size? There are many factors that enter into the statistics of sample size, and they have to do primarily with the statistical power you want for your study. We'll talk a lot more about this in later chapters when we discuss statistics, but for now, you need to understand what statistical power has to do with **sample size**. **Statistical power** is defined as the probability your research will identify a statistical effect when it does, in fact, occur in the population. You want your sample size to be large enough to give your study the ability to do just that—to detect a statistical effect when it actually occurs. Statistical power is determined by a combination of sample size, confidence level, margin of error, and the data itself resulting from the research. The sensitivity of your research to identify this statistical effect can be increased by increasing your sample size. In other words, the larger your sample, the more statistical power your study has. However, there's a limit as to how large you can make your sample. For cost and other practical considerations, you want your sample to be just large enough to have the statistical power you need. To determine what that is, you can conduct an *a priori* power analysis; to do this, you need to know your desired confidence level, your desired margin of error, and the data proportions (e.g., effect size) you expect to find in your study. Since you often won't know the data results you expect ahead of time, researchers use a general rule to calculate power and sample size. This rule assumes the largest sample size necessary to detect effect size. **Table 8.1** below gives what that sample size rule would be for each of several combinations of confidence level and margin of error. For example, if you are conducting a study and plan to set a confidence level of 95 percent and want to be able to detect differences at an error factor of ±5 percent, you would want to have a sample size of 400. If you are content with detecting differences at an error factor of ±8 percent, you can lower your sample size to 150.

sample size
The number of data sources that are selected from a total population.

statistical power
The probability that research will identify a statistical effect when it occurs.

Table 8.1. Sample Size Rules

	At a confidence level of:			
	80%	90%	95%	99%
With an error factor of:	**Your sample size should be:**			
± 5%	160	275	400	665
8%	64	100	150	260
±10%	40	70	100	170

For you math lovers in the class (yes, we know there are a few!), the formula for determining these sample sizes is:

$$n = \frac{(s^2)pq}{B^2}$$

In this formula, p and q are the two proportions (percentages) you'll be conducting your study to determine. Thus, this really contains circular reasoning, since you need to know what those proportions will be to determine your sample size, but you don't know what they are until you conduct your study. You can be more precise in determining sample size if you base these numbers on a pilot study or on previous research. However, for the purposes of the chart above, we used the most conservative estimate of proportions—we estimated that the proportions would end up being 50–50. B refers to the error factor ($\pm 5\%$, etc.), and s refers to the number of standard deviations from the mean your confidence intervals are. We haven't discussed this yet and won't until we get into statistics later, but for now know that (**Table 8.2**):

Table 8.2. Confidence Levels and Standard Deviations

A confidence level of	Is this many standard deviations from the mean
80	1.28
90	1.645
95	1.96
99	2.58

So, if you want to determine the sample size for an error factor of 5 percent, a confidence level of 95 percent, and proportions that are 50–50, your formula would be:

$$n = \frac{(1.96^2)(.5)(.5)}{.05^2}$$

$$n =$$

If you do the math, it comes to 384. We round to 400.

We said previously that there are many factors that enter into deciding the sample size. Strangely enough, the size of the population is *not* one of the factors that impacts the necessary sample size. Generally speaking, the size of your population is irrelevant to your desired sample size.

The only time the population size is important is if it is extremely small—so small that your sample size would be 5 percent or more of your population size (or when your population is less than 20 times larger than your sample). Then, there is a statistical correction for a small population. However, even this correction doesn't make much of a difference.

Again, for you math lovers, here's the formula for the correction:

$$\sqrt{1 - \frac{n}{N}}$$

You may remember from your statistics class that small n refers to your sample size and large N refers to your population size. So, let's say the earlier formula said you should have a sample size of 400, but your population size is only 4,000. If you apply those numbers to this formula for the small population correction, you'll end up with .95, which is the correction you should make to the sample size. Thus, .95 * 400 (the original sample size) is 380—and that's the sample size correction you would make.

You may have noticed that you can't use this formula if your population is smaller than your sample size, because you'll be trying to get the square root of a negative number and you can't do that. That's okay. First of all, if your population is that small, you may want to reconsider your desired confidence level and error factor, conduct a census, redefine your population, or consider a qualitative or case study method. Otherwise, you may feel better to note that Hamburg (1970), in his classic statistics textbook, states that "so long as the population is large relative to the sample, sampling precision becomes a function of sample size alone and does not depend on the relative proportion of the population sampled" (p. 290). In other words, it's what we said earlier—the size of your population is somewhat irrelevant to your desired sample size. Hamburg also notes that in the early days of statistics, researchers just arbitrarily sampled a percentage of their population—10 percent, for example. We don't generally recommend that, but you'll have to make some concession if your population is that small.

You may find it odd that population size is irrelevant to your desired sample size. The reason for this is that all populations, regardless of their size, fall into what is called a *normal distribution*. This means that, in any population, 95 percent of the responses will cluster around the average response, with a certain variability.

This is true if the population is 100 people or one million people. Since the sample is attempting to represent this cluster of responses, it doesn't matter how large the population is. We are only interested in sampling enough people to represent the curve of responses, regardless of the size of the population.

Sampling in Qualitative Research

Sampling Methods

In qualitative research, you are also sampling to represent the population. However, you don't want to represent the population numerically or in a way that you can predict numbers or proportions. You want to represent the sample behaviorally, or in a way that you can describe or understand the population.

While quantitative research typically involves large samples so you can make accurate predictions mathematically (little information about a lot of people), qualitative research typically involves small samples that you study in-depth (a lot of information about a few people). Qualitative researchers frequently also use convenience and volunteer samples, snowball and network sampling, but they also use other types of sampling methods.

purposive samples
Samples chosen for a particular purpose.

Purposive Sampling.

Qualitative samples are often **purposive samples**—samples chosen for a particular purpose. For example, in health-care research, you might want to conduct a focus group among residents of a battered women's shelter who have been receiving services for at least six months, so you would specifically choose people who meet that purpose or criteria. You might purposely choose people because they can serve as *informants*—people who can give you inside information about the group you're studying.

Karen Tracy (2007), for example, used a purposive sample in her case study of crisis communication in school board meetings. She studied meetings from one school board, but her unit of analysis was not school boards, it was meetings. Therefore, we need to see how she chose the meetings to analyze. She did not analyze all the meetings, but she analyzed three specific meetings, chosen because they "were the center of public attention" (p. 438). She also analyzed documents downloaded from the school board's website, as well as all relevant stories in the local newspapers during the time period under study. She determined relevance of documents and news stories based on whether they discussed the crisis issue.

In order to examine the question of what men think about gender roles and issues surrounding work-life, Tracy and Rivera (2010) recruited thirteen male executive gatekeepers to interview. Other forms of sampling simply wouldn't have been appropriate to answer this question. Remember that your questions should help determine your methods, including the best choices for sampling.

Martin (2004) also observed meetings—workplace meetings—to investigate the use of humor among women in middle management positions. She conducted research at one field site (a zoo) and sampled women who fit the desired characteristics (they were middle managers). She also studied the people who report to them and their male peers as informants. Her paper clearly states the limitations of this sampling method:

> *It is important to realize that the findings from this study are limited to the site and informants from which they are derived. For example, the behaviors exhibited by managers at The Zoo cannot be assumed to apply to non-white women, who may confront additional or very different constraints around humor usage and who may face entirely different forms of organizational paradox. (p. 153)*

quota sampling
A nonprobability (nonrandom) sampling technique that sets quotas for key categories to identify how many members of the sample should be put into those categories.

Yet, even though the findings may not be generalizable in a positivist sense, how might an interpretivist feel about the representativeness of the sample?

Quota Sampling.

Perhaps you want to talk to people who have been receiving services at the battered women's shelter for less than six months and people who have been receiving services for more than six months. You might conduct five in-depth interviews among people who meet each of those criteria. If you did this, you would be doing **quota sampling**—assigning quotas of interviews/focus groups to different groups. You'll notice that quota sampling is similar to stratified sampling, but stratified sampling is a random sampling method while quota sampling is conducted with nonrandom samples.

For example, Duke and Ames (2008) conducted a study to understand unplanned pregnancies among women enlisted in the U.S. Navy. They conducted fifty-two in-depth interviews at seven naval facilities. They used quota sampling, and in order to represent the different viewpoints adequately, they assigned quotas by gender, occupation (sailors versus other personnel), and location.

Maximum Variation Sampling.

Qualitative researchers also use several other sampling methods to ensure that their samples represent their populations in ways that meet their study objectives. **Maximum variation sampling** is a method that selects study participants to find examples that represent a wide range of characteristics that are present in the population and are of interest to the research. This sampling method is based on the "law of requisite variety," which says that any research study should represent the variety of characteristics present in the population. If you're studying street gang interactions, you might want to observe a range of different types of meetings or interactions.

Tracy (2004), for example, observed and interviewed correctional officers and staff to analyze organizational discourse. She "studied both male and female officers who worked 8- and 12-hour shifts and who represented a variety of ethnic backgrounds but were primarily white, black, and Hispanic" (p. 126). Assuming these characteristics represent the range of characteristics at the correctional facility, she used maximum variation sampling.

> **maximum variation sampling**
> *A sampling method that selects study participants who represent a wide range of characteristics that are present in the population and are of interest to the research.*

Theoretical Construct Sampling.

Theoretical construct sampling selects study participants who have characteristics that represent theories on which the study is based. For example, a researcher might wish to study medical teams through the lens of systems theory, and might select such teams based on their systemic properties (e.g., teams that interact with each other a great deal).

Klossner (2008) conducted a study to understand socialization among students in an athletic training program. She used theoretical sampling, specifically recruiting second-year students because they were in the middle of their educational experience, and she theorized that they would be at the third phase of professional socialization and their point of enrollment would enable them to have reciprocal social interaction.

> **theoretical construct sampling**
> *The selection of study participants who have characteristics representing theories on which a study is based.*

Typical and Extreme Instance Sampling.

Typical instance sampling would consist of sampling units (e.g., participants or meetings) who have characteristics typical of the population (e.g., a typical meeting), while **extreme instance sampling** would consist of sampling units who have characteristics quite different from the rest of the population (e.g., unusual interactions).

Davis (2009), in her ethnographic study of a hospice interdisciplinary team, sampled typical interactions between team members by attending various normal team meetings and health care visits.

Manatu-Rupert (2000), for example, used extreme instance sampling when she conducted a textual analysis of the depiction of black women in films by African American and non–African American filmmakers. She analyzed two films—Spike Lee's *She's Gotta Have It* and *Lethal Weapon*—chosen for their controversial representation of black women.

> **typical instance sampling**
> *Consists of sampling units who have characteristics typical of a population.*

> **extreme instance sample**
> *Consists of sampling units that have characteristics quite different from the rest of a population.*

Sample Size and Data Saturation

Determining sample sizes for qualitative research is quite different than for quantitative research. Remember, again, you're not trying to measure or predict anything with qualitative samples; you're trying to understand, explain, or describe. For that reason, qualitative researchers are more concerned with the *level of depth* of information than the number of participants about whom they're getting the information. Qualitative researchers sample until they reach what is called **data saturation**—until no new information emerges. Researchers typically begin with a planned sample size (maybe ten to twenty-five interviews, maybe monthly meetings over twelve months, maybe six to twelve months of field observations), then adjust this size as they collect the data, adjusting the size up if they determine they need more information, and adjusting down if they determine they are reaching saturation earlier than expected.

data saturation
Sampling until no new information emerges.

Guest, Bunce, and Johnson (2006) conducted a project about social desirability bias in health research among women from two West African countries, in which they attempted to determine the ideal sample size required for saturation to occur. Their study yielded thematic saturation at twelve interviews, but this may or may not hold for other dissimilar studies. Recommended sample sizes vary depending on the type of qualitative research conducted. These variations will be discussed in more detail in Chapter 14.

So What?

Whether you're conducting qualitative or quantitative research, whether you're approaching your research from a positivist or an interpretivist paradigm, your sample will be representative of something, and as a good researcher, it's your job to make sure it's representative of what you intend to study. Sampling procedures range from random, parametric samples that are representative of the population in a measurable, predictive sense to nonrandom, nonparametric samples that are representative of theories, behaviors, descriptions, or viewpoints. We'll talk in Chapter 9 about issues of validity, reliability, and credibility, but for now, know that a study is not valid, reliable, or credible if it doesn't represent whomever or whatever it's supposed to represent.

Glossary

Cluster sampling
A type of sampling method in which clusters, or groups (subsets of a population), are identified that are representative of the entire population, and are then sampled randomly within each cluster, letting each cluster represent the population.

Convenience sample
A group of people that is convenient to access.

Data saturation
Sampling until no new information emerges.

Extreme instance sample
Consists of sampling units that have characteristics quite different from the rest of a population.

Generalizability
Ensuring that a researcher's findings will apply to other people and situations that a study's sample supposedly represents.

Maximum variation sampling

A sampling method that selects study participants who represent a wide range of characteristics that are present in the population and are of interest to the research.

Network sampling

Using social networks to locate or recruit study participants.

Nonrandom sampling

Sample that is not generalizable to the population; sample that is not a random sample.

Proportional stratified sample

A type of sampling that uses a technique in which different subcategories of the sample are identified and then selected proportionate to their occurrence in the population.

Purposive samples

Samples chosen for a particular purpose.

Quota sampling

A nonprobability (nonrandom) sampling technique that sets quotas for key categories to identify how many members of the sample should be put into those categories.

Refusal rate

The number of people who refuse participation in a study.

Response rate

The proportion of people actually included in a sample, relative to the number of people who were attempted to be included.

Sample size

The number of data sources that are selected from a total population.

Sampling frame

A realistic version of your population; the ones you can identify and access.

Simple random sample

A basic sampling method where a group of subjects (sample) are selected for study from a larger group (population), and each member of the population has an equal chance of being chosen at any point during the sampling process.

Systematic random sample

A variation on random sampling in which a list of the entire sampling frame is assembled, a seed number is chosen, and participants are selected based on multiples of that seed number (for example, every 7th person on the list is selected).

Snowball sampling

This sampling method asks study participants to make referrals to other potential participants, who in turn make referrals to other participants, and so on.

Statistical power

The probability that research will identify a statistical effect when it occurs.

Stratified sample

A type of sampling that uses a technique in which different subcategories of the sample are identified and then randomly selected.

Theoretical construct sampling

The selection of study participants who have characteristics representing theories on which a study is based.

Typical instance sampling

Consists of sampling units who have characteristics typical of a population.

Unit of analysis

Sampling units.

Volunteer sample

Consists of people who are willing to volunteer for a study.

References

Davis, C. S. (2006). Sylvia's story: Narrative, storytelling, and power in a children's community mental health system of care. *Qualitative Inquiry, 12*(6), 1–24.

Davis, C. S. (2009). *Death: The beginning of a relationship*. Cresskill, NJ: Hampton Press.

Doerfel, M. L., & Taylor, M. (2004). Network dynamics of interorganizational cooperation: The Croatian Civil Society movement. *Communication Monographs, 71*(4), 373–394.

Duke, M., & Ames, G. (2008). Challenges of contraceptive use and pregnancy prevention among women in the U.S. Navy. *Journal of Qualitative Health Research, 18*, 244–253.

Eisenberg, E. M., Baglia, J., & Pynes, J. E. (2006). Transforming emergency medicine through narrative: Qualitative action research at a community hospital. *Health Communication, 19*, 197–208.

Guest, G., Bunce, A., & Johnson, L. (2006). How many interviews are enough? An experiment with data saturation and variability. *Field Methods, 18*(1), 59–82.

Hamburg, M. (1970). *Statistical analysis for decision making.* New York: Harcourt, Brace, & World.

Harrigan, M. M., & Braithwaite, D. O. (2010). Discursive struggles in families formed through visible adoption. *Journal of Applied Communication Research, 38,* 127–144.

Hennig-Thurau, T., Henning, V., Sattler, H., Eggers, F., & Houston, M. B. (2007). The last picture show? Timing and order of movie distribution channels. *Journal of Marketing, 71,* 63–83.

Hilari, K., & Northcott, S. (2006). Social support in people with chronic aphasia. *Aphasiology, 20*(1), 17–36.

Klossner, J. (2008). The role of legitimation in the professional socialization of second-year undergraduate athletic training students. *Journal of Athletic Training, 43*(4), 379–385.

MacLennan, A. F. (2005). American network broadcasting, the CBC, and Canadian radio stations during the 1930s: A content analysis. *Journal of Radio Studies, 12*(1), 85–103.

Manatu-Rupert, N. (2000). The filmic conception of the black female. *Qualitative Research Reports in Communication, 1*(3), 45–50.

Mannion, E. (2008). Alzheimer's disease: The psychological and physical effects of the caregiver's role. Part 2. *Nursing Older People, 20*(4), 33–38.

Martin, D. M. (2004). Humor in middle management: Women negotiating the paradoxes of organizational life. *Journal of Applied Communication Research, 32*(2), 147–170.

Samp, J. A., & Haunani Solomon, D. (2005). Toward a theoretical account of goal characteristics in micro-level message features. *Communication Monographs, 72*(1), 22–45.

Sarrafzadegan, N., Kelishadi, R., Esmaillzadeh, A., Mohammadifard, N., Rabei, K., Roohafza, H., Azadbakht, L., Bahonar, A., Sadri, G., Amani, A., Heidari, S., Malekafzali, H. (2009). Do lifestyle interventions work in developing countries? Findings from the Isfahan Healthy Heart Program in the Islamic Republic of Iran. *Bulletin of the World Health Organization, 87,* 39–50.

Siegel, T. (Producer), & Conquergood, D. (Director). (1990). [DVD]. *The heart broken in half.* Portland, OR: Collective Eye.

Smith, S. W., Rosenman, K. D., Kotowski, M. R., Glazer, E., McFeters, C., Keesecker, N. M., & Law, A. (2008). Using the EPPM to create and evaluate the effectiveness of brochures to increase the use of hearing protection in farmers and landscape workers. *Journal of Applied Communication Research, 36*(2), 200–218.

Tracy, K. (2007). The discourse of crisis in public meetings: Case study of a school district's multimillion dollar error. *Journal of Applied Communication Research, 35*(4), 418–441.

Tracy, S. J. (2004). Dialectic, contradiction, or double bind? Analyzing and theorizing employee reactions to organizational tension. *Journal of Applied Communication Research, 32*(2), 119–146.

Tracy, S. J., & Rivera, K. D. (2010). Endorsing equity and applauding stay-at-home moms: How male voices on work-life reveal aversive sexism and flickers of transformation. *Management Communication Quarterly, 24,* 3–43.

Wilson, S. R., Morgan, W. M., Hayes, J., Bylund, C., & Herman, A. (2004). Mothers' child abuse potential as a predictor of maternal and child behaviors during play-time interactions. *Communication Monographs, 71*(4), 395–421.

9

ENSURING VALIDITY, RELIABILITY, AND CREDIBILITY

CHAPTER OUTLINE

KEY TERMS

Alternate form reliability
Concurrent validity
Construct validity
Convergent validity
Credibility
Criterion validity

Data triangulation
Discriminant validity
Evaluator apprehension
Face validity
History
Instrumentation

Inter-coder reliability
Item-total reliability
Maturation
Member checks
Peer reviewer
Predictive validity

KEY TERMS (Continued)

Random error	Split-half reliability	Thick description
Reliability	Test-retest reliability	Validity
Reliability statistics	Testing	

CHAPTER OBJECTIVES

1. To understand the importance of validity, reliability, and credibility in social research
2. To know different techniques for ensuring validity, reliability, and credibility
3. To be familiar with validity, reliability, and credibility considerations in measurement and research
4. To understand validity, reliability, and credibility threats associated with research processes and procedures

- -

▼ # Thinking about the Quality of Your Observations

In Chapter 7, we discussed operationalizing your variables to make sure you are clear and consistent in terms of what it is that you are studying, and so that you and others can replicate the work you are studying. In Chapter 8, we discussed sampling appropriately so that you are representing what/whom you need to be representing. In this chapter we bring you face-to-face with thinking about other aspects of your research design. Specifically, you must think about your measures and observations in terms of their relative quality. We call these considerations **reliability**, **validity**, and **credibility**.

What Is Reliable? What Is Valid? What Is Credible?

reliability
The ability of a measure to produce the same results if replicated.

validity
Accuracy of a measure, in terms of measuring intended constructs or observations.

credibility
The believability of the research to the reader; how much the reader believes the research to represent participants' reality.

Why would you want to have the highest quality measures? Well, the answer to this question is pretty simple: The better your measures, the more confidence you can have in the conclusions you draw from your research, and the more confidence your audience has in your conclusions. If you think you are measuring one construct, and you are really measuring another, this will undermine your findings. Likewise, if you actually do measure the things you are interested in, but the measures sometimes work and sometimes do not, you will have difficulty in replicating your study—your findings will not be meaningful. Finally, if you write your analysis in such a way that readers do not believe your interpretations, your research will not be accepted.

Having a measure that replicates over and over again is necessary, but not sufficient, for good measurement. It could very well be measuring the incorrect concept and do a very good job of it. Measures have to be *reliable*—this is to say that they are able to produce the same results from the same people if repeated. But they must also be *valid*, or accurate, in terms of measuring their intended constructs or observations. Your textbook author Christine Davis is always on some sort of a diet. She used to own a scale that changed the results every time she stepped on it. If she didn't like what the scale said, she'd just get off and keep trying until she found the results she wanted. However, if another scale consistently said she weighed 500 pounds, it *would* be reliable; but if you had ever met her, you'd know it wasn't valid.

The measure also needs to be representative of whatever you say you're representing. A scale that reports Christine's weight may do so consistently, but it may or may not adequately represent my experience of being a person who fights her body weight. Finally, it needs to be *credible*. My scale may tell me I'm up a pound, but if my clothes are fitting more loosely, that may be a more credible report of my fitness or size.

As we will see, validity threats may be the greatest concern to a researcher in the positivist paradigm, who is trying to measure an objective reality, simply because there are many things that can go wrong in that measurement. Reliability is typically a question of designing good measures. With validity, a number of factors can affect your procedures in such a way as to distort your observations. These factors may be related to your sample, the design of the items, the procedures you perform in your study, or problems with research participants. Interpretivists may be more concerned with issues of representation and credibility—have I represented all viewpoints, have I adequately described the experience, and have I sufficiently interpreted the results?

Sound simple? Actually, this is far more complex than you might think. In fact, there are scholars in Communication and other disciplines who brand themselves as *methodologists*, or sometimes *psychometricians*, who spend their careers investigating new ways of developing quality measures and improving the techniques used for their assessment. Entire books have been written on estimating reliability and validity. This chapter is only a brief description of a multifaceted phenomenon, but it is essential to have a basic understanding as you begin to think about your own research.

Reliability ▾

Physical and Social Measurement

Measuring the length of a football field and measuring a person's degree of communication apprehension are two very different things. Measurement in the physical sciences is quite different from measurement in the social sciences and humanities, mainly in its degree of precision. The basic units of measurement we use to assess things in the observable physical world—feet, inches, ounces, pounds, miles, degrees Fahrenheit, and so on—are standardized, and are not likely to shift from measurement to measurement. A yard is always a yard, so if a football field is found to be 100 yards long, and you measure it again, chances are you will find it to be 100 yards long.

People, on the other hand, are different. The football field is just lying there motionless. People are in constant flux, paying varying degrees of attention, experiencing a myriad of thoughts and emotions that may affect their answers. Further, if you are working with people, then the concepts you are measuring are likely to be rather abstract, and you will have to use several measures that get at the construct in question. In other words, people sometimes change their responses from measure to measure, for reasons you haven't thought of, or perhaps even for no good reason at all. Asking a number of questions related to one of these abstracts concepts can give us an approximation – albeit an imperfect one – of what is going on.

Random Error

random error
A fluctuation in measurement.

This fluctuation in measurement is called **random error**. According to Nunnally and Bernstein (1994), one definition of reliability is freedom from random error. In other words, reliability refers to how repeatable a measure is from test to test. This could include how well it repeats when it is taken by different people, when alternative instruments are used to measure the same thing, or when incidental variation exists in the measures to an extent that is not cause for concern (see the section below on reliability statistics).

Types of Reliability

There are several ways to check if your measures repeat over different timeframes and groups of people. A few of them are described below.

Test-Retest. This is perhaps the simplest means of checking for reliability. In the **test-retest reliability** method, you simply give the same measure to the same people at two different times. If you don't expect a difference for any other reason, and the scores come out the same, then you can be fairly confident that you have a reliable measure.

test-retest reliability
A reliability method in which the same measure is given to the same people at two different times.

Consider this example. You could administer an IQ test to a group of students in a college classroom. For each student, you produce an IQ score estimating his or her intelligence. You then come back the next day and administer the test again. You would expect the scores to be exactly the same, since the test items are the same and it is highly unlikely that a student has suddenly become more intelligent overnight. If the scores turn out pretty much the same, then you can say with some confidence that the measure is reliable.

Of course, this seldom actually happens. For the same reasons related to random error mentioned above, the scores in our IQ example would probably fluctuate a little bit. This does not necessarily mean that the student taking the test has become more or less intelligent overnight. Rather, it probably means that the measure is not perfectly reliable. If it is not perfectly reliable, that's okay; most measures aren't. However, the scores should be pretty close. In a few pages we will discuss just how close they ought to be in order to have confidence that your instrument is reliable.

alternate form reliability
A reliability method where the order in which the items in a measure are presented affect the ways in which people respond.

Alternate Form. **Alternate form reliability** is a slightly more sophisticated way to think about reliability. In this test, different versions of the measure are used to determine whether the order in which the items in your measure are presented impact the responses. In this test, you start with a pool of people that you expect to score similarly on your instrument. You then take the same pool of items and rearrange them in different orders to create alternate forms of the same measure. If your measure is free from any reliability threats related to order of presentation, and your subjects are expected to score similarly, then the scores should be fairly similar across the different forms of the measure.

Perhaps the most common example of this takes place in the classroom. If you have ever taken a multiple-choice exam in a large classroom, then you have actually participated in an elaborate measure of your knowledge of the course material. Chances are your instructor developed different versions of the same exam, with the same items arranged in a different order in an attempt to discourage cheating. It should be the case that the average score on the exam is fairly similar between the two test forms, and the dispersion of these scores should be pretty close too (we will discuss central tendency and dispersion more in later chapters). If they are not, then the alternate form test has revealed that there may be reliability problems related to the order in which the questions were presented.

Split-Half. Of course, there are more sophisticated means of testing for reliability than simply giving the same test twice, or giving it to the same people with the items rearranged. While Communication researchers may use test-retest or alternate forms as a reliability test when developing a measure, they are much more likely to report more sophisticated techniques in their manuscript. These are known as *internal consistency methods*, and the first of them is called **split-half reliability**.

In split-half reliability, you randomly divide your measure in half. Of course, good measures should have multiple items (as we have previously discussed). Using some kind of randomizing technique (rolling dice, random number table, etc.), you randomly select half of the items on the scale and move them to make a second scale. Once you've split them, you now have two scales of items that were randomly selected from the scale you are actually using. *Correlation* is a statistical measure of similarity that refers to how closely related two variables are to each other, and you would expect these two new scales to be highly correlated; if they are, you can have confidence that your original scale is reliable. You could then repeat this random splitting over and over again, and the more often you produce this result the more confident you can be in the reliability of your scale.

split-half reliability
A means of evaluating internal consistency of a scale that compares one randomly selected half of a scale from the other randomly selected half of the same scale.

Item-Total. **Item-total reliability** is the second means of evaluating internal consistency. In this technique, you first create a score for each participant by summing each of the items. You then correlate each of the individual items with this sum score. The correlation between any one item on the scale, and the total of all items in the scale, should be fairly high. If it is, this would indicate to you that all items in the measure are doing just about the same job of measuring your construct. If you have a couple of items that have substantially lower correlations with the scale total, then they are probably not good items. You should remove them from the scale. You can probably see how this is similar in logic to split-half reliability; in this case, instead of correlating two different versions of the same scale, you are correlating individual items with the sum score across all of them.

item-total reliability
A means of evaluating internal consistency of a scale that compares the total score for a scale with individual item scores for the same scale.

Inter-Coder. There is another type of reliability that deals with the consistency of your measures, but does not look at how multiple subjects will respond to the

inter-coder reliability
An indicator of how similarly coders are coding content, both in terms of identifying units of analysis and in the contextual labels they ascribe to those units.

same scale. Rather, it deals with how multiple people will evaluate something that they observe. This is known as **inter-coder reliability**. It is used most often to determine the extent to which those working on a research project will evaluate things in the same way. In Communication research, it is perhaps most common in qualitative coding, content analysis, and observational research. *Coding* usually refers to the analysis of data (usually textual data) by categorizing it into thematic categories. In content analysis, for example, you will likely have multiple coders counting and categorizing content in order to process the data in a timely manner. In observational research, you might have multiple observers watching the same phenomenon, and making judgments about the categories into which certain behaviors or exchanges can be classified. In order to have confidence in the judgments that are being made by the coders or observers, you would first need to make sure that they were seeing things in more or less the same way. A rogue coder or inconsistency between coders could cause serious problems with your data.

Consider this example. The National Television Violence Study (Wilson et al., 1997) examined a massive amount of TV content—almost 10,000 hours—and sought to identify not only how often violence occurred, but also certain contextual elements that might be worrisome. In order to code this enormous amount of television content, more than fifty undergraduate coders were trained over a period of months in the definitions of violence, and in how to identify the risky portrayals with which they were concerned. While the content was being coded, each coder was given a reliability test every two weeks, in order to make sure all coders were still seeing things in the same way. Accomplishing this huge task in a timely manner required dozens of research employees. To get the job done in a scientifically rigorous manner, repeated checks for inter-coder reliability were necessary. Today, the NTVS is often held up as the *gold standard* of content analysis, partly due to its ability to maintain inter-coder reliability across such a large group of research employees.

Reliability Statistics

reliability statistics
Statistical tests that can show consistency between items, reflecting reliability of a scale.

Fortunately, there are **reliability statistics** that can be calculated and reported fairly easily. Since most of the techniques of assessing reliability deal with some calculation of consistency between items, researchers have developed a number of mathematical indicators of the reliability of a particular measure. Measures like a simple correlation coefficient, r, can be used to express split-half or item-total reliability fairly easily. Other internal consistency measures that are relied upon more frequently include: Cronbach's Alpha, the Kuder-Richardson formula (KR-20), and Cohen's Kappa. For identifying categories consistently, Scott's Pi (see Krippendorf, 1994) is commonly used to establish inter-coder reliability.

Cronbach's Alpha and KR-20 are used to measure the consistency of items in a list of items. Specifically, Cronbach's Alpha is an average of the correlations of pairs of items, using split-half reliability computed with a correlation coefficient. This is a highly regarded way to measure reliability in scales which measure attitudes, beliefs, or perceptions, when you are simply measuring the reliability of items in a scale. This measure is not appropriate for scales with right-wrong items, or when items should not have high intercorrelations between them (in which case a split-half reliability is not an appropriate measure) (Reinard, 2006). The KR-20 is used to provide estimates of internal consistency for scales when the items in the scale are scored as "passing" or "not passing," such as in a true-false comprehension test (Reinard, 2006).

Cohen's Kappa and Scott's Pi are used to determine agreement between coders or raters. An extension of Scott's Pi can be used when you are comparing the results of more than two coders. Both of these tests result in reliability coefficients that range from 0 to 1.00. In fact, all of these reliability statistics mentioned are based on correlations or coefficients that are designed mathematically to range between 0 and 1.00. A value of 1.00 indicates perfect agreement across all items in the measure, while 0 indicates no agreement at all. An acceptable reliability level is really kind of a subjective call; it depends on the degree of precision you wish to achieve with your measures. You may strive for perfect agreement, but most social researchers agree that perfect agreement is next to impossible when conducting research dealing with people. Unfortunately, people are not machines and, as this chapter points out, 100 percent precision is highly unlikely when examining human behavior. The conventional criterion is that a coefficient of about .70 is the minimum acceptable level of reliability, regardless of which coefficient you choose to use (Fleiss & Cohen, 1973; Krippendorf, 1994; Nunnally & Bernstein, 1994). This text will not expect you to compute these reliability coefficients yourself, as you can compute each of them in SPSS and other major data analysis programs. For now, it is more important that you know what reliability is, what techniques we use to estimate reliability, and what reliability statistic is appropriate for a given type of data.

• •

Validity ▼

Now that we have discussed the different techniques researchers use to establish what measures perform consistently if given to the sample of people twice, we must deal with whether they are actually measuring what they are intended to measure. As stated earlier in this chapter, reliability is necessary but not sufficient for good measurement; a measure can repeat itself with great reliability, yet tap into something completely different from what you think it measures.

Knowing What You Are Measuring

Validity, as a concept, is not nearly as cut and dried as reliability. To determine reliability, researchers typically pretest their measures to see if they hold together, and then conduct and report reliability coefficients to demonstrate the internal consistency of their measures. Validity is much subtler, and there is no magic coefficient that statistically indicates validity. Often, you have to design a study that includes one validity threat in order to avoid another. Validity really comes down to a matter of the researcher's common sense in executing measurement and design decisions, given the research questions she is asking and the validity threats with which she is most concerned. The validity of the measures and observations in any study are subjective and debatable, and researchers often engage in debate over the validity of each other's findings.

Face Validity

face validity
A type of validity consideration in which measures, or procedures, are looked at and questioned to see if they make sense at face value.

The simplest validity consideration is **face validity**. Face validity is simply looking at the measures, or looking at your procedures, and asking if they make sense at face value. As simple as this seems, you would probably be amazed at how often social researchers design measures and studies that violate face validity.

Here's an example. Let's say you wanted to design a measure of deceptiveness. You go to the drawing board and come up with twenty items that you believe measure deceptiveness. You give it to a group of college freshmen and discover that, for the most part, they are not deceptive at all. In fact, they appear to be the most honest group of people you have ever come across in your life. You conclude that they are all very trustworthy.

Do you see a problem here? You just asked people to answer a self-report scale concerning how deceptive they are. If you were a deceptive person, why would you answer these questions honestly? In fact, if you were someone who is prone to being deceptive, you would probably lie when responding to the items on the scale. So, honest people report that they are very honest, and deceptive people lie and report exactly the same thing. This is an example of poor face validity—even before administering the scale we should have known that it doesn't really measure deception. It didn't seem true "on the face of it." You really shouldn't have much confidence in your finding that everyone is honest because at face value it makes no sense.

Criterion Validity

criterion validity
A type of validity consideration that deals with how a particular measure holds up when compared to some outside criterion.

Another type of validity concern is **criterion validity**. Criterion validity deals with how a particular measure holds up when compared to other criteria, variables, or scales believed to measure the same construct. Criterion validity can be broken out into two subcategories: predictive validity and concurrent validity.

predictive validity
How well a measure predicts that something that will happen in the future.

Predictive Validity.　**Predictive validity** deals with how well a measure predicts that something that will happen in the future. You may design a measure that you believe gauges a construct that will predict future behavior; in this case, you'll want to know that it actually does. Probably the best-known examples of this are the standardized tests used in college and graduate school admissions.

When you took the SAT, you may have looked at the test items and wondered what in the world they had to do with anything. In actuality, the SAT and other standardized tests are remarkable pieces of psychometric research; across large populations, they predict performance in academic programs with tremendous precision. While there are always exceptions, on the whole, those who perform better on the SAT do better in college. The same goes for the GRE, the LSAT, and the MCAT, as those who do better on these exams do better in graduate school, law school, and medical school, respectively. This is why admission boards rely on them so heavily. Since they want the best prepared students they can get so their programs can be rigorous and train students well, they need to be able to predict success ahead of time. The predictive validity of standardized tests allows them to have confidence that they indicate academic preparation.

Concurrent Validity.   The other form of criterion validity is known as **concurrent validity**. Concurrent validity is how well your scale measures up against another scale that has been demonstrated to measure exactly the same thing. You may have a number of reasons for developing a scale that is slightly different, such as making the scale situationally specific, or shortening the scale to eliminate subject fatigue. In any case, you would want to make sure that the new version of a scale correlates very strongly with the old version. This is known as concurrent validity. You would probably want to pretest the scale, giving the same subjects the new scale and the old one, and correlating the scores to make sure that they are fairly similar.

concurrent validity
How well a scale measures up against another scale that has been demonstrated to measure exactly the same thing.

Construct Validity

Another broad category of validity is known as **construct validity**. Construct validity deals with logical relationships between variables. If your measures really get at what they are supposed to get at, then you can make certain predictions about their relationship with other variables with which they ought to have certain relationships (Kerlinger, 1986). If these relationships hold, then you can have a certain amount of confidence that your measure is valid in terms of its relationship to other constructs. Construct validity can be more specifically broken out into convergent and discriminant validity.

construct validity
The extent to which your variables are logically related to other variables.

Convergent Validity.   You may develop a measure and expect it to correlate positively with some other construct. You expect two constructs to be related, though not exactly the same thing. Sound confusing? Here's an example.

Lannutti and Lachlan (2007) thought it would be a good idea to develop a scale measuring people's attitudes toward same-sex marriage, since it might be a slightly different construct than other related ones (such as homophobia). They developed a thirty-two-item scale measuring the construct and found that it had strong reliability. Next, they expected it to correlate positively with a single item asking respondents if they would vote to approve a bill legalizing same-sex marriage in their state. Although attitudes toward same-sex marriage and willingness to vote in favor of it are not the same thing, logically they should be positively correlated. Sure enough, the researchers found that there was a strong correlation between favorable attitudes on the scale and willingness to vote yes on the hypothetical bill; thus, they concluded that their measure had strong **convergent validity**.

convergent validity
When two measures you expect to be related are shown to be positively statistically related.

Discriminant Validity.   Conversely, there are constructs with which you may expect your measure to be negatively related. Let's return to our same-sex marriage example from above. Lannutti and Lachlan (2007) also asked their participants to respond to a standardized test measuring homophobia. Logically, you would expect homophobes not to approve of same-sex marriage. Sure enough, the researchers found a strong, negative correlation between their new scale and the established scale measuring homophobia. While the constructs were not the

discriminant validity
When two measures you expect to be negatively related (opposite to each other) are shown to have a negative statistical relationship.

same, they found the expected negative relationship between them; thus, they concluded that their measure had strong **discriminant validity**.

Validity and Reliability Examples

Let's take a look at Rittenour and Martin's (2008) work on the Communication Based Emotional Support Scale (CBESS). The CBESS is a unidimensional scale and was previously determined to be reliable by the researchers who initially developed it, Weber and Patterson (1996).

From "Convergent Validity of the Communication-Based Emotional Support Scale" by C. E. Rittenour & M. M. Martin. *Communication Studies Vol. 59, No. 2,* January 7, 2008; reprinted by permission of the publisher (Taylor & Francis Ltd, http://wwwtandfonline.com).

communicated within the confines of those relationships warrants scholarly attention to the accuracy of its measurement.

Recognizing that previous scales focused on social support, a construct that primarily focuses on who is giving support and how that support produces positive outcomes, Weber and Patterson (1996) developed the Communication Based Emotional Support Scale (CBESS). This scale focuses on emotional support, incorporating the messages themselves and their emphasis on communicating care or concern as well as the communication networks from which these messages were created. Weber and Patterson created items that addressed qualities of concern, compassion, sympathy, esteem, and helpfulness. Starting with 20-items, they produced a 13-item scale that was internally reliable ($\alpha = .93$). The CBESS was positively correlated with relational solidarity and relationship quality, supporting the validity of the measure.

Communication-based emotional support has been studied in numerous types of relationships, including dating partners, superiors–subordinates, friends, spouses, and online support groups (Avtgis, 2000; Campbell & Wright, 2002; Merolla, 2004; Weber & Patterson, 1996; Wright, 2002). The CBESS was positively related to trust, commitment, relationship satisfaction, attributional confidence, and perceived understanding while negatively related to evoking jealousy (Avtgis, 2003; Cayanus, Martin, & Weber, 2004; Weber, Johnson, & Corrigan, 2004). Campbell, Martin, and Weber (2001) found that when superiors frequently used avoidance strategies, subordinates reported less emotional support, whereas when superiors frequently used approach strategies, subordinates reported more emotional support. When applied to online-support groups emotional support, when superiors frequently used approach strategies, sub-ordinates reported more emotional support. When online-support group superiors frequently used approach strategies, subordinates reported more emotional support. When applied to online-support groups, communication-based emotional support was negatively correlated with perceived stress, dominance, and formality and positively correlated with immediacy, similarity, receptivity, and equality among group members (Campbell & Wright, 2002; Wright, 2002). By correlating communication based emotional support with the aforementioned variables, these findings provide some construct validity and criterion-related validity of the scale. The purpose of this study was to further establish convergent validity by correlating the Communication Based Emotional Support Scale with other support scales.

As you can see from the excerpt from Rittenour and Martin's (2008) article, Weber and Patterson (1996) developed a thirteen-item scale that they determined had internal reliability of α = .93, based on a Cronbach's Alpha (α stands for "alpha"). Remember that reliability statistics range from 0.00 to 1.00, and researchers generally agree that anything over .70 is acceptable. Therefore, the CBESS appears to be a reliable scale. That means it measures whatever it measures consistently.

However, these data do little to tell us anything about the validity of the scale, or the extent to which it measures what it purports to measure. Rittenour and Martin report that Weber and Patterson found that "The CBESS was positively correlated with relational solidarity and relationship quality, supporting the validity of the measure" (p. 236). In other words, they're telling us that the measure has good convergent validity—it makes sense that emotional support would have a lot in common with relational solidarity and relationship quality. This is evidence that the scale is valid. They also cited several other studies that correlated emotional support (using the CBESS) with perceived stress, dominance, and formality (it was negatively correlated, as you would expect, providing discriminant validity), and with immediacy, similarity, receptivity, and equality (it was positively correlated, as you would expect, providing convergent validity). They claim (correctly) that these correlations provide additional evidence for the construct and criterion validity of the scale. However, they wanted to test the validity of the scale even further. They wanted to know if the CBESS also measured similarly to other scales—they wanted to "further establish convergent validity by correlating the Communication Based Emotional Support Scale with other support scales" (p. 237).

The following scales were used to establish the convergent validity of the CBESS: the Perceived Social Support - Friend Scale (PSS-Fr; Procidano & Heller, 1983), which measures participants' perceptions of their own needs for support as fulfilled by friends; the friend subscale of the Multidimensional Scale of Perceived Social Support (MSPSS; Zimet, Dahlem, Zimet, & Farley, 1988), which measures participants' perceived social support from friends; the Social Support Behaviors Scale (SSB; Vaus, Riedel, & Stewart, 1987) that measures perceived emotional, socializing, practical assistance, financial assistance, and advice/guidance dimensions of support; and the friend subscale of the Scales of Perceived Social Support (Macdonald, 1998) that measures participants' perceived social support from friends.

Although other support scales omit the two qualities that the CBESS takes into account—the supportive messages themselves and the interpersonal relationships

From "Convergent Validity of the Communication-Based Emotional Support Scale" by C. E. Rittenour & M. M. Martin. *Communication Studies Vol. 59, No. 2,* January 7, 2008; reprinted by permission of the publisher (Taylor & Francis Ltd, http://wwwtandfonline.com).

Their hypothesis was:

H₁: Individuals' scores on the CBESS are positively related to their scores on the Perceived Social Support–Friend Scale, the friend subscale of the Multidimensional Scale of Perceived Social Support, the Social Support Behaviors Scale, and the friend subscale of the Scales of Perceived Social Support. (p. 237)

They administered the scales in a survey to convenience sample of 209 students. What did they find? Their hypothesis was supported; they found statistically significant correlations between the CBESS and the other scales.

Results

The hypothesis predicted a positive correlation between scores on the Communication Based Emotional Support Scale and scores on the Perceived Social Support -Friend Scale, the friend subscale of the Multidimensional Scale of Perceived Social Support (MSPSS), the Social Support Behaviors Scale (SSB), and the friend subscale of the Scales of Perceived Social Support (Macdonald, 1998). The hypothesis was supported. Results of two-tailed *Pearson Product-Moment* correlations indicated significant relationships between the CBESS and the following: the Perceived Social Support – Friend Scale ($r = .72$, $p < .01$), the friend subscale of the Multidimensional Scale of Perceived Social Support ($r = .61$, $p < .01$), the Social Support Behaviors Scale ($r = .71$, $p < .01$), and the friend subscale of the Scale of Perceived Social Support ($r = .75$, $p < .01$).

Results of *Pearson Product-Moment* correlations indicated the following positive correlations between communication based emotional support and the subscales of the Social Support Behaviors Scale: emotional ($r = .76$, $p < .01$), socializing

Therefore, they established additional construct validity for the scale.

What if you're not developing a scale, you just want to use a measurement scale in a study you're conducting? Let's look at one more example.

Keaten and Kelly (2008) examined the relationship between family communication patterns, emotional intelligence, and reticence. To measure those three variables, they used three previously developed scales: the Revised Communication Patterns Scale (Ritchie & Fitzpatrick, 1990), the Emotional Intelligence Scale (Schutte et al., 1998), and the Reticence Scale (Keaten, Kelly, & Finch, 1997). They wanted to conduct valid research, so they had to choose scales that were themselves valid and reliable. One of the first things Keaten and Kelly do when they describe their study methods to us is tell us the reliability and validity statistics of the scales they used:

From "Development of an Instrument to Measure Reticence" by J. A. Keaten & L. Kelly, *Communiation Quarterly, Vo. 45, No. 1*, January 12, 1997; reprinted by permission of the publisher (Taylor & Francis Ltd, http://wwwtandfonline.com).

Measures

The questionnaire packet consisted of three instruments: (a) The Reticence Scale, (b) Emotional Intelligence Scale, and (c) the Revised Family Communication Patterns scale. The Reticence Scale (RS; Keaten, Kelly, & Finch, 1997) is a 24-item measure of reticence, employing a 5-point Likert scale (1 = Strongly Disagree to 5 = Strongly Strongly Agree). The RS measures six dimensions of reticence experienced in social situations: (a) feelings of anxiety ("I am nervous when talking"); (b) knowledge of conversational topics ("I know what to discuss"); (c) timing skills ("I say things at the time I want to say them"); (d) organization of thoughts ("I arrange my thoughts when talking"); (e) delivery skills ("I fluently say what I want to say"); and (f) memory ("I remember what to say when talking"). Scores for each of the six dimensions range from 1 to 21. Total scores range from 6 to 126; lower scores indicate lower levels of reticence, that is, less anxiety, fewer problems with knowledge, timing, delivery, and so on. The internal consistency of the RS has been consistently high ($\alpha > .90$) in prior studies (Keaten et al., 1997, 2000; Kelly et al., 2002). In this study, reticence was treated as a unidimensional construct by combining scores of the six dimensions. Using Cronbach's alpha, the reliability for the RS was .91.

The Emotional Intelligence Scale (EIS; Schutte et al., 1998) consists of 33 statements based on the emotional intelligence model developed by Salovey and Mayer (1990) and is measured using a 5-point Likert scale (1 = Strongly Disagree to 5 = Strongly Agree). The EIS has been shown to have a good internal consistency and test-retest reliability (Schutte et al., 1998). Validation studies indicated that scores on the EIS correlated with 8 of 9 theoretically related constructs, including alexithymia, attention to feelings, clarity of feelings, mood repair, optimism, and impulse control. The Cronbach's alpha for the EIS was .85.

The Revised Family Communication Patterns scale (RFCP; Ritchie & Fitzpatrick, 1990) measured participants' perceptions of family communication behaviors. The scale is composed of 26 statements comprising two dimensions: conversation orientation and conformity orientation. Items are measured on a 5-point Likert scale (1 = Strongly Disagree to 5 = Strongly Agree). Ritchie and Fitzpatrick (1990) reported that the internal consistencies of both dimensions were acceptable (conversation orientation, $\alpha = .84$; conformity orientation, $\alpha = .76$) and test-retest reliability of the scale was satisfactory (conversation orientation, $r = .81$; conformity orientation, $r = .80$). In the present study, the alpha reliabilities were .91 for conversation orientation and .83 for conformity orientation.

Problems with Participants and Procedures. To this point, we have discussed validity concerns that pertain directly to the measures we develop in our research. There are other threats to the validity of our research that deal less with the measures and more with what you do with them. Sometimes things go awry in our research procedures that make us wonder if we are measuring what it is that we think we are measuring. Below we will discuss a number of these threats known as *internal validity* threats. They call our observations into question not because our measurement is bad, but because some other factor we have not accounted for is affecting the responses (see Campbell & Stanley, 1963; Cook & Campbell, 1979).

HISTORY. Let's say you ask a number of subjects to report how they feel about driving under the influence. You survey men and women separately; men take the survey on a Monday, while women take it on Thursday. You look at the two groups and see noticeable differences between them. In fact, it appears as though women are much more disapproving of driving while impaired, and you conclude that there are differences between men and women.

Then you read the newspaper. As it turns out, a high-profile celebrity was seriously injured in an alcohol-related car crash on Wednesday night. Now you

history
A validity issue where something totally unrelated to your study happened at a particular time, and may have affected the responses.

may have a validity problem known as **history**; something totally unrelated to your study happened at a particular time and may have affected the responses. Are women really different than men in their disapproval of driving under the influence, or did this public event skew their responses? Maybe, maybe not. But the bottom line is that you don't know, because the data could be a product of gender differences or of what happened outside the lab. This limits the confidence you can have in your observations.

History can be a serious validity issue when conducting qualitative research (such as focus groups or observations), especially if you're studying naturalistic groups. Let's say you're conducting a focus group among employees in an organization to discuss how they feel about the company's latest health promotion campaign. Unbeknownst to you, a key employee was laid off the previous day. This could affect their reactions in the focus group, and you might mistakenly think their reactions are to the campaign, rather than to the layoff.

MATURATION. Another problem that can emerge in terms of the validity of your observations deals with the fact that subjects can change over time, otherwise known as **maturation**. This is especially problematic in long-term studies that track people over the course of months or years. Over time, people change both physically and psychologically. This can affect their responses to the measures you are interested in.

maturation
A validity issue dealing with the fact that subjects can change over time, which can affect their responses to the measures a researcher is interested in.

Let's say you are testing a new curriculum regarding public speaking. You ask college freshmen to take an instrument measuring their level of communication apprehension during the first week of classes. You then require them to take a Public Speaking class freshman year. You come back at the end of the year and give them the same measure. You notice that they are much lower in communication apprehension, and you conclude that your Public Speaking class was a huge success.

There is just one problem with this conclusion; lots of other things happened over the course of that school year, too. Generally speaking, many college students become more comfortable with strangers over the course of their freshman year, because they are forced to deal with roommates, classmates, professors, teaching assistants, a new town, and many other social interactions they were not forced to engage in back home. In effect, they grew and changed in a very natural way over the course of a year, becoming more comfortable around new people. So how confident can you be in your data that would otherwise indicate that your Public Speaking class was the source of this change? Not very.

In fact, the difficulty in understanding people's behaviors over time is one reason to choose qualitative research such as ethnography as a method, so you can attempt to capture and understand how people, their environment, their personality, and their lives interact in complex ways.

testing
A validity threat where if someone is more familiar or more comfortable with a series of questions or items, they may respond differently to them.

TESTING. Sometimes people respond differently when they see the same set of questions twice. If you are more familiar or more comfortable with a series of questions or items, you may respond differently. This validity threat is known as **testing**. Let's think back to our reliability example from a few pages ago, where we talked about creating alternate forms of the same exam. You could give a student one form of the exam, and then come back a week later and administer the test again. By simply comparing the scores, you might conclude that the student must have studied very hard that week, because their score on the test is much higher than it was the first time.

Think about it. If you could take any one of the exams in this class for a second time, would you do better on it? Probably. While it is certainly possible that you could become better versed in the material between time points one and two, it is also very likely that you will do better because *you know what the questions are going to be ahead of time*. This may be a bit of an extreme example, but it illustrates one instance in which completing an instrument multiple times may affect the results.

INSTRUMENTATION.   The flip side of testing as a validity threat is **instrumentation**. Instrumentation, as a threat, deals with differences that are observed at two different time points in which different instruments are used to assess the same construct. Let's use our exam example again.

You decide to give a student another exam on a particular section of material. Since you are concerned about testing as a validity threat, you give the student a different exam that covers the same chapter. It is not simply a different form of the same exam; it is an exam that has entirely different items drawn from the same chapter. You give it to the student, and he does much better on this version. Since you have controlled for testing, you conclude that he must have mastered the material the second time, because, after all, he did so much better and they are not the same items.

There is a very simple alternate explanation. The second exam was easier. In getting around testing as a threat, the use of different instruments means that the responses might differ simply as a function of measurement. So, which should you be more concerned with—testing or instrumentation? There is no easy answer, but it is a topic we will come back to when we discuss design.

Hawthorne Effect

Sometimes, you might be using valid and reliable instruments, but research participants engage in unpredictable behavior that threatens the validity of your observations or measures. The confidence that you can have in your findings may be inhibited by certain responses that participants have that are beyond your control. Broadly speaking, the tendency for participants to respond differently when they know they are being observed is known as the Hawthorne effect. Hawthorne effects can come in many varieties, but basically, they are instances in which research participants change their behavior or responses for no other reason than the fact that they know someone is watching. This is why it is considered a standard of validity for qualitative researchers to spend long periods of time in the field, so that study participants become accustomed to being observed and studied.

There are other more specific types of validity problems associated with participants. Take for example **evaluator apprehension**. If you have ever participated in laboratory research, you can probably relate to this. You walk into a laboratory and are greeted by a stranger who begins to ask you to do things you don't understand ("Sit over here . . . fill this out . . . wait until I come back. . . ." etc.).

instrumentation
A validity threat that deals with differences that are observed at two different time points in which different instruments are used to assess the same construct.

evaluator apprehension
When research participants become nervous or otherwise unsettled by the fact that they are in uncomfortable surroundings, which may limit their ability to concentrate or cause them to respond differently.

You are aware that you are being evaluated and that there are things going on that you don't know about. Are you being watched? What is it that they are looking for? Is this going to freak me out?

This is evaluator apprehension. Research participants may become nervous or otherwise unsettled by the fact that they are in uncomfortable surroundings. While laboratories procedures allow us controls that we might not have in the field or elsewhere, they are also artificial environments. This may limit the ability of participants to concentrate, or cause them to respond differently. Research participants may also respond differently if they decide that they know what you are looking for (whether they are right or wrong). If you bring participants into a laboratory, make them play *Grand Theft Auto*, then ask them questions about how aggressive they feel; they might figure out that you are studying aggression responses. Depending on whether they like you, they may change their responses to either give you what they think you are looking for, or the exact opposite. The propensity of subjects to figure out what you are doing, decide they don't like you, and give you dishonest answers is sometimes jokingly referred to as the "screw you" effect.

If you're conducting longitudinal research, you might lose participants during the course of a study. This is called *attrition*, or sometimes *mortality*, and it can be a real problem. Participants move away, decide to drop out of the study, or get bored. Large attrition rates can raise the same concerns that low sampling response rates raise—do the people who participate have the same thoughts and opinions as those who drop out? The best way to address this is to minimize the chances of people dropping out. If you're conducting a study in which you interview people every six months, keep in touch with them in between those times. Send them post cards, call, or e-mail them to remind them the next wave of research is coming up.

External Validity Threats

We've talked about internal validity threats—the possibility that you may not be measuring what you think you're measuring, either due to error in your measurement instrument, or errors in the way you're administering the study or in the way the participants are taking part in the study. There is also something called external validity threats, and this refers to how well your research represents your population. We discussed this at length in Chapter 8.

Ecological Validity Threats

The final type of validity concern we need to discuss is ecological validity. This refers to how well your study measures or reflects the real world. As we mentioned earlier, experimental designs, while allowing us to have precise controls, are a bit artificial. By way of comparison, the term *in vivo* means to conduct research in a natural setting. Research conducted in vivo has high ecological validity. Qualitative research, such as ethnographic research in which the researcher goes "into the field" to study people in their natural habitat, typically has very high ecological validity. Quantitative research such as laboratory experiments or surveys in which people are asked to recall prior behavior typically has low ecological validity. While they may have low ecological validity, laboratory designs can include checks for numerous internal validity threats. It really becomes a question of the priorities of the researcher.

Credibility ▼

In qualitative research, rather than thinking of *validity* and *reliability*, researchers refer to credibility: Is the research considered to be credible to the reader, and most importantly, do we believe that the research adequately represents participants' reality? (Creswell & Miller, 2000)

Member Checks

Qualitative researchers use several strategies to enhance the credibility of their research: member checks, data triangulation, thick description, and peer reviews are some examples. **Member checks** are opportunities for the researcher to test her findings, interpretations, and explanations within the culture she is studying. Member checks are conducted at the end of the study, before the analysis is finalized, and they are typically conducted through personal interviews, focus groups, or other forms of communication (e.g., e-mails) in which the researcher discusses preliminary findings with members of the culture under study. Member checks are usually conducted with some of your study participants, but sometimes they are not available, so member checks can also be conducted with others in the culture who were not involved in your research. Sometimes, member checks are conducted with both study participants and people outside your study to further add to the credibility of the research.

member checks
Obtaining feedback on your research findings from representatives of the population under study.

Data Triangulation

Another way to enhance credibility of qualitative research might be to employ **data triangulation**—conducting more than one form of data collection (e.g., observation and in-depth interviews and/or review of artifacts). Multiple forms of data collection can ensure multiple perspectives, and that's another way to enhance credibility—to make sure that all relevant perspectives are represented in the research. Richardson (2000) suggested that, rather than triangulation, qualitative researchers think of *crystallization*, like a prism in which multiple colors reflect from the whole. Crystallization, therefore, refers to conducting research in such a way that *all* perspectives, including the researchers' and all study participants', are fully fleshed out and reflected in the study.

data triangulation
Conducting more than one form of data collection to enhance the validity and credibility of your results.

Credible Data Gathering, Coding, and Writing

Another design issue related to credibility includes how long the researcher is in the field. Generally speaking, the longer the researcher is in the field, the more credible the research. Extended periods of fieldwork enhance the validity and credibility of qualitative research because long periods of observation yield trust, access to gatekeepers and informants, collaboration with participants, and rapport and allow the researcher time to check out their ideas and opinions. Most ethnographers, say Creswell and Miller (2000), spend from four to twelve months in a field site.

Credibility also depends on how well the data themes or categories are sufficiently saturated: Has everything been covered or are there themes that seem to have been left out? One other credibility consideration is whether the researcher writes the analysis in a persuasive manner (Creswell & Miller, 2000). In fact, Creswell and Miller suggest that reflexive writing in which researchers "self-disclose their assumptions, beliefs, and biases . . . that may shape their inquiry" (p. 127), along with rich, *thick description*, allow the reader to validate the findings for him or herself.

Peer Reviews

In some types of qualitative research, coding teams or research teams debrief and discuss the data, codes, and findings. A *peer reviewer*, say Creswell and Miller (2000), provides "support, plays devil's advocate, challenges the researchers' assumptions, pushes the researchers to the next step methodologically, and asks hard questions about methods and interpretations" (p. 129).

While qualitative researchers don't use the same validity and reliability terminology (or the same assumptions and frames of reference) as do quantitative researchers, qualitative research follows practices that ensure similar validity and reliability (See Table 8.1):

Table 9.1. Practices Qualitative Researchers Employ to Help Ensure Validity and Reliability

Qualitative Researchers Want	Qualitative Researchers Do
Internal validity	Use multiple sources of information; Discuss my analysis with my research collaborators and consultants; Conduct a member check of the analysis by discussing it with my research participants; Study my participants over time so that they will gain trust and comfort in the study and will behave in a natural manner as I observe and interview them.
Construct validity	Use multiple sources of information; Discuss my analysis with my research collaborators and consultants; Conduct a member check of the analysis by discussing it with my research participants; Compare the results with other studies looking at similar topics.

Divergent validity	Compare the results with other studies looking at similar topics.
External validity	Use multiple sources of information; Use multiple cases; Generalize to theory; Sample to represent population of interest.
Reliability	Study the participants over time; Use multiple cases and compare them in my analysis; Follow a consistent protocol for data collection, coding, and analysis; Use multiple sources of information; Discuss my analysis with my research collaborators and consultants; Conduct a member check of the analysis by discussing it with my research participants.

So What?

In this chapter, you have dealt with a number of issues pertaining to the quality of your measures, and the conclusions that can be drawn from your observations and measurements. In order to have confidence in your data, you must not only ensure the reliability of your measures, but also make sure that both the measures and the inferences drawn from them make sense in terms of validity, and make sure that these inferences are credible and representative. Good empirical research is that which is drawn from observations and techniques that are reliable, valid, and credible. Considering these factors before deciding upon a particular study design is critical in executing a quality study and generating useful knowledge.

Glossary

Alternate form reliability
A reliability method where the order in which the items in a measure are presented affect the ways in which people respond.

Concurrent validity
How well a scale measures up against another scale that has been demonstrated to measure exactly the same thing.

Construct validity
The extent to which your variables are logically related to other variables.

Convergent validity
When two measures you expect to be related are shown to be positively statistically related.

Credibility
The believability of the research to the reader; how much the reader believes the research to represent participants' reality.

Criterion validity
A type of validity consideration that deals with how a particular measure holds up when compared to some outside criterion.

Data triangulation

Conducting more than one form of data collection to enhance the validity and credibility of your results.

Discriminant validity

When two measures you expect to be negatively related (opposite to each other) are shown to have a negative statistical relationship.

Evaluator apprehension

When research participants become nervous or otherwise unsettled by the fact that they are in uncomfortable surroundings, which may limit their ability to concentrate or cause them to respond differently.

Face validity

A type of validity consideration in which measures, or procedures, are looked at and questioned to see if they make sense at face value.

History

A validity issue where something totally unrelated to your study happened at a particular time, and may have affected the responses.

Instrumentation

A validity threat that deals with differences that are observed at two different time points in which different instruments are used to assess the same construct.

Inter-coder reliability

An indicator of how similarly coders are coding content, both in terms of identifying units of analysis and in the contextual labels they ascribe to those units.

Item-total reliability

A means of evaluating internal consistency of a scale that compares the total score for a scale with individual item scores for the same scale.

Maturation

A validity issue dealing with the fact that subjects can change over time, which can affect their responses to the measures a researcher is interested in.

Member checks

Obtaining feedback on your research findings from representatives of the population under study.

Predictive validity

How well a measure predicts that something that will happen in the future.

Random error

A fluctuation in measurement.

Reliability

The ability of a measure to produce the same results if replicated.

Reliability statistics

Statistical tests that can show consistency between items, reflecting reliability of a scale.

Split-half reliability

A means of evaluating internal consistency of a scale that compares one randomly selected half of a scale from the other randomly selected half of the same scale.

Test-retest reliability

A reliability method in which the same measure is given to the same people at two different times.

Testing

A validity threat where if someone is more familiar or more comfortable with a series of questions or items, they may respond differently to them.

Validity

Accuracy of a measure, in terms of measuring intended constructs or observations.

References

Campbell, D., & Stanley, J. (1963). *Experimental and quasi-experimental designs for research.* Chicago: Rand-McNally.

Cook, T. D., & Campbell, D. T. (1979). *Quasi-experimentation: Design and analysis issues for field settings.* Boston: Houghton Mifflin Company.

Creswell, J. W., & Miller, D. (2000). Determining validity in qualitative research. *Theory into Practice, 39*(3), 124–130.

Fleiss, J. L., & Cohen, J. (1973). The equivalence of weighted kappa and the intraclass correlation coefficient as measures of reliability. *Educational and Psychological Measurement, 33,* 613–619.

Keaten, J., & Kelly, L. (2008). Emotional intelligence as a mediator of family communication patterns and reticence. *Communication Reports, 21*(2), 104–116.

Keaten, J. A., Kelly, L., & Finch, C. (1997). Development of an instrument to measure reticence. *Communication Quarterly, 45,* 37–54.

Kerlinger, F. (1986). *Foundations of behavioral research.* Fort Worth, TX: HBJ.

Krippendorf, K. (1994). *Content analysis: An introduction to its methodology*. Beverly Hills, CA: Sage.

Lannutti, P. J., & Lachlan, K. A. (2007). Assessing attitudes toward same-sex marriage: Scale development and validation. *Journal of Homosexuality, 53*(4), 113–133.

Nunnally, J., & Bernstein, I. (1994). *Psychometric theory*. New York: McGraw Hill.

Reinard, J. C. (2006). *Communication research statistics*. Thousand Oaks, CA: Sage.

Richardson, L. (2000). Writing: A method of inquiry. In N. K. Denzin & Y. S. Lincoln, (Eds.), *Handbook of qualitative research* (pp. 923–948). Thousand Oaks, CA: Sage.

Ritchie, L. D., & Fitzpatrick, M. A. (1990). Family communication patterns: Measuring intrapersonal perceptions of interpersonal relationships. *Communication Research, 17*, 523–544.

Rittenour, C. E., & Martin, M. M. (2008). Convergent validity of the Communication Based Emotional Support Scale. *Communication Studies, 59*(3), 235–241.

Schutte, N. S., Malouff, J. M., Hall, L. E., Haggerty, D. J., Cooper, J. T., Golden, C. J., & Dornheim, L. (1998). Development and validation of a measure of emotional intelligence. *Personality and Individual Differences, 25*, 167–177.

Weber, K. D., & Patterson, B. R. (1996). Construction and validation of a communication based emotional support scale. *Communication Research Reports, 13*, 68–76.

Wilson, B. J., Kunkel, D., Linz, D., Potter, W. J., Donnerstein, E., Smith, S. L., Blumenthal, E., & Gray, T. (1997). Violence in television programming overall: University of California, Santa Barbara study. In *National Television Violence Study* (Vol. 1, pp. 3–268). Newbury Park, CA: Sage.

RESEARCH UNDER THE QUANTITATIVE PARADIGM

SURVEY RESEARCH

10

CHAPTER OUTLINE

KEY TERMS

Cohort study
Cross-sectional survey
Evaluation research
Funnel format
Interview
Inverted funnel format

Longitudinal survey design
Market research
Panel study
Political polls
Researcher-administered questionnaires

Self-administered questionnaires
Survey design
Trend study
Tunnel format

Chapter Objectives

1. To become familiar with survey research
2. To understand survey measurement techniques
3. To examine common types of research design
4. To explore the advantages and disadvantages of interviews and questionnaires

▼ # Why Surveys?

Comedian Dave Barry once quipped, "If you surveyed a hundred typical middle-aged Americans, I bet you'd find that only two of them could tell you their blood types, but every last one of them would know the theme song from 'The Beverly Hillbillies'" (*The Quote Garden*, n.d.). *Late Night* host David Letterman said, "*USA Today* has come out with a new survey—apparently, three out of every four people make up 75% of the population" (*The Quotations Page*, n.d.). No doubt about it—survey research is popular in everyday society. In this chapter, we consider one of the most common types of research methodologies: surveys. We will consider why surveys are immensely popular; examine common survey research designs; explore survey measurement techniques, including questionnaire design; and scrutinize the pros and cons of different ways of administering surveys.

▼ # Survey Research

survey design
A method of asking research participants questions that provides researchers with a method of information gathering from a large number of people over a relatively short period of time.

For most of us, **survey design** is perhaps the most familiar research method, and may be the first method that comes to mind when we think about social research. When you fill out a teacher's evaluation at the end of the semester, a comment card at a restaurant, or even a profile on a dating website, you are completing a survey of one type or another. Surveys are popular in both proprietary and scholarly research for a variety of reasons. First, survey design provides researchers with a method of information gathering from a large number of people in a relatively short period of time. This allows you to gather a representative sample from a population of interest to you. Second, surveys are relatively inexpensive to administer. With Web-based applications, such as Survey Monkey (www.surveymonkey.com), Survey Share (www.surveyshare.com), and Qualtrics (www.qualtrics.com), the survey creation process has become even easier and more accessible. Third, this methodology involves a relatively straightforward research strategy. You ask people questions and analyze their answers. Fourth, surveys can include both quantitative questions and qualitative (open-ended) questions. Finally, since you can easily provide and administer identical questions to many participants, a well-written survey questionnaire is a reliable measurement technique.

Applications of Survey Research

Surveys have been widely used in communication research in many different ways. Macias, Springston, Lariscy, and Neustifer (2008) conducted a content analysis of 54 communication-related journals published from 1990 to 2002, and found that 565 studies used a survey methodology. Most survey research they found was conducted in the subfields of public relations, marketing, public opinion, advertising, and mass communication journals; however, 85 percent of the journals investigated had some survey research in them, indicating that most segments of our field use survey research at least some of the time.

You can use surveys to describe communication characteristics of participants for the purpose of theory building, or for generalizing about the population they represent. Other times, you utilize survey research to test theoretical predictions about the relationships between communication variables and other variables in a population of interest. You'll see in Chapter 11 that experiments in our field often use surveys as part of their design. In addition, a lot of communication research uses surveys to assess participants' attitudes, beliefs, and opinions, and to let participants retrospectively replay incidents, behaviors, and meanings. Market research surveys, political polls, customer satisfaction surveys, employee feedback surveys, and surveys designed to measure product perceptions and market position are all examples of ways surveys are used in business and industry.

Survey Research Measuring Attitudes. If you're designing a communication campaign to promote a product, service, or behavior, you're going to want to do an audience analysis—to determine what your potential audience already thinks, feels, or believes about your topic. You'd likely conduct a survey to find that out—it would give you a baseline understanding of where your audience stands at one point in time. Communication researchers also assess attitudes in surveys to develop, test, or apply theoretical concepts for both applied and scholarly research.

For example, Salmon, Park, and Wrigley (2003) conducted a survey research study among corporate spokespersons from 100 public companies to understand their perceptions of risk and bias toward optimism about the possibility of bioterrorism among corporate spokespersons. They tested five hypotheses:

H_1: Corporate spokespersons will tend to estimate their own organization's risk to be less than that of other organizations similar to their own.

H_2: Optimistic bias will be greater for referents that are more distant (e.g., other corporations in the United States) than for those that are proximate (other corporations in the state).

H_3: Corporate spokespersons who perceive their own organizations as low in vulnerability tend to show high optimistic bias.

H_4: Corporate spokespersons who perceive high severity of bioterrorism tend to show high optimistic bias.

H_5: Corporate spokespersons who perceive that their own organizations can control external events tend to show high optimistic bias.

A survey method was appropriate for these hypotheses because they were measuring participants' attitudes, beliefs, and perceptions. Salmon and colleagues (2003) used a purposive sampling method. They got a list (sampling frame) of the 100 largest privately and publicly held companies in the state from the Harris Michigan Industrial Directory (Carlsen, 2010). They called each company and got a list of 142 names of corporate spokespersons. They mailed out an introductory letter, then called each potential participant. If a participant refused, they called a second time five days later to see if the person had changed his or her mind. They ended up with a sample size of 72, which represents a 51 percent response rate.

Applying Weistein's concept of optimistic bias to risk perception, Salmon and colleagues (2003) designed their own measurements of bioterrorism awareness, perceived vulnerability, perceived severity, and perceived controllability using Likert-type scales. They used Weinstein's own measure of optimistic bias. Based on their statistical analysis (which we'll discuss in Chapter 13), Salmon et al. (2003) determined that there is a relationship between optimistic bias and perceived vulnerability and perceived severity, but not between optimistic bias and perceived control. What do you think are the pros and cons to their use of the survey method? What internal validity issues might they need to consider? How about external validity issues? How about ecological validity issues? How can they address these validity issues in future research? What can they do with this information?

Survey Research Measuring Retrospective Behaviors.   Some researchers use surveys to ask participants to report on retrospective, or past, behaviors. While asking participants to remember past events raises concerns about the accuracy of memory, this method does have the advantage of obtaining a recollection of an incident from the point of view of a participant. Here's an example of this use of surveys: Botta and Dumlao (2002) wanted to see if there was a relationship between conflict communication styles between fathers and daughters and eating disorders in the daughters. They had numerous hypotheses and research questions, all pertaining to that general topic (conversation orientation, conformity orientation, pluralistic, laissez-faire, and protective all referring to family communication styles; compromising, collaborating, avoiding, accommodating, confronting, and avoiding all referring to conflict styles):

H_1: Conversation orientation as encouraged by the father will be a significant negative predictor of anorexic and bulimic behaviors.

H_2: Conformity orientation as encouraged by the father will be a significant positive predictor of anorexic and bulimic behaviors.

H_3: Being raised by a pluralistic father will be a significant negative predictor of anorexic and bulimic behaviors.

H_4: Being raised by a protective father will be a significant positive predictor of anorexic behaviors.

H_5: Compromising as a way to respond to conflict will be a significant negative predictor of anorexic behaviors and a significant negative predictor of bulimic behaviors.

H_6: Collaborating as a way to respond to conflict will be a significant negative predictor of anorexic behaviors and a significant negative predictor of bulimic behaviors.

H_7: Avoiding as a way to respond to conflict will be a significant positive predictor of anorexic behaviors.

H_8: Accommodating as a way to respond to conflict will be a significant positive predictor of anorexic behaviors.

H_9: Confronting as a means of responding to conflict will be a significant positive predictor of bulimic behaviors.

H_{10}: Avoiding as a means of responding to conflict will be a significant negative predictor of bulimic behaviors.

RQ_1: Is being raised by a protective father, a laissez-faire father, or a consensual father a significant predictor of bulimic behaviors?

RQ_2: To what extent do family communication styles as encouraged by the father moderate the influence of a strong drive to be thin on anorexic and bulimic behaviors?

RQ_3: To what extent do conflict resolution styles between father and daughter moderate the influence of a strong drive to be thin on anorexic and bulimic behaviors?

To measure family communication patterns, Botta and Dumlao (2002) used Ritchie's 1991 Revised Family Communication Patterns (RFCP) instrument, a multidimensional Likert scale that has been shown to have high reliability—Cronbach's Alpha for conversation orientation was .91, and for conformity orientation was .86. To measure conflict styles, they used Rahim's Organization Conflict Inventory, a multidimensional Likert scale that also has been shown to have high reliability—avoidance conflict style ($\alpha = .85$), collaborating conflict style ($\alpha = .89$), compromising conflict style ($\alpha = .74$), confronting conflict style ($\alpha = .80$), and accommodating conflict style ($\alpha = .81$). They measured eating disorders using two scales: Garner and Olmsted's Eating Disorder Inventory and the Eating Attitudes Test, two Likert-type scales, both of which they report have high validity and reliability.

What are other methods they could have used to collect their information and address their hypotheses and research questions? Why do you think they chose surveys over other methods such as ethnography or experiments?

There are three additional applications of survey research we should also consider: political polls, evaluation research, and market research.

Political Polls.   One of the most common and readily available uses of surveys in the world today is in the form of **political polls**. It seems that every day leading up to an election, we are bombarded with a detailed account of who is leading whom in the run for a particular office. In fact, we have become so bombarded with polling data that data aggregation sites, such as Nate Silver's 538 (www.fivethirtyeight.com), have become popular resources for summary statements about what we can glean from the polls when taken together.

political polls
One of the most common and readily available uses of surveys. They provide a detailed account of who is leading whom in the run for a particular office during an election.

Oftentimes political poll surveys are conducted over the phone. The key to political polls and the validity of their findings rests upon the basic research method strategies used, the quality of sampling and sample size, the response rate, and as we will see shortly, even the types of questions asked.

Evaluation Research.

evaluation research
Research that is designed to assess the effectiveness of programs or products during development or after their completion.

Another type of survey research that many of you are already familiar with is the use of survey data in **evaluation research**. Evaluation research is designed to assess the effectiveness of campaigns, programs, or products either before (or while) they are being developed, or after their completion. The use of evaluation research for campaigns and programs allows practitioners and managers to develop more effective communication programs. A good example of evaluation research in organizational communication would be research designed to assess a new training program put in place in the organization. If you are a participant in the training, you might be asked to fill out a survey at the conclusion of the program, so the trainer can assess his or her success. In health communication, you might be interested in evaluating the relative success of a smoking cessation program or a new exercise regimen. You could even evaluate the success of a nutrition campaign such as the "5 a day" campaign that encourages Americans to eat five fruits and vegetables a day. This type of evaluation research is often called *summative research*, as it traditionally takes place after the program has run its course or the campaign is ending (Center & Broom, 1983).

Another type of evaluation research is known as *formative research*; this is simply evaluation research that helps the campaign or program manager develop a campaign or program, or evaluate it while it is ongoing (Atkin & Freimuth, 2000; Center & Broom, 1983).

The benefit of these types of evaluation research is that they allow you to identify ways in which the program or campaign can be refined and improved. The third type of evaluation research, *needs analysis*, is a mechanism for identifying problems experienced by a group of people by comparing what exists with what study participants want. For example, organizational employees might fill out a needs assessment survey to help management develop a new training program by comparing what existing training programs offer versus what employees want or need in a training program. This data is often used to guide in the development of communication interventions, such as skill training. Finally, the fourth type of evaluation research, *organizational feedback*, also utilizes survey design. Here, organizational members are asked to report on practices within the organization. You might be interested in surveying national insurance companies about the communication practices within their organization. You could use surveys to ask them about the use of different channels of communication, the quality of information provided, and even their preferred method of communication. The results can then be used for organizational improvement.

Market Research.

market research
Research that is designed to study consumer behavior.

Another common example of survey design comes in the form of **market research**. This is research designed to study consumer behavior, preferences, and opinions. The idea behind market research is that if you can determine what people consume, how often, and why, then you can predict future consumption (or at least market researchers can). Market research may question consumer reactions to a new product, interest in new products, and preferences for products and services. This type of research evaluates how satisfied consumers are with products and services, as well as explores persuasive strategies for advertising, product pricing, and even packaging. The most obvious example of market research in your world is likely to be a discount or frequent shopper card on your key ring, or the survey invitations issued to you on the receipt you receive from a local discount store. It seems marketers have many opportunities to gather data about your consumer behaviors. Did you really think the shopper card is to help you save money? What types of information do companies gather from your frequent shopper card? What marketing decisions could they make with it?

Design Concerns

Sampling. We discussed sampling in detail in Chapter 8, but let's review the types of sampling that are done in survey research. Because of the techniques used in administering surveys, researchers have the ability to conduct a truly random and representative sample if they have the necessary resources. Regardless of the type of survey you are designing, your design concerns are similar. One of your first concerns related to survey research design is selecting survey participants. To do this, you must have a sampling frame. Recall that a sampling frame is ideally a list of all members of a population, or at least it is the list you let stand in for your population. In some instances, an actual list of the population may be impossible to come by. At one time, telephone directories might have been a good choice; in today's world, this would be an incomplete sampling frame at best, because so many people use telephone numbers—cell phones, for example—that are not listed in directories. In fact, these days, we might argue that using a list of numbers from a telephone directory is only representative of, perhaps, older, less technologically savvy people, and there is evidence that the samples derived from telephone directories tend to skew toward older audiences. This is why many survey researchers are moving to random digit dialing—letting a computer randomly generate telephone numbers within an area code and exchange. Using random digit dialing, you're not limited to listed or land-line numbers, and, if you're looking for an overall population sample, your sample should be more representative. However you decide to sample, remember that your sample should represent your population as closely as possible. If you were interested in studying dating behaviors of college students at UCONN and UNC–Charlotte, you could likely contact the registrars of each of the schools and obtain a list of potential participants (with Institutional Research Board approval, of course). This list would be your sampling frame. If you're interested in why people voted for a particular candidate in an election, it would not make sense to poll people who didn't vote. Therefore, a sampling frame of all people—regardless of whether they voted—would not be very representative of the population you're interested in studying. You'd be better off using a list of registered voters, at least eliminating those who definitely couldn't have voted.

Many types of sampling can be used with survey design: random sampling, cluster sampling, stratified sampling, purposive samples, and even volunteer samples. What defines the best choice for a particular study? That's right, it's the research question. The question(s) and/or hypothesis(es) determine the technique you choose. For a review of best practices in making these decisions, take a second look at Chapter 8.

Cross-Sectional Design.

Another consideration and decision you must make early in the survey research design process is whether a cross-sectional or longitudinal design is best for your study. A **cross-sectional survey** describes the characteristics of a sample representing a population at one point in time. Think of it as a picture, or a snapshot. Researchers frequently utilize cross-sectional survey research because it's easy to collect data from a large number of people, in a short period of time, at a single time point. One researcher we know has, at times, been able to sample from the local jury pool. In just one afternoon, he collected nearly 500 surveys of a very wide sample of people who were appropriate for his research question. The Salmon et al. (2003) study mentioned earlier is an example of a cross-sectional study.

A cross-sectional design is great for describing the status quo—how things are right at one particular time point. However, there are some cautions to keep in mind. First, it is important to keep in mind the particular point in time when the survey was conducted. A friend of ours went through the Institutional Research Board and was approved to collect data on her project late one September. She was interested in studying different types of messages on brochures regarding breast self-exams. As she began her project, she realized that October, when she collected the majority of her data, happens to be Breast Cancer Awareness Month. Is there any chance that this particular month for data collection affected the outcome of her study? Absolutely. Data can be misleading if the survey is conducted at an unrepresentative time (see the discussion of History as a validity threat in Chapter 9).

An interesting example of the use of cross-sectional survey design comes from Lim and Teo (2009) who studied e-manners, or the level of respect communicated via e-mail communication in the workplace. They measured 192 employees in the financial services industry in Singapore at just one point in time. However, they caution that their results limit their ability to determine cause and effect despite some significant relationships between variables.

Cross-sectional surveys assume the variables and processes being studied have reached stability, but many variables and processes are constantly changing. For example, marital satisfaction, television viewing behavior, and communication apprehension are variables that have the potential to change over time. By the same token, you can't take one measurement at one point in time and assume causality. Consider the hypothesis that video game violence leads to an increase in aggressive behavior. If you measure both of these variables and find a positive correlation between them, can you conclude that video game violence caused aggressive behavior in your sample? No, you cannot. *Causal conclusions can never be drawn from cross-sectional data*. It is a lot like the question of which came first—the chicken or the egg. Do you know whether exposure to video game violence came before or after exhibiting aggressive behavior? Not if you only measure at one point of time. While a reasonable person might likely argue that watching violence causes aggressive behavior, it is possible that individuals with aggressive tendencies could choose to play violent video games. It is also equally likely that some other variable, such as family discipline, affects both video game playing and aggressive behavior.

The above is an example of the problems sometimes associated with confounds, or third variables, that we discussed at length in Chapter 7. Recall, a confounding variable is some third variable that explains the change in the dependent variable better than the independent variable. The independent and dependent variable may appear to be linked, while in reality they simply vary together because of some unmeasured confounding variable that is impacting both of them. Remember our crime and ice cream story in Chapter 7: crime and ice cream consumption may appear to be related, yet, in reality, both are correlated with heat. You should always try to anticipate potential confounds and eliminate them from the study design. Keep in mind that in cross-sectional designs you cannot evaluate change over time, so it is possible to demonstrate correlation but not causality.

Longitudinal Design.

In **longitudinal survey design**, you gather data from respondents at several points in time. This allows you to evaluate the impact of unusual or unique environmental events on a population, and assess whether a population's beliefs, attitudes, and/or behaviors are enduring or stable over time. One of the greatest strengths of longitudinal design is to allow you to examine causal relationships. You add this feature to survey research with a longitudinal design by determining whether A comes before B in time. You can only do this with a minimum of two measurements over some timeframe. There are three types of longitudinal research design: a trend study, a cohort study, and a panel study.

longitudinal survey design
A survey design that gathers data from respondents at several points in time.

TREND STUDY.

In a **trend study**, measurement occurs at two or more points in time, from different samples selected from the same population. This type of study is designed to identify changes or trends (thus the name) in people's beliefs about the variable of interest, or in the correlations between variables at different time points. An example of a trend study is the Gallup polls used during a presidential election. The Gallup organization, a premier research firm in the United States, draws a sample from all eligible U.S. voters and asks whom they plan to vote for in the upcoming presidential election. Each week they poll another group of people (sample) from this population (all eligible voters). Remember, the samples Gallup is taking are not the same people; they are merely samples from the same population. Keep in mind, though, that as your goal is comparison over time, you should be sampling from the same general population, at least. What if you sample first from the Socialists of America, second from the Students for Democratic Government, and third from the Young Republicans? Clearly, you cannot compare how people's attitudes changed over time because your sample would be very different each time. To compare trends, you must have comparable representative samples. What do you think are the pros and cons to trend studies?

trend study
Measurement occurs at two or more points in time, from different samples selected from the same population. This type of study is designed to identify changes or trends in people's beliefs about a variable of interest.

COHORT STUDY.

In a **cohort study**, responses from a specific subgroup of the population are identified and compared over time. In a cohort study, the key is that for some reason (relevant to your study) you are interested in

cohort study
A study in which responses from specific subgroups of a population are identified and compared over time.

studying a group of people that have some characteristic in common because of a historical marker of significance (i.e., lived through the Depression) or some other meaningful life event. For example, you might be interested in people born or graduated from high school in the same year. Simply put, a cohort is usually defined with respect to time or history.

Imagine for a moment you are interested in comparing how baby boomers talk about money and financial security over time. You decide to embark on a ten-year longitudinal study with a cohort design in which you measure attitudes and financial talk once every two years. You decide on a cohort study of baby boomers (individuals generally born from 1946 to 1964, who are currently between the ages 45 to 63). You sample persons 45 to 63 in 2009, another sample of individuals 47 to 65 in 2011, another sample of persons 49 to 67 in 2013, and so on. Although the *specific set of people* studied in each of these surveys would be different, each sample represents the cohort born between 1946 and 1964.

panel study
A study in which a sample is drawn from a population or universe and those same people or objects are measured at multiple points in time.

PANEL STUDY.   In a **panel study**, responses are obtained from the exact same people over time. Essentially, you draw a sample from your population, and measure those same people or objects at multiple points in time. This is also known as repeated measures. The most significant advantage of using a panel study is that it allows for true tests of causality, as it allows the researcher to look at correlations over time and rule out confounding variables.

If panel studies allow for true causal analyses, then why are they not used all the time? While there are important advantages to this type of design, it is not without serious disadvantages that warrant consideration. One important disadvantage of a panel study is that as you continue taking measurements over time, you may lose subjects. This is known as a high attrition rate, or as an issue of mortality (again, see Chapter 7). It is unlikely that you will literally lose participants due to death when conducting Communication research. It's more likely that participants will drop out of school, change address or contact information, or just become impossible to track down to measure at a subsequent wave of measurement (particularly if the study extends over a period of months or even years). Another major concern with attrition or mortality in a panel study is that you may not end up with enough participants in your study, and/or participants that do participate in all points of measure may somehow differ from participants who drop out of the study. This is not unlike our earlier comments on response rate. If you lose a large number of participants, perhaps there is something systematic about those who remain that call the generalizability of the findings into question.

Consider Segrin and Flora's (2000) study of students transitioning to college. They measured social skills and psychosocial problems at two points in time: during the end of the senior year in high school (wave 1), and again at the end of the first semester in college (wave 2). They found that (1) social skills interacted with stressful life events to predict changes in depression and loneliness, (2) people with lower social skills were predicted to make the transition to college with the worst psychosocial problems, and (3) people with lower social skills were more vulnerable to development of psychosocial problems than people with higher social skills. This all certainly makes sense and is a great use of a panel longitudinal survey method. However, what limitations can you identify with this method? What if the people with the poorest social skills dropped out by the second wave of interviewing? Would that make both waves of interviewing equivalent?

Consider another example of survey design. You might decide you are interested in studying family communication between children and their parents, paying particular attention to conflict. Your research question is this: Do parents believe conflict with their children increases as children move from elementary school through middle school and high school? How could you study this using a cross-sectional design? How could you study this same question using a longitudinal design? In a cross-sectional design, you would put together a questionnaire including a measure of conflict and ask parents of children in third, seventh, and eleventh grades to complete your survey. Or you could give one questionnaire to parents of eleventh-grade kids and ask them to fill out the questionnaire for their children when they were in third, seventh, and eleventh grades. In a longitudinal panel design, you could use the same questionnaire with the measure of conflict to assess parents with children currently in third grade, and then collect the same measurement again as their children entered seventh grade, and again four years later when their children were eleventh graders. What do you think are the pros and cons of each approach?

Measurement Techniques

Survey measurement techniques are what we call self-report. We discussed this in Chapter 7. Typically, in a survey you are asking the participants to tell you what they think or feel, and they are reporting on themselves. Do you think this is a good strategy? The obvious answer is it depends upon what you want to know. We will first consider some strategies for enhancing the strength of self-report data, before considering the disadvantages of self-report techniques. Self-report data is perhaps most commonly used (at least in positivist research), and when utilizing tight procedures, it can provide a clear and valid picture of some phenomenon of interest to the researcher.

To enhance the likelihood of obtaining valid self-report data, it is important that you clearly delineate why the study is important. Most questionnaires or surveys will include a statement on their cover sheet and their consent form detailing at least an abbreviated version of the main purpose of the study. While it may not be desirable to tell participants everything about the study purpose, they need to be given at least a general idea of what you're doing; if the subjects are given incomplete information in order to mask the intention of the study, then that needs to be revealed in some kind of debriefing statement. It is also essential that participants be informed of whether their data will be kept in confidence or will be anonymous. As we discussed in Chapter 5, it is important that the data is protected as though it was the researcher's own private information. Participants should be encouraged to give complete and accurate information when possible. We will discuss questions at length later, but participants should not be asked to respond to items that are irrelevant to them or their situation. You should also ensure that you consider the audience of the questionnaire before writing the statements and/or questions.

Self-report surveys are great for recording self-perception, covert or hidden behavior, beliefs, attitudes, opinions, and values. They might also be useful for questions of a personal nature, anything that might be considered private information. Self-report is also a strong technique for recording emotion or feelings; however, keep in mind that these have to be conscious thoughts and feelings you are interested in measuring.

As research questions ultimately guide your methodological choices, it is helpful to know what self-report surveys are particularly unsuccessful at measuring. First, self-report is a poor choice for unconscious behaviors and feelings, difficult to remember events, and things that happened in the distant past. Surveys are also a weak choice as a method of gathering data about abilities, skills (think communication competence), and socially undesirable behaviors—as individuals are often unlikely to report their own shortcomings or behaviors they may perceive as social undesirable.

▼ # Constructing a Survey Questionnaire

Writing Survey Questions

In designing survey questionnaires, one concern is how best to construct the questions. The first issue is the type of questions you can ask in a survey, which in turn depends upon the research question asked and/or hypotheses stated. You can ask questions about experience or behavior: How often do you talk with your mother? You can ask questions about opinions or values: Is television too violent? You may ask questions about feelings or attitudes: Do you like your new research methods textbook? You might ask questions about factual knowledge: How many drinks can you consume before your blood alcohol level goes over .10? You can ask questions about background or demographics: How old are you? What is your major? Where are you from?

Strategies for Questions.   While the initial criteria for writing and deciding upon what questions to ask in a research study come from the research questions or hypotheses, there are additional strategies for what questions work best. First, recent and important events are remembered more easily. For example, if you ask people to report on their television viewing behavior, asking them to report the previous day or week's behavior will produce more accurate data than asking about the distant past. People can recall past serious issues, but not past minor issues, and verbatim memory of minor issues can erode in as little as a few days. For example, you may not be able to recall whom you communicated with last Friday; yet most of you remember the first person you spoke with following the Boston Marathon bombings (which, at this writing, took place over three years ago). Another important strategy is that unpleasant and ego-threatening incidents tend to be reported inaccurately. In other words, parents underreport children's misbehavior, college students underreport unsafe sexual behavior, and almost no one admits to driving under the influence of alcohol (since it is both socially undesirable and a crime).

1. **Questions should be clear.**

   Creating good questions, at first glance, seems like an easy task; yet upon the first attempt, you will find this is a complex task and warrants much deliberation. Some guidelines can make the task easier. First and foremost, questions should be clear, using simple language participants can easily understand. Your word choice is dependent upon your audience. Just as you have been trained to consider your audience in public speaking, you need to give thought to your audience when writing a question for a survey. If you are surveying adolescents or engineers, the words you choose will differ. It is common for words to have multiple meanings, so you need to be sure that the interpretation you are thinking of is clear to the participants. For example, think about the word "drugs." Suppose you ask the question "Have you ever taken drugs?" What would people think you were asking about? On many research projects you might be talking about illegal substances, such as cocaine; however, in some health communication studies, you might be talking about prescription drugs. The key here is to be clear! If there is any doubt about what your question is asking, you need to write a better question.

2. **Questions must be about only one issue.**

   A second important guideline to follow when writing research questions is that the questions you write must be about only one issue. Questions that contain more than one issue are called *double-barreled* questions. Why should it matter if you ask questions containing more than one concept? Imagine that you ask the following question: "Do you like the education and social life at UNC–Charlotte?" In reality, a "Yes" tells you that the participant likes both the education and social life at UNC–Charlotte, while a "No" tells you that the participant dislikes both the education and social life at UNC–Charlotte. However, are these the only two possible answers? No. One might like the education and dislike the social opportunities at UNC–Charlotte, or one might dislike the education and like the social life at UNC–Charlotte. In any event, if you ask a double-barreled question, you can never be certain what the participant intended when he or she answered the question, or if they give a lukewarm answer that is indicative of conflicted opinions on the question. This will affect both the reliability and validity of the survey, compromise the measure's integrity, and thus impact the overall study.

3. **Questions should avoid biased wording.**

   Another guideline for good question construction is to avoid using wording that leads participants to particular outcomes. The actual wording of the question can dramatically change the outcome. Some common examples of this include starting questions and/or statements with phrases like "Wouldn't you agree . . ." or "Isn't it true . . ." A related guideline for question construction is to avoid language that is emotionally charged, as this can bias answers. A great example of emotionally charged language can be seen in the abortion debate. Regardless of what side you identify with, the language both sides use to talk about their perspective is emotionally provocative. Let's consider the debate language. Pro-choice groups equate legal abortion with free choice and a woman's control over her own body. They talk about being *pro-choice*, while they see the other side as being *anti-choice*. Similarly, pro-life groups equate legal abortion with murder, using phrases such as *pro-life* and *pro-abortion*. All of these terms, regardless of your own personal beliefs, are emotionally charged, and if used in a survey will likely result in difficulty in getting an unbiased response.

4. Questions should avoid making assumptions.
    The fourth guideline for question construction is to avoid making assumptions about your participant. So, while we suggested earlier you need to consider your audience when writing questions, here you want to move a step beyond that by asking participants questions that are relevant to them, and asking questions only when participants are informed about the topic. Do you take your pet to the vet for yearly exams? This question assumes the person answering the question has a pet. What do you think of Proposition 301? This question assumes the person answering the question knows what Proposition 301 is. Neither of these questions will provide accurate or reliable answers with the wrong participants. The solution to this problem often comes in the form of filter questions, which can assist in *filtering* out individuals who lack the appropriate knowledge or lack the appropriate conditions to answer the question at hand.

5. Questions should avoid offending participants if possible.
    Be careful how you phrase sensitive questions. Examples of sensitive topics are age and income. Suppose you ask such questions as "How old are you?" and "How much money do you make?" You will probably get an answer like "None of your business!" The best way around this is to list groupings of ages and income levels to follow your questions, such as: "In which of the following age categories do you fit?" and "In which of the following categories was your total household income before taxes last year?" It is also wise to place questions like these (especially those regarding demographics) at the very end of a survey; not only does this minimize the risks associated with offending the respondent, but they are easy questions to answer, so fatigue is not much of an issue.

Types of Questions

Before we leave the discussion of questionnaire writing, let's talk briefly about different types of questions. There are basically two types of questions: *closed-ended* questions and *open-ended* questions. A closed-ended question is one where you only give the respondent certain possible answers that his response must fit into—for example, a "yes/no" question, or the question "In which of the following age categories do you fit? Under 21; 21–34; 35–49; 50–64;

or 65 and over." Closed-ended questions are suited for eliminating interviewer interpretation, eliminating coding and editing interpretations, making recording of the data easier as the interview is being conducted, and ensuring consistency in interviewing. When you are using scales or similar measurement tools that we discussed earlier, you are usually using closed-ended questions.

However, sometimes closed-ended questions are not appropriate for the research questions that are being asked. What would happen with the closed-ended question "Do you believe the United States ought to enter into a treaty with Iran to eliminate long-range nuclear warheads?" Some people may simply say "yes" or "no." But others may wish to elaborate: "It depends on—if they will honor it, if they will allow independent inspections, and if they are willing to cease production now until the treaty is signed." In other words, "yes" and "no" may not be a sufficient choice of answers for some participants, and you'll need to allow for expanded answers. In this instance an open-ended question would make more sense.

Open-ended questions are suited when you need to measure a participant's level of knowledge, or playback of something, or detailed explanation of an opinion. Examples of open-ended questions are "Why do you say that?" and "What do you remember about _____?" and "What are your impressions of _____?"

Although we are not talking about *in-depth qualitative* interviewing (see Chapter 15), open-ended questions require some amount of probing and clarifying. A common weakness of inexperienced interviewers is poor probing. After the participant has seemingly finished what he or she is going to say, you would need to probe. For example, you may need to ask: "What do you mean by that?" or "What else do you remember?" or "Why do you say that?" A probe of "Do you remember anything else?" usually results in a "no." But if you ask, "What else do you remember?" often you will get more responses. It is also very important to probe for clarity. There is nothing more frustrating than reading over a questionnaire later and thinking, "I wonder what he or she meant by that." If you don't ask when he or she is there in front of you, you'll never know what he or she meant.

Structure and Arrangement of Questions

Of course, many researchers use already published and validated scales to build their questionnaires, instead of writing their own questions. As we alluded to earlier, there are scholars in Communication and other disciplines who focus their research entirely on developing and validating good measures that can be used by others. Most questionnaires in academic survey research are a combination of existing scales with newly written questions. However, whether compiling a questionnaire from existing scales or creating a completely new questionnaire, you have to make choices about the best way to structure and arrange your questions across the entire instrument. The three commonly used question formats are: tunnel, funnel, and inverted funnel formats.

> **tunnel format**
> *A type of question format in which questions tend to be similar in terms of breadth and depth throughout a questionnaire. Questions are organized by similarity and vary little in terms of depth.*

Tunnel Format. In the **tunnel format**, questions tend to be similar in terms of breadth and depth throughout the questionnaire. They are organized by similarity and vary little in terms of depth.

funnel format
A type of question format in which questions begin with broad, open-ended questions followed by narrow, more closed-ended questions.

inverted funnel format
A type of question format that generally begins with more closed-ended, narrow questions moving throughout the questionnaire to the most open-ended and broad questions.

Funnel Format. In a **funnel format**, the questions begin with broad, often open-ended questions followed by narrow, more closed-ended questions. Think of this as a format moving from general to specific.

Inverted Funnel Format. Finally, the **inverted funnel format** is the polar opposite of the funnel format. It generally begins with more closed-ended, narrow questions moving throughout the questionnaire to the most open-ended, broad questions. Think of this format as moving from specific to general.

How to Choose the Right Format.   As we have suggested throughout the book, the preferred questionnaire structure is the one best suited to your research question and/or hypotheses. Just as the questions determine the type of methodology that is best, the same components assist you in determining the most appropriate format for your question. For example, your author Ken Lachlan conducted a study of people's media dependencies and opinions of emergency information received following the collapse of a highway bridge in Minneapolis, Minnesota (Lachlan, Spence, & Nelson, 2010). When designing the instrument, he and his coauthors knew that they had to ask very specific questions about an incident that had happened about a week before the data collection. This included how they first heard of the bridge collapse, what sources they turned to for additional information, the types of information they received, and how satisfied they were with information that came from emergency managers, first responders, the mainstream media, and police. It also included questions concerning what the audience wanted to find out about most, and whether or not these needs were satisfied. Knowing that these were tough questions that required quite a bit of cognitive effect, they chose the inverted funnel format, putting these questions at the front of the survey. Easier questions, such as general media habits and demographics, went toward the end of the survey, since even a somewhat tired participant should be able to recall these things easily.

If you have ever answered a survey and thought, "I think I already answered that question," it may be that you have indeed answered a similar question—often one written that is the opposite of the first. For example, in McCroskey's (1982) Personal Report of Communication Apprehension Scale, one item states, "Ordinarily I am very tense and nervous in conversations," while another statement asks you to respond to the following, "Ordinarily I am very calm and relaxed in conversations." These items are written to minimize the tendency people have to start answering without much thought. This is called a *response set*. Reversing the polarity of some of the items on scales as you write is a good technique for avoiding a response set when participants complete your survey.

Survey Administration

When administering a questionnaire, researchers have choices to make about how best to deliver the material to the individual participating in the study or completing the questionnaire. This is known as questionnaire administration and we have three options: researcher-administered, self-administered, and interviews. In their content analysis of survey research in communication, Macias and colleagues (2008) found that the most common method of administration of surveys, by far, was mail (self-administered) surveys, used in 54 percent of research reviewed. Interviews over the telephone or in-person each were used in 11 percent of research reviewed. Web and fax surveys were rarely seen (only in 1% of studies reviewed).

Researcher-Administered.

In **researcher-administered questionnaires**, the researcher is present when the participant completes the survey questionnaire, usually in a group setting. When a person fills out her own survey instrument, regardless of whether the researcher is present at the time, the instrument is called a *questionnaire*. Researcher-administered surveys allow the researcher the opportunity of answering any questions participants may have. Another primary benefit to researcher-administered questionnaires is that, when administering questionnaires to a large group of people at one time, data collection is quick and efficient. However, the disadvantage to administering a survey in such a setting is that participants sometimes feel less anonymous, as the researcher is present. Another disadvantage of administering a survey to a group of people is that groups can sometimes bias an individual's own responses. We may answer the survey differently if we feel that the information can be tied to us or if we feel that there is the chance someone in the group may find out about our responses.

Self-Administered.

In the past, most **self-administered questionnaires** were either handed out and sent home or mailed; however, the advent of technology allows us to collect data in a self-administered questionnaire via the Internet. Macias et al. (2008) found that, on average, self-administered surveys via mail yielded a 42 percent response rate, via e-mail yielded a 30 percent response rate, and via fax yielded a 66 percent response rate. Mailing and allowing participants to take paper surveys home tends to decrease the response rate. In other words, the number of individuals who complete and return the surveys is consistently lower than if we had used researcher-administered questionnaires, regardless of the specific means of self-administration. For example, imagine that you are studying how stress impacts college student communication with roommates and you are using a longitudinal design. In the past, you might have sent home a packet with a questionnaire for both a student and her roommate to complete and return to the communication department. What are the odds that the surveys will be returned? More than likely, they will be excavated at the end of the semester, when the student cleans out the backseat of her vehicle before returning home for break. That will affect the outcome of your survey and diminish your response rate. Some researchers provide incentives to increase response rate. What incentives motivate you to respond to a survey request? Scholars may use extra credit, money, and/or gift cards to entice you to participate in their study and thus to increase their response rate. Sometimes, incentives appeal to some groups more than others and therefore can call into question the representativeness of the sample.

In their study on intensive care unit communication between physicians and nurses, Manojlovich, Antonakos, and Ronis (2012) were interested in communication's impact on patient outcomes. One part of their research design distributed surveys to 866 registered nurses; they collected 462, a response rate of 53.3 percent. Pretty good based on our discussion above. However, it is important to recognize that we don't know why the other 46.7 percent chose not to participate.

researcher-administered questionnaires
A researcher is present when a participant completes a survey.

relf-administered questionnaires
Surveys that are completed individually, with no researchers or other people present.

There may be something consistent about almost half of those approached to participate that then calls the generalizability of the findings into question.

A key advantage to self-administered questionnaires over researcher-administered questionnaires is that individuals completing the survey tend to be more honest in their answers as neither researchers nor others are present. This protects an individual's sense of privacy, ensuring that their data is anonymous. However, one of the trade-offs you make in self-administered questionnaires is that researchers are not present to answer any questions that may arise, so participants may guess at what you are asking them.

There are also pros and cons to conducting Web-based self-administered surveys. One large consideration for Web-based research is the representativeness of a sample that is able to access a questionnaire on the Web. There are still many people who don't have Internet access, or who are not comfortable with being on the Internet and thus might be less likely to complete a Web-based survey. Some research suggests that response rates for Web surveys are low, relative to other methods such as paper questionnaires (Couper & Miller, 2008). You can maximize representation of your sample by offering alternative modes of administration (Web and paper), but research suggests this also does not positively affect response rates (Couper & Miller, 2008). On the other hand, if your population is technologically savvy, a Web-based survey might be more attractive to them, and it is easier for you to work with since the data is already entered into a database ready for your analysis.

Interviews.   When the researcher asks the study participant the survey questions and records the responses, this is called an **interview**, and the researcher is called an *interviewer*. Interviewing can take place in person or over the phone. The survey instrument used in an interview is often called an *interview guide*, *interview protocol*, or *survey*. Essentially, what we are talking about here is a *quantitative* survey methodology, which differs from qualitative interviewing (which we cover in Chapter 14), and as such, utilizes a different set of rules. Macias and colleagues (2008) found that interviews conducted in person yielded on average a 79 percent response rate, the highest of all the methods they studied, and telephone interviews yielded a 61 percent response rate on average.

The first concern in this type of survey is the validity of interview data. Here, the validity of the data depends highly on how participants view the interviewer, as well as how effectively the interviewer manages the interaction. It is important to be capable of recording participants' answers unobtrusively, as well as knowing how to expand a person's answer with additional questions—also known as probing and clarifying.

The key to good quality interviews is the skill and training of the interviewers. There are, in fact, several validity threats related to interviewer issues. Interviewers can inadvertently create a personal attribute effect (when characteristics of the researcher—gender, for example—influences people's behavior) or unintentional expectancy effect (by influencing participants by letting them know the behaviors the interviewer desires, such as by smiling or frowning). When conducting an interview, it's important that you don't predispose a participant to answer in some set manner. When you write your questionnaire or survey protocol,

interview
A research practice with individual participants, or groups of participants, to obtain responses to survey questions by direct questioning.

disguise your questions so the respondent does not continually try to outguess you or anticipate the answer you want. Unskilled interviewers can damage the validity of a well-designed survey. They can bias participants' responses, they may record responses incorrectly, and they can misrepresent the goals and questions of the survey. All of these create problems with the validity of the research at hand. Often, these types of interviews are conducted by multiple interviewers; therefore, it is necessary that all interviewers are carefully trained to follow a written protocol, which details what questions will be asked in what order and how the entire interview will be conducted. Interviewers should be knowledgeable about the research, familiar with the interview questions, practice interviewing, and be skilled at building rapport with participants.

It is important that an interview gets off to the right start. Most people decide within the first few seconds whether they are willing to participate; therefore, the tone of the initial meeting and greeting with the researcher sets the tone for the rest of the interview process. A good interview should begin when the researchers introduce themselves to potential participants and identify the research entity they represent. They should identify the general research topic, explain any selection criteria for the study, and explain the time commitment participants must make. Finally, their role in the introduction of the interview is to convince the participant that his or her contribution is important to the research.

Interviews can be conducted either face-to-face or via telephone. We suspect future textbooks will have to consider survey-designed interviews that will be conducted via instant messaging, text messaging, and other similar electronic methods. The beauty of a face-to-face interview is that it provides nonverbal data and demographic information; however, we sacrifice time, expense, and a decrease in privacy and anonymity. As Opdenakker (2006, para. 3) points out, "Face-to-face interviews allow synchronous communication of time and place." As you have seen throughout this text, there is no perfect design; there is always some trade-off. That is true of telephone interviews, too! Using a telephone interview structure is less costly and time consuming and simultaneously increases privacy and anonymity; however, it sacrifices nonverbal data that cannot be collected. Yet, it has the added advantage of providing the opportunity to interview people over vast geographic distances. Telephone interviews can be difficult. A relatively new barrier to collecting data via the telephone is the "Do Not Call" list. This is a national registry where individuals can request to have their number listed, so solicitors and telemarketers are prohibited from calling. This severely limits the proportion of the population who is available via telephone, which brings the representativeness of a random telephone sample into question. An additional barrier to collecting data via the phone is that it is easy for individuals to make an excuse, avoid the call (thanks to caller ID), or even hang up in the middle of an interview. In addition, since cell phone numbers are typically not available via traditional directories, researchers must make additional effort to obtain a good cross-section of all numbers. However, telephone interviews are advantageous in that they do allow for "synchronous communication of time and asynchronous communication of place" (Opdenakker, 2006, para. 3).

There are both advantages and disadvantages to using interviews (researcher asking the questions and recording the answers) in place of questionnaires (in which participants fill out the instrument themselves). Interviews usually have a higher response rate than questionnaires. This is particularly true of self-administered questionnaires when the researcher is not present while the questionnaire is being completed. Another benefit of interviews, when compared to traditional survey design, is that you can minimize the number of "don't know" responses. The facilitator or interviewer can use a probe, asking the question in a different way or allowing the respondent to provide additional detail concerning their answer. Interviews also allow us to guard against misunderstandings. The interviewer or facilitator can clarify what she is asking. This provides more flexibility to your design, allowing for a deeper understanding.

In addition to recording verbal data when interviewing, an important advantage is that the interviewer can observe, as well as ask questions. Things such as race, age, and nonverbal communication cues can all be noted by the interviewer.

One example of face-to-face interviewing is the use of the Oral History Interview (OHI; Buehlman & Gottman, 1996; Buehlman, Gottman, & Katz, 1992; Krokoff, 1984). The OHI provides a useful tool for investigating perceptions about marriage as evidenced by how the couple communicates about their marital experience. The OHI is a structured interview that asks couples a series of open-ended questions about their relationship story; that is, the couple's dating and marital history, their philosophy of marriage, and how their marriage has changed over time (Buehlman & Gottman, 1996).

As a graduate student, interviewing for an oral history relational study, Heather Powell Gallardo interviewed a college-age dating couple using the OHI. As she interviewed this particular couple, their answers didn't seem to add up. They answered the questions, but there was something strange about the way they acted. After talking with another research assistant at the lab, who had watched the interview from the control room, she called the director of the study and let him know the concerns. When asked later, the couple admitted that they had never been in a relationship and just participated for the incentive (extra credit), even though there were alternative ways to earn the same incentive. Had she just had them fill out a self-administered questionnaire, it is unlikely she would have discovered their cheating, negatively impacting the validity of the study.

Thus far, we have detailed the strengths of interviewing over questionnaire survey techniques; however, interviewing is not without disadvantages. One major drawback to interviewing is that it can be very expensive and time intensive. While time and expense can be overcome, a more substantial problem with interviews is that they may be subject to problems associated with social desirability. Remember social desirability is the idea that we may fudge our answers to present ourselves in a positive light. As such, participants are often inclined to provide answers they think we want to hear—regardless of whether they are true. Face-to-face interviews are most affected by social desirability compared to other methodological options available to use. Some argue that interviewers, through the use of rapport, try to increase honest answers, whereas others argue that social desirability is still a major concern. In any case, while surveys provide at least some sense of anonymity, having to actually disclose information to a live person—whether face to face or over the phone—may impact social desirability effects.

When interviewing, we need to be certain that the interviewing is conducted in a consistent manner each time, regardless of who is interviewing the participants. Remember survey-designed interviews follow a detailed protocol and, while it is necessary to probe respondents for more complete answers, interviewers must follow the protocol consistently. This differs from qualitative interviewing techniques.

Relative Pros/Cons of Different Survey Methods

Table 10.1. The Three Main Methods of Administering Surveys

Mail Surveys (Self-Administered)		
When to Use	**Pros**	**Cons**
When you want to save money; When self-selection bias and low response rate are not problems; When you want to show participants something; When you don't have many/any open-ended questions; When the questions will be self-explanatory and easy to understand; When you have a large population so you can mail out many surveys (to account for low response rates); When you have ample time to conduct survey (to wait for questionnaires to be returned).	It is relatively inexpensive; It is relatively easy to do because you don't need trained interviewers to conduct the surveys.	Mail surveys generally have very low response rates (few people send them back). As a rule of thumb, for most mail surveys, you can expect a response rate anywhere from 2%–30%. This low response rate can cause: Bias (Do the people who returned the surveys have the same attitudes as those who didn't? Many researchers would say "no.") Invalid responses, because of too few people answering the questions; An inability to reach conclusions from the study because of the low return. It takes a long time to conduct a mail study, because you must allow time for mailing of materials and waiting for the return of the materials. Sometimes, you can wait weeks for the return of the surveys. Mail surveys do not allow you to "screen out" respondents. You are at the mercy of whoever opens the envelope and sends back the survey. You can ask for "only males between the ages of 18–24" to answer the survey. However, you have no control that this is who will actually do so.

How to Conduct Mail Surveys:

1. Define your population and sampling frame. Obtain a representative sampling frame.

2. Determine your desired sample size.

3. Determine your expected response rate (look at previous research or conduct a pilot study). From this, determine how many questionnaires you'll need to mail out. Be sure to account for wrong addresses and people who don't qualify for the study, as well as people who simply refuse or decline to participate.

4. Write your questionnaire. For a mail survey, all instructions must be "idiot proof"—crystal clear. The shorter the survey, the better your response rate will be.

5. Write a cover letter to be mailed with the survey. This letter should explain the purpose of the survey. It should ask for the respondent's assistance in this study. Think of a good reason why the person should help you. The more motivation you can give the respondents, the greater your response rate will be.

(Continued)

6. Make sure all your materials look as professional as possible. Letters on letterhead and envelopes with letterhead help response rates.

7. Always enclose a self-addressed, stamped envelope for return of questionnaire. No respondent is going to use his or her own money to return a survey to you. Have the envelope contents weighed at the post office to ensure that you have enclosed enough postage. Sending surveys out with "Postage Due" will not help your response rate.

8. Consider enclosing some type of incentive for filling out the survey: a $2 bill enclosed in each envelope works well. A promise to send $10–$25 when completed questionnaire is received also helps, but that requires the respondent to attach his or her name to the survey, which some are reluctant to do. Another incentive for some studies is to offer respondents a copy of the results.

9. Wait two weeks after mailing of materials. If not enough materials have been returned, do a second mailing to get more surveys.

10. Analyze the results.

Web-Based Surveys (Self-Administered)		
When to Use	**Pros**	**Cons**
When you want to save money; When self-selection bias and low response rate are not problems; When you want to show participants something that you can reproduce digitally; When you don't have many/any open-ended questions; When the questions will be self-explanatory and easy to understand; When you have a large population so you can invite many potential participants (to account for low response rates); When you are in a relative hurry, since participants can fill out a survey online and you get the results instantly.	It is relatively inexpensive; It is relatively easy to do because you don't need trained interviewers to conduct the surveys; Data is already entered and ready to be analyzed.	Web surveys have lower response rates than telephone or researcher-administered surveys. This lower response rate can cause: Bias (Do the people who returned the surveys have the same attitudes as those who didn't? Many researchers would say "no."). Invalid responses, because of too few people answering the questions; An inability to reach conclusions from the study because of the low return. Web surveys do not allow you to guarantee who actually answers the survey.

How to Conduct Web-based Surveys:

1. Define your population and sampling frame. Obtain a representative sampling frame.

2. Determine your desired sample size.

3. Determine your expected response rate (look at previous research or conduct a pilot study). From this, determine how many participants you'll need to invite. Be sure to account for wrong contact information and people who don't qualify for the study, as well as people who simply refuse or decline to participate.

4. Write your questionnaire and put it online, using a survey tool such as SurveyShare, Survey Monkey, or Zoomerang. All instructions must be "idiot proof"—crystal clear. The shorter the survey, the better your response rate will be.

5. Find a good way to invite participants, either in person or written. Personal invitations are more effective than cold mailings. When you invite them, explain the purpose of the survey. It should ask for the respondent's assistance in this study. Think of a good reason why the person should help you. The more motivation you can give the respondents, the greater your response rate will be.

6. Make sure all your materials look as professional as possible. Letters on letterhead and envelopes with letterhead help response rates.

7. Consider offering some type of incentive for filling out survey, but make sure that participants understand that an incentive mailed to them does not mean that you can connect their responses to their name.

8. Wait two weeks after inviting participants. If not enough surveys have been filled out, send a second invitation to get more surveys.

9. Analyze the results.

Telephone Surveys (Interviews)		
When to Use	**Pros**	**Cons**
When you want a more random, generalizable sample; When you have more money to spend (than for mail surveys); When you need to probe open-ended (discussion) questions; When you want to complete a large number of interviews in a relatively short period of time; When you want to project the sample to the population; When you have nothing to show respondent/nothing he or she has to see; When you need to "screen for" whom you want to interview.	Sample is more reliable, less problem with bias; Usually fairly high response rates; Can usually be done in a fairly short period of time; Responses are better because interviewers can probe for clarity and complete responses; Allows you to "screen" respondents/ determine if you do or do not want to talk to a respondent.	More expensive; Ideally, requires trained interviewers.

How to do Telephone Surveys:

1. Based on your RQ or H, determine who you want to talk to—determine if you want to set any special requirements (such as age, sex, product usage).

2. Find a sampling frame and obtain your sample.

3. Determine your expected response rate (look at previous research or conduct a pilot study). From this, determine how many people you'll need to call. Be sure to account for wrong phone numbers and people who don't qualify for the study, as well as people who simply refuse or decline to participate.

4. Write survey.

5. Determine who will do the interviewing.

6. Train interviewers (if you are not doing all the data collection yourself).

7. Conduct interviews. Make sure that you make calls at all times of day, at all days of week, to eliminate bias.

8. Analyze the results.

Here's a sample survey questionnaire with the brochure we used to explain the study to potential participants. It's designed to be a self-administered survey and was provided to participants over the Internet via a Web-based service called Survey Share. Participants were recruited via network sampling through students in a research methods class, and to address concerns about coercion, potential participants had to be assured that their participation or non-participation would not affect the student's grade.

"Study of Mental Health Attitudes, Knowledge, and Beliefs"
INFORMATION FOR POTENTIAL STUDY PARTICIPANTS

PROJECT OBJECTIVES

The "Study of Mental Health Attitudes, Knowledge, and Beliefs" project is designed to help us understand what the general public knows, thinks, and believes about mental healthcare patients and providers. The information we learn from this study will be used for research to help mental health providers understand how to most effectively communicate with patients and the general public.

THE RESEARCHERS

The data will be collected and analyzed by researchers at the University of North Carolina at Charlotte.

PARTICIPATION

For this research, we are inviting you to fill out an online survey. This should take no more than 15 minutes of your time. We will be asking you questions about what you think, believe, and know about mental illness.

PAYMENT AND STUDY TERMINATION

You will not be paid for filling out the survey. However, the Research Assistant student recruiting you will receive course credit for recruiting you. Once you have opened the Web page and submitted the ID number of the student recruiting you, the student has received credit, regardless of whether you continue filling out the survey.

Participation in this study is completely voluntary. Once you are taking part in the study, you can terminate your participation at any time.

CONFIDENTIALITY

The results of this study may be published. However, since your name will not be input anywhere on the survey, there is no way that identifying information about you would be included. We are bound by professional confidentiality agreements.

TO PARTICIPATE

If you are interested in participating in this study, please go to the following website: **http://www .surveyshare.com/survey/take/?sid=48210**

Please make a note of the ID number of the student who recruited you so he or she will get credit for your participation:

Once you are on the Web site, simply follow the instructions.

FOR MORE INFORMATION ABOUT THIS RESEARCH PROJECT, PLEASE FEEL FREE TO CONTACT:

DR. CHRISTINE DAVIS, DEPT. OF COMMUNICATION STUDIES, UNC–CHARLOTTE

Here's the survey for this same project. The Likert scale included in the questionnaire was derived from a validated, reliable scale of mental health literacy (Epps et al., 2007; Massey et al., 2008). Note the skip patterns in questions 15, 21, and 22, in which participants are instructed to only answer those questions if they are currently receiving mental health services. Also note the skip pattern in Q. 40, in which participants are told that if they have never received mental health services to skip to Q. 43. The consent form is part of the survey, and participants are told that if they fill out the survey, consent is presumed to be given.

**Thank you for your interest in participating in this study.
To continue, you MUST be 18 years old!!!!!**

Please give us the code number of the student who recruited you for this project: _____. The student has now been given credit for this assignment regardless of whether you continue with the survey.

Answering these questions should take you about 15 minutes. If you decide not to answer them, that's okay. Since you will not write your name anywhere on the survey, your responses will be completely confidential and anonymous. We will not know what you said, or even whether you filled out a survey.

Informed Consent Information:

The purpose of this study is to understand the attitudes, knowledge, and beliefs people have toward mental illness. The Primary Investigator (PI) of this project is Dr. Christine S. Davis, Dept. of Communication Studies at the University of North Carolina at Charlotte. If you have any questions or concerns, feel free to contact her at: 704-687-6638 or ctsdavis@email.uncc.edu

You may participate in this study if you are at least 18 years old. You will be asked to fill out an anonymous survey to indicate your agreement with statements concerning your attitudes, knowledge, and beliefs about mental illness. The survey should take no longer than 15 minutes to complete.

The project may involve risks that are not currently known. However, there are no known risks or benefits to study participants. Your information will be anonymous. Since the instructor, study PI, or the student who recruited you for this study will not know who is filling out the survey and who is not, the student's grade will not be affected by your either filling it out or not. There is a benefit to society in that the knowledge we are gathering will help us learn how to develop more effective healthcare messages.

If you choose not to fill out the survey, that is okay. By your entering the student's ID # at the beginning of this Web page, the student who recruited you has already been given credit, regardless of whether you continue with the survey. You are a volunteer. The decision to participate in this study is completely up to you. If you decide to fill out the survey, you may stop at any time. All data collected by the investigator will not contain any information that will link the data back to you or your participation in this study. The following steps will be taken to ensure this anonymity: Your name will never be entered on any of the survey materials.

UNC Charlotte wants to make sure that you are treated in a fair and respectful manner. Contact the university's Research Compliance Office (704-123-9999) if you have questions about how you are treated as a study participant. If you have any questions about the actual project or study, please contact Dr. Christine Davis, 704-123-9999, ctsdavis@email.uncc.edu

By continuing and filling out the survey, you are agreeing with the following statement: I have read the information in this consent form. I have had the chance to call or email the study PI with any questions about this study, and if I have, those questions have been answered to my satisfaction. I am at least 18 years of age, and I agree to participate in this research project. I understand that I can call or email the study PI to request a copy of this consent information.

Thank you for your participation!

1. Where do you get (or have you gotten) any information you have about mental health or mental illness?

[CHECK ALL THAT APPLY]

Case manager/family support coordinator	
Child welfare (DCF) worker	
Juvenile justice (DJJ) worker	
School: teacher, social worker, counselor, psychologist, other	
Counselor/therapist/social worker/psychologist/psychiatrist	
Medical doctor/pediatrician/nurse/brochures or other materials from my doctor/health-care provider/doctor's office	
Clergy members (pastor, priest, rabbi, imam, etc.)	
Family members	
Friends/neighbors/people I know socially/coworkers	
Human resources people at my job	
Media: television/movies/magazines/newspapers	
Internet	
From my own (or my child's) personal experiences	
Trainings/workshops for parents of children with mental, emotional, and behavioral disorders	
Other [PLEASE WRITE IN]	

The following questions are about your opinion, beliefs, and knowledge about mental health and about mental healthcare services. If you have never received mental health-care services (or do not currently receive any mental health-care services), please answer how you THINK you would feel if you ever had to receive mental health-care services.

When you're thinking of mental health-care providers and services, please think of counselors, therapists, psychologists, psychiatrists, social workers, school guidance counselors or psychologists, and school special education teachers or special education counselors.

PLEASE PUT AN "X" IN THE BOX THAT INDICATES YOUR LEVEL OF AGREEMENT WITH EACH OF THE FOLLOWING STATEMENTS:

	Agree Strongly	Agree Somewhat	Neither Agree nor Disagree	Disagree Somewhat	Disagree Strongly
2. I am capable of solving my problems.					
3. Any mental, emotional, and/or behavioral problems I may have can be successfully treated.					
4. I can control my behavior.					
5. Mental health treatments I may need to have are under my control.					
6. I have the right to receive any mental health *testing* I need (psychological, mental, or physical, etc.).					
7. I have the right to ask for mental health care help when I need it.					
8. I have the right to ask for all available mental health services in the community that I need.					
9. I have the right to *choose* what mental health services I will have.					
10. Having mental, emotional, and/or behavioral problems would *not* make me any less valuable to society.					
11. Mental, emotional, and/or behavioral problems in children or adolescents are ILLNESSES (not discipline issues).					
12. People with emotional, mental, and/or behavioral problems are still like everyone else.					
13. My opinions are important, regardless of any emotional, mental, and/ or behavioral problems I may have.					
14. Normal people can be mentally ill.					
15. [ANSWER IF YOU ARE CURRENTLY RECEIVING MENTAL HEALTH SERVICES] I understand any changes my mental health-care providers want me to make.					

(Continued)

	Agree Strongly	Agree Somewhat	Neither Agree nor Disagree	Disagree Somewhat	Disagree Strongly
16. I know what mental health resources and services are available for me if I need them.					
17. I know how to access all the mental health resources, services, and treatments available for me that I might need.					
18. I understand both the risks and the benefits of the alternative mental health-care treatments.					
19. I understand how to make an appointment with a mental health-care provider if I need to.					
20. I understand how to obtain mental health-care information I may need.					
21. [ANSWER IF YOU ARE CURRENTLY RECEIVING MENTAL HEALTH SERVICES] I understand how to juggle my mental health-care provider appointments and my other activities.					
22. [ANSWER IF YOU ARE CURRENTLY RECEIVING MENTAL HEALTH SERVICES] I understand how to fit my mental health-care treatments into my life.					
23. If necessary, I would be able to decide when I need to get a second opinion on my mental health care.					
24. If necessary, I would be able to decide whether the mental health-care treatments or services provided to me have worked well enough.					
25. I am able to decide when I need mental health help, assistance, or services.					
26. I am able to know when I need to make mental, emotional, and/or behavioral changes in my life.					
27. If necessary, I would be capable of asking my mental health-care providers questions.					
28. If necessary, I would be capable of expressing concerns to my mental health-care providers.					

	Agree Strongly	Agree Somewhat	Neither Agree nor Disagree	Disagree Somewhat	Disagree Strongly
29. If necessary, I would be capable of negotiating with my mental health-care providers to reach treatment or service solutions that are best for everyone.					
30. If necessary, I would be capable of asking for mental health-care help, services, treatments, and resources, in a way that gets me what I need.					

The following questions are for classification purposes:

31. What is your gender?
    a. Female
    b. Male

32. What is your race?
    a. American Indian or Native American
    b. Another race _____
    c. Asian or Pacific Islander
    d. Black or African American
    e. Multiracial _____
    f. White

33. Are you Hispanic?
    a. No
    b. Yes

34. What is your marital status?
    a. Divorced
    b. Living as married
    c. Married
    d. Never married
    e. Separated
    f. Widowed

35. What is the highest education level you have completed?
    a. Less than high school
    b. High school graduate or GED
    c. Vocational, technical, trade, or business school beyond the high school level
    d. Some college, but no degree
    e. Associate or Bachelor's degree
    f. Some graduate school
    g. Master's degree or higher
    h. Other (Please specify) _____

36. What best describes your work, school, or volunteer situation over the past year?
    a. Employed full time
    b. Employed part time
    c. Homemaker
    d. In the armed forces
    e. Other (e.g., volunteer worker, disabled) _____
    f. Resident of institution
    g. Retired
    h. Student
    i. Unemployed, looking for work
    j. Unemployed, on lay-off from job

37. Your health insurance is provided by:
    a. None
    b. Medicaid
    c. Medicare
    d. Private insurance (insurance through employer or purchase own)
    e. School insurance
    f. Other [WRITE IN] _____
    g. Don't know

38. Into which of the following age categories do you fall?
    a. 18–24
    b. 25–34
    c. 35–44
    d. 45–54
    e. 55–64
    f. 65+
    g. No answer

39. What mental health diagnoses have you ever been given?
    a. None
    b. Adjustment Disorder
    c. ADHD
    d. Depression
    e. Disruptive Disorder
    f. Other major psychiatric disorder
    g. Other: _____

40. In your entire life, how many years total have you received mental health-care services?
    a. Never received mental healthcare services (SKIP TO Q. 43)
    b. Less than one
    c. 1–4
    d. 5–9
    e. 10–14
    f. 15–19
    g. 20+

41. Are you receiving mental health-care services currently?
    a. Yes
    b. No

42. From whom have you ever received mental health-care services?
    a. Counselor
    b. Therapist
    c. Psychologist
    d. Psychiatrist
    e. Social worker
    f. School guidance counselor or psychologist
    g. School special education teacher or special education counselors
    h. Other: _____

43. Have you or anyone in your family ever experienced any of the following?

	Yes	No
a. Crime convictions	____	____
b. Physical abuse/violence	____	____
c. Psychiatric hospitalization	____	____
d. Running away	____	____
e. Sexual abuse	____	____
f. Substance abuse	____	____
g. Suicide attempts	____	____

So What?

Surveys will continue to be popular research tools; technology is contributing to their prevalence in assessing many different types of research questions and hypotheses, and there are many uses and advantages to this research method. We have examined survey design and many considerations a scholar must take into account when designing a questionnaire. You should know the difference between a cross-sectional and longitudinal design and when each is the appropriate study design. Survey-designed interviews have an important function in the assessment of many communication issues. Finally, we compared the uses, advantages, and disadvantages of using interviews and self-administered questionnaires. All methods and procedures have pros and cons and appropriate and inappropriate uses. The bottom line is—your research question or hypothesis drives what you do and how you do it. We will continue to revisit that notion in upcoming chapters.

Glossary

Cohort study
A study in which responses from specific subgroups of a population are identified and compared over time.

Cross-sectional survey
A survey design that describes the characteristics of a sample representing a population at one point in time.

Evaluation research
Research that is designed to assess the effectiveness of programs or products during development or after their completion.

Funnel format
A type of question format in which questions begin with broad, open-ended questions followed by narrow, more closed-ended questions.

Interview
A research practice with individual participants, or groups of participants, to obtain responses to survey questions by direct questioning.

Inverted funnel format
A type of question format that generally begins with more closed-ended, narrow questions moving throughout the questionnaire to the most open ended and broad questions.

Longitudinal survey design
A survey design that gathers data from respondents at several points in time.

Market research
Research that is designed to study consumer behavior.

Panel study
A study in which a sample is drawn from a population or universe and those same people or objects are measured at multiple points in time.

Political polls
One of the most common and readily available uses of surveys. They provide a detailed account of who is leading whom in the run for a particular office during an election.

Researcher-administered questionnaires
A researcher is present when a participant completes a survey.

Self-administered questionnaires
Surveys that are completed individually, with no researchers or other people present.

Survey design
A method of asking research participants questions that provides researchers with a method of information gathering from a large number of people over a relatively short period of time.

Trend study
Measurement occurs at two or more points in time, from different samples selected from the same population. This type of study is designed to identify changes or trends in people's beliefs about a variable of interest.

Tunnel format
A type of question format in which questions tend to be similar in terms of breadth and depth throughout a questionnaire. Questions are organized by similarity and vary little in terms of depth.

References

Atkin, C. K., & Freimuth, v. (2000). Formative evaluation research in campaign design. In R. E. Rice & C. K. Atkin (Eds.), *Public communication campaigns* (pp. 125–145). Thousand Oaks, CA: Sage.

Botta, R. A., & Dumlao, R. (2002). How do conflict and communication patterns between fathers and daughters contribute to or offset eating disorders? *Health Communication, 14*(2), 199–219.

Buehlman, K. T., & Gottman, J. M. (1996). *The oral history interview and the oral history coding system.* Mahwah, NJ: Erlbaum.

Buehlman, K. T., Gottman, J. M., & Katz, L. F. (1992). How a couple views their past predicts their future: Predicting divorce from an oral history interview. *Journal of Family Psychology, 5,* 295–318.

Carlsen, F. L. (Ed.). (2010). *Harris Michigan industrial directory.* Austin, TX: Harrisinfosource.

Center, A. H., & Broom, G. M. (1983). Evaluation research. *Public Relations Quarterly, 28*(3), 1–3.

Couper, M. P., & Miller, P. v. (2008). Web survey methods: Introduction. *Public Opinion Quarterly, 72*(5), 831–835.

Epps, C. S., Armstrong, M., Davis, C. S., Massey, T. O., McNeish, R., & Smith, R. B. (2007). *Development and testing of an instrument to measure mental health literacy*. Tampa, FL: Louis de la Parte Florida Mental Health Institute. University of South Florida.

Krokoff, L. (1984). The anatomy of blue-collar marriages (Doctoral dissertation, University of Illinois at Urbana-Champaign, 1984). *Dissertation Abstracts International*.

Lachlan, K.A., Spence, P.R., & Nelson, L. (2010). Gender differences in psychological responses to crisis news: The case of the I-35 collapse. *Communication Research Reports, 27* (1), 38–48.

Lim, V. K. G., & Teo, T. S. H. (2009). Mind your E-manners: Impact of cyber incivility on employees' work attitude and behavior. *Information & Management, 46*, 419–425.

Macias, W., Springston, J. K., Lariscy, R. A. W., & Neustifer, B. (2008). A 13-year content analysis of survey methodology in communication related journals. *Journal of Current Issues and Research in Advertising, 30*(1), 79–94.

Manojlovich, M., Antonakos, C. L., & Ronis, D. L. (2012). Intensive care units, communication between nurses and physicians, and patients' outcomes. *American Journal of Critical Care, 18*, 21–30.

Massey, O. T., Davis, C. S., Smith, R. B., Armstrong, M., & Vergon, K. S. (2008). *Refinement of an instrument to measure mental health literacy among caregivers and providers and a qualitative examination of interventions to enhance mental health literacy*. Tampa, FL: Louis de la Parte Florida Mental Health Institute. University of South Florida.

McCroskey, J. E. (1982). Oral communication apprehension: A reconceptualization. In M. Burgoon (Ed.), *Communication yearbook* (Volume 6, pp. 136–170). Beverly Hills: Sage.

Opdenakker, R. (2006). Advantages and disadvantages of four interview techniques in qualitative research. *Forum Qualitative Sozialforschung/Forum: Qualitative Social Research, 7*(4) <Electronic version>. Retrieved March 18, 2009, from http://www.qualitativeresearch.net/index.php/fqs/article/view/175/392

The Quotations Page. (n.d.). Retrieved June 15, 2009, from http://www.quotationspage.com/quote/706.html

The Quote Garden. (n.d.). Retrieved June 15, 2009, from http://www.quotegarden.com/tv-turnoff-week.html

Salmon, C. T., Park, H. S., & Wrigley, B. J. (2003). Optimistic bias and perceptions of bioterrorism in Michigan corporate spokespersons, Fall 2001. *Journal of Health Communication, 8*, 130–143.

Segrin, C., & Flora, J. (2000). Poor social skills are a vulnerability factor in the development of psychosocial problems. *Human Communication Research, 26*, 489–514.

QUANTITATIVE ANALYSIS OF TEXT AND WORDS: CONTENT AND INTERACTION ANALYSIS

11

CHAPTER OUTLINE

KEY TERMS

Chance agreement
Cluster sampling
Content analysis
Context units
Distributional structure

Interactive structure
Inter-coder reliability
Random sampling
Recording units
Sampling units

Scott's Pi
Sequential structure
Stratified sampling
Systematic sampling
Unitizing

CHAPTER OBJECTIVES

1. To understand what content analysis is and when it should be used
2. To understand how to select and unitize content
3. To understand how to train coders
4. To know how to analyze and interpret content analysis data

▼ # Exploring Quantitative Content Analysis

The February 11, 2006, edition of *The Charlotte Observer* (Germain, 2006) reported on a study of gender balance in top-grossing G-rated films from 1990 to 2004. The researchers, sponsored by the advocacy group Dads & Daughters, reported that male characters outnumbered females 3 to 1, with 28 percent of speaking characters being female and 17 percent of people in crowd scenes being female. What type of research did they conduct to determine this imbalance? A quantitative content analysis.

To this point, we have discussed measuring and evaluating human behavior using quantitative techniques such as surveys and experiments. We have discussed the ethics associated with conducting research involving human subjects, ensuring good measurement of human behavior, appropriate sampling techniques, and making sense of self-report data, among others. Communication researchers may be interested in other forms of data, however, that may not be derived from the reports or testing of research participants. While survey data can be informative, sometimes it's not appropriate given the research question or hypothesis—sometimes communication researchers would rather observe behaviors and make judgments about their observations independent of participant feedback. Still other times, communication researchers may be concerned with the nature of messages themselves, as opposed to how certain subjects may react to them.

content analysis
A quantitative methodology that allows researchers to quantify content, including the content of participant responses or the content of media texts.

In either of these instances, quantitative **content analysis** may be an appropriate analytic technique. As a methodology, content analysis allows researchers to quantify content—whether that means the content of participant responses, or the content of media texts. Quantifying the nature of content can answer numerous questions relevant to making sense of meaning.

Why Analyze Content?

There are two major circumstances under which it might make sense to conduct a content analysis. The first of these is most closely associated with mass media research. There is a long history in media research of attempting to quantify the nature of media content in terms of news themes, information presented, content that some may consider problematic, and so on. But why would someone want to make quantitative assessments of content?

Media researchers often talk about the *three-legged stool* of media effects research; the legs represent surveys, experiments, and content analysis. Of course, we have plenty of research linking media use with particular outcomes. Some have argued that violent television may make people more aggressive, that the consumption of political news leads to the polarization of attitudes, or that watching sexualized content may change one's opinions of one's partners. Experimental and survey media research has even identified particular contexts that may make people more or less susceptible to these effects. Repeated violence may lead to desensitization toward aggression, for example, while sexual content may be especially worrisome when combined with issues of power or dominance. One can easily think of anecdotal examples of this kind of content, but the social relevance of these findings can be ascertained only by answering the following question: "Exactly how often does this content really appear?" If the kind of content that engenders a specific effect seldom occurs, then it may not be relevant to our understanding of media and its impact on society. By contrast, if it occurs with great frequency, then we may be able to establish a case for concern.

For the media effects researcher, this is where content analysis comes in: by providing evidence that media content shown to have effects on audiences in the lab exists in the real world. Take for example the National Television Violence Study (NTVS) (Wilson et al., 1997). Wilson and colleagues assembled a thorough review of the experimental research on television violence, and identified numerous contextual features that mitigate the impact of violent content on aggressive attitudes and behaviors. These included the demographic attributes of perpetrators and victims, whether violence was rewarded or punished, whether it was repetitive in nature, whether there were weapons involved, and whether there were representations of blood and gore (just to name a few). They also came up with an operational definition of what constituted an act of violence, and looked at how often violent interactions took place and if any of these contextual features were commonplace. In analyzing thousands of hours of television content, they found that violence was fairly commonplace on network and basic cable, and that the types of violence shown to be problematic in experimental research were also fairly common. Thus, they showed evidence that the content found troublesome in the laboratory was readily available. As an aside, given the rigorous unitizing, sampling, and coding techniques they used, the NTVS is often held up as the *gold standard* in content analytic media research.

Content Analysis Versus Interaction Analysis

Content analysis makes sense in another context too. Instead of analyzing media messages, you may want to record the behaviors or interactions of participants and analyze the content. This type of analysis—often called interaction analysis—uses techniques similar to those of traditional content analyses, but looks instead at recordings of individuals or groups and how they may behave and exchange information. Interaction analysis is often used in conjunction with experimental research. While experimental procedures examining interpersonal interactions can produce data reflecting the feelings, attitudes, and opinions of the participants, having an unobtrusive measure of the nature of the interaction may also be very valuable to a researcher. In this way, communication researchers may be able to make quantitative assessments of both interpersonal interactions and group dynamics in ways that may get around the biases of the individual respondent.

In 2008, Stephens and Mottet conducted an experiment to test the effects of Web-based communication on training. They tested trainer-initiated interactions against trainee-initiated interactions in terms of their effect on instructional outcomes, including perceived credibility, goodwill, trust, vocal variety, competence, satisfaction, and learning. In order to measure the interactions (which served as the independent variable of their study), they conducted an interaction analysis. They operationalized two different levels (high and low) of interactivity with the two different groups controlling and initiating the interactivity (either the trainer or the trainee). Thus, they measured four conditions (see p. 241): high trainer-controlled interactivity where the trainer asked the trainees to participate in polls during the training event, low trainer-controlled interactivity where there was no request for trainee participation, high trainee-controlled interactivity where trainees were allowed to chat with one another prior to the Web conference, and low trainee-controlled interactivity where trainees did not chat with one another.

There are similar methodological considerations in both traditional content analysis and in interaction analysis. Both techniques involve the selection of content, unitizing, coding, and analysis. In either case, making quantitative assessments of the nature and frequency of a particular kind of content is the end goal. This chapter will outline some of the basic logic behind content analysis, and lay out the basic methodological procedures and considerations associated with this type of inquiry.

▼ # Content Structure

Distributional Structure

distributional structure
A type of content structure that deals with the number or frequency with which certain interactions take place in a certain timeframe.

Baxter and Babbie (2004) identify three basic types of content structure that can be elaborated on from content analysis. The first of these, **distributional structure**, deals with the incidence or frequency with which certain interactions take place in a certain timeframe. Smith, Lachlan, and colleagues (2003; 2004), for example, attempted to figure out how often acts of violence take place in popular video games. They sampled sixty popular video games (based on sales data across three leading home gaming platforms) and counted the number of times an act of violence took place. After adjusting for the ten-minute snippets of data they examined, they concluded that acts of aggression took place across their sample at a rate of *about thirteen acts of violence per hour on average—or more than three times* the frequency of violence on television found in the NTVS. This is an example of a statement concerning distributional structure; it answers the question of how often something happens.

Interactive Structure

interactive structure
A type of content structure that deals with the pattern of response types that may vary throughout an interaction.

Interactive structure, more applicable to interaction analysis, deals with the pattern of response types that may vary throughout an interaction. This type of analysis then becomes a case of analyzing who says what and to whom. By considering the nature of messages that are uttered, and considering who the senders and recipients of these messages are, the communication researcher can make numerous observations and claims about the relationships that are being established, reinforced, or undermined in a particular set of interactions.

Sequential Structure

Finally, there are questions of **sequential structure**. Typically, these types of questions have been associated with interaction analysis. They normally deal with an examination of the sequences of utterances, in order to make more sense of what is going on (Hirokawa, 1988). So, for example, examining an interpersonal exchange to evaluate how often a comment is followed by a slight, or how often a relational message is met with resistance, may be informative in painting a picture of the nature of the interaction. More recently, sequential analysis has found its way into traditional content analysis also. Lachlan and colleagues (2009) looked at the violence in professional wrestling telecasts, and were particularly concerned with the extent of violence in a given interaction. They used sequential analyses to determine that violence acts in this genre are almost always met with acts that are over-retributive in nature. As a result, fairly benign insults lead to full-scale bloodbaths in only a few exchanges, a pattern of violence, they claim, that is rather alarming. While nearly all wrestling viewers are aware that what they are watching is scripted, they argue that this pattern of over-retribution is troubling nonetheless.

sequential structure
A type of content structure that normally deals with an examination of the sequences of utterances in order to make more sense of what is going on.

• •

Content Analysis Logic　　　　　　　　　　▼

Content analysis, as a methodology, is unique in the degree to which the findings and the interpretation of those findings are related to the procedural decisions of the researcher (Krippendorf, 1980). This is because, to an extent, the researcher must *create* the framework for the data. The data are derived from a number of decisions the researcher must make concerning exactly what it is he or she wants to look at, where it might be found, and how it ought to be examined. The explicitness of these decisions and procedures must be clearly articulated in order for a reader to approach a content analysis with any sense of scientific scrutiny, as well as for anyone else who way wish to replicate the procedures in another context. Therefore, it is essential that the content analysis researcher make procedural decisions that make sense given the content under consideration and the questions that he wishes to answer.

As we walk through this decision-making process, it should become clear that content analysis is a different method than survey or experimental techniques. While other quantitative approaches have hard and fast rules regarding best procedures, the content analyst is often left to make judgment calls concerning exactly how to approach the content in question, what to look at, how to look at it, and how to make sense of the data. The first major issue that the content analyst must face, before proceeding any further, is the issue of what exactly it is that will be examined. This is a decision-making process called unitizing.

For example, interested in research on speech acts in computer-mediated communication, Carr, Schrok, and Dauterman (2012) analyzed status messages on Facebook. The abstract for their article explains:

A total of 204 status messages created by 46 participants were captured 3 times daily over 14 consecutive days. Content analysis of these data revealed that status messages were most frequently constructed with expressive speech acts, followed by assertives. Additionally, humor was integrated into almost 20% of these status messages. These findings demonstrate differences in how users express themselves in alternate media. Findings address implications for self-presentation in social networks and theoretical implications for computer-mediated communication research. (p. 176)

▼ Unitizing

unitizing
The process of deciding exactly what it is that should be observed.

Unitizing (Krippendorf, 1980) is the process of deciding exactly what it is that should be observed. This is not as easy as it seems. Are you primarily concerned with individual interactions? Individual scenes? Programs on the whole? Once you have made this determination, how do you define your units of analysis conceptually? What exactly defines a *scene*? Or an *interaction*? These are decisions the content analyst must consider carefully.

Sampling Units

sampling units
The units that are sampled from a larger population of content that you wish to examine.

The first unitizing decision that must be made by the content analyst is deciding upon **sampling units**. Sampling units are a determination of what type of content—in a broad sense—will be sampled or drawn from a population of similar content units. Let's take our wrestling example from above. Lachlan and colleagues (2009) wanted to look at violence in professional wrestling, so they decided that their sampling units would consist of episodes of *Monday Night Raw* and *WWE Smackdown*. While similar content could be found in other wrestling shows, they decided that these two shows were most representative of unedited, first-run wrestling content. They also decided that recording an intact season of each show would be a good idea, just as a snapshot of what was going on within the telecasts. To sum up the sampling unit, it is where you are going to go for your content.

Recording Units

recording units
The individual parts of a sampling unit the researcher is examining.

Recording units are a bit more complicated. According to Holsti (1969), recording units are the individual parts of a sampling unit that you may wish to quantify and analyze. Let's return to our wrestling example. Lachlan and colleagues (2009) decided to look at individual violent interactions in their analysis, in order to figure out whether violence escalated from interaction to interaction. To do this, they adopted the NTVS definition of a violent interaction, which is "any overt depiction of a credible threat of physical force or the actual use of such force intended to physically harm an animate being or group of beings. Violence also includes certain depictions of physically harmful consequences against an animate being/s that results from unseen violent means" (Smith et al., 1998, p. 30). Within each of their recording units (episodes of *Raw* and *Smackdown*), they identified individual violent interactions using this definition. They looked at each of these interactions to see what they contained in terms of context units.

Context Units

Context units are the types of content or contextual features that may appear in an individual recording unit. So, you may be able to identify a certain number of interactions that appear in a given sampling unit. You may then decide to look at the specific features of each of these interactions. These are known as context units.

Returning once again to our previous example, Lachlan and colleagues (2009) identified a number of context units within each of the recording units they identified. After identifying individual interactions as recording units, they then looked at each of these violent interactions and made a number of contextual judgments for each one. These included the number of acts of violence within each unit, the motive for violence, whether there were weapons and what types, and several others. The authors then combined their observations to make statements about the frequency with which violent actions occur (recording units) and the frequency with which violence escalated in terms of the number of acts committed from interaction to interaction (context units).

context units
The types of content or contextual features that may appear in an individual recording unit.

• •

Sampling   ▼

Like any quantitative procedure, issues of sampling become apparent when we are trying to figure out just how much we are going to examine and from where it will be drawn. As stated above, we talk about sampling units as the units that are sampled from a larger population of content that you wish to examine. Examining every issue of the *New York Times* would be a nearly impossible task; however, examining a sample of issues drawn from a particular timeframe may allow the content analyst to draw conclusions about the population in question, just as a sample of research participants may allow the experimentalist to draw conclusions about his or her population of interest. In other words, almost any research team would be overwhelmed by looking at an entire population of content, so content analysts, like behavioral researchers, almost always draw samples from larger populations of content.

Random Sampling

Random sampling involves the selection of a certain number of sampling units, at random, from the entire population of available sampling units. So in our *New York Times* example, your population of interest might be all issues from the 2008 calendar year. Instead of wading through over 300 issues of the paper, you could randomly select thirty from the calendar year using dice, a roulette wheel, a random number generator, or similar.

Stratified Sampling

Stratified sampling uses a technique in which different subcategories of the sample are identified and then randomly selected. To continue with our example from above, you may instead want to sample twenty-eight issues of the *New York Times*, but want an even distribution of days of the week. You would randomly sample four Mondays, four Tuesdays, four Wednesdays, and so on, to distribute the sample evenly across days of the week. Another example is commonly found in television content analysis, where a *composite week* is assembled. For example, Kunkel and colleagues (1999) randomly selected television content across different time slots and different days of the week, in order to assemble a sample of television content representing one week of programming, but drawn from numerous different weeks.

Systematic Sampling

systematic sampling
A type of sampling that is similar in logic to random sampling, but involves designating a timeframe ("k") and selecting every kth sampling unit within the population.

Systematic sampling is similar in logic to random sampling, but involves designating a timeframe ("k") and selecting every *kth* sampling unit within the population. In our *New York Times* example, one could select every eleventh issue of the *Times* for a given calendar year. This would allow for a sample that was drawn over the course of an entire year, but should be robust to any problems associated with sampling entirely from a particular day or a narrower timeframe that may not be representative of the year on the whole.

Cluster Sampling

Cluster sampling refers to the sampling of an entire group of sampling units. This is usually the case in which an entire population list is difficult or impossible to assemble. In this case, a group that has logical or natural boundaries is typically selected.

Take for example the Smith, Lachlan, and Tamborini (2003) content analysis. Smith and colleagues wanted to sample video game content. The problem was that they had no idea where to turn for a complete list of all available games. If they did have such a list available, they had no idea how to make sense of an appropriate sampling frame, since no one had attempted to quantitatively analyze video games before. So they felt their best course of action was to come up with a sample based on sales data. They sampled the top twenty selling games for each of the three major systems that were available at the time. While not a perfect sample by any stretch of the imagination, it at least allowed them to make statements about the games people were buying. Thus, without a true population list to draw from, a cluster technique was used to derive a sample that made sense.

· ·

▼ # Reliability

Once a sample has been assembled, the content analyst is left with the task of making sense of the data that has been collected. This typically involves turning to the recording and context units and making sense of them. Content analysis will first unitize the data by identifying the individual recording units (interactions, scenes, etc.) and then affix certain context categories to each recording unit. The frequency of these units, and the contextual elements associated with them, are later tallied for statistical analyses.

There is just one major problem with the process of identifying recording units and the content within them—time. Content analysts often have to analyze enormous amounts of data. The NTVS researchers, for example, had to unitize and code over 2,000 hours of television content. Further, if an individual researcher is responsible for unitizing and coding all of the content, she runs the risk of her own biases affecting the coding. Fortunately, there is a way to establish some degree of scientific objectivity while dramatically improving the efficiency of the coding process.

Coder Training

The solution is to assemble a team of independent coders. Content analysts will typically develop a coding protocol (Riffe, Lacy, & Fico, 1998). This is a document that details the operational definitions of everything in the study, including the sampling frame, the unitizing criteria, and the contextual definitions. They will then typically recruit and train a group of coders to make and record these decisions across multiple sampling units, breaking up the mass of content that has been harvested into easy to analyze chunks.

Inter-coder Reliability

What's critical in this process is making sure that all coders are analyzing content according to the definitions and criteria spelled out in the coding protocol. Content analysts will often meet with their coders numerous times, both in groups and in individual settings, and practice coding content that will not be included in the study itself. Typically, researchers will meet with their coder teams over and over again until they meet an acceptable level of agreement. This level of agreement, known as **inter-coder reliability**, is an essential component of the content analysis process (see Chapter 9). Inter-coder reliability is an indicator of how similarly the coders are coding the content, both in terms of identifying units of analysis and in the contextual labels they ascribe to those units.

inter-coder reliability
An indicator of how similarly coders are coding content, both in terms of identifying units of analysis and in the contextual labels they ascribe to those units.

Content analysts will typically train and retrain their coders until they reach an acceptable level of agreement across all coding categories. They will conduct reliability tests until it becomes apparent that the coders are examining the same content consistently. There are a number of ways of assessing reliability. The first is exact agreement. Let's say we have two coders. They are looking at ten newspaper clippings and evaluating whether each article contains a picture above the fold. This gives us a total of twenty judgments that the two coders have to make (See Table 11.1).

Table 11.1. Coders' Assessments of whether Newspaper Articles Have Pictures above the Fold

Coder A:	Y	N	Y	Y	Y	Y	N	Y	N	Y
Coder B:	Y	Y	Y	Y	N	Y	N	Y	N	Y

In this instance, sixteen of the twenty judgments made by the coders match. In terms of exact agreement, we might report an exact agreement of 80 percent between the two coders.

Of course, there is also the possibility that some of these could be due purely to chance. Since there are two response options and two coders, you would expect to get agreement due to chance one out of every four times, or 25 percent of the time. There are inter-coder reliability statistics that control for this kind of **chance agreement**. We discussed some of them in Chapter 9, but let's review them here. **Scott's Pi**, for example, is computed as follows:

chance agreement
The likelihood the two coders will agree on their coding judgments simply by chance.

scott's Pi
A statistical test measuring statistical reliability between coders.

$$Pi = \frac{\text{observed agreement} - \text{expected agreement}}{1 - \text{expected agreement}}$$

So in this case:

$$\frac{.80 - .25}{1 - .25} = \frac{.55}{.75} = .73$$

Similarly, Krippendorf's alpha (Krippendorf, 1980) uses a mathematical adjustment for chance agreement. But what exactly do these coefficients mean? If you remember back to our earlier discussion of reliability in measurement, you'll recall that .70 is generally accepted as the minimum level of acceptable reliability for scales. The same benchmark applies to inter-coder reliability in content analysis. While content analysts more typically report inter-coder reliability above .80, .70 is generally considered to be the minimum mark for having an acceptable level of reliability between coders.

● ●

▼ ## An Example of the Content Analysis Process

Let's return to our Smith et al. (2003, 2004) content analysis for a few minutes and walk through the process of designing and executing a content analysis. Consider this an *inside look* at one particular study. In the fall of 1999, these researchers and a few others at Michigan State University decided to launch a series of studies looking at the content and effects of violent video games. They were particularly interested in whether they could find any evidence that playing video games makes people respond aggressively when provoked. Of course, this question is only relevant if video games are, on the whole, fairly violent. Further, past research on media and violence has demonstrated that certain contextual features might be more likely to elicit aggressive responses. So when violence is presented as justified, committed by liked or attractive characters, goes unpunished, involves weapons, or is presented in an unrealistic manner these features can have particularly damaging effects on audiences. One member of the team had worked on the NTVS as a graduate student, so many of the coding and unitizing decisions were adapted from the procedures used in that earlier set of studies.

In order to address some of these issues, Smith et al. (2003, 2004) decided to come up with a content analysis that took a snapshot of the world of video games in terms of the frequency and context of violence. They were then faced with the problem of where to look. Generating a list of all available games for the three major platforms at the time (PlayStation, N64, and the Sega Dreamcast) would have produced an overwhelming amount of data. Taking a random sample from this list seemed like a bad idea, as well; what if they randomly selected games that no one played? In the end, the researchers decided to go with a systematic sample, selecting the top twenty selling games for each platform in order to get at the games people were actually playing.

The researchers were then faced with their second unitizing issue: recording units. They decided to look at the content on two levels, both by identifying individual scenes of violence and by making appraisals of certain games on the whole. Thus, from a unitizing standpoint they decided that there would be two levels of analysis: individual scenes and games on the whole. These were their recording units.

Context units then became the next consideration. As mentioned above, there are a number of contextual features that they believed might moderate the relationship between game playing and aggressive responses. So they decided that at the level of individual violent scenes, a number of context units would be identified. These included reasons for violence, the weapons used to enact violence, the type of violent act, the number of acts in a violent exchange, the depicted harm to the victim, the harm that would be likely in real life, and a number of characteristics of the perpetrator and victim.

The researchers then asked a number of research assistants to play these games from the *beginning* of the game, playing for a total of ten minutes. Keep in mind, we were living in an analog world in 1999; the audio and video signal was routed through a VCR and recorded for later use. In a short amount of time, they had their content; in fact, they had ten hours of it. Now they were faced with how to make sense of it all. Since the NTVS had recently received praise from scientists and policy makers alike, they decided to borrow heavily from their coding structure. The first thing that was necessary was to establish exactly what constituted a violent exchange. Borrowing from NTVS, they declared that in this study violence would be defined (operationalized) as "any overt depiction of a credible threat of physical force or the actual use of such force intended to physically harm an animate being or group of being[s]. Violence also includes certain depictions of physically harmful consequences against an animate being/s that results from unseen violent means" (Smith et al., 1998, p. 30). This is the first example of an *operational definition* in this study: a hard and fast definitional criterion for what is or is not. The researchers then went on to develop similar operational definitions for their context units. For example, for level of harm depicted, mild harm was defined as "an instance in which the victim makes a verbal or nonverbal depiction of harm without physical depiction," as opposed to extreme harm, which was described as instances in which "high bloodshed, severed limbs, visible entrails, or large-scale disfigurement" was depicted.

Realizing that the coding process would be time consuming and tedious, they then hired a number of research assistants to help with the coding. Over a period of a few weeks, the coders were trained to identify these features consistently. In order to train the coders, the researchers had to create a *codebook*, a brief list of the definitions used in the coding scheme. Below is the actual codebook used in the study:

Codebook for V2 Content Analysis—Fall 1999

Level 1 Data (Individual Acts)

1. Game: game number
2. System: gaming system (PS, N64, or DreamCast)
3. Rating: game rating (E, T, KA, or M)
4. Typ: type of violent act (behavioral act, credible threat, behavioral consequence)
5. Por: portrayal of *player* (first person) or *character* (character is pictured)

Reasons for Violence (coded as y/n):

6. Prolife: protection of life
7. Proprop: protection of property
8. Retal: retaliation
9. Anger: anger
10. Gain: personal gain
11. Mental: mental instability
12. Other: other/unknown
13. Means: the means through which the act is carried out
    - natural: natural means (punching, kicking, slapping, etc.)
    - unconventional: use of atypical instruments (frying pans, bowling pins, etc.)
    - handheld firearm (a pistol)
    - heavy weaponry: heavier firearms or weapons (machine guns, bazookas, flamethrowers, etc.)
    - bombs: an explosive or incendiary device
14. Numacts: number of acts in the interaction
15. Depharm: the degree of harm depicted
    - none: no harm is depicted
    - mild: character makes a verbal or nonverbal indication of harm, but not physically depicted
    - moderate: bloodshed, visible bruising, or visible injury
    - extreme: high bloodshed, severed limbs, visible entrails, or large-scale disfigurement
16. Likharm: how harmful this act would be if it occurred in real life
    - same as above
17. Sexaslt: does the interaction contain a sexual assault (y/n)

Victim and Perpetrator Demographics:

18. Victype: victim type (human, nonhuman, animal, etc.)
19. Vicgroup: victim grouping (single, multiple, unseen)
20. Vicsize: number of victims in group, if applicable
21. Vicsex: sex of the victim
22. Vicage: age of the victim
23. Viceth: ethnicity of victim

24. Vicgood: victim portrayed as good (y/n)
    - good: place needs of others ahead of themselves
    - bad: place own needs ahead of those of others
25. Vicphys: level of physical attractiveness of victim
    - victim is highly, moderately, or not attractive according to contemporary community standards
26. Vicprovk: sexual provocativeness of victim
    - high: victim is portrayed in such a way as to arouse game player
    - neutral: victim is not
27. Perptype: type of perpetrator
28. Perpgroup: grouping of perpetrator(s)
29. Perpsize: size of perpetrator group
30. Perpsex: sex of perpetrator
31. Perpage: age of perpetrator
32. Perpeth: ethnicity of perpetrator
33. Perpphys: physical attractiveness of perpetrator
34. Perpprvk: sexual provocativeness of perpetrator

Level 2 Data (Game Level)

1. Game#: game number
2. System: game system (PS, N64, DreamCast)
3. Rating: game rating
4. Type: game type (sports, racing, adventure, etc.)
5. Vthreats: number of verbal threats in the game segment
6. Pthreats: number of physical threats
7. Acts: number of behavioral acts
8. Cons: number of behavioral consequences
9. Total: total number of violent acts
10. Rewards: any rewards for violence (material rewards, praise, etc.)
11. Punish: punishment for engaging in violence
12. Range: close-up or long shot
13. Gore: graphicness of depicted gore
    - same as depicted harm above
14. Humor: humor associated with violence (y/n)

The coders were instructed to study this manual very closely. The research assistants underwent four weeks of intensive training to master all of the definitions and coding procedures. During this training, the coders participated in three reliability tests designed to assess the consistency of their coding judgments. Using an adjusted reliability formula for multiple coders, coders were trained to the point where Scott's Pi was found to be over .79 for all variables, indicating an adequate level of reliability. After the third training session the coders were turned loose on the sample and coded the video game recordings.

Each coder went through the tapes and identified individual violent acts. For each violent exchange that was identified, the coder used a *code sheet* to indicate the various features of each scene. Figure 11.2 is the actual code sheet that was used in the study.

To give you an idea of how time consuming content analysis can be, the study had a total of 1,389 acts of violence across the sixty games. In other words, the coders filled out this sheet al*most 1,400 times*. After coding all of the acts of violence in a particular game, they were then asked to fill out a final coding sheet indicating the overall nature of the game—their second recording unit.

Figure 11.1. Level 1 Code Sheet for Video Game Violence Study

Coding Sheet for Level 1 (Individual Acts of Violence)	
Game: _____	
System: _____	
Type of Interaction: ___ Verbal threat ___ Physical threat ___ Act ___ Consequence	
Portrayal: ___ Character ____ Player	
Reasons: ____ Protection of own life ____ Protection of property ____ Retaliation ____ Anger ____ Personal gain ____ Mental instability ____ Other/Unknown	**Means:** ____ Natural ____ Unconventional ____ Nonfirearm ____ Handheld firearm ____ Heavy weapon ____ Bomb
Number of Acts in Interaction: _____ 1 _____ 2–9 _____ 10–20 _____ 20+	
Depicted Harm: _____ None _____ Mild _____ Moderate _____ Extreme	
Likely Harm: _____ None _____ Mild _____ Moderate _____ Extreme	
Sexual Assault: _____ Yes _____ No	
Type:	**Victim:** ___ Human ___ Animal ___ Supernatural being ___ Anthropomorphised animal ___ Anthropomorphised supernatural being ___ Robot/Nonorganic	**Perpetrator:** ___ Human ___ Animal ___ Supernatural being ___ Anthropomorphised animal ___ Anthropomorphised supernatural being ___ Robot/Nonorganic
Grouping:	**Victim:** ___ Single ___ Multiple ___ Unseen	**Perpetrator:** ___ Single ___ Multiple ___ Unseen

Group Size:	___ 1	___ 1
	___ 2	___ 2
	___ 3–9	___ 3–9
	___ 10–99	___ 10–99
	___ 100+	___ 100+
Sex:	___ M	___ M
	___ F	___ F
	___ Can't tell	___ Can't tell
Age:	___ Child	___ Child
	___ Teen	___ Teen
	___ Adult	___ Adult
	___ Elderly	___ Elderly
	___ Can't tell	___ Can't tell
Ethnicity:	___ Caucasian	___ Caucasian
	___ African	___ African
	___ Hispanic	___ Hispanic
	___ Native American	___ Native American
	___ Asian/Pacific Islander	___ Asian/Pacific Islander
	___ Middle Eastern	___ Middle Eastern
	___ Can't tell/Nonhuman	___ Can't tell/Nonhuman
Good/Bad:	___ Good	___ Good
	___ Bad	___ Bad
	___ Can't tell/Neutral	___ Can't tell/Neutral
	Victim:	**Perpetrator:**
Physical Attractiveness:	___ High	___ High
	___ Average	___ Average
	___ Low	___ Low
	___ Can't tell	___ Can't tell
Sexual Provocativeness:	___ High	___ High
	___ Neutral	___ Neutral
	___ Can't tell	___ Can't tell

The researchers now had data concerning 1,389 individual acts of violence and the nature of sixty different games. They next began to pull the data apart to look at patterns of association between the variables. The details are perhaps a bit beyond the scope of this chapter, but the long and short of it is that the results showed that games for mature audiences feature violence more frequently (4.56 acts/minute) than those for general audiences (1.17/minute). When compared to general audience games, mature games were more likely to feature child perpetrators, graphic violence, the use of guns and other weapons, and violence that was depicted with unrealistic consequences.

Coding Sheet for Level 2 (Scene Level Variables)	
Game: _____	
System: ____ PlayStation2 ____ X-Box	
Rating: ____ E ____ T ____ KA ____ M	
Violent Acts: ____ Verbal threats ____ Physical threats ____ Behavioral acts ____ Behavioral consequences ____ **TOTAL**	
Rewards: ____ None ____ Praise from others ____ Self-praise ____ Material rewards	
Punishments: ____ None ____ Condemnation from others ____ Self-condemnation ____ Physical restraint ____ Physical violence	
Reasons: ____ Protection of own life ____ Protection of property ____ Retaliation ____ Anger ____ Personal gain ____ Mental instability ____ Other/Unknown	**Means:** ____ Natural ____ Unconventional ____ Nonfirearm ____ Handheld firearm ____ Heavy weapon ____ Bomb
View.ing Range: ____ Close-up ____ Long shot ____ Not shown	**Humor:** ____ Present ____ Absent
Blood and Gore: ____ None ____ Mild ____ Moderate ____ Extreme	

So What?

What have you learned from this chapter? Well, content analysis is a powerful tool for making sense of information exchanges that exist in the social world. These can come in the form of mediated information (content analysis) or interpersonal exchanges (interaction analysis). But in either case, you can use these analytic techniques to make empirical assessments of the nature of information exchange.

In this particular chapter, we have discussed the use of content and interaction analyses, and what types of research questions are best lent to these methodologies. We have examined different types of content, and the logic behind content analysis that leads to the production of data. We have explored techniques for sampling, unitizing, and evaluating the reliability of content data. Finally, we have walked through the logistics of the content analysis process, from initial conceptualization through data collection and analysis. It is our hope that this chapter illustrates the techniques and utility of content analysis in making sense of the social world. The chapter is also a logical segue into our next chapter, which deals with how to use surveys and quantitative observations to perform experiments.

Glossary

Chance agreement
The likelihood the two coders will agree on their coding judgments simply by chance.

Content analysis
A quantitative methodology that allows researchers to quantify content, including the content of participant responses or the content of media texts.

Context units
The types of content or contextual features that may appear in an individual recording unit.

Distributional structure
A type of content structure that deals with the number or frequency with which certain interactions take place in a certain timeframe.

Interactive structure
A type of content structure that deals with the pattern of response types that may vary throughout an interaction.

Inter-coder reliability
An indicator of how similarly coders are coding content, both in terms of identifying units of analysis and in the contextual labels they ascribe to those units.

Recording units
The individual parts of a sampling unit the researcher is examining.

Sampling units
The units that are sampled from a larger population of content that you wish to examine.

Scott's Pi
A statistical test measuring statistical reliability between coders.

Sequential structure
A type of content structure that normally deals with an examination of the sequences of utterances in order to make more sense of what is going on.

Systematic sampling
A type of sampling that is similar in logic to random sampling, but involves designating a timeframe ("k") and selecting every *kth* sampling unit within the population.

Unitizing
The process of deciding exactly what it is that should be observed.

References

Baxter, L. A., & Babbie, E. (2004). *The basics of communication research*. Belmont, CA: Wadsworth.

Carr, C. T., Schrok, D. B., & Dauterman, P. (2012). Speech acts within Facebook status messages. *Journal of Language and Social Psychology, 31(2)*. doi: 10.1177/0261927X12438535.

Germain, D. (2006, February 11). Few females in G-rated films: 3-to-1 gender imbalance found in study of 101 popular movies. *The Charlotte Observer (NC)*, 5E.

Hirokawa, R. Y. (1988). Group communication and decision making performance: A continued test of the functional perspective. *Human Communication Research, 14*, 487–515.

Holsti, O. (1969). *Content analysis for the social sciences and humanities*. Reading, MA: Addison-Wesley.

Krippendorf, K. (1980). *Content analysis: An introduction to its methodology*. Newbury Park, CA: Sage.

Kunkel, D., Cope, K. M., Maynard-Farinola, W. J., Biely, E., Rollin, E., & Donnerstein, E. (1999). *Sex on TV: Content and context*. Menlo Park, CA: Kaiser Family Foundation.

Lachlan, K. A., Tamborini, R., Weber, R., Westerman, D., Davis, J., & Skalski, P. (2009). The spiral of violence: Violent reprisal in professional wrestling and its dispositional and motivational features. *Journal of Broadcasting and Electronic Media, 53*(1), 56–75.

Riffe, D., Lacy, S., & Fico, F. G. (1998). Analyzing media messages: *Using quantitative content analysis in research*. Mahwah, NJ: Lawrence Erlbaum.

Smith, S. L., Wilson, B. J., Kunkel, D., Linz, D., Potter, J., Colvin, C. M., & Donnerstein, E. (1998). Violence in television programming overall: University of California, Santa Barbara study. In *National Television Violence Study (Vol. 3)*. Thousand Oaks, CA: Sage.

Smith, S. L., Lachlan, K., & Tamborini, R. (2003). Popular video games: Quantifying the amount and context of violence. *Journal of Broadcasting and Electronic Media, 47*, 58–76.

Smith, S. L., Lachlan, K. A., Pieper, K. M., Boyson, A. R., Wilson, B. J., & Tamborini, R. (2004). Brandishing guns in American media: Two studies examining how often and in what context firearms appear on TV and in popular video games. *Journal of Broadcasting and Electronic Media, 48*(4), 584–606.

Stephens, K. K., & Mottet, T. P. (2008). Interactivity in a Web conference training context: Effects on trainers and trainees. *Communication Education, 57*(1), 88–104.

Wilson, B. J., Kunkel, D., Linz, D., Potter, W. J., Donnerstein, E., Smith, S. L., Blumenthal, E., & Gray, T. (1997). Violence in television programming overall: University of California, Santa Barbara study, *National Television Violence Study* (Vol. 1, pp. 3–268). Newbury Park, CA: Sage.

12

EXPERIMENTS

CHAPTER OUTLINE

1. What Is an Experiment?
   a. Independent and Dependent Variables
      i. What Are Independent Variables?
      ii. What Are Dependent Variables?
   b. Good Questions for Experiments
2. Understanding Experimental Notation and Language
   a. Observation
   b. Induction
   c. Random Assignment
   d. Terminology
3. Designs and Validity
4. Preexperimental Designs
   a. One Shot Case Study Design
   b. One Group Pretest Posttest Design
   c. Static Group Comparison Design
5. Quasi-Experimental Designs
   a. Time-Series Design
   b. Nonequivalent Control Group Design
   c. Multiple Time-Series Design
6. True Experimental Designs
   a. Pretest Posttest Control Group Design
   b. Posttest-Only Control Group Design
   c. Solomon Four-Group Design
7. Factorial Design
8. Field and Natural Experiments
9. So What?

KEY TERMS

Baseline

Between-subjects design

Control group

Experimental group

Factorial design

Induction

Preexperimental designs

Posttest

Pretest

Quasi-experimental designs

Random assignment

Social experiment

True experimental designs

Within-subjects design

CHAPTER OBJECTIVES

1. To understand what experiments are
2. To understand the questions that can be addressed with experiments
3. To understand different types of experiments
4. To understand how different experiments address different validity threats

▼ # What Is an Experiment?

In Chapter 1, we talked about some of the general conceptions and misconceptions people have about social research. In particular, we talked about how people can readily think of examples of research in medicine, engineering, computer science, and so on, while they may have a more difficult time coming up with examples of social research. Social researchers also frequently perform experimental research, although usually without a white coat or a Bunsen burner. Communication scientists have relied upon experimental procedures since the birth of the discipline to answer a variety of questions concerning the ways in which people use and respond to information. Experimental designs have been used for decades to address how people respond to interpersonal interactions, mediated information, workplace dynamics, and interactions with computers. Of course, this raises the question of exactly what an experiment is, by definition.

social experiment
A procedure in which researchers take human subjects, do something to them, and observe the effects of what they did to them.

By definition, a **social experiment** is a procedure in which researchers take human subjects, do something to them, and observe the effects of what they did to them (Baxter & Babbie, 2004). This chapter will discuss some of the nuances associated with this seemingly simple procedure, including the use of subjects, random assignment, inductions, control groups, and multiple measures. More importantly, it will discuss how you can use these design elements to build confidence in your findings by ruling out particular validity threats.

Independent and Dependent Variables

Experimental researchers deal with independent and dependent variables (see Chapter 7). We use these terms to describe causes and effects. A variable is anything that can be measured or observed by the researcher. The independent versus dependent distinction is related to the researcher's involvement in the observation.

First, let's explain some concepts about variables in experiments. Remember that—for all research—variables can be measured through self-report, measured through other-report, or measured through observation. In an experiment, the independent variable can also be "manipulated" (we will get to inductions and manipulations shortly).

So, if—in your experiment—you are measuring a variable to determine beliefs, attitudes, or opinions, or to collect retrospective information about behavior or meaning, you would measure that variable using a *survey*. If, in your experiment, you are measuring a variable to analyze the content of media messages, you would measure that variable using a *content analysis*. Finally, if you are measuring a variable to analyze the content of an interpersonal message, you would measure that variable using an *interaction analysis*. So, to recap, surveys can be used as a stand-alone method, or as a way to measure a variable during an experiment. The same is true for interaction analysis.

What Are Independent Variables?   By definition, an independent variable is any observation that is controlled by the researcher. So, for example, you may

want to test the effectiveness of an antismoking public service announcement (PSA). You develop two types of PSAs, one that uses a fear appeal to attempt to scare people into compliance and one that does not. You then show the fear ad to one group of people and the non-fear ad to another group.

In this instance, the independent variable is the type of ad that is being shown. While the researcher will make the observation that a particular group saw one ad or the other, it was the researcher who decided which group would see which and what those messages would look like. Any differences in the responses of the participants might be attributable to this decision. This leads us to our next way of thinking about independent variables: they are causes. Independent variables are the things that are manipulated by the researcher in order to produce a particular outcome.

What Are Dependent Variables?   Dependent variables, on the other hand, are effects. They are observations made by the researcher that are not directly controlled by the researcher, but may be attributable to decisions surrounding the independent variable. In our example above, let's say the people who saw the fear appeal ad report that they are less willing to take up smoking. In this case, the dependent variable is willingness to take up smoking. It is the assumed result of a change in the independent variable.

Why do we call it a dependent variable? Because it is dependent on the independent variable. In short, independent variables are causes, while dependent variables are effects, or consequences.

Good Questions for Experiments

If you remember in Chapter 1, we talked about how social scientists use hypotheses to build theory, making educated guesses about the social world, and then testing those guesses through observation. In Chapter 6, we further discussed the formation of research questions and hypotheses, and how these may inform the selection of particular types of research design. As a classification of research design, experiments lend themselves best to particular types of questions. They are very useful for answering micro-level questions concerning responses to information. In particular, they lend themselves well to questions of *causation*. As we will see, this is because most experimental designs involve some kind of pretest; by examining someone before you expose her to a stimulus, then examining her again after the stimulus, you can argue to a certain extent that what you did to her may have caused any changes that you observe. So, if you are trying to answer a question such as: "Do video games *cause* people to respond more aggressively?" or "Does attractiveness *cause* people to disclose more information?" then an experimental design might be the way to go. Experiments are not particularly useful for descriptive purposes (since they are limited in the scope of phenomena they can address), nor are they particularly useful for drawing non-causal associations. They are, however, very useful for establishing causal relationships between independent and dependent variables.

Of course, it is not quite that simple. As we discussed in Chapter 9, there are a myriad of internal validity threats that can undermine a simple "X causes Y" statement. Non-spuriousness (making sure the independent variable is the only cause for the observed effect on the dependent variable) also becomes an issue, as it may be difficult to rule out alternative explanations ("third variables") that account for what you observe. Different types of experimental designs may be more or less effective at dealing with these concerns. In this chapter, we'll discuss different designs, what they might look like, and how well they may address these concerns and problems.

Experiments are used in business and industry as well as in scientific and social science research. When author Christine Davis worked for a marketing research firm, they frequently used an experimental design to test alternative advertisements. Following a pretest posttest control group design, they were able to determine if the test ad led to an increase in potential product usage.

▼ # Understanding Experimental Notation and Language

Before discussing different types of designs, it may be essential that we discuss the notation that is used when describing experimental procedures. We can identify three basic elements in an experimental design: observation, induction (or manipulation), and random assignment.

Observation

If you are reading the shorthand that scientists use to describe experimental designs, you will, at the very least, see a capital "O." This symbol is used to represent an *observation*. In communication research, this is typically some kind of written, spoken, or observed behavior or attitude. It is the basic building block of experimental design, which is after all a series of observations.

Induction

induction
What is done to a participant in an experiment.

You may also see a capital "X." This symbol is used to convey some kind of **induction**—an induction is what you *do* to the participant. So, in our video game example from above, this may be the part of the design where you make someone play a certain type of game. In a persuasion experiment, it may be a certain kind of argument that is delivered to the participant. In a television violence study, it may be a short film clip that you show. In any case, this is what you do to the participant, the independent variable, the effect of which you are examining.

Inductions are often incorrectly labeled as *manipulations*. Technically, an induction is only a manipulation if it actually works. The act of doing something to a participant, regardless of whether it affects them in any way, is more accurately referred to as an induction. In some fields, especially health communication, this is sometimes called an *intervention* or *treatment*.

Random Assignment

random assignment
The assignment of people at random to different groups in an experimental design.

You may also encounter a capital "R" in experimental notation. This refers to the **random assignment** of participants to different groups within your design. In a true experimental design, you would want to assign people at random to different groups. Why? Well, if we were concerned about ruling out spuriousness, you would want all the groups in your study to be as similar or comparable as possible. Similar how? It depends on your study, but certainly if you're studying health literacy you might want the two groups to have an equivalent distribution of education, and perhaps health status and/or experience with health-care providers. If you're studying employee productivity, you might want to make sure both groups are equivalent in terms of work experience and training. If you're studying the politeness level of communication on e-mail versus voice mail (see Duthler, 2006), you might want to make sure participants in both groups have equivalent distributions in terms of their relationships with the communication recipients. If you randomly assign people to groups—if everyone has an equal chance of being in a particular group, then (theoretically) they should be roughly the same. Of course, sometimes it is not logistically possible to have true random assignment. In these cases, you will sometimes see lines between conditions indicating that participants were not randomly assigned.

Terminology

There are also some key terms you should know in reading and understanding experiments. We just told you that you randomly assign participants to different groups. One of the groups is the group to whom you give the induction—this is called the **experimental group**. If you have more than one type of induction, you might have more than one experimental group. Ideally, you also have another group to whom you give no induction—this is called the **control group**. It's a group against which you can compare the experimental group. When you compare multiple experimental groups, this is known as a **between-subjects design**. When you only look at an experimental group, you call this a **within-subjects design**.

In many experiments, we measure the dependent variable both before and after exposure to the induction. The measurement before the induction is called a **pretest**, or **baseline** measurement. The measurement after the induction is called a **posttest**.

- -

Designs and Validity

If you remember in Chapter 9, we discussed a number of threats to validity that have to be taken into consideration when designing research. If you recall, there are a number of *internal validity* concerns that are relevant to the research process. These include history, or when something outside of the procedure takes place that skews your observations. Subjects may change over time, a process known as maturation. Testing describes the phenomenon in which participants respond differently as they become accustomed to your measures. Instrumentation refers to problems associated with using different measures to get at the same idea, and how well they measure the same things.

Fortunately, one of the advantages of the experiment is that in addition to allowing for causal statements, you can design studies in different ways to address each of these concerns. As we will see in the following descriptions, you

experimental group
The group of participants to whom you give the induction.

control group
A group that does not receive induction in an experiment.

between-subjects design
Designs comparing multiple groups.

within-subjects design
Designs looking at the same group multiple times.

pretest
An examination of someone before you expose him or her to a stimulus in order to argue, to a certain extent, that what was done to the subject may have caused any changes that are observed. Also called baseline measurement.

posttest
An examination or measurement conducted after administration of the induction.

baseline
An examination of someone before you expose him or her to a stimulus in order to argue, to a certain extent, that what was done to the subject may have caused any changes that are observed. Also called pretest.

can determine which of these issues concerns you the most, and design your study accordingly to rule it out as an internal validity threat. There is even one seldom-used design that rules out all of them. While no experimental design can ever rule out all plausible alternative explanations, thinking about internal validity concerns and designing a study appropriately can at least help you have more confidence in your findings.

▼ ## Preexperimental Designs

One Shot Case Study Design

The simplest possible design in this research family is known as the One Shot Case Study (Campbell & Stanley, 1963). In this design, there is only one group. You give participants some sort of induction and observe the results:

$$X \qquad O$$

For example, you could bring a group of participants into the lab and show them an ad for blue jeans. You could then pose a series of questions asking them about their likelihood to purchase the jeans. Since they seem to feel favorably toward the jeans, you conclude that the ad must have worked.

Do you see any problems here? There is no pretest, so you have no idea where the participants stood before seeing the ad. It is literally impossible to determine if your ad actually affected the results, since there is no measure of prior attitudes toward the product. The results could have come from anywhere: long-standing disposition toward the product, something that happened outside the laboratory, instrumentation that leads them in a certain direction, and so on. In this design, you really can't have any confidence in the results. As you can see, this experimental design doesn't account for anything in terms of validity concerns. In fact, it is almost never used. So why would we show you this design? Because it is a point of departure from which we can observe various means of ensuring against validity threats and providing results in which you can have more confidence.

Campbell and Stanley (1963) label these as **preexperimental designs**, since are either missing a pretest or a control group. Here are two more preexperimental designs.

preexperimental designs
Experimental designs that do not involve a true control group; no pretest, posttest, or control group.

One Group Pretest Posttest Design

Here is another example of a preexperimental design that lacks a control group:

$$O_1 \qquad X \qquad O_2$$

This is known as the One Group Pretest Posttest Design. It is a slight improvement over the One Shot Case Study. It still does not have a control group, so it is not possible to make comparisons between participants who did or did not receive the induction. But at least you can draw comparisons within this group of people in terms of where they stood before and after the induction. In our blue jeans example, you could ask people how they felt about the jeans, then show them the ad, then ask them again. You could then at least say that this group of people—whoever they are—did or did not feel more inclined to buy them.

Static Group Comparison Design

The final preexperimental design is the Static Group Comparison Design. This design looks just like the One Shot Case Study, except that you (kind of) add a control group:

$$X \quad O_1$$
$$O_2$$

Note that now, in addition to participants who get the induction, then take a posttest, you have added another group that takes the posttest without getting the induction. You can then compare those who get the induction to those who don't.

Returning to our example, you now have a second group: one that does not see the ad or take the pretest, but are simply asked about the jeans. Of course, there are still problems with this design. You can't really tell if people in the experimental group got used to your measures. If you run these groups at different time points, you can't tell if something outside the procedure affected the results. Most importantly, you don't know if these two groups felt differently about the jeans before the study.

• •

Quasi-Experimental Designs

This brings us to our next family of designs: the **quasi-experimental designs**. This term is used by Campbell and Stanley (1963) to describe designs that use pretests and posttests in more complicated ways, but that still lack random assignment. These designs are a marked improvement over the preexperimental, and while not perfect by any stretch, they are commonly used by communication researchers.

quasi-experimental designs
Experimental designs that use pretests and posttests in more complicated ways, but still lack random assignment.

Time-Series Design

The first of these is the Time-Series Design:

$$O_1 \, O_2 \, O_3 \quad X \quad O_4 \, O_5 \, O_6$$

This design is geared primarily to rule out history and maturation as validity threats. As you can see, you have several pretests, an induction, and several posttests. In our example, we could ask a group of people how they feel about the jeans several times over the course of a few weeks. We could show them the ad, then measure their attitude several more times over the course of a few weeks. Looking at the results, we could tell if the participants' attitudes were already shifting before seeing the ad, or perhaps find evidence that something happened outside the lab that would influence the results. There isn't really a control group, but we can at least detect other threats.

Nonequivalent Control Group Design

Here is another quasi-experimental design, and one that is actually used quite commonly—the Nonequivalent Control Group Design:

$$O_1 \quad X \quad O_2$$
$$O_3 \qquad O_4$$

For logistical reasons related to random assignment, communication researchers often use this design. As you can see, we now have a true control group; these are people who get both the pretest and posttest, but not the induction. If we are to rule out a number of validity threats, it should be the case that people in the test group change from pretest to posttest, but those in the control group should remain exactly the same. This helps control against instrumentation, testing, and maturation as design threats. It does not do too much to address history, and there may be selection problems since there is no random assignment, but at least three major threats are controlled.

Multiple Time-Series Design

In order to improve this design to account for history, we can add multiple measures and produce the following, the Multiple Time-Series Design:

$$O_1 \, O_2 \, O_3 \quad X \quad O_4 \, O_5 \, O_6$$
$$O_7 \, O_8 \, O_9 \qquad O_{10} \, O_{11} \, O_{12}$$

As you can see, this design combines the advantages of the last two. We now have controls in place for testing, instrumentation, and maturation, and we have added a history safeguard by collecting pretest and posttest measures at different times. It is still not a perfect design, though. The lack of random assignment is still a concern.

▼ # True Experimental Designs

true experimental designs
Experimental designs that randomly assign participants to both experimental and control groups.

Fortunately, there is another class of design that, by definition, introduces random assignment: true experimental designs. Campbell and Stanley (1963) define **true experimental designs** as those that randomly assign participants to both experimental and control groups. Through random assignment, the subject-related concerns we articulated in Chapter 9 should be pretty much avoided. If everyone in your population has an equal chance of being in any group, then problems like evaluator apprehension, Hawthorne effect, and selection problems should not be a concern. Over a large enough group, if these problems are present then they are at least equally distributed.

Pretest Posttest Control Group Design

One classic example of this type of design is the Pretest Posttest Control Group Design:

$$R \quad O_1 \quad X \quad O_2$$
$$R \quad O_3 \quad \quad O_4$$

Note that this looks a lot like the Nonequivalent Control Group Design we discussed earlier, but that it simply adds random assignment. In doing so, it takes care of subject-related problems. Many classic experimentalists rely heavily on this design, as it rules out most validity threats, but is still fairly economical in design.

Heimendinger and colleagues (2005) used this design in a study to test four alternative messages designed to increase fruit and vegetable consumption among callers to the National Cancer Institute's (NCI) Cancer Information Service (CIS). They conducted a baseline interview when the callers initially called CIS. They then randomly assigned each study participant to one of three experimental conditions (different messages promoting fruit and vegetable consumption) or to a fourth group, a control group which received a different message (unrelated to fruit and vegetable consumption). Finally, they did posttest interviews with all participants both five months and twelve months later. Here's something else to note about this study—the researchers used a survey interview format to gather the information pre and post intervention. Their surveys included several scales, including some Likert scales to test reactions to the messages.

Posttest-Only Control Group Design

Similar to the Pretest Posttest Control Group Design is the Posttest-Only Control Group Design:

$$R \quad X \quad O_1$$

In 2001, Lee and Guerrero wanted to see how people interpreted different types of interpersonal touch. They set up an experiment in which they videotaped dyads in an interaction that ended with one of nine types of touch (handshake, clasping hands, soft touch on the forearm, arm around the shoulder, arm around the waist, soft touch on the cheek, tapping the shoulder in a condescending manner, push against the shoulder, and no touch). In their paper, they refer to this videotape as a *stimulus material*, another name for intervention or induction. One hundred ninety-three students were randomly assigned one of the touch videotapes. After watching the video, students were asked to rate their impressions of the interaction. From this experiment, Lee and Guerrero determined that different types of touch lead to different interpretations in terms of affection, romantic attraction, flirtation, and love, but not in terms of trust or happiness. They also found that face touch was interpreted to be the most intimate type of touch. Their design was limited by validity concerns about consistency across the videotaped dyads (since their videos used two women and two men with various ethnic combinations), reactions to touch initiated by women versus men, and reactions to the ethnic mix of the dyads. Since their experimental design did not account for these possible affects, they tested for them statistically. Again, note that the dependent variables were measured using Likert scale measurements in a survey interview format.

In their study on whether there is a difference between which type of communication is presented first—computer-mediated communication (CMC) or face-to-face (FTF) in diverse teams, Triana, Kirkman, and Wagstaff (2012) used an experimental design with twenty-five teams of four people each (three men and one woman) receiving the CMC first, then FTF. Another twenty-five teams communicated first utilizing FTF, then CMC.

As you can see, these designs also involve random assignment, although the absence of pretest measures may undermine your confidence in the results to a certain extent.

Solomon Four-Group Design

Finally, there is a true experimental design that controls for all of the commonly identified internal validity threats. Those that study experimental methodology hold this design as the gold standard in experimental methodology. It is known as the Solomon Four-Group Design:

$$R \quad O_1 \quad X \quad O_2$$
$$R \quad O_3 \quad \quad O_4$$
$$R \quad \quad X \quad O_5$$
$$R \quad \quad \quad O_6$$

Note that this design involves four different groups. There is a test group that receives both a pretest and posttest. There is a posttest-only experimental group, which should allow comparisons to evaluate testing and instrumentation as threats. There is a true control group, which can be used to rule out maturation and history as potential threats. The capacity to rule these out is further improved with the addition of a posttest-only control group. Random assignment should take care of any subject-related problems.

You may be reading the description of this design and wondering two things. First, you may be wondering why we have just walked though nine different designs to arrive at one that controls for everything. Next, you may be wondering why all experimental researchers don't just use the Solomon Four-Group. If this design is so effective at ruling out validity threats, then why wouldn't everyone use it?

Take a look at the design for a minute. You will notice that of the four groups, only one gets a pretest, an induction, and a posttest. This is the group that you would use to test your hypotheses. The other three groups simply exist as checks against validity threats. This makes the design a bit cumbersome and impractical at times.

Let's return to our blue jeans ad from a few pages ago. Suppose you wanted to use the Solomon Four-Group to test the effectiveness of the ad. You randomly sample 200 people from your population, then you randomly assign those 200 people to each of your four conditions. How many people do you actually get to test the ad on?

Fifty. Yes, that's correct. In this particular example, you would have to run (test) 200 research participants in order to obtain the results of fifty. While you could have strong confidence in your results, you would have to spend time, money, and resources collecting data from 150 people that you can't use to test your hypothesis. This lack of economy then increases multiplicatively. If you wanted to gauge the responses of 250 people, you would have to run 1,000 to get 250.

Communication researchers, like all social researchers, do not have unlimited resources. Given the parameters in which they operate—balancing budgets, lab time, student labor, and participant availability—they can seldom use this near perfect design. They are much more likely to think about their research problems, consider the validity threats they are most concerned about, and choose a less complex design, accordingly. In truth, the Nonequivalent Control Group design and the Pretest Posttest Control Group design are much more commonly used, and do an adequate job of ruling out validity threats for the purposes of the communication researcher.

● ●

Factorial Design

▼

There's another *wrinkle* to conducting experiments. We've discussed experiments in which the induction either is or isn't. People either see the ad, or they don't. You may have noticed from our real-world examples it's also possible for the induction to have different levels or types. Or, alternatively, you might want to test more than one induction or independent variable at a time. Remember our example earlier of the Lee and Guerrero (2001) study testing reactions to different types of dyadic touch. Their independent variable had nine different levels, or types. In an attempt to account for any changes that might be a product of the gender of the observer, they conducted what is known as a **factorial design**. As we've stated earlier, their type of touch had nine levels. Gender of the observer, obviously, had two levels (male/female). This gave them a 9 × 2 factorial design (read "nine by two") in which each possible combination of these two factors and levels would be shown to the different groups. You can multiply these numbers

factorial designs
Analyses that involve multiple independent variables.

to tell you how many groups you would need to test all combinations of these factors (in this example, they needed 9 × 2, or 18, groups to test these factors). Here's how this 9 × 2 design would be notated:

$$R \quad X_{11} \quad O$$
$$R \quad X_{12} \quad O$$
$$R \quad X_{21} \quad O$$
$$R \quad X_{22} \quad O$$
$$R \quad X_{31} \quad O$$
$$R \quad X_{32} \quad O$$
$$R \quad X_{41} \quad O$$
$$R \quad X_{42} \quad O$$
$$R \quad X_{51} \quad O$$
$$R \quad X_{52} \quad O$$
$$R \quad X_{61} \quad O$$
$$R \quad X_{62} \quad O$$
$$R \quad X_{71} \quad O$$
$$R \quad X_{72} \quad O$$
$$R \quad X_{81} \quad O$$
$$R \quad X_{82} \quad O$$
$$R \quad X_{91} \quad O$$
$$R \quad X_{92} \quad O$$

This notation tells us that they had eighteen groups, randomly assigned, each of whom was exposed to a different experimental condition. Group one indicates that they viewed a videotape that includes level one of the touch (handshake) and the observer is categorized as level one on gender (male). Group two viewed a videotape that also uses the handshake but for whom the observer is female. Group three viewed a videotape that has the dyadic partners clasping hands, in which the observer is male. Group four viewed a videotape that has the dyadic partners clasping hands, in which the observer is female, and so on, through all eighteen groups. Of course, participants in each group would be administered the same interview after viewing the video. Using this design, we can easily determine which independent variable, and which combination of independent variables, affects the dependent variable. In case you are wondering, Lee and Guerrero (2001) found that male observers tended to find the touch gestures more flirtatious and indicative of love than did female observers, *regardless of the type of touch*. The authors could determine that these differences were accounted for by the gender of the observer and not by what type of touch they observed.

Communication-related studies frequently use a factorial design. Here's an example of one: Haumer and Donsbach (2009) conducted a study to see how a politician's nonverbal behavior influences his or her image. Using a mock television interview format, they tested viewers' reactions to politicians' communication. They had three independent variables, or factors: nonverbal behavior styles of the politician (active or passive), television host's reactions to the politician (negative, positive, or neutral), and television audience's reactions to the politician (negative, positive, or neutral). This gave them a $2 \times 3 \times 3$ factorial design. Their dependent variables (the effects they expected the independent variables to influence) were the viewers' perceptions of the politician's problem-solving competence, leadership abilities, integrity, and personal qualities. They, again, measured the dependent variables using Likert scale questions in an interview format. They had eighteen groups ($2 \times 3 \times 3$) with twenty participants in each. Each group viewed a different video, representing all eighteen possible combinations of the three factors. Note that this is a post-only design, as they did not conduct a pretest prior to administration of the intervention.

Field and Natural Experiments

▼

As we've shown you throughout this chapter, when we talk about experimental designs, we almost immediately think of laboratory experiments. There are other kinds of experiments that can take place outside of the laboratory. A *field experiment* takes place in a naturalistic environment, but nonetheless involves the manipulation of independent variables and some of the design concerns we have already voiced. *Natural experiments* also generally take place in naturalistic environments, but they do not involve variable manipulation—they simply involve analysis of naturally occurring variables. While field and natural experiments may not be as precise as laboratory experiments in terms of control, they are nonetheless valuable in evaluating causal relationships. In fact, they both have one major advantage over laboratory experiments—they have much higher ecological validity. Thus, external validity versus control is a major consideration when deciding whether to do your experiment in the field or in a laboratory.

Here's an interesting example of a field experiment. Argo, Dahl, and Morales (2008) used a field experiment to see how attractiveness affects consumer consumption. Rather than set up a laboratory experiment (can you think of how they might have designed that?), they conducted an experiment in an actual retail shopping environment. They hypothesized that the attractiveness of a person touching a product affects the level of interest another consumer has in purchasing that product. Simply stated, the research was conducted in a university bookstore, and the researchers set up a *confederate* sales clerk (an actor who was in on the experiment) and a *confederate* shopper and had the shopper confederate only handle a T-shirt. They compared shopper attractiveness to interest in purchasing the T-shirt. Note the independent variable (shopper attractiveness) and dependent variable (purchase intent).

In a classic example of a natural experiment, the 1986 research of Holak and Reddy used the 1970 ban against cigarette advertising on television and radio as an independent variable (pre-ban, post-ban). Since the real world had already administered the induction, they were able to test the effect of the television and radio advertising ban on cigarette pricing, advertising spending, and product demand (dependent variables) and found that the ban affected all three of those variables.

Of course, a field experiment such as this one lacks the kind of control one could have in the laboratory. In fact, field experimentalists are often left to make sense of data where they have to decide what constitutes an independent or dependent variable. Complex designs, such as those we described above, are seldom utilized simply because the researchers don't have much control over the environment. They do, however, allow for consideration of causal relationships in more naturalistic settings.

So What?

So what have we uncovered? We have discussed how communication researchers use experimental designs to answer research questions, and in particular we have discussed how micro-level, causal research problems lend themselves well to these types of designs. We then went on to discuss different types of research designs, and how you can build confidence in your findings by strategically using design to address particular internal validity threats. We have discussed the differences between laboratory and field experiments. And finally, we have discussed the ways in which the data derived from an experimental design can be analyzed and interpreted.

Of course, there is a major validity concern related to experimental designs that cannot be overlooked: the problem of external validity. While experimental designs are very useful for demonstrating causal relationships between independent and dependent variables, the extent to which these procedures mirror real-life behaviors may be problematic. This is especially the case with laboratory research. When you go home after class today, you may turn on the television. It is highly unlikely that a stranger will ask you to fill out a survey first, then ask you to fill one out again when you are done. When you talk to a friend, no one subsequently asks you to report how disclosive you found him or her to be. While experiments are very effective at establishing relationships between independent and dependent variables, the extent to which these findings generalize into real-life situations is questionable. Future chapters will detail some research methods that deal more with the experience of communication, as opposed to linear relationships between causes and effects. Again, we will see that the proposition of different questions begs the use of different methods.

Glossary

Baseline

An examination of someone before you expose him or her to a stimulus in order to argue, to a certain extent, that what was done to the subject may have caused any changes that are observed. Also called pretest.

Between-subjects design

Designs comparing multiple groups.

Control group

A group that does not receive induction in an experiment.

Experimental group

The group of participants to whom you give the induction.

Factorial designs

Analyses that involve multiple independent variables.

Induction

What is *done* to a participant in an experiment.

Preexperimental designs

Experimental designs that do not involve a true control group; no pretest, posttest, or control group.

Pretest

An examination of someone before you expose him or her to a stimulus in order to argue, to a certain extent,

that what was done to the subject may have caused any changes that are observed. Also called baseline measurement.

Posttest

An examination or measurement conducted after administration of the induction.

Quasi-experimental designs

Experimental designs that use pretests and posttests in more complicated ways, but still lack random assignment.

Random assignment

The assignment of people at random to different groups in an experimental design.

Social experiment

A procedure in which researchers take human subjects, do something to them, and observe the effects of what they did to them.

True experimental designs

Experimental designs that randomly assign participants to both experimental and control groups.

Within-subjects design

Designs looking at the same group multiple times.

References

Argo, J. J., Dahl, D. W., & Morales, A. C. (2008). Positive consumer contagion: Responses to attractive others in a retail context. *Journal of Marketing Research, 45*, 690–701.

Baxter, L. A., & Babbie, E. (2004). *The basics of communication research*. Belmont, CA: Wadsworth.

Campbell, D., & Stanley, J. (1963). *Experimental and quasi-experimental designs for research*. Chicago: Rand-McNally.

Duthler, K. W. (2006). The politeness of requests made via email and voicemail: Support for the hyperpersonal model. *Journal of Computer-Mediated Communication, 11*(2), article 6, http://jcmc.indiana.edu/vol11/ issue2/duthler.html

Haumer, F., & Donsbach, W. (2009). The rivalry of nonverbal cues on the perception of politicians by television viewers. *Journal of Broadcasting & Electronic Media, 53*(2), 262–279.

Heimendinger, J., O'Neill, C., Marcus, A. C., Wolfe, P., Julesburg, K., Morra, M., Allen, A., Davis, S., Mowad, L., Perocchia, R., Ward, J. D., Strecher, V., Warnecke, R., Nowak, M., Graf, I., Fairclough, D., Bryant, L., & Lipkus, I. (2005). Multiple tailored messages are effective in increasing fruit and vegetable consumption among callers to the Cancer Information Service. *Journal of Health Communication, 10* (Supplement 1), 65–82.

Holak, S. L., & Reddy, S. K. (1986). Effects of a television and radio advertising ban: A study of the cigarette industry. *Journal of Marketing, 50*(4), 219–227.

Lee, J. W., & Guerrero, L. K. (2001). Types of touch in cross-sex relationships between coworkers: Perceptions of relational and emotional messages, inappropriateness, and sexual harassment. *Journal of Applied Communication Research, 29*(3), 197–220.

Triana, M. d. C., Kirkman, B. L., & Wagstaff, M. F. (2012). Does the order of face-to-face and computer-mediated communication matter in diverse project teams? An investigation of communication order effects on minority inclusion and participation. *Journal of Business and Psychology, 27*, 57–70.

WRITING, ANALYZING, AND CRITIQUING QUANTITATIVE RESEARCH

13

CHAPTER OUTLINE

KEY TERMS

Central tendency

Confidence level

Correlation

Correlation coefficient

Inferential statistics

Leptokurtic peak

Mean

Measures of dispersion

Median

Mesokurtic peak

Mode

Multiple regression

Negative correlation

Negatively skewed

Platykurtic distribution

Population parameters

Positive correlation

Positively skewed

KEY TERMS (Continued)

Range	Skewness	Stepwise regression
Regression	Standard deviation	Variability
Significance testing	Statistical significance	Variance

CHAPTER OBJECTIVES

1. To understand how research questions, hypotheses, and variable type translate into appropriate statistical analysis methods
2. To understand how to conduct appropriate and accurate statistical analyses
3. To understand how to interpret statistical results
4. To understand how to read and understand statistical findings
5. To understand how to write, evaluate, and critique quantitative research reports

●●●

▼ Now That I Have My Quantitative Data, What Do I Do with It? Statistical Analysis of Quantitative Data

Know Your Variables, Research Questions, and Hypotheses

Just as your study method, sampling procedure, and data collection protocol all depend on your Research Questions (RQs) and/or Hypotheses (Hs), so does your data analysis. Thus, the first question you should ask yourself in determining how to analyze your findings is, "What did I set out to find or answer?" It's likely you set out to find or answer one of the following:

A. What do these people feel, believe, and think about "x"?
B. What does the rhetoric, language, text, visuals, and so on contain?
C. What does the communication between these people contain?
D. Does "A" cause "B"?
E. Are "A" and "B" related to each other?
F. Is "A" different from "B"?

Interestingly, pretty much all of the RQs and Hs you might have stated for your quantitative research could likely be summarized into one of three analytical goals: (1) to summarize or describe variables, (2) to compare two or more groups of people to see if they are the same or different, and (3) to see if two or more variables are related to each other. You'll use one or more statistical procedures to address these goals. What statistical procedures you use to address each of these goals depends entirely on what types of data you are testing. Remember in Chapter 7 when we discussed types of variables, we said that there are four levels of variables: nominal, ordinal, interval, and ratio. Nominal is the most basic level and it refers to categorical data (male, female). Ordinal is the next lowest level and it also refers to categories, but ordinal categories have an order to them, although the order does not refer to degrees or measurement of difference. Interval is the next level and while these categories have an order, they also have equal degrees of distance between the points. Ratio data is the highest level of data and it refers to measureable data, measurements on scales that have an absolute zero. Why is this distinction important? Because the statistical procedure you choose depends entirely on what you want to accomplish with it and the type of data you are working with.

To compute all of these statistics we're going to discuss in this chapter, you could compute them by hand, but—good news—researchers (almost) never do. We're going to illustrate how you can use a well-known statistical program—SPSS. We need to introduce this idea with a caveat. The great thing about SPSS is that it's very easy to compute statistics using it. The terrible thing about SPSS is how easy it is to compute statistics with it; it's very easy for somebody who doesn't really know what he or she is doing to misuse the program. Before using SPSS or any other statistical analysis program, you must be familiar with your data, your study H or RQs, and your analytical goals so that you compute the *correct* statistics. Remember the saying, "garbage in, garbage out." SPSS will compute (almost) anything you ask it to—but it is up to you to make sure the analysis you report makes sense.

We also want to give you one additional caveat. We are not attempting to introduce you to all the possible statistical procedures you might encounter in communication research journals, just the most commonly used ones, and the ones you are most likely to use in your Communication Research Methods course. In some cases, there are alternative statistical tests you could use in a given situation. We have attempted to reduce the complexity of this chapter by giving you our recommendation of the most commonly used, most popular, or most appropriate test for most situations. We are also not attempting to teach you everything you need to know about the theory, mathematics, and equations underlying each of the statistical methods we will be discussing. For most students, it's much more important to understand when to use a particular statistical test and how to interpret the results, than to know more advanced information on statistical tools. Finally, there are many very good statistics books available, and we encourage interested students to refer to them. Our favorite is Reinard's (2006), which focuses on statistics as they are used in communication research. In addition, the Babbie, Halley, and Zaino (2007) workbook on using SPSS in data analysis is a helpful addition to a statistics library, while Field (2015) offers an insightful (and often humorous) look into the connection between methods and SPSS analysis in quantitative research.

Okay, let's introduce you to SPSS. The first thing you'll need to do in using SPSS is to set up your variables. When you open SPSS, you'll be opening what looks like a blank spreadsheet-type page. This is your *data view*. In order to set up your variables, you'll need to click on the tab (see the bottom of the page in SPSS) for the *variable view*.

Let's set up the data for a very simple survey. For now, you can set up the variables without having any data collected yet, so let's just look at the survey.

Mental Health Literacy Attitudes Survey

1. How many children do you have? _____
2. I'd like to know how much you agree with each of these statements. For each one, please tell me if you agree strongly, agree somewhat, are neutral, disagree somewhat, or disagree strongly.

	Agree Strongly	Agree Somewhat	Neutral	Disagree Somewhat	Disagree Strongly
a. My child, family, and I have many strengths that enhance our health and well-being.					
b. I am sure that my child will be able to support him or herself when he or she grows up.					
c. I am capable of solving my or my family's problems.					
d. I am capable of being a good parent to all my children.					
e. I can survive any problems my child and family are going through.					

3. In which of the following categories does your total household income before taxes fall?
   a. $0–$15,000 _____
   b. $15,001–30,000 _____
   c. $30,001–$45,000 _____
   d. $45,001–$60,000 _____
   e. $60,001–$75,000 _____
   f. $75,001–$90,000 _____
   g. $90,001+ _____

Q. 1 (how many children do you have?) asks for ratio data. SPSS categorizes interval and ratio data together and codes it as *scale* data. We'll name this variable *children*, the data type is *numeric*, and way over on the right, the measure is *scale*. Q. 2 (the Likert scale for attitudes), as we know about Likert scales, is interval data. The last question could have been ratio data but we asked it as discrete categories. The categories have an order to them, and they would have equivalent distance except for the last category ($90,001+). Let's call it an ordinal scale. Here's how this data setup would look:

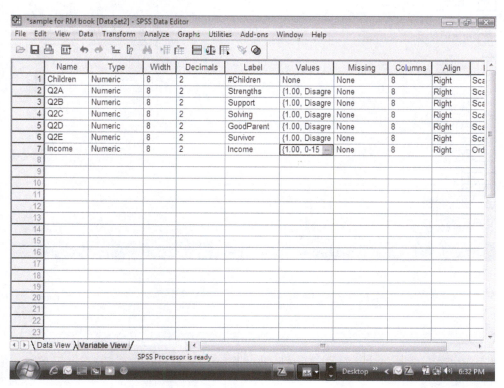

Notice you have to define your variable labels for questions 2 and 3.

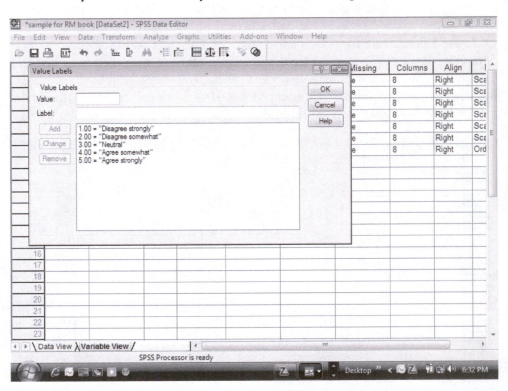

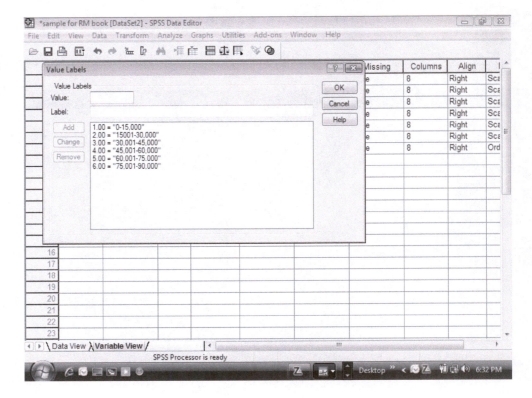

Now you're ready to input your data. We assigned numbers to the category labels in Qs. 2 and 3. So, for Q. 2, we said we would code "Strongly Agree" as a 5, "Agree Somewhat" a 4, "Neutral" a 3, "Disagree Somewhat" a 2, and "Disagree Strongly" a 1. Therefore, when you input the responses to those questions, you'll need to input the numbers corresponding to the answers. So, if someone answered Q. 2A with "strongly agree," you'd input a number 5. Here's what a sample input for 5 participants might look like:

SPSS Data Editor — sample for RM book [DataSet2]

	Children	Q2A	Q2B	Q2C	Q2D	Q2E	Income	var	var	var
1	3.00	4.00	1.00	5.00	5.00	2.00	1.00			
2	1.00	5.00	5.00	4.00	5.00	4.00	1.00			
3	4.00	4.00	3.00	3.00	4.00	5.00	2.00			
4	2.00	2.00	4.00	2.00	3.00	5.00	5.00			
5	2.00	1.00	2.00	2.00	2.00	3.00	3.00			

SPSS Processor is ready

This, by the way, is your data set. Now, let's talk about how you can analyze it.

Describing or Summarizing Your Variables

Descriptive statistics describe your findings in an easily understandable way. In describing your findings, you'll typically be describing two things about your data: its **central tendency**, and its **variability**.

Measures of Central Tendency. Measures of central tendency are called summary statistics, and they give us a number that represents the *typical* value of an array (distribution) of data. If you are working with nominal (categorical) data, you'll be looking for the **mode**. The mode is the most frequently occurring value in a data distribution. In our content analysis example that opened Chapter 11, we noted that researchers found that more men were depicted in G-rated movies than women. In other words, *men* was the modal category. Sometimes we have a tie between modes—a data distribution with two modes is *bimodal*, a distribution with three modes is *trimodal*, and a distribution with more than three modes

central tendency
Also called summary statistics. It is a measure that represents the "typical" number in an array (distribution) of data. Depending on the type of data you are working with, this can be the mode, median, or mean.

variability
Contrasted with central tendency, variability refers to the differences in our data, how wide the range is, and how far a given value might be from the measure of central tendency. Variability is another word for dispersion.

mode
The appropriate measure of central tendency for nominal data. The mode refers to the most frequently occurring value in our distribution. For example, a sample of communication studies students at UNC Charlotte might reveal that there are more female students than male students. Since the value "female" occurs more often in our data set, this value would be the mode.

median
A measure of central tendency that represents the exact center point of our data set when it's put in numerical order. The median is the appropriate measure of central tendency for ordinal data. For example, a data set consisting of scores of 1, 3, 5, 9, 17 would have a median of 5, since it is the center point of our array. The median can help control for outliers in our data sets as in the above example. Even though 17 is an extreme value, 5 is still our median. If there is an even number of participants, the two middle numbers will be "tied" and will be averaged together to get the median. The median is also sometimes used for higher levels of data than ordinal because it controls for outliers.

mean
A measure of central tendency; the arithmetic average, computed by adding the scores together and dividing by the total number of scores.

measures of dispersion
Measures that represent the distribution of scores in a data array. Dispersion can be thought of as statistics that represent differences in our data, whether it's the overall distance between the high and low scores (range), an average of how far the scores are from our mean (variance), or the standard deviation or square root of that variance.

is *multimodal*. The **median** is the appropriate measure of central tendency for ordinal data. This is the exact center point of a data set when it has been put in numerical order. For example, if five study participants rated their interest (on a scale of 1 to 10) in getting a dog as: 8, 2, 6, 7, 9; we could put their ratings in numerical order (2, 6, 7, 8, 9) and determine the median—the center point—to be 7. In an array of data with an even number of participants, two scores will be *tied* for the middle score and they would be averaged; thus, a data array of 2, 4, 6, 7, 8, 9 would present us with a tie between 6 and 7; the median would be 6.5. The median is also sometimes used for higher levels of data than ordinal because it controls for outliers. When we compute a mean (or arithmetic average), extreme scores can skew our measure. Since the median doesn't mathematically consider extreme scores (except to put them in order), it is much less likely to be skewed by outliers. This is why governmental and many other public polls and surveys report *median* income rather than *mean* income; people in extreme poverty or wealth are less likely to skew the data so that the measure is a more representative indication of the population as a whole. The last measure of central tendency is **mean**, and it is typically used for interval and ratio data. The mean is the arithmetic average, and is computed by adding the scores together and dividing by the total number of scores.

Frequencies and Visual Representation of Data.   While the measure of central tendency is an efficient way to summarize your data, a data set has much more information than that one number implies. So, researchers also use other measures to give information about the data distribution. For nominal or ordinal data, we might want to know the frequency of mentions, or observations, of each category. So, in our content analysis example, the researchers didn't simply say that *male* was the modal category; they also noted that, among the speaking characters in the movies, 28 percent were female and 72 percent were male. You might use a frequency table to show the frequency counts. You also might summarize the data array using a chart or graph. A pie or bar chart is most appropriate for nominal data, while a bar chart is best for ordinal data. Interval or ratio data could be depicted with a bar or a line chart.

Here's a frequency chart for our data:

	#Children			
	Frequency	**Percent**	**Valid Percent**	**Cumulative Percent**
Valid 1.00	1	20.0	20.0	20.0
2.00	2	40.0	40.0	60.0
3.00	1	20.0	20.0	80.0
4.00	1	20.0	20.0	100.0
Total	5	100.0	100.0	

Measures of Dispersion.   In addition to showing or depicting a summary or description of the data array, you might want to know more about the distribution of the scores. If you know the mean age of study participants is 20.4, you might want to know if most participants clustered around that mean (were all about that same age), or if their ages varied a lot. You might want to compute a **measure of dispersion**.

The **range** is the simplest measure of dispersion, and it simply refers to the distance between the highest and lowest scores, computed by subtracting the lowest score from the highest score. Thus, you might report that the mean age of participants was 20.4 and the range was 20.1, telling us that the ages ranged from about 10 to about 30. The **variance** is a measure that lets us know "on average, how far from the mean are the data?" (Reinard, 2006, p. 65). Specifically, the variance is the average distance of scores from the mean, squared. You might hear the variance also referred to as the average of the sum of the squares, because it's computed by squaring the deviation scores (how much each score deviates from the mean) and adding them, then averaging them (trust us on this mathematical computation). What does this mean, really? A high variance tells us that many of the scores are far away from the mean, and a low variance tells us that many scores are close to the mean. Since the variance is expressed in terms of the square of the scores, we translate it back into the original unit of measurement by taking the square root of the variance. This is called the **standard deviation**. For interval and ratio data, the mean and standard deviation are the two summary statistics most commonly reported. The standard deviation provides an estimate of how far a score typically falls from the mean.

All descriptive statistics can be computed in SPSS using the *analyze* command, and choosing *descriptive statistics*, then *descriptive*. The *options* box will let you select whichever descriptive statistics you choose to run.

range
A measure of dispersion that refers to the difference between the highest and lowest values in a data set. Calculated by subtracting the lowest score from the highest score. A data set with values between 1 and 29 would have a range of 28.

variance
A specific measure of dispersion that represents the average of how far our data is from our mean. Mathematically it is calculated by squaring the average distance of scores from the mean. It could also be referred to as the average of the sum of the squares, because it's computed by squaring the deviation scores.

standard deviation
One of the most commonly reported summary statistics for interval and ratio data is the square root of the variance. A measure of dispersion that represents the typical amount an entry deviates from the mean. Mathematically, it's the variance (the square of the average distance of scores from the mean) translated back into the original unit of measure by calculating the square root.

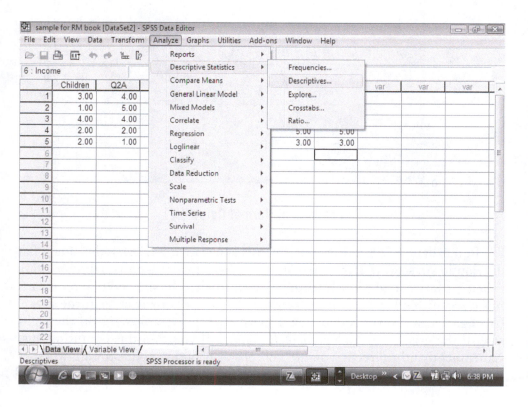

mesokurtic distribution
Having a normal bell shaped curve; a normal distribution of scores. This type of distribution has a moderate peak, representative of a normal number of scores in the middle of the distribution. A mesokurtic distribution also has a normal range with gradually sloping curves. When a mesokurtic distribution is perfectly centered, and not skewed in either direction, it is said to be normal.

platykurtic distribution
Indicates a flat distribution of scores (farther away from the mean than in a normal distribution). This type of distribution has a low peak, representing the fact that a relatively small number of scores are in the middle of the distribution. Platykurtic graphs also have a wide range, which represents a large amount of variance in scores.

positively skewed
More scores tend toward the left side of the graph, or lower than the mean.

negatively skewed
More scores are on the right side of the graph—or higher than the mean.

We see the mean number of children reported by people in our data set is 2.4, and the standard deviation is 1.14. This standard deviation isn't really very large, and you might recall from the data set that the individual scores mostly clustered around the mean of 2.4.

Descriptive Statistics			
	N	Mean	Std. Deviation
#Children	5	2.4000	1.14018
Valid N (listwise)	5		

By the way, you may recall from your statistics class that (approximately) all of the measures in a data set for a "normally distributed population (or sample)" occur within three standard deviations from the mean (+ or −), 95 percent occur within two standard deviations from the mean (+ or −), and 68 percent occur within one standard deviations from the mean (+ or −). You may also recall, this describes a *normal curve*, or a *bell-shaped curve*. A normal curve has what is called a **mesokurtic peak,** or mesokurtic distribution.

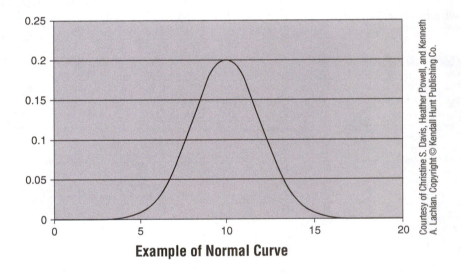

Example of Normal Curve

Courtesy of Christine S. Davis, Heather Powell, and Kenneth A. Lachlan. Copyright © Kendall Hunt Publishing Co.

In our data, SPSS tells us our kurtosis is negative (−.178), indicating a flat distribution of scores (farther away from the mean than in a normal distribution), called a **platykurtic distribution**. It's also **positively skewed**, which means more scores tend toward the left side of the graph, or lower than the mean. (A **negatively skewed** value would mean that more scores are on the right side of the graph—or higher than the mean). If you find this confusing, just remember that the direction of the "tail" of a distribution points toward whether it is positively or negatively skewed.

Descriptive Statistics					
	N	Skewness		Kurtosis	
	Statistic	Statistic	Std. Error	Statistic	Std. Error
#Children	5	.405	.913	–.178	2.000
Valid N (listwise)	5				

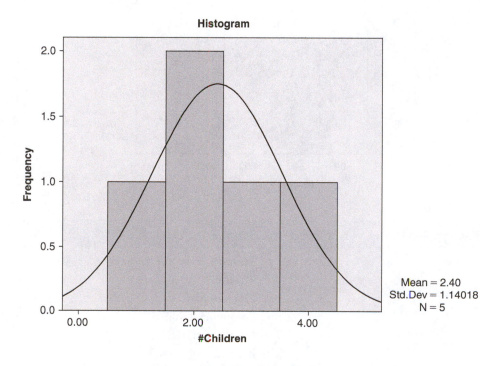

Histogram

Mean = 2.40
Std.Dev = 1.14018
N = 5

Courtesy of Christine S. Davis, Heather Powell, and Kenneth A. Lachlan. Copyright © Kendall Hunt Publishing Co.

leptokurtic distribution
A distribution of scores that has stronger consistency around the mean than in a normal distribution. This type of distribution has a high peak, representative of the fact that there are a large number of scores in the center of the distribution. Leptokurtic graphs also have a small range, showing that there is a relatively small difference or variance between scores.

Interestingly, our *income* data has a positive kurtosis (.536), indicating a distribution of scores that has stronger consistency around the mean than in a normal distribution, in what's called a **leptokurtic peak,** or leptokurtic distribution. This data also has a positive **skewness** value.

skewness
Either positive (lower than mean) or negative (higher than mean), is the uneven, sloping, or asymmetrical graph of scores. Refers to the condition that occurs when more scores tend to be higher than the mean (negative skewness), or lower than the mean (positive skewness).

Descriptive Statistics					
	N	Skewness		Kurtosis	
	Statistic	Statistic	Std. Error	Statistic	Std. Error
Income	5	1.089	.913	.536	2.000
Valid N (listwise)	5				

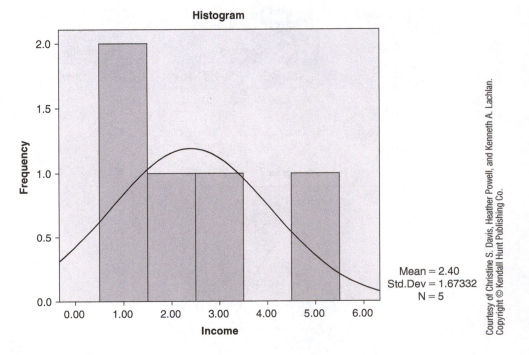

Mean = 2.40
Std.Dev = 1.67332
N = 5

What Type of Data Do You Have?	Summarize Data
Nominal	*Measures of central tendency:* Mode *Visual displays:* Frequency table Pie chart Bar chart
Ordinal	*Measures of central tendency:* Median *Visual displays:* Frequency table Bar chart
Interval/Ratio (Scale)	*Measures of central tendency:* Median Mean *Measures of dispersion:* Range Variance Standard deviation *Visual displays:* Bar chart Line graph

Comparing Groups to See if They Are the Same or Different

Okay, summary statistics are fine and you will see them reported in journal articles as researchers describe the sample or explain a finding. However, they're not why you went to the trouble of conducting your research. You conducted your research to answer a question or test a hypothesis. You might have conducted your research to see if two groups of people are the same or different on a characteristic or variable. We need to take a minute to explain *sameness* or *difference* in statistical terms. When we talk about statistical difference, we want to know if an observed (or measured) difference is due to *chance*, or due to a *real* difference. Remember our null hypothesis discussion from Chapter 6. The null hypothesis says that there is no difference. We are always testing for the null; always hypothesizing there is no difference. Why? Well, remember we rely on samples that represent the population. But, of course, samples can't represent the population 100 percent—we estimate the population characteristics (**population parameters**) based on the sample characteristics, and samples are subject to *sampling error*. You can never know for sure that a difference is due to a *true* difference rather than sampling error, so there's no way to test for that. However, you can test that there's *no* difference (the null hypothesis). Is this confusing? Remember eighth-grade geometry? You can't prove a theorem; you just continue to try to disprove them. It's the same principle. You can't prove there's a difference without conducting a census, which you decided not to do in the first place, so instead you try to prove the null hypothesis, which disproves your difference. If you can't disprove it, then it's likely to be true. How likely? Researchers talk in terms of the *probability* of there being a *true* difference. They call this a measure of **statistical significance**, and the method of answering these questions using statistics is known as **significance testing**. The types of statistics you use to do this are called **inferential statistics**, because you are drawing inferences about the population based on the sample.

Let's review some terms we discussed in Chapter 8 on sampling and sample size. Remember **confidence level** and margin of error? Our sample represents our population to a certain extent. The *confidence level* refers to the probability that I'm *close to correct* when I infer population characteristics based on my sample. How close I am to correct is the margin of error. Remember the marble experiment? A confidence level of 95 percent means that if I take 100 handfuls of marbles, 95 of those times, I will come up with the same number of black marbles that there actually are in the jar, within a margin of error. In other words, there is a 95 percent probability that my answer is pretty close to correct. If I have a 5 percent margin of error that means that my answer is within –5 or +5 percentage points of the *true* answer in the population. When we are conducting inferential statistics, we are estimating this margin of error. Not to confuse you, but margin of error is often called *confidence intervals*, and it's reported in SPSS as a *confidence coefficient*. It's found under "Analyze," "Descriptive Statistics," "Explore."

For our "number of children" variable, the mean was 2.4 and—at a 95 percent confidence level—the confidence interval ranges from .984 to 3.81, which means that there is a 95 percent probability that the *true* mean in the population is between .984 and 3.81.

population parameters
Population characteristics based on the sample characteristics.

statistical significance
The probability of there being a "true" difference between scores of a data set, as opposed to a perceived difference that may occur, but might in reality be simple "overlapping" of margins of error.

significance testing
Testing to determine the probability of there being a "true" difference between scores of a data set. Involves testing a null hypothesis in order to prove it, and therefore disprove the difference.

inferential statistics
The type of statistic used when gathering information about a population based on the sample. The type of statistics used with significance testing.

confidence level
Refers to the probability that I'm "close to correct" when I infer population characteristics based on my sample. How close I am to correct is the margin of error.

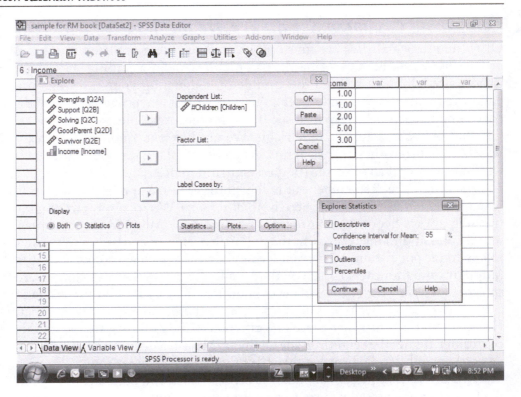

Descriptives		
		Statistic
Mean		2.4000
95% Confidence Interval for Mean	Lower Bound	.9843
	Upper Bound	3.8157

What does this have to do with statistically significant differences? Let's say we have a second sample: Perhaps we spoke to another group of five people, and their mean on this question was 2.9 and their confidence interval ranged from .83 to 4.15. We need to know if 2.4 versus 2.9 is a *true* difference (a statistically significant difference) or a difference due to chance (or sampling error). Let's draw a diagram of our two populations. The shaded areas represent their two confidence intervals. You can see that, even though their means are different, their confidence intervals have some overlap. Therefore, we cannot be certain that the two means are different. If the means of each sample are anywhere in their shaded areas, it's entirely possible that we could sample two means that are identical. We've found support for our null hypothesis—it's possible there's no difference between the two groups.

You can see that one way to determine if there is a difference between the means of two groups is to compute their confidence intervals and see if there is any overlap. There are, however, easier ways to do this. You can compute statistical tests that test for differences.

Group 1:

Group 2:

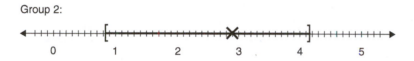

Nominal Data.

If you have a nominal variable and want to see if there is a difference between categories of this variable, you would use a one-sample Chi Square. This statistic is notated by the Greek symbol: χ^2. For example, we added a variable "experience with mental illness" to our survey data and we see that 60 percent of our sample has some experience with mental illness, while 40 percent do not.

Experience with Mental Illness				
		Frequency	**Percent**	**Valid Percent**	**Cumulative Percent**
Valid	No experience	2	40.0	40.0	40.0
	Some experience	3	60.0	60.0	100.0
	Total	5	100.0	100.0	

What we do not know at this point, however, if there is a *true* statistically significant difference between the 60 percent and the 40 percent. Since this is nominal data, the appropriate statistical test is a one-sample Chi Square. In SPSS, you access this test through "Analyze," "Non-parametric tests," "Chi Square."

Note that the expected values setting should be left on "all categories equal," since we have no reason (prior research, for example) to believe that all categories would not be equal. Thus, what we're testing in this statistical test is whether there is a difference between equal categories (50%–50%) and the proportions we observed in our sample (40%–60%). Here's the output of our statistical test:

Test Statistics	
	Experience with Mental Illness
Chi Square(a)	.200
Df	1
Asymp. Sig.	.655

SPSS reports our significance level as .655, but you need to know that in SPSS the significance is really reported for the *null* hypothesis. The value above (.655) is what's called the *p* value—the probability that the null hypothesis is true. The smaller the *p* value, the more likely the null hypothesis is *not* true, and the more likely our test hypothesis is true and there is a statistical difference.

What does this mean? Recall that our standard significance level is 95 percent, or 95 percent probability, and we said that a significance level of 95 percent means that there is a 5 percent probability ($p = .05$) that the difference is due to chance, or there is a 95 percent probability that the difference is a *true* difference. A *p* value of .65 means that there is a 65 percent probability that the null hypothesis is true, or that the difference is due to chance, which is much higher than our threshold of 5 percent. Therefore, we accept the null hypothesis that there is no difference. Another way to read this output table is to say that at a significance level of 95 percent, the *p* value stated above would have to be .05 or smaller (between .00 and .05) for us to say there is a statistically significant difference. Obviously, it's not, so we say that our research has found no difference in experience with mental illness.

What if we have a nominal variable (gender, for example) as our independent variable and we want to see if this differs on a nominal variable (whether subjects have experience with mental illness, for example) as our dependent variable? Let's write a hypothesis: There is a difference by gender in terms of experience with mental illness. This, by the way, is a two-tailed hypothesis because we're not implying directionality. If we instead were to hypothesize that men have more mental illness experience than women, we'd be making a one-tailed hypothesis. Since we have no prior research on which to base a one-tailed hypothesis, we're making a two-tailed one. Since our dependent variable is nominal, we'd use a two-variable Chi Square. In SPSS, you'll find this under "Analyze," Descriptive Statistics," and "Crosstabs."

Under "Crosstabs," you'll indicate the rows (groups) and columns (variables) you're testing, then select "Statistics" to say you want to compute a Chi Square.

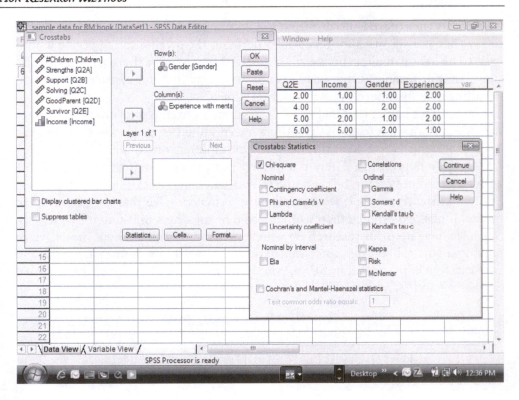

Normally, for nominal data, we look at the Pearson Chi Square p value. In our results, the p value for the two-sided Pearson Chi Square is .136. Since it is not between 0 and .05, we accept the null hypothesis that there is no difference between men and women on experience with mental illness. (An aside—if any cell has a zero value, we use the Fisher's Exact Test instead of the Pearson Chi Square. In this case, Fisher's Exact Test is .4 so we'd still accept the null.)

Chi Square Tests					
	Value	**df**	**Asymp. Sig. (2-sided)**	**Exact Sig. (2-sided)**	**Exact Sig. (1-sided)**
Pearson Chi Square	2.222(b)	1	.136		
Continuity Correction(a)	.313	1	.576		
Likelihood Ratio	2.911	1	.088		
Fisher's Exact Test				.400	.300
Linear-by-Linear Association	1.778	1	.182		
N of Valid Cases	5				

The Chi Square tests are nonparametric tests. Nonparametric tests are appropriate when your data is not continuous (that is, when your variables are not interval or ratio) and when you cannot assume you have a normal distribution of data (Reinard, 2006). Some have also suggested their use with very small samples, since normal distributions can generally not be assumed with samples smaller than twenty.

Ordinal Data. What if we want to determine if there are statistically significant differences between groups on ordinal variables? Perhaps you want to know if men differ from women on their income. In our study, income is an ordinal variable because we asked people to indicate the income group to which they belong rather than give us their exact income. To compare two groups on an ordinal variable, we would use another nonparametric test—the Mann-Whitney U Test—which is a test that looks at the equality of two distributions. In SPSS, you would find this test under "Analyze," "Nonparametric Tests," "2-Independent Samples." Note that they want you to define your independent variable groups. For our gender variable, we coded "men" a "1" and "women" a "2." That's what you would put for your definition of the groups.

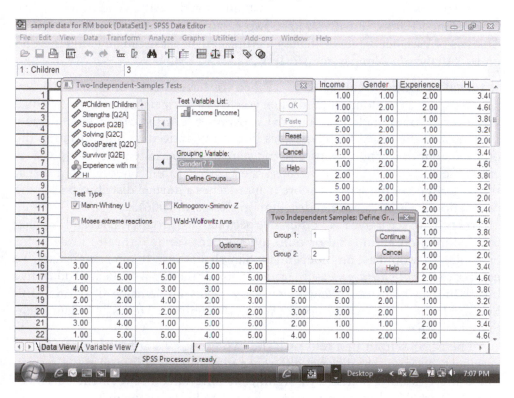

From our SPSS output, you can see there is not a statistically significant difference between men and women on income.

Test Statistics(b)	
	Income
Mann-Whitney U	1.500
Wilcoxon W	4.500
Z	–.889
Asymp. Sig. (2-tailed)	.374
Exact Sig. [2*(1-tailed Sig.)]	.400(a)
(a) Not corrected for ties	
(b) Grouping Variable: Gender	

If you are determining if there is a difference between three or more groups on an independent variable (that is, an ordinal variable), you would use the Kruskall-Wallis Test. If you're looking for differences between what's called *matched* or *related* groups (such as pre-post test), you'd use the Wilcoxon Matched Pairs Signed Ranks Test if you have two groups and the Friedman Two-Way Analysis of Variance for more than two groups. All of these can be found in SPSS under "Analyze," "Nonparametric Tests."

Interval or Ratio (Scale) Data.

When you have interval or ratio data, when your sample was randomized, and when you have a normal distribution and equal variances in your population, you can use parametric statistics. You should know that most of the time, if a scholar has interval or ratio data, she presumes the other assumptions and uses parametric statistics, especially if her sample sizes are sufficiently large. This is because the Central Limit Theorem states that the larger the sample size, the more it approaches a normal distribution—if the population itself has a normal distribution (Reinard, 2006).

If I want to see if there is a difference between two groups (males and females, for example) on an interval or ratio independent variable (health literacy, for example), we would use an Independent Samples T-Test. In our sample data, we computed a *health literacy* measure by determining the mean of the individual five health literacy questions. We will now see if males and females differ on health literacy. In SPSS, we would go to "Analyze," Compare Means," "Independent Samples T-Test."

The SPSS output first tells us if the two groups we are testing have equal variances, because that makes a difference in how we will interpret the results. Since there is not a statistically significant difference between the variances ($p = .286$), we'll look at the p-value for the two-tailed t-test when equal variances are assumed ($p = .756$). Clearly, we will accept the null hypothesis that there is no difference between men and women on health literacy.

Independent Samples Test						
		Levene's Test for Equality of Variances		t-Test for Equality of Means		
		F	Sig.	t	df	Sig. (2-tailed)
HL	Equal variances assumed	1.681	.286	.340	3	.756
	Equal variances not assumed			.429	2.271	.705

If we had related groups—again, a pre-post test—we wanted to compare on interval or ratio data, we would use a Paired t-Test, also found in SPSS under "Analyze," "Compare Means." If we wanted to see if three or more groups were different on one interval or ratio variable, we would use a one-way Analysis of Variance (ANOVA). If the p-value indicates a statistically significant difference between the groups, we would follow with what's called a post-hoc test to determine exactly where the difference can be found. We'd use the most powerful and most popular post-hoc test, the Tukey HSD post-hoc test, because it compares all pairs of means (Gravetter & Wallnau, 1986; Reinard, 2006; Williams, 1968). HSD stands for "honestly significant difference," and it computes a value that represents the minimum difference between means necessary for significance, then it compares each pair of means with that minimum difference. To compute a one-way ANOVA in SPSS, go to "Analyze," Compare Means," and "One-way ANOVA."

What Type of Data Do You Have?	Test for Differences between Groups
Nominal (Nonparametric)	*Analyze the distribution of the independent or dependent (nominal) variable:* Chi Square *Compare 2 or more (nominal) independent or dependent categories:* 2-variable Chi Square
Ordinal (Nonparametric)	*Analyze the differences between 2 groups on ordinal variable:* Mann-Whitney U Test *Analyze the differences between 3 or more groups on ordinal variable:* Kruskall-Wallis Test *Examine the differences between related (ordinal) scores:* Wilcoxin Sign Test (2 groups) Friedman 2-Way ANOVA (3 or more groups)
Interval/Ratio (Scale)	*Estimate parameters of interval/ratio variable:* Estimate confidence levels and margin of error *Examine differences between 2 unrelated groups on interval/ratio variable:* Independent samples t-test *Examine differences between 2 related groups on interval/ratio variable:* Paired t-test *Compare 3 or more groups on their distribution on one interval/ratio variable:* One-way analysis of variance (ANOVA) followed by a Tukey post-hoc test

Testing for Relationships (Association) between Two or More Variables

The last thing you might want to do with your data is to see if there is a statistical relationship between variables. When we say there is a relationship between variables, we are simply stating that when one occurs, the other tends to occur also. **Correlation** is the statistical test designed to test for linear relationships between variables when you have interval or ratio variables, and we'll discuss this in detail in a few pages. Because of this, people frequently refer to relationships between variables as *correlations* between variables.

Remember from Chapter 6, there are several types of relationships you can hypothesize and/or find: a positive linear relationship (when "A" goes up, "B" goes up), a negative linear relationship (when "A" goes up, "B" goes down), a curvilinear relationship (when "A" goes up, "B" goes up for a while, then as "A" continues to go up, "B" goes down—or some variation on that). The statistical tests you use to see if there is a relationship between variables are called *tests of association*.

Nominal Data. If both of your variables are nominal variables, or if one of your variables is nominal and the other is ordinal, we recommend you use Cramer's V. This can be used when there are either two or more than two categories for your variables, and it also adjusts for sample size. In SPSS, you'll find this test the same place you found the two-variable Chi Square, under "Analyze," "Descriptive Statistics," and "Crosstabs." As a matter of fact, Cramer's V is one of the options under the Chi Square function. It may appear that this statistic is the same as Chi Square, but while the Chi Square statistic only told us if there was a statistically significant difference between the two groups (male and female) on the independent variable (experience with mental illness), the Cramer's V statistic also gives us a value that indicates the strength of the relationship between the two variables, if there is one.

correlation
The statistical test designed to test for linear relationships between variables when you have interval or ratio variables. When one variable occurs, the other variable tends to be present as well.

Chi-Square Tests					
	Value	**df**	**Asymp. Sig. (2-sided)**	**Exact Sig. (2-sided)**	**Exact Sig. (1-sided)**
Pearson Chi Square	.139(b)	1	.709		
Continuity Correction(a)	.000	1	1.000		
Likelihood Ratio	.138	1	.710		
Fisher's Exact Test				1.000	.700
Linear-by-Linear Association	.111	1	.739		
N of Valid Cases	5				
(a) Computed only for a 2 x 2 table					
(b) 4 cells (100.0%) have expected count less than 5. The minimum expected count is .80.					

Symmetric Measures			Value	Approx. Sig.
Nominal by Nominal	Phi		−.167	.709
	Cramer's V		.167	.709
N of Valid Cases			5	
(a) Not assuming the null hypothesis.				
(b) Using the asymptotic standard error assuming the null hypothesis.				

The values of Cramer's V range from 0 to 1. A 0 value indicates there is no association between the two variables and a 1 indicates there is a high association between the two. Since our significance supported the null hypothesis it should not surprise us that the value for Cramer's V is very low also. Some have suggested a value of .10 as the minimal criterion for demonstrating a substantive association between the variables (Rea & Parker, 1992), with values between .10 and .20 indicative of an existing but weak relationship.

Ordinal Data. If both of your variables are ordinal, or if one of your variables is interval/ratio and the other is ordinal, we recommend you use the Spearman's Rho (also called Spearman Rank Order Correlation). It is subject to less error than other statistics (Williams, 1968), although Kendall's Tau (Kendall's Coefficient of Concordance) is preferred when you are testing interrater reliability on ordinal variables. In SPSS, Spearman's Rho and Kendall's Tau can both be found under "Analyze," "Correlation," and "Bivariate Correlation."

correlation coefficient *Indicated by the Greek letter r (pronounced "rho"). It is a number that represents the extent that variables are related or go together and the magnitude of their relationships. Correlation cannot identify causation. Just because two variables are related or vary together, we cannot determine whether one causes the other. The correlation coefficient ranges from +1.0 to −1.0. +1.0 indicates a positive relationship. −1.0 indicates a negative relationship. 0 indicates no relationship between the variables in question.*

Correlations				Income	HL
Spearman's Rho	Income	Correlation Coefficient		1.000	−.718
		Sig. (2-tailed)		.	.172
		N		5	5
	HL	Correlation Coefficient		−.718	1.000
		Sig. (2-tailed)		.172	.
		N		5	5

Note that in our example, the *p*-value for the statistical significance of the relationship between income (ordinal variable) and health literacy (ratio variable) is .172, which means we accept the null hypothesis.

There is also one additional piece of information to notice on this output table: the correlation coefficient. A **correlation coefficient** is indicated by the Greek letter *r* (pronounced "rho"). It is a number that represents the extent that variables are related or go together. It is important to note, however, that correlation does not have the capacity to distinguish between which variable comes first. In other words, correlation cannot identify causation. Just because two variables are related or vary together, we cannot determine whether one causes the other.

Correlations can range from +1.0 to –1.0. A +1.0 would indicate a perfectly positive relationship, a –1.0 indicates a perfectly negative relationship, and a 0 is indicative of no relationship between the variables in question. A correlation coefficient represents two pieces of information about any relationship: (1) the direction of the relationship, and (2) the magnitude of the relationship. The sign of the correlation, either positive or negative, indicates the direction of the relationship. If we have a **positive correlation**, this indicates that the two variables in question vary in the same direction. As one variable increases, so does the other variable, or as one variable decreases, so does the other variable.

positive correlation
Occurs when both variables vary in the same direction.

Consider an example. We could measure intelligence scores like IQ scores as well as reading ability. Would you predict a relationship between these two variables? Our hypothesis might be: As reading scores increase, so do IQ scores. This would be a hypothesis of association. Remember that the null hypothesis to this hypothesis is that there is no relationship between reading scores and IQ scores. So, using correlation we could test our hypothesis. This relationship predicts a positive relationship, as we predict scores will vary in the same direction—both increasing in this case. However, it is possible to have a positive relationship where both values decrease together.

On the other hand, a **negative correlation** occurs when one variable increases, while the other variable decreases, thus indicating two variables that vary in opposite directions. Consider another example: Reading ability and the time it takes to read a passage. In this case, we would hypothesize that the better your reading ability, the less time it will take you to read a passage. Here one score is increasing (reading ability) and the other variable is decreasing (time to read a passage), thus a negative correlation.

negative correlation
Occurs when one variable increases while the other variable de-creases, thus indicating two variables that vary in opposite directions.

A correlation coefficient also represents the magnitude of the relationship. If we take the absolute value (drop the sign in front of the number) of the correlation coefficient, the actual numerical value indicates the strength of the relationship. Remember that correlation coefficients range from –1.0 to +1.0, so if we drop the sign, the strength of the relationship is captured by the numerical value's closeness to 1.0. The larger the absolute value, the stronger the relationship. Essentially, this means that all of the variation in one variable is shared by the other variable. Thus, numbers closer to 1.0 are stronger than numbers closer to 0. Another way to think about this is that the stronger the relationship, the more the correlation coefficient deviates from zero, which essentially leads to the null hypothesis. The null hypothesis of correlation is simply that there is no meaningful association between two variables. In regard to the correlation coefficient, the null hypothesis is correlation = 0.

One of the most important considerations to make in being a critical consumer of research methods is to ask yourself how you interpret r. First you must answer the question of whether the statistic is significant; this can be identified by the significance column produced in SPSS. Second, what is the direction of the relationship (positive or negative)? What does that tell us about our variables and how they vary? The numerical value also communicates to us the magnitude or the strength of the relationship. This is generally subjective and may take into account special knowledge of the variables involved. However, there are some general guidelines from three different sources summarized in Reinard (2006, p. 95) that we'll replicate for you here:

Koenker (1961)	Losh (2004, citing G. Lutz)	J. Cohen (1988)
.80 to 1.00: Highly dependable relationship	1.00: Perfect	Above .371: Large
.60 to .79: Moderate to marked relationship	.76 to .99: Very strong	
.40 to .59: Fair degree of relationship	.51 to .75: Strong	
.20 to .39: Slight relationship	.26 to .50: Moderate	.243 to .371: Medium
0 to .19: Negligible or chance relationship	.11 to .25: Weak	.10 to .243: Small
	.01 to .10: Very weak	
	0: No relationship	

Ratio Data. We've explained the correlation coefficient to you when we discussed using Spearman's Rho correlation for ordinal data. For ratio data, you would use the Pearson Product Moment Correlation, which was, by the way, developed by Karl Pearson, an English mathematician. It, in effect, considers the relationship of two continuous (interval or ratio-level) variables, and was the first statistic to consider the effect size (Rodgers & Nicewander, 1988).

A Pearson Product-Moment correlation would be appropriate to see if there is a relationship between the number of children a person has and their level of health literacy. In SPSS, go to "Analyze," "Correlation," and "Bivariate Correlations." Remember to tell it if you're doing a one-tailed or two-tailed test.

Correlations			HL	#Children
HL	Pearson Correlation		1	−.092
	Sig. (2-tailed)			.882
	N		5	5
#Children	Pearson Correlation		−.092	1
	Sig. (2-tailed)		.882	
	N		5	5

In our example, the p-value for significance is .882, so we accept the null hypothesis. In addition, we see that the correlation coefficient is −.092, virtually zero, again telling us there is virtually no association between the two variables.

If you want to test for relationships between many variables at one time, you can compute a correlation matrix, which is one big table that gives you the correlation coefficient for all possible combinations of variables. To compute this, you simply select multiple variables under "Correlation."

Correlations		Strengths	Support	Solving	GoodParent	Survivor
Strengths	Pearson Correlation	1	.289	.783	.957	.023
	Sig. (2-tailed)		.638	.109	.011	.970
	N	5	5	5	5	5
Support	Pearson Correlation	.289	1	−.243	.121	.728
	Sig. (2-tailed)	.638		.694	.846	.164
	N	5	5	5	5	5
Solving	Pearson Correlation	.793	−.243	1	.912(*)	−.559
	Sig. (2-tailed)	.109	.694		.031	.327
	N	5	5	5	5	5
GoodParent	Pearson Correlation	.957(*)	.121	.912(*)	1	−.176
	Sig. (2-tailed)	.011	.0846	.031		.776
	N	5	5	5	5	5
Survivor	Pearson Correlation	.023	.728	−.559	−.176	1
	Sig. (2-tailed)	.970	.164	.327	.776	
	N	5	5	5	5	5

(*) Correlation is significant at the 0.05 level (2-tailed).

In this example, we computed a correlation matrix to see if there was a relationship between the different beliefs questions. There was a statistically significant relationship between beliefs in strengths and in being a good parent ($p = .01$) and beliefs in being able to solve problems and being a good parent ($p = .03$). The correlation coefficient (r) for the strengths/good parent relationship is .957 and for problem-solving/good parent is .912, both of which are awfully strong relationships whichever guideline you use.

Finally, there's one more thing you might want to look at as you look at relationships between interval or ratio variables: **regression**. Sometimes you want to take what you know about the relationship between "A" and "B" and use it to predict what new "B" values might occur given new values of "A" (Babbie, Halley, & Zaino, 2003; Williams, 1968). Regression looks at the pattern in a data distribution to make predictions about future patterns. The term refers to a *line of best fit* and is based on an algebraic equation (regression equation) that takes into account the regression line, the slope (the angle of the line), and the intercept (the point at which the line intersects the y-axis). The regression procedure finds the *line* that best fits your data distribution. We can construct a scatterplot of our HL/children correlation that approximates the overall relationship between the two variables. In SPSS, you would go to "Graphs" to create this plot. From "Graphs," go to "Scatter/Dot," then select "Simple

regression
For interval or ratio data, the procedure that looks at the pattern in a data distribution to make predictions about future patterns. This procedure finds the "line" that best fits your data distribution. This is also known as prediction. It is another way to look at relationships between interval or ratio variables. The term refers to a line of best fit and is based on an algebraic equation (regression equation) that takes into account the regression line, the slope (the angle of the line), and intercept (the point at which the line intersects the y-axis).

Scatter." You assign your dependent variable (in our case, health literacy) to the y-axis and your independent variable (in our case, number of children) to the x-axis. Now you have a graph that shows how your data distribution plots. Now, let's overlay the *best fit* regression line to see visually the relationship between the two variables. Double click on your graph and a chart editor will open. Under "Elements," select "Fit Line at Total." Here's what we come up with for our data:

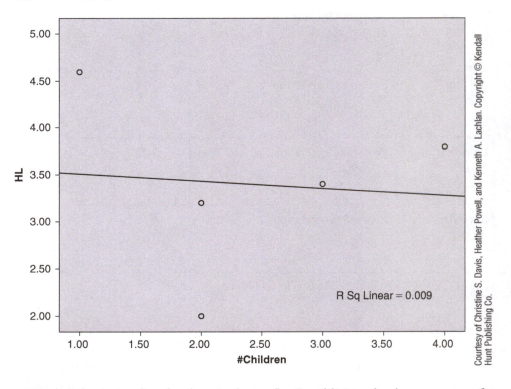

multiple regression
Represented by the symbol R, *this predicts the dependent variable's value from two or more independent variables. Used when testing curvilinear effects that can't be tested with linear correlation methods, and for testing the effects of extraneous variables.*

stepwise selection
A method of inserting independent variables into an equation for multiple regression. Each independent variable is subjected to a significance test, starting with the smallest p *value, and then proceeding to the next smallest and so on, until there are no more variables with statistically significant probabilities. Also called stepwise regression.*

You might notice that the slope is almost flat. In addition, the dots are pretty far away from the regression line. That makes sense, given our correlation data, which showed us that there was no statistically significant relationship between the two variables, and the r was $-.092$. The closer the dots are to the regression line, the stronger the association between the variables. In our case, the data points are pretty widely scattered throughout the graph, indicating the weakness of the association. You can, however, visually see the slight negative relationship between the two.

Researchers often use what's called **multiple regression** (symbolized by R) to predict the value of a dependent variable from two or more independent variables. Multiple regression is used when you want to test curvilinear effects that can't be tested with linear correlation methods and when you want to test interaction effects—the effect of additional or extraneous variables on your dependent variables. Researchers often use **stepwise selection** (also called stepwise regression) to insert their independent variables into the equation. In stepwise regression, the statistics program subjects each independent variable to a significance test. In the first modeling step, the variable with the smallest p value is used first for the model. In the next step, the variable with the next smallest *p* is used, and so on, until there are no more variables with statistically significant probabilities.

To illustrate this, let's add two more variables to our sample data. Let's hypothesize that in addition to the number of children, we think number of doctor's visits and age of participant might be associated with health literacy. We've also added additional cases (participants) so we have a large enough sample size to compute this data. Using SPSS, we went to "Analyze," "Regression," and "Linear." Under "Method," we chose "Stepwise." The first thing we find is that "Age" and "Number of doctor's visits" are the only variables that were entered in the stepwise method; the other variable (number of children) was removed from the model.

			Variables Entered/Removed(a)
Model	**Variables Entered**	**Variables Removed**	**Method**
1	Age	.	Stepwise (Criteria: Probability-of-F-to-enter <= .050, Probability-of-F-to-remove >= .100).
2	No. Doctor's Visits	.	Stepwise (Criteria: Probability-of-F-to-enter <= .050, Probability-of-F-to-remove >= .100).
(a) Dependent Variable: HL			

We next see a fairly strong (*r* = .988) and statistically significant (*p* = .00) association between "Age," "Number of Doctor's Visits," and "Health Literacy." We also see that most of that association occurs with "Age," and very little of the additional association occurred with the addition of the "Number of Doctor's Visits" variable to the model.

			Model Summary(c)					
Model	**R**	**R Square**	**Change Statistics**					**Durbin-Watson**
			R Square Change	F Change	df1	df2	Sig. F Change	
1	.987(a)	.973	.973	1755.429	1	48	.000	
2	.988(b)	.976	.002	4.632	1	47	.037	3.364
(a) Predictors: (Constant), Age								
(b) Predictors: (Constant), Age, No. Doctor's Visits								
(c) Dependent Variable: HL								

ANOVA(c)						
Model		Sum of Squares	df	Mean Square	F	Sig.
1	Regression	35.042	1	35.042	1755.429	.000(a)
	Residual	.958	48	.020		
2	Regression	35.128	2	17.564	946.439	.000(b)
	Residual	.872	47	.019		
	Total	36.000	49			

(a) Predictors: (Constant), Age

(b) Predictors: (Constant), Age, No. Doctor's Visits

(c) Dependent Variable: HL

We can see one final piece of information, and this may be the most interesting statistical finding yet. Partial correlation refers to the correlation with the dependent variable when the effects of the other variables are excluded. Note that the correlation between "Age" and "Health Literacy" is strong by itself, while the correlation between "Number of Doctor's Visits" and "Health Literacy" is not as strong by itself. This illustrates the interaction effects of the two variables working together.

Coefficients(a)						
Model		t	Sig.	Correlations		
				Zero-order	Partial	Part
1	(Constant)	−1.620	.112			
	Age	41.898	.000	.987	.987	.987
2	(Constant)	−.223	.824			
	Age	24.516	.000	.987	.963	.557
	No. Doctor's Visits	2.152	.037	.816	.300	.049

(a) Dependent Variable: HL

What Type of Data Do You Have?	Test for Relationships between Variables
Nominal	Cramer's V
Ordinal	Spearman's Rho
Interval/Ratio (Scale)	*Test for a statistically significant relationship between variables:* *2 variables:* Pearson-Product Moment Correlation *3 or more variables:* Correlation Matrix *Predict outcomes:* Regression analysis

Specific Uses of Statistical Analysis ▼

Content Analysis

In this section, we're going to show you how scholars have used different statistical methods in quantitative research and how they report their findings. First, let's look at some content analysis examples. The process of generating content analysis data is a lengthy one. As we showed you in Chapter 12, once you reach an acceptable level of reliability among coders, you go through the previously selected sampling frame and code the content to be included in the analysis.

In order to make sense of all of this, content analysts tend to provide extremely detailed discussion of both their methods and their findings. In crafting their method sections, content analysts will typically begin with a discussion of the sampling frame that was employed in the study, including the rationale for why this particular sample was used. They will then go on to discuss the recording units in the study, sometimes referred to as the unitizing process; again, they will typically offer a rationale as to why particular units of analysis were selected for inclusion in the study. They will then offer definitions and rationale for including the particular context characteristics they associate with individual recording units.

Reporting the findings of the analysis is pretty straightforward. As in most quantitative endeavors, content analysts begin their reports by developing a series of hypotheses or research questions relevant to the subject matter under consideration. Often, a simple set of descriptive analyses reporting the frequency of the occurrence of certain content units serves to accomplish this goal. Other times, more sophisticated statistical analyses are necessary, particularly when looking at the ways in which different content characteristics distribute throughout each other, or *hang together*.

Gordon and Berhow (2009) used quantitative content analysis to examine websites of universities to determine which types of universities used more dialogic features and if dialogic features in websites were associated with factors such as student retention and alumni giving. You can see from the excerpt from their journal article below that they reported descriptive statistics—means, standard deviations, and frequencies (percentages)—in great detail.

Reprinted from *Public Relations Review, Vol. 35, No. 2* by J. Gordon & S. Berhow, "University Websites and Dialogic Features for Building Relationships with Potential Students," pg. 151. Copyright 2009, with permission from Elsevier. ■

The mean dialogic score found across all universities types was 24.3 ($n = 232$, s.d. = 7.3). Results ranged from a high of 53.2 to a low of 6.8. Several of the most frequently observed features were related to the "usefulness of information" principle: All websites studied included pictures of students/campus and contact information. The two least frequently observed features associated with this principle were streaming video (26%) and streaming audio (7%).

Associated with the "ease of interface" principle, 95 percent of websites featured a search option and links organized by audience. Ninety-four percent featured links to admission information on their homepage. Breadcrumbs, a system that allows user to track one's depth into the page, appeared in only 20 percent of websites.

Related to the principle "generation of return visits," 96 percent of websites observed had a calendar of events, and 70 percent gave users the option of requesting more information by e-mail or mail. The least frequently observed features were RSS feeds and podcasts.

Items related to the "dialogic loop" principle had the some of the lowest scores among the categories. The most frequently observed dialogic loop feature was opportunity for user response, observed on 38 percent of the websites. Links for contacting admissions and sign-ups for an appointment or tour were observed 31 percent and 30 percent of the time. The least frequently observed feature, opportunity for voting, appears in 4 percent of websites.

Institutional type (national versus liberal arts) was examined in relation to dialogic score. National universities had a mean dialogic index score of 23.1 ($n = 124$. s.d = 6.8); liberal arts universities had a mean dialogic index score of 25.7 ($n = 108$, s.d. = 7.6). A *t*-test revealed that the differences between the two mean dialogic index scores were statistically significant, $t(229) = 2.80$, $p \le .05$. However, the practical difference between 23.1 and 25.7 on a 100-point scale is not impressive.

However, liberal arts colleges featured links for contacting admissions counselors more than twice as often as national universities, 45 percent and 19 percent respectively. Liberal arts colleges also more frequently featured online chats (17%), links to "about" information pertaining to the school (89%), FAQs (49%), blogs (21%), and self-explanatory image maps (90%). National universities were observed as more frequently featuring lists of majors and minors (66%), lists of clubs and activities (90%), and portal technology (44%) than liberal arts colleges. National universities utilized site maps (82%) more often than liberal art colleges.

Tier 3 institutions had the highest mean dialogic index score of the four tiers ($m = 26.03$, s.d. = 6.79), followed by Tier 1 institutions ($m = 25.07$, s.d. = 7.92) and Tier 2 ($m = 24.25$, s.d. = .95). Tier 4 had the lowest mean dialogic index scores ($m = 21.73$, s.d. = 6.52). A post hoc Bonferroni's test revealed that a meaningful difference did exist between the Tier 3 and Tier 4 mean dialogic index scores (df = 4.31; $p \le .01$)

The four principles composing the dialogic index score were examined by institution tier. Tier 3 institutions had the higher frequencies of dialogic features compared to Tier 1, 2, and 4 in all four principal categories. Tier 4 had the lowest frequencies of dialogic features in all four principle categories.

They then moved into more sophisticated statistical analysis to answer their research questions:

> *A post hoc Bonferroni's test revealed that a meaningful difference did exist between the Tier 3 and Tier 4 mean dialogic index scores (df = 4.31; p ≤ .01). . . . Pearson correlations were run between mean dialogic index score and each institutional variable (undergraduate enrollment, alumni giving, endowment, and retention rates). Some small correlations were found between two of the institutional variables, alumni giving (r = .180, p ≤ .05) and retention rate (r = .146, p ≤ .05). (Gordon & Berhow, 2009, p. 151)*

They evidently used an Analysis of Variance among the four tiers of institutions to see if there was a difference between the groups on the dialogic scores. When the ANOVA told them there was, they used a post-hoc test. We had recommended the Tukey test; they used the Bonferroni's test—an equally valid test. The post-hoc test found that the statistically significant difference found by the ANOVA was between Tiers 3 and 4. They then used the Pearson Product Moment Correlation to see if there was a relationship between the dialogic scores and undergraduate enrollment, alumni giving, endowment, and retention rates. They found that there was a statistically significant correlation between alumni giving and retention rate, and correctly noted that, based on the correlation coefficients, these were relatively small associations.

Survey Research

t-Test Example.

Salmon, Park, and Wrigley (2003) conducted a survey research study among corporate spokespersons from 100 public companies to understand perceptions of risk and bias toward optimism about the possibility of bioterrorism among corporate spokespersons. They tested five hypotheses:

From "Optimistic Bias and Perceptions of Bioterrorism in Michigan Corporate Spokespersons, Fall 2001" by Charles Salmon, Hyun Soon Park, & Brenda Wrigley, *Journal of Health Communication,* Vol. 8, No. 1; reprinted by permission of the publisher (Taylor & Francis Ltd, http://www.tandfonline.com).

H_1: Corporate spokespersons will tend to estimate their own organization's risk to be less than that of other organizations similar to their own.

H_2: Optimistic bias will be greater for referents that are more distant (e.g., other corporations in the United States) than proximate (other corporations in the state).

H_3: Corporate spokespersons who perceive their own organizations as low in vulnerability tend to show high optimistic bias.

H_4: Corporate spokespersons who perceive high severity of bioterrorism tend to show high optimistic bias.

H_5: Corporate spokespersons who perceive that their own organizations can control external events tend to show high optimistic bias.

Their measurements of bioterrorism awareness, perceived vulnerability, perceived severity, and perceived controllability used Likert-type scales, and Weinstein's measure of optimistic bias was a 0–10 scale.

They analyzed their data using a paired t-test and an independent samples t-test to test for differences between groups. Specifically, the groups they tested for their first hypothesis (H_1: Corporate spokespersons will tend to estimate their own organization's risk to be less than that of other organizations similar to their own) were their organization versus another organization. The groups they tested for their second hypothesis (H$_2$: Optimistic bias will be greater for referents that are more distant [e.g., other corporations in the United States] than proximate [other corporations in the state]) were distant organizations versus proximate organizations.

The groups they tested for their third hypothesis (H$_3$: Corporate spokespersons who perceive their own organizations as low in vulnerability tend to show high optimistic bias) were those who perceived their organizations as low in vulnerability versus those who perceived their organizations as high in vulnerability. The groups they tested for their fourth hypothesis (H$_4$: Corporate spokespersons who perceive high severity of bioterrorism tend to show high optimistic bias) were those who perceived low severity of bioterrorism versus those who perceived high severity of bioterrorism. Finally, the groups they tested for their fifth hypothesis (H$_5$: Corporate spokespersons who perceive that their own organizations can control external events tend to show high optimistic bias) were those who perceived that their organizations can control external events versus those who perceived their organizations cannot control external events.

From "Optimistic Bias and Perceptions of Bioterrorism in Michigan Corporate Spokespersons, Fall 2001" by Charles Salmon, Hyun Soon Park & Brenda Wrigley, *Journal of Health Communication, Vol. 8, No. 1;* reprinted by permission of the publisher (Taylor & Francis Ltd, http://www.tandfonline.com).

Optimistic Bias about Bioterrorism

On a scale from 1 to 10, respondents estimated the likelihood of vulnerability to bioterrorism to be 1.61 (*SD* = 1.76) for their own company, 2.64 (*SD* = 2.21) at a company like their own in Michigan, and 3.76 (*SD* = 2.77) at a company like their own in the United States. To assess the presence of optimistic bias in comparative risk judgments, a one-sample t-test was conducted. The results were significant at the .001 level and Hypothesis 1 was supported (for own company vs. similar Michigan company, t(69) = −5.01, *p* < .001; for own company vs. similar company in U.S., t(68) = −7.31, *p* < .001).

Next, to assess whether distance affects optimistic bias, a comparison was made of the mean difference between optimistic bias of respondents' own company vs. a company like their own in Michigan vs. a company like theirs in the U.S. A paired samples t-test was conducted and Hypothesis 2 was supported at the .001 significance level [t(68) = 6.78, *p* < .001]. That is, distance is positively related to the magnitude of optimistic bias.

Perceived Vulnerability

Corporate spokespersons who perceive their organizations low in vulnerability (*M* = −1.40, *SD* = 1.93) tend to show higher optimistic bias than those who perceive high vulnerability (*M* = −.53, *SD* = 1.25) to bioterrorism [t(67) = −2.27, *p* < .05]. Corporate spokespersons who perceive their own organizations low in vulnerability (*M* = −2.64, *SD* = 2.77) tend to show higher optimistic bias than those who perceive high vulnerability (*M* = −1.53, *SD* = 1.83) to bioterrorism [t(66) = −2.00, *p* < .05]. Thus, Hypothesis 3 was supported.

In the example above, you see they tested Hypotheses 1 and 2 using a one-sample t-test for Hypothesis 1 and a paired t-test for Hypothesis 2. Can you explain why they used those particular statistical tests?

Regression Example.   Here's another example of analysis of survey data: Botta and Dumlao (2002) wanted to see if there was a relationship between conflict and communication styles between fathers and daughters and eating disorders in the daughters. They had many hypotheses and research questions, all pertaining to that general topic (conversation orientation, conformity orientation, pluralistic, laissez-faire, and protective—all referring to family communication styles; compromising, collaborating, avoiding, accommodating, confronting, and avoiding—all referring to conflict styles):

H_1: Conversation orientation as encouraged by the father will be a significant negative predictor of anorexic and bulimic behaviors.

H_2: Conformity orientation as encouraged by the father will be a significant positive predictor of anorexic and bulimic behaviors.

H_3: Being raised by a pluralistic father will be a significant negative predictor of anorexic and bulimic behaviors.

H_4: Being raised by a protective father will be a significant positive predictor of anorexic behaviors.

H_5: Compromising as a way to respond to conflict will be a significant negative predictor of anorexic behaviors and a significant negative predictor of bulimic behaviors.

H_6: Collaborating as a way to respond to conflict will be a significant negative predictor of anorexic behaviors and a significant negative predictor of bulimic behaviors.

H_7: Avoiding as a way to respond to conflict will be a significant positive predictor of anorexic behaviors.

H_8: Accommodating as a way to respond to conflict will be a significant positive predictor of anorexic behaviors.

H_9: Confronting as a means of responding to conflict will be a significant positive predictor of bulimic behaviors.

H_{10}: Avoiding as a means of responding to conflict will be a significant negative predictor of bulimic behaviors.

RQ_1: Is being raised by a protective father, a laissez-faire father, or a consensual father a significant predictor of bulimic behaviors?

RQ_2: To what extent do family communication styles as encouraged by the father moderate the influence of a strong drive to be thin on anorexic and bulimic behaviors?

RQ_3: To what extent do conflict resolution styles between father and daughter moderate the influence of a strong drive to be thin on anorexic behaviors and on bulimic behaviors?

From "How do Conflict and Communication Patterns between Fathers and Daughters Contribute to or Offset Eating Disorders" by Renee Botta & Rebecca Dumlao, *Health Communication, Vol. 14, No. 2*, January 4, 2002; reprinted by permission of the publisher (Taylor & Francis Ltd, http://www.tandfonline.com).

To measure family communication patterns, conflict styles, and eating disorders, Botta and Dumlao (2002) used Likert scales. To analyze the data, they used a regression analysis because they had interval data (Likert scales) and they wanted to predict outcomes—to see if the independent variables (communication and conflict patterns) could predict (have a predictive relationship with) the dependent variable (eating disorders).

From "How do Conflict and Communication Patterns between Fathers and Daughters Contribute to or Offset Eating Disorders" by Renee Botta & Rebecca Dumlao, *Health Communication, Vol. 14, No. 2,* January 4, 2002; reprinted by permission of the publisher (Taylor & Francis Ltd, http://www.tandfonline.com).

The hypotheses and research questions were tested using hierarchical regression with anorexic and bulimic behaviors as the two criterion variables and the two FCP dimensions, the four conflict resolution styles, a drive to be thin, and the interactions as predictor variables.

H1 was supported for anorexic behaviors, but not for bulimic behaviors. Conversation orientation was a significant negative predictor of anorexic behaviors ($\beta = -.137$, $p = .046$) predicting 2 percent of variance, $F(3,206) = 1.05$, $p = .046$. Young women who do not appear to have a base of experience for talking things through with their fathers are more likely to engage in anorexic behaviors. Conversation orientation was not a significant predictor of bulimic behaviors ($\beta = -.073$, $p = .289$).

H2 was not supported for anorexic behaviors or for bulimic behaviors. Conformity orientation was not a significant predictor of anorexic behaviors ($\beta = .066$, $p = .374$). Conformity orientation was not a significant predictor of bulimic behaviors ($\beta = .052$, $p = .482$).

H3 was supported for anorexia. Young women from pluralistic families ($M = 1.85$, $SD = .64$) are less likely to be symptomatic of anorexia than those from other family types ($M = 2.08$, $SD = .76$), $t = -2.11$, $p = .036$. Fathers who encourage open communication while not encouraging conformity seem to provide a family environment that limits the development of anorexia. H3 was not supported for bulimia. Young women from a pluralistic family ($M = 1.91$, $SD = .60$) are no less likely to be symptomatic of bulimia than those from other family types ($M = 2.05$, $SD = .72$), $t = -1.36$, $p = .176$.

H4 was not supported. Protectives ($M = 2.05$, $SD = .71$) are no more likely to be symptomatic of anorexia than those whose fathers encourage other styles of family communication ($M = 1.99$, $SD = .73$), $t = 0.66$, $p = .511$). Fathers who do not encourage open communication while encouraging conformity do not seem to produce daughters who are more likely to engage in anorexic behaviors.

Results for RQ1 reveal young women with a laissez-faire father ($M = 2.07$, $SD = .82$) are no more likely to be symptomatic of bulimia than those of other fathers ($M = 1.99$, $SD = .65$), $t = 0.24$, $p = .813$. Young women with a protective father ($M = 2.05$, $SD = .73$) are no more likely to be symptomatic of bulimia than those with other fathers ($M = 1.99$, $SD = .65$), $t = 0.64$, $p = .521$. Young women with a consensual father

The excerpt above shows the results from their regression analysis. They used hierarchical regression, which is a method in which the researcher adds variables in a specified sequence, based on hypotheses or prior knowledge. You may notice they report their findings in terms of *beta weights*, indicated as β, which represent standardized regression coefficients (Reinard, 2006).

Experiments

Chi Square Example.   When we're discussing experiments, in thinking about our analyses, we must first think about the distinction between our independent and dependent variables. In the case of experimental designs, we are almost always looking to see if scores on some dependent variable change from group to group. Frequently, we will want to compare the mean of our dependent variable across these groups. Boster et al. (2009) conducted a field experiment to test a compliance gaining technique called *dump-and-chase* (DAC), which uses strategic persistence as a tactic. They tested the technique against other possible techniques. Their journal article reports on two different experiments conducted; we'll take a look at the first one. They randomly selected sixty pedestrians and approached them with a request using one of three compliance strategies: the test strategy, DAC; another compliance gaining strategy, called *door in the face* (DITF); and a placebo strategy (PI), which, like the two test conditions, also makes a request but gives an irrelevant reason for the request. Interestingly, they don't actually state a hypothesis or RQ, but a study objective: "The primary goal of this study is to test its effectiveness as a compliance-gaining technique relative to other techniques of known effectiveness" (p. 222).

Their independent variables are the compliance gaining techniques, nominal variables. Data on gender was also collected as additional independent variables. Their dependent variables are the participants' compliance with the request. The example below shows the results of their statistical tests, the Chi Square test of independence in which they tested to see if the three groups differed in terms of compliance. They found that, in fact, the DAC group had statistically significantly higher compliance than the other two groups.

Compliance rates for the target request are presented in Table 2. Overall, the three compliance rates differed from one another, χ^2 (2, $N = 60$) = 6.72, $p < 0.05$. A focused comparison indicated that the DAC technique resulted in a substantially higher compliance rate than did the DITF technique, χ^2 (1, $N = 40$) = 6.67, $p < 0.05$, $r = 0.41$, $OR = 6.00$. Additional focused comparisons showed that both the DAC and PI conditions, χ^2 (1, $N = 40$) = 0.90, *ns*, $r = 0.15$, $OR = 1.83$, and the

Table 2 Target Compliance Rate: Experiment 1

Compliance	Condition		
	DAC (%)	**DITF (%)**	**PI (%)**
Complied	12 (60)	4 (20)	9 (45)
Did Not Comply	8 (40)	16 (80)	11 (55)

Analysis of Variance Example.   In research looking at the effects of whether a person considers specific or abstract content and persons (when he thinks of violent video games) on his perceptions of the games, Ivory and Kalyanaraman (2009) set up a 2 × 3 factorial design between-subjects experiment. They tested two levels of content abstraction ("the most violent game with which you are familiar," and "games in general") and three levels of person abstraction ("other students in the United States," "other students on this campus," or "the person currently sitting nearest me") among 122 undergraduate students. They had three hypotheses, predicting that:

H_1: Perceptions of the effect of violent video games on aggression will differ by who they think is being effected—highest for people in the general U.S. population, next highest for other students at their campus, and lowest for specific persons in their class.

H_{2a}: Perceptions of the effect of violent video games on aggression will differ by type of game—highest for a specific game and lowest for violent games in general.

Or, the inverse of H2a:

H_{2b}: Perceptions of the effect of violent video games on aggression will differ by type of game—highest for violent games in general and lowest for a specific game.

Perceptions were measured using several nine-point Likert scales.

To test their first hypothesis, that perceptions of violent video games' effects on aggression will be highest for the general U.S. population, lower for other students on their campus, and lowest for individually selected, specific persons, they used a between-subjects ANOVA because they were testing differences between three or more groups. Their independent variable was "subject abstraction," which had three levels—"general U.S. population" was Level 1, "other students" was Level 2, and "individual specific students" was Level 3. Their dependent variable was "content abstraction," which had two levels of abstraction—"the most violent game with which you are familiar" was Level 1, and "games in general" was Level 2. Their ANOVA results indicated a p value of < .001; thus they reported a statistically significant difference between the three groups. Their reported statistics were: $F(2,116) = 8.54$, p < .002, $\eta^2_p = .128$. Remember that their hypothesis said that the perceived aggression would be highest for the group of "people in the general U.S. population," and it was ($M = 4.50$, $SD = 1.81$). They said it would be next highest for other students at their campus, and it was ($M = 3.43$, $SD = 1.85$). They predicted it would be lowest for specific persons in their class, and it was ($M = 2.93$, $SD = 1.72$). Thus, they rejected the null hypothesis (that there was no difference) and accepted their test hypothesis, H_1.

By the way, the F statistic they're reporting from their ANOVA is a statistic that refers to a probability distribution. SPSS reports this statistic and automatically finds the critical value of F that determines statistical significance. In their reporting of the findings ($F(2, 116) = 8.54$, $p < .001$), the 2 refers to the degrees of freedom between groups, and the 116 refers to the degrees of freedom in total. The 8.54 is the between-groups F statistic. Of course, the p-value is the probability of accepting the null hypothesis. Since you're not computing these by hand, you won't be using these numbers directly in the F formula, but you do report them as SPSS gives them to you. Their next information ($\eta^2 = .128$), is somewhat similar to a correlation coefficient, and refers to the effect size of each individual independent variable and a measure called *eta squared*. Their statistic means that 12.8 percent of the variance is contributed by each variable that contributes a significant difference (Reinard, 2006).

Recall that they set up a 2×3 factorial design, so they will be comparing six groups. To analyze this, they would have used a two-way ANOVA. Notice that, rather than reporting one F test, there are two different F tests reported. They report the *main effect* (the effect of one independent variable by itself) for content abstraction and report the direction of the difference ("specific game" condition has lower effects and "games in general" condition has higher effects). They also report interaction effects, or the effect of the two independent variables (content abstraction and person abstraction) interacting with each other (which they report was not statistically significant). In short, they found differences among those who considered different content abstractions, but found that consideration of person abstraction plus content abstraction did not make a difference over content abstraction alone. Note that they also found a statistically significant main effect for person abstraction, and their interaction analysis found that consideration of content abstraction plus person abstraction did not make a difference over person abstraction alone.

Writing Quantitative Findings ▼

General Information about Quantitative Writing

The preceding examples may make you think that writing up your research findings is a confusing process, but actually, writing quantitative research papers is pretty straightforward. Let's answer the first questions students always ask about papers: How long should it be? Typically, quantitative research reports in Communication are about twenty to twenty-five pages long, not counting title page, abstract page, references, or tables or figures.

The second question students might ask is: How do I write it? Your writing style will be relatively formal, much more formal than our writing in this textbook. You don't necessarily have to use the *one says* language (which admittedly is very hard to read and comprehend), but you do need to use formal English and proper grammar. It depends on the journal to which you're submitting the paper, but you might use the term "this research shows," or, alternately, "these researchers found," or "we found." Some journal editors cringe at giving *research* human characteristics (by being able to show us something), but others think that "we found" is too informal. Whichever level of formality you use, keep it consistent throughout your paper. Of course, as with any other paper you write, journals (and professors) expect your language to be free of any language that would be considered sexist or discriminatory in any way. Therefore, if you're referring to men and women, use the plural form or say "he or she" (or "she or he").

In quantitative research, you write with certainty. Remember, quantitative researchers are measuring objective reality, and if your study has been properly and appropriately conducted, you can write with the certainty of that objective reality. In quantitative reports, you might read phrases such as "the hypothesis was not supported," or "variable A is positively related to variable B," or "the preferred method is overwhelmingly. . . ." Unlike qualitative research reports (see our next section of the textbook), quantitative researchers are unlikely to use phrases such as "seems to," "indicates that," or "tends toward." Quantitative researchers are much more positive than that in reporting their objective reality.

Elements of the Paper

Introduction and Literature Review.   You'll start your paper with an Introduction. Usually, your Introduction will begin by telling us about the problem to be solved, the question to be answered, or at least the general topic you're examining. In the Introduction, you might tell us your RQ or hypothesis, or at least begin to build the argument for that. You'll explain why you chose to study this topic (this is more a discussion of the research building to this topic rather than your personal interest). You also want to answer the "so what" question by giving us data that convinces us of the relevance and significance of the topic. This is probably the most important part of your Introduction.

You might have a separate Literature Review, if you are building the case for your research on a good body of previous research or theory. If you are writing a shorter paper, or if there is very little prior research to report, your Literature Review might be part of your Introduction.

We discussed both of these sections of the paper in detail in Chapter 4, so we'll refer you to that chapter for more information.

RQs or H.   Your Introduction should flow right into your RQ or H section. If you properly built your argument from the beginning of your paper, you have stated in the Introduction: "This is the general topic area of my research"; in the Literature Review: "This is what's known about my research topic, and these are the theories and concepts on which I am building my project"; in the RQ/H section then: "Therefore, this is why I want to ask this question or test this hypothesis."

Sometimes, your H or RQ section is actually part of your Literature Review, if they are tightly based on the argument you are building in that section. In the example below, Salmon, Park, and Wrigley (2003) did just that in their paper on optimistic bias and corporate reactions to bioterrorism.

Harris & Middleton, 1994; Klar, Medding, & Sarel, 1996; Perloff, 1987; Weinstein & Klein, 1996; Whaley, 2000). Optimistic bias has been reported repeatedly to be greatest when subjects compared themselves to general others such as typical or average group members of the same age and gender (Taylor & Lobel, 1989; Weinstein & Klein, 1996; Wood, Taylor, & Lichtman, 1985).

However, more specific targets of comparison are proposed to have a different influence on optimistic bias. When participants are asked to compare their potential vulnerability with that of others, the illusion of invulnerability tends to be greater when people compare themselves with a close friend or an average college student than with their closest friend or family members (Chapin, 2000; Harris & Middleton, 1994; Klar et al., 1996; Perloff, 1987; Perloff & Fetzer, 1986). Therefore, as psychological distance increases (e.g., my closest friend, students in my class, students in my college, other students in the U.S., etc.), the degree of optimistic bias also tends to increase (Chapin, 2000). Perloff (1993) ascribed differential levels of optimistic bias to the difference in distance that may also reflect the heterogeneity and size of the audience or group (Perloff, 1993).

Based on the above discussion, the following research questions and hypotheses are proposed:

H₁: Corporate spokespersons will tend to estimate their own organization's risk to be less than that of other organizations similar to their own.

H₂: Optimistic bias will be greater for referents that are more distant (e.g., other corporations in the U.S.) than proximate (other corporations in the state).

Perceived Vulnerability, Susceptibility, and Controllability

According to prior research, optimistic bias is reportedly less a function of demographics such as age, gender, race, or education than of such psychological

From "Optimistic Bias and Perceptions of Bioterrorism in Michigan Corporate Spokespersons, Fall 2001" by Charles Salmon, Hyun Soon Park & Brenda Wrigley, *Journal of Health Communication, Vol. 8, No. 1*; reprinted by permission of the publisher (Taylor & Francis Ltd, http://www.tandfonline.com).

Method.   Your next section is where you describe—and justify—what you did and how you did it. When readers critique your research, it is the Methods section that will make or break their judgment. In this section, you will first tell us the population you are attempting to represent and how your sampling design ensured this representation. Explain your sampling design in detail—who you talked to and why they were selected; how you selected your sample; your sample size and justification for that size; when you collected your data and what data collection method you used; where you collected your data and how might that have affected validity and reliability; who specifically did the data collection, and how they were trained; and how reliability was insured. The participants should be described in enough detail that the reader can visualize them. If there was attrition, tell us the number of subjects who dropped out, the reasons for the attrition, and information about the dropouts, if available.

See below for a great example of a Method section from the Botta and Dumlao (2002) research.

From "How do Conflict and Communication Patterns between Fathers and Daughters Contribute to or Offset Eating Disorders" by Renee Botta & Rebecca Dumlao, *Health Communication, Vol. 14, No. 2,* January 4, 2002; reprinted by permission of the publisher (Taylor & Francis Ltd, http://www.tandfonline.com).

METHOD

Participants

After signing the required consent forms, 357 students from a university in the midwest and a university in the southeast completed questionnaires with established instruments to tap FCPs, conflict styles, and eating disordered behaviors along with other items that were part of another study. Because 90% of those with eating disorders are women (APA, 1994), men were excluded from analysis, reducing the sample to 220.

The sample was further reduced to the 210 participants who were younger than 24 years of age (90.5% of whom were 18–21 years of age) to reduce error due to forgetting what communication within the family was like when the participants lived at home.

Control Variables

Ethnicity was entered as a control variable due to differences in the rate of eating disorders among ethnic groups (e.g., Neff, Sargent, McKeown, Jackson, & Valois, 1997). Self-reported ethnicity resulted in 85.7% European American, 7.6% African or Caribbean American, 3.3% Latin American, 1.9% Asian American, 1.0% Native American, and 0.5% for whom their ethnicity was not indicated.

Family Communication

Ritchie's (1991) Revised Family Communication Patterns (RFCP) Instrument uses 16 items, each with a 5-point Likert scale ranging from 1 (strongly disagree) to 5

You'll also need to define your variables—all of them—all the ones you included in your RQ or H. In your Introduction and Literature Review sections, you should have given us the conceptual definition of your variables and you might also have shown us how other researchers have operationalized the same variables. Now it's time to tell us how, in your specific study, you operationalized your variables. Make sure all variables are clearly defined. Spell out for us which are independent and which are dependent.

Be specific about how you measured your variables—describe the scales or questions in detail so we could replicate them if we wished. If a published instrument was used, tell us the reliability and validity prior researchers (or scale developers) found with it, describe the scale in detail, and cite the appropriate reference(s). If an unpublished instrument was used, describe the traits that it was designed to measure, its format, and the possible range of scores. The whole instrument should also be reproduced in the Appendix of your paper. In addition to describing your measurement scales or instruments, all other details about your method—experimental procedures and other relevant information about how you conducted the study—should be described in sufficient detail so that the study can be replicated. The example below shows us how a relatively complex experimental design was explained in Boster and colleagues' 2009 study of compliance gaining strategies.

Used with permission of Taylor & Francis Group, from "Dump-and-Chase: The Effectiveness of Persistence as a Sequential Request Compliance Gaining Strategy" by F.J. Booster et al, *Communication Studies, Vol. 60, No. 3, 2009*; reprinted by permission of the publisher (Taylor & Francis Ltd, http://www.tandfonline.com).

Procedure

The 20 observations made in each message condition were divided equally across the four different locations (on a university campus, outside of a shopping mall, on the sidewalk of a suburban commercial district, and on the sidewalk of an urban business district). Furthermore, the 20 observations per condition were divided equally across three time periods (10:00am–1:00pm, 1:00pm–4:00pm, and 4:00pm–7:00pm). After selecting a location and time, the experimenter (E) followed the described sampling plan and selected an S. The E, observing unobtrusively, telephoned the identity of the S and compliance-gaining message condition to the C who was waiting out of sight and ready to approach the S. The C then approached the S, making eye contact, gesturing with the wave of a hand, and saying, *"Excuse me."* The C then delivered the assigned compliance-gaining condition. If the S complied with the request, the C entered the building, returned in 10 minutes and retrieved the bicycle before riding away to prepare for the next S. If the S did not comply with the C's request, the C rode away and prepared for the next S. In all cases, the S was debriefed and consent was obtained using an IRB-approved procedure.

Instrumentation

After the request, the E recorded the sex of the S and whether or not the S complied with the C's request. The C kept mental record of how many chases were used in the DAC condition and if the concession was presented in the DITF condition. The C reported these results to the E when preparing for the next S.

Results. Which brings us to the *meat* of your paper—the Results section. This is the statistics-heavy section. You might begin by telling us how you analyzed your variables. Remember, you're justifying this based on your RQs or Hs and the type of data you are working with, so make that clear in this section. Organize the Results section around the research hypotheses (or purposes or questions) stated in the RQ/H section; describe the analysis and results for the first hypothesis, then describe them for the second hypothesis, and so on. Say something such as, "for RQ$_1$, I analyzed the data using. . . ." Tell us what statistics you used and any other details we need to decide whether to agree with your findings. Standard statistical procedures need only be named; you do not need to show the formulas. Point by point, tell us what you found. You might say, "for H$_1$, I found these statistical results which supported (or did not support) the null hypothesis." Give us your percentages and numbers, results of your statistical tests, and a brief interpretation of those results. Raw scores are usually not reported; only the statistics based on them are reported. Present descriptive statistics first, usually starting with measures of central tendency and variability (or, for categorical data, starting with frequencies and percentages). See below for an example of the Results section in the Botta and Dumlao (2002) study on fathers' communication and eating disorders.

From "How do Conflict and Communication Patterns between Fathers and Daughters Contribute to or Offset Eating Disorders" by Renee Botta & Rebecca Dumlao, *Health Communication, Vol. 14, No. 2*, January 4, 2002; reprinted by permission of the publisher (Taylor & Francis Ltd, http://www.tandfonline.com).

The hypotheses and research questions were tested using hierarchical regression with anorexic and bulimic behaviors as the two criterion variables and the two FCP dimensions, the four conflict resolution styles, a drive to be thin, and the interactions as predictor variables.

H1 was supported for anorexic behaviors, but not for bulimic behaviors. Conversation orientation was a significant negative predictor of anorexic behaviors ($\beta = -.137$, p = .046) predicting 2% of variance, F(3,206) = 1.05, p = .046. Young women who do not appear to have a base of experience for talking things through with their fathers are more likely to engage in anorexic behaviors. Conversation orientation was not a significant predictor of bulimic behaviors ($\beta = -.073$, p = .289).

Watch your language as you present your results. You do not *prove* a hypothesis; your data or findings *support* or *do not support* your hypothesis (Reinard, 2006). Organize large amounts of data in tables and give each table a number and descriptive title (i.e., caption). In the text, describe the main conclusions to be reached based on each table and point out highlights that the reader may otherwise overlook. You do not need to discuss each entry in a table. Statistical figures (i.e., drawings such as histograms) should be professionally drawn and used sparingly in journal articles. Statistical symbols should be italicized. Use the proper case for each statistical symbol. Numerals that start sentences and that are less than 10 should usually be spelled out.

Discussion.   After you give us the results of your statistical testing and analysis, you then discuss them. This section is where you get to show off your analytical prowess and good mind for interpretation. In this section, discuss the highlights of the results. If there is room, give us either a brief summary of the study or a longer summary of what you did. Restate your hypotheses and tell us if they were supported by the data.

Take us back to the Introduction and Literature Review and remind us (yourself included) why you conducted this study in the first place. There was a reason you wanted to find something out. Now that you know whatever it is you found out, what does it *mean*? What does it mean for you? For society? For practice or policy? For the larger body of knowledge? What are the implications of the results? It is appropriate here to speculate about their meaning. Where is your data consistent and inconsistent with the literature you cited earlier? What does that mean?

Below is a good example of a Discussion section from the Salmon, Park, and Wrigley (2003) study of optimism bias and bioterrorism. Note how they tied the results to the events going on at the time and discussed how the timing of the study likely affected the results.

From "Optimistic Bias and Perceptions of Bioterrorism in Michigan Corporate Spokespersons, Fall 2001" by Charles Salmon, Hyun Soon Park & Brenda Wrigley, *Journal of Health Communication, Vol. 8, No. 1*; reprinted by permission of the publisher (Taylor & Francis Ltd, http://www.tandfonline.com).

Discussion

This is the only known study to document levels of awareness of the threat of bioterrorism in U.S. corporate spokespersons at the time of the September and October 2001 terrorism attacks. The findings indicate that levels of awareness of bioterrorism at that time were extremely low. The vast majority of corporate respondents were unaware of prior biological attacks in the United States, as well as differences between chemical and biological weapons, a distinction that has profound implications in terms of crisis response: biological organisms mutate and are potentially contagious, making them potentially far more hazardous to corporate security personnel. The finding that half of the respondents were still not aware of a bioterrorism event in the U.S. by Phase 2 of the data collection should, in fairness, be considered in the context that, at the time, the deaths attributed to anthrax were not definitively linked to terrorism.

As should be expected, corporate spokspersons admitted that they were largely unprepared for such a threat. Few had crisis management plans in place to deal specifically with the threat of terrorism. Most showed a strong preference to turn to state and local, rather than federal, authorities for information, and a preference for the telephone.

Often, researchers include study limitations (and perhaps strengths) in this section. We stated earlier that every method has its strengths and weaknesses. You made trade-offs when making each of your decisions. Now is the time to discuss those trade-offs and their implications to the research. Tell us: If you knew then what you know now, if you had to do it over again, what you would do differently. Perhaps you might want to suggest the next step in future research in this area; what specifically you would suggest. This section also acts as your concluding section, and every good Communication scholar knows that we use our Conclusion to remind our audience what you've just told them. Please note that it is inappropriate to introduce new data, new information, new results, or new references to literature in the Discussion and Conclusion section (Pyrczak & Bruce, 1992).

• •

Evaluating and Critiquing Quantitative Research ▼

When you are reading a journal article, proofreading your own research paper, or perhaps helping a fellow student by critiquing his or her research, what should you be looking for? What are the criteria for evaluating good quantitative research?

Not surprisingly, how you evaluate and critique a research study depends on the type of research it is. For all research, however, there are some general items you want to examine.

First, you want to take a look at the validity and reliability threats we discussed throughout this textbook and compare the design of the research against those threats. For example, was the sampling procedure subject to selection bias? Was the observation subject to the Hawthorne effect? Does the sample adequately represent the population?

You want to take a look at the sample size and determine if the study has sufficient statistical power to address the Hs and RQs. What's the quality of the instruments used? Did the researcher report validity and reliability statistics or have a good rationale for using these measurements?

Overall, you want to answer the following questions in a critique of quantitative research:

1. What was the reason for conducting this study?
2. What did the researcher intend to accomplish?
3. How were the participants selected and assigned? Which, if any, were lost and how did this affect validity and reliability?
4. Were the measurement instruments valid and reliable?
5. What was the study procedure? What did participants do? How were they measured? With what and by whom? Were testing conditions uniform? Were factors other than the independent variable operating?
6. How were the data analyzed? Was the analysis appropriate and accurate?
7. What were the major conclusions? Were they justified? Can the results be generalized? (Girden, 2001, p. 8)

When critiquing survey research, the two most important things you should look at are the validity and reliability of the questionnaire and measurements used, and the sample design. Because a survey especially is a methodology intended to generalize to a population, this last criterion is especially important. Here's a composite list of what Girden (2001) calls "caution factors when evaluating research" (p. 67):

Sampling Factors:

1. The sample frame
2. The criterion of exclusion
3. The response return rate (is it less than 70%)?
4. If the sample size is appropriately large for desired statistical power
5. The method used to contact nonresponders
6. The likelihood that characteristics of nonresponders introduced bias

Procedural Factors:

7. If participants were randomly assigned to groups or otherwise ensured group equivalence
8. If testing or observation was conducted throughout representative days, times, locations, etc.

Measurement Factors:

9. The nature of the questionnaire or measurement instrument (is it relevant to the purpose of the study?)
10. The reliability and validity of the questionnaire or measurement instrument

Data Collection Factors:

11. The number and characteristics of interviewers, observers, or data collectors
12. The training and supervision of interviewers

13. If interviewers or data gatherers do not affect participant performance; if appropriate, if test administrator was naïve with respect to study purpose

14. The uniformity of the interview setting or testing conditions

Analytical Factors:

15. If the analysis appropriately controls for extraneous variables

16. If appropriate statistical procedures were computed, appropriate to the variables and RQs or Hs

17. If statistical analysis was appropriately accurately performed and interpreted

(pp. 67, 96, 100, 219, 240)

We would like to add one additional area for evaluation criteria: ethics. It's important to determine if the study followed acceptable ethical procedures. Was the study conducted under the supervision of an institutional review board (IRB)? Were appropriate informed consent procedures followed? Were vulnerable populations properly protected?

So What?

In this chapter, we've pulled the book thus far together for you. We've shown you what to do with your data once it's collected, how to write it up once it's analyzed, and how to evaluate it once it's been written. We've shown you how researchers in the positivist paradigm—those who believe life can be measured and who want to do so—conduct research. We've shown you how quantitative researchers incorporate their ontology, epistemology, and axiology into research practice and how this carries through in the questions they ask, hypotheses they test, methods they design, data they collect, and statistics they use to analyze the results. It also carries into how they write their results and make their claims. In our next section, we'll show you how the other half lives—how qualitative researchers see their own research world.

Glossary

Central tendency
Also called summary statistics. It is a measure that represents the "typical" number in an array (distribution) of data. Depending on the type of data you are working with, this can be the mode, median, or mean.

Confidence level
Refers to the probability that I'm "close to correct" when I infer population characteristics based on my sample. How close I am to correct is the margin of error.

Correlation
The statistical test designed to test for linear relationships between variables when you have interval or ratio variables. When one variable occurs, the other variable tends to be present as well.

Correlation coefficient
Indicated by the Greek letter *r* (pronounced "rho"). It is a number that represents the extent that variables are related or go together and the magnitude of their relationships. Correlation cannot identify causation.

Just because two variables are related or vary together, we cannot determine whether one causes the other. The correlation coefficient ranges from +1.0 to –1.0. +1.0 indicates a positive relationship. –1.0 indicates a negative relationship. 0 indicates no relationship between the variables in question.

Inferential statistics

The type of statistic used when gathering information about a population based on the sample. The type of statistics used with significance testing.

Leptokurtic distribution

A distribution of scores that has stronger consistency around the mean than in a normal distribution. This type of distribution has a high peak, representative of the fact that there are a large number of scores in the center of the distribution. Leptokurtic graphs also have a small range, showing that there is a relatively small difference or variance between scores.

Mean

A measure of central tendency; the arithmetic average, computed by adding the scores together and dividing by the total number of scores.

Measures of dispersion

Measures that represent the distribution of scores in a data array. Dispersion can be thought of as statistics that represent differences in our data, whether it's the overall distance between the high and low scores (range), an average of how far the scores are from our mean (variance), or the standard deviation or square root of that variance.

Median

A measure of central tendency that represents the exact center point of our data set when it's put in numerical order. The median is the appropriate measure of central tendency for ordinal data. For example, a data set consisting of scores of 1, 3, 5, 9, 17 would have a median of 5, since it is the center point of our array. The median can help control for outliers in our data sets as in the above example. Even though 17 is an extreme value, 5 is still our median. If there is an even number of participants, the two middle numbers will be "tied" and will be averaged together to get the median. The median is also sometimes used for higher levels of data than ordinal because it controls for outliers.

Mesokurtic distribution

Having a normal bell shaped curve; a normal distribution of scores. This type of distribution has a moderate peak, representative of a normal number of scores in the middle of the distribution. A mesokurtic distribution also has a normal range with gradually sloping curves. When a mesokurtic distribution is perfectly centered, and not skewed in either direction, it is said to be *normal*.

Mode

The appropriate measure of central tendency for nominal data. The mode refers to the most frequently occurring value in our distribution. For example, a sample of communication studies students at UNC Charlotte might reveal that there are more female students than male students. Since the value "female" occurs more often in our data set, this value would be the mode.

Multiple regression

Represented by the symbol R, this predicts the dependent variable's value from two or more independent variables. Used when testing curvilinear effects that can't be tested with linear correlation methods, and for testing the effects of extraneous variables.

Negative correlation

Occurs when one variable increases while the other variable decreases, thus indicating two variables that vary in opposite directions.

Negatively skewed

More scores are on the right side of the graph—or higher than the mean.

Platykurtic distribution

Indicates a flat distribution of scores (farther away from the mean than in a normal distribution). This type of distribution has a low peak, representing the fact that a relatively small number of scores are in the middle of the distribution. Platykurtic graphs also have a wide range, which represents a large amount of variance in scores.

Population parameters

Population characteristics based on the sample characteristics.

Positive correlation

Occurs when both variables vary in the same direction.

Positively skewed

More scores tend toward the left side of the graph, or lower than the mean.

Range

A measure of dispersion that refers to the difference between the highest and lowest values in a data set. Calculated by subtracting the lowest score from the highest score. A data set with values between 1 and 29 would have a range of 28.

Regression

For interval or ratio data, the procedure that looks at the pattern in a data distribution to make predictions about future patterns. This procedure finds the "line" that best fits your data distribution. This is also known as prediction. It is another way to look at relationships between interval or ratio variables. The term refers to a *line of best fit* and is based on an algebraic equation (regression equation) that takes into account the regression line, the slope (the angle of the line), and intercept (the point at which the line intersects the y-axis).

Significance testing

Testing to determine the probability of there being a "true" difference between scores of a data set. Involves testing a null hypothesis in order to prove it, and therefore disprove the difference.

Skewness

Either positive (lower than mean) or negative (higher than mean), is the uneven, sloping, or asymmetrical graph of scores. Refers to the condition that occurs when more scores tend to be higher than the mean (negative skewness), or lower than the mean (positive skewness).

Standard deviation

One of the most commonly reported summary statistics for interval and ratio data is the square root of the variance. A measure of dispersion that represents the typical amount an entry deviates from the mean. Mathematically, it's the variance (the square of the average distance of scores from the mean) translated back into the original unit of measure by calculating the square root.

Statistical significance

The probability of there being a "true" difference between scores of a data set, as opposed to a perceived difference that may occur, but might in reality be simple "overlapping" of margins of error.

Stepwise selection

A method of inserting independent variables into an equation for multiple regression. Each independent variable is subjected to a significance test, starting with the smallest p value, and then proceeding to the next smallest and so on, until there are no more variables with statistically significant probabilities. Also called stepwise regression.

Variability

Contrasted with central tendency, variability refers to the differences in our data, how wide the range is, and how far a given value might be from the measure of central tendency. Variability is another word for dispersion.

Variance

A specific measure of dispersion that represents the average of how far our data is from our mean. Mathematically it is calculated by squaring the average distance of scores from the mean. It could also be referred to as the average of the sum of the squares, because it's computed by squaring the deviation scores.

References

Babbie, E., Halley, F., & Zaino, J. (2003). *Adventures in social research: Data analysis using SPSS 11.0/11.5 for Windows*, 5th edition. Thousand Oaks, CA: Pine Forge Press.

Babbie, E., Halley, F., & Zaino, J. (2007). *Adventures in social research: Data analysis using SPSS 14.0 and 15.0 for Windows*, 6th edition. Thousand Oaks, CA: Pine Forge Press.

Boster, F. J., Shaw, A. S., Hughes, M., Kotowski, M. R., Strom, R. E., & Deatrick, L. M. (2009). Dump-and-Chase: The effectiveness of persistence as a sequential request compliance gaining strategy. *Communication Studies, 60*(3), 219–234.

Botta, R. A., & Dumlao, R. (2002). How do conflict and communication patterns between fathers and daughters contribute to or offset eating disorders? *Health Communication, 14*(2), 199–219.

Field, A. (2015). *Discovering statistics using IBM SPSS statistics*. New York:

Girden, E. R. (2001). *Evaluating research articles: From start to finish*. Thousand Oaks, CA: Sage.

Gordon, J., & Berhow, S. (2009). University websites and dialogic features for building relationships with potential students. *Public Relations Review, 35*(2), 150–152.

Gravetter, F. J., & Wallnau, L. B. (1986). *Statistics for the behavioral sciences: A first course for students of psychology and education*. St. Paul, MN: West Publishing.

Ivory, J. D., & Kalyanaraman, S. (2009). Video games make people violent—Well, maybe not that game: Effects of content and person abstraction on perceptions of violent video games' effects and support of censorship. *Communication Reports, 22*(1), 1–12.

Pyrczak, F., & Bruce, R. R. (1992). *Writing empirical research reports: A basic guide for students of the social and behavioral science.* Los Angeles: Pyrczak.

Rea, L. M., & Parker, R. A. (1992). *Designing and conducting survey research.* San Francisco: Jossey-Boss.

Reinard, J. C. (2006). *Communication research statistics.* Thousand Oaks, CA: Sage.

Rodgers, J. L., & Nicewander, W. H. (1988). Thirteen ways to look at the correlation coefficient. *The American Statistician, 42,* 59–66.

Salmon, C. T., Park, H. S., & Wrigley, B. J. (2003). Optimistic bias and perceptions of bioterrorism in Michigan corporate spokespersons. *Journal of Health Communication, 8,* 130–144.

Williams, F. (1968). *Reasoning with statistics: Simplified examples in communications research.* New York: Holt, Rinehart and Winston.

RESEARCH UNDER THE QUALITATIVE PARADIGM

PART **4**

14

INTRODUCTION TO QUALITATIVE COMMUNICATION RESEARCH

CHAPTER OUTLINE

CHAPTER OUTLINE (Continued)

b. Significance Criteria
  i. RQ Criteria
  ii. Design/Methodology Criteria
  iii. Sampling Criteria
  iv. Data Collection Criteria
  v. Analysis Criteria

  vi. Writing Criteria
  vii. Credibility Criteria
7. So What?
8. Glossary
9. References

KEY TERMS

Active-member researchers
Advice questions
Aided account
Analytical notations
Artifact
Arts and humanities paradigm
Behavior or experience questions
Card pile sort
Clarifying
Co-constructed interview
Code list or codebook
Complete observer
Complete-member researchers
Constant comparison
Contrast question
Creative interviewing
Critical incident interviews
Crystallization
Data analysis
Data coding
Data saturation
Data transcription
Descriptive questions
Devil's advocate question
Dramatic or scenic method of writing
Emergent design
Emic
Epiphany interviews
Etic
Event analysis

Extreme instance sampling
Feeling question
Field notes
Field sites
Fieldwork
Focused observation
Frame analysis
Hypothetical question
Descriptive observation
In vivo
In-depth interviews
Inductive reasoning
Interpretive thematic analysis
Interpretive
Interview guide
Knowledge question
Life story interview
Material culture
Maximum variation sampling
Motive questions
Multivocality
Native-language questions
Naturalistic observation
Naturalistic
Negative case analysis
Observations
Observer-as-participant
Once-upon-a-time question
Opinion or value question
Oral history interviews
Participant observation

Performative texts
Peripheral-member researchers
Personal narrative interview
Polyphonic interviewing
Posing emergent ideas
Posing the ideal
Probing
Purposive sampling
Quotation questions
Reflexivity
Representation
Rhetorical paradigm
Schema analysis
Scratch notes
Selective observation
Sensitizing concept
Sensory question
Snowball or network sampling
Social constructionist paradigm
Social network analysis
Social science paradigm
Structural questions
Summary or traditional method of writing
Thematic analysis
Theoretical construct sampling
Time-line questions
Topical interview
Typical instance sampling

CHAPTER OBJECTIVES

1. To understand under what conditions, research questions, and study objectives qualitative research is appropriate
2. To understand the different approaches and paradigms to qualitative research and when each is appropriate
3. To understand the characteristics of the different approaches to qualitative research used in the field of Communication
4. To understand how qualitative research is collected, coded, analyzed, and reported

Qualitative Approaches to Research

Qualitative research is **interpretive**, as opposed to the more objective approach of quantitative research (Creswell, 2007). Recall that in quantitative research, something is either statistically significant or it's not, or the null hypothesis is either accepted or rejected. Qualitative research is—by design—much more attuned to inference, impressions, and a more inductive form of reasoning. Scholars using **inductive reasoning** discover patterns, make inferences, and draw conclusions from studying and observing certain phenomena in depth.

Qualitative research is appropriate to use when something needs to be explored (when not much is known about a topic) or when we need a complex, in-depth, detailed understanding about something, especially within its environment or context. We also use qualitative research to investigate a complex or sensitive issue that cannot be reduced to a simple, objective, quantitative study (Creswell, 2007). Many qualitative communication researchers study patterns, symbols, norms, rules, and assumptions in a culture to understand how people create meaning and how these meanings influence what people do and why they do it. Qualitative research methods are appropriate for communication studies researchers to use to describe or understand communication and interaction patterns, possibly within and between texts, dyads, groups, cultures, and contexts; to understand the influence of society, relationships, environment, or interactions on behavior; to closely examine interactive events in their natural settings; and to examine **reflexivity**—how your own thoughts, feelings, and behaviors interact with your research site and your research itself (Bochner & Ellis, 1992; Gill & Maynard, 1995).

In what ways do qualitative researchers study the things they study? They ask people, watch people, observe, participate, interview, review documents, and gather life histories, among other things. Qualitative research is **naturalistic**—it's often conducted *in the field* (qualitative researchers conduct **fieldwork** *in places called* **field sites**)—where participants live, work, and play. Qualitative research is often conducted **in vivo**—in a natural setting; qualitative researchers observe interactions, talk to people, or participate in events as they are happening. The *data* for qualitative research consists of communication that is word-based (transcripts, quotes, field notes, and texts), behaviorally based (observations, interactions, and actions), and emotion based (feelings, emotions, and thoughts).

interpretive
A research perspective in which understanding and interpretation of the social world is derived from one's personal intuition and perspective.

inductive reasoning
Reasoning that discovers patterns, inferences, and conclusions from studying and observing certain phenomena.

reflexivity
Acknowledgement of a researcher's positionality in relation to the study, study topic, and the study participants; addressing how one's own thoughts, feelings, and behaviors interact with his or her research site and his or her research itself.

naturalistic
Research that is conducted in the field or where participants live, work, and play.

fieldwork
Conducting observations in natural settings.

field sites
Groups, organizations, or cultures in which research is conducted.

in vivo
Research that takes place in a natural setting.

emergent design
A study design in which methods (including sampling, data collection, data protocols, coding, and analysis) are revised as the study emerges and progresses.

representation
In qualitative research, the concept that the qualitative sample should adequately represent the population under study to provide in-depth understanding of the experience.

multivocality
A form of writing that frequently includes multiple voices; it might be written from different points of view (including researchers and multiple stakeholders or participants).

etic
An approach to research that is more deductive and is based on a pre-existing concept or theory.

emic
An approach to research that is more inductive and based on the partici-pants' point of view and on the findings resulting from the study itself.

inductive reasoning
Reasoning that discovers patterns, inferences, and conclusions from studying and observing certain phenomena.

Qualitative researchers typically use an **emergent design**, revising the study (including sampling, data collection, data protocols, coding, and analysis) as the study emerges and progresses (Creswell, 2007).

Qualitative Communication Research Paradigms

In Chapter 2, we discussed the basic research paradigms that represent the different metatheoretical considerations: positivitism, interpretivism, and the critical perspective. Remember that people who follow the positivist paradigm tend toward the realist end of the metatheoretical spectrum. Positivists believe that reality is orderly, fixed, measureable, and objective. Positivists typically use quantitative methods because those are the methods that allow them to measure variables objectively. Qualitative researchers tend to follow more critical and/or interpretive paradigms. The interpretive paradigm values **representation** and **multivocality**, and believes that reality is subjective and interpreted. The critical perspective—which critiques power and values social change that alleviates power imbalances—can lean toward an objective or an interpretive stance, but critical scholars most frequently follow an interpretive worldview because this allows them to share and critique power and voice in their research. Some qualitative research takes what's called an **etic approach**; in that researchers base their research on a pre-existing concept or theory. This approach is more **deductive** and is said to move from the theory to the application, as research from an etic approach might seek to show the application of a specific theory (Montegut, 2017). Other qualitative research takes an **emic** approach. Research from this perspective is more **inductive** and the researcher bases his/her research on the participant's point of view and on the findings resulting from the study itself. This research is said to move from application to theory, because—as in grounded theory—a theory (or understanding) is grounded in the data itself (Scarduzio, 2017).

Qualitative research in the field of Communication Studies can be further broken down into four main perspectives: the **rhetorical paradigm**, the **social science paradigm**, the **social constructionist paradigm**, and the **arts and humanities paradigm**. These approaches overlap, and many qualitative scholars follow more than one approach, sometimes in the same study. Regardless of what paradigm is being used, the method used must be the right one for the issue being studied. If there is a specific research question based on a theoretical concept, then it might be more appropriate to use a more social science or social constructionist approach. If the study is attempting to let the reader vicariously experience a phenomenon through multiple senses, then it might be most appropriate to use a more arts-based method, like poetry or performance (Davis, 2014).

Social Science Paradigm

You can see in Figure 14.1 that communication scholars who do focus groups, grounded theory, thematic analysis, or discourse analysis tend to follow more of a social science paradigm. Qualitative researchers in this paradigm see research as

Figure 14.1. Four Main Perspectives for Conducting Qualitative Research in Communication Studies.

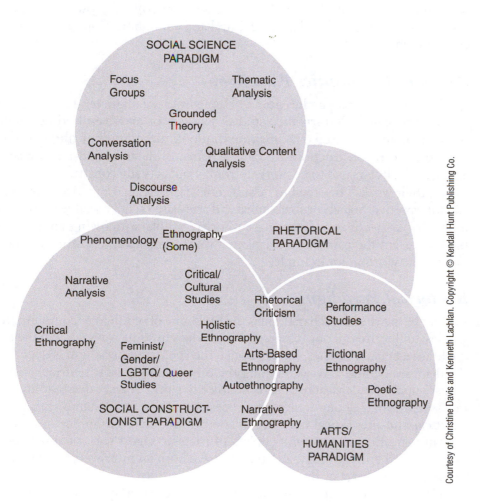

Courtesy of Christine Davis and Kenneth Lachlan. Copyright © Kendall Hunt Publishing Co.

rhetorical paradigm
A research paradigm that focuses upon a wide variety of texts in order to gain a deep understanding of the message within the communication process, to connect that understanding to broader practical and theoretical concerns related to human communication and the human condition in general.

social science paradigm
A research paradigm in which researchers see research as a systematic investigation and tend to believe in a reality that is more observable and better understood objectively.

social constructionist paradigm
A research paradigm that believes that shared meaning is constructed through our cultural systems and focuses on culturally situated action and interaction through which meanings and interpretations are socially, historically, temporally, and culturally constructed. Qualitative researchers in this paradigm tend to see research as a social construction of meaning.

arts and humanities paradigm
A research paradigm in which researchers tend to see research as a performance and tend to use art or performance to understand the world in an embodied and holistic manner.

a systematic investigation. Qualitative researchers following a more social science stance, even though they fall on the interpretivist end of the metatheoretical paradigms, tend to believe in a reality that is more observable and better understood objectively. People who do grounded theory or some kinds of discourse analysis are looking to identify meaning which exists within the communication act or text they are studying, although they realize the meaning they identify is subject to interpretation.

Social Constructionist Paradigm

Narrative scholars, narrative ethnographers, narrative auto-ethnographers, gender scholars, and people who do critical or cultural analysis, on the other hand, tend to follow a social constructionist paradigm, believing that shared meaning is constructed through our cultural systems and focusing on culturally situated action and interaction through which meanings and interpretations are socially, historically, temporally, and culturally constructed (Gergen, 1991). Qualitative researchers in this paradigm tend to see research as a social construction of meaning. Scholars under this perspective tend to conduct research that addresses questions about what ideas are being socially constructed; how they are being socially constructed; and what the cultural and communication systems are that construct meaning.

Arts and Humanities Paradigm

Qualitative researchers in the Arts and Humanities paradigm tend to see research as a performance. Performance studies scholars or arts-based ethnographers often favor an arts-based or humanities outlook, although they might also lean toward a social constructionist mental schema. Both social constructionist and arts-based scholars end to be more upfront about actually constructing meaning within their work. They tend to be subjectivists, to believe knowledge is relative and interpretive. Social constructionist and arts-based scholars value representing multiple perspectives and sharing authority. Scholars following an arts-based model present their findings in artistic ways—dramatic compositions or poetic or creative writing, for example.

Rhetorical Paradigm

And, since the rhetorical paradigm is the backbone of our field of communication studies, undergirds all our research, and overlaps in some ways with all the other qualitative epistemologies, in this model, the rhetorical paradigm is depicted in the diagram behind and overlapping the other paradigms. Rhetorical criticism focuses upon a wide variety of texts in order to gain a deep understanding of the message within the communication process, to tie that understanding to broader practical and theoretical concerns related to human communication and the human condition in general. Scholars of rhetoric take a social constructionist ontology and epistemology, and tend to have both an interpretivist and critical axiology at the heart of their work.

Of course, it is very common for scholars to overlap these paradigms in a single study—to conduct focus groups and analyze them using a feminist standpoint, for example, or to use grounded theory as a method but also employ a rhetorical concept for the analysis. Arts and humanities scholarship typically takes a critical/cultural analytical stance. We'll talk more about that when we discuss each of these methods individually.

Interpretive Research

Most qualitative communication researchers at least tend toward an interpretive stance. Even qualitative researchers with a more social science orientation lean toward a social constructionist bent in their ontology. Most qualitative scholars are likely to believe reality is constructed through interpersonal and cultural communication, and, as we study things, we influence those things by the act of studying them. Qualitative researchers perceive reality as not being completely objective and as being subject to interpretation. Now, how strongly a scholar believes and utilizes this determines where s/he falls on the social science-social constructionist-arts/humanities diagram. Qualitative scholars with different metatheoretical perspectives have different emphases on reflexivity, on the importance and style of writing, on being systematic, and so on.

● ●

General Characteristics of Qualitative Research

Despite these differences, qualitative scholars have more in common than differences. Qualitative researchers conduct research that is **naturalistic**—they study communication in at least a somewhat natural setting. They are interested in understanding how people see, experience, and behave in the world, and they are interested in representing that understanding. And qualitative scholars use similar tools to collect data—observation, participation, interviews, focus groups, document reviews, and so on. Like all scholars, qualitative communication scholars conduct research to answer specific questions and solve specific problems. We will discuss the role of research questions, theory, data collection, ethics, reflexivity, sampling, and writing for each method specifically in subsequent chapters. Here, however, are some general thoughts on how each of these characteristics looks in qualitative research in Communication Studies.

naturalistic
Research that is conducted in the field or where participants live, work, and play.

Research Questions or Study Objectives in Qualitative Research

Qualitative research is goal directed in that all scholars begin their study with at least a general sense of where they are headed with their research and—at least generally—what they want to find out. All qualitative researchers start with a specific problem or question, although sometimes it is simply to "understand x." The study objective or research question might be explicit or implicit, it might be stated or unstated, it might be broad or narrow, clear or vague, and it might change throughout the course of the research or it might stay the same. However, all qualitative researchers start with a question or problem in mind. Qualitative research lets us understand, describe, and get close to the people or contexts we're studying. It lets us understand how people see the world. Qualitative research answers questions such as: What is going on here? How do *they* do it? What does it mean to them? How do they interpret what it means to others? How can we describe and interpret how they act, what they tell us they know, and how they justify their actions?

The Role of Theory in Qualitative Research

Like scholars from all social science disciplines, qualitative scholars in Communication Studies use theory in some way in their research. Scholars from more social science orientations reflect a specific theoretical base in their research question and study design. They use theory as a foundation for their research, and their research question, sampling, data collection, and analytical decisions all stem from that theoretical base. In contrast, a scholar from a more social constructionist or arts-based focus might take a very different view of theory. Here is a quote from Ron Pelias, an arts-based performance studies scholar: "I don't really think about theory in the beginning. I launch into whatever interests me, which might be a

purposive sampling
A method of sampling in which the researcher selects participants based on their having experienced the phenomenon or issue under study.

theoretical sampling
Choosing a sample based on the people, events, groups, and so on who can shed light on a theory being investigated.

maximum variation sampling
A sampling method that selects study participants that represent a wide range of characteristics that are present in the population and are of interest to the research.

typical instance sampling
Consists of sampling units who have characteristics typical of a population.

extreme instance sampling
Consists of sampling units that have characteristics quite different from the rest of a population.

snowball or network sampling
This sampling method asks study participants to make referrals to other potential participants, who in turn make referrals to other participants, and so on.

data saturation
The collection and analysis of data until no new categories of theories are identified.

detail of my life or somebody else's life or some interaction. Then once I'm in the details of the project and reading and thinking conceptually and theoretically, that's when for me the theory comes in" (Pelias, qtd. in Davis, 2014, p. 32). Like Pelias, many interpretive scholars from more social constructionist or arts-based paradigms tend to use theory as an explanation—in order to understand what they have observed in their data or in order to explain their findings at the writing stage. Other scholars might start with a foundational theory and use or develop the same or another theory as explanation. For all, theory provides a way of thinking about, seeing, and understanding the phenomena being studied.

Sampling in Qualitative Research

In qualitative research, a sample size depends on the scope and objectives of the study (Starks & Trinidad, 2007). Most qualitative methods rely on **purposive sampling** methods, looking for participants who have experienced the phenomenon or issue under study (Starks & Trinidad, 2007). Depending on the study objectives, qualitative research projects might also use other sampling methods, most of which are discussed in Chapter 8, such as **theoretical construct sampling, maximum variation sampling, typical instance sampling,** or **extreme instance sampling.** Potential participants may be identified through **snowball** or **network sampling.** In the next several chapters, we'll discuss how this might be done in specific qualitative methods.

Sampling is one area in which qualitative scholars of different metatheoretical paradigms differ from each other. Davis (2014) describes this difference in terms of the "closeness of the relationship between the scholar and his/her research participants. Some scholars use themselves as their sample. These scholars collect data through observation, and capture it in field notes. Other scholars choose people with whom they are in a relationship as their sample, and their data consists of observation and/or informal conversations. They capture their data in field notes, and possibly via tape recording. Other scholars choose people they don't know as their sample, and use more formal methods such as interviews or focus groups for their data collection. Their data capture consists of audio and/or videotaping" (Davis, 2014, p. 134). Sample size in qualitative research depends on a process called **data saturation.** Data saturation refers to the point in data collection at which no new information is emerging. When you have reached data saturation, you typically collect a small amount of additional data to be sure nothing new is discovered, then you can conclude it is time to complete your fieldwork.

Data Collection in Qualitative Research

Data collection for qualitative researchers can be a thoroughly planned, well-thought-out endeavor for scholars on the social science end of the field, and can be more of a serendipitous emergent process for scholars taking a social constructionist or arts-based direction. Organizational communication scholar Sarah Tracy takes a social scientific approach to her qualitative research and, as she says, "you have to make some decisions upfront about data collection. Am I going to work with diaries? Am I going to bring people together in focus groups?

Am I going to do one-on-one interviews? . . . Doing the kind of qualitative research I do, that planning process has to be done upfront more than I might do if left to my own devices." (Tracy, qtd. in Davis, 2014, p. 35).

Carolyn Ellis and Buddy Goodall, both of whom take a more social constructionist approach to research, describe a study design that emerges as it evolves: "For me, it's a constant process of decision making. . . . I have to see what works and then I get involved in ethical considerations and what's working for the people who are my participants. Ideas keep coming to me along the way about . . . what data to collect, what's important, what isn't. I don't have a plan usually in the beginning, I kind of go in and get messy and try to figure out, . . . first, what am I looking for, next, what can we create together, then what's the best way to do it. Also taking into account I always hope my research will somehow be positive for the people I'm working with. So it has to be done in interaction with them" (Ellis, qtd in Davis, 2014, p. 34). Buddy Goodall suggests you can "write the best plan you can but you realize as soon as you're in the field it'll probably change. . . . You can't really anticipate all of the situations or questions that may come up but you can guess. You can do the best guess work you can . . . but there will be other things and probably even more interesting things that emerge in the field you probably didn't anticipate and I think that's part of it" (Goodall, qtd. in Davis, 2014, p. 35).

Chris Poulos, whose research flows between a social constructionist and an arts-based paradigm, describes his approach to data collection as "intuitive, following my instincts. Sort of decision on the spot rather than pre-planned decisions of any kind. . . . I call it a much more accidental approach; life presenting itself to me and then turning itself into a text. Sometimes I feel like I'm the channel for that" (Poulos, qtd. in Davis, 2014, p. 35). Finally, Ron Pelias who conducts arts-based research using an ethnodrama approach, says, "I start my initial writing process with a blank sheet of paper in front of me. I start scribbling, trying to find some kind of organizational scheme, some kind of scaffolding that might hold the subject together. The data collection for me is a way of going about the business of completing that scaffolding. So, once I have the scheme then I know what I need to go gather, whether that's interviewing or digging into my own experiences or doing additional research or whatever. I really can't proceed until I have that scaffolding in place" (Pelias, qtd. in Davis, 2014, p. 36). Regardless of their orientation to planning ahead, qualitative scholars typically collect data through observation, interviewing (group or individual), document analysis, and/or archival or artifact analysis. Scholars frequently use multiple methods of data collection in order to achieve **crystallization**—the process of reviewing multiple sources of data to capture a full, rich, multivocal, and nuanced view of the phenomenon under study (Ellingson, 2009; Richardson, 2003).

Observations. Qualitative researchers use **observations** to gain insight into the obligations, constraints, motivations, and emotions that participants experience as they complete everyday actions. You can observe events, interactions, or phenomena. You can observe normal everyday happenings, or special, unusual, or one-time events. You might observe people shopping, or eating, or working.

crystallization
The process of reviewing multiple sources of data to capture a full, rich, multivocal, and nuanced view of the phenomenon under study.

observations
A way to gain insight into the obligations, constraints, motivations, and emotions that participants experience as they complete everyday actions.

naturalistic observation
Observation in natural settings.

participant observation
When a researcher is participating in the life of others, but is still observing as a naïve outsider who doesn't understand exactly what's going on and needs to ask, explore, and try on the experience.

complete observer
Researchers who have little to no interaction with the people being observed.

peripheral-member researchers
Researchers who have some level of involvement with a group without core group involvement.

active-member researchers
Researchers who become involved with central activities of the group but do not fully commit themselves to the group.

complete-member researchers
Researchers who study settings in which they are already members or with which they are already affiliated.

descriptive observation
A type of observation that is usually done when the researcher is first in the field, in which the researcher observes everything, no matter how small, and takes notes on all details and observations.

You might, for example, observe patients, families, and providers interacting in a hospital setting, or families and friends at a child's birthday party. You could observe a family dinner or shoppers at the mall. You can observe systematically or accidentally, formally or informally. Observations help us understand the complex, lived experience of human beings. Qualitative researchers conducting studies such as ethnography, case study, phenomenology, and others often use observational techniques in natural settings, which is why it is sometimes called **naturalistic observation**. Observation in natural settings is also frequently referred to as fieldwork (Angrosino & de Pérez, 2003). Often, observation is referred to as **participant observation** because you are participating in the life of others. Regardless of your level of participation, it's typically considered ideal to take the stance of a naïve outsider who needs to explore deeply and try on the experience (Rock, 2007). As an observer, you might observe a few times, or—preferably—you might observe multiple times over a long period of time, likely months, maybe years.

TYPES OF OBSERVERS. Observation can be formal or informal. You can, for example, simply hang out. Or you can become more involved—become a volunteer, join a group, move in. Some ethnographers take on the role of **complete observer**, in which they have little to no interaction with the people being observed. This is done rarely, however, partly due to the incompatibility of informed consent procedures with lack of interaction with participants, and partly because researchers recognize that there really is no such thing as no-interaction or true objectivity. Researchers need to be aware that the very act of observing a setting will in fact influence and change behaviors of the people being observed (the Hawthorne effect, discussed in Chapters 7 and 12). Many researchers instead do **observer-as-participant**, in which the researcher interacts casually with participants, but still remains primarily an observer and does not become a member of the group being studied.

Other researchers take on the role of **peripheral-member researchers**, researchers who have some level of involvement with a group without core group involvement. **Active-member researchers** become involved with central activities of the group but do not fully commit themselves to the group. **Complete-member researchers** study settings in which they are already members or with which they are already affiliated (Angrosino & de Pérez, 2003).

TYPES OF OBSERVATIONS. There are several ways to observe. In **descriptive observation**, usually done when you are first in the field, you observe everything, no matter how small. You take notes on all details and observations. In **focused observation**, conducted after you've been in the field for a while, and after you've had a chance to start ruminating on what you are finding out and thinking about the data you've been collecting, you start to narrow your focus somewhat. You still take field notes on most things you are observing, but you can ignore some phenomena you have decided (based on your emerging analysis) are irrelevant to your study. In **selective observation**, as your time in the field is winding down, you concentrate on certain activities, again based on additional analyses, interviews, coding, and so forth (Angrosino & de Pérez, 2003).

Alternatively, in methods such as conversation analysis and discourse analysis, rather than taking field notes during the observation, researchers videotape and/or audiotape the event or interaction and then transcribe it word for word, adding information on nonverbal behavior and paralanguage.

WHAT OBSERVERS OBSERVE. What specifically do you observe? People—who is involved and who is not involved; the setting, the context, or the scene; and your impressions. Of course, remember that you are communication researchers, so you're observing communication—communication acts or interactions; how, when, and where they communicate; and what their communication might mean. Some qualitative scholars focus their observations on the 5 Ws and 1 H: who, what, when, where, why, and how. In terms of what to write down, you could respond to these questions:

WHO: Who is there (and not there)?

WHAT: What are they doing? What else is going on?

WHEN: When are you there? When are things happening? How long are things taking to happen? Is there is temporal difference in when things happen and don't happen?

WHERE: Where are you? What does it look like?

WHY: What motivations are you perceiving in the people you are observing?

HOW: How are people doing what they are doing? How are people communicating?

It's also helpful to focus on your five senses (vision, hearing, smell, touch, taste) as you observe. This would take the form of responding to these questions:

VISION: What are you seeing? Who is there (not there)? What else is there (not there)? What colors do you see? Is it dull or bright? Clear or hazy? Near or far away?

HEARING: What are people saying? What other sounds do you hear? Are they loud or soft? Near or far away? Clear or garbled?

SMELL: What do you smell? Are the smells pleasant or unpleasant? Sweet or sour? What do the odors have to do with how you (and people in the field) experience the phenomena?

TOUCH: What does it feel like? It is hot or cold? Wet or dry? Hard or soft? Rough or smooth? What emotions are you experiencing? What emotions do the people around you seem to be experiencing?

TASTE: What taste is in your mouth as you are in the field? What does that say about how you (and people in the field) experience the phenomena?

Of course, what you are observing specifically depends on your research question.

FIELD NOTES. How do you remember what you're observing? You take **field notes**. Field notes are taken in all sorts of ways: notebook, sketch pad, tape recorder, video recorder, laptop, even napkins, or, when necessary, the palm of

---

focused observation
A stage in qualitative observation which occurs after the researcher has been in the field for a while and begun preliminary analysis, in which the researcher begins to narrow his/her focus and ignores some phenomena that are irrelevant to his/her study.

selective observation
A stage of observation which occurs as the researcher's time in the field is winding down, in which the researcher concentrates on certain activities and on additional analyses, interviews, coding, and so forth that correspond to the meanings emerging from the data already collected.

field notes
A record of what was meaningful during an observation.

your hand. Field notes are a record of what was meaningful. They include mental observation, note taking during or after the observation, recording during or after, and journals or diaries highlighting your impressions as you interact in the field. Write it down, record it, remember it—the only rule is to do what you need to do so that you can vividly recall it later. You'll usually write rough notes, often called **scratch notes**, then embellish those notes soon after for more detailed field notes.

Here's an example of field notes your author Christine Davis took for research on hospice in which she observed hospice team meetings and interactions with patients (Davis, 2010). She was an **observer-as-participant**. She took brief notes in a notebook during most of the hospice team meetings she attended, and she dictated more detailed field notes into a small tape recorder after the meeting was over. Notice how the field notes represent a sort of stream-of-consciousness notation of her descriptive observation. She noted everything, since at this point she didn't know what the point of her analysis was going to be.

scratch notes
Rough notes that are embellished upon shortly after an observation.

observer-as-participant
A method of observation in which the researcher interacts casually with participants, but still remains primarily an observer and does not become a member of the group being studied.

> *Field notes following shadowing nurse C. with A. Ironically as I'm driving here the song "Spirit in the Sky" is playing and that makes me think of A. as I think of her corner table with all the religious icons, her candles, she's always got at least one candle burning, some of the candles are in Virgin Mary decorated vases or glasses. She's got a statue of Virgin Mary that's got neon lights that blink surrounding her. That's always kind of in the background of the room, a lot of beadwork and candles around. She's rearranged her bed this time, I haven't seen her in a while. She recently finished a chemotherapy treatment and is just blown up. Evidently that's partly due to the chemotherapy and partly due to the fact that her cancer has spread; she's got a huge mass, that's involving the bladder and the kidneys and the nurse verified later that it's also spread to her spine and she also has a compression fracture in her spine. The dr told her that since the cancer was in the bladder, that's causing a lot of her swelling. Her abdomen is huge. Very tender to the touch. She and the nurse talked about her pain. She described her pain as being centered in the abdomen and hips and was a sharp stabling pain that's going on and on that's aggravated by movement or activity. When she took her pain medication and lay down and relaxed that seemed to help. She also later talked about a pain that was shooting up her back from her hips and abdomen and later she talked about another pain in her abdomen that was a tearing pain and the nurse verified that was probably due to the mass pressing against all sorts of organs. She's having a great deal of nausea, vomiting, after her last chemo she just stayed in bed for 3 days, she was all worn out. When the nurse met with her, she sat down on the side of her bed, held her hand the entire time, actually had her hand on her arm the entire time, after a lot of questions about the pain, asked her to rate her pain on a scale of 1 to 5, asked her about nausea symptoms, questions about how often she urinated and how often she moved her bowels, to see what, she explained later, to see what organs were being affected, symptoms from the cancer and from the chemo I think also. She talked her about do you want to continue the chemo because of the side effects, and the pt said yes, they agreed that the side effects went on for 3 days but was helping a lot of the symptoms, was shrinking the primary tumor in the cervix and so that's alleviating symptoms. A. said that her leg which had been all swollen, was that went down with them chemo, so she's willing to take*

> *3 days of misery for another 3 weeks of feeling better before her next bout with chemo. She also said the Dr. said that with the cancer in the bladder that was also contributing to the blood clots and that would continue as well, and she's been in the hospital recently to have a screen put in for blood clots. The Dr. and nurse practitioner evidently went out week before last to straighten out her medication so she seems to be doing better. She was so sick after the chemo that she was not well enough to say she was out of her pain medication so she's been taking it max. so the nurse sat on her bed, asked her a lot of medical questions, asked her a lot of questions about if she's taking care of her kids, are her daughters helping out at all, is she standing up for herself. A. did say that she was in bed for 3 days, she sent the kids out of the room and didn't do anything and the daughters seemed to at least leave her alone. It's not clear if they understand how sick she is but they at least seem to at least be leaving her alone. Also, she said when her boyfriend's over there, they don't leave the kids with her, they look in the room, see the boyfriend there, and leave her alone. So she seems to be doing some things to stand up for herself. The nurse talked about, if she wanted to go into the hospice home after her next bout with chemo, just to get some relief, and have somebody to take care of her. A didn't respond, didn't look to me like she was pleased with the idea; it looked to me like she was not pleased with the idea, but she didn't respond one way or the other. They are seeing her twice a week now*

In-Depth Interviews.   Many qualitative researchers from all three traditions frequently use **in-depth interviews** as a method for collecting data. In qualitative research, think of the interview as an opportunity for the co-construction, exchange, and negotiation of ideas, information, and meaning. Instead of asking specific questions with pre-set responses as in quantitative surveys or interviews, qualitative interviews use an **interview guide** which typically consists of a list of topics to discuss or a topic outline. In-depth interviews resemble conversations between equals who systematically explore topics of mutual interest. Interviews are opportunities for participants to describe their worlds, in concert and negotiation with researchers. Such interviewing involves co-constructing a narrative with a participant—to understand his or her history and version of the story and the ways that he or she makes sense of his or her actions in the context of his or her cultural narratives. The goal of qualitative interviewing is to establish rapport with participants and to understand and learn from participants. When interviewing, qualitative researchers seek to understand participants' perspectives on an experience, because remember, in qualitative research, we want to retrieve experiences, gain insight, obtain information, obtain descriptions, foster trust, understand sensitive relationships, or create discourse to analyze (Fontana & Frey, 2003; Fontana & Prokos, 2007; Madison, 2005; Roulston, deMarrais, & Lewis, 2003; Silverman, 2003). Interviews can help us understand a phenomenon: They can help us identify it, discover it, and explain it; we can listen to participants' thoughts, ideas, feelings, and behaviors about it. Interviews can let us understand participants' natural attitudes, life experiences, preferences, intentions, and behaviors, and in doing so, we can better understand their language, knowledge, and experience (Fontana & Prokos, 2007).

in-depth interviews
Opportunities for participants to describe their worlds in concert and negotiation with researchers. Such interviewing involves co-constructing a narrative with a participant—to understand his or her history and version of the story and the ways that he or she makes sense of his or her actions in the context of his or her cultural narratives.

interview guide
An outline or list of topics or general questions to guide the in-depth interview.

Qualitative interviews are usually audiotaped and later transcribed, although if noticing nonverbal behaviors is also important you might prefer to videotape the interview. Word-for-word transcriptions let you analyze both what was said and how it was said (paralanguage and vocal disfluencies, for example). Alternatively, you can take notes instead of tape recording, but that does not allow you to attend to specific communication strategies in your analysis.

Here's an excerpt from an interview with a hospice chaplain in a study concerning the experience of hospice (Davis, 2010). Notice how it sounds like a natural conversation.

I take a bite of cake as Father Logan and I chat. "So, would you say hospice is a spiritual organization?" I ask.

He pauses for a minute and then responds thoughtfully. "I do not agree with this dichotomy between the spiritual and the secular. As I understand life, and from a biblical perspective, all of life is spiritual. Sitting here talking to you is an act of spirituality. Taking care of a patient physically, medically, is an act of spirituality because the body is as much of a person as the soul. You can't really take care of one part separate from the other. They are intertwined."

I nod. "You know, it seems to me somehow, by addressing the physical, hospice actually takes care of the spiritual." He licks a bit of icing off his fork, then leans forward, gesturing with his fork as he talks. "That gets back to hospice's philosophy of health care, which is holistic. I think the patients appreciate us because they feel loved and valued. Somebody cares."

"One of the things I notice is how you all touch the patients. I see a lot of hugging and touching."

"Yeah," he agrees. "One of the first things I noticed when I started with hospice is all the touching that goes on, among the hospice worker, the patient, and the caregiver. Touching people on the shoulder, rubbing their back."

"Do you do that much?"

"When I go to visit a patient, I might touch them on the back. If they're bad off, I'll make sure I rub their hand or their arms. Because touch communicates love and care."

I think of my dad when he was sick and how much touching meant to both of us. I nod.

He continues. "There are thousands of nerves in the skin. Touching speaks volumes to the patient and the caregiver. By the family seeing you touch the patient in some way, their burden is eased as well." (pp. 35–36).

TYPES OF INTERVIEWS. Interviewing can be structured, semi-structured, or unstructured. Most qualitative interviews in communication studies are fairly unstructured and open ended. In unstructured interviews, you discuss with participants their (and perhaps your) inner thoughts and feelings. You modify the interview as you go along. You would think of this type of interview as a guided conversation. Your goal is to be dialogic and interactive, understanding each other at a deep level of meaning (Fontana & Frey, 2003).

A **life story interview** documents all the significant streams of a person's life, to provide understanding of the larger cultural or historical frames. This can take a linear narrative form (what happened next), or can be more performative (tell me a story, or role play this situation). Full life history interviews are rare, but often aspects of a life might be examined in an interview. Life story interviews often look at turning points or disjunctures in a person's life as a way of studying identity, conflicts, and so on. **Oral history interviews** capture people's stories about their lives. Oral history is a person's recounting of a significant historical moment in their life, and would ask the participant to "give me your experiences of this historical time or event." A variation, a life history interview, takes place over several days in multiple sessions as people go about their everyday lives and give oral reports about their experiences. A **personal narrative interview** is a person's recounting—telling a story about—an event, experience, or point of view. A **topical interview** consists of a person's discussion of a topic, program, issue, or process. In **polyphonic interviewing**, the voices of the participants are recorded with minimal influence from the researcher and are reported separately (from each other) as individual voices, multiple perspectives, and differences between each are highlighted rather than glossed over. **Epiphany interviews** are interviews in which people tell about certain moments in their lives that are turning points, participants' transformational, existential moments in their lives. They provide rich, meaningful data.

Critical incident, episode analysis, account analysis, and protocol analysis interviews all ask participants to tell about a specific experience in a specific context, for example, "Tell me about a good day at work or school." In this type of interview, participants might reconstruct a scene, complete with dialogue/role playing, and the interviewer might ask questions such as "What did you mean when you said that?" or "What were you thinking when that happened?

Some qualitative researchers use what's called a **co-constructed interview**, an interview that is a collaboration between researcher and participant—the researcher and participant are full partners in the interview. The conversation between them is as important as the response given by the participant. **Creative interviewing** is adaptive to situations. These types of interviews may consist of multiple sessions over many days. They may be more intimate and dialogic, or may include shared stories between researchers and participants (Fontana & Frey, 2003; Madison, 2005).

TYPES OF QUESTIONS.

There is an almost unlimited list of types of questions you can ask in qualitative research. The purpose in giving you this list isn't as much to make you memorize lists, but to tweak your curiosity and generate ideas for your interview processes. Remember, too, that while the questions you ask are important, your questions will evolve and improve as you spend more time in the field.

---

life story interview

A type of interview that documents all the significant streams of a person's life, to provide understanding of the larger cultural or historical frames.

oral history interviews

A type of interview that captures people's stories about their lives.

personal narrative interview

A type of interview in which the participant recounts—tells a story about—an event, experience, or point of view.

topical interview

A type of interview that consists of a person's discussion of a topic, program, issue, or process.

polyphonic interviewing

A type of interview in which the voices of the participants are recorded with minimal influence from the researcher and are reported separately (from each other) as individual voices and multiple perspectives, and differences between each are highlighted rather than glossed over.

epiphany interviews

Interviews in which people tell about certain moments in their lives that are turning points; participants' transformational, existential moments in their lives.

critical incident interviews
Interviews in which participants are asked to tell about a specific experience in a specific context.

co-constructed interview
An interview that is a collaboration between researcher and participant—the researcher and participant are full partners in the interview. The conversation between them is as important as the responses given by the participant.

creative interviewing
Interviews that may consist of multiple sessions over many days, which may be more intimate and dialogic, or may include shared stories between researchers and participants.

Here are some of the types of qualitative interview questions mentioned in the literature:

→ **Advice questions:** Asking participants to give advice to a person in a similar situation, yielding information on beliefs or understandings.

→ **Aided account:** Use of video, picture, or graphics to ask questions about specific experiences.

→ **Behavior or experience questions:** Asking for more information about an action or behavior.

→ **Contrast question:** Asking for unlike comparisons in order to understand something by understanding what it is not. For example, "What's the difference between 'a' and 'b'?"

→ **Descriptive questions:** Asking participants to recount (in detail) or recreate a phenomenon or experience, like a verbal tour of the phenomenon.

→ **Devil's advocate question:** Why should "a" happen or not happen?

→ **Feeling question:** Ask participant to discuss how they feel or are emotionally affected by a phenomenon.

→ **Hypothetical interaction:** What would you do if "x" did "y"?

→ **Knowledge question:** Asking a participant for specific factual information about a topic and how one attains this type of information.

→ **Motive questions:** What were you trying to accomplish, why do you think he or she said that?

→ **Native-language questions:** What do the terms mean, who uses them, when, in what context, and so on.

→ **Once-upon-a-time question:** Asking participants to narrate an experience related to a phenomenon.

→ **Opinion or value question:** Asks a person to discuss a belief or judgment they have about an issue.

→ **Posing emergent ideas:** It's sounding like "this" is going on, how does that resonate with your own experience?

→ **Posing the ideal:** Describe the ideal—organization, situation, state of affairs, goals, and so on.

→ **Quotation questions:** Giving participants a direct quotation from another interview or observation and asking for their feelings or opinions about it.

→ **Sensory question:** Attempting to understand how a participant experiences a phenomenon from a sensory point of view (what do they see, hear, feel, taste, smell).

→ **Structural questions:** Questions that require explanation and explore contextual information (how does something work? how do you—the participant—structure knowledge?). For example, "What are all the different ways to do this?" or "What are all the stages/ranges?"

→ **Time-line questions:** What happened next? (Fontana & Frey, 2003; Madison, 2005).

INTERVIEWING TIPS. While the questions you ask are important, your attitude and stance during the interview are equally important. When going into an interview, you should display excitement, naïveté, active and sympathetic listening, awareness of status differences, patient **probing** and **clarifying**, and also an inquiring mind—the strong desire to find out and understand the answers to the questions you are asking (Fontana & Frey, 2003; Madison, 2005).

Here are some general interviewing tips:

- Start with ice-breaker questions.
- Move on to more general questions.
- Depending on study objectives and RQs, you may share your opinions with participants, or you may not.
- Remember that the goal is to create shared meaning; you want to observe nonverbal behaviors that are also communicating meaning in the interview.
- Keep the interview questions natural and conversational.
- Avoid irrelevant questions and topics.
- Listen for slang, jargon, and so forth—ask participants to explain terms to you to help you understand them; avoid using slang yourself unless you know the participant understands it.
- It's okay to be broad in your questions, but make sure both you and the participant are clear what you are asking about.
- Ask one thing at a time.
- Don't embarrass your participant.
- Keep the questions in a flow.
- Order or group the questions in a logical sequence.

probing
Posing follow-up questions in an interview to encourage participants to provide further information.

clarifying
Posing follow-up questions in an interview that fill in gaps of understanding.

LISTENING IN AN INTERVIEW. Good interviewing requires good listening skills. I'm sure you remember these skills from your Introduction to Communication class, but let's review them anyway. Good listening involves listening for both content and feelings. You exhibit good listening skills through appropriate eye contact and body language and through, frankly, intent listening. It's important to listen carefully enough that you know when you have received a complete response and when you have not. When you have not, or when the person's response raises additional questions (which it often will), you should probe and clarify. Often, in in-depth interviewing, probing and clarifying yield the most meaningful information of the entire interview.

PROBING AND CLARIFYING. When do you probe and clarify? When the person says something that can have more than one meaning (e.g., nice, perfect, boring, attractive, exciting, convenient, lovely, unusual, different), you should ask him or her to define the term by asking, "What does *nice* mean to you?" or "What do you mean by *nice*?" When the person gives you a generalization ("Everybody likes ice cream,"), you might ask, "What do *you* like about it?" When she is vague ("Sometimes I think about it"), you would ask her to be more specific ("Tell me about a specific time you thought about it"). When he contradicts something he said earlier, you might say, "I'm confused. Maybe I misunderstood, but didn't you say earlier _____ ?" When she needs to elaborate, you can ask, "Tell me more about that." You might need her to say more, and you can give her a silent probe with a questioning look (raised eyebrows, frown, head tilt), hand gestures (roll hands for "tell me more"), or a head nod. If he seems to need encouragement to continue talking, you can say, "I see!" or "Uh huh," or you can ask, "And then?" or "What happened next?" To get additional facts or a more accurate understanding, you can ask, "Can you clarify that for me?", "Could you describe that once more? I'm not sure I understand.", "What do you mean by that?", "Help me understand.", "I'm unclear how you came to that conclusion. Can you tell me more?", or "I've lost you. Can we go back to _____ ?"

To show you understand, or to help him label his feelings/experiences, you can probe or clarify for feelings by saying, "You feel that _____ ", "At that point you were feeling _____ ", "You were [angry] at that moment . . .", "I can hear the [sadness] when you tell that story . . .", "I can sense the [frustration] you must have felt," or "If I understand correctly, you're feeling _____ ".

To check your meaning and interpretation and to show you are listening and understanding, you can say, "As I understand it, you _____ ", "Am I right in saying that this is the way you see this situation?", "If I were to say _____, would I be on target?", "Would it be accurate to say you thought _____ ?", or "If I understand how you see this situation, it's _____ ?"

To help her define a situation, explore aspects, or examine attitudes, you can ask, "What led you to make that particular decision?", "How would you describe the problem as you see it now?", "How would you assess the situation at this point in time?", "What values might have prompted you to take that action?", or "What is the key issue for you right now?"

Probe and Clarify

1. When the person says something that can have more than one meaning
2. When the person gives you a generalization
3. When the person contradicts something he or she said earlier
4. When the person needs to elaborate
5. If the person needs encouragement to continue talking
6. To show you understand
7. To help the person label his or her feelings/experiences
8. To check your meaning and interpretation
9. To show you are listening
10. To help the person define a situation, explore aspects, or examine attitudes

---

CHALLENGES TO INTERVIEWING. Just because we said that qualitative interviewing resembles a conversation, please do not think that if you can converse, you automatically can interview. Interviewing is more difficult than it looks. One reason is that, despite your best intentions and preparation, you never know ahead of time exactly what will happen in an interview. Our questions and our participants' responses are always more ambiguous than we think they will be. You have to be flexible and prepared for anything (Fontana & Frey, 2003; Roulston et al., 2003).

Roulston and colleagues (2003) interviewed student interviewers and gathered information on the challenges they faced in their first interviews. They had lots of challenges. They encountered unexpected participant behaviors such as participants who were late to the interview. The room was noisy, and the environment was distracting to both the researcher and the participant. Participants were uncomfortable with the note taking or tape recording of the interview. The interviewers didn't receive the responses they expected to receive. They had difficulty being flexible in terms of going where the participants' answers took them. They didn't know how much to talk, or they talked too much or not enough. They had difficulty being mentally present throughout the interview and were unable to attend to what the participant was saying. They had difficulty keeping the conversation related to the research topic. They were uncertain about what they were really asking or really wanting to find out from the interview. They had problems asking questions that were clear and concise. They had difficulty dealing with emotionality of the participants. They had trouble asking difficult questions. They couldn't create rapport in the interview. Finally, they felt overwhelmed by everything they had to do at once during the interview. What went well among the student interviewers was turning the interview into a conversation in which participants were relaxed and open.

Interviewing Challenges

1. Participants late to the interview
2. Distracting, noisy environment
3. Discomfort with note taking or tape recording
4. Unexpected responses
5. Being flexible
6. Talking too much or not enough
7. Being mentally present throughout the interview
8. Keeping the conversation related to the research topic
9. Determining what they really wanted from the interview
10. Asking clear and concise questions
11. Dealing with participant emotionality
12. Asking difficult questions
13. Creating rapport in the interview
14. Being in control of everything they had to do at one time in the interview

---

There are other potential errors you need to guard against as well. Make sure you give the participant enough time to give you a complete answer. Don't interrupt participants before they've given you a complete response. Learn to live with silence while your participant is thinking and pondering your question.

Remember to ask only one question at a time. Make sure your questions are clear. Guard against half-listening and missing an opportunity to probe appropriately. Be careful not to "feed" answers to participants or put words in their mouth. And, definitely, don't talk down to participants.

DATA TRANSCRIPTION.   Raw data in qualitative research consists of your interview and focus group transcripts, detailed field notes from observations and interviews, texts themselves, and any field notes you take from reading and examining texts and artifacts. Just as your data in quantitative research must be reliable and valid, so must your qualitative data, although that takes on a different meaning in qualitative research.

The most important, yet challenging, task in preparing your data is properly transcribing interviews and focus groups. When transcribing, it is important to keep all words and punctuation as close as possible to the actual speech. As you're typing, you need to type the text as close to the participants' natural speaking voices as possible. The text should be a verbatim account; do not edit or reduce text. Many researchers suggest including mispronunciations, slang, grammatical errors, nonverbal sounds (laughs, sighs), and background noises in your transcripts. If you also have a videotape of your interview, focus group, or observation, it's easiest to transcribe the dialogue from the audiotape, then fill in nonverbal communication (eye contact, body language, facial expressions, description of the environment, silence or pauses) from the video. Or, these can be noted in field notes while you are there. If so, you may want to merge the two (transcript of dialogue with notes on visual nonverbal), because it may assist your analysis to have both of these things on the same file.

When you're transcribing, keep participants' identities anonymous. When you come to a person's name or other identifying piece of information in a tape, type a _____, or substitute his or her role in the study (e.g., parent or teacher). So, for example, if a participant in a focus group uses the name of a teacher, saying: "Mrs. Smith praised my child," you would type, "Teacher praised my child," or " _____ praised my child."

CHALLENGES TO TRANSCRIPTION.   There are numerous challenges to transcription. Transcription is tedious and boring. It is an intensive, tough, lonely, and tiring task. You've got to approach it with an inquiring mindset—keep up your excitement about delving deeply into your data. The primary challenge is in understanding what people are saying. People talk in incomplete sentences and they overlap speech (talk over each other). In addition, you might be dealing with poor tape quality and distracting or disturbing background noises. Also, it's not always clear when punctuation is necessary, and sometimes (oral) punctuation makes a big difference in the meaning of a sentence. Even misunderstanding or dropping words can change the meaning of a message (McLellan, MacQueen, & Neidig, 2003; Roulston et al., 2003). Many scholars hire people (frequently, students) to transcribe their tape recordings. However, it is a good idea to transcribe at least some of your own interviews or tapes so you can get a feel for what is going on.

Texts and Artifacts. In ethnography, phenomenology, case study, and grounded theory, analysis of texts and other artifacts of material culture supports the interviewing and observation. In addition, rhetorical scholars, cultural ethnographers, and researchers utilizing content analysis study texts, as well as **artifacts-as-texts**. Researchers have been known to study clothing and personal adornment (hair, makeup, jewelry); architecture, buildings and grounds, and decorating; garbage bags; personal memorabilia; documents (corporate, personal); memos; logs, diaries, and journals; records (health records, driver's licenses, building contracts, bank statements, other legal or formal records); visual or audio media (songs, photographs, video); evidence of cultural rituals (wedding programs, marriage certificates) and behavior (shopping); cultural symbols (regalia, cemeteries, memorials, tombs, art); and community and social artifacts (roads, transportation) (Charmaz, 2006; Hodder, 2003). Denzin (2008) offers a critical examination of the painting *The Grand Canyon of the Yellowstone*; he explores historical documents surrounding this piece. In her piece on torch songs—songs about unrequited love—Holman-Jones (1999) explored her own experience with and about questions surrounding torch songs.

There are many good reasons for analyzing text, documents, and artifacts—called **material culture** by Hodder (2003): Access is easy, cost to access is low, information may differ from other data collected (allowing you to triangulate or crystallize your data), they allow you to understand the perspectives of others and to pay attention to your own understandings of and experiences with those same texts, and texts endure and give historical insight and social context (Charmaz, 2006; Grbich, 2007; Hodder, 2003). Because text is written, it is an artifact that is capable of transmission, manipulation, and alteration, being used in different ways through time, and can thus acquire new and different meanings over time. Texts and artifacts are "material traces of behavior" that are left behind and give a different insight than interviews or personal communication. What people say is often very different than what people do, and texts and artifacts were constructed to *do* something. "They can be understood only as what they are— . . . produced under certain material conditions . . . embedded within social and ideological systems . . . designed specifically to be communicative and representational" (Hodder, 2003, pp. 157, 160).

artifact
An object of study that represents material culture, such as adornment, or environmental or cultural objects.

material culture
Physical evidence of a culture; cultural artifacts.

Ethics in Qualitative Research ▼

Human Subjects Protection

In Chapter 6, we talked about research ethics. Participants whom you interview should sign informed consent forms. Participants with whom you interact in observations should also sign consent forms if their personal information is identifiable or if they are included as data in an identifiable manner. But there is more to research ethics than consent forms. Qualitative research has its own particular ethical issues, primarily around the relationships qualitative researchers frequently develop with their research participants. Scholars conducting this type of research tend to conduct research with participants in vulnerable situations, on topics that are sensitive, traumatic, or emotional, and the act of collecting data among a person or groups of people over a long period of time (the mark of good qualitative research) leaves participants (and researchers) open to emotional vulnerability and emotionality. The key issue is that all qualitative scholars, even scholars who conduct autoethnographic work (research about themselves or their own lives), work with research participants because even a personal story includes other people, even if just peripherally.

Caring for Participants

Ethics in qualitative research necessarily involves issues of trust, ethical recruiting of participants, and adequately and appropriately giving voice to participants and representing their experiences (Davis, 2014). Qualitative scholars have numerous strategies to ensure they treat their participants, themselves, and their data in an ethical manner. The first is to be aware and intentional about the impact of the research on the participant. Because qualitative research includes in-depth probing, participants can be vulnerable to emotional and social distress. Thus, not every question should be asked, and not everything a participant says or you observe should be included in the analysis. As Davis (2014, p. 40) notes, "maybe some points don't need to be made."

Reflexivity

Qualitative researchers reflexively seek to understand their participants' points of view and their own points of view, and further understand how their own standpoints affect their research. Reflexivity is a term that refers to acknowledgement of a researcher's positionality in relation to the study and the study participants. All qualitative scholars have some degree of reflexivity. Rather than seeking the objectivity and detachment quantitative researchers value, qualitative researchers acknowledge their own subjectivity and include that either formally or informally in their analysis and consideration of the research. Qualitative researchers acknowledge that research is biased and infused with their own values and assumptions, and, rather than trying to remain objective, take those biases into account during the research process. In fact, a researcher's subjectivity frequently becomes part of the data to be analyzed and written about.

Participants as Co-Researchers

Qualitative researchers frequently treat participants more as equal research partners than study subjects, and this is an ethical choice to shift the balance of power between researchers and participants. A participant as research partner might suggest questions to ask or events to observe, and might assist in coding and analyzing the data, and writing up the findings. Some scholars purposely engage in a relationship with their participants, in order to be able to empathize with and more deeply understand the people they are studying.

Analyzing and Writing Qualitative Research

All qualitative research includes some sort of analytical interpretation. In an arts-based project, the analysis itself might be understated or subtly understood. Research from a social constructionist or arts-based orientation might be written as a narrative, a poem, or a script. Arts-based research might have explicit analytical sections or the analysis might be implied in the content, manner, and style of writing. An arts-based paper might let the poem or script or narrative convey the meaning and leave it to the reader to interpret the point for him/herself (letting the reader become a partner in the co-construction of the paper's message).

A social science paper, on the other hand, would be more likely to make specific claims and support those claims with exemplary pieces of data in the form of illustrative snippets from interviews or field notes. A social science based qualitative research report would look similar to its quantitative cousin—it would have clearly delineated sections similar to that of a quantitative paper (Introduction, Literature Review, Research Question, Methodology, Analysis, Discussion, Conclusion).

Regardless of the type of research project and the manner in which the analysis is undertaken, all types of research have some sort of analysis—involving some method to study the data and sort for patterns and themes. Sometimes the sorting process is explicit and systematic; other times it is intuitive. Sometimes the analysis involves separate steps and sometimes the patterns and themes become apparent in the writing process itself.

Coding

In quantitative research, you reduce your data into something manageable through the use of summary and descriptive statistics: mean, median, and mode; and standard deviation, variance, and range. In qualitative research, you reduce your data into something manageable through the use of **data coding**, or categorizing the data.

data coding
The process of categorizing the data to make it manageable and understandable.

There are several different, specific ways of coding, some with highly specified and rigorous steps and some taking a more general approach to data categorization. Regardless of the type, coding generally consists of a multistep process that involves: 1) reading through the data and making analytical notations; 2) developing a code list; 3) coding your data.

Reading the Data and Making Analytical Notations.
The first stage of any coding process is to take one or more passes through your transcripts, recordings, field notes, and texts, and reading through the data multiple times as you jot down initial thoughts and ideas about the emergent themes and meanings. The initial and multiple passes through your data are crucial; it's important to immerse yourself in the data so you can begin to develop interpretive impressions. You can be in this stage for a long time, and in most qualitative research projects, you would immerse yourself in your data and begin making initial interpretations while you are still collecting your data. You are ready to move on to the next

stage of coding and analysis when you can answer this question: "What are you finding out?" When you can answer that, you have moved from notes jotted in the margins of the transcripts to more complete thoughts and ideas. Here's an example of **analytical notations** in the field notes from the hospice research I conducted (Davis, 2010). Note that in these notes, I am beginning to form thoughts about what is going on and what meaning I might be able to make from it.

analytical notations
Note taking in the early stage of coding and analysis in which the researcher is beginning to form thoughts about what is going on and what meaning he/she might be able to make from it.

> *They then talked about new admissions again talking about the people as people, kind of almost gossiping about them in a good sense. Talking about their situations, kind of by the RN's talking about the physical, went into talking about what they called readmits, some of this was interrupted by when the dr came in and he also did a little bit of chatting and gossiping and kind of friendly conversation about the pts, not only having the symptoms but also the pts as people and personalities and relationships and talking in those terms. Later on, in an interesting contrast, the female nurse practitioner came in about the first ½ of her section was pretty cut and dried, almost staccato voice, boom boom boom. And I noticed that when the RN's responded to her, they were speaking very clinically, very symptom oriented, it was a very interesting contrast. The doctor actually took what the nurses said and took their recommendations and seemed to defer to them. the nurse practitioner actually argued with them on 1 or 2 cases. And really seemed to be barking orders as opposed to working collaboratively. It was an interesting contrast between the Dr. and the nurse practitioner.*

code list or codebook
An organized listing of your categories and codes and the rules for documenting and applying them.

constant comparison
A stage of coding in which you refine the code list by looking for similarities and differences in the data and the emerging categories. Through multiple passes with the data, each new idea is compared to existing categories and categories are continually combined, divided, and sorted into themes (codes).

negative case analysis
A stage of data coding in which the researcher searches for negative cases, or cases that do not fit his/her emerging coding scheme, in order to refine the coding categories.

Developing a Code List.   This first step is followed by a step in which you review your notations and begin to build a **code list or codebook**, which is an organized listing of your categories and codes and the rules for documenting and applying them. A completed codebook would include a detailed description of each code, inclusion and exclusion criteria, examples of text for each code, and examples of text that would *not* fall in each code. Codebooks are developed and refined as the study progresses. As you move through your coding process, you might turn some themes into subthemes, you might delete other themes, and you might refine or combine other categories (Ryan & Bernard, 2003). Using a process called **constant comparison**, you refine the code list by looking for similarities and differences in the data and the emerging categories. Through multiple passes with the data, each new idea is compared to existing categories and categories are continually combined, divided, and sorted into themes (codes). As you conduct a **negative case analysis**, searching for negative cases, or cases that do not fit your emerging coding scheme, you continue to add and refine categories until all cases in your data (or almost all) fit into a category or code (Smulowitz, 2017).

Here's part of the codebook for the hospice research project conducted by Christine Davis (2010).

1. Introductions
   a. My introduction to team
   b. Patient's introduction to terminal illness

2. Deepening
    a. Getting used to team
    b. Patient getting used to illness
3. Coming to terms
    a. Becoming part of the team
    b. Patient's coming to terms with illness
4. Endings
    a. Leaving the team
    b. Leaving patients
5. How does hospice construct humanness
    a. Dignity
    b. Free will
    c. Individual responsibility
    d. NOT perfect
    e. Respect and acknowledge feelings

Coding your Data.   Finally, the last step in coding is to connect actual data (lines of discourse, quotes, words, portions of narrative or text) to each code. In this step, you will somehow mark or tag your text according to the category in which it belongs (Ryan & Bernard, 2003). Some people do this by hand, highlighting text and writing next to it a number corresponding to the category. Many researchers use coding software—NVivo is a commonly used one—to perform this step. Instructions on how to use NVivo can be found at:

Windows:

http://download.qsrinternational.com/Document/NVivo11/11.2.1/en-US/NVivo11-Getting-Started-Guide-Pro-edition.pdf

Mac:

http://download.qsrinternational.com/Document/NVivo11forMac/11.2.0/en-US/NVivo-for-Mac-Getting-Started-Guide.pdf

Tutorials on how to use NVivo can be found at:

Windows:

https://www.youtube.com/playlist?list=PLNjHMRgHS4Fcx3NfpKsaqXuGdcxI9y-Qa

Mac:

https://www.youtube.com/playlist?list=PLNjHMRgHS4FfTN-GoztTaPLshavAb0NxR

A final word about coding software—many companies offer free demos and/or student discounts for the software. A free trial version of NVivo can be obtained here:

http://www.qsrinternational.com/trial-nvivo

Here's where you can purchase the student license for NVivo:

Windows: http://www.qsrinternational.com/products/nvivo/pro/education/new/nvivo11prostulicense12mon

Mac: http://www.qsrinternational.com/products/nvivo/mac/education/new/nvivoformacstulic12mon

A word of caution: Statistical software like SPSS computes your statistics for you. However, coding software does not code your data for you. The software just gives you a way to record your codes that provides an easily sorted output so that analyzing them is much easier than sifting through your coded data by hand.

Card Pile Sort Approach to Coding.   Another approach to data sorting is to use a **card pile sort**. You would go through your field notes and interview transcripts and write all the answers to the research question you find in the data. Write each answer on a separate index card, then put them in piles according to semantic groupings (which ones seem to have similar meanings). You would sort and resort the piles, merging and subdividing the piles until no further subdivision is possible. You might first sort by variations, layers, or dimensions. You might then classify each of these into subgroups or types. The list of piles becomes your code list or codebook (Davis, 2014; Grbich, 2007).

Methods of Categorizing

Thematic Analysis.   Regardless of whether you use written notation or sort piles, you need a method of categorizing. The most common coding method is a **thematic analysis**, a method of categorizing your data into thematic categories. How you select your categories depends on your research question (RQ), study objectives, and method or approach to your research. You may have come into your research with a **sensitizing concept**. Perhaps you knew you wanted to study the use of certain types of language (gendered language, for example). Your coding categories would then reflect the different categories of gendered language. Perhaps you wanted to understand a lived experience; in this case, you might code more openly, letting the data itself suggest themes and categories. Perhaps you had a series of RQs; for each RQ, you would use a sorting technique to find all the possible responses found in the data to that question. You might sort the data by responses related to a particular issue (Grbich, 2007).

Analysis by Sensitizing Concepts.   There are many categorization schemes based on sensitizing concepts derived from your RQ, study approach, or your data.

Frame analysis.   **Frame analysis** consists of sorting your data by the interpretive frames within which we construct meaning and understanding. For example, I might see the world through multiple frames such as parent, professor, and writer. Or I might make sense of an illness situation through the frames of physical sensations or pain, cost or financial parameters, lifestyle or ability to maintain daily activities, and so on (Grbich, 2007).

Social network analysis.   **Social network analysis** consists of sorting by the relationships involved in a group. For example, in a health-care team meeting, you might observe relationships between the case manager and the caregiver, between the case manager and the health-care provider, or between the caregiver and the health-care provider (Grbich, 2007). Your code list might then consist of:

Case manager-caregiver relationship

Case manager-health-care provider relationship

Caregiver-health-care provider relationship

card pile sort
A method of data sorting in which the researcher puts individual codes on index cards and sorts and resorts the piles, merging and subdividing the piles until no further subdivision is possible.

thematic Analysis
A method of categorizing data into thematic categories.

sensitizing concept
Initial ideas, concepts, or interests to pursue and sensitize people to ask certain kinds of questions and look for certain kinds of information during data coding.

frame analysis
A sensitizing concept in data coding in which the data is sorted by interpretive frames within which we construct meaning and understanding.

social network analysis
A sensitizing concept in data coding in which the data is sorted by the relationships involved in a group.

Event analysis. In **event analysis**, you might sort by the perspectives of a specific event represented in the interview accounts (person one's perspective, person two's perspective, and so on). You might also use codes that represent structural aspects of the event (time, space, location, context, culture, etc., depending on what emerges from your data) (Grbich, 2007).

Schema analysis. **Schema analysis** consists of close reading of texts or discourse, in which you look for clues in the discourse that tell you what people might be thinking or believing that would cause them to say what they are saying. You would want to pay specific attention to their patterns of speech, key words and phrases, use of metaphors, and repetition of ideas. You might be looking for participants' personal semantic networks—repetitive ideas associated with people's assumptions or meanings. You would also need to look at what is not said—these reflect assumptions people make about what "everyone knows" (Grbich, 2007).

Interpretive thematic analysis. In **interpretive thematic analysis**, you code with your analysis in mind. As you read through your data, themes begin to emerge. You begin clustering categories, grouping for similarities, always keeping in mind your analysis, presentation, readership, and audience. As you build these categories, you would examine the emerging topics within each category. You would compare and contrast each topic with the other topics in a cluster, looking for overlapping topics, distinctions, topics that should be moved to a different cluster, and topics that should be eliminated. You adjust your topics and clusters as you identify linkages and themes. These themes then guide your analysis (Madison, 2005).

Analyzing Qualitative Data

Coding is the process of labeling your raw data and finding patterns and themes. **Data analysis** is the process of taking those patterns and themes and understanding the meaning, concepts, and propositions that stem from the themes. Analysis bridges the gap between your data, your codes, and your written report. Of course, as a good researcher you will be mentally and informally analyzing the data as you move throughout your study, but when you're finished coding, and before you start writing, it's a good idea to take a step back and do some analytical thinking and note taking on your research. This step consists of memo writing in which analytical interpretation lends a structure to the process. As with every other step in your research, this step will reflect your research questions or study objectives. In this stage, you are attempting to answer your RQs, using your data and the coding of your data to do so. So, you're looking at your themes, and asking yourself what they mean (in terms of answering your RQs and objectives), as you build your conclusions and inferences. You're looking for first order explanations (what you think is going on), as well as second order explanations (what your research participants think is going on). You're looking for patterns within and between categories, comparing your emerging findings with existing theories to see where your data might agree with, expand upon, or change theory. You are seeking to understand meaning as it is created from within the data. You will build ideas and theories inductively as you move from coding to analysis. As you continue to immerse yourself in the data, you will tune into ideas that

event analysis
A sensitizing concept in data coding in which the data is sorted by the perspectives of a specific event represented in the interview accounts.

schema analysis
A sensitizing concept in data coding in which the data is sorted through a close reading of texts or discourse, in which you look for clues in the discourse that tell you what people might be thinking or believing that would cause them to say what they are saying.

interpretive thematic analysis
A sensitizing concept in data coding in which you code with your analysis in mind.

data analysis
The process of taking patterns and themes from the data to understand the meaning, concepts, and propositions that stem from the themes.

inform what meanings you make of your data. Your final step will be to refine, communicate, support, explain, and substantiate your ideas, as you write them in your report (Charmaz, 2000).

As you build ideas and refine them, you might discuss them with your informants, or key study participants. This might take place as formal member checks (interviews or focus groups with study participants or people who are similar to study participants to get their feedback on your findings), or they might be more informal conversations. Here's an example of a conversation I (Christine Davis) had with two key informants in my children's mental health research (Davis, 2013, pp. 169–171). You might note that one of the key conclusions I came up with in this project was that the team used communication to construct hope for themselves and the family. Can you see how that idea was beginning to develop?

Two weeks later, I have a chance to discuss my ideas about the research with Nancy and Alan. We're at Jason's Deli again. I eat here at least once a week. I munch on salad as we talk.

"One of the things that I'm trying to do with this research," I explain, "is to not be the expert, imposing my opinion on the rest of the team. I want this to be a partnership between me and the team. One of the things I'm discovering is how hard it is not to play the expert role. I wonder if it's hard for you and all the other professionals on the team, to have the family be a real true partner on the team."

Nancy answers first. "The more frequently the team meets, the better it is to have them be viewed as a full partner. It's much better that there is a team, because otherwise they're asking me for things. This way, I can say wait for the team to decide instead of being the gatekeeper. I also think the team realizes their partnership more when they meet regularly."

Alan nods. "We've talked about this before. You have a situation of power, no matter what. If you're just talking about us being case managers, I don't even think about it anymore, being the professional versus the family, because we just do what we need to do to get things better."

"But isn't the power differential still there, even if you don't think about it?" I protest.

"To complicate matters," Nancy adds, "the financial assistance fund puts them in a subservient role since they have to ask for it, and it's the state's money. We have to make decisions that are not just about adhering to the family's choice. A good example is the situation with the gas. I can't as an administrator just hand them the money because she wanted to go specifically to another, more expensive, company 'cause she was mad at the first company. By statutes, I had to say no, and that was a power decision. But I don't know that power necessarily needs to be looked at as something that is either inherently positive or negative. It's how you use it."

> *"How about the other professionals on the team?"*
>
> *"That depends. As far as the regular team members, I don't know that I've been aware of any abuse of power or anything like that. The school psychologist definitely came over as the big expert, talking about a lot of negative things," Alan says.*
>
> *"He didn't really understand our team," Nancy adds. "He was just invited that day as a guest."*
>
> *"I don't think it was his fault," Alan responds, "but he came over powerfully and very negatively. I don't think it was his intention to do that, but at the same time I don't think he saw that family with the level of respect that the team members that know them do."*
>
> *I nod. "I felt that he de-humanized them. Would you agree with that?" Alan smiles. "I think that's what I just said."*
>
> *"I've been noticing how the family, especially Kevin, seems to be doing better, and I wonder why you think that is," I ask.*
>
> *Nancy sits forward. "I've thought a lot about this. We've given them more structure. The family financially isn't able to go a lot of places, and with the behavioral rewards, they now they have something to look forward to every week. On Monday, they're already looking forward to what they're going to do on Saturday, and so they have a hope of things getting better."*

Another way you might verify your findings is with a data conference, a process that involves discussing your preliminary analysis with other scholars in your field. In the data conference, you would discuss the research process itself and then present and defend your claims. The scholars discuss, critique, and revise the findings (Braithwaite, Allen, & Moore, 2017).

Writing Qualitative Findings

How you write your findings depends entirely on the research paradigm under which you are operating. For all types of qualitative research, you will continue to keep your study objectives and RQs in mind as you write your paper.

Summary or Traditional Method of Writing. Caulley (2008) lists two basic ways to write qualitative research reports. One is the more traditional method. Caulley calls this the **summary method of writing**, in which you give the reader summaries of what happened and what you discovered in your research. Research that is social science based, and some research under the social constructionist and rhetorical paradigms, is usually written in this style. You will base your paper on a claim that consists of the theme or thread that forms the *backbone* of your paper. You'll likely include both description and analysis, perhaps using verbatim quotes to support your claim(s). Quotes from your transcripts of field notes serve as evidence for your claim. Many researchers include recommendations where appropriate—for future research, for organizations, and so on. We will describe how to write this type of research paper in the next two chapters.

summary or traditional method of writing
A method of conveying the results of a research project that provides summaries of what happened and what the researcher discovered in his/her research.

Dramatic or Scenic Method of Writing.

The second way to write your qualitative findings is the **dramatic or scenic method of writing**, what Caulley (2008) calls *creative nonfiction* writing. Ethnographic researchers in communication studies frequently use this style of writing for their findings.

In this style of writing, you would actually show a scene of what happened rather than describe it or tell about it. This is more compelling reading. Usually written in present tense, this style of writing is more action-oriented. It's often written as a series of scenes connected by a series of narrative summaries. Depending on the research and on your style of writing, sometimes there will be more narrative summaries than scenes, and other times there will be more scenes than narrative summaries.

Writing Performance Texts.

Performative and artistic styles of writing allow for creative opportunities to communicate your study results. More and more, ethnographies in communication studies are written as **performative texts**. It's important to remember, however, that your findings drive your writing, not the other way around. For example, you might want to use a poetic method of writing the results because you feel that represents a more evocative style of communicating that reminds you of your research participants or scene. You might use ethnodrama to communicate the dramatic nature of the phenomenon you studied. In her research on funeral communication, Davis (2008) wrote her findings as a liturgy to communicate the ritualistic elements found in her research. This style of writing lets you use the style itself as a statement of resistance—as a way of using the text itself to suggest different ways of being, reflecting, and seeing the world, and as a way to possibly create change in society. A good performance text offers a way for the audience to relive the experience through the eyes of the writer or performer. Poetry and other creative forms of writing and presenting engage the listener's body to let the reader feel the world you're studying. Ethnographic drama can allow conflicting voices to be heard, can give voice to people or things whose voices are normally silenced, and can recreate emotionally laden experiences. Done well, this type of research contributes to our understanding of your research and of our world, has aesthetic merit, is reflexive, has emotional and intellectual impact, and expresses and embodies a lived experience (Denzin, 2003; Richardson, 2003).

dramatic or scenic method of writing
Also called creative nonfiction writing, it is often written as a series of scenes connected by a series of narrative summaries.

performative texts
More evocative style of communicating research results, using art-based tools such as poetry or ethnodrama.

▼ ## Evaluating and Critiquing Qualitative Research

When evaluating your own qualitative research or when critiquing qualitative research you read in journals, there are several lists of criteria that serve as good guides. However, the criteria for qualitative research from a more social science tradition differs from the criteria for narrative research or for more arts-based work. In fact, many qualitative researchers would argue that the idea of criteria itself raises ethical issues around voice, credibility, and marginalization of different epistemologies (Bochner, 2000; Richardson, 2000a). All "qualitative researchers strive for understanding," (Creswell, 2007,

p. 201), "but of course that looks different in different research projects" (Davis, 2014, p. 51).

Here are some useful criteria to consider in your own qualitative research:

Ethical Criteria

As with all research, qualitative projects should adhere to a set of ethical criteria. They should have IRB oversight and should follow IRB procedures such as preventing or minimizing harm to people involve in the study, appropriately obtaining informed consent from participants, and safeguarding the confidentiality and privacy of participants unless they have the participants' permission to identify them. The research benefits should outweigh the risks or cost to the participants. Researchers should show respect for their research participants when they interact with them and as they represent them. Vulnerable participants should be safeguarded (Davis, 2014; Tracy, 2010).

Significance Criteria

Tracy suggests that a research project should consider "a worthy topic, rich rigor, sincerity, credibility, resonance, significant contribution, . . . and meaningful coherence" (Tracy, 2010, p. 839). In other words, is the topic of significance to someone or something? Does it add to our understanding of the world (Richardson, 2000b)? Does it make a difference, or a contribution to our field (Goodall, 2008a)? Does it represent people who are marginalized; does it address critical issues of power (Denzin, 2000)? Does it move people or open up a conversation, or is it useful to somebody or something (Davis, 2014)?

RQ Criteria.   Did the researcher appropriately define the scope of the problem? Does the research have significance for society/academia? Was the research problem formally, clearly, and concisely stated? Does the research question flow from a theory if that is appropriate? Does the research question fit into the ongoing conversation in the literature? Does the study design appropriately address the research question (Davis, 2014; Tracy, 2010)?

Design/Methodology Criteria.   Was the design the most appropriate for the RQ? Is the study externally valid? What were the major limitations of the design? Were the limitations acknowledged by the researcher and taken into account in interpreting the results? If appropriate, was the study based on productive theoretical concepts (Tracy, 2010)?

Sampling Criteria.   Was the target population identified and described? Were eligibility criteria specified? Were the sampling selection procedures appropriate and clearly described? How adequate was the sampling plan in yielding a representative sample? Were there factors that affected the representativeness of the sample? Were possible sample biases identified and accounted for in the study? Was the sample size sufficient?

Data Collection Criteria.   Was the data itself productive and was the data collection rigorous (Tracy, 2010)? Did the RQ lend itself to the type of data collection? Did the data collection adequately cover the complexities of the problem under study? Who collected the data? Were data collectors qualified? How were they trained? How was the data gathered? Was it potentially distorted?

Analysis Criteria.   Was the coding sufficient, correct, and appropriate? Was an appropriate amount of quotes and supporting evidence reported? Was the information appropriately summarized and clear? Were the findings adequately supported? Were the findings appropriately tied to theory and concepts (if applicable) and does do the findings inform theory or constructs? Are the claims made appropriate for the methods used? Are the claims valid for the study reported (Davis, 2014)?

Writing Criteria.   Was the research written in a clear, concise manner? Was it well organized? If it was a narrative, was the writing action-oriented and evocative? Is it aesthetic? Did it show rather than tell? Is it evocative? Did the writing include thick description? Was the writing sufficiently reflexive? Did the writing reflect the findings, tone, and concepts you wanted to convey? Was anyone's voice left out that should have been included? Does it remind me of things in my life or does it help me better understand things in the participants' lives? Does it help me better understand certain theories or concepts? (Bochner, 2000; Davis, 2014; Denzin, 2000; Ellis, 2000).

Credibility Criteria.   Does the research make sense? Tracy asks, is it "honest, [self-reflexive], and transparent" (2010, p. 841)? Does it sound like something you can trust? Is it plausible (Tracy, 2010)? Does it have verisimilitude—does it seem to be true? In qualitative research of all kinds, the descriptions should be sufficiently rich that they are believable; the paper should offer enough description, detail, variety, evidence, and/or support so we could believe it, understand it, and see it through multiple dimensions. In other words, there should be "sufficient evidence to support the claims" (Goodall, 2008a, p. 139).

In the next three chapters, we will describe how to apply each of these characteristics and criteria to specific research methodologies.

So What?

As stated earlier in this chapter, these descriptions and categorizations are not mutually exclusive. In communication studies, it would be common for a study to be thought of as a feminist narrative ethnography, for example. It is also common for an ethnographic study to use grounded theory as a coding and analysis method, or for an ethnography to be reported as a case study. A textual analysis might very well take a critical focus, and phenomenological research might be written as a narrative. You might conduct a phenomenological ethnography in which you use ethnographic methods to understand lived experience. What is important is that the method(s) or approach(es) used be appropriate to the RQ or study objectives and that the researcher employ accepted, ethical procedures to carry out the study.

Good qualitative research is rigorous. This means that good qualitative research is reflexive. Good qualitative researchers engage in empathy, respect, and rapport toward their research participants and care about the research practices they use. They are accountable for their actions and are aware of the ethics of their practices. Good qualitative researchers remember that all knowledge is partial. They are open to the unexpected and unanticipated, and are also open about their research procedures, findings, and their claims, boundaries, and limits. Good qualitative researchers are fully engaged in the research process (Davies & Dodd, 2002). And, as Lincoln and Cannella (2004) claim, qualitative research is rigorous in that "it makes its premises, biases, predilections, and assumptions clear up front" (p. 181). We would argue, it also works appropriately within the limits and opportunities those premises, biases, predilections, and assumptions represent. It is also rigorous in that it explores and documents lived experience (Lincoln & Cannella, 2004); immerses itself in the culture, text, or discourse under study; points out societal oppression and control; and gives voice to marginalized people (Lincoln & Cannella, 2004).

Now that we have described the main types of qualitative research used in the field of Communication Studies and the general ways in which qualitative research is conducted, we will move to Chapters 15, 16, and 17 in which we discuss specific types of qualitative research under the four main qualitative paradigms.

Glossary

Active-member researchers
Researchers who become involved with central activities of the group but do not fully commit themselves to the group.

Advice questions
Interview questions that ask participants to give advice to a person in a similar situation, yielding information on beliefs or understandings.

Aided account
Use of video, picture, or graphics to ask questions about specific experiences.

Analytical notations
Note taking in the early stage of coding and analysis in which the researcher is beginning to form thoughts about what is going on and what meaning he/she might be able to make from it.

Artifact
An object of study that represents material culture, such as adornment, or environmental or cultural objects.

Arts and humanities paradigm
A research paradigm in which researchers tend to see research as a performance and tend to use art or performance to understand the world in an embodied and holistic manner.

Behavior or experience questions
Interview questions that ask participants for more information about an action or behavior.

Card pile sort
A method of data sorting in which the researcher puts individual codes on index cards and sorts and resorts the piles, merging and subdividing the piles until no further subdivision is possible.

Clarifying
Posing follow-up questions in an interview that fill in gaps of understanding.

Co-constructed interview
An interview that is a collaboration between researcher and participant—the researcher and participant are full partners in the interview. The conversation between them is as important as the responses given by the participant.

Code list or codebook
An organized listing of your categories and codes and the rules for documenting and applying them.

Complete observer
Researchers who have little to no interaction with the people being observed.

Complete-member researchers

Researchers who *study* settings in which they are already members or with which they are already affiliated.

Constant comparison

A stage of coding in which you refine the code list by looking for similarities and differences in the data and the emerging categories. Through multiple passes with the data, each new idea is compared to existing categories and categories are continually combined, divided, and sorted into themes (codes).

Contrast question

A question that asks for unlike comparisons in order to understand something by understanding what it is not. For example, "What's the difference between 'a' and 'b'?"

Creative interviewing

Interviews that may consist of multiple sessions over many days, which may be more intimate and dialogic, or may include shared stories between researchers and participants.

Critical incident interviews

Interviews in which participants are asked to tell about a specific experience in a specific context.

Crystallization

The process of reviewing multiple sources of data to capture a full, rich, multivocal, and nuanced view of the phenomenon under study.

Data analysis

The process of taking patterns and themes from the data to understand the meaning, concepts, and propositions that stem from the themes.

Data coding

The process of categorizing the data to make it manageable and understandable.

Data saturation

The collection and analysis of data until no new categories of theories are identified.

Data transcription

Written representation of spoken (and/or nonverbal) language from audio or video recordings of interviews or other data collection efforts. Used in qualitative research for coding and analysis.

Descriptive observation

A type of observation that is usually done when the researcher is first in the field, in which the researcher observes everything, no matter how small, and takes notes on all details and observations.

Descriptive questions

Questions that ask participants to recount (in detail) or recreate a phenomenon or experience, like a verbal tour of the phenomenon.

Devil's advocate question

A question that asks why should "a" happen or not happen?

Dramatic or scenic method of writing

Also called creative nonfiction writing, it is often written as a series of scenes connected by a series of narrative summaries.

Emergent design

A study design in which methods (including sampling, data collection, data protocols, coding, and analysis) are revised as the study emerges and progresses.

Emic

An approach to research that is more inductive and based on the participants' point of view and on the findings resulting from the study itself.

Epiphany interviews

Interviews in which people tell about certain moments in their lives that are turning points; participants' transformational, existential moments in their lives.

Etic

An approach to research that is more deductive and is based on a pre-existing concept or theory.

Event analysis

A sensitizing concept in data coding in which the data is sorted by the perspectives of a specific event represented in the interview accounts.

Extreme instance sampling

Consists of sampling units that have characteristics quite different from the rest of a population.

Feeling question

A question that asks participants to discuss how they feel or are emotionally affected by a phenomenon.

Field notes

A record of what was meaningful during an observation.

Field sites

Groups, organizations, or cultures in which research is conducted.

Fieldwork

Conducting observations in natural settings.

Focused observation

A stage in qualitative observation which occurs after the researcher has been in the field for a while and begun preliminary analysis, in which the researcher begins to narrow his/her focus and ignores some phenomena that are irrelevant to his/her study.

Frame analysis

A sensitizing concept in data coding in which the data is sorted by interpretive frames within which we construct meaning and understanding.

Hypothetical question

A type of research question that asks participants what would you do if "x" did "y"?

In vivo

Research that takes place in a natural setting.

In-depth interviews

Opportunities for participants to describe their worlds in concert and negotiation with researchers. Such interviewing involves co-constructing a narrative with a participant—to understand his or her history and version of the story and the ways that he or she makes sense of his or her actions in the context of his or her cultural narratives.

Inductive reasoning

Reasoning that discovers patterns, inferences, and conclusions from studying and observing certain phenomena.

Interpretive thematic analysis

A sensitizing concept in data coding in which you code with your analysis in mind.

Interpretive

A research perspective in which understanding and interpretation of the social world is derived from one's personal intuition and perspective.

Interview guide

An outline or list of topics or general questions to guide the in-depth interview.

Knowledge question

A question that asks a participant for specific factual information about a topic and how one attains this type of information.

Life story interview

A type of interview that documents all the significant streams of a person's life, to provide understanding of the larger cultural or historical frames.

Material culture

Physical evidence of a culture; cultural artifacts.

Maximum variation sampling

A sampling method that selects study participants that represent a wide range of characteristics that are present in the population and are of interest to the research.

Motive questions

A type of interview question that asks the participant, "What were you trying to accomplish, why do you think he or she said that?"

Multivocality

A form of writing that frequently includes multiple voices; it might be written from different points of view (including researchers and multiple stakeholders or participants).

Native-language questions

A type of interview question that asks the participant, "What do certain terms mean, who uses them, when, in what context, and so on?'

Naturalistic observation

Observation in natural settings.

Naturalistic

Research that is conducted in the field or where participants live, work, and play.

Negative case analysis

A stage of data coding in which the researcher searches for negative cases, or cases that do not fit his/her emerging coding scheme, in order to refine the coding categories.

Observations

A way to gain insight into the obligations, constraints, motivations, and emotions that participants experience as they complete everyday actions.

Observer-as-participant

A method of observation in which the researcher interacts casually with participants, but still remains primarily an observer and does not become a member of the group being studied.

Once-upon-a-time question

A type of interview question that asks participants to narrate an experience related to a phenomenon.

Opinion or value question

A type of interview question that asks a person to discuss a belief or judgment they have about an issue.

Oral history interviews

A type of interview that captures people's stories about their lives.

Participant observation

When a researcher is participating in the life of others, but is still observing as a naïve outsider who doesn't understand exactly what's going on and needs to ask, explore, and try on the experience.

Performative texts

More evocative style of communicating research results, using art-based tools such as poetry or ethnodrama.

Peripheral-member researchers

Researchers who have some level of involvement with a group without core group involvement.

Personal narrative interview

A type of interview in which the participant recounts—tells a story about—an event, experience, or point of view.

Polyphonic interviewing

A type of interview in which the voices of the participants are recorded with minimal influence from the researcher and are reported separately (from each other) as individual voices and multiple perspectives, and differences between each are highlighted rather than glossed over.

Posing emergent ideas

A type of interview question in which the participant is asked questions related to member checking or analysis, such as, "It sounds like 'this' is going on, how does that resonate with your own experience?"

Posing the ideal

A type of interview question that asks participants to describe the ideal—organization, situation, state of affairs, goals, and so on.

Probing

Posing follow-up questions in an interview to encourage participants to provide further information.

Purposive sampling

A method of sampling in which the researcher selects participants based on their having experienced the phenomenon or issue under study.

Quotation questions

A type of interview question in which participants are given a direct quotation from another interview or observation and asked for their feelings or opinions about it.

Reflexivity

Acknowledgement of a researcher's positionality in relation to the study, study topic, and the study participants; addressing how one's own thoughts, feelings, and behaviors interact with his or her research site and his or her research itself.

Representation

In qualitative research, the concept that the qualitative sample should adequately represent the population under study to provide in-depth understanding of the experience.

Rhetorical paradigm

A research paradigm that focuses upon a wide variety of texts in order to gain a deep understanding of the message within the communication process, to connect that understanding to broader practical and theoretical concerns related to human communication and the human condition in general.

Schema analysis

A sensitizing concept in data coding in which the data is sorted through a close reading of texts or discourse, in which you look for clues in the discourse that tell you what people might be thinking or believing that would cause them to say what they are saying.

Scratch notes

Rough notes that are embellished upon shortly after an observation.

Selective observation

A stage of observation which occurs as the researcher's time in the field is winding down, in which the researcher concentrates on certain activities and on additional analyses, interviews, coding, and so forth that correspond to the meanings emerging from the data already collected.

Sensitizing concept

Initial ideas, concepts, or interests to pursue and sensitize people to ask certain kinds of questions and look for certain kinds of information during data coding.

Sensory question

A question that attempts to understand how a participant experiences a phenomenon from a sensory point of view (what do they see, hear, feel, taste, smell).

Snowball or network sampling

This sampling method asks study participants to make referrals to other potential participants, who in turn make referrals to other participants, and so on.

Social constructionist paradigm

A research paradigm that believes that shared meaning is constructed through our cultural systems and focuses on culturally situated action and interaction through which meanings and interpretations are socially, historically, temporally, and culturally constructed. Qualitative researchers in this paradigm tend to see research as a social construction of meaning.

Social network analysis

A sensitizing concept in data coding in which the data is sorted by the relationships involved in a group.

Social science paradigm

A research paradigm in which researchers see research as a systematic investigation and tend to believe in a reality that is more observable and better understood objectively.

Structural questions

A type of interview question that requires explanation and explores contextual information (how does something work? how do you—the participant— structure knowledge?). For example, "What are all the different ways to do this?" or "What are all the stages/ranges?"

Summary or traditional method of writing

A method of conveying the results of a research project that provides summaries of what happened and what the researcher discovered in his/her research.

Thematic Analysis

A method of categorizing data into thematic categories.

Theoretical sampling

Choosing a sample based on the people, events, groups, and so on who can shed light on a theory being investigated.

Time-line questions

A type of interviewing question that asks participants what happened next.

Topical interview

A type of interview that consists of a person's discussion of a topic, program, issue, or process.

Typical instance sampling

Consists of sampling units who have characteristics typical of a population.

References

Angrosino, M. V., & de Pérez, K. A. M. (2003). Rethinking observation: From method to context. In N. K. Denzin & Y. S. Lincoln (Eds.), *Collecting and interpreting qualitative materials* (pp. 107–154). Thousand Oaks, CA: Sage.

Bochner, A. (2000). Criteria against ourselves. *Qualitative Inquiry, 6*(2), 266–272.

Bochner, A., & Ellis. C. (1992). Personal narrative as a social approach to interpersonal communication. *Communication Theory, 2*, 65–72.

Braithwaite, D., Allen, J., & Moore, J. (2017). Data conferencing. In J. Matthes, R. Potter, & C. Davis (Eds.). *International encyclopedia of communication: Methods of communication research*. Hoboken, NJ: Wiley-Blackwell.

Caulley, D. N. (2008). Making qualitative research reports less boring: The techniques of writing creative nonfiction. *Qualitative Inquiry, 14*(3), 424–449.

Charmaz, K. (2006). *Constructing grounded theory: A practical guide through qualitative analysis*. Thousand Oaks, CA: Sage.

Creswell, J. W. (2007). *Qualitative inquiry and research design: Choosing among five approaches*. Thousand Oaks, CA: Sage.

Davies, D., & Dodd, J. (2002). Qualitative research and the question of rigor. *Qualitative Health Research, 12*, 279–289.

Davis, C. S. (2010). *Death: The beginning of a relationship*. Cresskill, NJ: Hampton Press.

Davis, C. S. (2014). *Conversations about qualitative communication research: Behind the scenes with leading scholars*. New York, NY: Left Coast Press/Routledge.

Davis, C. S. (2008). A funeral liturgy: Death rituals as symbolic communication, *Journal of Loss and Trauma, 13*(15), 406–421.

Denizin, N. K. (2008). Drawn to Yellowstone. *Qualitative Research, 8*, 451–472.

Denzin, N. K. (2000). Aesthetics and the practices of qualitative inquiry. *Qualitative Inquiry, 6*(2), 256–265.

Denzin, N. K. (2003). The practices and politics of interpretation. In N. K. Denzin & Y. S. Lincoln (Eds.), *Collecting and interpreting qualitative materials* (pp. 458–498). Thousand Oaks, CA: Sage.

Ellingson, L. (2009). *Engaging crystallization in qualitative research: An introduction*. Thousand Oaks, CA: Sage.

Ellis, C. (2000). Creating criteria: An ethnographic short story. *Qualitative Inquiry, 6*(2), 273–277.

Fontana, A., & Frey, J. H. (2003). The interview: From structured questions to negotiated text. In N. K. Denzin & Y. S. Lincoln (Eds.), *Collecting and interpreting qualitative materials* (pp. 61–106). Thousand Oaks, CA: Sage.

Fontana, A., & Prokos, A. H. (2007). *The interview: From formal to postmodern*. Walnut Creek, CA: Left Coast Press.

Gergen, K. J. (1991). *The saturated self: Dilemmas of identity in contemporary life*. New York: Basic Books.

Gill, V. T., & Maynard, D. W. (1995). On labeling in actual interaction: Delivering and receiving diagnoses of developmental disabilities. *Social Problems, 42*(1) 11–37.

Goodall, H. L. (2008). Twice betrayed by the truth: A narrative about the cultural similarities between the Cold War and the Global War on Terror. *Cultural Studies <–> Critical Methodologies, 8*(3), 353–368.

Grbich, C. (2007). *Qualitative data analysis: An introduction*. Los Angeles, CA: Sage.

Hodder, I. (2003). The interpretation of documents and material culture. In N. K. Denzin & Y. S. Lincoln (Eds.), *Collecting and interpreting qualitative materials* (pp. 155–175). Thousand Oaks, CA: Sage.

Holman-Jones, S. (1999). Torch. *Qualitative Inquiry, 5*, 280–304.

Lincoln, Y. S., & Cannella, G. S. (2004). Qualitative research, power, and the radical right. *Qualitative Inquiry, 10*(2), 175–201.

Madison, D. S. (2005). *Critical ethnography: Methods, ethics, and performance*. Thousand Oaks, CA: Sage.

McLellan, E., MacQueen, K. M., & Neidig, J. L. (2003). Beyond the qualitative interview: Data preparation and transcription. *Field Methods, 15*(1), 63–84.

Montegut, L. E. (2017). Etic approach to qualitative research. In J. Matthes, R. Potter, & C. Davis (Eds.). *International encyclopedia of communication: Methods of communication research*. Hoboken, NJ: Wiley-Blackwell.

Richardson, L. (2000). Introduction—Assessing alternative modes of qualitative and ethnographic research: How do we judge? Who judges? *Qualitative Inquiry, 6*(2), 251–252.

Richardson, L. (2000). Writing: A method of inquiry. In N. K. Denzin & Y. S. Lincoln (Eds.), *Handbook of qualitative research* (2nd ed., pp. 923–943). Thousand Oaks, CA: Sage.

Richardson, L. (2003). Writing: A method of inquiry. In N. K. Denzin & Y. S. Lincoln (Eds.), *Collecting and interpreting qualitative materials* (pp. 499–541). Thousand Oaks, CA: Sage.

Rock, P. (2007). Symbolic interactionism and ethnography. In P. Atkinson, A. Coffey, S. Delamont, J. Lofland, & L. Lofland (Eds.), *Handbook of ethnography* (pp. 26–38). Los Angeles, CA: Sage.

Roulston, K., deMarrais, K., & Lewis, J. B. (2003). Learning to interview in the social sciences. *Qualitative Inquiry, 9*(4), 643–668.

Ryan, G. W., & Bernard, H. R. (2003). Data management and analysis methods. In N. K. Denzin & Y. S. Lincoln (Eds.), *Collecting and interpreting qualitative materials* (pp. 259–309). Thousand Oaks, CA: Sage.

Scarduzio, J. A. (2017). Emic approach to qualitative research. In J. Matthes, R. Potter, & C. Davis (Eds.). *International encyclopedia of communication: Methods of communication research*. Hoboken, NJ: Wiley-Blackwell.

Silverman, D. (2003). Analyzing talk and text. In N. K. Denzin & Y. S. Lincoln (Eds.), *Collecting and interpreting qualitative materials* (pp. 340–362). Thousand Oaks, CA: Sage.

Smulowitz, S. (2017). Constant comparison. In J. Matthes, R. Potter, & C. Davis (Eds.). *International encyclopedia of communication: Methods of communication research*. Hoboken, NJ: Wiley-Blackwell.

Starks, H., & Trinidad, S. B. (2007). Choose your method: A comparison of phenomenology, discourse analysis, and grounded theory. *Qualitative Health Research, 17*(10), 1372–1380.

Tracy, S. J. (2010). Qualitative quality: Eight "big-tent" criteria for excellent qualitative research. *Qualitative Inquiry, 16*(10), 837–851.

SOCIAL SCIENCE QUALITATIVE APPROACHES TO COMMUNICATION RESEARCH

15

CHAPTER OUTLINE

KEY TERMS

Axial coding	Ethnography	Informants
Bounded unit	Ethnomethodology	Metacodes
Bracketing	Field site	Negative case analysis
Case study research	Fieldwork	Open coding
Conversation analysis	Focus groups	Phenomenology
Discourse analysis	Gatekeeper	Sensitizing concepts
Ethnography of communication	Grounded theory	Theoretical sampling

CHAPTER OBJECTIVES

1. To understand the different approaches to qualitative research under the social science paradigm, and when each is appropriate
2. To understand the characteristics of the main methods of qualitative research under the social science paradigm
3. To learn how to design and conduct research under the social science paradigm

▼ # Social Science Paradigm

Qualitative researchers under the social science paradigm see research as a systematic investigation. They believe that reality is discoverable, observable, and understandable. While they do view their research endeavors reflexively—understanding their own role in the interpretation of meaning in an experience—they also tend to focus primarily on understanding as it derives from the standpoint of other people who are the focus of their research.

Ethnography

Some types of Ethnography (Chicago school, ethnomethodology, ethnography of communication). Ethnography, simply put, is the study of a culture. Communication ethnography is the study of communication in a culture. Ethnography is characterized by immersion in a culture—called **fieldwork**—in order to fully understand beliefs and practices in context. This immersion usually occurs through observations, various types of participation, and formal interviewing and informal conversations. Ethnography frequently makes use of key participants, called **informants**, who can act as co-researchers and help the researcher explain and make sense of the culture (Atkinson, Coffey, Delamont, Lofland, & Lofland, 2007). Within the method called *ethnography* are many subareas, which we will explain in more detail here and in subsequent chapters. You may notice as you look through these descriptions that the areas sound as if they might overlap. In fact, they do, but researchers usually begin their research at one of the traditions.

Chicago School of Ethnography.   The **Chicago School of Ethnography** was developed by sociologists at the University of Chicago between 1917 and 1942. The Chicago School of Ethnography focused on reflexive interactional communication to understand how people use communication for sense-making (Deegan, 2007). This perspective on ethnography was grounded in the theory of social interactionism, a communication theory that studies interrelationships between relational participants by understanding that meaning resides not in the individuals, but in their negotiated everyday interactions, and by understanding the interrelationships between individuals, the larger community, and their social experience (Reusch & Bateson, 1951; Blumer, 1969; Goffman, 1959, 1967; Laing, 1961; Mead, 1934). The Chicago School of Ethnography studied urban settings and marginalized people. Their studies were characterized by informal conversational language depicting everyday life. They researched hobos and gangs, juvenile delinquency, small town life, race relations, and mental disorders (Deegan, 2007). Although this form of ethnography was founded by sociologists, their emphasis on interaction and meaning forms the basis of our interpersonal communication field today.

Ethnomethodology.   Developed by Harold Garfinkel in 1967, **ethnomethodology** focuses on understanding the lived experience and lived practices from the point of view of those within the experience (Pollner & Emerson, 2007). Researchers following this approach use participant observation to attend to what interactional participants think is important or accountable (able to be noticed and accounted for). Ethnomethodology studies interactions in everyday life and attempts to understand ordinary unnoticed interactions. Ethnomethodologists suggest that researchers "make the familiar strange," or seek to see meaning in the ordinary. They also stress reflexivity, which they refer to as the meaning constructed in an interaction while the action is taking place (Pollner & Emerson, 2007). **Conversation analysis**, the study of everyday talk (discussed later in this chapter) is associated with ethnomethodology (Ten Have, 2007).

---

ethnography
The study of a culture.

fieldwork
Immersion in a culture through observations, various types of participation, and formal interviewing and informal conversations.

informants
Participants who can act as co-researchers and help the researcher explain and make sense of the culture.

ethnomethodology
A type of ethnography that focuses on understanding the lived experience and lived practices from the point of view of those within the experience.

conversation analysis
An investigation of social interaction between humans, most especially of everyday, ordinary conversation.

Ethnography of Communication.

Ethnography of communication, also called "ethnography of speaking," was developed in the 1960s by John Gumperz and Dell Hymes to study speech events in the context of community (Keating, 2007). Their research focused on the meaning resulting from shared beliefs, values, and social interaction in a culture. They looked at specific speech exchanges and their social meaning—actual language use in context. **Ethnography of communication** is characterized by its focus on communication competence, or the social rules, norms, skills, and structures that a communicator needs to be able to follow in order to communicate appropriately in a specific speech community. This method is also characterized by its use of speech acts, speech events, speech situations, and speech communities as units of analysis. Unlike other types of ethnography that focus on everyday speech, ethnography of communication focuses on routine or ritualized forms of communication in a society (e.g., ceremonial events). Hymes created an analytical schema termed "SPEAKING," in which the researcher systematically addresses a culture's Setting, Participants, Ends, Act sequence and topic, Key, Instrumentalities, Norms of interaction and interpretation, and Genre. This framework allows the researcher to understand a speech act from the point of view of the specific case being studied and the larger culture.

ethnography of communication
The study of speech events and their meaning in a culture.

Appropriate Research Questions Answered by Ethnography.

Ethnography in the field of Communication Studies is appropriately used in research designed to understand, describe, or explain communication in a culture or cultural group. Ethnographic research methods allow scholars to immerse themselves in a culture in order to deeply comprehend how communication in a culture operates. Ethnography answers "how" questions and focuses on the communication process rather than the outcomes or motivations.

The Role of Theory in Ethnographic Research.

Theory is used in two very different ways in research projects: either as an overarching ontological position driving the project's design from its conception, or as specific explanatory theories utilized at the project's conclusion. Most ethnographic studies begin from a theoretical position which is frequently understood rather than stated, and which derives from an overarching social constructionist and/or critical ontology. In ethnographic research from the social science paradigms, other theoretical constructs are frequently pulled in during the analysis as explanatory theories to help clarify the findings and to tie the research back to the scholarly conversation.

Sampling in Ethnography.

There are as many sampling strategies in ethnographic research as there are types of ethnographic research. An ethnography that takes a **grounded theory** stance might utilize theoretical sampling, or an ethnography that has a **phenomenological** approach might sample purposively for phenomenological understanding. Other ethnographies might want people who represent different types of experiences, so they might use typical instance, maximum variation, or extreme instance sampling. Many ethnographies are methodologically **case studies** and might study only one culture or field site, but even with small samples or single site samples, all ethnographers typically

grounded theory
A systematic approach to understanding and analyzing participants' lives.

conduct long periods of fieldwork (up to twelve months of observations—or more) and multiple forms of data collection of many participants in that one site.

Selecting and accessing a field site. Ethnographic research samples within **field sites**—within groups, organizations, or cultures. The type of field site you choose will depend, again, on your research question or study objectives. Christine Davis, for example, has conducted ethnographic research at a hospice organization (Davis, 2010) and within a children's mental health system of care (Davis, 2014). If you wish to study communication within an organization, you might select one specific organization to study based on the same factors on which you'd base your sample selection—your initial theoretical construct, the amount of variability you want at your site, if you want an organization that is typical, or if you want an organization that is atypical.

Once you've determined what type of site you wish to study, you need to gain access to the site. Most ethnographers, for example, gain access to the site through **informants**. Sometimes it's as simple as knowing someone at the site—the higher the rank, the better. Other times, you need to make an appointment with management (if it's an organization) or a respected group member or leader, then sell yourself and the project. You'll need to get past the organizational **gatekeepers**, and you may not always know who they are until after you think you have approval to conduct the research. Ironically, Christine Davis, while writing this book chapter, was attempting to collect data within a field site—a local children's mental health system of care. She thought she had permission from the people in charge of giving her referrals to potential study participants, but after she began trying to collect data, the research was blocked by a gatekeeper higher up in the site she had not known to contact. As of this writing, she is attempting to gain access to another alternative site. In naturalistic research, you have to be flexible and prepared for changes and setbacks.

Frequently, rather than being given carte blanche approval, access is negotiated. For example, I might want to observe child and family team meetings, and to do that, I might ask to be given names of all caregivers of children to obtain their permission to attend. The gatekeeper might tell me that I can only attend meetings of children with one kind of disorder, but not another (because of concerns about risk or their different funding requirements for different diagnoses). Perhaps the site might want to give me access, but only if I provide them with copies of my videotapes of the meetings for their training purposes; however, that would go against IRB guidelines for anonymity. Instead, I might offer to give them de-identified typed transcripts and also offer to conduct training for them based on the study findings. As in any negotiation, it's important to think about what's in it for the site—how the risks (and perceived risks) can outweigh the benefits. At the very least, you might be inconveniencing people at the site, and in health-related sites gatekeepers might be concerned that your presence will affect provision of care. You need to address these concerns up front.

Once you have access to a site and before you start formal data collection, it's a good idea to familiarize yourself with the environment. Do some informal hanging out. If it's an organization, take a tour. If it's a town, study a map. Ask the gatekeepers or informants to brief you on what to expect and how to act.

field site
Group, organization, or culture in which research is conducted.

gatekeeper
A person who controls access to a field site.

Actually, that's one of the key roles of the informants—they are people who are in the culture or site you wish to study who are willing to act as a guide and translator of cultural practices and jargon or language (Fontana & Frey, 2003).

You may have to gain access only once, such as accessing a health-care organization. Or you may have to gain access each time you talk to new participants, such as talking to people in a public place such as a shopping mall, or attending a series of health-care team meetings for which you have to get access for each meeting separately. In his study on cigar smokers' rationalization of smoking behaviors, Desantis (2003) spent time in the same cigar shop over a matter of years, for a total of six hundred hours of fieldwork.

You have to decide how to present yourself—as a student, a professor, or one of the participants. This is an important consideration, and one that will shadow you throughout the study. You may want the respect (and cooperation) of the professionals or managers at your site, but you need the rapport and trust of the employees, patients, or members at the site, as well. It's a fine line. Desantis (2003) was first a cigar shop regular prior to engaging in both participant observation and interviewing. This allowed him a type of privileged access to be both friend and researcher to the others he studied.

To get good information, you need to be in the field (involved with the site) long enough to gain the trust of the study participants. This will occur over time as they become familiar with you. You also have to establish rapport with study participants in order to get good trustworthy information. How you access the site affects both of those factors.

Ethical Concerns Specific to Ethnographic Research. In Chapter 6, we talked about the ethical issues to be considered in data collection, but we'd like to remind you of a few of them now. In most qualitative research, you must obtain informed consent from study participants before conducting data collection. This is easy enough when conducting in-depth interviews. However, it becomes problematic when doing observations or when taking field notes in public places. The general rule is that if a person is identifiable to anyone (including you), you must obtain informed consent from him or her. If you are observing a group, every person in the group must give consent in order for you to observe them. What if you are observing in a large site such as an organization? There's no way you can get every organization member to give consent. That may not be practical, but you must get consent from the people you will be doing any identified interaction with. That doesn't mean that you need consent if you're just going to say "hello" when passing someone in the hallway, but you do need consent if you plan to have a long conversation with a person, and especially if you plan to write about a person specifically (identified or not) in your findings.

How you identify participants in your report is also an important ethical decision. Sometimes you will be reporting their comments anonymously or they will be identified by role (e.g., mother or provider). Other times, you might give them pseudonyms. Other times, they might give you permission to use their real names. Make sure each person in the study is clear up front how his or her name will be used. Also make sure everyone understands fully if you will be using actual quotes, narratives, stories, or other information that may identify him or her.

Sometimes, the ethical thing to do is to let those involved read the report before it's finalized so they can flag any passages they think might blow their cover.

Data Collection in Ethnography.

Data collection for ethnographic research under the social science paradigm uses fieldwork, which typically involves observation, in-depth interviewing, and perhaps document analysis to immerse oneself in the field site. Chapter 14 talked about how to observe and conduct in-depth interviews.

Analysis in Ethnography.

Ethnographic research under the social science tradition uses coding schemes such as card sorts or interpretative thematic analysis to analyze the hundreds of pages of field notes and interview transcripts. Chapter 14 described how to do a thematic analysis of qualitative data. Alan DeSantis (2003), whose ethnography of cigar smokers was described earlier in this chapter, uses a card sort technique. His process is to take transcriptions of the interviews and his field notes, and divide the transcripts and field notes into segments by theme or idea. He then puts each segment on a note card and moves the note cards around as he looks for patterns and recurring themes. As patterns emerge, he sorts and re-sorts the cards, keeping the emerging themes in mind (Davis, 2014).

Writing Ethnographic Findings.

Ethnographic reports under the social science paradigm have much in common with quantitative research reports. In this style of writing, you will make sure you specifically address your RQ or study objectives and include rich illustrative examples that support each of your findings—give enough detail to help the reader understand the coding process and support your themes with quotes or excerpts. You will demonstrate how the themes relate to each other and provide adequate amounts of evidence to support your claims. Finally, you will present the results in an understandable, well-organized manner (Ponterotto & Grieger, 2007). Traditionally written qualitative research reports typically follow an outline that looks like this:

A. Title page (1 page)
B. Abstract (1 page, 100–200 words)
C. Introduction (may include literature review or literature review may be a separate section) (6–7 pages)
D. Research questions or study objectives (1 paragraph)
E. Methods (6–7 pages)
F. Results (6–7 pages)
G. Discussion (5–6 pages)
H. Limitations and suggestions for future research (1/2 page)
I. References (3 pages)

Review Chapter 4 for more information on how to write a title page, abstract, and literature review. Your final paper picks up where that chapter left off.

The Introduction should introduce us to your topic, describe the nature of the situation, and provide an overview of the selected topic. Use this as an opportunity to justify your research and your selection of the topic, and preview what good reading the paper will do. Show us how your research furthers scholarly understanding of communication or responds to a need in society. Describe the prevalence of the problem you're solving, and the implications for individuals, families, organizations, and/or society at large. Focus your research by indicating why others should be interested in the selected topic. Convince the audience that the topic is worthy of study. Include a literature review that justifies your topic, introduces relevant theory, summarizes previous research done in the area, and leads us to your specific research and your argument and claim.

The conclusion of your introduction should be that *this* certain type of research is needed on *this* specific topic. That should lead us right into your research questions or study objectives.

In your Methods section, you will describe in detail what methodology you used. You may need to cite research to justify why you chose the method you chose; at the very least it should be clear how your method specifically addresses your research questions or study objectives. You'll need to define and describe your population and sample. Tell us what your sampling design is. Who did you talk to? How many people did you talk to? When/where/how? How did you select your sample? How, where, what, and when did you observe? How did you enhance credibility, crystallization, and ethics? What are your variable(s) and how did you define them conceptually and operationally? What information did you gather? What sensitizing concepts did you use? How did you code and analyze the results?

Sometimes, the Results and Discussion sections are merged together. Usually, the Results section explains and describes the themes, with supporting quotes or snippets from your transcripts or field notes serving as evidence for each one. You would use the Discussion section, then, to give your *big picture* analytical opinion on what this all means, how it answers your RQs, and how it is important to your community or to society. This is where you would show us that your study has social validity—the social value or importance of the topic to society (Ponterotto & Grieger, 2007).

In the final section, you would let us know what limitations you see for your research. Maybe you would do things differently if you had to do it over—perhaps you weren't able to sample as broadly as you would have liked, or perhaps, in retrospect, you would have liked to have spent more time in the field. Then, suggest future research for us—what future research might your study point to? This is your chance to justify your next research project.

It's easy to get carried away when writing up qualitative research. Since your evidence can be quite wordy and long, if you try to include all the good pieces of evidence, your paper could easily reach 50 to 100 pages! For journal articles, you want to end up with a paper that is 25 to 35 pages long, not counting the title page, appendix, and references. Therefore, you'll need to balance providing evidence for your claims with only including the most persuasive evidence. For example, if you're organizing your paper thematically, with quotes to support each theme, include enough quotes to support but not too many—usually two to three good quotes for each theme should suffice.

Examples of Ethnography.   In the Chicago School tradition, Smith (2008) conducted a long-term ethnography of professional wrestling, looking at the ways wrestlers use interactions in the ring and the gym to give meaning to their physical suffering and pain. He analyzed the ways wrestlers use their bodies in the context of pain and what their interactions say about the meaning they bring to their pain. Other examples of traditional ethnographies include Desantis's exploration of the health and wellness rationalizations some cigar smokers make (Desantis, 2003), and Way's and Tracy's 2012 ethnography of communication at hospice.

For an example of ethnomethodology, we can look at the research of Frers (2009), who looked at how patients' medical files are used as one part of doctor-patient interactions to organize medical discussions, control access to information, establish boundaries, distribute medical access, and create meaning.

One example of Ethnography of Communication is Gerry Philipsen's 2000 study analyzing a controversial speech given by the president of his university in which a portion of the president's speech was termed by some people as being racist. Philipsen worked through a systematic process of thoroughly collecting information about the speech act, then coding the event by going through each element of the SPEAKING schema and, for each, determining how specific elements of the speech act address each category of the schema (Davis, 2014).

Ethnography of Communication has been used to study classroom interactions between teachers and students, language usage in various cultures and countries, and politeness and formality (Keating, 2007). Phillips (2009) followed the tradition of ethnography of communication as she studied the African American gang practice of writing while dancing. She discussed how gang members use this writing with their feet as a form of language expression to perform racial politics. Some other interesting applications of Ethnography of Communication include studying the use of music in the workplace (Korczynski, 2011) and the experience of Mexican American fathers and mothers who had gone through the death of a child (Russell-Kibble, 2011).

Ethnography is a frequently used tool in consumer products marketing research. In fact, there are numerous marketing research companies that specialize in this method. Ethnographic research allows the researcher (and, by extension, the manufacturer) to obtain a more profound examination of a consumer's experience with the product or product category (Burrows, 2014). One research firm, Ethnographic Insight, describes their research as "examin[ing] how consumers actually use and experience your products and services to determine their patterns of usage, current level of satisfaction, unmet wants and needs, and suggestions for improvement" (Ethnographic Insight, 2015, n.p.). As for scholarly research, ethnography as a method provides an in vivo understanding of a phenomenon, rather than relying on a person's retrospective self-report of motivations and behaviors. Thus, it has much more ecological validity than, for example, surveys or even in-depth interviews. Because ethnographic researchers can compare a consumer's actual behavior with his/her self-report of behavior, and can observe nuances in behaviors that people do not see in themselves, researchers can identify contradictions and gaps in understanding (Burrows, 2014).

▼ Focus Groups

Focus group research is a methodology that is known by its method of data collection. Focus groups are in-depth group discussions on a specific situation or topic of interest, made up of five to twelve participants and a moderator (or two co-moderators). They provide participants a forum to discuss differing perspectives. Developed in the 1950s by sociologist Robert Merton and psychologist Paul Lazerfeld, the first focus groups were used for media testing. They have been used primarily in the marketing field for decades, but they have been more recently (re)discovered by social scientists.

Historically, focus groups are held in a small face-to-face group. Today, focus groups held via telephone, Skype, and other electronic means are more and more popular. Focus groups are either conducted with a group of people who are strangers to each other, or among a group of people who know each other (also called natural groups or bona fide groups). A group can meet one time only or regularly over a period of time. A trained facilitator leads the group session, typically follows a semi-structured moderator's guide, and asks in-depth and open-ended questions (Davis, 2016).

There are many advantages to focus groups. The foremost advantage is that you can see group interaction in action. Focus groups can be a forum to provide a voice to marginalized groups. In some ways, focus groups are more naturalistic than some other data collection methods, in that they tap into the usual *modes of communication* and *everyday social practices* that constitute people's social lives—they mirror social interchange in a relatively naturalistic way. For communication scholars, focus groups are studied in the context of interactions with others—human experience is constructed within specific social contexts—so you can watch the process of collective sense-making through interactions of participants. Also, with focus groups, the relationship between the researcher and the participants is less hierarchical—the balance of power shifts from the researcher to the participants in a focus group. Of course, focus groups are inherently biased due to the interactional nature of method and this interaction should always be factored in as part of the analysis.

Appropriate Research Questions Answered by Focus Groups.

Focus groups can be used as a stand-alone methodology but they are also commonly used as one of multiple qualitative methods of data collection in ethnographic or grounded theory research—typically to triangulate or crystallize data from observations, in-depth interviews, artifact analysis, case reviews, document reviews, and/or expert panels. Focus groups are also sometimes included in a mixed method design for quantitative research (Davis, 2016).

Focus groups hold the unique position of providing two types of information—they are naturalistic because they involve naturally occurring communication practices and social interactions, but they are held in a laboratory setting. Focus groups yield retrospective and metacommunication information as participants look back over past behaviors, and also provide an opportunity to observe naturalistic group discourse as it occurs in the focus group itself (Davis, 2016).

In social science research, especially in communication studies, the objective of focus groups is to better understand group dynamics, and in these contexts, focus groups are used primarily for exploratory or phenomenological (to understand *lived experience*) research. You might use focus groups with ethnographic, phenomenological, and grounded theory research, as well as for action research, **case study research**, **discourse analysis**, or content analysis.

Also salient for communication research, focus groups are specifically useful to listen to people talk in a group, to listen for group-generated language, to listen to people bouncing ideas off of each other, and to listen to how people influence each other.

case study research
An in-depth study of a particular case (or multiple cases).

discourse analysis
The study of spoken or written discourse.

The Role of Theory in Focus Group Research.
As with ethnographic research, a focus group project begins with an overarching theoretical basis which may be explicit or implicit, and which may simply relate to the researcher's ontology. Focus groups might also be designed to reflect theories related to group processes, such as systems theory, social network theory, social constructionism, or structuration theory. The facilitation itself might take into account group dynamics through theories such as symbolic interactionism or nonverbal communication concepts (Davis, 2016). Explanatory theories inform the analysis always in scholarly research and sometimes in industry research.

Sampling in Focus Group Research.
Remember that in qualitative research you are sampling to represent the population in terms of understanding their perspective or giving voice to them. Most focus group research uses purposive sampling methods (Davis, 2016), which means that people are chosen to fit certain characteristics. Groups may consist of people who have little in common, or people who have a lot in common (or who know each other), but homogeneous is not necessarily better—it may be advantageous to watch people disagree with each other or have to explain themselves. Prospective participants are identified and invited to attend. Although sample size in qualitative research is related to data saturation (you are done collecting data when you are not gathering new information), in focus group research it's a good idea to set out planning to conduct 2 or 3 group sessions for each participant category. You should plan to over-invite about 25% more people than you want to attend to account for people who cancel or don't show up. Participants, especially for commercial research, are typically paid a stipend for participation—usually in the form of a gift card in amounts ranging from $25 to $50. Participants are more likely to attend if you offer them an incentive, and sometimes academic research participants are offered an inducement for participation (sometimes an amount as low as a $5 gift card), but this is not always necessary if the funding is not available (Davis, 2016).

Data Collection in Focus Groups.
Corporate focus group research typically uses a formal focus group facility with a one-way mirror and sophisticated audio and video recording equipment. However, academic focus groups are usually held in more naturalistic settings such as a conference room at a place of business, hospital, or library; a private room in a restaurant; or a university classroom. In these types of settings, academic researchers have to bring our own audio and video recording equipment. It's a good practice to bring backup equipment.

In a formal focus group facility, the room is typically set up in a conference room layout. In alternative locations, you frequently have the option to arrange the room as you wish. This is actually an important consideration, as the size and shape of the seating arrangement affects interactional patterns (Fern, 2001). The participants should be sitting close enough to each other to develop a sense of intimacy and collegiality but not so close that spatial boundaries are breached. Because of this, long rectangular conference tables are actually the least desirable seating arrangements because of the distance between the two ends of the table. The best choice for a setup, if you can accomplish this, is a small square or round table or even a pseudo-living room layout (Davis, 2016).

The facilitator's skills are key for a successful discussion, but most of the success of a focus group discussion depends on planning ahead of time. Planning the facilitation itself is perhaps the most important step. Focus groups traditionally use in-depth techniques, such as nondirective interviewing, loosely structured questions, indirect approaches to asking questions, and nonverbal questioning; and projective techniques such as visualization or role playing, to focus on getting interactive discussion. However, two of the most important features of facilitation are to be a good listener and to be familiar with your facilitation guide.

The facilitation guide consists of an outline of topics that might be discussed and potential questions that might be asked, in the order they might be addressed. The guide is always written to address the study objectives, and it typically includes an outline and suggested order but the facilitator has the discretion to let the group discussion itself determine what to ask and when (Davis, 2016).

The focus group itself generally has four main stages (Fern, 2001; Stewart et al., 2007):

1. 8–10 minutes: Introduction
2. 10 minutes: Rapport-building
3. 60 minutes: In-depth investigation
4. 8–10 minutes: Closure

In addition to asking straightforward (but open ended) direct questions about your topic, you can also use various projective exercises, assignments or interventions to probe more deeply into the phenomena under discussion. Some exercises you could use include:

Collage exercise: Bring materials for participants to create a collage (magazines, glue, poster board) that depicts your topic. Be sure to debrief.

Mock shopping: Give participants fake money and index cards representing alternative products. Instruct them to shop as a group and observe their deliberation.

Sentence completion: Read participants the beginnings of sentences (related to your topic) and ask them to complete the sentence.

Metaphor comparison: Ask participants to compare a product to a common item such as a car or movie (Davis, 2016).

You should use no more than one or two of these exercises in each project; more than that is too unwieldy to facilitate. It's a good idea to vary the ways you're asking for information and it's also helpful to list many more questions than you intend to use. It's good to have options in front of you while you're facilitating. That way, if one question doesn't work, you can ask it another way (Davis, 2016).

Here's a sample facilitation guide from Davis (2016, pp. 40–44):

MODERATOR'S GUIDE

TOPIC: Needs Assessment Project among the Center of Hope for People in Need Clients

Separate Groups for:

2 groups: Clients involved in therapy services

2 groups: Clients involved in caregiver support groups

2 groups: Clients involved as volunteers

AS PARTICIPANTS ARRIVE, STUDENT RESEARCHERS WILL CONSENT THEM AND HELP THEM MAKE NAME CARDS.

I. INTRODUCTION: (5:00)

A. Hi, my name is _____ and I'm your moderator for today's discussion. We'll be here for 1 ½ hours, and the subject of our conversation is The Center of Hope for People in Need and the needs of our community. Our purpose is to simply get your reactions to some topics we'll be discussing.

B. I'm a graduate student at State University, so I'm working as an outside consultant—I don't work for The Center of Hope for People in Need, so my role here is to understand you and your opinions, not to represent any particular organization.

C. Feel free to make any comments—negative or positive—about any of the things we will be discussing today. This is a free flowing discussion, and there are no wrong answers.

D. For those of you who haven't been in a group like this before, I'd like to give you some information:

1. This room has been specially equipped for this meeting. We'll be audio and video taping this meeting so that I can write an accurate report—not of who said what, but "what got said." Your name will not be used in the report.

2. I'll be encouraging all of you to participate, even if each one of you doesn't answer each and every question.

3. Please, for the sake of our having clear tapes, and for getting as much information as possible, speak one at a time, in a voice as loud as mine. And, please avoid side conversations with each other.

4. Everyone doesn't have to answer every single question, but make sure I hear from each of you today as the session progresses.

5. I realize that it's possible that some of our conversation may be difficult for some of you. Feel free to take part in the parts of the conversation you feel comfortable with, and be quiet during any parts of the conversation you feel uncomfortable with. Feel free to express any feelings or emotions you may have about anything we're talking about.

6. You do not need to address all of your comments to me to get them on the table. You can respond directly to someone who has made a point. If you end up having a discussion back and forth between yourselves, that would be great. It's my job to get us back on track if we get off topic.

7. Say what is true for you, even if you are the only one who feels that way. Don't let the group sway you, and don't sell out to a group opinion or a strong talker.

8. The restroom is down the hall. If you need to, please feel free to step outside for a moment if you need to, please just rejoin us just as soon as you can. If you want to get up to get a refill of your drink, or seconds on food, feel free to do that.

II. WARM-UP: (5:00)

A. Now, I'd like to give each one of you a chance to introduce yourself. One thing all of you have in common is that you have had personal experience with The Center of Hope for People in Need. As an introduction, could you please mention your first name, very briefly tell how long you have been using CHPN services, and tell us what CHPN services you are using or have used? This can be brief; we'll have an opportunity to talk more about our experiences throughout the meeting if you want.

1. I'll start . . . Introduce myself.

2. (Go around the table-remind them of what we want them to say).

III. GENERAL IMPRESSIONS OF FINANCIAL, HEALTH, OR SUPPORT ISSUES: (10:00)

A. Who do you rely on for support when you or someone in your family has a serious financial, health, emotional, problem?

B. Other than CHPN, what agencies support people with problems like these?

C. What is most important to you in dealing with your problems?

D. What are your and your family's beliefs toward people who have financial, health, or emotional needs?

E. What are your and your family's attitudes towards people who receive help from an organization like CHPN?

F. What are your opinions of our community's financial, health, or emotional needs?

IV. INITIAL IMPRESSIONS OF CHPN SERVICES: (10:00)

  A. Before you had the financial, health, or emotional needs, had you heard of CHPN?

    1. What had you heard?

    2. What were your impressions?

  B. When you first had your financial, health, or emotional needs, how were CHPN services introduced to you?

    1. What were you told? Who told you? How did they tell you?

    2. What was it that made you interested in accepting CHPN's services?

      i. What was it that you wanted CHPN to do for you and your family?

V. UNDERSTANDING OF CHPN PROGRAMS: (10:00)

  A. Explain the CHPN services to me.

    1. How do they work?

    2. What do they offer?

    3. How does a person qualify for services?

    4. What types of services are provided?

  B. How well do you think you understand CHPN's programs and services?

    1. Who explained CHPN services to you?

    2. What did they tell you?

    3. How did they explain it?

    4. What did they tell you, that made you interested in using CHPN services?

VI. EXPERIENCE WITH CHPN SERVICES: (15:00)

  A. What has your experience with CHPN services been like?

  B. What is it like to be a CHPN client?

  C. How satisfied are you/are you with the services you are receiving from CHPN?

    1. What specifically makes you satisfied/not satisfied?

  D. What is your main impression NOW of CHPN?

    1. What specifically makes you say that?

    2. Give a specific example/tell a specific story of why you say that?

VII. ATTITUDES TOWARDS CHPN: (15:00)

  A. (Brainstorming Exercise) What words come to mind when you think of CHPN? Name everything you think of. Discuss answers.

  B. I'd like to ask you to complete some sentences. I'm going to read you the beginning of the sentence, and I'd like you to call out the first thing that comes to your mind. Discuss answers.

    1. CHPN provides me with . . .

    2. To me, CHPN represents . . .

3. Using CHPN makes me . . .
4. My family would say that CHPN is . . .
5. My favorite story about CHPN is . . .
6. My best experience with CHPN is . . .
7. My worst experience with CHPN is . . .
8. The worst thing about working with CHPN is that . . .
9. The best thing about working with CHPN is that . . .
10. I will always wish that CHPN . . .
11. I will always be grateful that CHPN . . .
12. One thing I would change about CHPN services is . . .

VIII. FACTORS IMPORTANT IN FINANCIAL, HEALTH, EMOTIONAL NEEDS: (15:00)
   A. (BRAINSTORM) What factors or characteristics do you think are important in addressing the financial, health, and emotional needs in our city?
   B. When a person or organization is addressing the financial, health, and emotional needs in our city, what factors should they be considering?

IX. What positive things do you think can come from our discussion today?
   1. For CHPN?
   2. For our community?
   3. For your family?
   4. For you personally?

X. CLOSE:
   1. (Go around table): Tell us one positive thing resulting from this discussion today.

XI. THANKS FOR ATTENDING AND ACKNOWLEDGEMENT OF PARTICIPATION

Focus group moderating or facilitating. The moderator is the instrument of research in focus groups—the importance of the moderating role cannot be overemphasized. As you are facilitating the in-depth discussion, you are attending to many different things at the same time: who is talking, how much each person is talking, and to whom they are addressing their comments. Qualities of a good moderator include:

- Expresses warmth and empathy
- Appears kind, yet firm
- Is actively involved
- Pays close attention
- Is a good listener
- Pursues understanding of meaning and intents
- Demonstrates unconditional positive regard
- Links trains of thoughts and divergent comments

- Demonstrates incomplete understanding (sophisticated naïveté)
- Expresses interest in new ideas

A good moderator encourages all group members, demonstrates flexibility, demonstrates sensitivity and respect, demonstrates a research orientation (a questioning mind), is a quick starter and initiator, demonstrates quick thinking, has stamina (facilitating focus groups is tiring!), displays an appropriate sense of humor, and shows a genuine interest in what participants have to say.

Focus group moderators need to exhibit unconditional positive regard as you show respect for an opinion without appearing to reinforce it. You should also, as appropriate, exhibit listening skills, probe for clarity, practice flexibility by following up on unexpected issues, practice sensitivity to the emotional level of discussion, encourage the expression of different opinions, respond to nonverbal signals as well as verbal communication, and be attentive to both process and content.

Ethical Concerns Specific to Focus Group Research. There are specific ethical concerns to be taken into consideration when designing a study using a focus group methodology. The first is the confidentiality of the information discussed. Because participants will be sharing information in front of others, you can't promise participants confidentiality nor anonymity and you must remind them of that when you consent them. Because of the group nature of this method, you must protect against group coercion when consenting participants. Participants in focus groups are typically consented multiple times: first, when invited to the session; second, privately when they arrive at the session (this is when they sign the consent form); third, at the beginning of the group when participants are reminded of the consent parameters during introductions (Davis, 2016).

Insuring security of the audio or videotapes of the sessions is paramount to confidentiality. In addition, participants in focus groups are especially vulnerable to group coercion or pressure to disclose information participants may not have intended to disclose. Creating a safe environment in which participants can share painful and emotional experiences is a challenge that must be met in any focus group, but you should be especially aware of this in groups in which the topic is sensitive or in which group discussion leans toward deeper disclosure. Since focus groups, especially for academic purposes, frequently invite participants to discuss emotionally difficult experiences, participants can potentially become emotionally distressed and you should take measures to alleviate this (e.g., letting the participants choose whether or not they want to respond to a topic, making sure participants know they can leave the session if they need to, providing appropriate referrals to counselors, etc., if necessary) (Davis, 2016).

Analyzing Focus Groups. The coding and analysis process for a focus group project typically follows a five step procedure:

1. Transcription of video or audio tape recordings of the sessions (transcribing both verbal utterances and nonverbal behaviors);
2. An initial read-through of the transcripts while making analytical notations;
3. A first coding pass, usually called open coding;

4. A second coding pass in which categories or findings are combined, broken apart, and re-categorized, usually called constant comparison;

5. One or more additional analytical passes in which bigger picture ideas, speculations, or conclusions are formulated and connected to pre-existing theory, contexts, or concepts in a way that addresses the research questions and provides guidance to the client or research project (Davis, 2016). Many focus group analyses use coding methods such as thematic, categorical, or content analysis to code and analyze focus group data, but Davis (2016) suggests using discourse analysis in order to be able to take into account the important interactional quality of focus groups. We will discuss this method of analysis later in this chapter.

Writing/Presenting the Findings of Focus Group Research. In focus group research, the final analysis is typically organized in a "claim—explanation—supporting evidence" format, with each coding category functioning as the claim and 1 to 3 short excerpts from the transcript operating as supporting evidence for that claim. Given the social science ontology of most focus group research, the paper is usually organized around the categories described earlier in the chapter.

Scholarly Examples of Focus Group Research. In academic research, focus groups can be used for application or evaluation of theories, or to study applied contexts of theories. They are used for exploratory tasks such as creating messages, collecting information, identifying beliefs, discovering attitudes, explaining processes, and generating thoughts, feelings, and behaviors. They are also used for experiential (or phenomenological) tasks, such as observing natural attitudes, life experiences, preferences, intentions, and behaviors, or understanding language, knowledge, and experience. With focus groups, you can gain insights into attitudes, beliefs, motives, behaviors of participants, explore how people act, behave, think—you can observe their behavior in process, hear reactions to ideas, and see things from a different (the participants') perspective.

Here's an excerpt from a focus group held as part of an ethnographic study with a children's mental health-care team, as they metacommunicate about their team communication (Davis, 2014, pp. 138–144):

We start with the collage exercise.

"This is a collage that represents this team," I explain. "Your impressions of the team. I brought new magazines this time," I say, referring to the fact that they did the same exercise in the previous focus group.

"Did you say nude magazines?" Mr. Camelini asks incredulously.

"This is getting interesting!" says Margie, the Center for Children and Families' therapist who is helping videotape the meeting.

After some joking, the group settles down quickly to the task, looking through magazines, cutting, and gluing. Alan, Nancy, and Peggy help clear off lunch debris. Alan stands to reach magazines. Jane, Mr. Stewart, Mr. Camelini, Peggy, and Nancy sit comfortably as they look through magazines. Alan puts his magazine down and holds out his hand.

Without a word being exchanged, from across the table, Peggy hands him scissors. There is some chatter about the magazine pictures.

Peggy asks, "Did we do this wrong last time so we have to do it again?"

"No!" I protest. "I thought it was so interesting, I wanted to do it again!"

Jane shows Peggy a picture.

Alan and Mr. Stewart compare pictures. Alan asks him, "You want me to put that in? Where do you want to put it?"

"We're trying to get in Kevin's mind!" Mr. Stewart responds.

"That's a good one!" Alan comments.

Jane studies a page. "45 Top Descriptions of Kids. All You Need to Know," she reads out loud.

"We should cut it out and paste it in your office," Peggy offers.

Mr. Camelini stands up and picks up a glue stick.

"This is more fun than taking pictures," Alan comments, referring to his videographer role in the last focus group.

I notice that Jane and Peggy are chatting. Mr. Camelini is working on his own, slightly away from the table.

The intercom blares, "The fire alarm will be going off. Please disregard it." Nobody seems to pay the message any attention. The fire alarm never does go off.

. . .

I watch as a poster begins to form. In the top center a headline says "Lifetime." There is a picture of a broken teacup with a band aid mending the break. In the center is a Lexus. I see a tossed salad. A picture of a room, neat as a pin, with hardwood floors and perfectly lined up files. A cartoon of a woman comforting a young boy, with a young girl crying in the background. "Hope" reads one headline. "Walls" in another. A mirror. A satellite. A young boy waiting for a ball to come down from the air. A picture of two boys in a classroom, raising their hands, with a headline "Education," and a sub-head "Concern. Worldwide." Another headline, "Oh, I wish. . . ." Small girls playing soccer, great effort showing on their faces. Finally, a headline that reads: "Deeper Into the Mind-Bending Universe Than You've Ever Been: A Guide in Plain English." That would make a good title for my book, I think to myself.

"Okay," I say. "Explain to me what we've created. What are we saying about our team here?"

"In the center I put the Lexus," Mr. Camelini answers first. "When we first met, we didn't know each other and we were pulling in different directions, but now we're a fine-tuned machine, moving along," he explains.

"Ooh," I respond. "You guys are a Lexus now. Cool. What else is here?"

"I put a salad," says Nancy, "'cause I think of this as healthy for ourselves and for the family."

Jane and Mr. Stewart are flipping through magazines. Alan and Mr. Camelini watch them. Peggy gets up to get a soft drink.

Nancy leans forward and points to the poster. "This is a person doing his own thing and going his own way, and this is a group of people all working together to get to the goal." She looks at Alan and watches his reaction. He studies the board for a minute.

"Soccer players. Great," I comment.

"Get to the goal. That's neat," says Alan.

"Literally, get to the goal," I respond.

"Since we're close to the last day of school," Alan says, "I found this headline of concern about education. This other picture would represent a radar, that we're still trying to listen very carefully and figure out what's going on. This other picture represents a goal that the family has, their house."

Mrs. Stewart comes back in the room and gets a drink. She looks over the poster and dabs glue under the corners of one of the pictures.

"What's the coffee cup?" I ask.

"It's broken. The band-aids are there to help," says Peggy.

"Anything else up there we haven't talked about?" I ask.

"Oh, I wish," says Jane, with feeling.

"Oh I wish," I repeat, momentarily confused, then I see the phrase on the poster. "Right."

"They wish for a lot of things," says Jane.

"There's the most important right there," adds Mrs. Stewart, pointing to the "Lifeline" headline.

"You can wish, you can hope," Jane adds.

. . .

"That's great. What's the cartoon?" I wonder.

"That reminded me of when Kevin was in here with us today," Nancy answers. "We all have a different perspective of him. This person on the team is going one way, another person is going another way, but we can all bring our perspective. Kevin can bring his and help us to understand some of the things he's thinking about. The team has a common goal from different perspectives." I notice that everyone is leaning forward, listening to her intently.

I glance at my watch and move quickly to my next question. "What's it like being a member of this team?"

"Complicated is the best word I can come up with," Mrs. Stewart responds. She is still standing, leaning against the back of her chair.

"In what way?" I ask.

"Well," she answers, looking around the table at everyone, "we're all trying to figure out what's driving Kevin, what his ultimate motives are, and so far we're coming up empty. It's hard to come up with the answers if you don't know the question."

Mr. Stewart leans back in his chair and puts his hands behind his head. "Yeah!" he responds.

Mrs. Stewart continues, "That's basically what it is. What's making Kevin do this, and then how do we solve it? It's like trying to put the cart before the horse," she explains in a serious tone, as if she's teaching a classroom of children.

"What was the question?" Peggy asks, as everyone laughs.

"What's it like being a member of this team?" I answer, then smile. "But you could answer any question you feel like answering."

"I got off from thinking about what she was saying," Peggy says. "One of the things that I get from the team is that so often, when I'm working with families, I feel like I'm by myself."

The door opens and the woman from the front office comes in and whispers something to Mrs. Stewart, who says 'okay,' then sits down in her chair.

Peggy continues, "Then I'm running around trying to connect everybody, and having everyone at the table really helps do that. We're all communicating at the same time and we all see what happens at the same time. For me, being part of the team really makes me feel less alone in what I'm trying to do."

The door opens again, then closes.

"I would mirror that. I agree," says Alan.

Mr. Stewart responds. "We agree. 'Cause a lot of times we feel like we're alone, trying to deal with this. But with the group, we don't feel so alone."

. . .

"I feel some frustration," says Mr. Camelini, seemingly ignoring the diversion at the other side of the table. "On one hand, it's great to have parents here, but like Mrs. Stewart said, I'm not sure how much progress we've made. When I'm in these meetings, I'm always torn; I want to be in the classroom."

"It's taking time away from your class," I acknowledge.

"Yes."

"We very much appreciate your . . ." Alan starts to say.

"Spending a lot more time with one student than I am with the others," Mr. Camelini interrupts.

Mrs. Stewart sits forward. "Like I said, Kevin's complicated. Finding out why he does what he does would make dealing with him so much easier, but we wind up with more questions than we have answers." Her hands are expressive and everyone is listening attentively to her. "One minute we think we know why Kevin does some of what he does, and then the next minute that whole idea is shot out of the water because he's done something worse than what he had done before. That's what makes this whole situation complicated for everyone. . . ."

Peggy interrupts. "I do think it's frustrating because sometimes when we're trying to figure out why, we can get stuck there. One of the good things about a team is that if we do get stuck, there's always someone that can pull us out a little bit. We may never know why, but there's people, yourself included," she looks at Mrs. Stewart, "who know what works and doesn't work. So in that way I think a team approach is good. Sometimes it's frustrating because team involvement slows down the pace. So we have to have everybody on board from the beginning."

Alan nods. "It's one of those balance things. Sometimes, if you were just working on your own, it would be so much faster; 'cause it's just you doing it with the family, where with a team it does take longer to get everybody on board."

Peggy continues. "But who's to say that with the team approach we don't get where we're going, maybe a little slower, but maybe a little more lasting than you would with individuals?"

When the door opens again, Jane looks up and leaves the room. When Jane returns a moment later, she walks over to Mr. Camelini, shows him a paper, and steps back out of the room.

Mrs. Stewart jumps in. "They say too many cooks spoil the broth, but in this instance, I think the number of cooks actually makes the broth better, because they're each putting in a separate ingredient and not the same thing. No two people are going to put in the same idea, or look at something the same way."

"This is a good team," Alan says.

I ask my next question. "If you guys were making a movie of this team, what would the movie be like? Where would it take place?"

"I think the location we're at right now would be perfect," Mrs. Stewart answers. "The whole school environment."

"Documentary," Alan comments.

"Who would be there?" I ask.

"People like us," Mrs. Stewart says.

"Except Mr. Stewart would be called Julius Caesar," Alan interjects.

"Not hardly. I'm no Cleopatra!" Mrs. Stewart says.

"Demi Moore would play me," I say as everyone laughs. "What would be happening?"

"Exactly what is happening now," Mrs. Stewart answers. "Discussing what's the best way to help Kevin. Find out what's eating him, and what we can do to put a halt to it."

Nancy agrees. "I really like that idea. I was thinking the same thing. I think it would be real interesting if we were making a movie, to have this be part of it. Then, we'd follow Kevin through his whole day, starting at home, coming to school, going to class, riding the bus back home; brief little segments of each one, and then us as a team coming together with Kevin and talking about it." Everyone is nodding.

"Movies have to have a plot," I say. "What would the plot be?"

Peggy answers first. "The first thing that came to my mind was The Bad News Bears."

There's a knock on the door again, but no one comes in.

"That sounds like Kevin sometimes!" Mrs. Stewart says, laughing.

Peggy continues. "They're just a mess, with the whole sports theme, and the story is about the team and where they came from and where they went."

"The second one, Breaking Training," Mrs. Stewart adds.

"I haven't seen that one." Nancy says.

"They play baseball," Peggy explains. "Somebody winds up having to put a group of kids who can't do much of anything together to play ball, and they have nothing. They don't have uniforms. I don't remember who was in charge of them."

"Who was in charge of them?" Mrs. Stewart says thoughtfully.

"I want to say Rodney Dangerfield. No?" Peggy thinks.

"No, that was another soccer movie," Alan says. *"It wasn't Walter Matthau, was it?"* he asks.

"I think it was. Yeah, it was Walter Matthau," Mrs. Stewart confirms.

Peggy continues. *"But anyway, through the course of the movie, they are a really good little ball playing team and they learn a lot about each other."*

I ask, *"Movies have to have dialogue. What would people be saying?"*

Alan answers, *"They wouldn't be saying just stuff about Kevin. 'Cause I don't think this is just all about Kevin. It's about your whole family,"* he says to the Stewarts.

Jane comes back into the room and returns to her seat at the table.

"It's about the entire family and the group itself," Mrs. Stewart says.

"How they interact with us," Mr. Stewart adds.

"I'm not even sure that Kevin would be the star," Alan thinks.

"Who's the star?" I ask.

Mrs. Stewart answers, *"Actually, I think the entire team."*

"An ensemble," Alan says. *"Just like Friends."*

"But the entire team would be the actual stars of the movie," Mrs. Stewart says.

Peggy speaks up. *"I was thinking of the show 24. Every hour you see is an hour in the day, and there's 24 hours and there's 24 shows. It's a drama. I think it's in a hospital."*

"He's a spy," Alan remembers.

"A spy. Even though we're not that exciting, I see it focusing on different parts of us, like Mr. Camelini in the classroom, you two at home, and individual therapy," Peggy says.

Mrs. Stewart interjects. *"I can give a good example too. Like CSI. They got two different cases going on at once, but they go back and forth between what one group is doing to solve this, to what this second group is doing, and sometimes the two overlap. They become one case instead of two separate ones. Basically, that's exactly what's going on here. We have the team at school, then we have us at home, and when we come together at school, the two overlap into one. So it's a two-part thing. CSI actually fits the bill best because they have two cases going on at the same time."*

"What would people be looking like, body language and facial expressions?" I ask.

"A variety," Peggy answers. *"I don't think we could pin that down. Even when one person's talking, everybody's reacting differently. Sometimes I'm listening, sometimes I'm not. I might look like I'm listening, I might not be."* Everyone laughs.

Mrs. Stewart says softly, *"That's perfect. We have laughter. We all have concerns about Kevin, but in different ways."*

Industry Examples of focus group research.

The best known use of focus groups is for marketing, advertising, or consumer research, to determine consumer needs or to pretest advertising concepts. Author Christine Davis was a market research consultant for 18 years, and in that time she conducted thousands of focus groups for many different uses. One type of study she frequently conducted was a needs assessment, to help companies understand the needs and motivations of their consumers. In marketing and communication research (particularly media research), focus groups are especially useful to let you discover factors that may motivate purchase, product use, brand loyalty, or product trial; understand how people use a product or service, or how they perceive a communication act; understand the attitudes and values associated with product use, purchase, brand loyalty, and so on; understand how groups interact or communicate as a group; understand how people influence each other through language and conversation; and get ideas for language, visuals, and imagery to use in communication efforts. Other common uses of focus groups are to gather feedback among a company's employees or to test messages for political candidates. Focus groups can be an eye opening experience for corporate clients because they let corporate management or marketing executives actually hear a consumer speak about the product or product category in his/her own words (Davis, 2016).

▼ # Grounded Theory

The process of **grounded theory** was originally developed by Barney Glaser and Anselm Strauss (Glaser & Strauss, 1967; Strauss & Corbin, 1990), but most communication studies researchers who use grounded theory use a constructivist approach to grounded theory developed by Kathy Charmaz (2000), so we will discuss Charmaz's version here.

Appropriate Research Questions Answered by Grounded Theory Research.   The goal of grounded theory, says Charmaz, is to learn "what our research participants' lives are like. We study how they explain their statements and actions, and ask what analytic sense we can make of them" (2000, pp. 2–3). Grounded theory seeks to understand interaction within social practices and the resulting meaning (Starks & Trinidad, 2007). Grounded theory is appropriate for research questions that focus on experiences over time within a social context (Creswell et al., 2007).

The Role of Theory in Grounded Theory Research.   There are two main ideas incorporated into grounded theory: We are developing theories that are grounded in the data and that surface through the **theoretical saturation** of categories (we collect and analyze the data until no new categories of theories are identified); and our design is *emergent*—we analyze, collect data, reanalyze, interpret, and change our design as we go along. The process of grounded theory allows for surprises, fresh ideas, and exploration (Charmaz, 2006). The theories derived in grounded theory are explanations of social processes—grounded theory answers the question of "How does the social process of 'X' happen in the context of this environment?" (Starks & Trinidad, 2007). The focus of a grounded theory analysis is to develop a social model or theory (Creswell et al., 2007).

theoretical sampling
Choosing a sample based on the people, events, groups, and so on who can shed light on a theory being investigated.

Sampling in Grounded Theory Research.   Grounded theory typically uses a **theoretical sampling** method—you choose your sample based on the people, events, groups, and so on who can shed light on the theory you are investigating. As you collect your data, your theory may change and, as a result, your sampling design may change also. In grounded theory, you're done when you're done—when you've collected enough data to understand and explain the full complexity of the culture you're studying; when you have detailed descriptions of the ways that participants view the world; when you fully understand underlying issues, changes over time, and multiple viewpoints; when you can develop analytic categories; and when you understand differences and nuances in your data (Charmaz, 2006). Grounded theory is more interested with immersion in a culture than in sample size. In a grounded theory study, achieving understanding and rapport with our participants is more important than the number of participants we talk to. Having said that, however, grounded theory often has larger sample sizes than other qualitative methods because it uses theoretical sampling, involving participants with different experiences to compare and explore different aspects. In grounded theory, the sample size is complete when the study reaches *theoretical saturation*—when no more theories or constructs emerge by the data. Grounded theory research typically uses samples ranging from ten to sixty participants (Starks & Trinidad, 2007).

Data Collection in Grounded Theory Research.

Researchers conducting grounded theory typically use observation and in-depth interviews in which participants describe their experiences (Starks & Trinidad, 2007). Grounded theory involves a systematic process of synthesizing data throughout the course of a study (Charmaz, 2006). In grounded theory, researchers observe social processes in their natural environments, which help them see the effect of the environment on behavior and meaning (Starks & Trinidad, 2007). Since, in grounded theory, you shape and reshape your data collection and refine your study design as you try out tentative concepts, theories, and analysis throughout your study, you might return to the field to observe different things, explore additional questions or experiences, or otherwise move along your ideas as they emerge (Charmaz, 2006). Field notes in grounded theory might include descriptions of both individual and collective behaviors, much detail including stories and observations, processes you consider to be significant, things that participants tell you they consider to be interesting or problematic, participants' language use, scenes and contexts, and analytical thoughts and ideas. Observations in a grounded theory project focus on processes—what is related to what else, what are the practices in the site, how are people organized, and what are the social networks. In grounded theory, you will be looking for data that lets you compare across time, across categories, and between concepts. In grounded theory research, think of fieldwork as an opportunity to "dig into the scene" (p. 23).

Grounded theorists begin their research with **sensitizing concepts**—initial ideas, concepts, interests to pursue and sensitize you to ask certain kinds of questions and look for certain kinds of information. These sensitizing concepts give you a starting point for data collection but they are only a starting point in grounded theory—you let the data help you develop your thoughts, theories, and ideas and you follow those as you refine your study. Therefore, interview guides in grounded theory are open ended and emergent, subject to change as the study—or the interview—progresses (Charmaz, 2006).

sensitizing concepts
Initial ideas, concepts, interests to pursue and sensitize you to ask certain kinds of questions and look for certain kinds of information.

Grounded theory interview questions center around the central question of grounded theory, "What's happening here?" Grounded theory interviewing will be formed by what you've observed in the field, as you ask participants questions about meanings, processes, and control related to actions and behaviors you've seen. A grounded theory interview will consist of a few good open-ended questions that let your participant do most of the talking, yielding an in-depth exploration of the participant's experience. Questions such as: "Tell me about," "How," "What," and "When" are useful in helping participants give rich responses. Grounded theory interviewing investigates taken-for-granted aspects of life to understand participants' meanings, intentions, and actions.

Coding and Analysis in Grounded Theory Research.

Coding in grounded theory follows a very specific, rigorous process. In fact, grounded theory's coding process is among the most systematic and rigorous coding processes in qualitative research.

In grounded theory, coding begins when you collect your first piece of data. As you code and collect your data, you start to define and categorize the data. You interact with the data and pose questions while coding and collecting. Your emerging interpretations shape your data collection (who you talk to, what you attend to, what you ask them) as well as your data coding. This starts the chain of theory development, which also emerges as you work with your data.

In grounded theory, data collection, coding, and analysis are simultaneous. As the issues become clearer and more specific, researchers can hone in on participants' issues, interests, and concerns with more specificity. The interviewer is an active participant in the process. Grounded theory uses multiple interviews to delve deeper into salient topics.

Grounded theory coding takes into account the relationships between the data and the categories. In grounded theory, codes and categories are mutable (changeable) until late in the project, but coding in grounded theory research actually begins as soon as you begin collecting your data.

As you collect your data, you do **open coding**—initial coding of data and jotting down emerging themes, thoughts, ideas, or concepts. This process will continue throughout your data collection and will create sensitizing concepts that will inform your data collection efforts.

When you have completed data collection, you finalize your open coding to do what's called **axial coding**: creating codes that connect categories (called **metacodes**). As you refine your axial codes or metacodes, you go through a process of **negative case analysis**—constantly comparing existing codes with new data, adding new codes (or revising existing codes) until all cases of data are accounted for in the coding scheme. You're done creating categories when you reach **theoretical saturation,** when no new themes or meanings are derived.

Writing Grounded Theory Findings.

Grounded theory research is often organized thematically, with each concept or theme supported by snippets of quotes from interviews or field notes. The theories themselves might be explained in a diagram or in a written explanation (Starks & Trinidad, 2007).

Examples of Grounded Theory Research.

Here is an example of a grounded theory paper. Note how the paper is organized by theme, with each

---

open coding
Initial coding of data and jotting down emerging themes, thoughts, ideas, or concepts.

axial coding
Creating codes that connect categories.

metacodes
Overarching coding categories that connect lower level categories or themes.

negative case analysis
A stage in coding in which you constantly compare existing codes with new data, adding new codes (or revising existing codes) until all cases of data are accounted for in the coding scheme.

theme supported, in this case, both by literature and by supporting quotes (Becker, Ellevold, & Stamp, 2008, p. 96). Becker, Ellevold, and Stamp (2008) used a grounded theory framework to analyze self-report interview and observation data about defensive communication among romantic couples. They developed a theory of defensive communication that they illustrated through narrative.

Relational Concerns. The final contextual condition influencing the process of defensive communication is relational concerns, which comprises romantic partners' underlying anxiety about the relationship. The two main relational concerns pertain to uncertainty and identity. Participants in dating relationships expressed concerns about relational uncertainty that often colored the process of defensive communication. For example, Christy and Derek, a dating couple, experienced defensiveness when Derek joked about her dating someone else.

D: Um, we went [to the restaurant] and we go out to eat a lot, but it had been a week or two weeks since we were even there. And then umm, we sat in this one booth and we sat in this booth once before but it was like maybe a month ago. We sit down and she was like we sat in the same seat. So she got a little nickname from me and I chuckled and I was like you must be getting me confused with one of your other ones because we didn't even come here yesterday let alone sitting in this booth.

I: How do you feel you were approaching the situation when talking with her?

D: Umm, in a light joking manner because we I mean, we were just hanging out at that time. I mean I knew how she felt about me and vice versa but that is as deep as it went. I mean if she was with someone else, there was nothing I could say or do about that. So it was mostly in a joking manner.

I: Did you suspect that maybe she had been there with someone else?

D: Yeah. She is smart, okay? And I can understand that there is some knuckle head who can't remember this or that, who we were sitting at a table and we got the same table that we were sitting in yesterday. I mean I don't think that I had even her the day before you know, and that is what makes me think that maybe it was. (5:I:B:147–172)

Uncertainty often resulted from jealousy about the partner's fidelity or interest in another person, threats of relationship termination, lack of relational maintenance, or unclear

phenomenology
The study of experience, in order to understand, in great depth, the nature, essence, and meaning of that experience.

Phenomenology

Phenomenology—developed by Max van Manen and others, and based on the philosophies of Edmund Husserl and Martin Heidegger—is the study of experience, in order to understand—in great depth—the nature, essence, and meaning of that experience. **Phenomenology** is "an encounter" with real life, says Vagle (2014, p. 12), in that phenomenologists practice their craft through embodied engagement and relationship with their experiences. Phenomenologists study an experience from within the experience as they examine "how it is to

phenomenology
The study of experience, in order to understand—in great depth—the nature, essence, and meaning of that experience.

BE in the world" (Vagle, 2014, p. 21). Van Manen refers to phenomenological inquiry as "surrendering to a state of wonder" (2014, p. 15).

Appropriate Research Questions Answered by Phenomenology.

Unlike other interpretive methods that study the social construction of meaning in an experience, or that reflexively examine an experience in light of our own interpretations and experiences, the goal of phenomenology is to understand an experience as it is lived, uncontaminated by other theories or assumptions. One of the key aspects of phenomenological inquiry is to undertake a systematic identification of the researchers' preconceived ideas and thoughts, in order to be able to focus on understanding the experience with an open, blank mind (called **bracketing**). As Starks and Trinidad (2007) explain it, "phenomenology contributes to deeper understanding of lived experiences by exposing taken-for-granted assumptions about [our] ways of knowing" (p. 1373). Phenomenologists' sole focus is on the experience itself—not the people in the experience except in terms of how they live through the experience, not the construction of the experience, not the interpretation of the experience—but the pure experience, to understand how it is experienced from within. As Vagle (2014) states,

> *Phenomenologists . . . study how things are being and becoming. . . . The phenomenologist . . . is not studying the individual but is studying how a particular phenomenon manifests and appears in the lifeworld. . . . The "unit of analysis" in phenomenology is the phenomenon, not the individual (pp. 22–23).*

Phenomenologists study the fundamental essence of an experience. Phenomena and experiences studied by phenomenologists might include things like "confusion, respect, despair, hope, resistance, being in love" (Vagle, 2014, p. 27), and they ask questions like, "how does someone find him/herself in a state of being in love?" Other phenomenologists might study an experience such as a healthcare experience or an educational experience, and might ask, "how is this experienced as the people are living through the experience?" The key to phenomenological understanding is to see everyday lived experience "as if we are seeing it for the first time" (van Manen, 2014, p. 43).

Sampling in Phenomenology.

The first step in phenomenology is to choose the experience you wish to study. Van Manen (2001) suggests selecting an experience that is "something you really care about and want to question" (p. 58). You then have to identify how you can enter into the experience and sample to that aim.

Phenomenological research typically has small samples, because phenomenologists are not looking to sample from a wide range of experiences—they want detailed information about a very specific experience. Phenomenological research typically uses sample sizes from one to ten participants (Starks & Trinidad, 2007); people who have experienced the phenomena under study. For that reason, phenomenological research typically uses purposive sampling or theoretical construct sampling.

Data Collection in Phenomenology.

Phenomenologists seek to understand embodied experience, to understand a phenomenon as completely as if they had experienced it themselves (Starks & Trinidad, 2007). Data collection in

bracketing
In phenomenology, identification of the researchers' preconceived ideas and thoughts, in order to be able to focus on understanding the experience with an open, blank mind.

phenomenology seeks to identify specific concrete instances of how someone experiences the phenomenon.

Phenomenologists frequently gather data through in-depth retrospective interviews or focus groups in which participants are encouraged to relive, explain, and describe experiences in great detail. Phenomenological interviewing would include non-structured interviews that you can follow up on to understand the participant's experience. You would return to each participant multiple times to make sure you fully understand (Grbich, 2007).

Sometimes phenomenologists use their own personal experiences for analysis, and these accounts are similar to autoethnographic accounts. Researchers conducting phenomenology might also use observation methods in which they observe people in their natural environment participating in the phenomenon under study in order to gain information about their lived experience and resulting meaning (Starks & Trinidad, 2007). Phenomenologists also use document or artifact data (Creswell et al., 2007; Starks & Trinidad, 2007). Regardless of the type of data included in a study, phenomenologists utilize what Grbich (2007) calls "bathing in the experience as it occurs" (p. 88).

Analysis in Phenomenology.   Coding in phenomenological research uses a systematic procedure that categorizes specific statements into "clusters of meaning" that represent the phenomena. In phenomenological analysis, as you are collecting the data, you begin to form ideas about patterns, relationships, and connections. You use written descriptions to uncover the essence of the phenomenon through different layers of interpretation. You identify key themes that occurred as you yourself interacted with your participants, or with your data itself (Grbich, 2007; Starks & Trinidad, 2007; van Manen, 2001).

Phenomenological coding and analysis uses a multistep process:

1. Thoroughly review your text, field notes, and interview transcripts.
2. Make analytical notations as you read through the data, line by line.
3. Ask follow-up questions to participants to clarify thoughts and ideas.
4. Read through the data a second time, line by line, and make further analytical notations.
5. Follow up with participants again to clarify.
6. Read through the data a third time, line by line, and make analytical notations.
7. Begin to identify categories of meaning related to the RQ by reflecting on "the essential themes which characterize the experience" (van Manen, 2001, p. 58) and construct a code list of these themes.
8. Isolate natural meaning units (phrases with a single meaning) and add these to the code list.
9. Write and rewrite the themes and categories as you deeply reflect on the experience. Consider both the "parts and whole" (van Manen, 2001, p. 60)—the essential themes that contribute to the experience.
10. Select themes that are central to the experiences of participants and write a descriptive comment about each theme.

11. Write a narrative about the participants' experiences with the phenomenon and relate it to the interpretive themes you selected.

12. Collect these narratives and themes and combine them into related field of interconnections.

13. Rank the themes in terms of frequency and intensity.

14. Group themes into subthemes and metathemes.

15. Identify additional or overriding themes that explain the phenomena.

16. Write a narrative about the phenomenon, including your own personal experience with the phenomenon, description of the phenomenon from the literature, and your interpretive themes from your research.

17. Distill the narrative into one final description to form your conclusion.

Writing the Findings in Phenomenology. Phenomenological analysis consists of thick descriptions of the phenomena that are then categorized into units or themes to describe the *essence* of the experience (Creswell et al., 2007; Starks & Trinidad, 2007). Phenomenological studies are often reported as narratives, perhaps as blended accounts from different participants' points of view, often written to allow the reader to experience the phenomenon (Starks & Trinidad, 2007). A phenomenological narrative will typically be rich and detailed and clearly communicate the experience under study. As Starks and Trinidad (2007) explain, "By the end of the story the reader should feel that she has vicariously experienced the phenomenon under study and should be able to envision herself . . . coming to similar conclusions about what it meant" (p. 1376). In phenomenology, the final narrative may use more poetic or other creative forms of writing to distill the experience. Regardless of the manner in which phenomenological findings are written, phenomenology always balances "verbatim excerpts, paraphrasing, and your descriptions/interpretations" (van Manen, 2001, p. 98).

Examples of Phenomenology. Following is an excerpt from a phenomenological paper (Beabout, Carr-Chellman, Alkandari, Almeida, Gursoy, Ma, Modak, & Pastore, 2008, pp. 218–219) about the perceptions of New Orleans educators on the process of rebuilding the school system after Hurricane Katrina. You can see this paper was written as a more traditional paper, organized around themes with quotes for supporting evidence.

From "The Perceptions of New Orleans Educators on the Process of Rebuilding the New Orleans School System after Katrina" by Brian Beabout et al, *Journal of Education for Students Placed at Risk, Vol. 13, No. 2, January 4, 2008;* reprinted by permission of the publisher (Taylor & Francis Ltd, http://www. tandfonline.com).

Findings

Our findings indicate that a wide range of factors have influenced educators' perspectives on this unique process of drastic school change. Among others, comments addressed topis ranging from district communication and leadership, the need for accountability, the lingering challenges of the pre-Katrina system, and concerns about working conditions. This variety is consistent with our view of schools as complex social systems. Viewed through the lens of chaos theory, three dominant themes emerge: the current culture of uncertainty in New Orleans, a mix of hope and cynicism for the future, and the lack of revolutionary change. A detailed analysis of these three themes and their relation to chaos theory follows.

Current Culture of Uncertainty

In 2005 and early 2006, the uncertainties of living in post-Katrina New Orleans have included disrupted mail, spotty communication, unreliable utility services, disrupted social networks, skyrocketing housing costs, and increased violent crime. These factors have lent a mood of indeterminacy to life in New Orleans, a feeling that has deeply affected educators living there. This uncertainty, felt by educators tasked with reform, can be described on several different levels: the citywide level, the school system level, and the school site level.

The Road Home: Citywide Uncertainty

Predicting student enrollment is a task central to the planning of any school district (Hartman, 1999). The extreme uncertainty surrounding the return of New Orleans' population has remained a topic of intense interest in the rebuilding process (Hill & Hannaway, 2006; Ritea, 2007; Troeh, 2006; Warner, 2005). With returning children a key determinant for how much funding is available for hiring teachers and opening school buildings, the future of the school system rests on the decisions of thousands of New Orleans families displaced by the storm across the state, the region, and the nation. As educators discussed their experiences with change, the impossibility of estimating how and when the population would return figured large in their comments: Again, the whole problem and the most confusing thing is that nobody really knows what the whole system and the whole city will be like in the next 12 months . . . . We have a staff meeting and we talk about doubling or tripling enrollment. How many students can our school handle? How many faculty would we have to hire? What would it look like? What classes would we offer? You know, I can't honestly imagine everything because all of the variables make me imagine chaos (Charter School Teacher).

Merrill and Grassley (2008) studied the experiences of overweight female patients to understand their encounters with health-care services and providers from their points of view. They used what's called a "hermeneutic phenomenological approach," which refers to the interpretation of lived experience. They used face-to-face interviews with eight women, and analyzed the data using a framework commonly used by phenomenologists, Van Manen's lifeworlds of lived space, lived body, lived time, and lived relations.

Case Study   ▼

The key thinkers in case study research are Robert Stake and Robert Yin. A **case study** is an in-depth study of a particular case (or multiple cases). A case is defined as a *bounded unit*, and could be a person, a group, an organization, a culture, or a community.

Appropriate Research Questions Answered by Case Studies.   Case study research is appropriate for research questions that focus on an in-depth understanding of a specific issue or example (Creswell et al., 2007). With a case study, the objective is to understand that case fully or to use that case to understand an issue or a theory.

Sampling in Case Study Research.   Sometimes a researcher will use multiple cases to compare cases, but often a case study will have a sample size of one—one case. Sampling is not really a concept used in case studies, at least not in the traditional sense. While a case is defined as a **bounded unit**, determining what the exact bounds of your case are may not be as easy as you might think. A case certainly can consist of one individual (if that person exemplifies a phenomenon or issue you want to study), but a case may also be an organization, a program, an event or activity, a time, or a process. Sometimes, your *case* may be the same as a *research site* (see the next section), especially if you are studying organizations or groups. Before you decide on your sampling strategy, you need to make sure you're clear on the bounds of your case—what qualifies as being *in* the case, and what is *out*? Case studies use purposive sampling strategies, cases chosen specifically for their characteristics related to the issues you are studying. While you may likely be studying one case, in order to understand that case fully, you might do many observations over time, conduct multiple interviews with many different people, and look at quite a few records. As with ethnography and phenomenology, the hallmark of case study data collection is to immerse yourself in the case until you have reached saturation—until no new insights, understandings, or descriptions occur (Baxter & Jack, 2008).

It's also possible to do a multiple case study, when you want to compare one organization or program with another, for example, or when you want to replicate a case to understand the situation under study even more fully or understand the situation from different nuances or angles. Again, sampling or sample size is not really the relevant question to ask here. Instead, you want to determine what it is you are trying to compare or replicate. If, for example, you want to understand how Medicaid versus non-Medicaid health-care providers communicate with patients, you might want to use as one case a health-care clinic that takes Medicaid, and, as a second case, one that does not (Yin, 2009).

Data Collection in Case Study Research.   A case study is similar to ethnography in that it uses an immersion method to understand the case fully. As with ethnography, case studies typically involve multiple data sources such as observation, in-depth interviews, and, perhaps, artifact analysis. The rigor in this method comes from the immersion in the case—the amount of time spent in the field and the ability of the researcher to describe, understand, and explain the case fully and completely.

Analysis and Reporting Case Study Research.   Analysis of a case study typically focuses on description and understanding, although categorization of concepts or themes might be done as well (Creswell et al., 2007). Typically, a case study is written as an extensive narrative about each individual case (Flyvbjerg, 2011). You might report on each case (Simons, 2014):

1. Summary of the case
2. Description of the context of the case, including interview excerpts, observations, and other information from the case that will support your interpretations

bounded unit
A specific case in case study research.

3. Analysis of the case
4. Conclusions or implication of the case

The narrative should include sufficiently thick description that elucidates the level of complexity in the case. Flyvbjerg (2011) refers to this narrative as a "virtual reality" (p. 312) of the case. Sometimes, a case study might use more arts-based forms such as paintings, poetry, photography, collage, or performance, to communicate about a case (Flyvbjerg, 2011; Simons, 2014).

Examples of Case Study Research. Huang Chua (2009) used an analysis of two case sites to compare restrictions on speech in virtual communities and the contradiction between these restrictions and collective identity.

Discourse Analysis

▼

Discourse analysis is a methodology that is known by its method of analysis. Discourse analysis—the study of spoken or written discourse—studies speech acts—from the content of the discourse, to its delivery (paralanguage, speech, grammar), to its context, and the meaning deriving from each of these, to understand how people use language to construct ideas, meanings, and identities (Starks & Trinidad, 2007). Discourse analysis is a broad term that actually refers to a wide variety of methods of analysis (Manning & Kunkel, 2014; Scharp & Thomas, 2017). Discourse analysis examines meaning from the level of everyday talk (speech acts) through the systemic—or social—contextual levels (Davis, 2016; Schart & Thomas, 2017; Tracy & Robles, 2013).

Discourse analysis might focus on relational roles in the interaction; language use, exchange, or persuasion strategies; conversational turns; interactional and relational history of the participants; and nonverbal strategies. Discourse analysis takes a wide view of the context of the interaction. While both **conversation analysis (CA)** and discourse analysis focus on the specific utterances (or discourse) and the meaning resulting from it, they differ in terms of their primary focus. CA focuses primarily on how people talk, while discourse analysis focuses on how that talk constructs meaning.

conversation analysis (CA)
An investigation of social interaction between humans, most especially of everyday, ordinary conversation, called in CA "talk-in-interaction."

Research Questions Addressed by Discourse Analysis. Discourse analysis studies communication from everyday discourse to social or cultural discourse. Discourse analysis, then, can address research questions that reach from the micro perspective (how specific interactional and communication patterns construct meaning), to the macro perspective (how cultural contexts and social structures influence meaning). In addition, many studies look at both of those levels in order to understand how the cultural and discursive practices interact with each other (Davis, 2016; Scharp & Thomas, 2017).

Data Collection in Discourse Analysis. For a discourse analysis, researchers observe speech-in-action (Starks & Trinidad, 2007) and ideally record the actual discourse used, giving a well-rounded picture of discourse and meaning. Data collection in discourse analysis involves ways of finding discourse—recorded transcripts of conversations, interviews, or focus groups are ideal, as are transcripts from Internet messaging or chat groups and perhaps discursive texts such as letters, e-mail, or journal accounts. It's helpful to include notations of nonverbal communication in the transcripts as well. Field notes of discourse are also sometimes used, albeit they are less than ideal. Observation of discourse and the resulting transcripts might be supplemented by in-depth interviews in which the study participants discuss meaning related to the discourse (Scharp & Thomas, 2017; Starks & Trinidad, 2007).

Coding in Discourse Analysis.   Discourse is analyzed through a *close look* at the communication, especially at its significance, activities, identities, relationships, politics, connections, sign systems, and knowledge, to understand how language constructs social realities (Starks & Trinidad, 2007). Discourse analysis examines verbal speech (both what is said and what is not said), paralanguage and nonverbal cues, and the social and cultural context of the discourse in order to understand how the discourse and its context construct meaning and understanding (Davis, 2016).

You might begin your analysis by examining attitudes, meanings, and understandings as they are articulated in the discourse. You might then examine how these attitudes, meanings, and understandings are constructed through specific communication acts, such as turn-taking; grammatical, social, and cultural conventions and variations on language; conversational contexts and interpretations; and patterns of utterances and responses (Silverman, 1993; Wooffitt, 2005). You might also study the social structures and systems of meaning as they relate to relational sense-making practices (Davis, 2016; Tracy & Robles, 2013).

Coding in discourse analysis involves identifying meaning, themes, and roles constructed through language and finding examples of the ways in which language constructs that reality. This typically involves categorizing the discourse into themes, statements, arguments, challenges, or ideas, and connecting these categories to their historical, social, economic, and/or political context. You would especially look for places the discourse has disunity and discontinuity and try to identify where the limits of the discourse are (Grbich, 2007; Starks & Trinidad, 2007). Tracy and Robles (2013) offer these discursive elements to consider in discourse analysis:

1. Person-referencing practices, or how people refer to others or themselves in conversation, and how these practices construct ideas about social identities.

2. Speech acts, or how people use language to perform actions such as directives (to get a person to do something); representatives (to describe a situation); commissives (to establish intent); expressives (to express feeling); and declaratives (to transform social identities).

3. Paralanguage, or how the way people talk contextually constructs meaning.

4. Language selection, or how people choose the use of one language over another.

5. Interaction structures, including turn taking (the ways in which speaker changes occur), which is related to identity, power, and context.

6. Directness style, or ways in which direct or indirect communication reflect relationships.

7. Narratives, or the ways in which the stories we tell construct and reflect our relationships.

8. Stance indicators, or the ways in which a person might indicate which states of being are normal or abnormal.

(Davis, 2016, p. 86).

Writing Discourse Analysis Findings.   Final analyses for discourse analysis typically use descriptions of the language and discourse and a discussion of the ways in which this language constructs meaning (Starks & Trinidad, 2007). A discourse analysis is written as a discussion of the outcomes of language, supported by evidence from the participants' narratives to explain how language was used to construct meaning (Starks & Trinidad, 2007). It might be written thematically or topically, or in a narrative format.

Examples of Discourse Analysis.   Elliott Mishler (2007) used discourse analysis to look at the way time is constructed through language of sexual abuse survivors in a way that allowed them to re-story their past and construct new identities for themselves. The example below is of a critical discourse analysis by De Melo Resende (2009, p. 373), on the discourse in a Brazilian apartment building meeting about homeless people in the vicinity.

De Melo Resende, V., *Discourse and Society*, Vol. 20, No. 3, pp. 373, copyright © 2009 by Sage Publications, Inc. Reprinted by Permission of Sage Publications, Ltd.

Although the phrase 'homeless people' appears in the text only once, it is clear that this is the theme of the circular. Further, although the reference to 'homeless people' is a general reference, in the first paragraph ('as causas que levam os moradores de rua a permanecerem mais tempo em um só lugar'/'the causes that led the homeless people to remain longer in one place'), the rest of the text makes it clear that the focus is on this one specific group. However, this specification is not done explicitly, rather, it is taken as understood. The group in street circumstances is referred to through pronominalization ('eles', 'deles'/'they', 'them'). This pronominal representation of the group implies a dichotomic division 'we' versus 'them' (especially in *their* remaining near to *our* building' ['a permanência *deles* perto do *nosso* prédio'], my italics). This indicates the group's social exclusion and the negating of the problem: the real problem is not their street circumstances but 'their remaining near our building'.

An evaluation of the group is made through the structuring of assumptions. See the excerpt highlighted in example (2), original bold:

(2) . . . as causas que levam os moradores de rua a permanecerem mais tempo em um só lugar **é a facilidade de obterem as coisas básicas necessárias como: comida, roupas, calçados e dinheiro, sendo este último transformado nas drogas que utilizam.**
Gostaria também de colocá-los a par, uma informação, passada na reunião, de que existem duas ou três pessoas recentemente libertadas da penitenciária e que estão ainda na condicional, entre eles.

. . what leads homeless people to remain longer in one **place is the fact that it is too easy to obtain basic goods such as food, clothing, shoes and money, the**

Another example is from Deborah Tannen's discourse analysis of narratives told by women in interviews about their sister (Tannen, 2008, p. 217).

From "'We've Never Been Close, We're Very Different': Three Narrative Types in Sister Discourse" by Deborah Tannen, Narrative Inquiry, Vol. 19, No. 2, pp. 217. With kind permission by John Benjamins Publishing Company, Amsterdam/Philadelphia. www.benjamins.com

I encountered a similar use of dialogue in another woman's account of a problematic sister—in this case, the speaker's own. This conversation, too, was with a woman I was meeting for the first time. She began by rolling her eyes when she answered in the affirmative my question about whether she had a sister. She then established the big-N Narrative that would drive everything else she told me: She and her sister did not have a good relationship because of her sister's selfishness and self-centeredness. In particular, the sister did not fulfill family responsibilities but relied on her (older) sister, the speaker, to do everything. To support this evaluation of her sister, the speaker told me a small-n narrative: when their father was nearing the end of his life and the family was gathered by his bedside, her sister decided to leave. "You'll be there," she said. "You can tell me what's happening."

In this instance, too, the coherence principle of the big-N Narrative driving the speaker's discourse was a sister's callousness, selfishness, and failure to fulfill responsibilities as a family member. The specific event recounted—the sister's departure at the time of their father's death—was a small-n narrative that supported the big-N Narrative or theme: my sister and I are not close because she is irresponsible and selfish. As in the previous example, the big-N Narrative is motivated by the Master Narrative that sisters are expected to be close. In this example, as in the one immediately preceding, the key involvement strategy was constructed dialogue, which was effective because it capped and helped create a scene that dramatized the speaker's point. The word "dramatize" is not only metaphoric; it captures the sense in which framing discourse as someone's speech is not passive "reporting" of words uttered by another but rather

▼ Conversation Analysis (CA)

Conversation analysis was developed by Harvey Sacks and Emanuel Schegloff and was influenced by the work on interaction of Erving Goffman and Harold Garfinkel's ethnomethodology (Ten Have, 2007). CA is an investigation of social interaction between humans, most especially of everyday, ordinary conversation, called in CA "talk-in-interaction" (p. 4).

Appropriate Research Questions Answered by Conversation Analysis.   Conversation analysts record natural interactions and then listen for context and structure. The goal of CA is to explain *how* people talk with each other.

In conversation analysis (CA), there are three assumptions of conversational organization:

1. Talk is action—language conveys a message.
2. Action is structurally organized—single acts are organized into sequences.
3. Talk creates and sustains intersubjective reality—conversation creates meaning. (Perakyla, 2005).

Sampling in Conversation Analysis. Like discourse analysis, conversation analysis (CA) might have a very small sample size, depending on the study objectives. Sometimes a single conversational event might be sufficient; other times, more discourses might be required to compare across people or settings (Starks & Trinidad, 2007). Sometimes in CA, sampling is thought of as collecting a specimen, and you would want one or more specimens that are representative of the category you are studying (Ten Have, 2007). Both CA and discourse analysis studies would be likely to use purposive sampling and might, depending on the research question or study objectives, use maximum variation or typical instance sampling.

Data Collection in Conversation Analysis. CA does not usually use interviews as a source of data, since CA considers interviews to be too subject to the researcher's manipulation or construction, and CA seeks to analyze more pure forms of natural conversation (Ten Have, 2007). Thus, CA does not use observation per se, especially with field notes, but instead CA uses recordings of natural interactions (Ten Have, 2007).

Transcription in Conversation Analysis (CA). In CA, it is especially important to transcribe both what is said and how it is said. When transcribing and analyzing conversations in CA, it's also important to remember CA's reminder that the transcription is not the data, the transcription is just a way to capture the actual data—the conversation. In CA, tapes are transcribed as "actual words as spoken" and "sounds as uttered" (Ten Have, 2007, p. 98). Conversation analysis researchers look at characteristics of talk, such as pacing, turn-taking, delivery, words, sounds, silences or spaces, overlapped speech and sounds, volume, and other verbal and nonverbal details. CA transcription accounts for identification of participants (by first name, initial, random letter, or role); words as spoken; sounds as uttered (e.g., hmm, tch, eh); spaces and silences; overlapped speech and sounds; and pacing, stretches, stresses, and volume. Ten Have suggests transcribing in rounds: Start with a transcription of the words, go back through and add the sounds, go back through and add spaces and silences, and so on.

CA is especially known for its unique form of transcription that provides detail on turn-by-turn conversation sequences and structure. For example, brackets in transcripts indicate where conversational turns overlap with each other. Numbers in parentheses indicate elapsed time (pauses) between utterances. Underscoring indicates stress in pitch. A period indicates a fall in tone. Arrows indicate a raising or lowering of pitch. Colons indicate prolonging of a sound. Equal signs indicate no gap between lines. A degree sign means that the utterance is relatively quiet. A question mark indicates a rise in tone, and so on. Reading—and writing—CA transcripts is an art and a skill.

Ten Have (2007, p. 96) gives the following excerpt of a CA transcript:

1. Maude: I says well it's funny; Missi:z uh: ↑ Schmidt ih you'd think she'd help<.hhh

2. Well (.) Missiz Schmidt was the one she: (0.2) assumed respo:nsibility for the three

3. specials.

4. (0.6)

5. Bea: Oh ↓ *::. °°M-hm, °°=

Coding in Conversation Analysis (CA).

CA does not use categorization as data reduction, per se. Rather, coding and analysis in CA identifies *devices* used by conversational participants and discusses and describes those devices. CA coding consists of identifying speech characteristics such as: types of statements (assertions, declarations, directives, commissives, or expressives); turn taking, gaps, and pauses between speakers; and structural and verbal and nonverbal patterns. CA coding and analysis consists of detailed transcriptions of conversations (using CA notations described above) and a sense-making process within an episode of talk, using your intuitive sense to interpret what certain types of speech characteristics mean (Grbich, 2007).

Rather than forming categories, CA utilizes an inductive process in which you work back and forth between your transcript and your analysis. This involves a three-step process in which you (1) identify sequences of related talk, (2) examine how the speakers take on certain roles or identities through their talk, and (3) look for outcomes of the talk and work backward to trace the way that outcome was produced (Silverman, 2003).

Writing CA Findings.

CA writing typically does not include much in the way of theoretical or literature discussions, and tends, instead, to provide detailed discussion of the transcripts and the meaning resulting from the communication patterns. A CA report usually involves use of extensive transcripts as data evidence (Grbich, 2007). The following gives a great example of a CA analysis as it uses the unique CA notation in the text (Good & Beach, 2005, p. 573).

The first extract to be analyzed comes from Kristine's seventh birthday party and represents a prototypical gift-opening sequence, as described in Figure 2. Kristine is sitting in a chair by the side of the pool, with a stack of wrapped gifts to her right. Her grandma is behind her and Mom is to Kris's left, holding a pad of paper and writing down what each gift is and whom it is from. Immediately in front of Kristine is a group of girls sitting in the pool, watching Kristine open the gifts. Although they are in the pool, they still create their own little intense focus cluster to watch the opening and see the gifts. Dad is seen walking back and forth through the scene, cleaning up wrapping papers and helping to entertain the guests. It is clear, then, that the gift-opening system involves more than just the birthday girl and the gifts she is opening.

Extract (1) begins at the moment Kris picks up a gift. This excerpt occurs five and one-half minutes into the gift-opening portion of the party and displays Kris opening a gift from Judy, a friend who has been going back and forth between the pool and Jacuzzi, about 30 feet away:

(1) *SDCL: Birthday Party: Age 7*
    ((Grma = Grandma; Wen = Wendy))
1. Kris: [((Selects and holds gift))
2. Kris: [Who's this one fro[m?
3. Kim: [JUDY!

Examples of Conversation Analysis. In their study on public discourse surrounding the Young Women's Christian Association of America decision to reverse its mandate on single-sex membership, Harter, Kirby, and Gerbensky-Kerber (2010) drew upon nearly six years of public discourse as their sampling. In a study on joint laughter in workplace meetings, Kangasharju and Nikko (2009) found through conversational analysis that shared laughter can be used by leaders to create a positive work environment, as well as help remediate issues and reduce tension associated with those issues.

As the example above illustrates, Good and Beach (2005) used CA to analyze gift giving in children's birthday parties. They looked at gift opening activities as interactional and embodied actions. Characteristic of CA, they specifically identified "an extended summons–answer sequence involving initiation of a gift-opening, enthusiastic response cries, positive assessments of the gifts, the offering and prompting of thanks, and related actions" (p. 565). They noted that the rituals constitute a "complex social system where adults model and facilitate the construction and integration of past, present, and future relationships" (p. 565).

· ·

Qualitative Content Analysis ▼

Chapter 11 talked about quantitative content analysis, in which researchers count and measure characteristics within a message. Content analysis can also be used as a qualitative method. Qualitative content analysis describes elements in a message, often mass media messages (television or film, advertisements, news stories). This method is different from other types of textual analysis or coding in that, in content analysis, code categories are determined before you begin collecting data. Your research question sets up your categories—perhaps you want to see ways that women are depicted in a popular television show, for example, so you might have a coding scheme that consists of four codes: villain, victim, survivor, and rescuer. Content analysis coding schemes can be somewhat more complex than this, but content analysis uses a finite number of categories. While content analysis describes the content of a text, or what message a text conveys, rhetorical criticism (discussed in Chapter 17) focuses on the structure of a text, or how the text conveys that message.

Sampling in Qualitative Content Analysis. Sampling in qualitative content analysis depends completely on your research question or study objectives. If, for example, you want to know how doctors are depicted in the television show *House*, you might actually randomly sample ten episodes from the 2008 season and analyze them. If you want to understand how Martin Luther King Jr. constructed hope in his famous "I Have a Dream" speech, you would be studying the population—that one speech.

Coding in Qualitative Content Analysis. A key characteristic of coding in content analysis is that your codes are developed ahead of time.

Rather than emerging from the data, they instead reflect your literature review, theory, and RQ. For example, if you think that children's television programming perpetuates stereotyped gender roles, you might code the characters in television shows by a predetermined typology of such roles (e.g., mother, housewife, businessperson). Qualitative content analysis might categorize the texts by content, context, linkages, possible interpretations, purpose, or meaning.

In a research project studying social support in children's mental health treatment team meetings, Christine Davis created the following content analysis code list to determine what types of social support are observed in meetings. The list of types of social support was derived from literature research on the topic, and it was developed when she designed the study, before she ever looked at the data.

1. Instrumental: Helping or doing things for him or her
2. Emotional: Emotional support
3. Informational: Providing information
4. Tangible: Material aid or giving him or her things or money
5. Positive social interaction: Companionship
6. Affectionate: Love and affection
7. Esteem: Raising his or her self-esteem
8. Network: Connecting the person to others
9. Listening: Nonjudgmental listening support
10. Emotional challenge: Challenging recipient to evaluate his or her attitudes, values, feeling
11. Reality confirmation support: A person similar to the recipient thus confirms the recipient's view of the world
12. Task appreciation support: Acknowledging the recipient's efforts and expressing appreciation for work
13. Task challenge support: Challenging way of thinking about task or activity to stretch, motivate, or lead recipient

In content analysis, **inter-coder reliability** is an important concept, and usually two coders code the data, then compare the percentage of agreement between coders. Inter-coder reliability of 70 percent to 80 percent is usually considered to be acceptable (Grbich, 2007).

Chen (2008) used a qualitative content analysis to analyze a Chinese TV drama, *The Gobi Mother*, a highly popular television show in China. She identified several themes that helped explain the success of the show: fate and faith; favor and face; foes, friends, and family; home, happiness, and harmony despite harsh circumstances. She concluded the main character's use of a sincere, simplistic, and down-to-earth communication style as resistance to prestige, power, and position was a key to the show's success.

So What?

In Chapter 14, we discussed many of the different epistemological approaches to qualitative research. In this chapter, we discussed the research that is conducted under the social science paradigm. Qualitative researchers under this paradigm see research as a systematic investigation of an observable reality, and they seek to understand an experience deeply and from the point of view of the participants. As you can see, the methods under this paradigm are in some ways very similar and in other ways very different. Differences in approaches to data collection and analysis reflect the different research questions and study objectives each method addresses. Regardless of the approach and type of qualitative research being used, all qualitative research should be conducted using careful, rigorous, systematic, and ethical practices.

Glossary

Axial coding
Creating codes that connect categories.

Bounded unit
A specific case in case study research.

Bracketing
In phenomenology, identification of the researchers' preconceived ideas and thoughts, in order to be able to focus on understanding the experience with an open, blank mind.

Case study research
An in-depth study of a particular case (or multiple cases).

Conversation analysis
An investigation of social interaction between humans, most especially of everyday, ordinary conversation.

Conversation analysis (CA)
An investigation of social interaction between humans, most especially of everyday, ordinary conversation, called in CA "talk-in-interaction."

Discourse analysis
The study of spoken or written discourse.

Ethnography of communication
The study of speech events and their meaning in a culture.

Ethnography
The study of a culture.

Ethnomethodology
A type of ethnography that focuses on understanding the lived experience and lived practices from the point of view of those within the experience.

Field site
Group, organization, or culture in which research is conducted.

Fieldwork
Immersion in a culture through observations, various types of participation, and formal interviewing and informal conversations.

Focus groups
Focus groups are in-depth group discussions on a specific situation or topic of interest, made up of five to twelve participants and a moderator.

Gatekeeper
A person who controls access to a field site.

Grounded theory
A systematic approach to understanding and analyzing participants' lives.

Informants
Participants who can act as co-researchers and help the researcher explain and make sense of the culture.

Metacodes
Overarching coding categories that connect lower level categories or themes.

Negative case analysis
A stage in coding in which you constantly compare existing codes with new data, adding new codes (or revising existing codes) until all cases of data are accounted for in the coding scheme.

Open coding
Initial coding of data and jotting down emerging themes, thoughts, ideas, or concepts

Phenomenology

The study of experience, in order to understand, in great depth, the nature, essence, and meaning of that experience.

Phenomenology

The study of experience, in order to understand—in great depth—the nature, essence, and meaning of that experience.

Sensitizing concepts

Initial ideas, concepts, interests to pursue and sensitize you to ask certain kinds of questions and look for certain kinds of information.

Theoretical sampling

Choosing a sample based on the people, events, groups, and so on who can shed light on a theory being investigated.

References

Atkinson, P., Coffey, A., Delamont, S., Lofland, J., & Lofland, L. (2007). *Handbook of ethnography*. Thousand Oaks, CA: Sage.

Bamberg, M. (1997). Positioning between structure and performance. *Journal of Narrative and Life History*, 7, 335–342.

Baxter, P., & Jack, S. (2008). Qualitative case study methodology: Study design and implementation for novice researchers. *The Qualitative Report*, 13(4), 544–559.

Beabout, B., Carr-Chellman, A., Alkandari, K., Almeida, L., Gursoy, H., Ma, Z., Modak, R., & Pastore, R. (2008). The perceptions of New Orleans educators on the process of rebuilding the New Orleans School System after Katrina. *Journal of Education for Students Placed at Risk*, 13(2), 217–237.

Becker, J. A. H., Ellevold, B., & Stamp, G. H. (2008). The creation of defensiveness in social interaction II: A model of defensive communication among romantic couples. *Communication Monographs*, 75(1), 86–110.

Blumer, H. (1969). *Symbolic interactionism: Perspective and method*. Berkeley: University of California Press.

Burrows, D. (2014, 9 May). How to use ethnography for in-depth consumer insight. *Marketing Week*. Retrieved from https://www.marketingweek.com/2014/05/09/how-to-use-ethnography-for-in-depth-consumer-insight/

Charmaz, K. (2000). Grounded theory: Objectivist and constructivist methods. In N. Denzin & Y. S. Lincoln (Eds.), *Handbook of Qualitative Research* (pp. 509–535). Thousand Oaks, CA: Sage.

Charmaz, K. (2006). *Constructing grounded theory: A practical guide through qualitative analysis*. Thousand Oaks, CA: Sage.

Creswell, J. W., Hanson, W. E., Clark, V. L. P., & Morales, A. (2007). Qualitative research designs: Selection and implementation. *The Counseling Psychologist*, 35(2), 236–264.

Davis, C. S. (2010). *Death: The beginning of a relationship*. Cresskill, NJ: Hampton Press.

Davis, C. S. (2014). *Conversations about qualitative communication research: Behind the scenes with leading scholars*. New York, NY: Routledge.

Davis, C. S. (2014). *Communicating hope: An ethnography of a children's mental health care team*. New York, NY: Routledge.

Davis, C. S. (2016). *Focus groups: Applying communication theory through design, facilitation, and analysis*. New York, NY: Routledge.

Deegan, M. J. (2007). The Chicago School of Ethnography. In P. Atkinson, A. Coffey, S. Delamont, J. Lofland, & L. Lofland (Eds.), *Handbook of Ethnography* (pp. 11–25). Thousand Oaks, CA: Sage.

De Melo Resende, V. (2009). "It's not a matter of inhumanity": A critical discourse analysis of an apartment building circular on "homeless people." *Discourse and Society*, 20, 363–379.

DeSantis, A. D. (2003). A couple of white guys sitting around talking: The collective rationalization of cigar smokers. *Journal of Contemporary Ethnography*, 32(4), 432–466.

Ethnographic insight. (2015). Retrieved from http://www.ethno-insight.com/ourservices_2.html

Fern, E. F. (2001). *Advanced focus group research*. Thousand Oaks, CA: Sage Publications.

Flyvbjerg, B. (2011). Case study. In N. K. Denzin, & Y. S. Lincoln (Eds.). *The SAGE handbook of qualitative research*, 4th Ed., pp. 301–316. Thousand Oaks, CA: Sage.

Fontana, A., & Frey, J. H. (2003). The interview: From structured questions to negotiated text. In N. K. Denzin & Y. S. Lincoln (Eds.), *Collecting and interpreting qualitative materials* (pp. 61–106). Thousand Oaks, CA: Sage.

Frers, L., (2009). Space, materiality, and the contingency of action: A sequential analysis of the patient's file in doctor-patient interactions. *Discourse Studies, 11*(3) 285–303.

Glaser, B. G., & Strauss, A. L. (1967). *The discovery of grounded theory: Strategies for qualitative research*. Chicago: Aldine Publishing Company.

Goffman, E., (1959). *The presentation of self in everyday life*. Garden City, NY: Doubleday.

Goffman, E., (1967). *Interaction ritual: Essays on face-to-face behavior*. Garden City, NY: Doubleday.

Good, J. S., & Beach, W. A. (2005). Opening up gift-openings: Birthday parties as situated activity systems. *Text, 25*(5), 565–593.

Grbich, C. (2007). *Qualitative data analysis: An introduction*. Los Angeles, CA: Sage.

Harter, L., Kirby, E., & Gerbensky-Kerber, A. (2010). Enacting and disrupting the single-sex mandate of the YWCA: A poststructural feminist analysis of separatism as an organizing strategy. *Women & Language, 33*, 9–28.

Huang Chua, C. E. (2009). Why do virtual communities regulate speech? *Communication Monograph, 6*(2), 234–261.

Kangasharju, H., & Nikko, T. (2009). Emotions in organizations: Joint laughter in workplace meetings. *Journal of Business Communication, 46*, 100–119.

Keating, E. (2007). The ethnography of communication. In P. Atkinson, A. Coffey, S. Delamont, J. Lofland, & L. Lofland (Eds.), *Handbook of ethnography* (pp. 285–301). Thousand Oaks, CA: Sage.

Korczynski, M. (2011). Stayin' Alive on the factory floor: An ethnography of the dialects of music use in the routinized workplace. *Poetics, 39*, 87–106.

Laing, R. D. (1961). *Self and others*. London: Tavistock.

Manning, J., & Kunkel, A. (2014). *Researching interpersonal relationships: Qualitative methods, studies, and analysis*. Los Angeles: Sage.

Mead, G. H. (1934). *Mind, self, and society*. Chicago: University of Chicago Press.

Merrill, E., & Grassley, J. (2008). Women's stories of their experiences as overweight patients. *Journal of Advanced Nursing, 64*(2), 139–146.

Mishler, E. G. (2007). Narrative and identity: The double arrow of time. In A. de Fina, D. Schiffrin, & M. Bamberg (Eds.), *Discourse and identity*. New York: Cambridge University Press.

Perakyla, A. (2005). Analyzing talk and text. In N. K. Denzin & Y. S. Lincoln (Eds.), *The Sage handbook of qualitative research* (pp. 869–886). Thousand Oaks, CA: Sage.

Philipsen, G. (2000). Permission to speak the discourse of difference: A case study. *Research on Language and Social Interaction 33*(2), 213-234.

Ponterotto, J. G., & Grieger, I. (2007). Effectively communicating qualitative research. *Counseling Psychologist, 35*(3), 404–430.

Pollner, M., & Emerson, R. M. (2007). Ethnomethodology and ethnography. In P. Atkinson, A. Coffey, S. Delamont, J. Lofland, & L. Lofland (Eds.), *Handbook of ethnography* (pp. 118–135). Thousand Oaks, CA: Sage.

Ruesch, J., & Bateson, G. (1951). *Communication: The social matrix of psychiatry*. New York: Norton.

Russell-Kibble, A. (2011). *Mexican American parents' perceptions of cultural influences on grieving the death of their child*. (Unpublished doctoral dissertation). University of Arizona, Tucson, Arizona.

Scharp, K. M., & Thomas, L. J. (2017). Discourse analysis. In J. Matthes, R. Potter, & C. Davis (Eds.). *International encyclopedia of communication: Methods of communication research*. Wiley-Blackwell.

Silverman, D. (2003). Analyzing talk and text. In N. K. Denzin & Y. S. Lincoln (Eds.), *Collecting and interpreting qualitative materials* (pp. 340–362). Thousand Oaks, CA: Sage.

Simons, H. (2014). Case study research: In-depth understanding in context. In P. Leavy (Ed.), *The Oxford Handbook of Qualitative Research*, pp. 455–470. New York, NY: Oxford University Press.

Smith, R. T. (2008). Pain in the act: The meaning of pain among professional wrestlers. *Journal of Qualitative Sociology, 31*, 129–148.

Starks, H., & Trinidad, S. B. (2007). Choose your method: A comparison of phenomenology, discourse analysis, and grounded theory. *Qualitative Health Research, 17*(10), 1372–1380.

Stewart D. W., Shamdasani, P. N., & Rook, D. W. (2007). *Focus groups: Theory and practice* (2nd ed.). Thousand Oaks, CA: Sage.

Strauss, A., & Corbin, J. (1990). *Basics of qualitative research: Grounded theory procedures and techniques.* London: Sage.

Tannen, D. (2008). "We've never been close, we're very different": Three narrative types in sister discourse. *Narrative Inquiry, 19*(2), 206–229.

Ten Have, P. (2007). *Doing conversation analysis: A practical guide.* Los Angeles, CA: Sage.

Tracy, K., & Robles, J. S. (2013). *Everyday talk: Building and reflecting identities.* New York, NY: Guilford.

Vagle, M. D. I2014). *Crafting phenomenological research.* London, UK and New York, NY: Routledge.

Van Manen, M. (2001). *Researching lived experience: Human science for an action sensitive pedagogy.* London, UK and New York, NY: Routledge.

Van Manen, M. (2014). *Phenomenology of practice: Meaning-giving methods in phenomenological research and writing.* London, UK and New York, NY: Routledge.

Way, D., & Tracy, S. J. (2012). Conceptualizing compassion as recognizing, relating, and (re)acting: A qualitative study of compassionate communication at hospice. *Communication Monographs, 79*(3), 292–315.

Wooffitt, R. (2005). *Conversation analysis and discourse analysis: A comparative and critical introduction.* Thousand Oaks, CA: Sage.

Yin, R. K. (2009). *Case study research: Design and methods.* Thousand Oaks, CA: Sage.

16

SOCIAL CONSTRUCTIONIST AND ARTS-BASED QUALITATIVE APPROACHES TO COMMUNICATION RESEARCH

CHAPTER OUTLINE

KEY TERMS

Arts and humanities scholarship

Autoethnographers

Autoethnography

Co-constructed interviewing

Collaborative research

Communication activism

Community-Based Participatory Research (CBPR)

Creative analytical practices

Critical scholars

Critical scholarship

Digital ethnography

Dramatic or scenic method of writing

Embodied practice

Ethnodance

Ethnodrama

Ethnotheatre

Fiction as method

Grounded theory

Hegemonic cultural practices

Holistic ethnography

Interactive interviewing

Introspective fiction

Marginalized and silenced voices

Narrative scholars

Performance ethnography

Performance studies

Performative writing

Personal narrative

Poetic ethnography

Presentational knowing

Reflexive writing

Relational ethics

Representation

Social constructionism

Thematic analysis

Thick description

Visual ethnography

Voice

Writing as a method of inquiry

CHAPTER OBJECTIVES

1. To understand the different approaches to qualitative research under the social constructionist and arts-based paradigms, and when each is appropriate
2. To understand the characteristics of the main methods of qualitative research under the social constructionist and arts-based paradigms
3. To learn how to design and conduct research under the social constructionist and arts-based paradigms

• •

▼ Social Constructionist Paradigm

Characteristics of Research Under the Social Constructionist Paradigm

While all qualitative research—including research from the social science paradigm—leans toward an interpretive metatheoretical perspective and builds on some amount of a social constructionist belief system, research under the social constructionist paradigm takes the theoretical concept of social constructionism even farther. Qualitative researchers under the social constructionist paradigm specifically study how ideas, realities, and experiences are socially constructed through communication; they recognize that their own presence in a field site in itself socially constructs its own reality; and they see their writing and reporting as itself a social construction.

Therefore, scholarship in this paradigm tends toward the critical and the narrative. **Critical scholars** (feminist, gender, LGBTQ, queer, critical, and cultural scholars) examine how power is constructed through communication. Narrative ethnographers and **narrative scholars** look at how our personal and cultural narratives construct ideas, identities, and experiences. **Autoethnographers** study how their own personal experiences are constructed through communication and interaction interpersonally and culturally. As we said in Chapter 14, scholars taking a social constructionist stance toward research tend to conduct research that addresses questions about what ideas are being socially constructed; how they are being socially constructed; and what the cultural and communication systems are that construct meaning.

Autoethnography and Personal Narratives

While the term itself was introduced several decades earlier, Ellis and Bochner (2000) are known for the development of **autoethnography** in communication studies in the 1990s (Adams, Ellis, & Holman Jones, 2017). Recall that ethnography is the study of a culture; autoethnography is a type of ethnography in which you are an integral part of the culture you're studying. Autoethnography is to ethnography what autobiography is to biography. Autoethnographers use their own personal experiences to reflect upon, distinguish, and question cultural practices. It's a merging of the personal and the cultural (Adams, Ellis, & Holman Jones, 2017). While more traditional ethnographical research allows the researcher to observe and understand a culture at a deep level but from a distance, autoethnography lets the researcher understand a culture even more deeply, because it is an understanding that derives from within the culture. Autoethnography is usually written in the first person voice ("I"), and Ellis and Bochner (2003) identify many different forms of autoethnographic writing, including short stories, poetry, fiction, novels, and fragmented and layered writing (p. 209). Since most autoethnographic writing involves some sort of narrative writing, scholars frequently use the term "**personal narrative**" to describe autoethnography.

Ellis and Bochner (2000) describe five forms of autoethnography:

1. Reflexive ethnographies that provide researchers an opportunity to critique the experiences of a particular cultural community.

2. Native ethnographies in which ethnographers reflect on their own membership in a historically marginalized or mysterious culture.

3. Complete-member-researcher/ethnographies where a member of a culture reports on that culture for outside interpretation.

4. Literary autoethnographies in which writer/researchers describe their culture to those unfamiliar with the culture.

5. Personal narratives that are critical autobiographical stories of experiences. They provide the audience an opportunity to access and interpret those experiences to make sense of society.

Appropriate Research Questions Answered by Autoethnography.   The appropriate research questions for autoethnography are similar to those

critical scholars
Feminist, gender, LGBTQ, queer, critical and cultural scholars, who examine how power and control are constructed through communication.

narrative scholars
Scholars who study how our personal and cultural narratives construct ideas, identities, and experiences

autoethnographers
Scholars who study how their own personal experiences are constructed through communication and interaction interpersonally and culturally.

personal narrative
A narrative form of autoethnographic writing.

for ethnographic research: to understand cultural practices from within the experience itself. Adams, Ellis, and Holman Jones (2017) list several purposes of autoethnographic research:

1. To speak against **hegemonic cultural practices**;
2. To explain a cultural phenomenon from the point of view of someone inside the experience;
3. To take a political position in favor of **marginalized and silenced voices**;
4. To offer rich description of everyday experiences;
5. To write and publish work that is accessible to a non-academic audience.

(Adams, Ellis, & Holman Jones, 2017).

Personal narratives can provide insight into historical events and social movements. For instance, the civil rights movement sparked interest in slave narratives. The second wave of the women's movement also produced interest in women's life stories and experiences, particularly as the silenced group.

The Role of Theory in Autoethnographic Research.

Autoethnographic projects usually begin with a personal transformative experience that the scholar wants to investigate and understand (Adams, Ellis, & Holman Jones, 2017). Thus, a project idea stems from an experience rather than a theory. Theory frequently is brought in during the analysis stage when the researcher begins to connect the personal to the cultural. Of course, autoethnographers frequently use the concept of **social constructionism** as a theoretical basis for their research overall.

Ethical Concerns Specific to Autoethnography.

The most important issue related to the ethics of autoethnography is that you cannot write about your own experiences without including other people who are involved in that experience or whose own experiences overlap with yours (Ellis, 1999; Tullis, 2013). As Tullis (2013) and many other people point out, these "others" in your research may include your family members or partners, friends, colleagues, community members, and strangers. Metta (2013) talks about "the permeable self" (p. 503), a concept that addresses the fact that my story necessarily overlaps with and changes through other people. Confounding this issue is that most autoethnographic accounts are written retrospectively, using techniques to facilitate memory recall. Thus, any informed consent given by a study participant would have to be given retrospectively, and many research ethicists consider retrospective consent to be coercive (Tullis, 2013). Tullis (2013) argues, however, that this viewpoint is unrealistic and overly restrictive, and instead suggests that consent be procured as early in the process as possible. While you may not be able to obtain consent before an event occurs, you should certainly obtain consent before writing about that event, and you should—if possible—offer people included in your writing an opportunity to read and comment on what you have written.

An issue related to the inclusion of other people in your personal narrative is that frequently, anonymity cannot be promised to people who are written about in your autoethnography (for instance, if I identify someone as my spouse, it

hegemonic cultural practices
Practices that create and maintain the hidden power in a society.

marginalized and silenced voices
In a culture, people who—relative to people in positions of power and privilege—do not have agency or power to participate or be heard.

social constructionism
A perspective suggesting that communication is the vehicle through which reality is understood, constituted, and represented, and it is through communication that beliefs and meanings are constructed and negotiated.

is impossible to offer him/her anonymity). Instead, scholars suggest ensuring that what you write will not harm the people about whom you are writing, and that you should check in with your participants frequently to be sure they continue to be willing to be included—what Ellis (2009b) calls "process consent" (p. 310). In fact, researchers should maintain an open dialogue about ethical concerns throughout the course of an autoethnographic project (Ellis, 2007; Tullis, 2013). Sometimes, participants' identities can be disguised by changing names, de-identifying, fictionalizing, or merging characters, and that should be decided on in conversation with participants (Davis, 2010; Tullis, 2013). Other times, it might be desirable to co-write your narrative with one or more of your participants—in effect, turning the researcher hierarchy upside down and changing the role of study participants to co-researchers.

Since other people included in autoethnographic accounts are frequently people with whom you have a relationship, there is the issue of what Carolyn Ellis (2009b) calls "relational ethics" (pp. 308–309). **Relational ethics** refers to the responsibility you as a researcher might have to friends and partners about whom you write, or to study participants with whom you develop a relationship throughout the course of a research project. Maintaining a relationship with people about whom you are writing and with whom you are critiquing your writing requires finesse and courage and takes attending to the ongoing maintenance of mutual trust and respect between you and the people about whom you are writing (Adams, Holman Jones, & Ellis, 2013). Finally, autoethnographers should consider any harm that might befall themselves in disclosure of difficult, embarrassing, or vulnerable incidents. Not all stories should be shared (Tullis, 2013).

relational ethics
The responsibility of a researcher who has friends and partners about whom s/he writes, or study participants with whom s/he develops a relationship throughout the course of a research project.

Another issue to consider in narrative ethnography is the question of **voice**—whose voice is being privileged in the telling of a story (Tullis, 2013). Researchers often take on an authoritative voice; that is, they interpret the narration, but that is frequently not the most ethical way to present another's voice or standpoint. Related to the issue of voice is the issue of **representation**—how can we represent the voice of another person in an ethical and respectful manner? It's important to remember that when I write about another person's experience, it is not a representation of his/her experience but it is my interpretation of that experience. This is why many researchers employ autoethnography, co-constructed ethnography, or reflexive ethnography—to include the other person's own voice in the co-construction of the interpretive narrative.

voice
A concept related to personal and cultural agency and repetition, referring to cultural status, embodiment, and privilege.

representation
An ethical consideration of how the voice of another person in a research project is represented in an ethical and respectful manner.

Sampling and Data Collection in Autoethnography.

Autoethnographers might write about mundane everyday experiences, or they might write about turning points, traumatic events, or significant times in their lives. Autoethnographers sample from their own personal experiences by writing field notes of events of their past relying on emotional recall (Ellis, 2009a) and journaling, and taking field notes and journaling about events as they are happening. Ellis (2009a) describes emotional recall in comparison with Strasberg's method acting:

> To give a convincing and authentic performance, the actor relives in detail a situation in which she or he previously felt the emotion to the enacted. I place myself back into situations, conjuring up details until I was immersed in the event emotionally (p. 108).

co-constructed interviewing
An in-depth interviewing technique in which the interview is collaborative, dialogic, interactive, and open-ended.

interactive interviewing
A type of interviewing that involves multiple participants and researchers who share their stories and personal experiences with the goal of co-authoring an autoethnographic project.

grounded theory
A systematic approach to understanding and analyzing participants' lives.

Thematic analysis
A method of categorizing data into thematic categories.

writing as a method of inquiry
An approach to qualitative analysis in which the researcher thinks about the meaning of what s/he is studying as s/he is writing and thus the analysis and writing stages might be one and the same.

As far as a personal narrative might include other people, data collection might include reflexive types of interviewing. **Co-constructed interviewing** and **interactive interviewing** are two such types of interviewing. Co-constructed interviewing is an in-depth interviewing technique in which the interview is collaborative, dialogic, interactive, and open-ended. In a co-constructed interview, the lines between researcher and researched are blurred and both are seen more as equal conversational partners who share their mutual expertise, hold equivalent power and authority, open up to a constructive conversation, blur their roles, and consider the ethical responsibilities of their relationship. This type of interview is marked by the inclusion of voice among people whose voice may not have traditionally been highlighted or counted (Patti & Ellis, 2017). Interactive interviewing similarly involves multiple participants and researchers who share their stories and personal experiences with the goal of co-authoring an autoethnographic project. Because this type of interviewing by necessity involves sharing and vulnerability, participants have to be open to the process and have to trust that it will lead to deeper understanding and respect (Phillips, 2017).

Analysis in Autoethnography. Sometimes the autoethnographic narrative is broken up thematically, and in those cases, more traditional thematic coding (as described in previous chapters) might be used. The final result might include sections of **grounded theory** or **thematic analysis** with supporting literature. The study might make claims based on the themes and narrative snippets or excerpts might be used to illustrate the claims. However, as we've stated, frequently the organization takes a more narrative or creative bent, and the analysis is more organic and understated. In these cases, the writing itself is evocative, written much as a creative writing work might be written, usually with the addition of some sort of cultural, critical, or analytical discussion woven into the text. Some forms of autoethnographic research seek to represent the data through narrative, description, or other arts-based forms. Sometimes these narratives, poems, or works of art are based on themes derived from coding the data as we've described above; other times, the narratives are organized chronologically or for aesthetic reasons, and no formal coding scheme is used.

Many autoethnographers talk about Laurel Richardson's (2000) concept of **writing as a method of inquiry**, in which they think about the meaning of what they're studying as they're writing. Thus, the analysis and writing stages might be one and the same. In the same vein, autoethnographers often speak of interpretation, rather than analysis. Chris Poulos explains the distinction:

> *If you can buy into a kind of social constructionist's view of identity, then you can understand we're always engaging our world actively in a kind of ongoing co-construction project with our peers, then you can see that every story, everything that happened, is subject to some kind of interpretation. . . . My interpretive process comes down to, organic, I'm interpreting as I'm writing . . . I also have a sense of where I'm going . . . I have a sense of the direction I'm going in, but I don't quite know how it's going to end . . . I know when I get there, this is the end* (Davis, 2014, p. 254).

Carolyn Ellis sees analysis as creating a story that creates conversations with the reader, and with which others can relate (Davis, 2014). Since autoethnography is usually written as a narrative, the analysis happens as the writer creates narrative coherence. Buddy Goodall, in Davis (2014), describes the process:

> *It's in the writing itself where I'm actually sitting down at the computer and composing a story I actually come to understand what I'm writing about . . . For me it's very much connecting the dots. It's also a narrative trajectory I'm interested in . . . For me, it's very much a story I'm after. How should this be told?* (pp. 89-90).

Narrative ethnography is typically written in the first person, in an evocative, active voice. One key characteristic of this type of research is the re-storying of the researcher's and/or participants' stories into a chronological narrative with plots, time, place, and scene (Creswell, Hanson, Clark, & Morales, 2007). Autoethnographic scholars frequently use a **dramatic or scenic method of writing**, or, what Caulley (2008) calls **creative nonfiction** writing. In this style of writing, you would actually show a scene of what happened rather than describe it or tell about it. This is more compelling reading. Usually written in present tense, this style of writing is more action-oriented. It's often written as a series of scenes connected by a series of narrative summaries. Depending on the research and on your style of writing, sometimes there will be more narrative summaries than scenes, and other times there will be more scenes than narrative summaries.

In research that involves other people, the narrative writing approach blends narratives from other participants' points of view with narratives from the researcher's own point of view. Researchers using the narrative approach also include autoethnographic narratives on their own personal reflections on issues raised in the course of doing the research. Good writing of this style is an evocative narrative, reminiscent of a novel, with characters, plot, action, and movement that uses plot and character development to illustrate themes.

When you write up qualitative research findings using a dramatic or scenic method, you want to use realistic details; concrete nouns with concrete adjectives that appeal to the senses (sight, sound, smell, taste, touch); words that imply emotion; conversations to convey emotion and to pull the reader into the story; and active verbs (he ate the cake) rather than passive verbs (the cake was eaten). Narrative writing involves the use of **thick description** (Geertz, 1973), which refers to an immersive writing technique in which researchers include rich details, vivid language, and specific quotes to connect culture, environment, behaviors, theory, and meaning. In this method, your writing should include thick description about details, contexts, emotions, relationships, feelings, history, voices, actions, and meanings. Adequately describe the research participants so your reader can actually see them. Use **reflexive writing**—include yourself and your biases, frames of reference, and personal connections to the topic in the writing. How can you write such detail? By capturing it in your field notes. Write detailed notes about the environment and context. You never know what details you might want to use later. Write detailed notes about dialogue, or—even better—record the dialogue so you can use it later. Open and close the writing with a narrative, the first narrative to set the stage and the second to conclude it (Caulley, 2008; Ponterotto & Grieger, 2007).

dramatic or scenic method of writing
A creative, nonfiction method of writing that is often written as a series of scenes connected by a series of narrative summaries.

thick description
An immersive writing technique in which researchers include rich details, vivid language, and specific quotes to connect culture, environment, behaviors, theory, and meaning.

reflexive writing
Writing that includes the researcher and his/her biases, frames of reference, and personal connections to the topic in the writing.

Examples of Autoethnography. Carolyn Ellis, among many other scholars, is known for writing narrative autoethnographies, studies which use narratives about her own life to make critical statements about the larger culture in which she is a part. For instance, in a piece called "Katrina and the Cat: Responding to Life's Expendables" (Ellis, 2007), she used a personal story of rescuing an injured cat to relate to the situation of poor people in New Orleans, Louisiana, in the aftermath of Hurricane Katrina. The story leads to the questions of whether she adequately cared for the cat and whether we as a society adequately care for people who need our help.

Using analysis of narratives, Davis (2008), in "Final Stories: The Ultimate Sensemaking Frame," analyzed stories told by her mother prior to her death, and Montalbano-Phelps (2003) conducted an analysis of narratives of domestic violence survivors, identifying several major themes within those narratives. Using narrative ethnography in "A Family Jigsaw Puzzle: Secrets and Gaps," Davis (2009) used a narrative approach to tell a story of secrets within her family of origin. Davis (2010, pp. 75–76), for example, wrote her hospice ethnography as a narrative. The sample below gives you an example of rich, detailed narrative writing (Davis, 2010, p. 2).

2   *Chapter One*

her husband, John, died 15 years earlier. She doesn't like being in the hospital, not one bit. It brings back too many unhappy memories. Since John's death, she has tried to remain optimistic and upbeat, especially in front of her daughter, Katherine. But today she has a bad feeling. They're doing a biopsy to check out some pain she has been having. "Just a routine precaution," the doctor said. But she has a bad feeling. A really bad feeling.

"Hey, honey, what do you say we get out of here and you take me over to the mall?" Marian asks the aide who's wheeling her out of her hospital room down the hall toward the operating room.

He laughs loudly and repeats her question. "Take you to the mall!" He laughs again as he continues pushing her. She can feel her pulse quickening, her breaths becoming shallower. The blanket covering her is soft, and she feels its weight as she shivers underneath it. Cold, she feels cold, down to her bones. The cold comes from deep within her and mingles with her fear as it spreads from her toes to her stomach to her throat. They're moving quickly, and Marian looks up at the ceiling tiles as they float by. White square after white square. Row after row of tiles in a white checkerboard pattern. White checkerboard merges into the tops of white walls. People walking by are a blur of flesh-colored faces above white jackets. White. White everywhere.

"Here you are," the aide says, as he parks the stretcher in what looks like a small empty cubicle. "This is a holding room. You're going to wait here until they're ready for you." He pauses at the edge of her sight. "Good luck."

She looks around. More white tiles, more white walls on each side of her. A gray curtain, pulled back, on the wall in front of her feet. Beyond, she can see what looks like a nurse's station. The nurses' desk area is light gray, the lights are dim, and the room is empty. It looks brand new, clean, with no evidence of a person anywhere. No papers, no clutter, no coffee cups. She is in here alone, and it feels like a ghost town.

Marian takes a deep breath and closes her eyes.

Critical and Feminist Ethnography

Critical ethnography, as with all critical methodologies, is the study of power and control. Critical ethnographers, like all other ethnographers, view positivist objectivity as a myth, and acknowledge their own biased viewpoints and backgrounds inherent in their research. Critical ethnography is often an action-oriented method in which participants see the possibility of their participation resulting in changes to social problems. **Critical scholarship** overlaps with other methods, in that it is a lens through which to view a research topic much more than a method in and of itself. Critical scholars may use, for instance, ethnographic or autoethnographic methods, rhetorical methods, or performative methods with the distinction that their research question, study design, analysis, and writing look at issues of oppression, social justice, and power—most specifically, how power is constructed and reified through cultural communication and social systems. Critical ethnographers and autoethnographers examine their experiences from the viewpoints of everyday life within social contexts such as stigma and privilege (Boylorn & Orbe, 2014). Critical scholars are engaged scholars, which means they have as their scholarly goal to gain social impact and facilitate social change through the study of symbolic and material discourse (Harter, Dutta, & Cole, 2009).

critical scholarship
A lens through which to view a research topic in order to question issues of oppression, social justice, and power— most specifically, how power is constructed and reified through cultural communication and social systems.

Appropriate Research Questions Answered by Critical Ethnography.
Critical ethnography is the practice of ethnography for the purpose of exposing and critiquing cultural intersections of power (Foley & Valenzuela, 2007; McDonald, 2017) such as race, class, gender, ethnicity, sexual identity, and dis/abilty identity (Meade, 2017), and position such as nationality, age, or spirituality (Boylorn & Orbe, 2014). Critical scholarship studies taken-for-granted social structures and symbols and dominant discourses to understand how power in a society is constructed. As critical scholars, feminist communication scholars, for example, look at how conceptions of gender are constructed through discourse, language, communication (verbal and nonverbal), messages, or texts. Feminist scholars critique the ways in which cultural discourses privilege gender and voice and call attention to the significance of women's ways of knowing (Breede, 2017). As another example, queer studies scholars also critique cultural practices and identify the significance of gender and sexual ambiguity (Adams & Holman Jones, 2017). Queer scholarship, by definition, confronts the way our culture sets and maintains hegemonic and sexist values for relational, gendered, and sexual behaviors (Adams & Holman Jones, 2017), and in so doing, questions and critiques many forms of social norms and expectations.

How Critical Ethnography Uses/Incorporates Theory.   Critical scholarship
utilizes critical traditions such as neo-Marxism, cultural studies, postmodernism, and poststructuralism, and refers to critical theorists such as philosopher Karl Marx, feminist and gender theorist Judith Butler, philosopher Michel Foucault, critical theorist Walter Benjamin, and philosopher Jacques Derrida, among too many others to name, as a framework for their research—foundational theories through which to design their study, and as explanatory theories to analyze their findings. Much feminist scholarship, for instance, commences from: "both a Foucauldian and postmodern feminist sense of power and resistance, sex and

gender, agency, and passivity. Foucault's unique contribution was to question how discourses and associated practices came to be accepted as true or legitimate, and how these normalized discourses become objects for thought, to reimagine power as a productive force and to question the normalizing, long established, and societal practices associated with bias and the development of an ethic of the self (Foucault, 1972; 1973; 1995; Motion & Leitch, 2007). Foucault's work was especially important in understanding power as it is experienced and conveyed in everyday practices and discourses, and a Foucauldian perspective examines the biopolitics that use the body as a field for power, control, and discipline (Deveaux, 1994; Foucault, 1972; 1973; 1995)" (Davis, 2014, p. 105).

Ethical Concerns Specific to Critical Ethnography.

Critical scholarship is itself an ethical response to cultural and ideological positions that exploit, marginalize, and privilege certain groups and categories of people. Thus, critical scholars specifically attend to issues of **representation** and **voice** (who has the power to represent another's voice), **embodied practice** (the idea that the researcher's personal and bodily experiences are essential to understanding the culture under study), **collaboration** (research participants are co-researchers with equivalent power to the researcher), and the power positionality between the researcher and the research participants (Meade, 2017).

embodied practice
The idea that the researcher's personal and bodily experiences are essential to understanding the culture under study.

Data Collection in Critical Ethnography.

Today's critical ethnographers utilize qualitative methods such as ethnography, autoethnography, arts-based research, and related methods that give them access to the understanding of voice and privilege (Breede, 2017b; Farmer & Chevrette, 2017). Critical ethnography is frequently characterized by conversational, informal interviewing; collaborating with participants; reader-friendly writing; and offering participants the opportunity to edit or give feedback on transcriptions and findings (Foley & Valenzuela, 2007).

Analysis and Writing in Critical Ethnography.

Critical ethnographers write and analyze their findings with an eye for examining marginalization, resistance, and social justice. Critical scholars specifically look at the social construction of power dynamics in cultural discourse. Critical scholars frequently employ Derrida's framework of deconstruction in which they critique the hidden meanings in social discourse, cultural practices, and social structures (McDonald, 2017). Queer scholarship, for instance, critiques construction of identity; deconstructs the way language creates and reifies gender, sexual, and ethnic binaries; and questions the discursive nature of our bodily identities (Adams & Holman Jones, 2017).

Critical scholarship frequently entails co-creation of texts with participants and sometimes involves political activism activities (Meade, 2017). Critical scholarship advocates for social change (Adams & Holman Jones, 2017; Breede, 2017b; McDonald, 2017). Reporting of critical methods frequently utilizes non-traditional formats that legitimate alternative voices and forms. For example, critical autoethnography is typically written in an evocative narrative format that might or might not implicitly invoke overt analysis (Boylorn & Orbe, 2014), and other critical scholarship is frequently written in arts-based or performative formats to privilege oral forms of knowing and understanding.

Communication Activism and CBPR.

Taking critical scholarship to the next level are the related methods **communication activism** and **Community-Based Participatory Research (CBPR).** Communication activism is a movement of research that is specifically aimed toward social justice goals. Communication activism works with community partners to address specific real-world problems and issues and achieve potential solutions (Breed, 2017a). CBPR research uses critical methods in collaboration with community stakeholders to achieve social change through full and equal partnerships and coalitions between researchers and community collaborators (Huffman, 2017; Tapp, de Hernandez, & Smith, 2017).

Examples of Critical and Feminist Ethnography.

Winkle-Wagner (2008) conducted a critical ethnography to study the way black undergraduate college women negotiated identity as they navigated issues of feminism, race, and gender. She used ethnographic methods to look at how these women constructed strength, assertiveness, and empowerment at a predominantly white college.

Generally, Foucauldian feminist scholarship (see Trethewey, 1999, for example) explores women's gendered embodiment of self within social, personal, and professional identities. Other feminist scholars, for example, see women's issues, such as anorexia, as a function of gendered discourse and power (see Moulding, 2006; Whitehead & Kurz, 2008). Feminist scholars use many methods to study these issues, including ethnography, autoethnography, and phenomenology. Trethewey, for example, used in-depth interviews to look at the ways women "discipline their bodies" as they adorn, carry, and size their bodies in socially acceptable ways.

Holistic Ethnography

Holistic ethnography is a social constructionist method that seeks to understand the multidimensional and interdependent aspects of reality by moving through multiple passes through a phenomenon. Similar to embodied meditation, holistic ethnography intentionally directs attention to the sensory, the bodily, the emotive, and the dialogic. Davis (2014) describes this approach as "more like cross-training; a whole body experience" (p. 13). She says:

> *I suggest conducting research by moving through the senses: from the body—the ears and eyes, touch and taste; to the mind, and, finally, the heart. Only when you have immersed yourself into your research from top to bottom; inside and out; through your body, mind, and spirit; can you fully understand the experience* (pp. 13–14).

Holistic ethnography intermingles the Cartesian divide between mind, body, and spirit in a holistic manner that acknowledges the complexity of real life and juxtaposes "emotion, compassion, empathy, embodiment, and the corporeal" (Breede, 2017c). This method involves combining a narrative approach—by understanding the stories inherent in the experience; an intellectual approach—by mentally sorting and pondering the meaning of the experience; and a heart-felt approach—by connecting with your feelings and emotions as you unite with the experience (Davis, 2014). In many ways, holistic ethnography is similar to an embodied meditation practice, "a conscious awareness of experience in which the researcher intentionally and variously focuses her attention on physical sensations,

---

communication activism
A movement of research that is specifically aimed toward social justice goals in which researchers work with community partners to address specific real-world problems and issues and achieve potential solutions.

community-based participatory research (CBPR)
Research that uses critical methods in collaboration with community stakeholders to achieve social change through full and equal partnerships and coalitions between researchers and community collaborators.

holistic ethnography
A social constructionist method that seeks to understand the multidimensional and interdependent aspects of reality by moving through multiple passes through a phenomenon, intentionally directing attention to the sensory, the bodily, the emotive, and the dialogic.

emotions, contemplation, and dialogue to contribute to deep sensemaking and critical examination" (Davis & Breede, 2015, p. 77), with the goal of obtaining a deeper dialogic understanding of the phenomenon. This method begins with data collection and moves through introspection, interpretation, and writing by a four-step process:

1. Focusing on the sensory and sensual embodied nature of the experience;
2. Focused reflection and contemplation on the feelings and emotions related to the experience;
3. Focusing on the intellectual meaning and connections behind the experience;
4. Focusing on dialogic discussion, connection, and voice through engagement with the experience.

This holistic approach to intellectual pursuit and understanding lets the researcher more fully and completely critically examine cultural practices and results in deep understanding, engaged empathy, and ethical representation (Breede, 2017c; Davis & Breede, 2015).

Davis and Breede (2015) describe how this process might work in a project:

Step 1: Embodied Knowledge: Visit field sites multiple times. Take field notes as you move your attention through your senses—sight, hearing, feeling, tasting, smelling—from both the positive and the negative (what do you see and not see, etc.). Focus on each sense for a period of time and attune to specific sensory details such as depth, intensity, and so on. Turn your field notes into narratives about the experience. This process expands the way you experience the world and engages yourself holistically into the experience.

Step 2: Access your emotions related to the experience through focused reflection, meditation, and writing. Free association or poetry writing can be helpful in this step.

Step 3: Brainstorm for all the ways in which this experience connects with different times in history, theoretical perspectives, social roles, places, and areas of focus. Intersect the phenomena with various social and cultural contexts and stretch your thinking to make intuitive jumps and create patterns and analogies.

Step 4: Share your experience with others (co-researchers, study participants, classmates, and colleagues) through a dialogic conversation in which you jointly create new connections and meanings.

Digital and Online Ethnography

digital ethnography
A type of ethnography used to investigate communication in digitized spaces.

A discussion of ethnographic methods would not be complete without including the rapidly growing interest in digital and online methods of ethnography. **Digital ethnography** is a method used to investigate communication in digitized spaces.

Digital ethnography involves ethnography of an online or computer-mediated field site, such as a virtual space, chat room, blog, discussion forum, online gaming, or social media site, among many, many others (Kaur & Dutta, 2017).

Appropriate Research Questions for Digital Ethnography.

In many ways, digital ethnographic methods are similar to those for ethnographic research in face-to-face sites. The research question, as with other ethnographic research, would be to seek to understand communication in that site. In digital ethnography, the online space is viewed as a culture within which to study social and interpersonal interactions (Kaur & Dutta, 2017). Since the researcher would typically be participating in the digital space, digital ethnography would appropriately be autoethnography or at least reflexive ethnography in many instances (Gatson, 2011).

Ethical Considerations for Digital Ethnography.

The issue of public versus private space is an ethical consideration in digital ethnography. Having access to a site does not insure that site is a public space. Many of the interactions occurring in a site may be considered private and may therefore require informed consent, which may be difficult to obtain in a space in which participants' identities are anonymous. Revealing private information without consent from online sources may cross legal as well as ethical boundaries. At the least, in most cases, you should inform the online group that you are conducting research before beginning to collect data (Kaur & Dutta, 2017). Gatson (2011) points out that "the site of the online ethnography necessarily pushes the definitional boundaries of generally accepted concepts such as self, community, privacy, and text" (p. 515).

Digital ethnography involves types of data collection which should be considered private but may not obviously be so. For instance, reading online content may not feel as if you are crossing ethical boundaries, but in this type of environment it would probably be considered participant observation, and if the person posting that content had a reasonable expectation of privacy, you should obtain informed consent before using it (Gatson, 2011). Many scholars consider that if a site requires membership or passwords to access, it is considered private and informed consent must be obtained. Even in more public sites, anonymity and confidentiality must be assured before inclusion of materials, and informed consent may be required if the researcher's participation would influence or connect with other group members.

Data Collection in Digital Ethnography.

Depending on the site specifics, data collection would most likely include participant observation, but may also include interviews, focus groups, and archival research. Participant observation in digital ethnography would likely include visits to chatrooms, discussion groups, or virtual reality sites, and would involve immersion in the digital sites through visiting the sites, participating in the site activity, and writing about the experience.

Data collection in digital ethnography has its own set of challenges. Determining the boundaries of an online site may be problematic (Gatson, 2011). The anonymity of digital sites and the enactment of multiple identities must be taken into account in terms of how they interact with the discourse under study (Kaur & Dutta, 2017). As participants in the online community of study, researchers also should be reflexive about the power differentials between community members and the loss of control once posts are submitted (Gatson, 2011).

Analysis and Reporting in Digital Ethnography.

In many ways, digital ethnography research would be analyzed similarly to other types of ethnography. However, there are additional considerations. Digital spaces may be studied at multiple levels—the interactional level, the community level, and the social (critical and cultural) level of cyberspace (Kaur & Dutta, 2017). Analysis may involve critical issues related to online access and power (Gatson, 2011).

Examples of Digital Ethnography.

Kozinets (2002) discusses the use of "netnography" (p. 61), or online ethnography, for marketing research purposes. As we mentioned, ethnography of online or digital spaces has many of the same methodological considerations as face-to-face ethnographic methods. Marketing research netnography studies online communities such as message boards, Web pages, and chat rooms, for the purpose of understanding "an unprecedented level of access to the heretofore unobservable behaviors of interacting consumers" (Kozinets, 2002, p. 63). Kozinets suggests a less involved and more unobtrusive observation method than participation; he suggests lurking to simply observe (and code and analyze) online texts and messages. Kozinets gives as an example a netnography of an online community related to coffee consumption. Researchers used this method to understand the culture of coffee drinkers, their motivations for making coffee decisions, brand perceptions and preferences, and details about the practical aspects of their consumption.

Kozinets also raises the same ethical issues mentioned earlier, about the ambiguous distinctions between private and public spaces in online communities; he recommends disclosure and insuring confidentiality and anonymity to address ethics concerns.

▼ # Arts-Based Paradigm

Characteristics of Research Under the Arts-Based Paradigm

arts and humanities scholarship
In this type of research paradigm, scholars tend to see research as a performance.

Qualitative researchers in the **Arts and Humanities** paradigm tend to see research as a performance. The method of reporting (narrative, poetry, performance, artwork) the research has a three-fold purpose: to present the findings in a manner which represents and evokes the aesthetic of what you are trying to communicate; to challenge, resist, and transform the more traditional hegemonic methods of representing reality; and to bridge academic writing and lay writing (Davis, 2014; Pelias, 2014). Performance-based scholarship reflects the dramatistic paradigm—the belief that everyday life is a performance and thus must be understood through the frame of a performance. This type of scholarship also reflects a social constructionist belief system as the scholars enter into that construction themselves through their work. As a Performance Studies scholar, you can write your work as a script and perform it in a theater. You can write poetry or create artwork. You might perform your research as radical street or public performances, such as rallies, puppet shows, marches, vigils, choruses, clown shows, or ritual performances. You might do a co-performance in which you bring the audience into the text and invite them to share the experience with you. You can advocate for a specific cause by creating an exhibition out of something that has happened; asking people to confront something that they normally don't think about or interact with; showing an idealized version of reality, or depicting traditional, culturally shared beliefs or values. You might create a documentary to depict your research. What all of these forms of scholarship have in common is an attention to the aesthetic way of knowing—to the sensorial (through the senses), intuitive, and imaginative ways in which knowledge is experienced and understood (Harter, Ellingson, Dutta, & Norander, 2009).

Performance Studies

In **performance studies**, researchers represent cultural experiences by observing and reenacting culturally situated communicative acts to reflect an interpretation of cultural practice through human expression. The communicative act performed can either be a cultural text or an ethnographic account, which is why performance studies are sometimes known as **performance ethnography** because they represent a culture through performance. Performance ethnography creates an appreciation for representation of others by enabling the actor to fully embody the others' experience. Pelias (2014) says that this type of knowledge "welcomes the body in to the mind's dwellings" (p. 11). This embodiment of cultural practice also results in a critical observation of knowledge (Alexander, 2005). In other words, when I perform your actions as if I were you, I can more fully understand your experience and your situation. In addition, when you see my performance, you can more fully understand yourself and others. In the performance, the audience is allowed to see others related to how they see themselves. For this reason, performance studies combine theory and praxis (practice or normal behavior) as they perform theory and make it alive to the audience (Holman Jones, 2000). In addition, the evocative nature of performance studies scholarship "opens up space, . . . allows me to say some things I can't quite say any other way" (Pelias, in Davis, 2014, p. 293). Performative work makes the "text alive in the present," suggests Denzin, in Davis (2014, p. 268).

Performance ethnography is considered a standpoint epistemology because it is a particular moment of knowing that allows participants and the audience to understand themselves and others through and as the other. In conducting performance studies, it is important to balance your everyday experiences with your commentary on the subjects. As a performance studies scholar, you would practice reflexivity. You would clearly define yourself in relation to the people being portrayed, your research intentions, and your prior knowledge. Since it is impossible to separate life stories from those cultural, social, and political contexts that influence experiences; and since cultural, social, and political contexts impact the performance itself (actors, setting, audience perspectives) (Holman Jones, 2000), performance studies reflect culture and experience. Performance studies research reflects the complexities of real life and human experience, and seek to represent multiple realities, experiences, and perspectives (Pelias, 2014). In addition, works written and presented performatively create space for alternative voices (Davis, 2014).

performance studies
A method in which researchers represent cultural experiences by observing and reenacting culturally situated communicative acts to reflect an interpretation of cultural practice through human expression.

performance ethnography
Representation of a culture through performance.

Performance studies are also a critical method because they shed light on cultural hegemony by identifying dominant characters who regulate norms in situational and environmental membership. Alexander (2005) notes that as a moral discourse, performance studies fill the gaps between the known and the unknown, as well as the self and others.

Performance based scholarship is also an empathetic form of scholarship because it, says Pelias (2014), "encourage[s] us to see and to define situations by their unique human and spiritual poetic, the interpenetrations of self, Other, and context, by our complexity and interdependence rather than by some simpler linear or causal logic" (p. 12). Performative writing lets each of us take each other's perspective and discover each other's experiences.

Performance studies contributes to the understanding of social life as a whole, by examining the intent of social behavior, and considering the moral and theoretical assertions inherent in the action. Performative writing is a form of critical research, as it challenges politics and power and uncovers issues of social justice (Pelias, 2014). Holman Jones (2000) highlights the value of performance in social activism (i.e., women's movement, civil rights, AIDS activism, etc.). Such performance asks the audience to examine critically the issue at hand. Performance matters because it is action in the world, and voice is intrinsically tied to experience. Performance studies creates a space to critically examine social systems; motivates performers with rhetorical currency to make social changes; urges audience members, as a collective unit, to make changes; and teaches audience members to recognize social disparities and work to liberate the oppressed (Madison, 1998).

Ethnodrama and Ethnotheatre

ethnodrama
The presentation of data in staged performance, with a plot, characters, dialogue, and stage movements, in which scripts are derived from the researcher's field notes, interview transcripts, document analysis, and journal entries, etc. put together in a dramatized account.

ethnotheatre
The performance of the researcher's experience.

Ethnodrama is a written play script with a plot, characters, dialogue, and stage movements. Scripts are derived from your field notes, interview transcripts, document analysis, and journal entries, etc., which you put together in a dramatized account (Grbich, 2007; Saldaña, 2011). **Ethnotheatre** involves the performance of the researcher's experience. The performance may be scripted or improvisational, live or mediated (Saldaña, 2011). For both ethnodrama and ethnotheatre, the script or performance is derived directly from the research fieldwork. The performative method of reporting is used when it is the most appropriate method to relay the study findings, typically when the researcher wants to convey the performative aspect of a cultural or personal experience.

Research Questions Appropriate for Ethnodrama and Ethnotheatre.
Ethnodrama scholarship is appropriately used for studies that seek social justice, social change, or social awareness; for research that strives to represent a historical or cultural experience; for research that aims to give marginalized people a voice; for writing that seeks to create space for alternative voices and alternative ways of knowing; and for scholarship that works toward an intellectual, emotional, and aesthetic result (Marsh & Davis, 2017; Saldaña, 2011).

Ethical Issues in Ethnodrama and Ethnotheatre.
Ethnodrama shares ethical concerns with other ethnographic methods. The primary matter to attend

to is to obtain informed consent from anyone who might end up being depicted in your script, no matter how peripheral to the action they may be. There is also the question of how to represent other people in your work. Saldaña (2011) suggests giving your participants drafts as you are writing and inviting them to rehearsals so that they can suggest ideas regarding staging and representation.

Data Collection in Ethnodrama and Ethnotheatre.

Ethnodrama derives from ethnographic research methods, so scholars use participant observation, personal experience, interviews, and document analysis to collect their data. Since you will be closely representing verbal and nonverbal communication, as well as environmental and aesthetic details, it is important to use documentation methods that collect detailed accounts of the experience. Ethnodramas are "character-driven stor[ies]" (Saldaña, 2011, p. 36), so you should make sure you capture detailed information about the people you may include in the script.

Analysis in Ethnodrama and Ethnotheatre.

The analytical process is much more intuitive in performative writing than in less arts-based forms of research. Stacy Holman Jones, for example, writes with themes in mind but those themes emerge organically as she begins thinking about her ideas (see Holman Jones in Davis, 2014). She describes her analytical process as:

> *"I have a feeling about it. The thing that happens for me is, something will start taking hold; it's like knitting. Then you can knit up around it, when you're in the flow of doing it. You get into a rhythm and things start happening"* (Davis, 2014, p. 309).

Ron Pelias similarly begins with an emerging idea and adds theoretical "scaffolding" (Davis, 2014, p. 282) around which to build a story. Pelias analyzes through the method we described earlier as "writing as a method of inquiry," in which analytical ideas emerge through the writing process.

Writing Ethnodrama and Ethnotheatre.

Saldaña (2011) suggests the following ways to write an ethnodrama:

1. Write a script by using dialogue and stage direction directly from interview recording or transcripts.
2. Taking poetic license to adapt data from field notes or interviews into an aesthetically pleasing script.
3. Fictionalizing data from field notes or interviews (e.g., creating a composite character) for aesthetic or ethical reasons.
4. Adapt published accounts from historical documents into a script.
5. Utilize multiple sources of information to embellish or create a script.
6. Write a script based on your own personal memories and experiences.
7. Compile a collection of thematically related scripted performances from a company of actors and perform as scripted performances, improvisational performances, choral speaking, poetry, dance, or song.

Frequently, following an ethnodrama performance, open discussions between audience and performers can occur to facilitate dialogue and understanding (Grbich, 2007).

Performative Writing

performative writing
Writing that is written in a manner that is meant to be read aloud or performed.

A variation on performance studies or performance ethnography is **performative writing**, writing that is written in a manner that is meant to be read aloud or performed. All types of performative writing have as their goal to create an aesthetic account that depicts the essence of everyday performances in life (Pelias, 2014). Liamputtong and Rumbold (2008) call this type of research **presentational knowing**, referring to expressive forms of performative arts-based research methods. Performative writing and creating—what Richardson (2003) calls **creative analytical practices**—turns your text into an evocative artistic representation.

presentational knowing
Ways of knowing based on expressive forms of performative arts-based research methods.

Performative writing involves writing thick description, including specific details of the experience, depicting the experience so deeply that it rings true with the reader, and telling a good story (Pelias, 2014).

creative analytical practices
A form of performative writing and creating that turns text into an evocative artistic representation.

Examples of Performative Writing.
Pelias's (2002) study of his relationship with his son is written as a play script, and Pelias calls this method a "strategy of writing that lets the heart be present" (Ellis et al., 2008, p. 257). Holman Jones's (1999) performative ethnography using Billie Holiday's blues lyrics to illustrate her reasoning is an example of performative writing, and Davis's (2008b) work "A Funeral Liturgy," about funeral rituals, is written as a liturgy meant to be read aloud, responsively. The following two samples give you examples of performative writing (Davis, Delynko, & Cook, 2010, p. 509; Holman Jones, 2011, p. 328).

Glory days.
Sharing, showing,
weaving a pattern of dreams and hope,
rebirth and resurrection.
Understanding. And
connection.
Not all survived.
Some problems intruded.
Some dreams eluded.
Some voices stayed voiceless.
and some's status are erased
We offer insight into
lives we cannot relate to.
To say,
these are not others.
They are not
them.
They are us.
We offer stories to show
men without homes are still
men.
Men ill,
can try again.

Literature and Theoretical Basis

Stigma

Two-thousand, one hundred ninety-
six
nameless, faceless, homeless deviant others.[6]
Careful!
They may be dangerous!
Disruptive!
Unasthetic![7]
Remember:
God helps those
who help themselves!
Homeless aren't.
Homeless don't.[8]
They:
Are lazy.
Won't work
Can't relate.
Can't
relate.[9]
They are
Runaways
From abused homes
With trust issues,
Support issues,
Deviant peers
Isolation,
Depression.[10]
Drug abuse: Cause? Effect? Both.
Social environment. Poverty.[11] Disability.[12]

Undesirable difference[1]
Undesirable
  Other[2]
Outgroups.
Out,
  groups!
Out,
  other![3]
Out of sight,
  out of mind.
    Out of their mind,
      out of our mind.
    Discounted deviant.
    Social death.
    Disconfirmed.
    Socially liminal.
    Socially ambivalent.[4]
Dedicated to preserving the social order through providing an example of unacceptability for the rest of society[5]

Homelessness

According to the National Alliance to End Homelessness, in January 2005, there were 10,765 homeless people in North Carolina, 2,196 in Mecklenburg County.

They are
  Alone.[13]
They have
  Each other.
    Well, some of them do
some of the time.
    Closeness.
    Aloneness.

Poverty

Income:
  The cost of participating in our social system[14]

Standpoints

Social memberships.
  Views of the world.
    Perspectives of others
      about others.
Folk history
  of oppressed group.
Oppositional voice
  from the standpoint
    of the opposition.

---

328   *S. Holman Jones*

"Grandma, I want to you to know how your love made me." Her eyes open again, now pale blue water. You watch each other, waiting.

  Pulse, push, breathe. Pulse push
  breathe. Pulse, push breathe. Her eyelids
  fall, closing embrace.

Door

Your husband looks at you and his silent questions pierce your skin. You breathe in sharply and push out the words, "I need to tell you something." He clenches his jaw. He nods. You lose your nerve. "Let me take a shower and then we'll talk." He turns and leaves the bedroom.

You undress and step into the scalding water. You stand there, breathing and willing yourself to stop, to put your arms out and break the fall, to be still. You let the water flow over you until it runs cold. You dry yourself, get dressed, and meet him on the sidewalk.

You walk several blocks without speaking. He looks at you, willing you to meet his gaze. He waits. You let the momentum of your movement still your pulse and quiet the fear rising in your throat. You say that you have fallen for her.

He drops to his knees on the sidewalk. He says, "Jesus." He stays down and you say you are sorry again and again. You wait. He puts his palms on the ground and pushes up, then begins walking away. You follow. He is angry, hurt, incredulous. He asks you what this means. You say you don't know. He asks you if you still love him. You say you don't know. He asks you if you want to stay in the relationship. You say you don't know. He asks you if this means you're a lesbian. You say you don't know.[25]

You wait. He stares hard at you, then lowers his head. "I don't know *you*. I don't even recognize you." You hear something—a faint clicking sound—and turn your head. It could have been anything—a leaf falling, a twig snapping.

> One door slamming
> shut and another opening
> suddenly makes sense.[26]

You see your chance, your choice. You say, "Yes."

Hold

> He insists: *you* call
> the social worker and say,
> "the adoption's off."

You agree, trying to diffuse his anger and sadness and ignore your own. But each time you pick up the phone to call, the recriminating sound of the dial tone taunts you. You push the receiver back into its cradle. With each failed call, your husband

Poetic Ethnography

poetic ethnography
A form of ethnography in which texts are written as poetry, synthesizing the most important and salient meaning, symbolism, and interpretation into poetic lines, using poetic rhythms to convey speech, incorporating pauses, repetitions, narrative strategies, and rhythms in the speech into the poem.

Texts might be written as poetry (**poetic ethnography**), synthesizing the most important and salient meaning, symbolism, and interpretation into poetic lines, using poetic rhythms to convey speech, incorporating pauses, repetitions, narrative strategies, and rhythms in the speech into your poem. Poetry is meant to be read aloud, and thus is a performative method, with all the critical and representational possibilities of performance.

Many narrative ethnographers and autoethnographers—Stacy Holman Jones and Laurel Richardson come to mind—sometimes write portions or all of their autoethnographic narrative as poetry. There are several reasons you might use poetry to convey your ethnographic experience. As an alternative form of expression, poetry is an act of resistance against traditionally hegemonic positivist language of the academy. Therefore, poetry is often seen as more closely aligning with standpoints of color and feminist standpoints. Poetry removes the academic language that so often creates a divide between the academy and a lay audience, so poetry can be seen as more accessible. Poetry is a language of emotion and it's possible to convey an idea in a poem that cannot be sufficiently conveyed in prose. The emotions conveyed through poetry can be more clearly understood than with prose (Maynard & Cahnmann-Taylor, 2010). As Richardson stated, "Poetry can touch us where we live, in our bodies" (1993, p. 695). Poetry as an alternative form of expression offers another way to represent our experience. Poetry represents reality in its disorganized and chaotic state (Maynard & Cahnmann-Taylor, 2010).

Poetry as method requires attention to rhythm, form, image, and metaphor (Cahnmann-Taylor, 2008). For ethnographers, the rhythm of the verse comes directly from the rhythm of the spoken word of the study participants. Each of your participants' spoken voices has a unique cadence or way of talking. You can capture the rhythm of that voice and write the character's dialogue as poetry that represents their speech, using line breaks, punctuation, and white space to depict speech (Cahnmann-Taylor, 2008). Richardson describes this process as she describes her poem about a woman named Louisa May: "I used only her words, repetitions, phrases, hill-southern rhythms, and narrative strategies, such as multi-syllabic words, embedded dialogues, and conversational asides" (p. 696).

Poetry in ethnographic research can be free-form or can be structured. Stacy Holman Jones sprinkles poetry throughout her autoethnographic work as a way to engage the reader and capture a deep level of philosophical and intellectual insight (in Davis, 2014). She uses poetic structures as haiku and the related form haibun, and suggests that the structure encourages freedom: "Haiku are really interesting to work with; they are so restrictive . . . they're structured in a way that can kind of release your mind into these really amazing expansive ideas" (Davis, 2014, p. 300).   Poetry or poetic prose can incorporate images and metaphors from your field notes to convey feelings, emotions, and description (Cahnmann-Taylor, 2008).

Fiction as Method

You might write a fictionalized narrative account (**fiction as method**) (Denzin, 2003; Richardson, 2003). **Introspective fiction**, including fictionalized narrative accounts, poetry, and reflections, can bring research to life, ensure representation, heighten aesthetics, deepen meaning and understanding, and ensure anonymity of participants (Davis & Ellis, 2008; Davis & Warren-Findlow, 2012). Fictionalized accounts have a long history in ethnographic scholarship, and fictional ethnography is an extension of the practice of narrativising ethnographic or autoethnographic findings. As you turn your field notes and interview transcripts into a narrative, there are always questions to ask and decisions to be made in order to maintain narrative continuity and ensure anonymity of participants' identities. You need to decide, for example, if you will disclose participants' identities or if you use will pseudonyms or change identifying details, or create composite characters (Davis & Ellis, 2008). Since you will likely take literary license and change some details to write a narrative—creating a coherent storyline, forming a plot, and simplifying the characters—you are to some degree fictionalizing your account. As you analyze and write any ethnographic account, you reduce thousands of pages of data into a short paper or report, thus interpreting, editing, and reducing (Davis & Warren-Findlow, 2011). In that way, as Carolyn Ellis claims, "all ethnography is interpretive and thus is fiction" (in Davis & Ellis, 2008, p. 107).

Other research takes fictionalization further. There might be times you wish to create dialogue or exchanges in a narrative, for example, that fill in gaps in the storyline or provide explanatory information. You might want to include poetry or other alternative formats in order to add literary style, create dramatic tension, or represent the information alternatively (Davis & Warren-Findlow, 2011; Davis & Ellis, 2008).

Davis and Ellis (2008) describe their process in creating fictionalized dialogue and scenes:

> I used autoethnographic elements introspectively, adding elements from my own personal stories that resonated with my fieldwork experience. . . . I created introspective accounts of emotions shared between me, the study participants, and the characters in my story. For example, I used my own knowledge, based on my own hospital experienced and interactions with my dying parents, to fill in gaps of information where my interviews and

fiction as method
A fictionalized narrative account.

introspective fiction
A form of data presentation which includes fictionalized narrative accounts, poetry, and reflections, with the goals to bring research to life, ensure representation, heighten aesthetics, deepen meaning and understanding, and ensure anonymity of participants.

observations did not yield details I needed to create a coherent story. I used introspection to put myself into my characters and to embody them as I filtered my fieldwork reflections through my own personal experiences, situations, thoughts, and feelings evoked by the reflections. I wrote from a sense that experience is universal as well as particular and that there were commonalities among my experiences and the people in my study (p. 104).

The appropriate question for fictionalized ethnography is not IS this true, but rather, "could [it] be true, [does] it make sense?" (Davis & Ellis, 2008, p. 104). The goal in this process is to represent the exeperience as you understand it from your immersion in it. Fact and representation are "not oppositional," suggests Ellis (Davis & Ellis, 2008, p. 107). "All research is storytelling," suggests Rambo (Davis & Ellis, 2008, p. 112), because it's an interpretation of your experience. All research generalizes, and fiction as method generalizes as universval experiences resonate with the reader (Davis & Warren-Findlow, 2011).

This method addresses issues of authenticity, voice, and representation. As Davis and Warren-Findlow (2011) say,

Narrative is never identical to experience. Narratives are imaginative respresentations, but good narrative research is transparent, reflexive, appropriate, and honest (Davis & Warren-Findlow, 2011, p. 570).

It also considers issues of aesthetics. As Mitch Allen, publisher of qualitative research, states in Davis & Ellis's 2008 article about this method, "you're got to be able to think like a scholar and write like a novelist" (p. 107).

Documentary, Video, or Visual Ethnography

Unlike digital or online ethnography which studies digital or online texts, or types of rhetorical criticism which study visual images as text, visual ethnography uses visual images to represent experience. **Visual ethnography** uses photographic and video images rather than, or in addition to, words, in order to represent an experience through image. Visual ethnography refers to any visual medium used to represent a community or experience. Scholars use media such as still photography; film, video, or documentary representation; and hypermedia (Pink, 2007).

Image-based ethnography crosses aesthetic, intellectual, and social boundaries to explore and represent experience (Pink, 2007). Image-based research reflects a way of knowing that is different from verbal responses. Images construct a more embodied and sensory way of knowing and understanding. Images mirror our bodies and as such replicate a more corporeal sense of an experience than words. Images also, however, are independent of the body and thus are constructed representations and interpretations (MacDougall, 2005; Sherman, 2015). Image-based ethnography uses the unique qualities of the medium to construct ideas about the experience being studied. Image-based ethnography articulates ways of "looking and being" (MacDougall, 2005, p. 5), rather than ways of judging, thinking, or explaining. Visual ethnography has the dual purposes of representation and aesthetics and requires attention to both (Cole, Quinlan, & Hayward, 2009; Quinlan, Smith, & Hayward, 2009; Mathew, 2014); however, it's important to remember that "film is the tool and ethnography is the goal" (Heider, 1976, p. 4).

Documentary ethnographies involve an interaction between the researcher and the experience being studied, the production process, and the audience

visual ethnography
A type of ethnography which uses photographic and video images rather than, or in addition to, words, in order to represent an experience through image.

(Mathew, 2014). Moving between these elements requires several decision stages. Ethnographic filmmaking is generally understood to be a non-fictional undertaking, although most scholars acknowledge that documented reality is always interpreted and constructed (Mathew, 2014). Image-based ethnographies are typically collaborative endeavors, involving at minimum the researcher or research team, the study participants, and a cinematographer (Sherman, 2015). Sometimes, visual ethnographies are collaborative endeavors between the filmmaker and the study participants. Frequently, participants are invited to suggest ideas, narrate the story, and give feedback on rough cuts (Mathew, 2014). Visual ethnographers frequently include their study participants as partners in the filmmaking effort, and this inclusion not only makes important social justice statements but also "transform[s] oppressive and stereotypical representations of people when they arise from the daily experiences of social actors who assert agency over—and participate in—representations of themselves and their own lives" (Cole, Quinlan, & Hayward, 2009; p. 80).

Filmmakers' decisions about who and what they document make a difference in the construction of the reality they are depicting (Sherman, 2015). Ethnographers might shoot a large amount of footage and visual images, but s/he can only use a small percentage of them in the final product (Heider, 1976). The decision, then, in terms of what to use, is, in essence, a sampling decision, as the images selected become representative of a community or experience as a whole. Some filmmakers focus their images on people who have been traditionally marginalized; others select spokespersons. Some people are selected because of their ability to explain a phenomenon and others because they lend specific physical characteristics. Sometimes, a person is included because h/she is a friend of the filmmaker. Some filmmakers choose people based on their uniqueness, others because of their ordinariness (Sherman, 2015). Sometimes inclusion decisions require a trade-off between aesthetics and the ethics of representation. For instance, a more aesthetic camera angle might not appropriately or fairly depict a person or experience (Cole, Quinlan, & Hayward, 2009). It's important to remember that who is excluded is as much a statement as is who is included (Heider, 1976).

Despite this visual way of knowing, suggests MacDougall (2005), image-based claims are indefinite (MacDougall, 2005) and easily manipulated. Thus, another decision to be made is the "mode of looking [with the camera] . . . —a responsive camera observes and interprets its subject without provoking or disturbing it. It responds rather than interferes. An interactive camera, on the contrary, records its own interchanges with the subject. A constructive camera interprets its subject by breaking it down and reassembling it according to some external logic" (MacDougall, 2005, p. 4). Including the researcher interacting with participants in the video addresses methodological and ethical issues of reflexivity, voice, and inclusion (Heider, 1976). A camera angle of shooting down on people might have connotations of inferiority or status (Heider, 1976).

Another decision regards framing. Framing is the process of selecting what images, subjects, and camera angles are to be included and in what manner they are included. Framing is related to meaning-making—the ways in which the ethnographer represents and constructs reality. Filmmakers use "visual rhetoric" (MacDougall, 2005, p. 5) of camera shots, scenes, appearance, and editing. Films, say MacDougall (2005), are "a form of looking" (p. 6) and they necessarily represent the ethnographer's "Truth" (Heider, 1976, p. 63), or understanding.

Another decision to be made is about sound. A film-based ethnography can have external narration, "sound-over voices of those being filmed" (p. 212), or sync-sound. Varying the sound provides different ways of conveying the ideas in the film. The ability of the participants to articulate verbally needs to be a consideration, as well as how various accents or dialects might come across to the audience. Narration can be used for analysis, although some documentary ethnographers frown on this because it distracts from the action in the film (Sherman, 2015).

Filmmaking has ethical considerations related to voice and representation. The filmmaker is ultimately in control and "what he or she does with the data has ethical accountability" (Sherman, 2015, p. 210). Film can be distorted, biased, and manipulated in ways that are more powerfully depicted than the written word. Visual ethnography tells a story, and the researcher has a responsibility for how s/he tells the story.

Great examples of visual ethnography include the Emmy-award-winning documentaries by Harter, Shaw, Quinlan and others, on arts-based medical interventions (Harter, Shaw, Quinlan, Ruhl, & Hodson, 2015; Harter, Shaw, & Quinlan, 2016; Harter, Quinlan, & Shaw, n.d.). This series of three feature-length documentaries explores the Arts in Medicine Program at MD Anderson Cancer Center, the DooR to DooR performance art program at the University of North Carolina hospitals, and the Creative Abundance art workshops for people with disabilities. The beauty of these films is their use of an arts-based method to explore and represent arts-based programs.

Other Types of Arts-Based Research Methods

Ethnodance
An arts-based form of representation which uses dance to convey the meaning of an experience.

In arts-based research methods, you might present your research as works of art, recreating the essence of the experience into an art form—painting, sculpture, music. Arts-based scholars use drawings to explore the complexity of human experience (Guillemin & Westall, 2008); others use dance (**ethnodance**) to uncover and explore knowledge and meaning (Cancienne & Bagley, 2008); and others use music to understand the construction of meaning (Aldridge, 2008) and provide insights into social understandings (Daykin, 2008).

So What?

For the past several chapters, we've shown you how your ontological, epistemological, and axiological perspectives manifest in a specific research methodology and research project. We've shown how knowledge can be defined, understood, and studied through many different and equally valid approaches. Regardless of your metatheoretical paradigm, as you move through your project, keep in mind the goal of all types of qualitative research—to describe communication (in all forms) and to understand that communication constructs or creates ideas, reality, and outcomes.

Glossary

Arts and humanities scholarship
In this type of research paradigm, scholars tend to see research as a performance.

Autoethnographers
Scholars who study how their own personal experiences are constructed through communication and interaction interpersonally and culturally.

Autoethnography
A type of ethnography in which the researcher is an integral part of the culture s/he is studying.

Co-constructed interviewing
An in-depth interviewing technique in which the interview is collaborative, dialogic, interactive, and open-ended.

Collaborative research
A research project in which research participants are co-researchers with equivalent power to the researcher.

Communication activism
A movement of research that is specifically aimed toward social justice goals in which researchers work with community partners to address specific real-world problems and issues and achieve potential solutions.

Community-Based Participatory Research (CBPR)
Research that uses critical methods in collaboration with community stakeholders to achieve social change through full and equal partnerships and coalitions between researchers and community collaborators.

Creative analytical practices
A form of performative writing and creating that turns text into an evocative artistic representation.

Critical scholars: Feminist, gender, LGBTQ, queer, critical and cultural scholars, who examine how power and control are constructed through communication.

Critical scholarship
A lens through which to view a research topic in order to question issues of oppression, social justice, and power—most specifically, how power is constructed and reified through cultural communication and social systems.

Digital ethnography
A type of ethnography used to investigate communication in digitized spaces.

Dramatic or scenic method of writing
A creative, nonfiction method of writing that is often written as a series of scenes connected by a series of narrative summaries.

Embodied practice
The idea that the researcher's personal and bodily experiences are essential to understanding the culture under study.

Ethnodance
An arts-based form of representation which uses dance to convey the meaning of an experience.

Ethnodrama
The presentation of data in staged performance, with a plot, characters, dialogue, and stage movements, in which scripts are derived from the researcher's field notes, interview transcripts, document analysis, and journal entries, etc. put together in a dramatized account.

Ethnotheatre
The performance of the researcher's experience.

Fiction as method
A fictionalized narrative account.

Grounded theory
A systematic approach to understanding and analyzing participants' lives.

Hegemonic cultural practices
Practices that create and maintain the hidden power in a society.

Holistic ethnography
A social constructionist method that seeks to understand the multidimensional and interdependent aspects of reality by moving through multiple passes through a phenomenon, intentionally directing attention to the sensory, the bodily, the emotive, and the dialogic.

Interactive interviewing
A type of interviewing that involves multiple participants and researchers who share their stories and personal experiences with the goal of co-authoring an autoethnographic project.

Introspective fiction
A form of data presentation which includes fictionalized narrative accounts, poetry, and reflections, with the goals to bring research to life, ensure representation, heighten aesthetics, deepen meaning and understanding, and ensure anonymity of participants.

Marginalized and silenced voices
In a culture, people who—relative to people in positions of power and privilege—do not have agency or power to participate or be heard.

Narrative scholars
Scholars who study how our personal and cultural narratives construct ideas, identities, and experiences.

Performance ethnography
Representation of a culture through performance.

Performance studies
A method in which researchers represent cultural experiences by observing and reenacting culturally situated communicative acts to reflect an interpretation of cultural practice through human expression.

Performative writing
Writing that is written in a manner that is meant to be read aloud or performed.

Personal narrative
A narrative form of autoethnographic writing.

Poetic ethnography
A form of ethnography in which texts are written as poetry, synthesizing the most important and salient meaning, symbolism, and interpretation into poetic lines, using poetic rhythms to convey speech, incorporating pauses, repetitions, narrative strategies, and rhythms in the speech into the poem.

Presentational knowing
Ways of knowing based on expressive forms of performative arts-based research methods.

Reflexive writing
Writing that includes the researcher and his/her biases, frames of reference, and personal connections to the topic in the writing.

Relational ethics
The responsibility of a researcher who has friends and partners about whom s/he writes, or study participants with whom s/he develops a relationship throughout the course of a research project.

Representation
An ethical consideration of how the voice of another person in a research project is represented in an ethical and respectful manner.

Social constructionism
A perspective suggesting that communication is the vehicle through which reality is understood, constituted, and represented, and it is through communication that beliefs and meanings are constructed and negotiated.

Thematic analysis
A method of categorizing data into thematic categories.

Thick description
An immersive writing technique in which researchers include rich details, vivid language, and specific quotes to connect culture, environment, behaviors, theory, and meaning.

Visual ethnography
A type of ethnography which uses photographic and video images rather than, or in addition to, words, in order to represent an experience through image.

Voice
A concept related to personal and cultural agency and repetition, referring to cultural status, embodiment, and privilege.

Writing as a method of inquiry
An approach to qualitative analysis in which the researcher thinks about the meaning of what s/he is studying as s/he is writing and thus the analysis and writing stages might be one and the same.

References

Adams, T., & Holman Jones, S. (2017). Queer studies. In J. Matthes, R. Potter, & C. Davis (Eds.). *International encyclopedia of communication: Methods of communication research*. Wiley-Blackwell.

Adams, T., Ellis, C., & Holman Jones, S. (2017). Autoethnography. In J. Matthes, R. Potter, & C. Davis (Eds.). *International encyclopedia of communication: Methods of communication research*. Wiley-Blackwell.

Adams, T., Holman Jones, S., & Ellis, C. (2013). Conclusion: Storying our future. In S. Holman Jones, T. E. Adams, & C. Ellis (Eds.). *Handbook of autoethnography*. (pp. 669–677). Walnut Creek, CA: Left Coast Press.

Aldridge, D. (2008). Therapeutic narrative analysis: A methodological proposal for the interpretation of musical traces. In P. Liamputtong & J. Rumbold (Eds.), *Knowing differently: Arts-based and collaborative research methods* (pp. 205–228). New York: Nova Science.

Alexander, B. K. (2005). Performance ethnography: The reenacting and inciting of culture. In N. K. Denzin & Y. S. Lincoln (Eds.), *The Sage handbook of qualitative research* (pp. 411–441). Thousand Oaks, CA: Sage.

Boylorn, R. M., & Orbe, M. P. (Eds.). (2014). *Critical autoethnography: Intersecting cultural identities in everyday life*. Walnut Creek, CA: Left Coast Press.

Breede, D. (2017a). Communication activism. In J. Matthes, R. Potter, & C. Davis (Eds.). *International encyclopedia of communication: Methods of communication research*. Wiley-Blackwell.

Breede, D. (2017b). Feminist research/feminist methods. In J. Matthes, R. Potter, & C. Davis (Eds.). *International encyclopedia of communication: Methods of communication research.* Wiley-Blackwell.

Breede, D. (2017c). Holistic ethnography. In J. Matthes, R. Potter, & C. Davis (Eds.). *International encyclopedia of communication: Methods of communication research.* Wiley-Blackwell.

Cahnmann-Taylor, M. (2008). Poetry in qualitative research. In L. M. Given (Ed.). *The SAGE Encyclopedia of Qualitative Research Methods*, Volume 2, pp. 637–640. Thousand Oaks, CA: Sage.

Cancienne, M. B., & Bagley, C. (2008). Dance as method: The process and product of movement in educational research. In P. Liamputtong & J. Rumbold (Eds.), *Knowing differently: Arts-based and collaborative research methods* (pp. 169–186). New York: Nova Science.

Caulley, D. N. (2008). Making qualitative research reports less boring: The techniques of writing creative nonfiction. *Qualitative Inquiry, 14*(3), 424–449.

Cole, C. E., Quinlan, M. M., & Hayward, C. C. (2009). Aesthetic projects engaging inequities: Documentary film for social change. In L. M. Harter, M. J. Dutta, & C. E. Cole (Eds.). *Communicating for social impact: Engaging communication theory, research and pedagogy.* pp. 79–90. Cresskill, NJ: Hampton Press.

Creswell, J. W., Hanson, W. E., Clark, V. L. P., & Morales, A. (2007). Qualitative research designs: Selection and implementation. *The Counseling Psychologist, 35*(2), 236–264.

Davis, C. S. (2008). A funeral liturgy: Death rituals as symbolic communication, *Journal of Loss and Trauma, 13*(15), 406–421.

Davis, C. S. (2009). A family jigsaw puzzle: Secrets and gaps. *The International Review of Qualitative Research, 1*(4), 433–452.

Davis, C. S. (2010). *Death: The beginning of a relationship.* Cresskill, NJ: Hampton Press.

Davis, C. S. (2014). *Conversations about qualitative communication research: Behind the scenes with leading scholars.* New York, NY: Routledge.

Davis, C. S., & Breede, D. C. (2015). Holistic ethnography: Embodiment, emotion, contemplation, and dialogue in ethnographic fieldwork. *The Journal of Contemplative Inquiry, 2*(1), 77–99.

Davis, C. S., & Ellis, C. (2008). Autoethnographic introspection in ethnographic fiction: A method of inquiry. In P. Liamputtong & J. Rumbold, *Knowing differently: Arts-based and collaborative research*, pp. 99–117, Hauppage, NY: Nova Science.

Davis, C. S., & Warren-Findlow, J. (2011). Coping with trauma through fictional narrative ethnography: A primer. *Journal of Loss and Trauma, 16*, 563–572.

Davis, C. S., & Warren-Findlow, J. (2012). The mystery of the troubled breast: Examining cancer and social support through fictional narrative ethnography. *Qualitative Communication Research, 1*(3), 291–314.

Daykin, N. (2008). Knowing through music: Implications for research. In P. Liamputtong & J. Rumbold (Eds.), *Knowing differently: Arts-based and collaborative research methods* (pp. 229–244). New York: Nova Science.0 0

Denzin, N. K. (2003). The practices and politics of interpretation. In N. K. Denzin & Y. S. Lincoln (Eds.), *Collecting and interpreting qualitative materials* (pp. 458–498). Thousand Oaks, CA: Sage.

Deveaux, M. (1994). Feminism and empowerment: A critical reading of Foucault. *Feminist Studies, 20*, 223–248.

Ellis, C. (1999). Heartfelt ethnography. *Qualitative Health Research, 9*, 669–683.

Ellis, C (2007). Telling secrets, revealing lives: Relational ethics in research with intimate others. *Qualitative Inquiry, 13*, 3–29.

Ellis, C. (2009a). Renegotiating *Final Negotiations*: From introspection to emotional sociology. In C. Ellis, *Revision: Autoethnographic reflections of life and work* (pp. 95–120). Walnut Creek, CA: Left Coast Press.

Ellis, C. (2009b). Writing revision and researching ethically. In C. Ellis, *Revision: Autoethnographic reflections of life and work* (pp. 303–318). Walnut Creek, CA: Left Coast Press.

Ellis, C., & Bochner, A. (2000). Autoethnography, personal narrative, reflexivity: Researcher as subject. In N. Denzin & Y. Lincoln (Eds.), *The handbook of qualitative research* (2nd ed., pp. 733–768). Thousand Oaks, CA: Sage.

Ellis, C., & Bochner, A. P. (2003). Autoethnography, personal narrative, reflexivity: Researcher as subject. In N. K. Denzin & Y. S. Lincoln (Eds.). *Collecting and interpreting qualitative materials* (pp. 199–258). Thousand Oaks, CA: Sage.

Ellis, C., Bochner, A., Denzin, N., Lincoln, Y., Morse, J., Pelias, R., & Richardson, L. (2008). Talking and thinking about qualitative research. *Qualitative Inquiry, 14*(2), 254–284.

Farmer, M., & Chevrette, R. (2017). Critical theory and research. In J. Matthes, R. Potter, & C. Davis (Eds.). *International encyclopedia of communication: Methods of communication research.* Wiley-Blackwell.

Foley, D., & Valenzuela, A. (2000). Critical ethnography: The politics of collaboration. In N. K. Denzin & Y. S. Lincoln (Eds.), *The Sage handbook of qualitative research* (pp. 217–234). Thousand Oaks, CA: Sage.

Gatson, S. N. (2003). The methods, politics, and ethics of representation in online ethnography. In N. K. Denzin & Y. S. Lincoln (Eds.). *Collecting and interpreting qualitative materials* (pp. 513–527). Thousand Oaks, CA: Sage.

Geertz, C. (1973). *The interpretation of cultures.* New York, NY: Basic Books.

Grbich, C. (2007). *Qualitative data analysis: An introduction.* Thousand Oaks, CA: Sage.

Guillemin, M., & Westall, C. (2008). Gaining insight into women's knowing of postnatal depression using drawings. In P. Liamputtong & J. Rumbold (Eds.), *Knowing differently: Arts-based and collaborative research methods* (pp. 121–140). New York: Nova Science.

Harter, L. M., Dutta, M. J., & Cole, C. E. (Eds.). (2009). *Communicating for social impact: Engaging communication theory, research and pedagogy.* Cresskill, NJ: Hampton Press.

Harter, L. M., Ellingson, L. L., Dutta, M., & Norander, S. (2009). The poetic is political . . . and other notes of engaged scholarship. In L. M. Harter, M. J. Dutta, & C. E. Cole (Eds.). *Communicating for social impact: Engaging communication theory, research and pedagogy.* pp. 33–46. Cresskill, NJ: Hampton Press.

Harter, L. M., Shaw, E., & Quinlan, M. M. (2016). *Creative abundance.* Athens, OH: WOUB Center for Public Media.

Harter, L. M., Quinlan, M. M., & Shaw, E. (n.d). *Acoustics of care.* Athens, OH: WOUB Center for Public Media.

Harter, L. M., Shaw, E., Quinlan, M. M., Ruhl, S. M., & Hodson, T. (2015). Beautiful remedy. Athens, OH: WOUB Center for Public Media.

Heider, K. G. (1976). *Ethnographic film.* Austin, TX: University of Texas Press.

Holman Jones, S. (2000). Autoethnography: Making the personal political. In N. K. Denzin & Y. S. Lincoln (Eds.), *The Sage handbook of qualitative research* (pp. 763–791). Thousand Oaks, CA: Sage.

Huffman, T. (2017). Participatory/action research/CBPR. In J. Matthes, R. Potter, & C. Davis (Eds.). *International encyclopedia of communication: Methods of communication research.* Wiley-Blackwell.

Kaur, S., & Dutta, M. J. (2017). Digital ethnography. In J. Matthes, R. Potter, & C. Davis (Eds.). *International encyclopedia of communication: Methods of communication research.* Wiley-Blackwell.

Kozinets, R. V. (2002). The field behind the screen: Using netnography for marketing research in online communities. *Journal of Marketing Research, 39,* 61–72. doi:10.1509/jmkr.39.1.61.18935

Liamputtong, P., & Rumbold, J. (2008). *Knowing differently: Arts-based and collaborative research methods.* New York: Nova Science.

MacDougall, D. (2005). *The corporeal image: Film, ethnography, and the senses.* Princeton, NJ: Princeton University Press.

Madison, D. S. (2005). *Critical ethnography: Methods, ethics, and performance.* Thousand Oaks, CA: Sage.

Marsh, J. S., & Davis, C. S. (2017). Ethnodrama and ethnotheatre. In J. Matthes, R. Potter, & C. Davis (Eds.). *International encyclopedia of communication: Methods of communication research.* Wiley-Blackwell.

Mathew, W. (2014). Reality in ethnographic film: Documentary vs. docudrama. *Visual Anthropology, 27*(1–2), 17–24.

Maynard, K., & Cahnmann-Taylor, M. (2010). Anthropology at the edge of words: Where poetry and ethnography meet. *Anthropology and Humanism, 35*(1), 2–19.

McDonald, J. (2017) Critical methods. In J. Matthes, R. Potter, & C. Davis (Eds.). *International encyclopedia of communication: Methods of communication research.* Wiley-Blackwell.

Meade, M. R. (2017). Critical ethnography. In J. Matthes, R. Potter, & C. Davis (Eds.). *International encyclopedia of communication: Methods of communication research.* Wiley-Blackwell.

Metta, M. (2013). Putting the body on the line: Embodied writing and recovery through domestic violence. In S. Holman Jones, T. E. Adams, & C. Ellis (Eds.). *Handbook of autoethnography.* (pp. 486–509). Walnut Creek, CA: Left Coast Press.

Miller, L. (2008). Foucauldian constructionism. In J. A. Holstein & J. F. Gubrium (Eds.), *Handbook of constructionist research* (pp. 251–274). New York: Guilford.

Motion, J., & Leitch, S. (2007). A tool box for public relations: The oeuvre of Michel Foucault. *Public Relations Review, 33*(3), 263–268.

Moulding, N. (2006). Disciplining the feminine: The reproduction of gender contradictions in the mental health care of women with eating disorders. *Social Science & Medicine, 62*(4), 793–804.

Patti, C., & Ellis, C. (2017). Co-constructed interview. In J. Matthes, R. Potter, & C. Davis (Eds.). *International encyclopedia of communication: Methods of communication research*. Wiley-Blackwell.

Pelias, R. J. (2014). *Performance: An alphabet of performative writing*. Walnut Creek, CA: Left Coast Press.

Phillips, J. (2017). Interactive interviewing. Co-constructed interview. In J. Matthes, R. Potter, & C. Davis (Eds.). *International encyclopedia of communication: Methods of communication research*. Wiley-Blackwell.

Pink, S. (2007). *Doing visual ethnography*. Thousand Oaks, CA: Sage.

Ponterotto, J. G., & Grieger, I. (2007). Effectively communicating qualitative research. *Counseling Psychologist, 35*(3), 404–430.

Quinlan, M. M., Smith, J. W., & Hayward, C. (2009). This car seems to be alive—Perspectives on the documentary Plan F. *Journal of Research in Special Educational Needs, 9*, 59–61.

Richardson, L. (1993). Poetics, dramatics, and transgressive validity: The case of the skipped line. *The Sociological Quarterly, 34*(4), 695–710.

Richardson, L. (2000). Writing: A method of inquiry. In N. K. Denzin & Y. S. Lincoln, (Eds.), *Handbook of qualitative research* (pp. 923–948). Thousand Oaks, CA: Sage.

Richardson, L. (2003). Writing: A method of inquiry. In N. K. Denzin & Y. S. Lincoln (Eds.), *Collecting and interpreting qualitative materials* (pp. 499–541). Thousand Oaks, CA: Sage.

Saldaña, J. (2011). *Ethnotheatre: Research from page to stage*. Walnut Creek, CA: Left Coast Press.

Sherman, S. R. (2015). *Documenting ourselves: Film, video, and culture*. Lexington, KY: University Press of Kentucky.

Tapp, H., de Hernandez, U., & Smith, H. (2017). Community based participatory focus groups. In J. Matthes, R. Potter, & C. Davis (Eds.). *International encyclopedia of communication: Methods of communication research*. Wiley-Blackwell.

Trethewey, A. (1999). Disciplined bodies: Women's embodied identities at work. *Organization Studies, 20*(3), 423–450.

Tullis, J. A. (2013). Self and others: Ethics in autoethnographic research. In S. Holman Jones, T. E. Adams, & C. Ellis (Eds.). *Handbook of autoethnography*. (pp. 244–261). Walnut Creek, CA: Left Coast Press.

Whitehead, K., & Kurz, T. (2008). Saints, sinners and standards of femininity: Discursive constructions of anorexia nervosa and obesity in women's magazines. *Journal of Gender Studies, 17*(4), 345–358.

Winkle-Wagner, R. (2008). Not feminist but strong: Black women's reflections of race and gender in college. *The Negro Educational Review, 59*(3–4), 181–195.

RHETORICAL APPROACHES TO COMMUNICATION RESEARCH

Contributed by Robert Westerfelhaus, Ph.D.

CHAPTER OUTLINE

KEY WORDS

Aristotelian rhetoric
Burkean criticism
Critique
Cultural criticism
Dramatism
Ethos
Extra text
Guilt-redemption rhetoric
Logos
Mortification

Mythical analysis
Narrative coherence
Narrative fidelity
Narrative paradigm
Norms of perfection
Pathos
Primary texts
Rhetoric
Rhetorical criticism
Scapegoating

Secondary texts
Semiotics
Sign
Subtext
Texts
The American monomyth
The hero's journey
The heroine's journey
Transcendence

CHAPTER OBJECTIVES

1. To understand the different rhetorical approaches to textual analysis
2. To understand the characteristics of the main methods of rhetorical criticism
3. To learn how to design and conduct different types of rhetorical criticism

▼ # Characteristics of Rhetorical Criticism

rhetorical criticism
The study of the ways that written or spoken language (such as speeches, books, images, performances, texts, and films), in their historical and cultural context, work—to persuade, instruct, inform, entertain, arouse, engage, and convince.

texts
Any communicative message, such as an advertisement, book, film, speech, etc.

As a method of communication inquiry, **rhetorical criticism** focuses upon a wide variety of **texts**. These texts may be oral messages delivered by speakers in real time to live audiences, such as lectures, sermons, and political speeches. Often, rhetorical critics rely upon print and recorded versions that preserve such oral presentations after they have been delivered. Written texts also attract the attention of rhetorical critics. These include novels, poems, short stories, and all manner of fictional and nonfictional literature. In addition, the scope of rhetorical inquiry encompasses texts disseminated via the mass and social media, including advertisements, blogs, comic books, films, magazines, musical recordings, podcasts, radio talk shows, television series, videogames, websites, etc. Rhetorical critics also look at texts collected via ethnographic methods, such as the stories workers share with one another within an organization. Put simply, rhetorical critics engage a wide and diverse range of texts.

A basic conception of human communication, the Shannon-Weaver model, depicts a process in which a sender sends a message to a receiver via some medium. In examining texts, rhetorical criticism focuses primarily upon the message within the communication process. This is not to say, however, that such criticism ignores those who send or receive messages. They too are important but are typically treated as secondary considerations viewed primarily in relation to the shared texts they create and consume. There are some good reasons why rhetorical critics prefer to focus upon texts rather than those who produce them or the audiences to which they are directed. One reason is that neither senders nor receivers are fully aware of the full range of rhetorical methods embedded within and informing their mutual communication, and consequently they are not able to articulate how or why they manage to influence others or be influenced. Of course, if communicators could do so there would be no purpose in producing rhetorical criticism, which would then only serve to point out the obvious. Another reason texts are privileged by rhetorical critics can be inferred from the kind of texts they traditionally study, which are typically fixed in some way like books or films. These can be more easily shared and studied by critics than such ephemeral phenomena as casual conversations. The emerging social media might serve to expand the range of texts rhetorical critics examine.

▼ # Appropriate Research Questions Answered by Rhetorical Criticism

Rhetorical criticism involves close readings of texts. These readings look beneath the surface and beyond the obvious. The goal is to obtain a deeper understanding of the text, or some important aspect of it, than one gains from a merely superficial reading; and to tie that understanding to broader practical and theoretical concerns related to human communication in particular and the human condition in general. In examining texts, rhetorical criticism traditionally seeks to answer questions regarding communicative influence. How is such influence exercised explicitly and implicitly? Who does that influence affect? Who benefits and who does not? And how: culturally, economically, politically, and socially? What do texts reveal and what do they conceal? How? And why?

Data in Rhetorical Criticism

The texts rhetorical critics examine are not data per se, but rather the sources from which data are drawn for analysis. Such data include narrative threads, quotations culled from dialogue, descriptions (from written and oral texts), depictions (from visual texts), and other words and images. The principal sources from which rhetorical data are derived are the **primary texts** that critics examine, the very texts listed in the first paragraph of this section. Another important source of data is what John Fiske (1987) refers to as **secondary texts**. These are separate texts that comment upon and refer back to a primary text. For example, a rhetorical critic examining the 2012 film *The Avengers* might also look at reviews of the film or interviews with the film's creative team (its actors, director, producer, and writer) broadcast on radio or television or published in newspapers, magazines, and online websites. The rhetorical critic might also pay attention to materials that Robert Alan Brookey and Robert Westerfelhaus (2002) call **extra text**. These are texts made possible by contemporary technology that accompany and are sometimes embedded within primary texts, such as the extra features included in many DVDs and videogames: alternate endings, deleted scenes, promotional material, voice-over commentary, interviews with the creative team, Easter eggs (hidden features), etc.

In examining primary and secondary texts the goal of rhetorical criticism is not to be blandly descriptive, but rather to offer new insights regarding the text and understandings of human communication made possible through systematic analysis. Such critical analysis, also referred to as **critique**, is guided by rhetorical theory, which provides critics with a lens through which to view the texts they are examining. Theory suggests what texts to examine, which textual features should be looked at, and how best to interpret them. Several major rhetorical theories and their approaches to criticism are featured later in this section.

primary texts
The principal sources from which rhetorical data that critics examine are derived.

secondary texts
Separate texts that comment upon and refer back to a primary text.

extra text
Texts made possible by contemporary technology that accompany and are sometimes embedded within primary texts, such as the extra features included in many DVDs and videogames: alternate endings, deleted scenes, promotional material, voice-over commentary, interviews with the creative team, Easter eggs (hidden features), etc.

Writing Rhetorical Criticism

In writing rhetorical criticism, rhetoricians conventionally begin their essays or book-length monographs by identifying the specific text, texts, or textual genre that will be the focus of their critical analysis (e.g., *The Avengers*, the Marvel Cinematic Universe film franchise, or films featuring superheroes). Next, they argue why the chosen text is worthy of critical analysis. Such arguments might point to the text's cultural, economic, political, or social impact; note its influence upon the content or form of other similar texts; cite it as an illustrative example; observe that the text is the first of its kind or unique in ways that set it apart as special; or claim that critique of the text will address gaps in communication

critique
Critical analysis which is guided by rhetorical theory, which provides critics with a lens through which to view the texts they are examining.

scholarship and contribute new knowledge about human communication. Making the argument that the chosen text is significant is important, as there is no good reason for rhetorical critics or their readers to invest time and energy in critiques of texts with marginal influence and from which little to no new practical or theoretical knowledge about rhetoric can be gleaned. Critics then identify which rhetorical theory and what associated method they will use to critique the text they have chosen to examine and explain why this is the best—or at least an appropriate—approach. Having defined what they will critique, and why and how, critics then engage in the critique itself. This analysis is the meat of any critical essay. Critics typically conclude a study by acknowledging the strengths and weaknesses of their critique and discussing what it teaches us about the text and about human communication in general. They explain how insights derived from their analysis help to extend, refine, revise, or refute existing theory. And, they end by suggesting future directions for similar research that draw from and build upon the critique they have just presented.

▼ Aristotelian Rhetoric

As with many other intellectual pursuits, the origins of rhetorical theory—at least as it is practiced in the Western world—can be traced back to ancient Greece, and most especially the city-state of Athens during the 4th and 5th centuries BCE. In the Athenian democracy, the small select group of elite males who were fully enfranchised were not only permitted but were actually required by law to participate actively in political processes and judicial proceedings. Those who opted not to participate were punished. Successfully running for office, getting legislation passed, and defending oneself in court or prosecuting another relied then, as now, upon effective public speaking skills that few people naturally possess but must acquire through training and practice.

To satisfy demand for instruction regarding how to speak effectively in public venues, teachers who called themselves Sophists offered their services to those affluent elites who could afford to pay them. Naturally Sophists needed the understanding of how persuasion works offered by rhetorical theory in order to provide their students with effective means of making arguments that would win court cases and political debates. Their opponents charged the Sophists with seeking to win arguments at the expense of truth. Indeed, their critics claimed that they taught their students how to make weaker arguments appear to be the stronger through the use of rhetorical tricks. The Sophists' alleged disregard for the truth is why Socrates (c. 470 BCE–399 BCE) and his most famous pupil, Plato (c. 428 BCE–c. 348 BCE), criticized them and viewed their artful use of rhetoric with suspicion. This same suspicion is reflected in contemporary dismissals by some of polished and professional legal, political, and other discourse as mere rhetoric, which they see as a bag of linguistic tricks the clever employ to deceive the naïve.

Plato's most famous student, Aristotle (384 BCE–322 BCE), did not share his teacher's suspicion of and disdain for rhetoric and those who made positive, productive use of it. In his groundbreaking work, *On Rhetoric*, Aristotle (2006) combines the Greek concern for the practical with their interest in the theoretical. This work, arguably the first to examine systematically any aspect of human communication, offers a theoretically informed practical guide to effective public speaking. In that work, Aristotle famously defined **rhetoric** as the art of determining all available means of persuasion for any given case. Persuasion is the attempt by one communicator to get another to agree with him or her. Given that he was writing for and in response to the needs of the Greek culture in which he lived, it is not surprising that Aristotle concentrated his attention upon persuasion in relation to the three types of oral presentations that dominated public speaking in his day: forensic (legal), deliberative (political), and epideictic (ceremonial). Over time, the scope of rhetorical criticism has come to include inquiry into all forms of communicative influence, and the type of texts examined has expanded well beyond the narrow confines of public speeches.

According to Aristotle, **ethos**, **logos**, and **pathos** are key considerations in crafting persuasively effective speeches. In contemporary public speaking classes and textbooks, these terms are typically referred to as speaker credibility, logical argument, and emotional appeals. Aristotelian rhetorical criticism takes into consideration one, two, or all three when examining a text in order to evaluate its potential persuasive effectiveness. Speaker credibility takes into account an orator's character, her honesty, her experience and expertise regarding the subject about which she is speaking, her perceived honesty, and her apparent good will toward the audience. Logical appeals include classical deductive and inductive arguments, as well as discussions informed by analogies and precedents, and regarding correlation, cause and effect, and comparative advantage. Emotional appeals evoke anger, envy, fear, love, pride, and patriotism, etc. Like biological science, which can be used to cure diseases or create lethal weapons of mass destruction, the methods of persuasion identified by Aristotelian rhetoric are in themselves morally neutral tools that can be used for good or ill. Both Adolf Hitler and Martin Luther King, Jr. were gifted public speakers. Both moved audiences and influenced events. But one used his rhetorical gifts in the service of evil, and the other to promote positive political and social change.

Aristotle's ideas dominated the field of rhetoric for more than two millennia. Evidence of his continued influence can easily be found in most if not all contemporary public speaking textbooks, which contain his insights regarding excellence in public speaking. However, little criticism published by today's rhetorical scholars is exclusively Aristotelian in the traditional sense. Still, his approach to criticism is not a mere relic of the past, as we can see in James G. Shoopman's (2011) use of Aristotelian rhetorical categories to examine how theological conservatives came to dominate the internal politics of the Southern Baptist Conference.

rhetoric
The art of determining all available means of persuasion for any given case.

ethos
Speaker credibility, e.g., an orator's character, her honesty, her experience and expertise regarding the subject about which she is speaking, her perceived honesty, and her apparent good will toward the audience.

logos:
Logical argument; classical deductive and inductive arguments, as well as discussions informed by analogies and precedents, and regarding correlation, cause and effect, and comparative advantage.

pathos
Emotional appeals which target emotions such as anger, envy, fear, love, pride, and patriotism, etc.

aristotelian rhetoric
Examines how logical arguments, emotional appeals, and perceptions of speaker credibility are employed as persuasive tools.

Narratives and Rhetorical Criticism

Walter Fisher (1984) dubbed our species as *Homo narrans*: that is, he defines storytelling as essential to our human nature. There is much evidence to support Fisher's view, as storytelling is indeed central to our shared human experience. We certainly use stories extensively. We use them to connect with one another. When old friends get together after being separated for a few years, they reestablish their relationship by retelling old stories about their shared past, and bring one another up to date by sharing new stories regarding what they have done since last they last met. When couples begin their relationships they use stories to get to know and bond with one another. We also use stories to entertain ourselves and others. We enjoy telling jokes, reading novels, attending plays, viewing films and television shows, and playing video games that have a narrative structure. In addition, we use stories to advance arguments. Prosecutors tell stories intended to convince judges and juries to convict defendants, while defense lawyers use stories in the hopes of gaining an acquittal for their clients. Politicians rely upon stories to garner votes. And, we use stories to make sense of the world we inhabit and to define our place within it. The Judeo-Christian Bible, Islamic Koran, Hindu Mahabharata, and other sacred texts use mythic narratives to offer religious adherents answers to some of life's most profound questions. Clearly, stories play a significant role in our personal and collective lives, and for that reason they are texts worthy of serious and sustained rhetorical analysis.

As a means of judging stories themselves, and in making judgments based upon them, Fisher (1984) proposes his **narrative paradigm**, which examines stories in terms of their **coherence** and fidelity. A narrative that is coherent is consistent, has characters that behave believably, and lacks puzzling gaps, perplexing contradictions, and gross exaggerations. Narrative fidelity is judged by the extent to which a story rings true in confirming and conforming to our own values, beliefs, and lived experience. The story might indeed be true, and it might not. As is often the case, we cannot independently verify the veracity of story via video or eyewitness testimony. But we can reject as true stories that lack fidelity. Whether knowingly or not, television's popular Judge Judy evaluates the claims of litigants who appear on her show using criteria outlined by Fisher. In rendering her judgements, she takes into account the coherence of the stories they tell and their fidelity to probable truth. So too do police officers when interrogating suspects. And so do we in our day-to-day encounters with one another. Fisher's narrative paradigm has not proven to be particularly heuristic; that is, it hasn't inspired much original research that makes use of its theoretical lens. However, it has practical and pedagogical value, as Melissa Hobart (2013) demonstrates in a classroom exercise she developed in which she has students use Fisher's criteria for determining narrative probability to assess dubious Internet warnings, urban legends, and other suspicious stories; and in doing so, she also teaches her students the practical value of being rhetorically literate.

Fisher's narrative paradigm is not the only rhetorical means of examining stories. Mythical analysis is another method used by rhetorical critics. Myths are narratives that may or may not be literally true in terms of the details of their storylines, but which convey deeper truths about the human condition. In doing so, myths are cultural treasures that conserve and pass on traditional wisdom. One influential method of mythic rhetorical criticism is offered by Joseph Campbell (1904–1987). Drawing upon the work of Swiss psychologist Carl Jung, Campbell (1949) identified a popular narrative monomyth that informs stories both old and new from diverse cultures across time and throughout the world. Central to

narrative paradigm
Proposed by Fisher (1984), the criteria by which to examine stories in terms of their coherence and fidelity.

narrative coherence
A narrative that is coherent is consistent, has characters that behave believably, and lacks puzzling gaps, perplexing contradictions, and gross exaggerations.

narrative fidelity
The extent to which a story rings true in confirming and conforming to our own values, beliefs, and lived experience.

mythical analysis
Rhetorical analysis of myths, narratives that may or may not be literally true in terms of the details of their storylines, but which convey deeper truths about the human condition and which conserve and pass on traditional wisdom.

this narrative pattern is a formula, which he calls **the hero's journey**, found in stories ranging from traditional fairytales and folktales from the past to today's popular series of Harry Potter books and films. George Lucas famously patterned the first three films of his Star Wars epic after this mythic formula.

A simplified version of the elaborated hero's journey that Campbell (1949), first outlined in *The Hero with a Thousand Faces*, begins with a call to adventure, in which a hero is summoned from the mundane world in which he or she lives and charged with accomplishing an impossible mission that involves a difficult journey. To accomplish the task, the hero is given aid in the form of supernatural gifts and/or a wise mentor. Additional help and helpers may appear later. Along the course of the journey the hero faces dangers and encounters trials, but eventually manages to accomplish the mission, after which he or she returns home transformed by the adventure. Many academic studies and popular reviews make use of Campbell's hero's journey. Wilson Koh (2009), for example, points out how that mythic pattern shaped the plot and contributed to the commercial success of the 2002 film *Spider-Man*.

Another and more distinctively American approach to mythic criticism is that of the **American monomyth** described by John Shelton Lawrence and Robert Jewett (2002), which adheres to the following formula:

> *A community in a harmonious paradise is threatened by evil; normal institutions fail to contend with this threat; a selfless superhero emerges to renounce temptations and carry out the redemptive task; aided by fate, his decisive victory restores the community to its paradisiacal condition; the superhero then recedes into obscurity. (p. 6)*

Although there are notable exceptions, the American monomyth typically celebrates lone male heroes. It what has become something of a cliché, at the end of Western films that adhere to this mythic pattern the hero "rides off," as does Alan Ladd in *Shane*, John Wayne in *True Grit*, and Clint Eastwood in the "Man with No Name" Western Trilogy. Like the hero's journey, the American monomyth has informed much rhetorical criticism. According to Mark Poindexter, (2008) the ABC documentary *The Path to 9/11* derives much of its emotional power from tapping into the American monomyth. As a contrast to the masculine radical individualism of the conventional American monomyth, Maureen Murdock (1990) points to a narrative that she refers to as **the heroine's journey**. Females who undertake a heroine's journey do so in collaboration with others. Buffy the Vampire Slayer and Xena the Warrior Queen are examples of popular culture heroines whose heroic quests are collaborative adventures.

the hero's journey
A narrative formula described by Fisher which is characterized by a hero, a call to adventure, a supernatural gift or wise mentor, dangers and trials, and ultimate transformation.

the American monomyth
A narrative formula described by Fisher which is characterized by celebration of lone male heroes.

the heroine's journey
A narrative formula which is characterized by females who undertake a heroine's journey in collaboration with others.

Burkean Criticism

Kenneth Burke (1897–1993) is arguably the most important rhetorical theorist produced in the United States. His many remarkable scholarly accomplishments are rendered even more impressive by the fact that he never earned a college degree. Burke's approach to rhetorical criticism is indebted to insights derived from his extensive reading from a wide range of disciplines, including anthropology, economics, literary criticism, psychology, and sociology. Today international, national, and

Burkean criticism
Also called dramatism, a form of rhetorical criticism which views our shared human experience as an ongoing drama.

dramatism
A form of rhetorical criticism which views our shared human experience as an ongoing drama.

norms of perfection
In Burkean criticism, a third source of social tension in which the social order imposes impossible ideals regarding achievement, beauty, wealth, etc.

guilt-redemption rhetoric
In Burkean criticism, the idea that because guilt, regardless of its source, threatens the social fabric it must be purged and redeemed; and thus requires a rhetorical means of redeeming guilt.

mortification
In Burkean criticism, a method of redeeming guilt in which one claims responsibility for social tension and accepts the consequences of that admission.

transcendence
In Burkean criticism, a method of redeeming social tension in which one redefines the source of guilt so that it no longer produces social tension.

regional associations of communication scholars have divisions devoted exclusively to the work of Burke and those influenced by him. The Kenneth Burke Society publishes a journal featuring contemporary applications of Burkean rhetorical criticism. **Burkean criticism** is also a regular feature in other peer-reviewed academic journals within and outside the field of communication studies.

Burke's (1935, 1945, 1961, 1966) rhetorical theory is referred to as **dramatism** because it views our shared human experience as an ongoing drama. A central feature of this drama and a major concern of Burke is the presence of social tension, which he refers to as *guilt*. According to Burke, guilt has several sources. One source is law. Laws are rules, some formal and many not, that impose order and thus make it possible for small groups such as families and large collectivities like the citizens of a nation to live together without devolving into chaos. The same rules that promote social harmony also have the potential to threaten it. Some people inadvertently violate a rule from ignorance or inattention, as when we exceed the posted speed limit unknowingly. Others do so on purpose because they think they will benefit from doing so, as in the case of a thief, or because they fundamentally disagree with the rule, such as those who organized and ran the underground railroad that helped enslaved African Americans escape forced bondage.

Hierarchical structures, which are based upon and perpetuate relative social rank, are a second source of social tension. Conspicuous examples of such structures include the academy, the military, and such religious traditions as Hassidic Judaism and the Roman Catholicism. Other hierarchical arrangements are less formal. Some of these are based upon easily measurable traits, such as age or wealth, others upon more subjective criteria like perceived beauty. Hierarchies of any kind foster social tension through discontent, envy, competition, and inequitable distribution of benefits and rewards. Those at the top of a hierarchy face fierce competition from those situated below them. Those at the bottom fight to better their position. And those in between must contend with pressure from above and below them. This ongoing struggle is a fertile source of social tension.

Norms of perfection are a third source of social tension. The social order imposes ideals regarding achievement, beauty, wealth, etc. These ideals are rarely achieved and many are frankly impossible. Only a few students earn a 4.0 GPA; but flawless beauty, however defined, is virtually unobtainable. Infomercials exploit our discontent and insecurity regarding how much we weigh or how little we earn and promise to remedy our perceived deficiencies through purchase of the products they promote.

Because guilt, regardless of its source, threatens the social fabric, it must be purged and redeemed; and thus the **guilt-redemption cycle**. Burke identifies three rhetorical means of redeeming guilt. **Mortification** is one method. Through mortification one claims responsibility for social tension and accepts the consequences of that admission. A criminal confesses to her crime and pays the penalty. One friend apologizes to another for an offense and makes amends. A politician accepts blame for the negative consequences of a policy failure and resigns from office.

Transcendence is another rhetorical means of redeeming social tension. Transcendence does so by redefining the source of guilt so that it no longer produces social tension. In 1920, the Eighteenth Amendment was added to the U.S. Constitution. It prohibited "the manufacture, sale, or transportation of intoxicating liquors" within the United States. This prohibition caused a great deal of social tension since many people still wanted to sell or consume alcoholic beverages although doing so was now illegal. Gangs in Chicago and other cities fought to control the production and sale of bootleg booze, resulting in the kind of violence represented by the St. Valentine's Day Massacre. Consumers of bootleg booze not only risked being arrested, but also becoming blind, paralyzed, or even dying as a result of drinking inferior bootleg beverages containing methanol (wood alcohol), which is poisonous to humans. In 1933, the Twenty-first Amendment repealed prohibition. This redefinition of the legality of alcoholic beverages did much to assuage the social tension caused by prohibition, but it caused other forms of social tension including deaths related to alcoholism or drunk driving.

Scapegoating is yet another means of redeeming social tension. Scapegoating involves blaming a person, group, thing, or things as the cause of social tension, whether actually responsible or not, and often making the scapegoat pay the consequences. Scapegoating can be as benign as blaming your dog for a missed homework assignment or as heinous as Hitler's accusations against and treatment of the Jews, whom he wrongly blamed for Germany's losing World War I and its unfavorable treatment at the hands of the victors. In an early and influential essay entitled "The Rhetoric of Hitler's Battle," Burke (1939) argued that in scapegoating Jews Hitler exploited an us and them antithesis with the intent of rhetorically erasing regional and other divisions among the German people by creating a common enemy against whom he hoped they would rally and join forces. Burke's conception of scapegoating has informed numerous rhetorical studies, such as Theodore F. Sheckels (2009) study of South African President Thabo Mbeki's strategic scapegoating of "The West" as a means of deflecting attention away from his own controversial position regarding the crisis of HIV/AIDS within his country. In addition, Burke's dramatism in general has influenced scholarship within those disciplines which influenced him, such as anthropology, psychology, and sociology. A prominent example is the work of sociologist Hugh Dalziel Duncan (1968a, 1968b), who saw communication as central to our shared human experience. He made extensive use of Burke's dramatistic process and pentad as keys to understanding the creation and maintenance of social order. Burke's pentad, the five characteristics on which he analyzed a message, include the act (the specific message), the purpose of the message, the agent or person communicating the message, the agency or medium of the message, and the scene or context of the message.

scapegoating
In Burkean criticism, a method of redeeming social tension which involves blaming a person, group, thing, or things as the cause of social tension, whether actually responsible or not, and often making the scapegoat pay the consequences.

cultural criticism
A type of rhetorical criticism practiced by scholars who are feminists, Marxists, members of ethnic and linguistic minorities, and those whose gender or sexual identities are outside of the mainstream; criticism that is often offered as a means of pointing out injustices, methods of marginalization, and forms of oppression as these are expressed and supported by various texts.

Cultural Criticism   ▼

Rhetorical critics who are feminists, Marxists, members of ethnic and linguistic minorities, and those whose gender or sexual identities are outside of the mainstream often offer **cultural criticism** as a means of pointing out injustices, methods of marginalization, and forms of oppression as these are expressed and supported by various texts. Critics working within the critical-cultural tradition are unapologetically subjective in their approach to scholarship. Their goal, frankly, is to bring about positive cultural, political, and social change. In this respect, such criticism differs from the traditional approach to social scientific inquiry which values objectivity, neutrality, and—at least in theory—an indifference to the results of experiments and others means of collecting data. The goal of such inquiry is simply to discover the truth about the phenomenon being studied.

Cultural criticism does not offer its own distinctive method, but instead relies upon a range of rhetorical tools in critiquing texts and the social structures they reflect and support. Two common approaches to cultural criticism are to point out absences in a text or textual tradition and to critique those representations that are present. Vito Russo's (1987) landmark *The Celluloid Closet: Homosexuality in the Movies* is a classic example of such criticism. The book served as the basis for a 1996 documentary, simply titled *The Celluloid Closet*, which was written and directed by Rob Epstein and Jeffrey Friedman and produced by Lily Tomlin. These two works highlight the conspicuous absence of gay women and men, as well as overtly gay content of any kind, from Hollywood films for decades after such was forbidden by the Motion Picture Production Code (often referred to as the Hays Code) introduced in 1930. Both the print and film critiques offer numerous examples to illustrate how when included in a film LGBT characters were usually consigned to play the roles of comedic foils, depraved and dangerous criminals, and psychologically disturbed individuals. Lesbians were stereotypically depicted as butch, gay men as effeminate.

Irony is another tool in the arsenal of cultural rhetorical criticism. In a scene from the 1959 film *Pillow Talk*, featured as an illustrative example in the documentary film version of *The Celluloid Closet*, Rock Hudson pretends to be gay by lifting his pinky finger while drinking, feigning interest in food recipes and fashion, hinting he is a momma's boy, and talking and moving in an exaggerated fashion. At the time the scene was filmed, Hudson was a closeted gay man whose public persona was that of a virile all-American male, the kind of masculine cliché that men wanted to be and women wanted to be with. In the *Pillow Talk* scene he was, ironically, portraying a heterosexual male pretending to be stereotypically gay when in fact he was gay man pretending in public to be stereotypically straight.

Another focus of cultural criticism is the identification and explication of **subtext**.

subtext
An implicit message inserted within a text.

Subtext is not immediately obvious to a casual consumer of a text, but is rather an implicit message inserted within the text. Sometimes subtext is slowly revealed to attentive members of a text's audience, and at other times subtext is directed toward a select group within the broader audience that possesses unique subcultural knowledge required to recognize and understand the subtext, which is either invisible to or misunderstood by most members of the social mainstream. The documentary version of *Celluloid Closet* points to multiple examples of subtextual messages, such as a scene from Howard Hawks' classic 1948 Western film, *Red River*, in which two cowboys—Matt Garth (Montgomery Clift) and Cherry Valance (John Ireland)— demonstrate their shooting prowess and casually talk about their guns in ways that are sexually suggestive. Cherry addresses Matt, "That's a good-looking gun you were about to use back there. Can I see it?" In response, Matt first looks into Cherry's eyes and then hands him his gun. He asks, "And you'd like to see mine?" Cherry gives Matt an appraising glance, and then says approvingly: "Nice! Awful nice!" Gazing first at his pistol and then at Matt he provocatively asks: "You know, there are only two things more beautiful than a good gun: a Swiss watch or a woman from anywhere. You ever had a good Swiss watch?" The banter continues in a similar vein. On the surface, it seems the two men are discussing their guns; but below the surface the dialogue has a decidedly phallic subtext.

When it comes to subtext, not everyone involved in the making of a text is necessarily aware of its presence, which is one strength of rhetorical criticism that might make use of but need not solely rely upon authorial interviews. Critics sometimes see what a text's authors—and audience—might be blind to. In the documentary version of *The Celluloid Closet*, Gore Vidal is interviewed regarding a scene he scripted for the 1959 Hollywood epic film *Ben-Hur*, in which the title character, played by Charlton Heston, shares a toast with his childhood friend, the Roman soldier Messala, played by Stephen Boyd. In toasting, the two men link arms and deeply and directly gaze into each other's eyes with a lingering intensity that suggests far more than mere male friendship. Boyd was informed of the gay subtext before filming, while Heston was not.

Rhetorical critics offering cultural criticism regarding gender and sexuality are prolific. They have much to write about given the many changes that have occurred in American society, such as recognizing the legality of gay marriage, which changes they helped bring about. They are not alone in critiquing and changing society. Rhetorical scholars writing as and about women, African Americans, Asians, and Hispanics, and others have also been busy critiquing absences and representations. There are abundant examples. In one feminist study Susan J. Douglas (1995) offers a critique that points out how mass media depictions of woman during the second half of the 20th century encourage female empowerment while simultaneously encouraging them to keep to their socially prescribed scripts. In another, Carol J. Clover (1993) argues that the character of the clever and resourceful "last girl," who is often the sole survivor in horror films, serves to subvert gender expectations through the celebrating of her proven power. Examples of cultural criticism that focuses upon ethnic and racial issues include critiques by Eric King Watts and Mark P. Orbe (2002), who argue that Budweiser's exploitation of purportedly "true" African American culture in the "Whassup" commercials both reflects and perpetuates white ambivalence toward that culture; Murali Balaji and Tina Worawongs (2010), who challenge the sexualized subservience of Asian females paired with white males in television advertisements; and Debra Merskin (2007), who applauds the inclusion of a Latina in the popular television series *Desperate Housewives*, but charges that the character of Gabrielle represents—albeit in a more subdued form—the stereotype of the hot-Latina female.

semiotics
Semiology in Europe, the science of signs.

sign
The smallest unit capable of conveying meaning.

• •

Semiotics

Semiotics, or semiology as it is known in Europe, is defined as the science of signs. As conceived by semioticians, **signs** are the smallest unit capable of conveying meaning. In focusing upon signs and how they are collectively organized, semiotics examines the means through which meaning is created, shared, and sometimes contested. Semiotic theory traces its origin back to two theoreticians working independently—and indeed in ignorance—of one another: American pragmatic philosopher Charles Sanders Peirce (1839–1914) and Swiss linguist Ferdinand de Saussure (1857–1913).

A conventional sign is rendered meaningful by pointing beyond itself to some object. To illustrate, McDonald's Golden Arches and the Nike Swoop are meaningful in that they represent a popular fast food franchise and a multinational athletic gear corporation; in doing so, these famous brand logos function as signs in the semiotic sense. Peirce (1991) developed several sign typologies. The one most often cited distinguishes signs based upon how they relate to the objects they represent. Icons are meaningful through their resemblance to the object they represent. Through visual likeness a portrait iconically represents its subject. A caricature does so by exaggerating recognizable traits. Indices (plural for index) derive their meaning from an existential connection to that which they represent. Smoke is an index of fire; symptoms are indices of an illness; and GPA is an index of a student's academic performance. Symbols are rendered meaningful through cultural convention. There is neither a natural nor necessary connection between a symbol and what is represents. Thus, the linguistic symbols *alkalb*, *chien*, dog, *gǒu*, *Hund*, and *perro* all represent the same canine mammal in Arabic, French, English, Chinese, German, and Spanish respectively.

Signs do not function independently of one another; instead, their use and the meanings ascribed to them are governed by codes. Codes are arranged according to two axes: the paradigmatic, which organizes content; and the syntagmatic, which governs the use of that content. Languages are semiotic codes, with vocabulary constituting the paradigmatic axis and grammar the syntagmatic rules regulating the construction of sentences, which words go with which, in what order, etc. In English adjectives typically go in front of the nouns they modify, while in Spanish the reverse is true. Thus, *white house* in English is rendered *casa blanca* (house white) in Spanish. Other semiotic codes operate similarly. Meals are not only nutritional but meaningful events. Our culture's culinary code defines what animals and plants are edible (paradigmatic content) and what foods are eaten in connection with what others, in what order, and in what context (syntagmatic rules). To illustrate: those of us in the United States who are not vegan or vegetarian view beef as edible, but few of us would eat horse as the French do or dogs as they do in China and Korea even though they too are sources of animal protein. And unlike us, observant Hindus reject beef. If you order beef at an expensive restaurant, you typically pair it with a red and not white wine, as well as some form of starch, such as a potato or rice. Consumption of beef would be preceded by appetizers and salad and followed by dessert. The meal would be served on fine china with silverware on a linen table lit by candlelight. The consumption of beef from a fast food franchise's drive-thru window follows a different coded pattern, and is interpreted differently as well.

In their book *Social Semiotics*, Charles Hodge and Gunther Kress (1988) tie semiotic systems with the historical settings and socio-cultural contexts that inform them and to which they give expression. An example of such research is provided by Alfredo Tenoch Cid Jurado (2016), who looks at these ties with respect to identity construction associated with the production and consumption of spicy foods in Mexico, Italy, and Texas. In another study, Fabio Parasecoli (2011) examines what occurs when tourists bring their own set of semiotic expectations regarding food with them as they travel. Spaghetti as served in Italy is frequently quite different from what tourists expect based upon their culinary experiences back home, which may lead to confusion and disappointment.

Rhetorical Criticism in the Workplace ▼

Rhetorical criticism has much practical benefit to offer organizations, their members, other stakeholders, and those who study professional communication from an academic perspective. This is a relatively recent focus of rhetorical study, but one that makes sense. After all, as Richard E. Crable (1990) argues, organizations are inherently rhetorical. Data used in critiques of rhetoric by and about organizations include printed texts such as directives, memoranda, and all manner of internal and external communication; digital and taped recordings; e-mails, websites, and other social media; and stories and other oral communication collected via ethnographic means.

The range of organizations and organizational practices examined by rhetorical critics and scholars working in collaboration with them is wide and diverse, as can be seen from the following illustrative examples of subjects studied: crisis management (Johnson & Sellnow, 1995), maternity leave (Meisenbach, Remke, Buzzanell, & Liu, 2008), public relations (Ihlen, 2011), restructuring (Erkama & Vaara, 2010), sports (Boyd & Stahley, 2008), websites (Sillince & Brown, 2009), and intercultural rhetoric in relation to professional communication (Thatcher, 2012).

So What?

While these critiques offer valuable theoretical insights of interest to academics, they also have an eye toward practical application. In this respect the rhetorical critics listed above, and many others like them, are continuing the tradition begun long ago by Aristotle. In doing so, they not only teach us how we can most effectively influence others, but also how others attempt to influence us. This knowledge, which benefits us personally as well as professionally, is especially useful in navigating today's global village, with its pervasive mass and social media.

We hope that throughout this book you've been inspired to conduct research for yourself. We trust you've learned how to be a critical consumer of all types of research, as well as learned how to appreciate all types of research for the strengths and limitations they bring to the researcher's toolkit. Thanks for sticking with us. Where are you on the stages of learning? Think about how much more you know now than you did in the beginning of the semester. Congratulations! You've made it through Communication Research Methods!

Glossary

Aristotelian rhetoric
Examines how logical arguments, emotional appeals, and perceptions of speaker credibility are employed as persuasive tools.

Burkean criticism
Also called **dramatism**, a form of rhetorical criticism which views our shared human experience as an ongoing drama.

Critique
Critical analysis which is guided by rhetorical theory, and which provides critics with a lens through which to view the texts they are examining.

Cultural criticism
A type of rhetorical criticism practiced by scholars who are feminists, Marxists, members of ethnic and linguistic minorities, and those whose gender or sexual identities are outside of the mainstream; criticism that is often offered as a means of pointing out injustices, methods of marginalization, and forms of oppression as these are expressed and supported by various texts.

Dramatism
A form of rhetorical criticism which views our shared human experience as an ongoing drama.

Ethos
Speaker credibility, e.g., an orator's character, her honesty, her experience and expertise regarding the subject about which she is speaking, her perceived honesty, and her apparent good will toward the audience.

Extra text
Texts made possible by contemporary technology that accompany and are sometimes embedded within primary texts, such as the extra features included in many DVDs and videogames: alternate endings, deleted scenes, promotional material, voice-over commentary, interviews with the creative team, Easter eggs (hidden features), etc.

Guilt-redemption rhetoric
In Burkean criticism, the idea that because guilt, regardless of its source, threatens the social fabric it must be purged and redeemed; and thus requires a rhetorical means of redeeming guilt.

Logos:
Logical argument; classical deductive and inductive arguments, as well as discussions informed by analogies and precedents, and regarding correlation, cause and effect, and comparative advantage.

Mortification
In Burkean criticism, a method of redeeming guilt in which one claims responsibility for social tension and accepts the consequences of that admission.

Mythical analysis
Rhetorical analysis of myths, narratives that may or may not be literally true in terms of the details of their storylines, but which convey deeper truths about the human condition and which conserve and pass on traditional wisdom.

Narrative coherence
A narrative that is coherent is consistent, has characters that behave believably, and lacks puzzling gaps, perplexing contradictions, and gross exaggerations.

Narrative fidelity
The extent to which a story rings true in confirming and conforming to our own values, beliefs, and lived experience.

Narrative paradigm
Proposed by Fisher (1984), the criteria by which to examine stories in terms of their coherence and fidelity.

Norms of perfection
In Burkean criticism, a third source of social tension in which the social order imposes impossible ideals regarding achievement, beauty, wealth, etc.

Pathos
Emotional appeals which target emotions such as anger, envy, fear, love, pride, and patriotism, etc.

Primary texts
The principal sources from which rhetorical data that critics examine are derived.

Rhetoric
The art of determining all available means of persuasion for any given case.

Rhetorical criticism
The study of the ways that written or spoken language (such as speeches, books, images, performances, texts, and films), in their historical and cultural context, work—to persuade, instruct, inform, entertain, arouse, engage, and convince.

Scapegoating
In Burkean criticism, a method of redeeming social tension which involves blaming a person, group, thing, or things as the cause of social tension, whether actually responsible or not, and often making the scapegoat pay the consequences.

Secondary texts

Separate texts that comment upon and refer back to a primary text.

Semiotics

Semiology in Europe, the science of signs.

Sign

The smallest unit capable of conveying meaning.

Subtext

An implicit message inserted within a text.

Texts

Any communicative message, such as an advertisement, book, film, speech, etc.

The American monomyth

A narrative formula described by Fisher which is characterized by celebration of lone male heroes.

The hero's journey

A narrative formula described by Fisher which is characterized by a hero, a call to adventure, a supernatural gift or wise mentor, dangers and trials, and ultimate transformation.

The heroine's journey

A narrative formula which is characterized by females who undertake a heroine's journey in collaboration with others.

Transcendence

In Burkean criticism, a method of redeeming social tension in which one redefines the source of guilt so that it no longer produces social tension.

References

Aristotle. (2006). *On rhetoric: A theory of civic discourse* (2nd ed.) (G. A. Kennedy, Trans.). New York: Oxford University Press.

Balaji, M., & Worawongs, T. (2010). The new Suzie Wong: Normative assumptions of White male and Asian female relationships. *Communication, Culture & Critique, 3*(2), 224-241.

Boyd, J., & Stahley, M. (2008). Communitas/corporatas tensions in organizational rhetoric:

Finding a balance in sports public relations. *Journal of Public Relations Research, 20*(3), 251-270.

Brookey, R. A. & Westerfelhaus, R. (2002). Hiding homoeroticism in plain view: The *Fight Club* DVD as digital closet. *Critical Studies in Media Communication, 19*(1), 21- 43.

Burke, K. (1935). *Permanence and change: An anatomy of purpose*. New York: New Republic.

Burke, K. (1939). The rhetoric of Hitler's battle. *The Southern Review, 5*, 1-21.

Burke, K. (1945). *A grammar of motives*. New York: Prentice-Hall

Burke, K. (1961). *Rhetoric of religion: Studies in logology*. Boston: Beacon Press.

Burke, K. (1966). *Language as symbolic action: Essays on life, literature, and method*. Berkeley: University of California Press.

Campbell, J. (1949). *The hero with a thousand faces*. New York: Pantheon Books.

Clover, C. J. (1993). *Men, women, and chain saws: Gender in the modern horror film*. Princeton, NJ: Princeton University Press.

Crable, R. E. (1990). "Organizational rhetoric" as the fourth great system: Theoretical, critical, and pragmatic implications. *Journal of Applied Communication Research, 18*(2), 115- 128.

Douglas, S. J. (1995). *Where the girls are: Growing up female with the mass media*. New York: Three Rivers Press.

Duncan, H. D. (1968a). *Communication and social order*. New York: Oxford University Press.

Duncan, H. D. (1968b). *Symbols in society*. New York: Oxford University Press.

Erkama, N., & Vaara, E. (2010). Struggles over legitimacy in global organizational restructuring: A rhetorical perspective on legitimation strategies and dynamics in a shutdown case. *Organization Studies, 31*(7), 813-839.

Fisher, W. R. (1984). Narration as human communication paradigm: The case of public moral argument. *Communication Monographs, 51*, 1–22.

Fiske, J. (1987). *Television culture*. New York: Routledge.

Hodge, R. & Kress, G. (1988). *Social semiotics*. Ithaca, NY: Cornell University Press.

Hobart, M. (2013). My best friend's brother's cousin knew this guy who . . .: Hoaxes, legends, warnings, and Fisher's narrative paradigm. *Communication Teacher, 27*(2), 90-93.

Ihlen, Ø. (2011). On barnyard scrambles: Toward a rhetoric of public relations. *Management Communication Quarterly, 25*(3), 455-473.

Johnson, D., & Sellnow, T. (1995). Deliberative rhetoric as a step in organizational crisis management: Exxon as a case study. *Communication Reports, 8*(1), 54-60.

Jurado, A. T. C. (2016). The culinary and social-semiotic meaning of food: Spicy meals and their significance in Mexico, Italy, and Texas. *Semiotica, 2016*(211), 247-269.

Koh, W. (2009). Everything old is good again: Myth and nostalgia in *Spider-Man. Continuum: Journal of Media & Cultural Studies, 23*(5), 735-747.

Lawrence, J. S., & Jewett, R. (2002). *The myth of the American superhero*. Grand Rapids, MI: Wm. B. Eerdmans.

Meisenbach, R. J., Remke, R. V., Buzzanell, P., & Liu, M. (2008). "They allowed": Pentadic mapping of women's maternity leave discourse as organizational rhetoric. *Communication Monographs, 75*(1), 1-24.

Merskin, D. (2007). Three faces of Eva: Perpetuation of the hot-Latina stereotype in *Desperate Housewives. Howard Journal of Communications, 18*(2), 133-151.

Murdock, M. (1990). *The heroine's journey: Women's quest for wholeness*. Boston: Shambhala.

Parasecoli, F. (2011): Savoring semiotics: Food in intercultural communication, *Social Semiotics, 21*(5), 645-663

Peirce, C. S. (1991). *Peirce on signs: Writings on semiotic by Charles Sanders Peirce*. Chapel Hill: The University of North Carolina Press.

Poindexter, M. (2008). ABC's *The Path to 9/11*, terror-management theory, and the American monomyth. *Film & History, 38*(2), 55-66.

Russo, V. (1987). *The celluloid closet: Homosexuality in the movies* (rev.ed.). New York: Harper & Row.

Sheckels, T. F. (2004). The rhetoric of Thabo Mbeki on HIV/AIDS: Strategic scapegoating? *Howard Journal of Communication, 15*(2), 69-82.

Shoopman, J. G. (2011). Rhetorical tools in modern religious conflict: Aristotelian rhetoric and framing in the Southern Baptist conservative resurgence. *Florida Communication Journal, 39*(2), 23-33.

Sillince, J. A., & Brown, A. D. (2009). Multiple organizational identities and legitimacy: The rhetoric of police websites. *Human Relations, 62*(12), 1829-1856.

Thatcher, B. (2012). *Intercultural rhetoric and professional communication: Technological advances and organizational behavior*. Hershey, PA: IGI Global.

Thomlin, L. (Producer), Epstein, R., & Friedman, J. (Directors). (1995). *The celluloid closet* [Motion picture]. United States: Sony Pictures Classic.

Watts, E. K., & Orbe, M. P. (2002). The spectacular consumption of "true" African American culture: "Whassup" with the Budweiser guys? *Critical Studies in Media Communication, 19*(1), 1-20.

APPENDICES

Appendix A

Writing Research Proposals

1. *Introduction:* Introduce us to your topic and tell us why you are interested in studying it. You may introduce us to any theoretical or conceptual framework you plan to use for your research project. State upfront the specific aims of this project. You can explain them in detail later in the proposal, but give us a preview of what we're about to read.

2. *Rationale:* Justify your selection of the topic. Convince the audience that the topic is worthy of study, that it is interesting and significant.

3. *Literature Review:* Use your literature review to further develop your idea to convince us that research on the topic is necessary, and your proposed way of conducting the research is the best way to do it. Make sure your literature review is comprehensive and, again, points to your project as the next missing piece of information. Use the literature to explain your theoretical or conceptual framework.

4. *Research Questions, Study Objectives, or Hypotheses:* What, specifically, will this study address?

5. *Methodology:* Your method should be justified by your Research Questions; be very specific in terms of what you will be doing. You want to be sure the methods used are appropriate for your research questions, and that what you propose to do is feasible and doable.
   a. *Method:* Which method or approach will you use (be specific)?
   b. *Population:* How have you operationalized your population?
   c. *Sample:* What is your sampling design and how does it represent the population?
   d. *Information to be Collected or Instruments to be Used:* Justify the selection of the instruments and discuss their validity, or explain how you chose the information to be gathered.
   e. *Validity, Reliability, Credibility, Crystallization:* How will you ensure study quality?
   f. *Ethics:* How will you ensure ethical treatment of your study participants?
   g. *Variables:* What are your main variables and how have you conceptualized and operationalized them?

6. *Analysis Plans:* How do you plan to analyze the data? What statistical tests will you use to test your hypotheses? What coding and analytical method will you use?
   (Morse, 2003; Sandelowski, 2003)

7. *Limitations and Suggestions for Future Research:* What will this study not allow you to do? What future research does this study suggest?

8. *Time/Duration of Project:* Include a timeline outlining each step of your proposed research.

9. *Appendix*
   a. Copy of instrument or study protocol
   b. Consent form
   c. IRB application

References

Morse, J. (2003). A review committee's guide for evaluating qualitative proposals. *Qualitative Health Research, 13*(6), 833–851.

Sandelowski, B. (2003). Writing a qualitative proposal. *Qualitative Health Research, 13*(6), 781–820.

Appendix B

[CAREGIVER CONSENT]

Dept. of Communication Studies
9201 University City Blvd.
Charlotte, NC 28223

Informed Consent for
Children's Mental Health Child and Family Team
Meeting Communication Study

Project Title and Purpose:

You are invited to participate in a research study titled "Children's Mental Health Child and Family Team Meeting Communication Study." This is a study to look at communication in child and family team meetings between your providers and your family. I want to use this information to help providers better communicate with families.

Investigator(s):

This study is being conducted by Christine Davis in the Department of Communication Studies at the University of North Carolina (UNC)–Charlotte.

Description of Participation:

As part of this research study, I would like to attend your upcoming child and family team meeting. I'd like your permission to observe and videotape the meeting and ask you and the other people attending the meeting to fill out a short questionnaire at the end.

Length of Participation:

The only time you will spend on this study is time you will already be spending in attending the meetings plus the extra 15 minutes to fill out the questionnaire at the end. If you decide to participate, this will be one of 25 meetings observed, and you will be one of 25 caregivers participating.

Risks and Benefits of Participation:

There are no known risks to participate in this study. However, there may be risks that are currently unforeseeable. There are no direct benefits to you, but the benefits of participating in this study are helping improve communication between providers and caregivers and families. In addition, I will give you $25.00 as appreciation for your participation, and if your child attends, I will give him or her $5.00.

Volunteer Statement:

You are a volunteer. The decision to participate in this study is completely up to you. If you decide to be in the study, you may stop at any time. You will not be treated any differently if you decide not to participate or if you stop after you have started. The information you provide will not affect the services your child and family are getting now or in the future. Taking part in the study is completely up to you, and even if you decide during the meeting that you no longer want to participate, you can just let me know. The meeting will be held and you will receive services whether or not you choose to participate in this research.

Anonymity:

The data collected, including the videotape and the questionnaire, will not contain any identifying information or any link back to you or your participation in this study. The following steps will be taken to ensure this anonymity: your name will not be written down anywhere but the consent form. The consent form will be kept separate from the videotape and the questionnaire. Names will not be used when transcribing the videotape.

Fair Treatment and Respect:

UNC–Charlotte wants to make sure that you are treated in a fair and respectful manner. Contact the University's Research Compliance Office at 704-687-9999 if you have any concerns about how you are treated as a study participant. If you have any questions about the project, please contact Dr. Christine Davis, Department of Communication Studies, UNC–Charlotte, 9999 Colvard, 9201 University City Blvd., Charlotte, NC 28223, 704-687-9999, xxx@uncc.eduw

Participant Consent:

I have read the information in this consent form. I have had the chance to ask questions about this study, and those questions have been answered to my satisfaction. I am at least 18 years of age or an emancipated minor*, and I agree to participate in this research project. I understand that I will receive a copy of this form after it has been signed by me and the principal investigator.

_____   _____   _____

Participant Name (PLEASE PRINT)   Participant Signature   DATE

_____   _____

Investigator Signature   DATE

*Emancipated Minor (as defined by NC General Statute 7B-101.14) is a person who has not yet reached his or her 18th birthday and meets at least one of the following criteria: (1) has legally terminated custodial rights of his or her parents and been declared emancipated by a court; (2) is married, or (3) is serving in the armed forces of the United States.

Appendix C

How Your Objective, Research Question, and/or Hypothesis Relates to Your Methodology

If your objective, research question, and/or hypothesis is:	Then your chosen method should be:
To test causation	Experimental design (Chapter 12)
To assess (measure) beliefs, attitudes, opinions; to collect (measure) retrospective information about behavior, meaning	Survey (Chapter 10)
To analyze (in a measureable way) the content of messages such as media messages; to measure how information is exchanged through text or media messages	Quantitative content analysis (Chapter 11)
To analyze (in a measurable way) the content of interpersonal messages; to measure how information is exchanged interpersonally	Interaction analysis (Chapter 11)
To understand, describe, explain communication in a culture or cultural group	Ethnography (Chapters 14 and 15)
To describe and understand group discourse/conversation in action	Focus groups (Chapters 14 and 15)
To describe or understand communication as it relates to behavior within social situations and multiple realities	Grounded theory (Chapters 14 and 15)
To understand, describe, explain meaning within lived experience	Phenomenology (Chapters 14 and 15)
To describe or understand communication as it relates to illustrative case(s)	Case study (Chapters 14 and 15)
To study spoken or written discourse—speech acts—from the content of the discourse, to its delivery (paralanguage, speech, grammar), to its context, and the meaning deriving from each of these, to understand how people use language to construct ideas, meanings, and identities	Discourse analysis (Chapters 14 and 15)
To describe and understand interpersonal social action in sequences of utterances and interaction as agents of action and activity	Conversation analysis (Chapters 14 and 15)
To analyze (in a descriptive way) the content of messages such as media messages	Qualitative content analysis (Chapters 14 and 15)
To understand, describe, and explain communication in a culture in which the researcher is an integral part; to write personal narratives about a culture in which the researcher is an integral part	Autoethnography and Personal narratives (Chapters 14 and 16)
To describe or understand communication as it relates to power and gender in a culture, often to achieve social change and/or social justice goals	Critical and feminist ethnography/ Community Based Participatory Research, Cultural criticism (Chapters 14 and 16)

Continued

If your objective, research question, and/or hypothesis is:	Then your chosen method should be:
To understand the multidimensional and interdependent aspects of reality	Holistic ethnography (Chapters 14 and 16)
To investigate communication in digitized spaces	Digital and online ethnography (Chapters 14 and 16)
To observe and reenact culturally situated communicative acts to reflect an interpretation of cultural practice through human expression	Performance studies (Chapters 14 and 16)
To write in an aesthetic manner to turn your text into an evocative artistic representation	Performative writing, Poetic ethnography, Fiction as method, Ethnodance (Chapters 14 and 16)
To perform the researcher's and/or participant's experience, often to seek social justice, social change, or social awareness; to represent a historical or cultural experience; to give marginalized people a voice; to create space for alternative voices and alternative ways of knowing; and to work toward an intellectual, emotional, and aesthetic result	Ethnodrama and Ethnotheatre (Chapters 14 and 16)
To use photographic and video images rather than, or in addition to, words, in order to represent an experience through image	Documentary, video, or visual ethnography (Chapters 14 and 16)
To understand how symbols act on people—the ways that written or spoken language (such as speeches, books, images, performances, texts, and films), in their historical and cultural context, work—to persuade, instruct, inform, entertain, arouse, engage, and convince	Rhetorical criticism (Chapter 17)
To study the persuasive ability of a text by Aristotle's criteria	Aristotelian criticism (Chapter 17)
To understand the narrative or mythic elements in a text	Narrative criticism (Chapter 17)
To study how our symbolic actions construct our ideas of reality, based on Burke's ideas of social tension	Dramatistic criticism; Burkean criticism (Chapter 17)
To point out injustices, methods of marginalization, and forms of oppression as these are expressed and supported by various texts	Cultural criticism (Chapter 17)
To understand how reality is constructed through the use of symbol systems (signs, symbols, codes)	Semiotics (Chapter 17)

Appendix D

Statistics Decision Chart

What type of data do you have?	What do you want to do?		
	Summarize Data	Test for Differences between Groups	Test for Relationships between Variables

Nominal	Look at measures of central tendency:
	    Mode
	Display data visually:
	    Frequency table
	    Pie chart
	    Bar chart
		Analyze the distribution of the independent or dependent variable:
		    Chi Square
		Compare 2 or more independent or dependent categories:
		    2-variable Chi Square
			Cramer's V

Ordinal	Look at measures of central tendency:
	    Median
	Display data visually:
	    Frequency table
	    Bar chart
		Analyze the differences between 2 groups:
		    Mann-Whitney U Test
		Analyze the differences between 3 or more groups:
		    Kruskall-Wallis Test
		Examine the differences between related scores:
		    Wilcoxin Sign Test
			Spearman's Rho

Interval/Ratio (Scale)	Standardize your data
	    Z-Scores
	Determine measures of central tendency:
	    Median
	    Mean
	Determine measures of dispersion:
	    Range
	    Variance
	    Standard deviation
	Display data visually:
	    Bar chart
	    Line graph
		Estimate data:
		    Estimate confidence levels and margin of error
		Examine differences between 2 unrelated groups:
		    Independent samples t-test
		Examine differences between 2 related groups:
		    Paired t-test
		Compare 3 or more groups on their distribution on one variable:
		    One-way analysis of variance (ANOVA) followed by a Tukey ad-hoc test
		Compare 3 or more groups and their differences over time:
		    Repeated measures ANOVA followed by a Tukey ad-hoc test
			Test for a statistically significant relationship between variables:
			    2 variables:
			    Pearson-Product Moment Correlation
			    3 or more variables:
			    Correlation Matrix
			Predict outcomes:
			    Regression analysis

Appendix E

Style Manual Summary (APA, MLA, Chicago)

APA Style	
Journal Article	Bastien, D. T., & Hostager, T. J. (1992). Cooperation as communicative accomplishment: A symbolic interaction analysis of an improvised jazz concert. *Communication Studies, 43*(2), 92–104.
Book	Anderson, H. (1997). *Conversation, language, and possibilities: A postmodern approach to therapy*. New York, NY: Basic Books.
Book Chapter in an Edited Book	Charmaz, K. (2000). Grounded theory: Objectivist and constructivist methods. In N. K. Denzin & Y. S. Lincoln (Eds.), *The handbook of qualitative research* (pp. 509–535). Thousand Oaks, CA: Sage.

MLA Style	
Journal Article	Bastien, David T., and Todd J. Hostager. "Cooperation as Communicative Accomplishment: A Symbolic Interaction Analysis of an Improvised Jazz Concert." *Communication Studies*, vol. 43, no. 2, 1992, pp. 92–104.
Book	Anderson, Harlene. *Conversation, Language, and Possibilities: A Postmodern Approach to Therapy*. Basic Books, 1997.
Book Chapter in an Edited Book	Charmaz, Kathy. "Grounded Theory: Objectivist and Constructivist Methods." *The Handbook of Qualitative Research*, edited by Norman. K. Denzin and Yvonna S. Lincoln. Sage, 2000, pp. 509–35.

Chicago Style	
Journal Article	David T. Bastien, and Todd J. Hostager, "Cooperation as Communicative Accomplishment: A Symbolic Interaction Analysis of an Improvised Jazz Concert. *Communication Studies*, 43, no. 2 (1992): 96.
Book	Harlene Anderson, *Conversation, Language, and Possibilities: A Postmodern Approach to Therapy* (New York: Basic Books, 1997), 493.
Book Chapter in an Edited Book	Kathy Charmaz, "Grounded Theory: Objectivist and Constructivist Methods," in *The Handbook of Qualitative Research*, ed. Norman K. Denzin and Yvonna S. Lincoln, (Thousand Oaks, CA: Sage, 2000), 509.

INDEX